BAILLIE-KI-PALTAN

BEING

A History of the 2nd Battalion, Madras Pioneers

1759–1930

LIEUTENANT-COLONEL H. F. MURLAND

The Naval & Military Press Ltd

Reproduced by kind permission of the Central Library,
Royal Military Academy, Sandhurst

Published by
The Naval & Military Press Ltd
Unit 10, Ridgewood Industrial Park,
Uckfield, East Sussex,
TN22 5QE England
Tel: +44 (0) 1825 749494
Fax: +44 (0) 1825 765701
www.naval-military-press.com
© The Naval & Military Press Ltd 2005

In reprinting in facsimile from the original, any imperfections are inevitably reproduced and the quality may fall short of modern type and cartographic standards.

PREFACE.

The records of the old IV Pioneers covering the period up to 1903 were originally published for private circulation in 1922, and have now, at the request of the Commandant and Officers of the Regiment, been revised, and brought up to the year 1930.

Since the publication of the original edition, much additional information has been forthcoming, and it has been found necessary to re-write the greater part of the history.

This battalion of the old Coast Army is, with two nearly contemporaneous exceptions, the oldest regiment in India, having had an uninterrupted history of upwards of 170 years, and I think that its records may well be left to speak for themselves.

H. F. M.

Preface to the Edition of 1922.

This compilation is an attempt to place on record as much as has so far been traced of the history of the IV Madras Pioneers (now the 64th Pioneers). The original records having most unfortunately been lost, the narrative is necessarily very incomplete, and while there are, of course, numerous histories extant of the various campaigns in which the regiment took part, it is altogether impossible to reproduce the atmosphere, or replace the personal element, which only a contemporary account can supply.

The objection may be raised that a great deal has been included which has no direct connection with the regiment, and that such extraneous matter as the disaster to Colonel Baillie in 1780 might well be omitted. The whole aim, however, of printing these records has been to assemble as many facts as possible, however loosely strung together, which may have even a slight connection with the regiment or may seem to possess any interest for those serving with it, and to put them in print in the hope that some better qualified person with access to the military records of Fort St. George may one day supplement what is here recorded, and produce a connected story worthy of the subject.

If the dryness of this chronicle should lead anyone to imagine that the subject is necessarily a dull one, the shortcomings of the compiler are entirely responsible. A narrative of our early struggles in India must always possess an interest for those who have any connection with the country where these stirring events took place.

H. F. M.

CONTENTS.

	PAGE.
Battle Honours	viii
Introductory Note	1
PART I.—Services of the Regiment, 1759—1930	3—256
Affairs in the Carnatic, 1748—1759	4
Chapter I.—The 5th Battalion Coast Sepoys, 1759—1769	7
Chapter II.—The 5th Carnatic Battalion, 1769—1770	
The 4th Carnatic Battalion, 1770—1784	39
Chapter III.—The 4th Madras Battalion, 1784—1796	77
Chapter IV.—The 1st Battalion, 4th Regiment of Madras Native Infantry, 1796—1824	95
Chapter V.—The 4th Regiment of Madras Native Infantry, 1824—1883	147
Chapter VI.—The 4th Regiment of Madras Native Infantry (Pioneers), 1883—1885	
The 4th Regiment of Madras Infantry (Pioneers), 1885—1901	
The 4th Madras Pioneers, 1901—1903	169
Chapter VII.—The 64th Pioneers, 1903—1921	
The 2nd Battalion, 1st Madras Pioneers, 1922—1929	
The 2nd Battalion, Madras Pioneers, 1929—1930	189
PART II.—Orders and Changes affecting the Regiment, 1759—1930	257—368
PART III.—Colonels of the Regiment	371
British Officers of the Regiment	372
Alphabetical Index of British Officers	466
Warrant Officers and Sergeants	471
PART IV.—Indian Officers of the Regiment	473
PART V.—Pioneer Work of the Regiment, 1883—1930	499
Bibliography	594
Reviews of the 1922 Edition	598

MAPS AND PLANS.

General Map of India

Plan of the Battle of Porto Novo (1781)

Plan of the Battle of Pullalur (1781)

Plan of the Battle of Sholinghur (1781)

Plan of the Action near Virakanellur (1781)

Plan of Hyder's Attack on 13th January 1782

Plan of the Battle of Arni (1782)

Map illustrating the Mysore Wars

Plan of the Battle of Assaye (1803)

Plan of the Battle of Argaum (1803)

Map illustrating the Campaign of 1803

Map showing part of Coorg

Map of the Chin Hills

Map showing part of Mesopotamia

Map of Country between Shaikh Saad and Shumran Bend

Map showing the position of the Harnai Railway

Map showing part of Hkamti Long

Besides, numerous maps and plans in the text.

Battle Honours.

The following are the battle honours of the Corps of Madras Pioneers, after the re-organisation in 1929, when the three Madras Pioneer Battalions, *viz.*, 1st (later the 61st [K.G.O.] Pioneers), 4th (later the 64th Pioneers), and 21st (later the 81st Pioneers) were united in one Corps.

"*Sholinghur.*"

"*Carnatic.*" "*Mysore.*" "*Seringapatam.*"

The Plume of the Prince of Wales. **The Royal and Imperial Cypher.**

The Elephant.

"*Assaye.*" "*Seetabuldee.*" "*Nagpore.*"

"*Ava.*" "*Pegu.*"

"*Central India.*" "*Afghanistan 1878—80.*"

"*Burma 1885—87.*"

"*Punjab Frontier.*" "*Tirah.*"

"*China 1900.*" "*Afghanistan 1919.*"

The Great War.

"*Kut Al Amara 1917.*" "*Baghdad.*"

"*Mesopotamia 1916—18.*"

"*Persia 1918.*" "*N. W. Frontier, India, 1915.*"

"*Baluchistan 1918.*"

"*Kilimanjaro.*" "*E. Africa 1914—18.*"

The 2nd Battalion was granted an Honorary Colour for the Battle of Assaye.

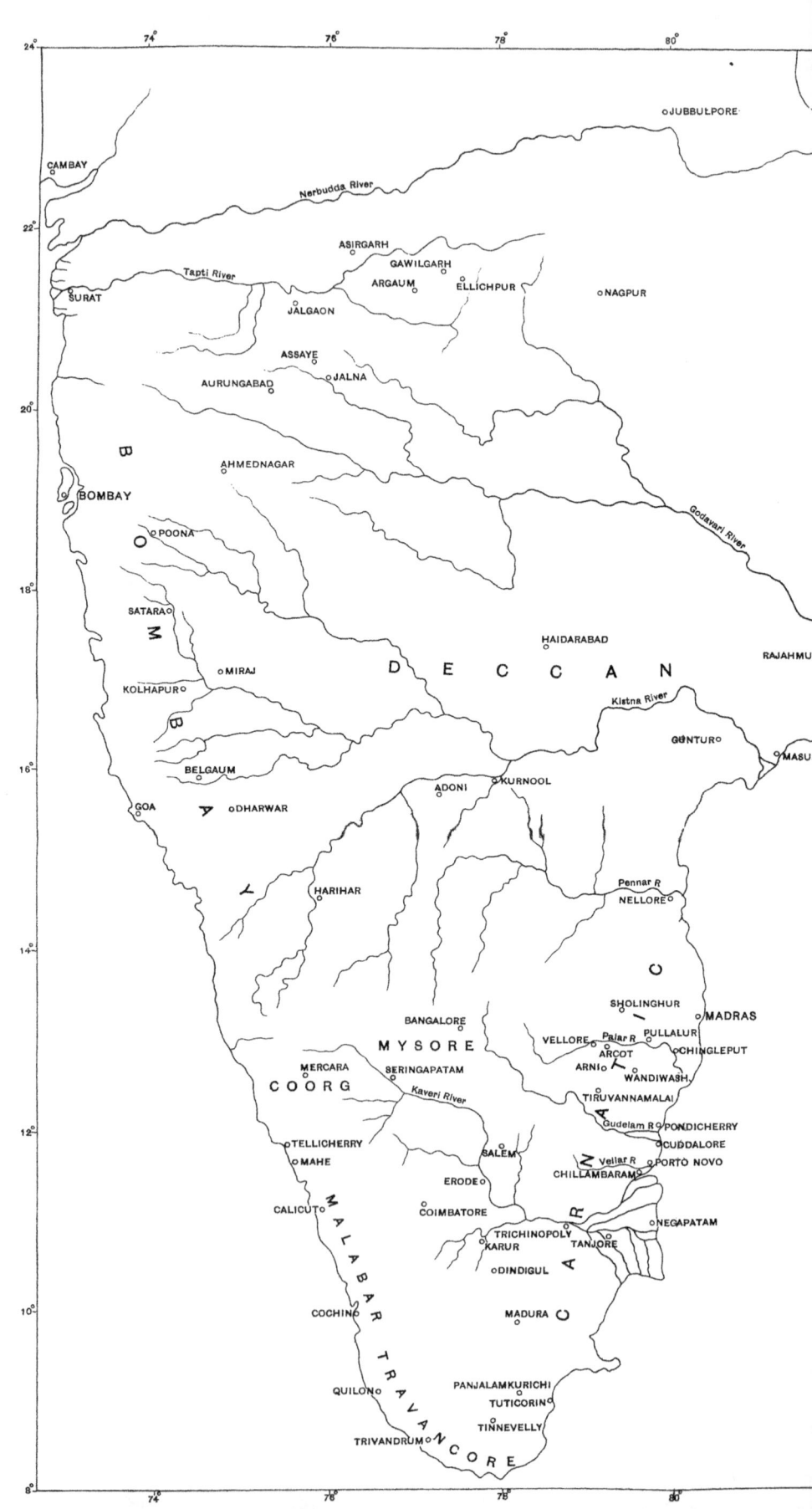

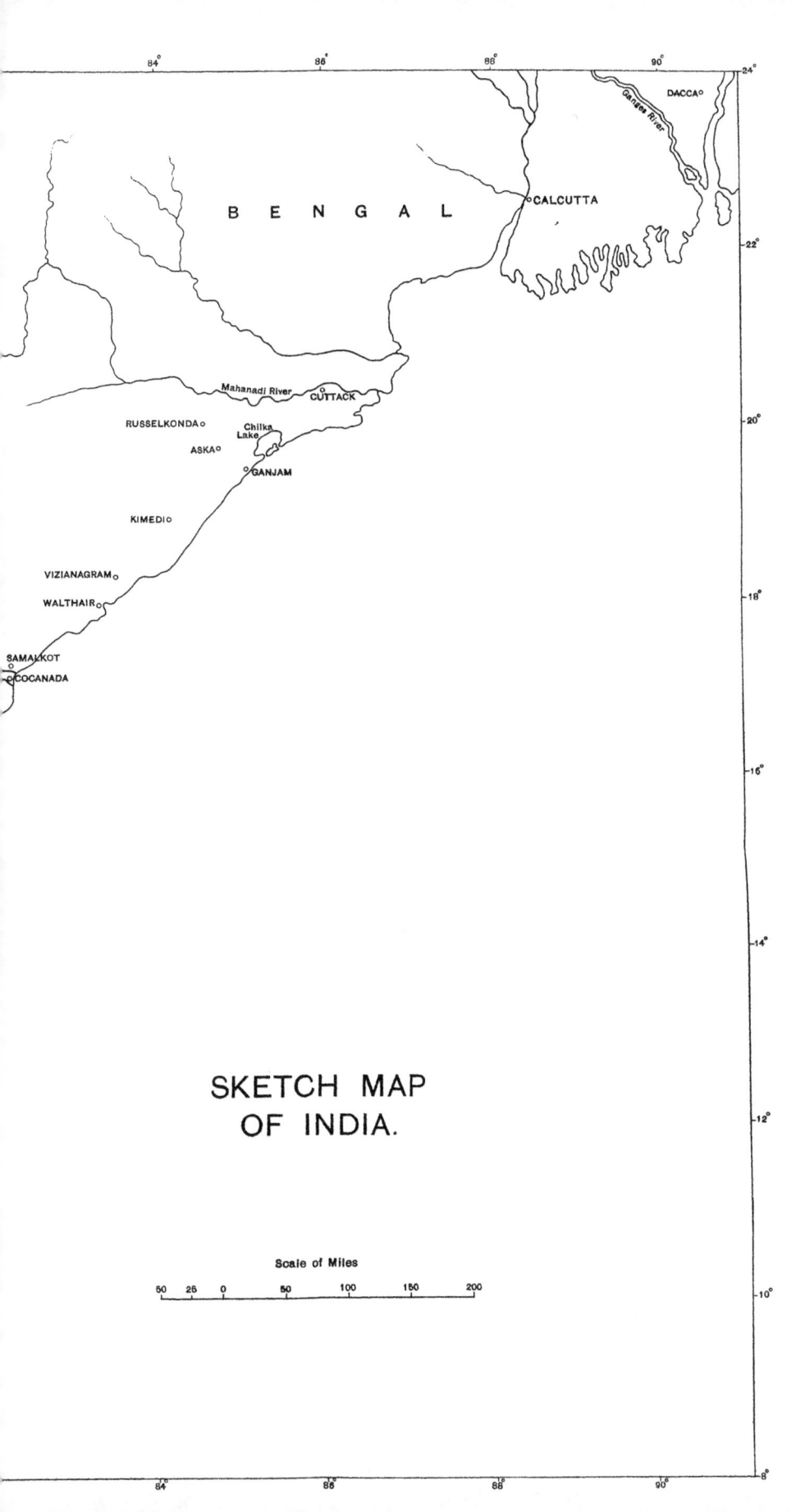

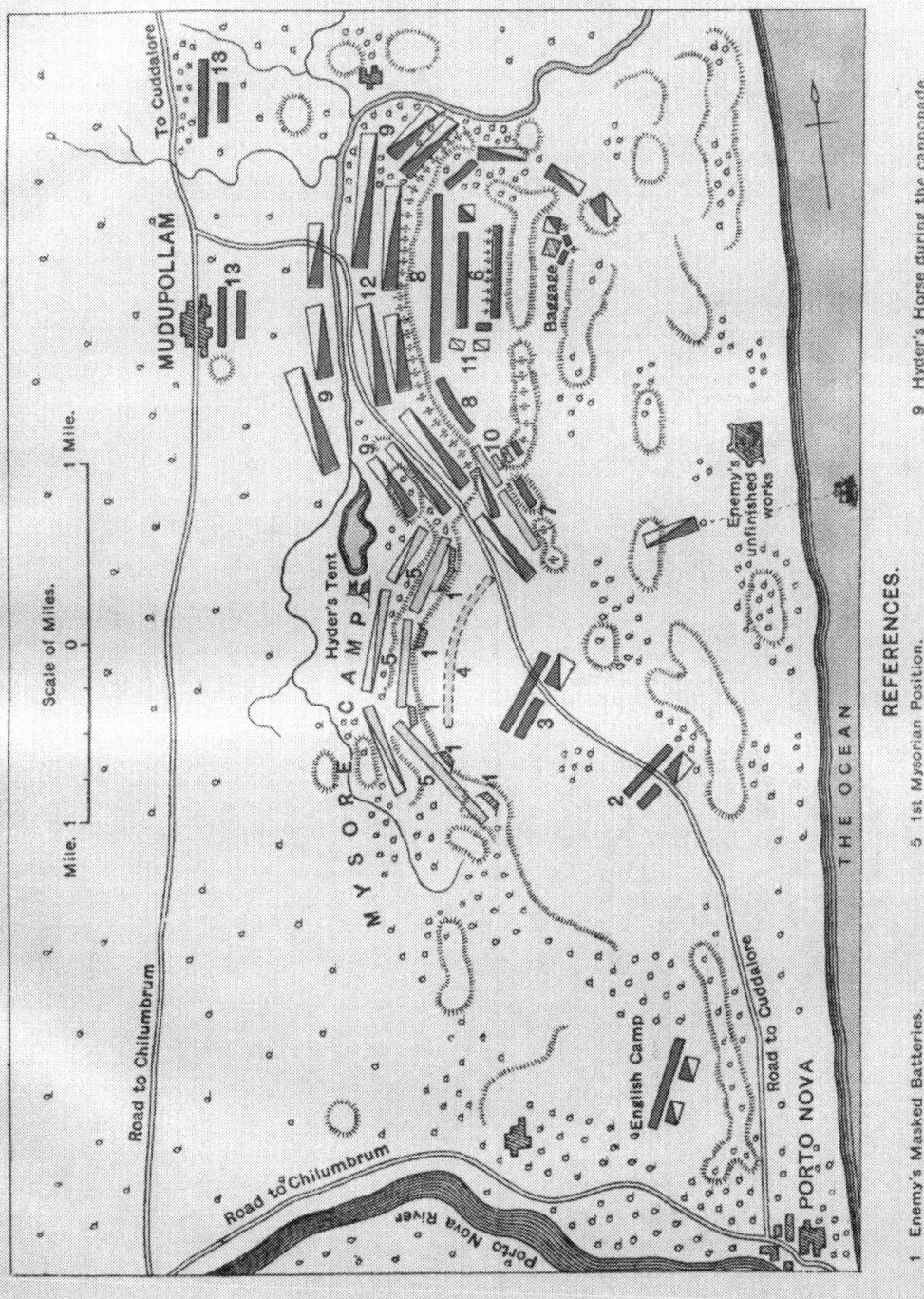

THE BATTLE OF PORTO NOVA.

REFERENCES.

1 Enemy's Masked Batteries.
2 1st Position of English advancing.
3 2nd do
4 Irregular Horse covering Masked Batteries.
5 1st Mysorian Position.
6 1st English Line during cannonade.
7 2nd do
8 2nd Position of Hyder's Infantry.
9 Hyder's Horse during the cannonade.
10 Attempt on the Hill by Hyder's Grenadiers.
11 Kiram Sahib's attempt to charge.
12 Hyder's Position during the action.
13 English Camp after the Battle.

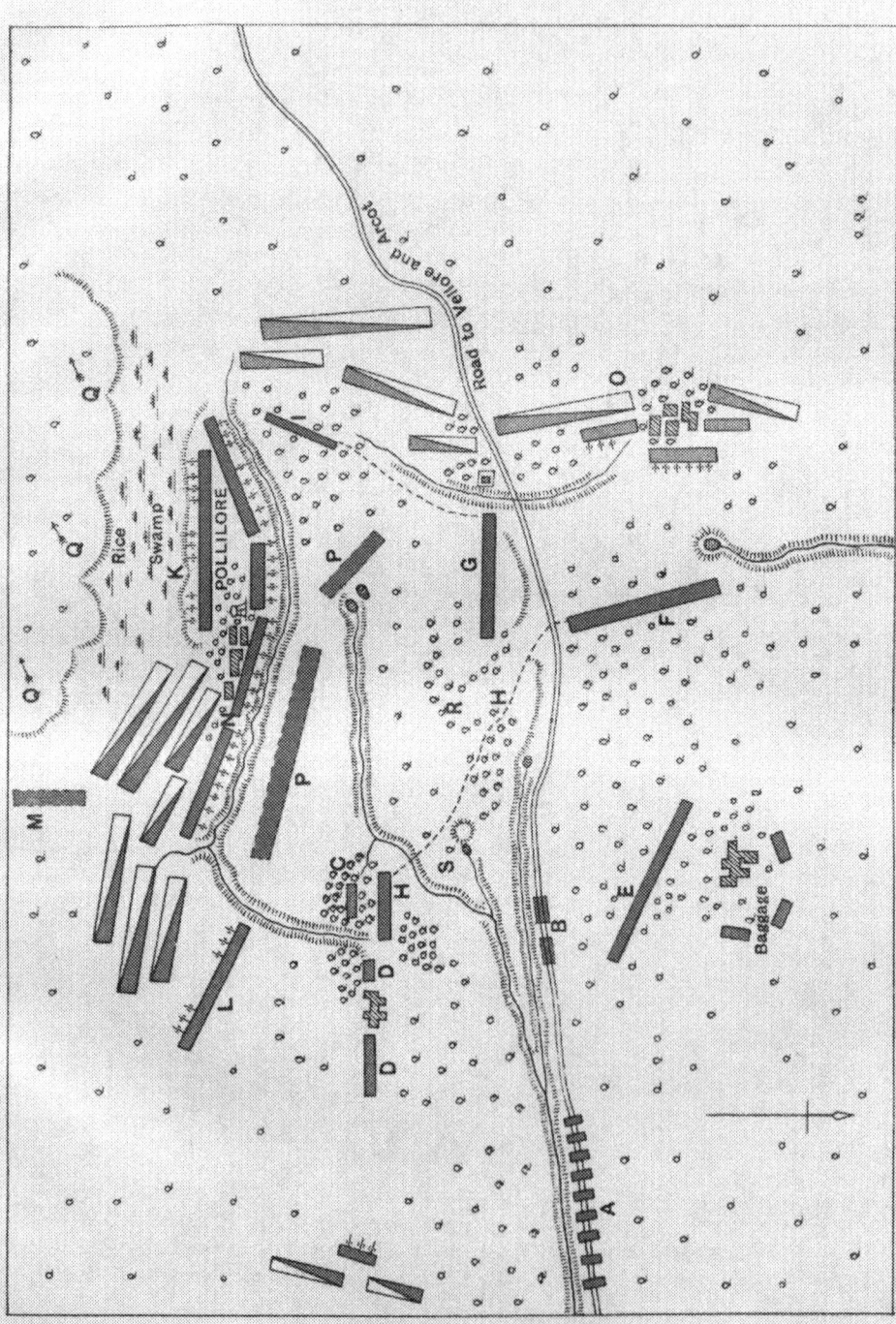

THE BATTLE OF POLLILORE.

REFERENCES.

A English Army on the march in the morning.
B Advanced Guard when fired upon.
C The Tope. occupied by the Advanced Guard.
D Col. Pearse's First Position.
E First Line First Position.
F do   Second Position.
G First Line Third Position.
H Col. Owen's march to the left.
I 2nd Bde. advances on Pollilore.
K First Line Cannonading the fugitives
L Col. Pearse's First advance.
M Col. Pearse in pursuit of the enemy and his Camp that night.
N Hyder's Position.
O Tippoo's Corps.
P English Camp that night.
Q Flying enemy.
R Place where Col. Baillie was defeated.
S Tree where Sir Eyre Coote reconnoitred the Enemy.

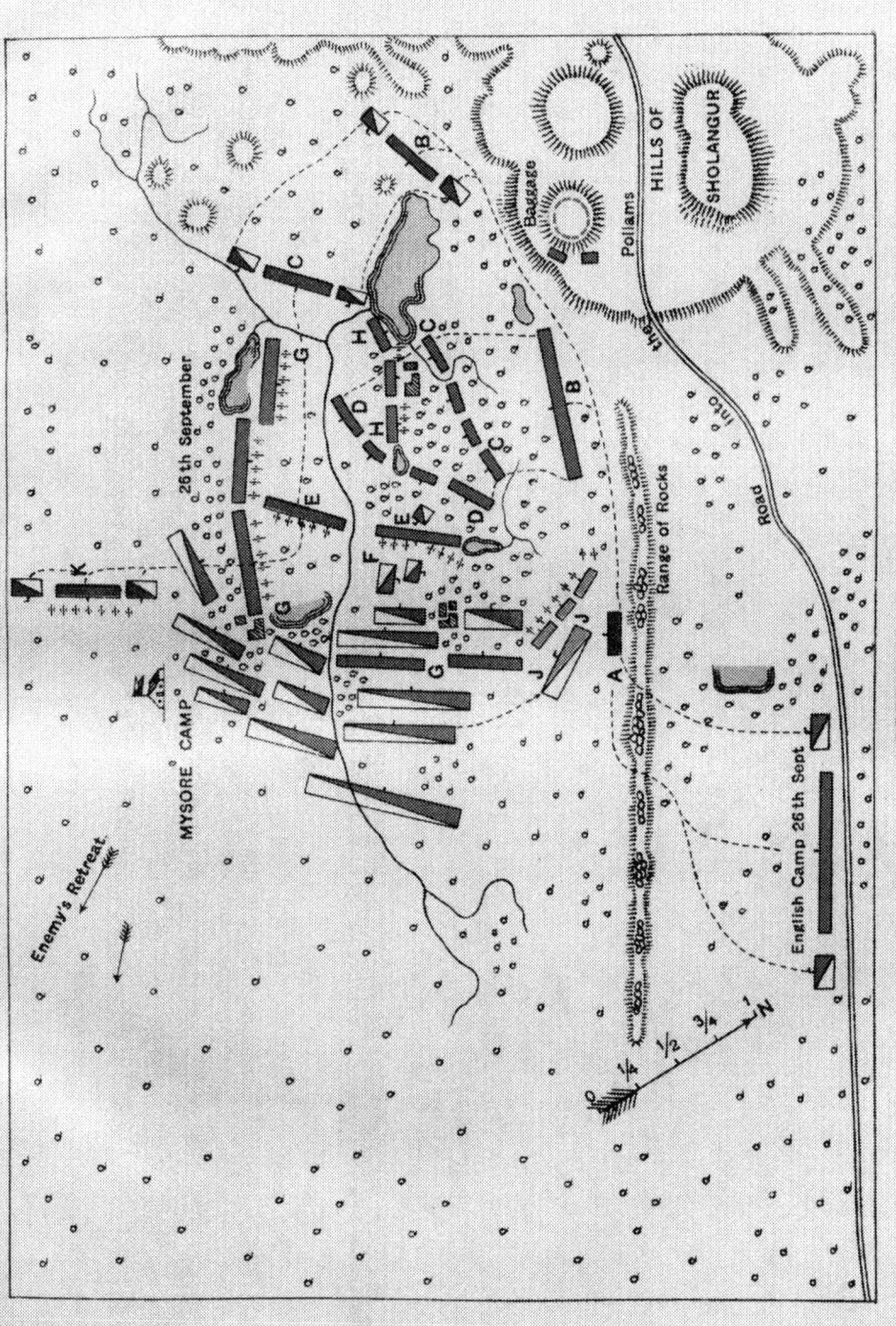

THE BATTLE OF SHOLANGUR.

REFERENCES.

A Route and position taken by 2nd Bde. in morning.
B First position of Army formed for action.
C Second position of line advancing irregularly.
D Third position of line advancing.
E Fourth and last position, with.
F Enemy's Cavalry charging.
G Enemy's Grand line of Infantry.
H Advanced Corps of Enemy who began attack.
J Tippoo's corps charging line and cannonading left flank and baggage.
K 2nd Brigade cannonading retreating Enemy at sunset.

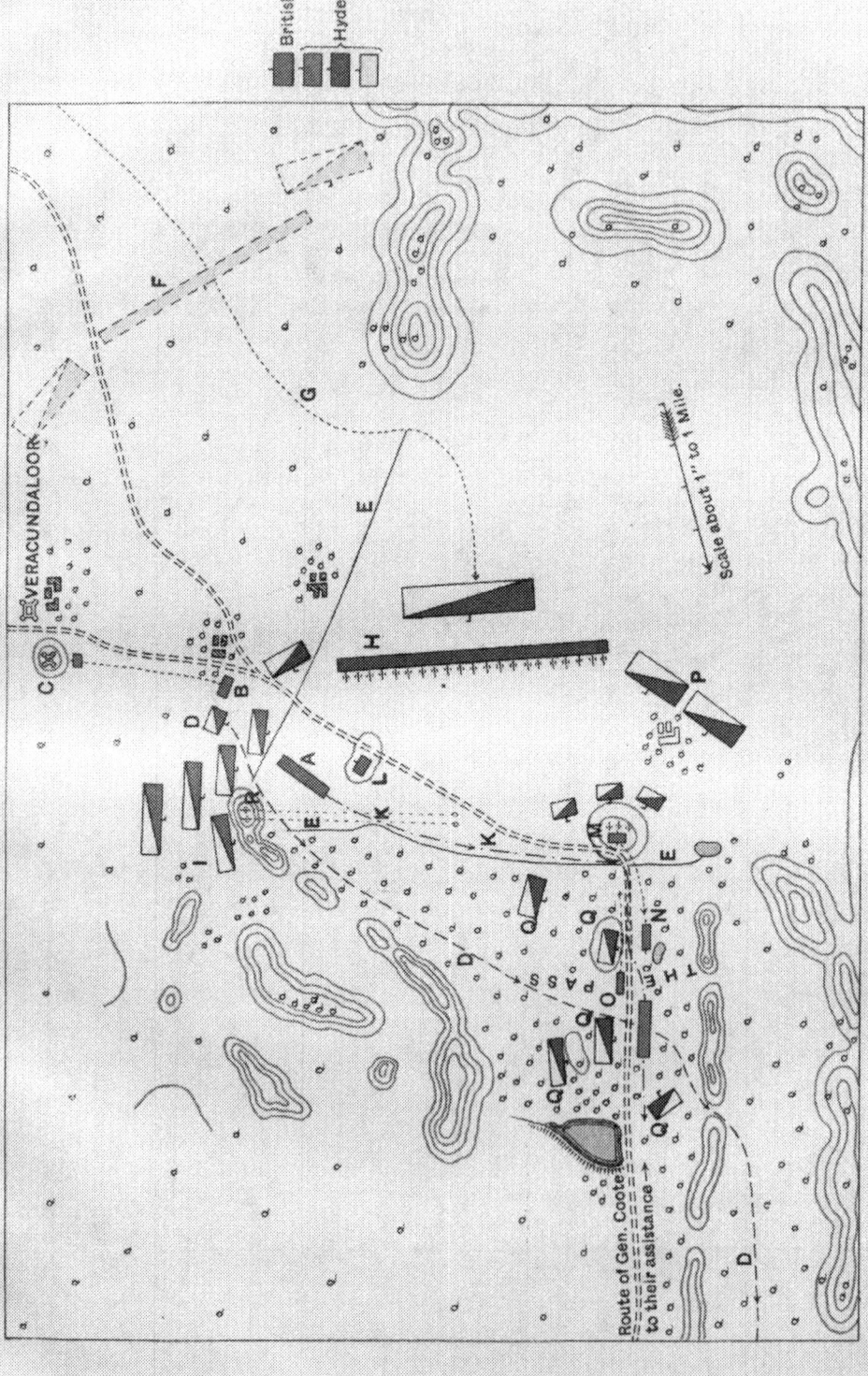

ROUGH SKETCH OF THE ENGAGEMENT AT THE PASS OF VERACUNDALOOR.

REFERENCES.

A Encampment of the Detachment.
B Picquet, with one Company on.
C A little Fort on a Rock.
D Cavalry, ordered to retire early, as being too few to be of Service.
E Broken down walls of loose Stones.
F First appearance of Enemy, whence they advanced rapidly by G to H
I Enemy's Cavalry advancing to plunder baggage.
K Our march towards the Pass.
L Battalion formed to cover the rear.
M Bn. and Guns posted to defend the Pass.
N The same Bn. retreating, abandoning one gun.
O Eur. Grenrs. and 21st Bn. going back to retake gun.
P Large bodies of Horse charging line & impeding retreat.
Q Parties of Horse that entered the Pass by another route and attacked briskly on all sides.
R Two guns of the enemy that enfiladed the line of March.

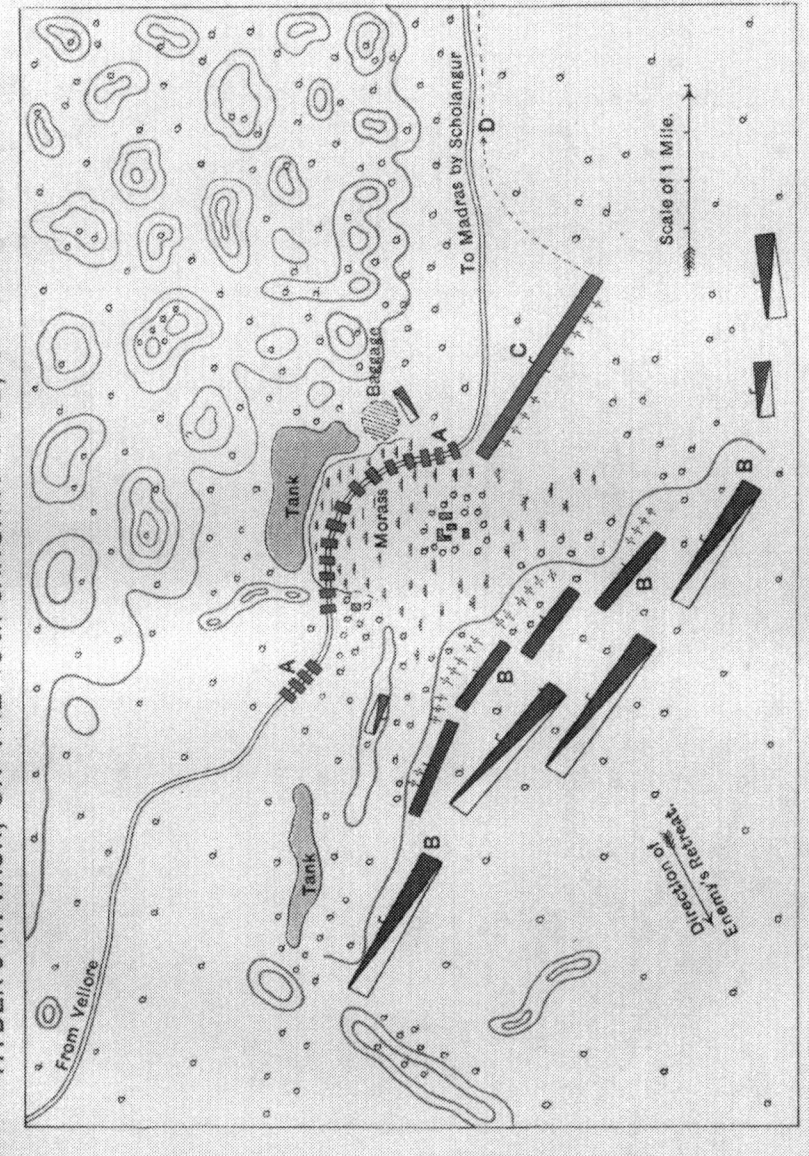

HYDER'S ATTACK, ON THE 13th JANUARY 1782, ON SIR EYRE COOTE.

REFERENCES.

A Entangled position of the British troops upon their march when first attacked in the morass.
B Position of the Enemy's line and Guns.
C The British formed in order of battle, after crossing the morass.
D The British Army continues the route to Madras.

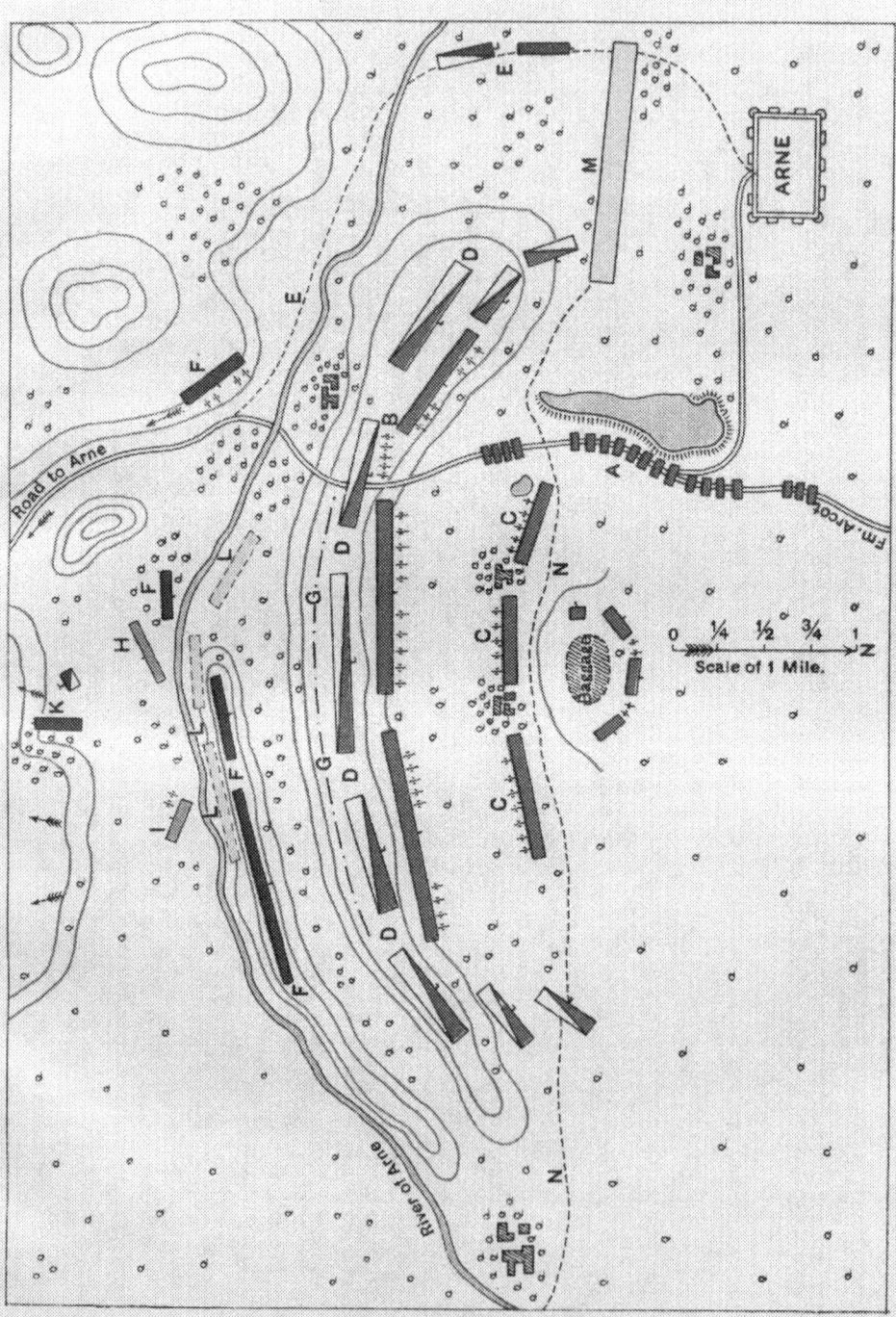

THE BATTLE OF ARNE.

REFERENCES.

A The British Army upon its march.
B First guns opened upon our rear.
C Retrograde motion of the Army in forming the line.
D Advance and order of battle of the enemy.
E Succour thrown into Arne during the action.
F Rally of the enemy to renew the Cannonade on
G The British line halted until the Baggage came up.
H The Grenrs. and 73rd Regt. in rapid pursuit of the enemy, take 7 tumbrils in the river, while at
I A Battn. of Bengal Sepoys seizes a gun in the river, both afterwards Cannonading.
K The Battn. which had abandoned them.
L Halt of the Army.
M Camp before Arne after the battle.
N Route back to Madras.

⟵ Retreat of the enemy.

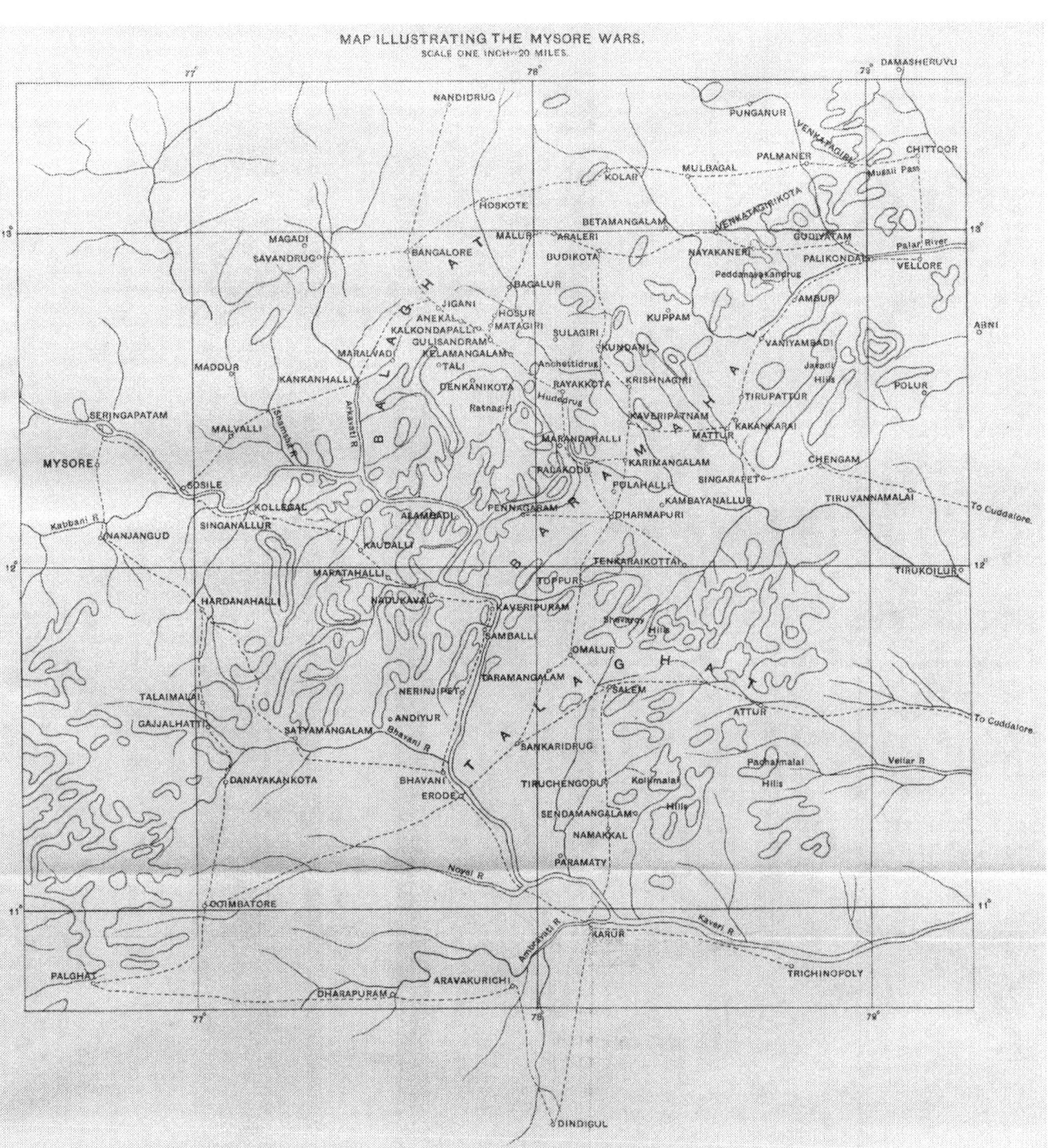

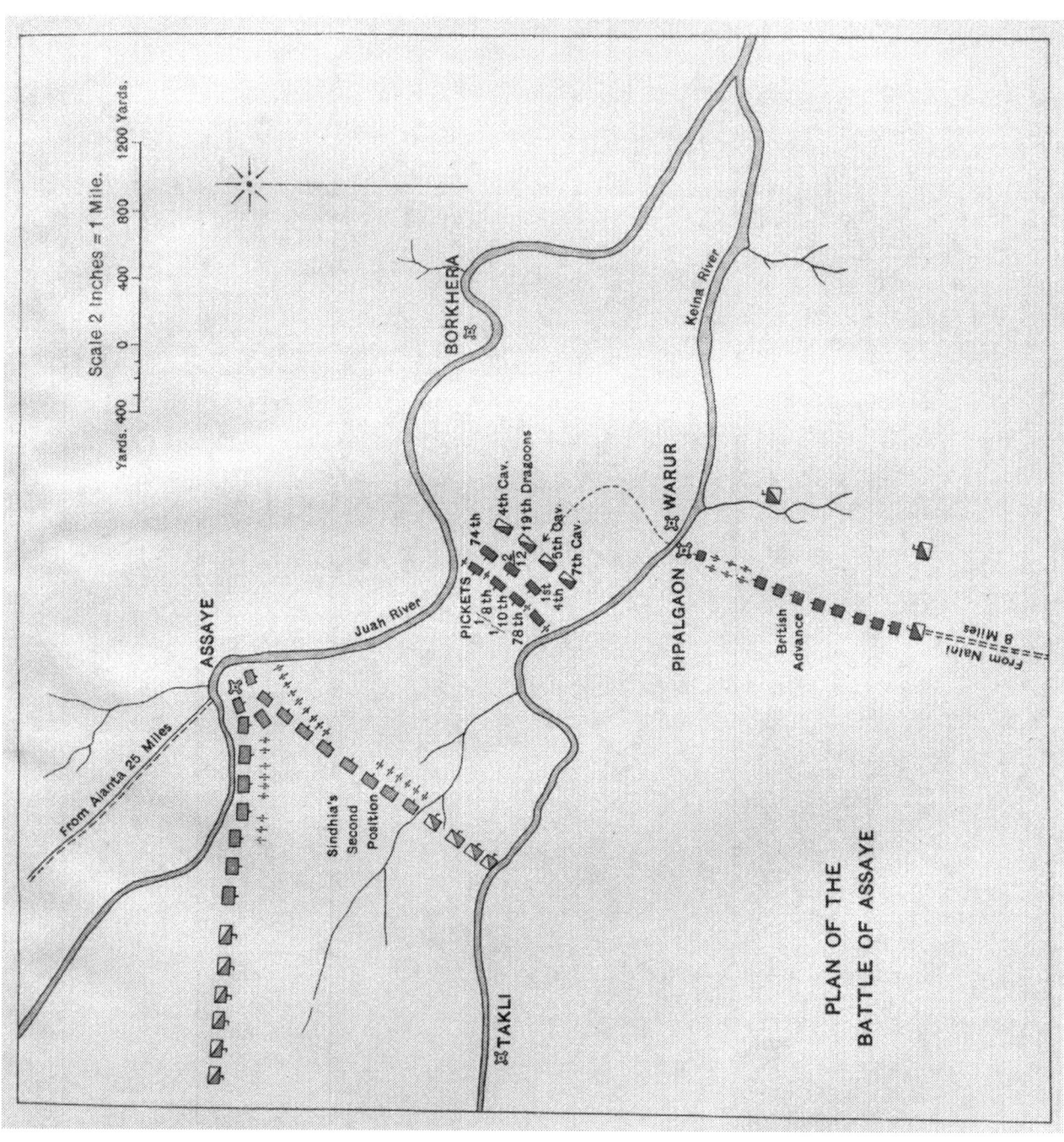

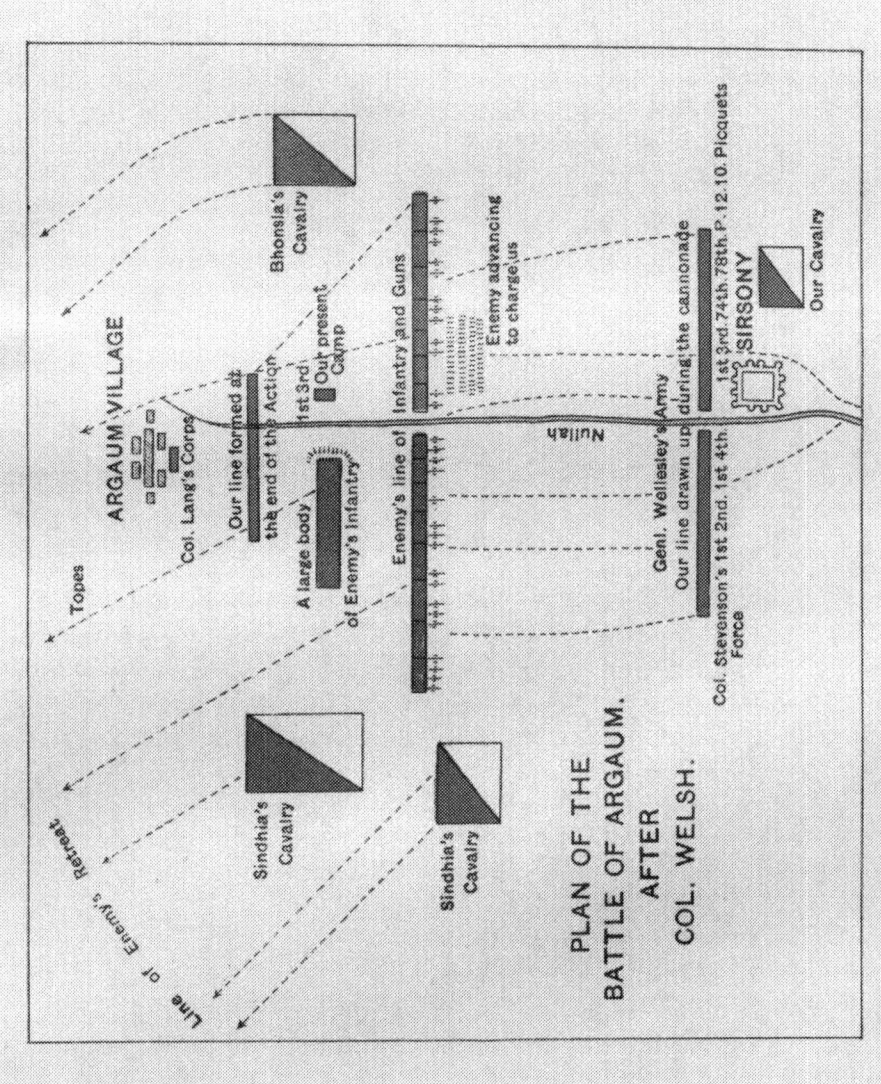

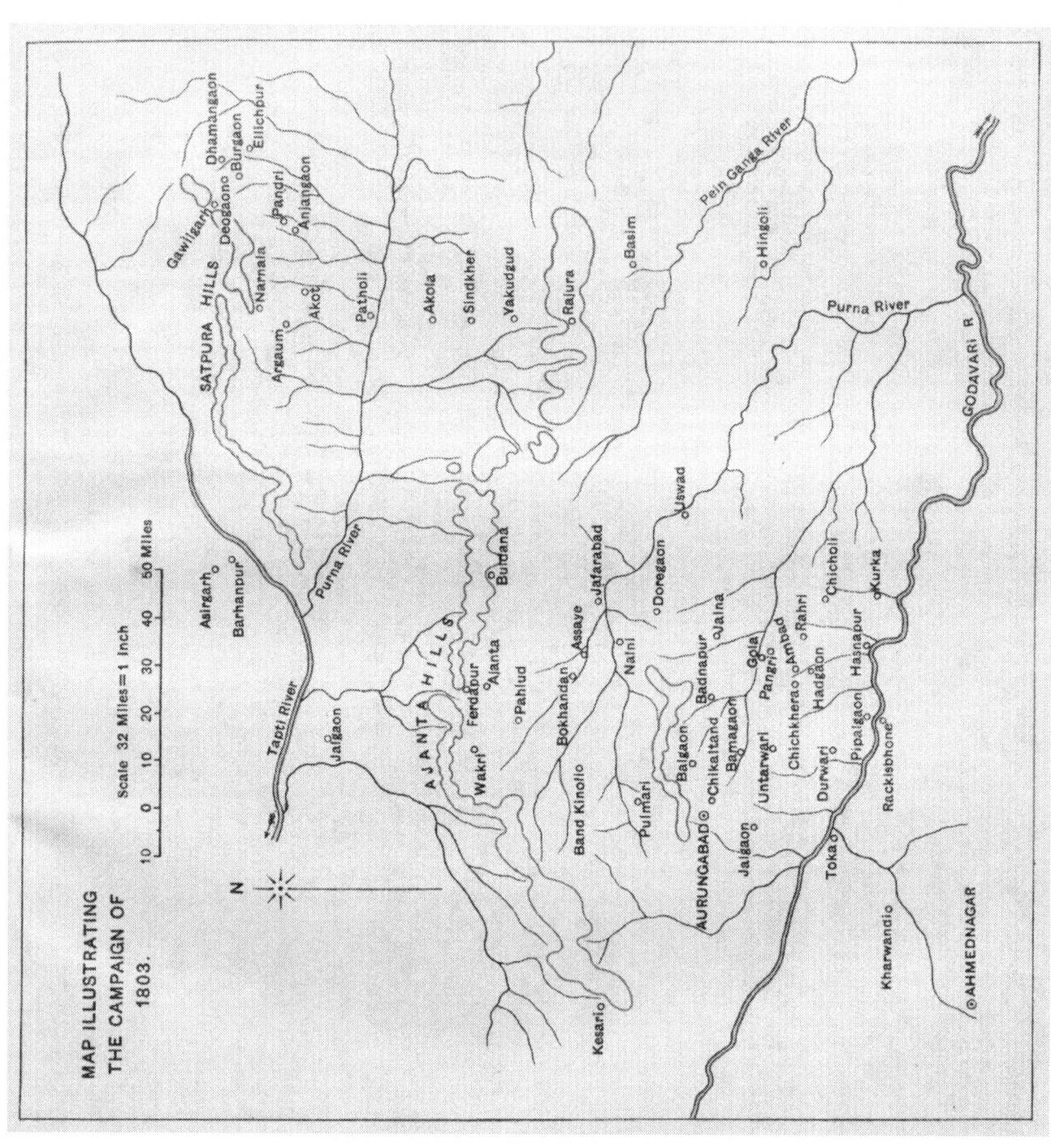

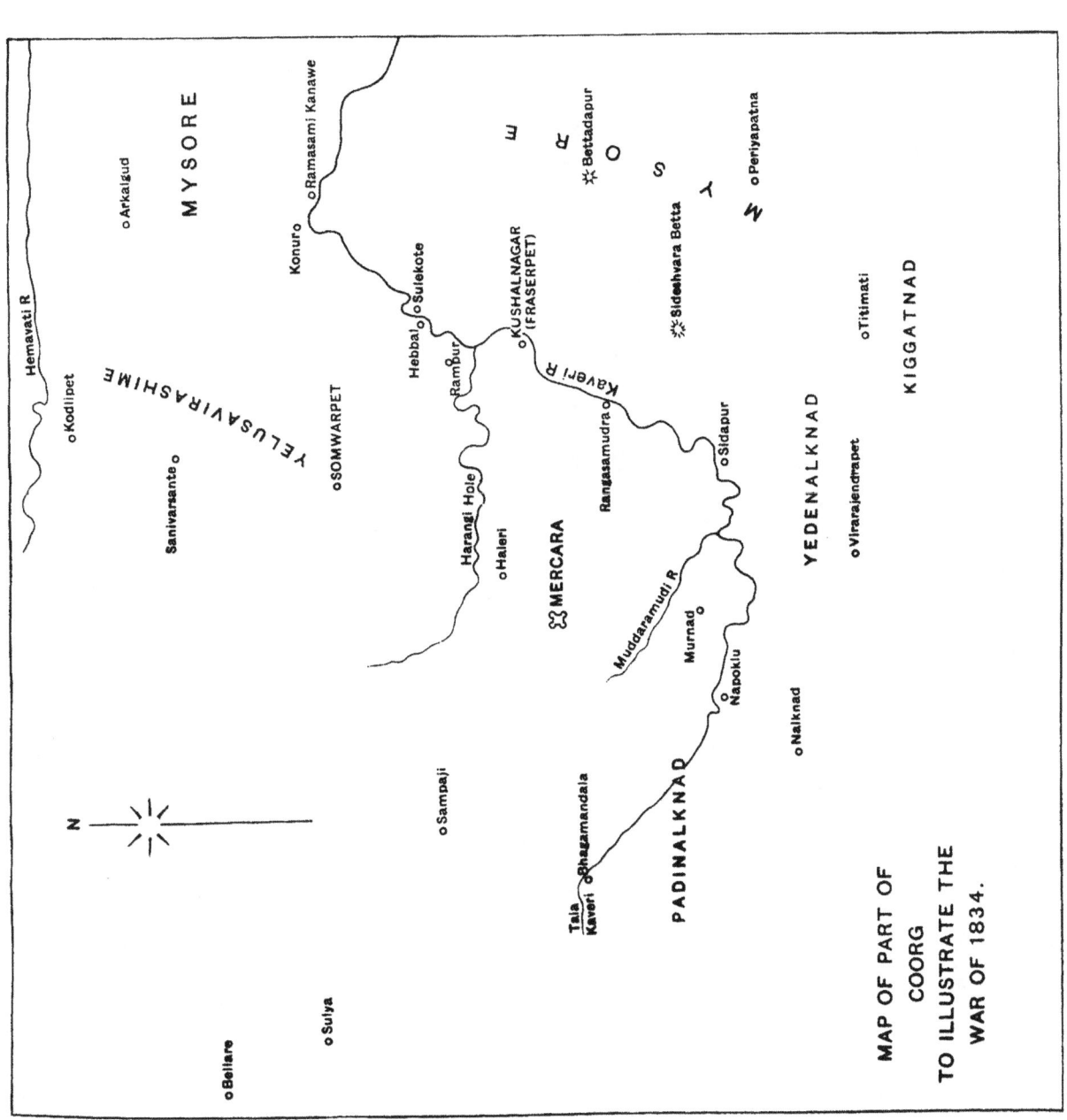

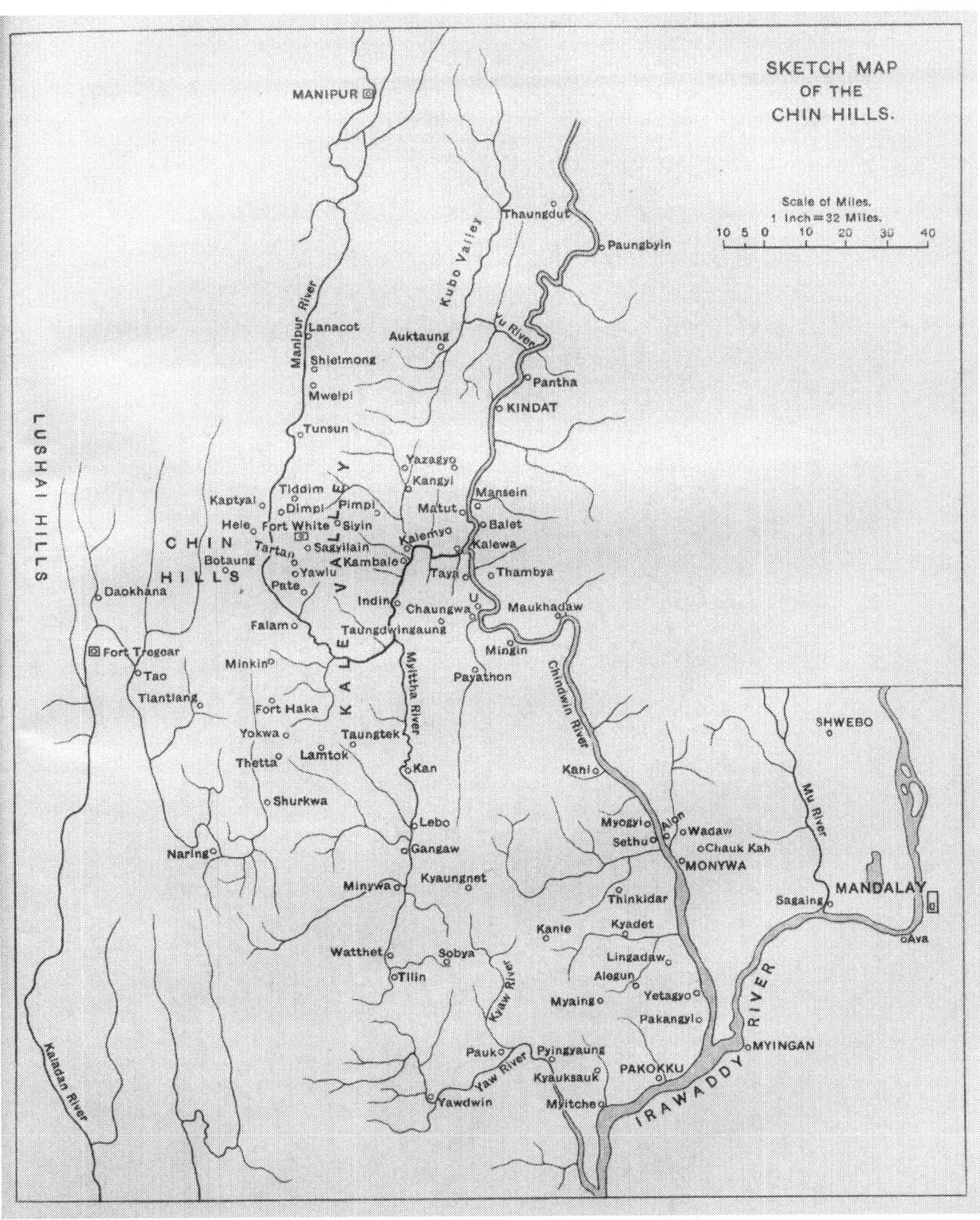

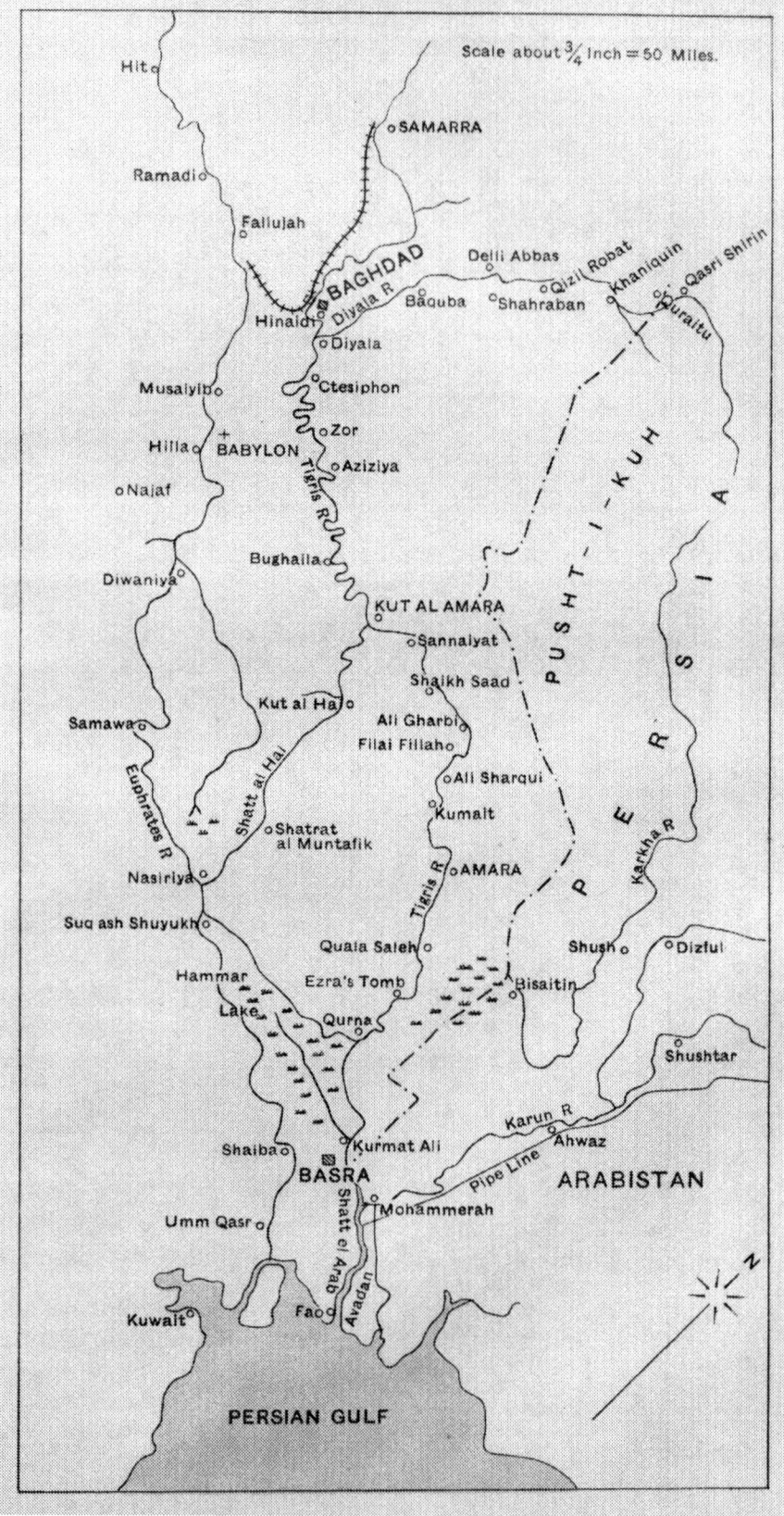

MAP OF COUNTRY BETWEEN SHAIKH SAAD AND SHUMRAN BEND.

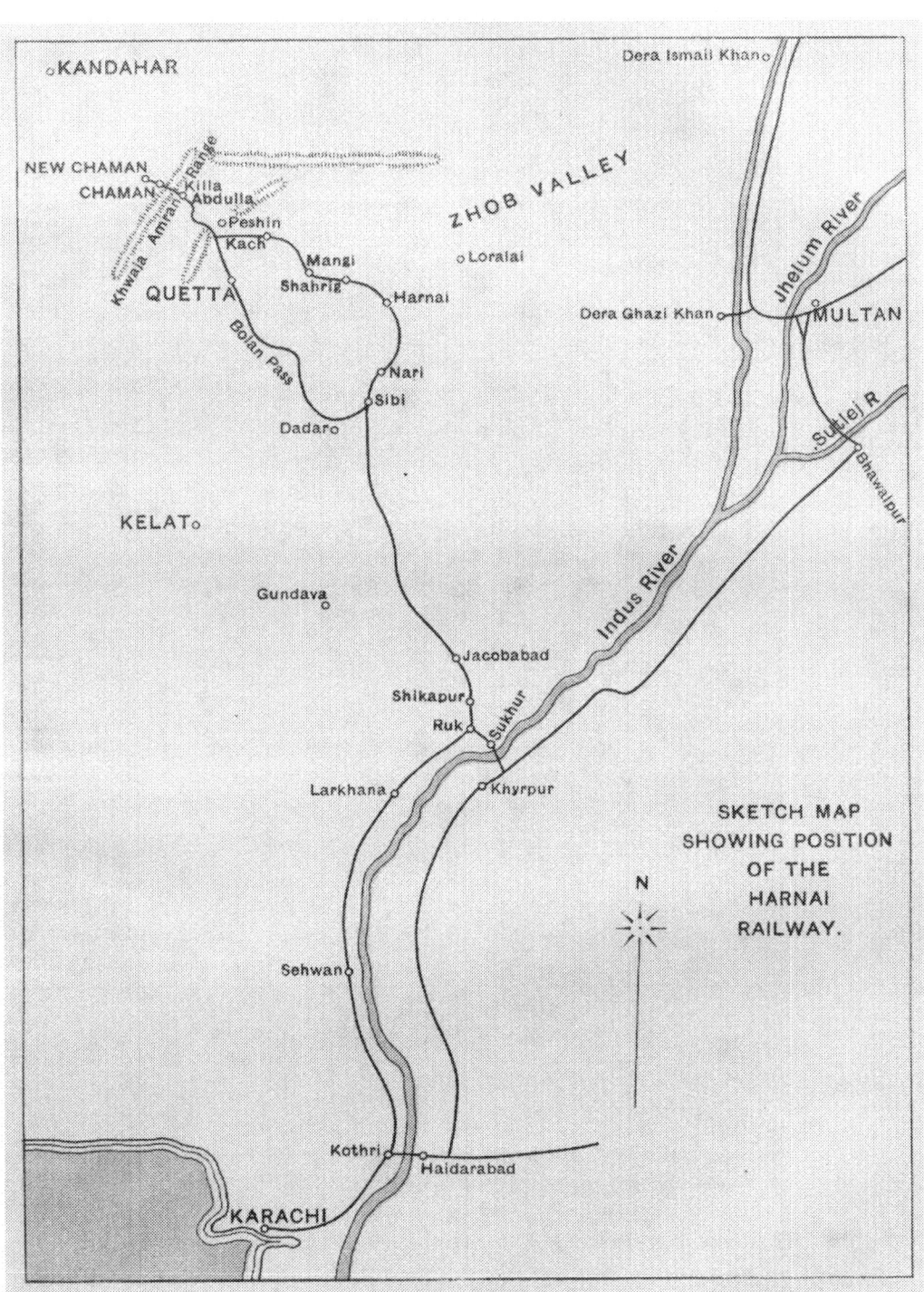

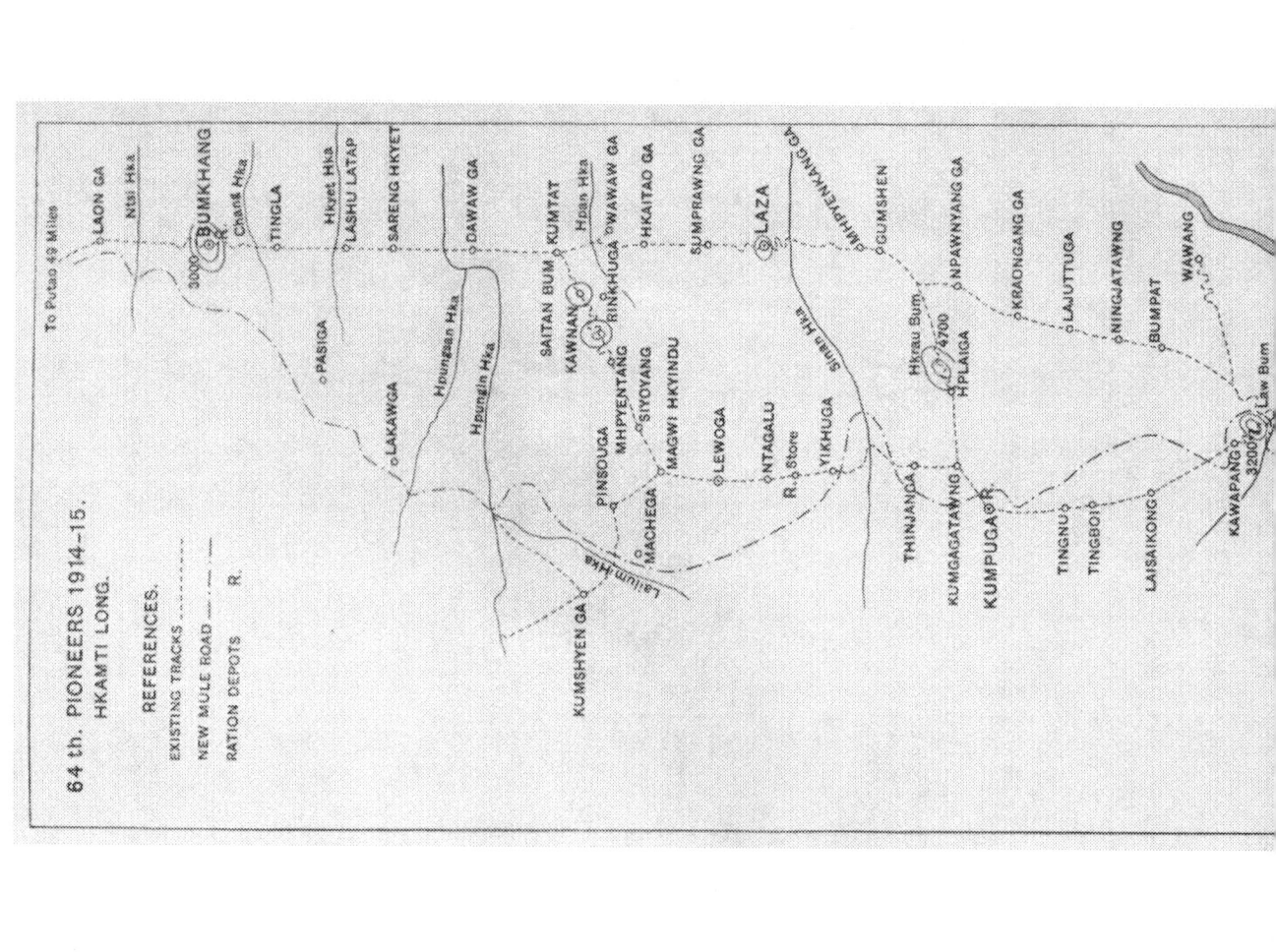

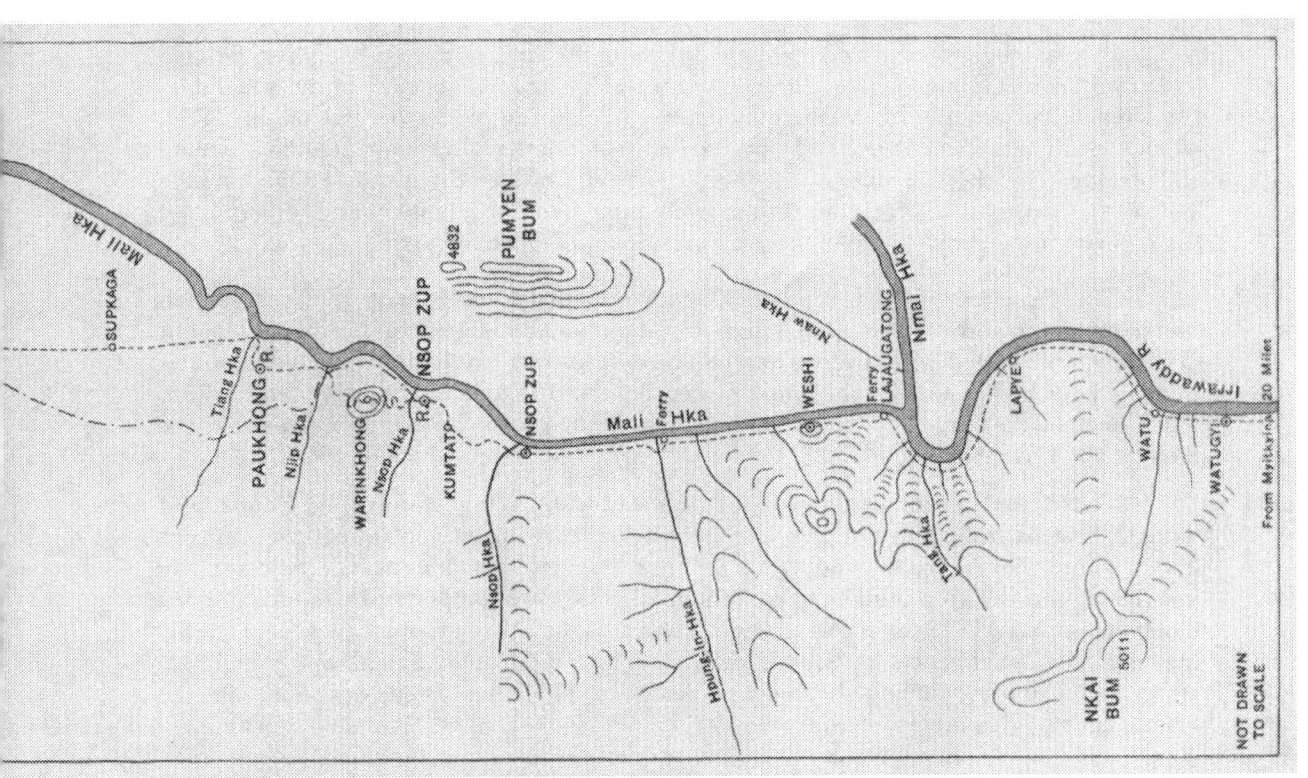

Introductory Note.

In 1744, war having been declared between England and France, the British, who had been established on the Coast of Coromandel, since 1639, found themselves unsupplied with any means of defence and, in September 1746, the town of Madras fell an easy prey to a French force under La Bourdonnais despatched from Pondicherry. The Government of Madras, thus left with only Fort St. David to represent the possessions of the Company in the Carnatic, hastily began to raise troops, and thus commenced the history of the Madras Army.

1746.

It may be noted that, though this was the first effort made by the British to form into disciplined bodies the raw material which was so abundantly available, the French had already made a commencement some few years before as, in 1739, when Pondicherry was threatened by the Mahrattas, the Governor, Dumas, armed and trained in the European manner some four or five thousand Muhammadans and, in the words of Fortescue, "thus was conceived, in danger and emergency, the embryo, now grown to such mighty manhood, of a Sepoy Army."

The first parties of sepoys raised were formed into irregular bodies, each under the command of a native chief of its own, which were entirely without discipline and armed with almost every weapon known to history. The composition of these bodies was of the most mixed description and it was not until 1758, when men were urgently required, that it occurred to Government to enlist the men of the Carnatic.

These early representatives of the Madras Army were called Peons, and were at first of little use, but, as the result of careful selection of the officers under whom they were placed, and constant service in the field, they rapidly improved, and Major Stringer Lawrence, who had been appointed Commander-in-Chief in January 1748, testified to their good conduct throughout the severe fighting against the French at Cuddalore in 1748, and round Trichinopoly in 1753, while their devotion during the siege of Arcot in 1751 has been described in the vivid pages of Macaulay.

In 1756, when Calcutta had been taken by the Nawab, the Madras Government, which had sent all the troops who could possibly be spared to assist the Government of Bengal, found itself faced with a war against the French, and without troops to meet the emergency. Fort St. David was captured on the 2nd June 1758, and the French then advanced to besiege Madras, which had been restored to the British in 1749, by the Treaty of Aix-la-Chapelle.

1756.

In August 1758, the Sepoys were formed into regular companies of 100 men each, with a due proportion of Native Officers, Havildars and Naicks, and, on the 4th December of that year, it was resolved by Government that these independent companies (which were known by the names of their Native Commandants) should be formed into four battalions, with an European subaltern

1758.

to each, and a captain to command the whole. Two battalions are shown as forming part of the garrison of Fort St. George on the 18th December, but without any remark to show how they were officered, and the following entry, from the diary of the siege of Madras, dated the 12th January 1759, appears to show that it was from that date that these battalions were definitely formed, and placed under the command of a British Officer:—

1759.

"It being found impracticable to maintain that Order and regularity amongst the Sepoys under their own Commandants as the Nature of the Service requires, and as there is reason to believe they may be made more usefull by being put under the command of a Carefull European Officer, Lieutenant Charles Todd is therefore appointed to that Command."

Part I.

CHAPTER I.

THE 5th BATTALION COAST SEPOYS.

September 1759—15th June 1769.

Affairs in the Carnatic.
1748—1759.

Before commencing the records of the regiment it would appear necessary to give a short account of the political situation in the Carnatic. The following two genealogical tables will make it easier to understand the relationships of the various persons who claimed to be Nawab of the Carnatic or Subadar of the Dekkan.

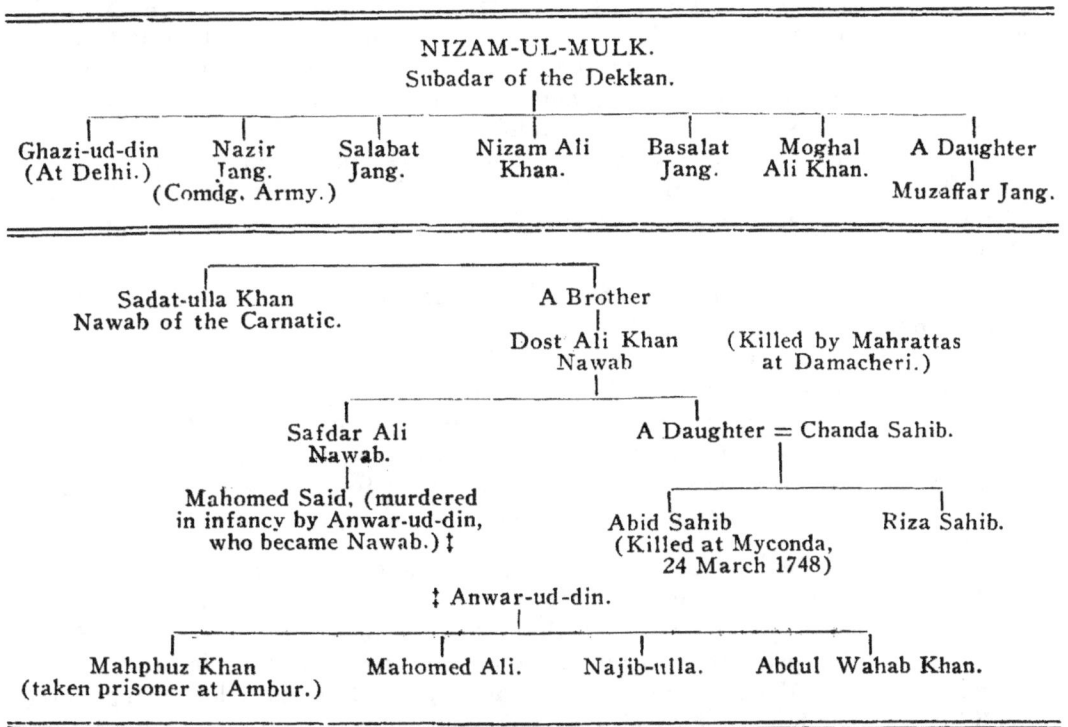

On the 24th March 1748, Nizam-ul-Mulk, who held the Subadarship of the Dekkan under the King of Delhi, died, and the succession was claimed by Muzaffar Jang (otherwise called Hidayat Mohiyuddin). His cause was espoused by Chanda Sahib (Husain Dost Khan), a claimant to the Nawabship of the Carnatic, who, obtaining from M. Dupleix, head of the French settlements in the Carnatic, the assistance of some French troops under M. D'Auteuil, defeated and slew Anwar-ud-Din at the battle of Ambur on the 23rd July 1749. Mahomed Ali, son of Anwar-ud-Din, escaped and took refuge in Trichinopoly, until he was joined by Nazir Jang, who had marched from the north, and Major Stringer Lawrence with a British detachment of 600 men. The rival forces were about to fight when a mutiny amongst his French officers compelled Muzaffar Jang to throw himself upon the mercy of Nazir Jang, and his army dispersed, whilst Chanda Sahib retreated with the French to Pondicherry.

In 1750, the French under M. Bussy* defeated Mahomed Ali, whom the British, disgusted with his prevarications, had abandoned, and captured the fortress of Gingee. On the 5th December, Nazir Jang was slain near Gingee, and Muzaffar Jang was proclaimed Subadar of the Dekkan, whereupon Mohamed Ali fled to Trichinopoly. In January 1751, a conspiracy in his army caused the death of Muzaffar Jang, and Salabat Jang was elevated in his place. In February, Trichinopoly was closely besieged by Chanda Sahib, and the siege was only raised by the capture, and historical defence, of Arcot by Captain Clive, and with the assistance of 1,000 Mahratta horsemen sent by Morari Rao.

In February 1752, induced by the promises of Mahomed Ali, Nanjaraj, the Dewan of Mysore, arrived at Trichinopoly from Seringapatam, and was followed by Morari Rao from Gooty, and the Rajah of Tanjore. On the 15th March, Stringer Lawrence arrived from England, as the first Commander-in-Chief in India, and superseded Clive, who had just inflicted a severe defeat on the enemy. A detachment under Clive defeated and captured D'Auteuil, and Chanda Sahib, deserted by his followers, surrendered himself to Monaji, the Tanjore General, by whom he was treacherously murdered. The French army then surrendered to Lawrence.

Dupleix now conferred the office of Nawab on Riza Sahib and prepared to support him with troops, but the French were completely defeated by Lawrence at Bahur, and shortly afterwards Clive reduced the French garrisons at Covelong and Chingleput, but was then compelled by ill-health to return to England. Meanwhile Mahomed Ali and Nanjaraj had fallen out, and the latter was attacked, on the 23rd December 1752, by Captain Dalton, who was commanding at Trichinopoly, but after a temporary success the latter was forced to withdraw, and by March 1753 Trichinopoly was completely blockaded.

While these events were passing, Salabat Jang had, with the permission of the Moghal, entered Aurungabad in October 1752, and procured the death of his brother Ghazi-ud-din, by poison. Dupleix, finding that the appointment of Riza Sahib had not been productive of any advantage, transferred the office of Nawab to Murtaza Khan of Vellore, and early in January 1753, prepared a strong force, which included the horsemen of Morari Rao, to wage war against the British and Mahomed Ali.

Space will not permit of even a brief resumé of the struggle for Trichinopoly, which lasted for the next two years, and which covered the name of Stringer Lawrence with glory. On one occasion (26th June 1753), with only 1,000 men, he won a brilliant victory over 30,000 French and Mysoreans, which showed the quality of the material from which the Madras Army was subsequently to be formed.

In January 1755, a treaty was concluded between Mr. Saunders (Governor of Madras, 1750-55) and M. Godeheu, who had superseded Dupleix on the

---

* Charles Joseph Palissier, Marquis de Bussy Castelnau (1718-85). He was absent from India between 1760 and 1782, when he returned, and died at Pondicherry in 1785.

2nd August 1754. Nanjaraj refused to be bound by this treaty and continued to make efforts against Trichinopoly, but was compelled to withdraw by the advance on Mysore of Salabat Jang's army. He returned too late to avert the capitulation of Seringapatam, from which Salabat Jang withdrew, after exacting his arrears of revenue as Subadar of the Dekkan.

In 1756, war was once more declared against the French, but nothing of importance occurred in the South during this year, the British reinforcements intended for the Carnatic being diverted to Bengal, owing to the loss of Calcutta, and the dreadful massacre of the Black Hole.

In the meantime, Mahphuz Khan, the elder brother of Mahomed Ali, who had been living at Fort St. David under the protection of the British, compromised with Mahomed Ali for the Government of Madura and Tinnevelly. Haidar Ali was now (1757) making himself felt as the chief power in Mysore, and Mahphuz Khan displayed his French sympathies by soliciting his aid to expel the British from those provinces. Haidar accordingly marched South, but was completely defeated at the Nattam Pass by Mahomed Yusuf, Commandant of the English Sepoys, who were marching from Trichinopoly to Madura. In this year, Salabat Jang, whose authority was upheld by a French detachment under Bussy, succeeded in counteracting the intrigues of his brothers Basalat Jang and Nizam Ali, and the latter was compelled to flee to Burhanpur.

In 1758, the position of affairs was most serious for the British on the Coast. Not only were all the brothers of Mahomed Ali—Mahphuz Khan, Najib-ulla, and Abdul Wahab Khan—conspiring against the British, but on the 28th April, Lally arrived from France with a powerful force, and the danger of the position was quickly shown by the fall of Fort St. David on the 2nd June. Lally next turned his attention to Tanjore, but the descent of a British squadron on Karikal, after a favourable action with the French squadron, caused him speedily to retreat to Pondicherry. On the 12th December, he moved against Madras, and opened the siege of Fort St. George on the 17th but, owing to scarcity of supplies, and the operations of small bodies of troops on his lines of communications, he was obliged to raise the siege on the 17th February 1759.

Meanwhile a force sent from Bengal into the Northern Circars, under Colonel Forde, had captured Masulipatam, by a brilliant feat of arms, on the 7th April 1758, and compelled Salabat Jang to make a treaty by which the French were to be expelled from the Dekkan. This treaty was, however, vitiated by subsequent disagreements. The French now once more changed their policy, and Lally appointed Riza Sahib to be Nawab of the Carnatic.

When Colonel Lawrence, whose health had again become impaired, proceeded to England in 1759, Major Brereton succeeded him and carried out his operations with considerable skill, but in September failed with great loss to capture Wandiwash.

This brings us up to the date when the regiment was raised, and it is hoped that enough has been written to furnish a key to the succeeding narrative.

1759.

The Formation of the Battalion.

When the siege of Fort St. George was raised, on the 17th February 1759, Government once more turned its attention to the condition of its Sepoys, and three members of the Select Committee—Major Stringer Lawrence, Charles Bourchier and John Pybus—drew up a scheme, which was sanctioned in September 1759, for the formation of a sepoy force of 7,000 men, organised in seven battalions, and disposed as follows:—

Madras	.. 2 Battalions.
Trichinopoly	.. 2 Battalions.
Conjeeveram	.. 2 Battalions.
Chingleput	.. 1 Battalion.

Two battalions being already in existence, five battalions were formed at once, in compliance with this order, and it is with the third of these, that is to say, the 5th Battalion (which later became the 4th) that we have now to deal. Other battalions were raised shortly afterwards, and by February 1767, the number had risen to sixteen.

The 5th Battalion of Coast Sepoys, thus raised, in accordance with the orders of Government, in September 1759, was probably one of the two battalions raised for service at Trichinopoly, in view of the fact that it is shortly afterwards found stationed at that place. As first raised, the battalion was composed of nine companies, each 115 strong, and including one Grenadier Company.

As regards the officer by whom the battalion was raised, it might be supposed that it was Captain Baillie, from the fact that the old name of the regiment, by which it is still known to old sepoys, is "*Baillie-Ki-Paltan.*" It appears, however, from the records, that Lieutenant William Baillie only transferred from H. M. 89th Highland Regiment to the Company's service in 1764, on the departure to England of the King's troops serving in Madras, and as, further, it is known that the Officer Commanding the battalion in the earlier campaigns of 1761-64 was Captain George Airey, an officer who entered the Company's service as an Ensign on the 26th March 1754, it seems highly probable that the latter officer originally raised the battalion.

The name "*Baillie-Ki-Paltan*" probably arose from the fact that that officer commanded the battalion from 1765 to 1771, which was a long period for those times, and the association of his name with the regiment was no doubt confirmed by the melancholy disaster with which his name was connected in later years.

1759-61.

Coote's Campaign in the Carnatic.

Immediately after the formation of the six battalions of which the establishment was now composed, the army was ordered into the field to take part in the operations against the French. Whilst there had been no time for them to be properly drilled and disciplined and they consequently played but a minor part in this campaign, it would not seem proper to omit all mention of events at which the new battalions were present, even though it be not possible to trace the movements of any individual corps.

Colonel Coote, who had been appointed to the command of the army in the Carnatic, arrived at Madras on the 27th October 1759, and joined the troops, who were in cantonments for the rains at Conjeeveram, on the 21st November. His arrival at once put a better complexion on the state of affairs. On the 25th November, he marched towards Arcot, with a view to deceiving the French as to his intentions, while on the same day he detached Major Brereton towards Wandiwash. Brereton captured the petta at Wandiwash by assault on the 27th November, and Coote, who had seen nothing of the enemy in the neighbourhood of Arcot, made a forced march and joined Brereton on the 28th. On the 30th, the fort was delivered up without the necessity of assaulting it, the casualties of the British during the short siege only amounting to 5 men wounded.

Capture of Wandiwash and Karunguli.

As the French, who were at Settupati, had made no attempt to interfere with his movements, Coote next resolved to attack Karunguli, another strong fort, which was commanded by Colonel O'Kenelly, an Irishman in Lally's regiment. On the 4th December, the petta was occupied, and Coote opened fire on the fort on the 6th. On the 10th, the garrison surrendered, the French marching out with their arms, whilst the sepoys were disarmed and set free. The British loss was only one officer and three men killed.

The loss of these places showed Lally the necessity of concentrating his forces and accordingly he called in all his detachments and assembled his army at Arcot. Early in January 1760, Coote also arrived in the neighbourhood of Arcot, and both sides occupied themselves for some time in bidding against each other for the services of Morari Rao who, with a horde of Mahratta horsemen, was ravaging the whole country.* In this competition the French were successful, and the Mahrattas, to the number of about 3,000, joined the French camp.

On the 10th January 1760, Lally marched from Arcot and moved in the direction of Tiruvattur but, halting before he reached that place, he made a sudden

---

* These freebooters were conducting their operations with so much success that cattle were sold at the time at the rate of seven or eight for a rupee!

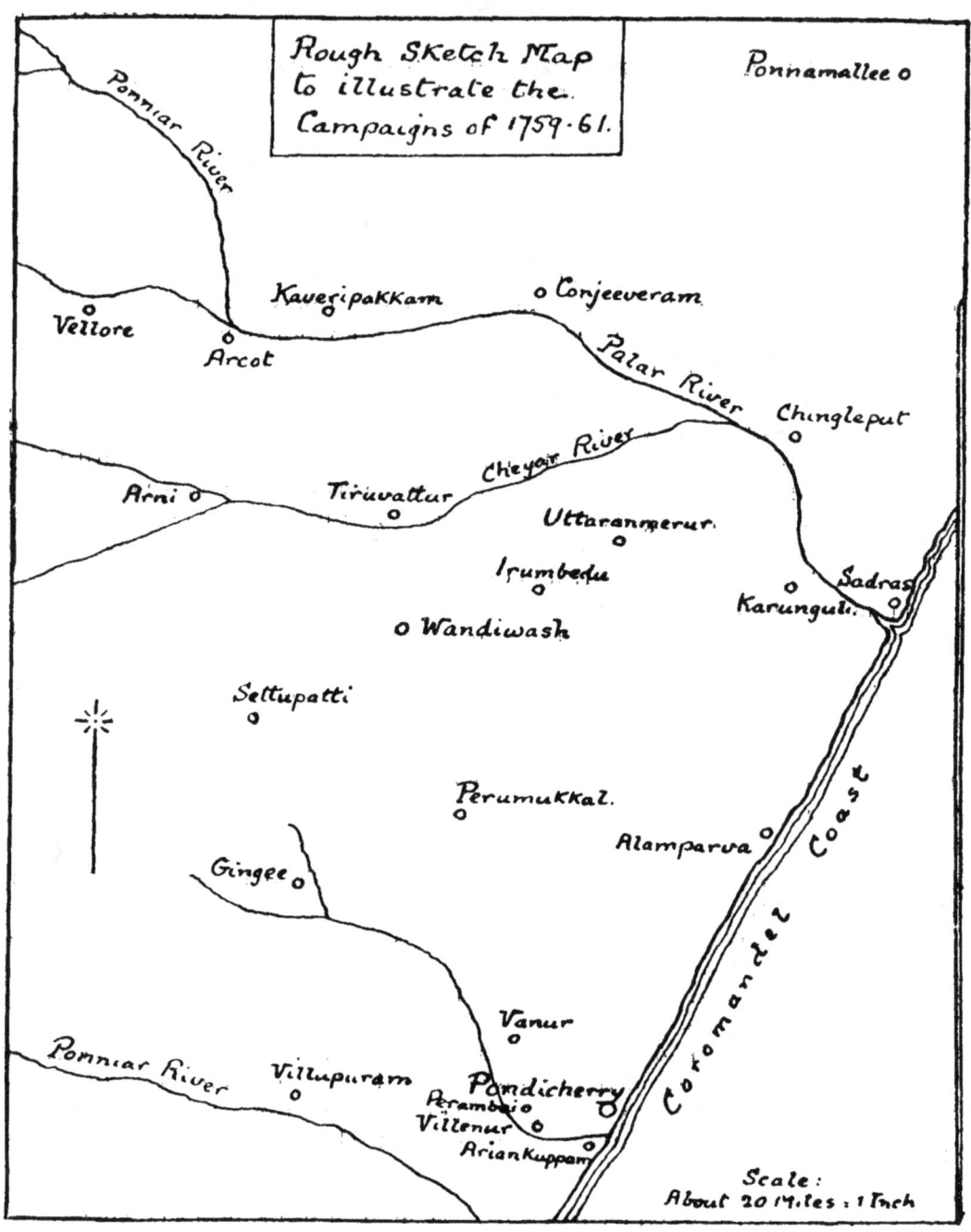

dash on Conjeeveram, hoping to seize large supplies for his army. Being disappointed, however, in this expectation, he marched to Tiruvattur, where he arrived on the 13th January:

Meanwhile Coote, on observing Lally's movements from Arcot, sent his baggage to Kaveripakkam on the 11th January, and marched some distance along the Palar river, but, on receiving the news of Lally's advance on Conjeeveram, he hastened to that place, where he arrived on the 13th January after the French had withdrawn to Tiruvattur.

On arrival at Tiruvattur, Lally, contrary to—or perhaps because of—the advice of Bussy, with whom he was on very bad terms, decided to keep the attention of the British Commander occupied with part of his army while he attempted to capture Wandiwash with the remainder. He marched, therefore, with a detachment on the 14th January, leaving Bussy with the main body at Tiruvattur, and reached Wandiwash on the same day, where he at once occupied the petta and began to prepare batteries to reduce the fort.

On the 15th January, Coote moved from Conjeeveram towards Wandiwash and camped at Uttaranmerur on the 17th. His intention was to wait until Lally was committed to the siege, so that he could have his choice of attacking either the troops employed on the siege or the covering force. Bussy saw through this design but his advice to Lally to desist from the siege and keep his force together was in vain. On the 17th January, Lally heard of Coote's movements from Bussy, but would not at first believe him. Eventually, however, he gave Bussy a free hand, and the latter at once joined him before Wandiwash. Batteries were opened against the fort on the 20th January, and on the 21st, Coote marched from Uttaranmerur with his cavalry to make a reconnaissance. On learning from Captain Sherlocke, commanding at Wandiwash, that the main rampart was breached, he ordered his infantry to march at once, sending the baggage to Karunguli, and his force was assembled at Irumbedu, 7 miles from Wandiwash, on the night of the 21st.

Battle of Wandiwash 22nd January 1760. At sunrise on the 22nd, Coote marched on Wandiwash, and soon came in touch with the enemy's cavalry, who were quickly driven off, mainly by a detachment of sepoys. Coote then proceeded to form up his army. This consisted of 1,900 Europeans, of whom 80 were cavalry, 2,100 Sepoys, 1,250 Native cavalry, and 26 field pieces, and was formed up in three lines. In the first line were Coote's and Draper's Regiments and the Company's two European battalions, with 1,800 Sepoys equally divided on either flank of the Europeans; in the 2nd line were the 300 grenadiers of the army, with 200 Sepoys on either flank; and in the 3rd line were all the cavalry. Lally's force consisted of 2,200 Europeans and 10,300 Sepoys.

It is not intended to give here a detailed account of the brilliant and decisive victory which Coote now proceeded to gain over the combined forces of Lally and Bussy. The brunt of the fighting passed entirely between the Europeans of both armies, and after the cannonade commenced the native troops took no part in the battle. When it was over, Orme tells us that " the Commandants of the English

Sepoys complimenting Colonel Coote on his victory thanked him for the sight of such a battle as they had never seen."

Twenty-four pieces of cannon were taken, besides large quantities of ammunition and stores, and the French lost 200 Europeans killed, besides 160 taken prisoner. Amongst the latter was Bussy who, on being led to the second line, asked who the troops he saw were. " On being answered 200 grenadiers, the best men in the army, who had not fired a shot; he clasped his hands in surprize and admiration, and said not a word." He was permitted by Coote to proceed to Pondicherry on parole.

In the British army 63 Europeans were killed and 124 wounded, while the Sepoys had only 22 killed and 47 wounded, and those mostly in the cavalry. In Madras the victory caused " joy almost equal to that of Calcutta on the victory of Plassey."

From Wandiwash, the French fled through Settupatti to Gingee, and shortly afterwards retreated to Pondicherry. This town was first occupied by the French, under François Martin, in 1674. It was taken by the Dutch in 1693, but restored to France in 1697 by the Treaty of Ryswick, when Martin was again sent out as Governor. He died in 1706, and after a period of misfortunes, the trade of Pondicherry revived about 1725, under Beauvallier de Courchant. Joseph François Dupleix (1679-1754) was at Chandernagore in 1730, and Pondicherry was governed in succession by Lenoir and Dumas, but Dupleix succeeded the latter in 1741. It was unsuccessfully besieged by the British, under Admiral Boscawen, in 1748.

Coote, who had to await the arrival of his baggage, marched to Settupatti, which surrendered to him on the 29th January 1760, and on the 5th February, commenced the siege of Arcot, which fell on the 10th. On the 29th February, Tiruvannamalai capitulated to a detachment under Captain Stephen Smith, and Coote marched to Perumukkal ("Permacoil") which, after an unsuccessful assault had been made, surrendered on the 4th March. On this occasion the Sepoys, who lost 40 killed and 70 wounded, displayed great resolution. "These troops," says Orme, "had never behaved so well." On the 7th March, Coote reconnoitred the outskirts of Pondicherry, and on the 12th, received the surrender of the fort of Alamparva.

Further Successes.

On the 4th April, Villupuram was taken by a detachment of Sepoys under Captain Wood, and on the 5th, Karikal surrendered to an expedition sent by sea under the command of Major Monson, who was temporarily in command owing to Coote's illness. The Nawab of Arcot, who had been escorted from Trichinopoly by Captain Joseph Smith, was present with Major Monson. On the 16th April, Vanur ("Valdore") surrendered to Coote, who had resumed command of the main army, and on the 19th Chillambaram fell to Monson, who joined Coote on the 3rd May.

Haidar Ali joins the French.
Lally now sent to solicit the aid of Haidar Ali, who ordered Makhdum Ali, then engaged in the conquest of the Baramahal, to proceed to Pondicherry, and that chief accordingly marched to Tayaga-durgam, which with Gingee was the sole place of importance left to the French in the province of Arcot, and thence to Pondicherry, where a treaty was ratified with the French on the 27th June 1760. This alliance came as a great surprise to the Madras Government, and the surprise was not rendered any more agreeable by what followed.

On the 17th July, a force under Major Moore, which had been detached by Coote to oppose Makhdum Ali, fell in with the whole Mysore army near Tiruvadi, and was completely routed, the remnants of the force taking refuge in the fort at Tiruvadi. This disaster was counterbalanced by Coote's capture of the fort of Villenur, just as Lally was marching out from Pondicherry to relieve it. The Sepoys behaved very well on this occasion. Orme says that of all his successes Coote deemed this the most fortunate, because least expected—

"When the English colours were raised on the rampart......the change was received with the curses of every man in the French army. All the line stopped involuntarily and at once, stricken by horror; and Mr. Lally, more confounded than any, immediately ordered the whole to retreat under the guns of Ariancopang."

On the 31st July, Coote was reinforced by 600 men from England, which brought his force up to a strength of 2,000 Europeans and 6,000 Sepoys, and in August he settled down in a position between Perambai and Villenur.

Blockade of Pondicherry.
The "bound-hedge" of Pondicherry, enclosing an area of about seven square miles, extended in a curve of fifteen miles round the town, and was strengthened by four large redoubts, called respectively, from north to south, Madras, Valdore, Villenur and Ariankuppam (or "Ariancopang"). Coote decided that before attacking these defences it was necessary first to capture the fort of Ariankuppam, which was separated from Pondicherry by the river, and, to assist this project, a force of 400 marines was landed at Cuddalore from the fleet on the 27th August. The plan was abandoned owing to the protests of Major Monson, but Lally heard of the intention and resolved to surprise the British camp. The attempt was made on the 4th September, but failed with considerable loss to the French, M. D'Auteuil being among the prisoners.

News now arrived from England that Major Monson had been appointed Lieutenant-Colonel, with prior date to Colonel Coote, so the latter went to Madras, intending to return to Bengal.

On the 8th September, Monson attacked the Valdore and Villenur redoubts, and both were taken, with a loss of 115 Europeans killed and wounded, the Sepoys having very few casualties. Monson had his leg broken during the attack. The attack on the Villenur redoubt, which was held by the regiments of Lovaine and Lally with ten pieces of cannon, was entirely composed of Company's troops, and was commanded by Joseph Smith, now a Major, and senior officer of the Company's troops on the Coast, of whom Orme says, " wherever he commanded, affection to the man conspired with duty to the officer." An attempt made by the French on the following day to re-capture the redoubts was nearly successful, Monson's successor, Major Robert Gordon, being an officer " whose talents were inadequate to the general command." On the 13th September, the French withdrew from the Ariankuppam redoubt, after partially blowing it up.

Coote resumes Command. Colonel Coote, who had not yet left Madras, now consented to resume the command, and rejoined the camp on the 20th September 1760. On the 1st October, the Madras redoubt, the last of the four still in the hands of the French, was taken by Coote and Joseph Smith. The French re-captured it the same night but " Subahdar Coven Naig " formed up the Sepoys who had been driven out, and re-took it with great gallantry soon afterwards.

In October, Coote allowed the French to send their women and children to the Dutch and Danish settlements. Little was done during this and the succeeding month, owing to heavy rain. On the 27th November, Lally turned all the natives out of Pondicherry, to the number of 1,400. Coote refused to let them through his lines, and they remained between the two forces for eight days, without other food than the roots of grass, when Coote, seeing that Lally was inflexible, let them go.

Throughout December, a cannonade had been kept up against the walls, chiefly with the object of wearing down the garrison, which was reduced to a pound of rice a day for each man, with meat only very occasionally. Heavy rain frequently interrupted the bombardment, and on the 30th December, a storm of great violence wreaked destruction among the ships of the fleet, and caused great damage on shore. The fleet was, however, able to resume the blockade before Lally could obtain any supplies from outside.

On the 5th January 1761, a redoubt called St. Thomas, erected by Lally opposite that of Ariankuppam, was captured, but lost again on the 6th. The Governor of Madras, Mr. Pigot, arrived on the 9th, and by this time the Nawab, by a promise of 20 lakhs of rupees, had succeeded in winning over the Mahrattas, with whom Lally was negotiating, thus depriving the French of their last hope of assistance from outside.

Fall of Pondicherry. On the 10th January, fresh batteries were opened, and trenches were commenced on the 13th. On the 16th, Lally surrendered, and the garrison of 1,100, who showed strong evidences of their privations, laid down their arms. The British flag was hoisted on Pondicherry on the following day, under a salute of 1,000 guns. Great quantities of arms and ammunition were taken, besides 500 pieces of cannon and 100 " mortars and howits." Lally* was sent off to Madras, his departure being witnessed by his officers, who took the opportunity of displaying the hatred they felt for him—

> "A hue was set up by the whole assembly, hisses, pointing, threats, and every abusive name; but the escort prevented violence."

Dubois, Commissary of the French King, was less fortunate. On meeting with a similar reception, he challenged his detractors—

> "One Defer stepped out, they drew, and the second pass laid Dubois dead. who was 60 years of age, short-sighted, and always wore spectacles. No one would assist his servants to remove and bury the corpse."

The fortifications of Pondicherry were demolished and orders were given for the reduction of the remaining French settlements in India. On the 4th February, Tayaga-durgam capitulated to Major Preston, and on the 9th Mahé fell to Major Hector Munro, while the surrender of Gingee to Captain Stephen Smith on the 5th April "left not a single ensign of the French nation avowed by the authority of its Government in any part of India."

As we have seen, the new Sepoy battalions had behaved very well during this campaign and, whether actively engaged or not, they were present at many brilliant demonstrations of how war should be conducted—a lesson by which they were not slow to profit in later years. Towards the end of 1761, the gradual growth of discipline began to become evident and, animated by the example of their officers, they grew more confident, and were soon able to take their place in the ranks with the Europeans.

---

* The fall of Pondicherry marked the close of a remarkable career. On his return to France the public indignation against Lally resulted in a trial for high treason. With his usual indiscretion and intemperance he treated his judge with haughtiness and contempt. After a trial lasting 18 months he was moved to the Bastille. "Here in the morning of the 9th May 1766, his sentence was read to him; he threw up his hands to heaven, and exclaimed, Is this the reward of 45 years service? and snatching a pair of compasses, which lay with maps on his table, struck it to his breast, but it did not pierce to his heart; he then gave loose to every execration against his judges and accusers. His scaffold was prepared, and his execution appointed for the same afternoon: to prevent him from speaking to the spectators, a large gag was put into his mouth before he was taken out of prison, when he was carried in a common cart, and beheaded on the Greve. He perished in the 65th year of his age"

It may not be generally known that this celebrated French General, Thomas Arthur, Count Lally de Tollendal (1700-1766), was an Irishman, being a son of Sir Gerard O'Lally of Tullindally near Tuam. I have seen an account of him which states that his name was merely a corruption of "O'Mullaly," but I believe this to be incorrect. He distinguished himself greatly at the battle of Fontenoy.

1761.

Capture of Vellore.

The first occasion on which we find the 5th Battalion of Coast Sepoys mentioned by name as taking part in operations in the field, was in 1761, when six companies of the regiment, 601 strong, were employed with the force sent against Vellore in that year.

On the fall of Pondicherry, on the 16th January 1761, the Government of Madras applied to the Nawab of the Carnatic for 50 lakhs of rupees, to meet the expenses of the campaign. The Nawab, himself in equal difficulties, was unable to pay this amount, but requested that assistance might be given to him to force certain of his tributaries to discharge the arrears of revenue which he stated were due to him. To this the Madras Government agreed, and began to make preparations accordingly.

In September 1761, a force was assembled at Arcot, under the command of Colonel John Caillaud, who in the previous year had been commanding the army in Bengal, and with 2nd Captain Smith* in command of the native troops. The force advanced on Vellore, where it arrived on the 28th September, and waited for stores. Negotiations were opened with the Killadar, Mortiz Ali Khan, but no settlement could be arrived at, and the Killadar withdrew to the Fort on the 12th October.

On the 13th October, the batteries opened fire at a distance of 400 yards, and the trenches were commenced. On the 16th, the wall was breached and a sap run up to the ditch in order to fill it in, this operation entailing a loss of 2 officers and 20 men wounded. On the same day, the Killadar's family was captured while trying to escape from the fort. Operations in the ditch were continued from the 17th to the 20th October, and on the 22nd, the petta was stormed and captured with little resistance. It was then discovered that the chief obstacle to taking the fort was the breadth and depth of the ditch and a successful attempt was made to drain it partially, the water having been lowered a foot by the 17th November.

---

* *2nd Captain Smith.*—When the five fresh battalions were raised in 1759, the seven battalions then existing were each placed under the command of a Subaltern, and three Captains were appointed over the whole—one to reside at Madras, one in the field, and one at Trichinopoly. In accordance with this order, Captain Charles Tod (or Todd) (who had raised the first two battalions) was placed in command at Madras; Captain Stephen Smith was appointed Second Captain; and Captain Richard Smith was given the command at Trichinopoly. From this it seems clear that the 2nd Captain Smith mentioned above was Stephen Smith. Richard Smith, originally a Purser's mate, became a Captain and A.D.C. to Stringer Lawrence in 1758, and a Major in 1762.

On the 16th November, Captain Leigh, the only Engineer officer, was killed, but Major Call arrived on the 4th December, and two others on the 10th. The enemy had meanwhile destroyed the gallery which had been constructed over the ditch, but on the 4th December, the Killadar expressed a desire to come to terms, and on the 11th, he determined to give up the fort to the Nawab, and sent Vakils to Arcot. The attack was, however, carried on, and it was decided to fill in the ditch uncovered, a passage to the foot of the breach being completed by the 24th December. On the 26th, the Killadar gave in and surrendered, and the operations were concluded.

I have not been able to discover what the casualties of the regiment were.

In November 1761, Major-General Lawrence returned from England, and resumed the Command-in-Chief of the Army.

1762.

Early in 1762, the force under Colonel Caillaud moved against Nellore and in February, captured the fort. No returns have been found, but presumably the same six companies of the 5th Battalion were engaged in this operation.

The request of the Nawab having thus been complied with, the districts of Vellore and Nellore were handed over to him, and a division was made of the revenue between him and the Company.

In June 1762, news arrived in Madras that war had been declared against Spain, and on the 1st August following, a force was despatched against Manilla which included a party of 650 sepoys made up from different battalions. On the departure of this expedition, the 5th Battalion was detailed to form part of the garrison of Trichinopoly, where 500 of the 1,100 French prisoners then in the hands of the British were confined.

About the end of this year, Mahomed Yusuf Khan, renter of Madura and Tinnevelly, broke out in open rebellion, but no steps were taken against him until the following year.

1763—1764.
The Campaign against Mahomed Yusuf.

Before entering on an account of the campaign against Mahomed Yusuf it will be as well to trace a rough outline of the previous history and services of that remarkable man, who gave the Madras Government such cause for anxiety during the next two years.

Mahomed Yusuf Khan first took service with the British in 1752, when he enlisted under Clive. During 1754 and 1755, he frequently distinguished himself and in Orme's History his services in escorting convoys to Trichinopoly in the former year are thus referred to:

> "In this service they were much assisted by the activity and vigilance of Mohomed Issoof, an excellent partizan whose merit had raised him from a Captain of a Company, to be Commander-in-Chief of all the sepoys in the English service, into which he first inlisted under Captain Clive, a little before the battle of Covrepauk (in February 1752). He was a brave and resolute man, and cool and wary in action, and capable of stratagem; he constantly procured intelligence of the enemy's motions, and having a perfect knowledge of the country, planned the marches of the convoys so well, that by constantly changing the roads, and the time of bringing the provisions out of the woods, not one of them was intercepted for three months."

In April 1754, he fell under suspicion of plotting with the Mysoreans, but succeeded in clearing his name and, consequent on a strong letter of recommendation from Major Lawrence, Government granted him a commission as Commandant of all the sepoys in the Company's service. Early in the following year he was presented with a gold medal bearing the arms of the Company on one side and on the other the following inscription:—

> "To Mahomed Isouf Cawn Behauder, Commander of the Honourable English Company's Sepoys, this medal is given by the Honorable the Governor and Council of Fort St. George as a reward to courage, and to preserve to posterity the name of a brave soldier, a skilful officer, and a faithful servant."

In 1756, Mahomed Yusuf was ordered to assist Mahfuz Khan, brother of the Nawab of the Carnatic, who was in charge of the districts of Madura and Tinnevelly, with a party of sepoys, and took part in numerous engagements with the Polygars, while in November 1757, he defeated the redoubtable Haidar Ali at the Nattam Pass. Towards the end of 1758, he was recalled to Madras and did good service in cutting up convoys on their way to Lally's camp when the latter was before Madras.

In 1759, he took part in the action at the Mount between Caillaud and Lally Tollendal on the 9th February, and also in the successful assault on Conjeeveram in the following April. In May, Government having persuaded the Nawab to allow him to rent the districts of Madura and Tinnevelly, he returned to Madura and renewed his operations against the Polygars of those districts.

In December 1760, a force under his orders drove back the Mysoreans, who had advanced from Dindigul and taken a number of forts in the neighbourhood of Madura.

In 1761 and 1762, Government again succeeded in procuring for him a further lease of the two districts from the unwilling Nawab, who looked upon Mahomed Yusuf with the greatest suspicion. As early as 1756, Captain Caillaud had expressed an opinion to the effect that Mahomed Yusuf was harbouring the design of making himself an independent ruler, but these suspicions seem to have subsequently disappeared.

In July 1762, however, a report was received from Captain Preston, who was commanding at Trichinopoly, that Mahomed Yusuf was purchasing arms in great numbers, and was making further additions to his already large force of 6,000 sepoys and 300 horse; also that some thousands of workmen were employed in strengthening the fortifications of Madura. Further, towards the end of that year news was received that Mahomed Yusuf had commenced operations against the King of Travancore, and had begun to raise additional troops in Tanjore.

On receipt of this information, Government, now thoroughly alive to the danger of permitting this display of independence, ordered Mahomed Yusuf to return to Madras at once, but instead of complying with this order, he hoisted French colours on all the forts in his possession.

This occurred in February 1763, and in June Government issued orders for a force to be assembled for the subjugation of this unruly officer.

First Siege of Madura. At the commencement of hostilities against Mahomed Yusuf the force at the disposal of that officer in Madura was estimated at 5,000 Sepoys, 7,000 Colleries, 1,700 Black Horse, 200 Europeans, 12 Field Pieces and 2 Howitzers, while he also had under his command in other places some 5,000 Sepoys and 8,000 Colleries, besides a few Horse.

The British force which assembled at Trichinopoly, under the command of Colonel Monson, was altogether 9,913 strong, including the 1st, 3rd, 4th, 5th and 9th Battalions of Coast Sepoys, of which the 5th Battalion was commanded by Captain George Airey.

On the 2nd August, Colonel Monson commenced his march, while on the 6th Major Preston, the 2nd-in-Command, who had been sent on in advance, encamped 15 miles from Madura. On the 11th, the first encounter took place with the enemy, when a reconnoitring party was driven in by a greatly superior force with a loss of 150 sepoys killed and wounded and 40 missing, and 200 stand of arms captured. The enemy also lost heavily. On the 20th, one of the outer forts was captured and on the 23rd, the rebels abandoned Tirumbur and the Vallichinattam and Onnasatram forts. On the 28th, Monson advanced from Tirumbur and found Mahomed Yusuf encamped under the walls of Madura, and about the same date Mr. West with 2,000 of the Nawab's troops occupied the Nattam Pass.

On the 2nd September, when the British force was encamped at Teppakulam in the suburbs of Madura, Monson went out in person with the European cavalry, two or three hundred black horse, a battalion of sepoys, a European picket and two guns, with a view to reconnoitring the west of the fort, but was driven in by a superior force with considerable loss, Lieutenant Stevenson being killed, Captain Donald Campbell wounded and taken prisoner, and 15 European cavalry killed and wounded.

During September, great difficulty was experienced owing to the monsoon floods but, on the 24th, fire was at last opened on the fort. However, after five days it was found that practically no impression had been made and on the 27th October, it was decided that owing to the shortage of ammunition it was useless to continue the siege. On the 3rd November, Monson reconnoitred the ditch and finally decided to raise the siege, and on the 5th, after a vain attempt at negotiation with Mahomed Yusuf, the force began to fall back on Tirumbur, about six miles East of Madura. On the 18th November, Colonel Monson went to Trichinopoly, leaving Major Preston in command.

No precise record of the casualties during these operations has so far been discovered, but they appear to have been heavy, and Vibart records that, on the 24th October alone, 84 wounded sepoys arrived in Trichinopoly.

Owing to the refusal of the 96th Regiment to march, Major Preston was compelled to remain at Tirumbur throughout the month of December, but on the 29th of that month he moved to Audakotavam near the Teppakulam.

Early in 1764, Mahomed Yusuf opened negotiations with the Government, and expressed regret for his former conduct, and on the 12th January he was offered security for his life and property on terms which included the surrender of Madura, and all other forts and arms in his possession, and payment of arrears due. These terms were refused, and operations were accordingly recommenced.

In the meantime Mahomed Yusuf repaired the fortifications of Madura, keeping 3,000 men continually at work and, by the 15th January 1764, the place was completely restored.

Second Siege of Madura. On the 26th January 1764, Major Charles Campbell, the senior officer of the Company's troops, was appointed to the command, and took over from Major Preston on the 13th February, the latter taking command of the strong fort of Sikandarmalai, some 6 miles south on the road to Tinnevelly. On the 26th February, a Monsieur Riquet, commanding the French Hussars, deserted to the British with 41 of his men.

By the 2nd March, Madura was completely invested and one or two minor forts in the neighbourhood had been captured, and shortly afterwards Captain Hart took Chinampetta by storm, with a loss of Ensign Carty killed and 15 men wounded. About the same time three Lieutenants—Hunterman, Ward and Philips—were dismissed the service for " unreasonable and unmilitary " conduct, of which we are not given the particulars.

On the 27th March, Captain Fitzgerald, whilst reconnoitring towards the Teppakulam, was charged by Mahomed Yusuf's Horse, and routed them with a loss on the British side of 5 European troopers, 10 natives and 15 horses killed and wounded.

Meanwhile Preston, who had marched towards Palamcotta on the 16th March, captured Sundavandi, and on the 5th April, reached Ganigudam, when he was ordered to return to Madura by the 20th April, leaving a detachment before Palamcotta. On his return to Madura, Campbell attacked one of the redoubts and took it with trifling loss, but was forced to abandon it as it was too near the fort to be held.

On the 29th April, at noon, five redoubts were stormed by Campbell on one side and Preston on the other, with a loss of 34 Europeans and 30 Sepoys killed and wounded. The enemy lost heavily and five guns were captured. The siege was now undertaken in earnest, and by the 10th June the batteries were ready to open on the fort.

On the 14th June, the enemy made a sally, but were repulsed with a loss of Captain Smith, Lieutenant Maitland and 4 Europeans killed, and 10 wounded. On the 16th, Lieutenant Whithear and 2 Europeans were killed and 5 wounded. On the 20th, the mines for blowing in the counterscarp of the ditch were sprung, and the fausse braye was then breached, Mr. Hamilton (Engineers) being killed on this day and Ensign Bowman wounded. It was expected that the place would be stormed on the 22nd, but the assault was postponed till the 26th, owing to heavy rain. Between the 22nd and 24th, 8 Europeans were killed and 2 officers and 13 men wounded.

Early on the morning of the 26th, the assault was delivered in three divisions, but all three attacks were repulsed with loss. The right attack was led by Major Preston, who was mortally wounded, and the left by Major Wood, while the centre, of which the 5th Battalion appears to have formed part, was presumably commanded by Major Campbell himself. The failure of the assault was due to the heavy rain of the preceding few days, which had made the ditch so wet and muddy that it was extremely difficult to cross, and in traversing it all the ammunition was rendered useless so that, though the troops pushed on and in many places succeeded in getting to the top of the tower, they only had their bayonets to depend on, which were of little use against the long pikes of the enemy who, hurling down quantities of stones, grenades and shells, had so much the advantage that it was found impossible to ascend the breach.

Besides Major Preston, the attackers lost Captain Bullock and Ensign Vashan killed, and Captains Kirkpatrick and Fitzgerald, and Lieutenants Wear, Owen, MacDonald and Bruce wounded. 150 Europeans and 50 sepoys were also killed and wounded, and many men were injured by stones.

Owing to heavy rain, it was decided not to attempt another assault, but to endeavour to reduce the place by investing it closely. On the 19th July, Lieutenant Robert Kelly took Varadagiri, which commanded several passes into Travancore. By the 5th August, the garrison of Madura was beginning to suffer from want and, in September, Mahomed Yusuf made several attempts to come to terms, but refused the conditions imposed. On the 13th October, a letter was received from Monsieur Marchand to say that he had made Mahomed Yusuf a prisoner and offering to give up the fort. Accordingly, at 6 p.m. on the 14th October, Madura was handed over and Mahomed Yusuf and his family were taken prisoners. On the day following—to the great discredit of the British—Mahomed Yusuf was hanged as a rebel by order of the Nawab. On the 18th October, Campbell set out for Palamcotta, leaving Wood in command at Madura, and on the 23rd, Palamcotta was surrendered, which closed the campaign, Campbell then returning to Madura.

It is to be regretted that the close of this campaign was sullied by the execution of a brave enemy. Recent research tends to show that Mahomed Yusuf was as much sinned against as sinning, and Colonel W. Fullarton, one of the ablest commanders the Carnatic has seen, bears witness to the excellence of his administration in these words:—

> "While he ruled those provinces his whole administration denoted vigour and effect: his justice was unquestioned—his word unalterable,—his measures were happily combined and firmly executed;—the guilty had no refuge from punishment..........On comparing the state of that country with his conduct and remarks, I found that wisdom, vigour and integrity were never more conspicuous in any person of whatever climate or complexion."

So far no casualty lists of these campaigns have come to light, so it is not possible to say what were the losses of the 5th Battalion. They must, however, from the nature of the fighting, have been considerable.

With regard to the *Colleries* mentioned above, these were of the caste now known as "Kallars," who are a caste of thieves, formerly engaged in stealing cattle. The following contemporary extracts concerning them may be of interest. Orme says:—

> "These are a people who, under several petty chiefs, inhabit the woods between Trichinopoly and Cape Comorin: their name in their own language signifies Thieves, and justly describes their general character, which however has differences in different parts of the country. Those to the north of Madura are almost savage: their weapon is a pike 18 feet long, with which they creep along the ground, and use it with great address in ambuscades; but the principal service they render to an army is by stealing or killing the horses of the enemy's camp."

He also gives the following amusing illustration of their character:—

> "When booty is the object, they regard danger and death with indifference, of which the English officers themselves saw a very striking example, whilst they were besieging the French and Chundasaheb in Seringapatam. Of the party of Colleries employed at that time by the English to steal the enemy's horses, two brothers were taken up and convicted of having stolen, at different times, all the horses belonging to Major Lawrence and Captain Clive; the prisoners did not deny the fact; but being told that they were to be

hanged, one of them offered to go and bring back the horses in two days, whilst the other remained in prison, provided that both should be pardoned. This proposal being agreed to, one of them was released; but not appearing in the stipulated time, Major Lawrence ordered the other Collery to be brought before him, and asked him the reason why his brother had not returned, bidding the prisoner prepare for death if the horses were not produced before the next evening; to this the Collery with great composure replied, that he was surprised the English should be so weak as to imagine that he or his brother ever had any intentions of restoring so valuable a booty, which would make the fortunes of their whole family; seeing they had it in their power to retain it, at no greater expence than his single life, which had often been hazarded for a single meal; he added, that the English could not blame them for having contrived the escape of one of the two, when both, if unavoidable, would willingly have died rather than restore the horses. The man uttered this ridiculous apology with the appearance of so much indifference to the fate that threatened him, that it moved both the laughter and compassion of the audience; and Captain Clive interceding with Major Lawrence, he was dismissed without any punishment."

Mr. T. Turnbull, writing of them in 1817, says:—

"The Colleries are said to be in general a brave people, expert in the use of the lance, and in throwing the curved stick called the *vullarce tadee*."

1765.

From the end of 1764 till June 1767, detachments of the army were employed in reducing to submission the Polygar Chiefs of the Central and Southern Carnatic, but I have not found it possible to discover what part, if any, the regiment took in these operations.

In November 1765, the ten Native Battalions were reorganised, each battalion being placed under the command of a Captain, and having a Lieutenant and an Ensign in addition. It is probable that on this occasion Captain Baillie was given command of the 5th Battalion.

1766.

In April 1766, Major-General Lawrence retired, and was succeeded as Commander-in-Chief by Brigadier-General Caillaud.

Early in this year, the King of Delhi having granted the Northern Circars to the British, a force was sent under Caillaud to take possession of those districts, which were then held by the Nizam. The latter threatened to retaliate by invading the Carnatic. The Madras Government, alarmed at this, deputed General Caillaud to negotiate. Eventually, on the 12th November, the Nizam agreed to cede the disputed territory, with the exception of Guntur, in consideration of an annual tribute and the assistance of a detachment of troops who, it was tacitly understood, were to support the Nizam in an attack on Haidar Ali.

In September of this year Colonel Joseph Smith arrived from England, and early in 1767, he became Commander-in-Chief in place of General Caillaud, who had resigned. This Joseph Smith was a son of Joseph Smith, a former Gunner of Fort St. George. He became an Ensign on the 3rd October 1749; Captain in 1754; and Major in 1760.

1767.

The Campaign against Haidar Ali.

In order to carry out the recent arrangement made with the Nizam by General Caillaud, Colonel Smith was selected to proceed to Haidarabad and arrange the details of the co-operation, and on the 20th January 1767, an agreement was made by which a British force was to assemble on the River Kistna, and march with the Nizam's army against Bangalore. A detachment was accordingly assembled, consisting of some 750 Europeans and the 1st, 2nd, 3rd, 5th and 8th Battalions of Coast Sepoys, of which the 5th Battalion, under Captain William Baillie, had marched from Vellore.

The ostensible plan of campaign was that Nizam Ali, in conjunction with Mahadeo Rao and the Mahratta Army, assisted by the British force, was to invade Mysore and attack Haidar Ali, but in March 1767, the latter bought off the Mahrattas, who evacuated Kolar on the 11th May and moved towards Poona.

Meanwhile Nizam Ali, who had been joined by Colonel Smith's force, was approaching the Mysore frontier, and was continually being incited by Haidar to join him in an attack on the British and Mahomed Ali. Colonel Smith soon began to perceive that treachery was intended, and his suspicions were confirmed when the army entered Mysore in May, and he found that Nizam Ali accorded it the treatment of a friendly country.

All his warnings, however, were disregarded by the Council at Madras, and at length the British Army moved towards its own frontier and, having joined a small force which had moved westward from Madras, endeavoured to strengthen the frontier by occupying various places in the Baramahal, including the mud forts of Vaniyambadi, Kaveripatnam and Tirupatur, which were placed under the command of Major Bonjour.

An attempt was also made to take the strong fort of Krishnagiri, but the assault was repulsed with loss on the 3rd June. On this occasion Krishnagiri was defended by a German adventurer named Constantin, "a native of Andernac on the Rhine, in the electorate of Cologn," and being the first German to whom I have found reference at this early date in South India, it is of interest to read what the author of "*The History of Ayder Ali Khan* (1784)" has to say about him:—

"He came to India with Ficher's troop in 1754; and married a Portuguese, by whom he had a very beautiful daughter; he was serjeant when M. Hughel commanded the Europeans in Ayder's army. The officers discovered that, together with his wife, he was in treaty with the Nabob about selling his daughter: they regarded this transaction as an infamous piece of business, that would disgrace all the Europeans in the army. M. Hughel sent for him, to enquire concerning the design laid to his charge, which he denied. A young officer in the army offered to espouse the girl; and the father received the proposal with gratitude. M. Hughel, in favour of the marriage, at the same time promoted the father; but that very night the parents sold their daughter to Ayder, for fifty thousand rupees; and Ayder sent them into the country of Benguelour. Constantin has ever since that time lived at a distance from the army. After the brave defence of the fortress of Krishnagiri, the inhabitants of the flat country brought their most valuable effects, and deposited them in the place for security: he opened the boxes and cabinets, taking out the richest property, to a vast amount, and escaped to Goa; from whence he went to Bombay, and afterwards to Europe. Ayder's French surgeon affirms that the girl has since told him that she esteemed herself fortunate in being sold to the Nabob; as her father and mother might have made a more shameful traffic with her, if she had staid with them."

Towards the end of May, Nizam Ali, followed by Haidar at a distance of two days' march, approached the Baramahal, and everyone, with the exception of the fatuous Madras Council, was well aware that the two forces were on the point of combining in an attack on the British army, which had stationed itself in occupation of the passes which gave ingress to the Carnatic by the Baramahal.

At the time when General Smith commenced to withdraw to the Carnatic, he left Captain Baillie and three battalions (presumably including Baillie's own battalion, the 5th) with the Nizam. These battalions were greatly in arrear of pay, and it was feared that either Haidar or Nizam Ali would endeavour to persuade them to mutiny, so General Smith sent a detachment under Captain Cosby to take a sum of money to Captain Baillie's camp. The detachment carried out this service successfully, marching 350 miles in 13 days, including two days' halt at Baillie's camp. On coming to an agreement with Haidar, Nizam Ali permitted Baillie's battalions to withdraw unmolested.

1767.
The Campaign against Haidar Ali and Nizam Ali

At the opening of the campaign, Colonel Smith's forces consisted of 16 guns, 30 European Cavalry, and 100 of the Nawab's irregular horse, who were a greater danger to their friends than to their foes, with 800 European and 5,000 Native Infantry, including the 5th Battalion.

Nizam Ali had 30,000 Cavalry, 10,000 Infantry and 60 guns; and Haidar's army consisted of 12,860 Cavalry, 18,000 Infantry and 49 guns.

Hostilities were commenced on the 25th August, when a force of cavalry under Makhdum Ali, Haidar's brother-in-law, swooped down through one of the passes near Krishnagiri which was unguarded by, and indeed unknown to, the British, and drove off the majority of the cattle of the army, causing at the same time considerable loss to Colonel Smith's cavalry, which had moved out from his camp at Kakankarai. The loss of his cattle so crippled Colonel Smith's force that he was unable to move till the 28th and in the meantime Haidar besieged and captured Kaveripatnam, which was defended with great gallantry by Captain McKain and two companies of the 3rd Battalion who, after repulsing two assaults by Haidar's best troops, was forced to capitulate on the 27th.

On the 30th August, Colonel Smith reached Singarapet, to which place he had marched with the object of effecting a junction with a British corps, under Colonel Wood, which was on its way from Trichinopoly, and had received orders to await him at Tiruvannamalai. Urged by the reproaches of Nizam Ali, Haidar now began to press upon the British rearguard which, on the 31st August, was passing along a narrow forest road, but on the 1st and 2nd September, the country became more open, and the column was continually attacked by parties of horse while the camp by night was assailed by flights of rockets.

The Battle of Chengam, September 3rd*, 1767. The next day's march was in a south-easterly direction, and traversed a defile between hills, with a fordable river crossing the road obliquely at its entrance. Colonel Smith did not move at his usual hour, but waited until noon when, having kept his tents standing as long as possible with a view to deceiving the enemy as to his intentions, he sent forward his baggage as rapidly as possible, and followed himself with the main body.

The order of march was, firstly a battalion of sepoys in column of companies, then the Nawab's cavalry which, as stated before, was quite useless, and then the baggage, protected by a battalion of sepoys in column of files on either

---

* Colonel Wilson, following Colonel Smith, says the 2nd September. Wilks gives the 3rd and thought Smith had made a mistake, and Fortescue and Vibart follow him.

flank: at a short distance behind, the main body followed, with the flank companies forming a rearguard.

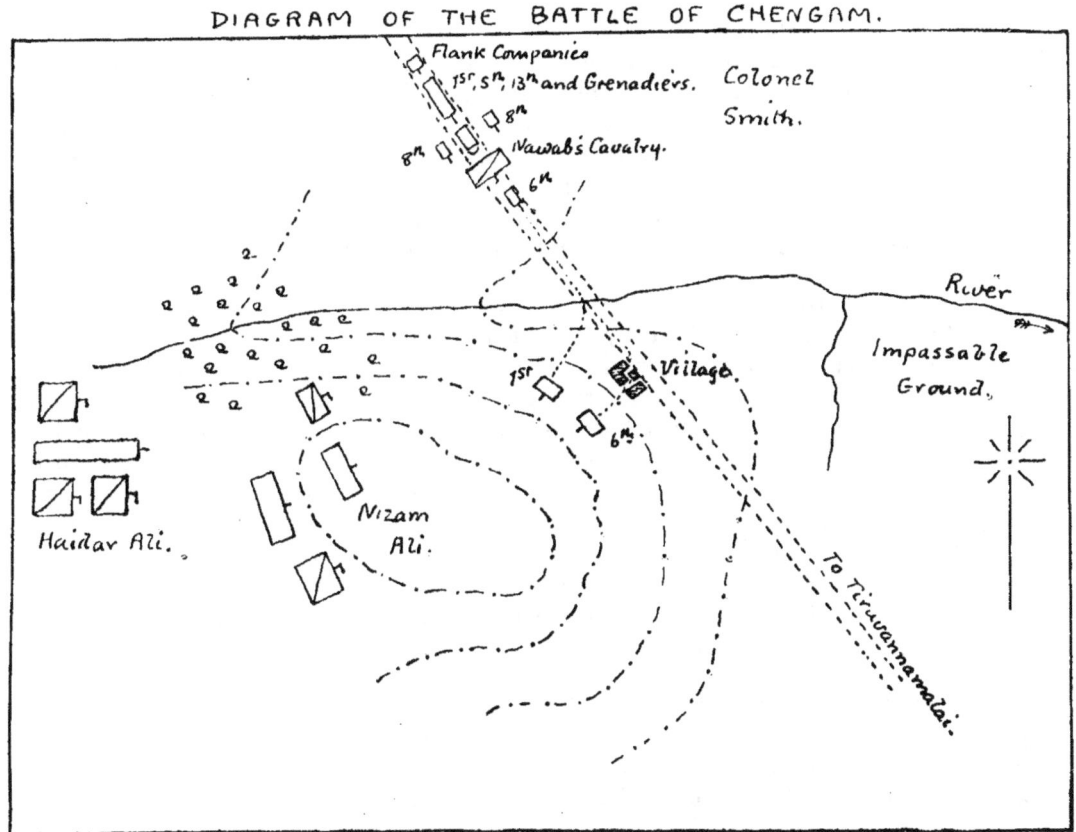

DIAGRAM OF THE BATTLE OF CHENGAM.

Haidar, who perceived that the main object of the British was to get their baggage safely through the defile, moved from the west on a hill, or rather a series of hills, which commanded the road and which, with a village at its foot, was the key of the pass, and was already occupied by a force of Nizam Ali's under the command of Rakhun-ud-Daulah, his Prime Minister, and a few Mysore troops. One of the advanced corps (the 6th Battalion), commanded by Captain Cosby, was ordered to clear this village, which was accordingly carried at the point of the bayonet. Finding himself annoyed from the hill, Captain Cosby proceeded to drive the enemy from the hill itself, while the advance guard pursued its way and cleared the pass. Observing from the top of this hill the rapid approach of Haidar's army, Captain Cosby reported it to Major Bonjour, commanding the advance guard, and asked leave to call up the leading corps of the main body under Captain Cowley (1st Battalion), to occupy the hill before he left it to rejoin the advance guard, a suggestion which was approved and which contributed largely to the success of the day.

Meanwhile Colonel Smith, on receiving a report from Captain Cosby, perceived the necessity of haste and, disregarding the fire of the rapidly advancing enemy, pushed on until the head of his column reached the corps on the hill, when he faced to the right and confronted Haidar, who now saw, when too late, his mistake in not forestalling his enemy on the hill. Nevertheless he made several determined attacks in mass, himself on foot at the head of his best troops, but was unable to dislodge the British sepoys, and suffered enormous losses, his killed alone being estimated at 2,000 and he himself being slightly wounded, while Colonel Smith's casualties only amounted to 170 killed and wounded. The confederates, foiled in the attempt to take the hill, now kept up a heavy but ill-aimed fire of musketry and guns and made a further endeavour to break through the line by working through the woods on their left, but without success.

Meanwhile the British rearguard had been long delayed by the two last guns, which had been attacked by the enemy while crossing the river, but on its arrival and junction with the main body, the whole line, led by the Grenadier Battalion, which, as was usual at that time, had been formed by taking two companies from each of the six battalions present, and was commanded by Captain Baillie of the 5th Battalion, moved forward and completely routed the immense army of the confederates. The enemy were pursued till sunset and abandoned two guns which, however, Colonel Smith was unable to carry off. In the fighting on this day Captain Baillie and the Grenadier companies of the 5th Battalion distinguished themselves greatly and the remainder of the battalion, with the other battalions engaged, in Colonel Smith's words "performed their duty to the utmost in the posts they were stationed in."

Unfortunately during the action the enemy's cavalry had broken in on the baggage and captured the whole of the supplies of rice, and Colonel Smith found himself in the unpleasant position of having to march forthwith, lest the enemy might again intercept his march while his army was starving.

Except for a halt of two hours after midnight, the retreat was continued throughout the night, and for the greater part of the following day, and when the army reached Tiruvannamalai they had, in the quaint wording of Colonel Smith's report, " Marched 27 hours without the least refreshment for man or beast who were never unloaded in the midst of this fatigue, the troops were chearfull though extenuated, and I can, with the utmost pleasure assure the Honourable Board that during the action every corps of sepoys behaved with a regularity scarce to be expected, and with as much firmness as could be wished."

It will be seen from the above that the sepoy battalions might now be said to have "found themselves," and in the battle of Chengam the Madras Army really received its baptism of fire as, though it had been engaged in minor operations for some years previously, it was not until this battle that it was called on not only to fight, but to manœuvre as a disciplined force, and as Wilson justly points out, in this and in the succeeding battle at Tiruvannamalai the close fighting was done entirely by sepoys.

It is of interest to note that Colonel Wilks records, on the 7th September, one of the rare instances* known in India of the desertion of a British Officer, a Lieutenant Hitchcock, and goes on to state that "the army afterwards learned with delight that the traitor was suspected, and sent to prison, where he lingered in infamy, and died unpitied."

On his arrival at Tiruvannamalai, Colonel Smith found to his disgust that, in spite of the reiterated declarations of Mahomed Ali that there were ample supplies in that place, there was not a single grain of rice, and only a small supply of paddy.

On the 8th September, Smith was joined by Colonel Wood, unmolested by the allies, who were busied in mutual recriminations over the results of their late unsuccessful engagement. Wood's force consisted of 540 Europeans, parts of the 7th, 10th and 11th Sepoy Battalions, and 8 guns. Soon after his arrival, the army was compelled by scarcity of provisions to proceed to the eastward, whence it returned on the 14th in time to prevent an attack by the enemy on Tiruvannamalai, where the stores and sick had been left, and drove off with some loss a corps of 10,000 horse which, with the battering guns, encamped some six miles N. W. of the British position.

Colonel Smith now deemed himself sufficiently strong to act on the offensive and moved out to attack the enemy on the 15th, but found them unapproachable owing to a large morass, and was compelled to return to Tiruvannamalai, for food, on the 16th.

The rains were now approaching and, as the army found itself in the unfortunate position of being compelled to forage for supplies within a short radius round Tiruvannamalai, not being able to move far owing to the hospital and stores being unguarded in that place, it was decided by a Council of War that the stores should be moved to Chittapet, a place of some strength garrisoned by the Nawab, while the army went into cantonments at Arcot or Vellore, where supplies were more plentiful. This, however, did not coincide with the views of the Madras Council, who wished Colonel Smith to remain in the neighbourhood of Tiruvannamalai, which he accordingly did.

Meanwhile the intention of the confederates, who were aware of the straits to which the British army was reduced, was to wait until the enemy was weakened by want and then make an attack. This plan was, however, frustrated owing to fortunate finds by the British of subterranean stores of grain which, with further reinforcements from Madras, placed Colonel Smith in even stronger condition than before. His army now consisted of 34 guns, 1,400 European and 9,000 Native Infantry, 30 European Cavalry, and 1,500 of the Nawab's very indifferent horse. With this force the 5th Battalion of Coast Sepoys was still serving.

---

* Another case had occurred in 1761 when a Captain Coulson disappeared with a small party of 50 sepoys, and was supposed to have taken service with Haidar.

Nizam Ali, who had become wearied of these operations, now insisted on greater activity, and accordingly a strong force, accompanied by 16 guns, was moved forward to a position in front of Colonel Smith's left, on which a cannonade was opened. This position was covered by an impassable morass in which Haidar hoped that the British would become entangled under the fire of his guns and musketry. Colonel Smith, who was unaware of this morass, moved forward his left which was, of course, at once checked by that obstacle, but its nature could now be more closely observed, and Colonel Smith saw that while it extended indefinitely to his left, it appeared only to extend on his right as far as the foot of a hill, behind which was stationed a large part of the allied army, and he decided to move to his right and endeavour to get round the enemy's left flank.

The Battle of Tiruvannamalai, September 26th, 1767.

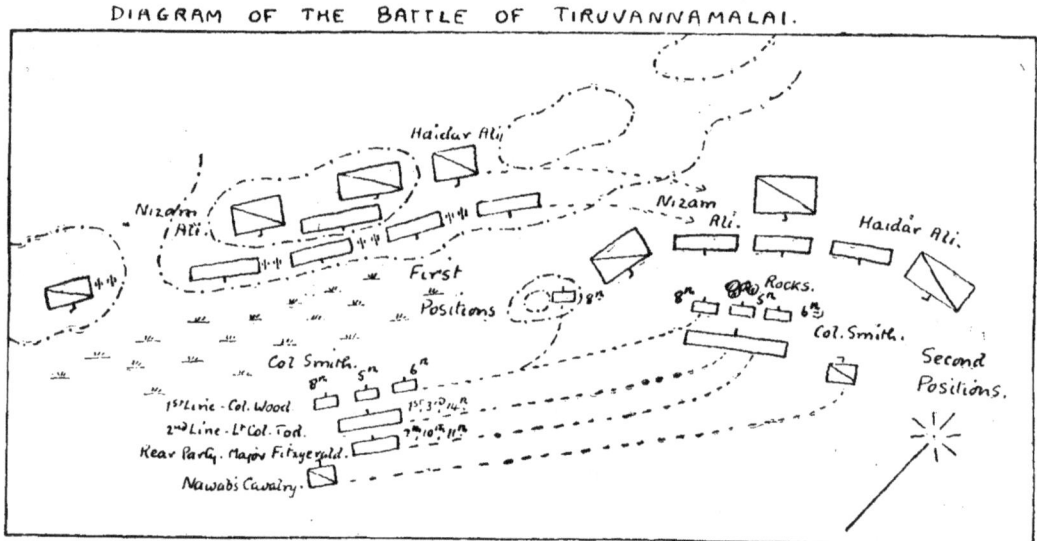

DIAGRAM OF THE BATTLE OF TIRUVANNAMALAI.

The direction on which he was now moving was north-east, and the confederates, who were still labouring under the delusion that the British troops were reduced to the last extremity for want of food, at once jumped to the conclusion that they were retreating on Arcot, and accordingly moved hastily forward to fall upon their flank and rear. To their mutual surprise, the two forces suddenly met and almost ran into each other on rounding the hill. The confederates made a hurried movement to occupy the hill, but Captain Cook's (8th) Battalion got there before the enemy and driving them back from the summit, secured a point of support for the left of the line.

A large body of the enemy's best infantry was moved forward to occupy a strong position among some rocks on the plain, but before they were fully in occupation Captain Cook's (8th), Baillie's (5th), and Cosby's (6th) Battalions, who were much inferior to the enemy in number, were pushed forward and, in Colonel Smith's words, "advanced with such rapidity, and gave so brisk a fire that the enemy's sepoys could not stand it, but were obliged to quit their posts and run." The left of the British Army now rested on this point, the line deploying opposite the main masses of the enemy, who had occupied a hill from which they commanded the British, and annoyed them considerably with their guns. Immense bodies of cavalry, with sepoys in the intervals, formed a crescent which seemed about to envelop Colonel Smith's inferior force, but no order to charge was given to them, while the British Artillery caused great destruction in their ranks. The cause of this inaction was that Haidar, with his chiefs, was completely disconcerted by the failure of his original plan, and the majority of his guns were still in their old positions on his right, where they were useless.

The tremendous disparity in numbers did not shake the courage of the sepoy battalions and, as Colonel Smith says, "did not prevent our men from marching on with a firmness that will ever do them honour, for, notwithstanding all efforts from cannon, musketry, rockets and horse, they could not discompose our lines."

The steady fire of the British was most effective, and though the infantry and guns continued to maintain their ground, the cavalry fled in disorder, and Haidar, who from the first had realized that the battle was lost, and now saw the firm advance of Colonel Smith, began to draw off his cannon and begged Nizam Ali to do the same. The latter, however, who did not see so clearly as his ally the dangerous position of affairs, refused to do so until it was almost too late, and the utmost efforts were necessary to save them. Darkness now fell, and the British were compelled to halt, having driven the enemy off the ground and taken nine cannon.

The following extract from Colonel Smith's report testifies to the gallantry with which this action was fought, and shows that the disciplined valour of the Madras sepoy, first displayed at Chengam, was now firmly established:—

"It is now my duty and my happiness to pay a just tribute to merit: Seconded as I was by Field officers, who conducted themselves so as to deserve everlasting honour, I have been enabled to obey your commands and drive the most formidable enemy that ever attacked us out of the Carnatic. I cannot omit giving great applause to the inferior officers, who executed with the greatest spirit and gallantry every order they received. Their zeal and bravery will, I am confident, ensure them your protection and favour on every occasion. The soldiers' steadiness at this critical conjuncture was so remarkable (and many of them recruits too) that I am firmly of opinion every man would have sacrificed his life or have conquered. Your officers of sepoys and their Battalions deserve more praise than I can express, for I never saw men behave with more resolution and intrepidity than those I have the honour to command. Those who distinguished themselves most conspicuously were the 1st, the 5th commanded by Lieutenant Bowman (as Captain Baillie commanded the Sepoy Corps of Grenadiers), the 6th and 8th Battalions. . . . . ."

During the night, Nizam Ali fled to the west through the pass of Singarapet, leaving his army to look after itself, and Haidar made arrangements for the withdrawal of his forces, which were well on their march before the disorganised army of his ally was ready to start. Colonel Smith arranged for a midnight attack on the enemy's camp, to be led by the Grenadier companies under Major Fitzgerald, and followed up by the remainder of the army, but the guide, who was a spy of Haidar's, led them to an impassable swamp, and they were compelled to return to camp.

At daybreak on the 27th, a fresh start was made and, on ascending the hill to their front, the pleasing spectacle presented itself to them of the whole confederate army in full retreat along the road. Following up as rapidly as possible, the British army soon converted the retreat into a rout and added to their spoils no less than 41 guns, 14 more being subsequently found concealed in the jungle. The operations of the day only ended when the troops were exhausted, and Colonel Smith was unable to continue the pursuit on the day following owing to the unfortunate necessity of retiring to procure supplies.

In this important victory the British only lost 150 men killed and wounded, the losses of the enemy amounting to 4,000, together with 64 guns and a large quantity of stores of every kind except rice, which the British army required more than anything else. One of the first results of the victory was the hasty withdrawal of Tippu Sultan, then plundering in the outskirts of Madras, who hastened to join his father.

Colonel Smith now proceeded to Madras to endeavour to make some arrangement for the more efficient provisioning of his army in future, after cantoning his forces at Vellore, Conjeeveram, Wandiwash, and Trichinopoly. In selecting these places he made a great mistake in having his detachments so far apart, though the blame should be placed rather on the shoulders of the Council of Madras than on his, as that wretched body made no attempt whatever to assist the army with provisions or transport, and it was in consequence impossible to maintain a large body of men in any one place.

Haidar, who, with Nizam Ali, had established his army at "Calaimuttoor"* in the Baramahal, was not slow to take advantage of this dispersion. On the 5th November, he took Tirupattur, and on the 7th, Vaniyambadi, thence proceeding to Ambur on the 10th. Here he compelled Captain Calvert, who was in command, to withdraw from the lower fort on the 15th but, after a siege lasting 26 days, was forced to retire on the 6th December, on the approach of the British army under Colonel Smith, who had been compelled by Haidar's activity to withdraw his forces from cantonments.

The whole of the British army was assembled at Vellore, with the exception of Colonel Wood's division at Trichinopoly, which was ordered to Tiruvannamalai so as to enter the Baramahal by the pass of Singarapet. On the 7th December, Colonel Smith reached Ambur and moved off in pursuit of Haidar whom he found on the following day at Vaniyambadi, Nizam Ali having moved further to the south. After offering but a slight resistance, Haidar retreated and the British followed as far as Tirupattur, but were then compelled to halt—as usual, owing to want of supplies. The confederates retired on Kaveripatnam and Colonel Smith,

---

* This I believe to have been the village of Mattur.

having effected a junction with Colonel Wood, proceeded to that place, which, however, he found too strong to attack.

A rising in Malabar, and operations by the Bengal Army towards Haidarabad now caused the confederate armies to break up, and on the 14th December, Haidar despatched his guns and baggage to the west, Nizam Ali's army withdrawing on the 18th. Whilst these arrangements were being carried out, they were covered by active operations on Colonel Smith's supply columns.

Action at Singarapet. December 29th, 1767.

Against one of these columns, escorted by the 1st Battalion, under Captain R. V. Fitzgerald, which was expected from Tiruvannamalai by the pass of Singarapet, Haider moved in person on the 29th December, with 4,000 select horse, 2,000 infantry, and 5 guns, confident of obtaining an easy conquest over a single battalion without guns and hampered by a large convoy. Colonel Smith, however, had strengthened the escort by a reinforcement under Major Thomas Fitzgerald of 500 horse, the Grenadier Companies of the 1st and 2nd Regiments, and the 5th Battalion of Coast Sepoys, with two guns. Haidar being unaware of this, attacked with great energy and, charging in person at the head of his cavalry, was received with a most unexpectedly hot fire, had his horse shot under him, and received a bullet through his turban, his force being driven off with loss. The fact that many of his best officers perished evinced an effort of more than usual determination, and the repulse was most creditable to Major Fitzgerald, who commanded the united detachments, and the small force under him.

As regards the part played by the 5th Battalion in this sharp engagement, Major Fitzgerald says in his despatches:—

"HYDER NAIGUE, judging that dispapointing the army of this supply would benefit him in proportion to the distress it would be attended with to us, moved in person with the flower of his troops to intercept it. About 5 yesterday evening he attacked us with more resolution than I ever saw his men show on any occasion......His horse made a most resolute charge on the 5th Battalion which stood firm on its ground......"

This campaign was brought to an end by a treaty between Nizam Ali and the British on the 23rd February 1768, Mahomed Ali also being included in the negotiations, and Haidar with his main army proceeded to the West Coast, where events which do not come within the scope of this narrative demanded his attention.

1768.

Renewal of the Campaign Against Haidar Ali.

On the departure of Haidar, the British army was formed into two divisions, that under Colonel Smith, which included the 5th Battalion, proceeding to Kaveripatnam, and thence northwards to Palikondai near Vellore, returning at the instance of the ever-interfering Council to waste valuable time in the blockade of Krishnagiri, which was surrendered on the 2nd May. Meanwhile the second division under Colonel Wood was engaged in reducing the numerous forts in the provinces of Salem, Erode, Coimbatore and Dindigul, of which Dharmapuri and Erode were taken by assault while Tenkaraikottai, Salem, Attur, Namakkal, Satyamangalam, Danayakankota, Gajalahatti, Kaveripuram, Coimbatore, Palghat, Dharapuram, Aravakurichi and Dindigul surrendered.

Colonel Smith was now afflicted by the addition to his force not only of two members of Council, Messrs. Call and Mackay, but also of the Nawab, a most objectionable arrangement which was bound to cause dissensions in the councils of the army. Call was a Colonel in the Engineers, who held the contract for the supplies and transport of the army, in the profits of which all the other members of Council, except the Governor, had a share. The first action of these Field Deputies was to insist on an escort of 200 Europeans and 5 battalions of sepoys, with a large proportion of artillery, which seriously weakened Smith's army.

On the 8th June, Colonel Donald Campbell, with the advanced division of the army, which included a detachment of the 5th Battalion, moved from Krishnagiri and ascended the pass of Budikota, and on the 16th of that month, reduced the mud fort of Venkatagiri-Kota three marches to the northward. Sending back a detachment to open up the road to Vellore, which accomplished its object by the capture of the rock of Peddanayakandurgam at the pass of that name, he then proceeded another two marches to the north and occupied the lower fort on the droog of Mulbagal, but found that the rock was too strong for its capture to be attempted by open assault. The provincial commander, however,—Jafar Husain Khan,—who was in occupation of the rock, opened secret negotiations for its surrender, but as the garrison remained faithful to Haidar, this had to be accomplished by treachery.

Colonel Campbell accordingly moved off to Kolar, leaving a detachment at Mulbagal and, on the 23rd June, Captain Mathews (16th Bn.), disguised as a Subadar, with two companies of sepoys, gained access to the upper fort under the pretence that they were a party of recruits for Haidar's army, and attained their object without bloodshed, the garrison being too much surprised to offer any resistance. On the same day Colonel Campbell reached Kolar and carried forward regular approaches against that place, the garrison surrendering at discretion on the 28th June.

Makhdum Sahib was now reported to be at Bagalur, some 18 miles to the south-west, and Captain Cosby (6th Bn.) was sent with a detachment which inflicted some slight loss on him, but it was found useless to pursue his active horse.

Hosur. Colonel Campbell having rejoined Colonel Smith's force at Araleri, on the 3rd July, the combined force, with which the whole of the 5th Battalion was now serving, moved on Hosur by way of Bagalur, and besieged that place, which fell on the 11th, a detachment under Cosby subsequently taking possession of Anekal and Denkani-Kota. The usual difficulties of supply detained the army at Hosur for some time, and meanwhile negotiations were opened with Morari Rao which resulted in that chief supplying a force of 3,000 horse and 2,000 irregular infantry, the two forces effecting a junction at Hoskote, two marches to the north, on the 4th August. On the same day Haidar returned to Bangalore, and on the 9th, his light horse commenced to harass the British camp. On the night of the 22nd, a sudden attack was made on Morari Rao's camp which was some distance from that of the British, but after confused fighting the enemy sustained a repulse.

The division of Colonel Wood was now ascending from the Baramahal and on the 3rd September, Haidar made a move towards the south with a view to cutting him off. Colonel Smith expected that Colonel Wood would reach Budikota on the 5th September, and move towards Malur on the 6th but, rendered anxious by his ignorance of Haidar's movements, left his baggage at Malur on the 5th and on the 6th marched on Budikota, having with him the 1st and 2nd European regiments, the 1st, 3rd and 5th battalions of Coast Sepoys, and Achmuty's Bengal battalion. Colonel Wood's route led through a long defile, the direction of which lay north-west for some miles and then turned due west at a comparatively open spot where another road led off to the north-east. Haidar, expecting Colonel Smith to await reinforcements at Malur, had taken up a position to the north-east of this spot with the intention of enfilading Colonel Wood's column on the march, his own retreat in case of failure being open to the north-east. Early in the morning Colonel Smith sent out scouts to the tops of the hills which lay between him and Haidar, who reported to him that both Haidar's and Colonel Wood's forces were in sight, moving in the directions described. Perceiving that he could reach the angle of the defile before Haidar, Colonel Smith sent messengers to Colonel Wood informing him of his intentions and was just arriving at his objective when, to his indignation, and to the surprise of Haidar, who at once retired, a regular *feu-de-joie* was heard in the defile, which Colonel Wood had had the folly to fire on receiving the news of Colonel Smith's approach. A pursuit of Haidar was commenced, but it was too late and had no result. Colonel Smith having in no measured terms given Colonel Wood his opinion of his idiotic conduct, the latter resigned his command, and his division, now placed under Colonel Lang, was ordered to continue the pursuit in the direction of Betamangalam, while Colonel Smith was to move to Kolar. Finding, however, that Haidar got more and more distant, the pursuit was given up, and the British army returned to Kolar, leaving a garrison at Murgamalai two marches to the north.

Haidar now opened negotiations with the British, offering to pay ten lakhs of rupees and to cede the Baramahal, but these terms were foolishly refused by the Madras Government, and the campaign was continued.

Mulbagal. In October Haidar recaptured Mulbagal, thanks to the Field Deputies who, in Colonel Smith's absence, had removed the regular garrison and left only a company of Mahomed Ali's, and on the 3rd of that month Colonel Wood, who had resumed his command in September, hastened there, and occupied the lower fort, but was beaten off with loss in an attempt to storm the rock. On the next day some of the enemy's troops appeared and Colonel Wood, who marched out against them with a small force, found himself opposed by Haidar's whole army and, after fighting of the most desperate description, was only saved by a stratagem of Captain Brooke's* by which the enemy were led to believe that Colonel Smith, for whose name they now had considerable respect, had arrived with his division. In this action the British lost 8 officers and 229 rank and file killed and wounded, while the enemy lost over 1,000. Colonel Wood sent messengers to Colonel Smith, then at Kolar, who, marching on the 6th October, arrived near Mulbagal on the 7th, when Haidar withdrew his army. On the 14th, the two divisions moved northwards, and spent the remainder of the month in vain endeavours to force Haidar to a general action.

On the 5th November, Haidar appeared at Kolar and cannonaded the pettah but, finding Colonel Campbell on the alert, retired two days later. This news, however, compelled Colonel Smith to return to Kolar on the 8th, whence he was summoned on the 14th, ostensibly to assist in the deliberations of the Council but really, according to the belief of the time, to give Colonel Wood an opportunity of distinguishing himself in the field. The 5th battalion had served with the division of Colonel Smith throughout the operations just described, but it has not yet been discovered what part they played in those which will now be briefly traced, though it seems highly probable that they formed part of the force under Major Fitzgerald.

Bagalur. On the 16th November, Colonel Wood, now—to the misfortune of the Army— reinstated in command of a division, marched to the relief of Hosur, which Haidar had commenced to besiege, the rest of the Army remaining at Venkatagiri-Kota under the command of Major Fitzgerald. Bagalur was reached on the 17th, and in the pettah of that place the baggage and stores were left, besides two 18-pounders and Colonel Wood then moved to Hosur, where he arrived on the 18th, too late to make a night attack on the enemy as he had proposed. On the previous evening Haidar had withdrawn his troops from the siege and, waiting until he saw Colonel Wood's force entering Hosur, moved round in his rear and marched to Bagalur where he succeeded in capturing the two 18-pounders and a quantity of stores, besides inflicting considerable loss on the detachment under Captain Alexander (Nawab's troops) to whom the baggage had been entrusted. He then got safely away before Colonel Wood's hasty return from Hosur.

---

* This officer belonged to the Bengal Battalion, and was afterwards Governor of St. Helena.

On the 20th, Colonel Wood again marched to Hosur, where he left some provisions, and on the next day marched back again through Bagalur to Araleri, which lies between Bagalur and Kolar. On the 22nd, Haidar suddenly reappeared and opened a cannonade from twelve heavy guns which Colonel Wood sustained without making the least attempt to attack the enemy, and suffered a loss in consequence of 1 Captain, 6 Subalterns, 20 Europeans and 200 Sepoys, killed and wounded. During the night Colonel Wood marched again, severely harassed by the enemy, who renewed their attacks in the morning, but just as it was becoming probable that he would suffer a disaster which would make his previous misfortunes appear trifling, the arrival of Major Fitzgerald, who had hastened by forced marches from Venkatagiri-Kota, compelled the enemy, who imagined that it was Colonel Smith's force and had no desire to encounter that energetic officer, to retire to the south-east. Colonel Wood was now so despondent, and his troops so disheartened, that nothing could be done, and Major Fitzgerald made representations to the Commander-in-Chief which resulted in orders being sent for Colonel Wood to proceed to Madras under arrest, his successor, Colonel Ross Lang, assuming the command early in December. It may be added that Colonel Wood, who, as Fortescue says, "did indeed display an incompetence worthy of his patrons," was tried in 1769 for misappropriation and misconduct in the field, and cashiered.

The position of affairs now began to look threatening for the British. Fazal-ulla-Khan, who had been ordered by Haidar to move from Seringapatam with a large army, descended the passes of Kaveripuram and Gajalhatti in the middle of November, and rapidly captured the latter place and numerous others, while Coimbatore fell by treachery, on the 29th of the month. On the 6th December, Haidar himself descended into the Baramahal by the pass of Palakodu, and thence proceeded southwards through the pass of Toppur.

Apprised of these events, Colonel Lang despatched Major Fitzgerald in that direction with a division "composed of the best troops of the army," which marched on the 10th December. The 5th was one of the five select battalions of sepoys included in this force. Colonel Lang himself remained at Venkatagiri-Kota with very few troops while Major Fitzgerald followed Haidar as rapidly as possible, but had the misfortune to be invariably one day too late. Haidar in consequence retook in rapid succession all the forts held by the weak British detachments with which, in his folly, Colonel Wood had garrisoned them, including Dharmapuri, Tenkarai-Kottai, Omalur, Salem, and Namakkal. As Major Fitzgerald approached the Kaveri he learnt that Haidar was about to cross that river to the east of Karur and intended to march on Trichinopoly and Tanjore, leaving Fazal-ulla to invest Karur and Erode. Knowing that the latter place had a good garrison whereas Trichinopoly was almost defenceless, Fitzgerald decided to march to protect Trichinopoly, but Haidar, perceiving this movement, proceeded in the opposite direction, took Karur on the 19th December, and after meeting and almost annihilating a detachment under Captain Eccles Nixon, invested Erode, which was surrendered on the 25th by Captain Orton, under disgraceful circumstances. Captain Orton, it may be remarked, was subsequently tried and cashiered. Haidar next moved on Kaveripuram,* where Captain Faisan was forced to capitulate after a fine defence and was, in defiance of the terms of surrender, sent to the dungeons of Seringapatam, together with the garrison of Erode. The fall of the latter place on the 31st December closed the events of the year.

---

* Wilks says Kaveripuram; Vibart says Kaveripatnam; the former is probably correct.

1769.
Conclusion of the War with Haidar Ali.

Fazal-ulla-Khan was now sent to Dindigul to operate against the provinces of Madura and Tinnevelly, while Haidar crossed the Kaveri and marched eastwards. Major Fitzgerald, who was at Mansurpet near Madura, marched northwards to intercept Haidar and oppose his advance on Madras, but the latter, turning first north-east and then south-east, eluded him and marched down the Coleroon, exacting a tribute of four lakhs from the Raja of Tanjore. He then returned to the tract which Fitzgerald, for want of provisions, had had to abandon and retire on Cuddalore.

The command of the army was resumed by Colonel Smith at Chittapet on the 1st February 1769, and the pursuit of Haidar was recommenced, but the Madras Government opened negotiations for peace, and sent Captain Brooke to interview Haidar, who, however, refused the terms offered. Further negotiations resulted in a twelve days truce, from the 22nd February, but on the 6th March, hostilities were once more renewed. After much manœuvring on both sides, Haidar, who was hard pressed and feared that he might be forced to fight a general action with disastrous consequences, resolved to attempt to bring the war to a favourable conclusion by a bold stroke and, on the 29th March, he suddenly appeared with 6,000 horse and 200 foot within five miles of Madras, having marched 130 miles in three and a half days, and demanded that Mr. Josias Du Pre, one of the Members of Council, should be sent to him to negotiate terms of peace.

By this time, Colonel Smith was rapidly approaching in pursuit of Haidar and, on the 31st March, reached Vandalur, within 12 miles of the Mount, but the Council, at the instance of Haidar, and fearing an attack on the Black Town, strictly forbade him to come within 25 miles of Madras, and on the 2nd April*, a treaty was finally concluded. The terms of the treaty do not appear to have been disadvantageous to the British, but the circumstances under which it was made gave it the appearance of having been "dictated at the gates of Madras," and caused great dissatisfaction.

While the negotiations were pending, Colonel Lang appears to have missed a fine opportunity of striking an effective blow at the enemy, by failing to make an attack on the crowded masses of Haidar's main army, when they were entangled in the passes of Attur and Chengam.

The 5th Battalion of Coast Sepoys, which had, as has been seen, played a prominent part in the events of the preceding two years, was, on the 16th June 1759, when the native troops were divided into "Carnatic" and "Circar" battalions, re-named the 5th Carnatic Battalion, and appears to have spent the remainder of that year, after peace had been concluded, in garrison at Trichinopoly.

---

* Colonel Wilson gives the 3rd April, but Vibart says the 2nd.

Part I.

CHAPTER II.

THE 5th CARNATIC BATTALION
16th June 1769—August 1770.

THE 4th CARNATIC BATTALION
August 1770—October 1784.

1770.

On the 2nd July 1770, Major-General Coote, who had been appointed Commander-in-Chief in India, arrived in Madras, but the Council having decided that the commission of Mr. Du Pre as Commander-in-Chief in Madras was superior to General Coote's, that officer sailed in disgust for England in October, and was succeeded by General Joseph Smith.

About August in this year, the Army was formed into two Carnatic, and one Circar, brigades, and the 3rd or Madras Battalion was reduced, the 5th Battalion being consequently renumbered and now becoming the 4th Carnatic Battalion. Captain Baillie was still in command.

1771.

Operations Against Tanjore.

Early in 1771, the Nawab, Mahomed Ali, asked for the assistance of the British in compelling the Raja of Tanjore to acknowledge his suzerainty. The Raja had refused as he felt himself strengthened by the presence of the Mahratta Army then invading Mysore. Haidar Ali had in vain demanded the co-operation of the British against the Mahrattas as promised in the treaty of 1769. It was this indefensible treatment of Haidar Ali by the British which finally estranged that prince and made him, till his death, their bitterest enemy.

The Court of Directors being themselves of the opinion that it was most unreasonable that the Raja of Tanjore should hold the finest part of the country without contributing to its defence, it was decided that assistance should be given to Mahomed Ali, and accordingly in August a force was assembled at Trichinopoly under the command of General Smith, which included the 4th Carnatic Battalion.*

In September, the march was commenced against Tanjore, and at 10 a.m., on the 16th of that month, the army arrived in heavy rain before the fort of Vallam, a few miles to the south-west of Tanjore, and at the same time the Tanjore cavalry appeared. As soon as the weather cleared, Matthews' cavalry and the Grenadier Corps were sent against the Tanjorines, of whom it is recorded that "the instant we began to speak from the mouths of our sixes they set out for Tanjore." The pettah was then occupied and, on the 20th September, a battery was opened against the fort, which was garrisoned by about 1,200 men. At midnight, Colonel Bonjour, advancing to the breach with some Europeans and a battalion of sepoys, found the fort deserted. On the 23rd September, the army encamped 3 miles E. by S. of Tanjore, and preparations were begun for the siege.

---
* Captain Baillie was appointed Brigade-Major of the General Staff of this force, so it is not at present known who was in command of the battalion.

On the 1st October, the garrison made a very determined sortie, which lasted for over four hours, and was eventually repulsed with loss. On the 2nd, a battery was opened, but was found to be ineffective, so, on the 11th, another opened fire within 370 yards of the walls. The defenders kept up a heavy fire from the fort and caused many casualties, while great difficulty was experienced in mining owing to the hardness of the soil and continuous heavy rain.

By the 27th October, a practicable breach was completed, and preparations were made for an assault on the following day, when General Smith received a letter from the Nawab to say that he had come to an agreement with the Raja, and hostilities consequently ceased, the principal condition of the agreement being the payment of a large sum of money to the Nawab.

In these operations the army suffered considerably, one authority stating that they amounted to 158 Europeans and 281 sepoys killed and wounded, a total of 439, while Vibart says that the casualties were 143 killed and 403 wounded, a total of 546. The casualties of the 4th Battalion were 14 sepoys killed, and Lieutenants Barton, Campbell and Davis; one Sergeant, 3 Jemadars, 1 Havildar, 2 Naicks, and 16 sepoys wounded.

During the siege, the army was greatly distressed for want of provisions, as is shown by the following letter, dated the 17th October, from General Smith to Captain Cosby:—

Dear Cosby,—I have received your several letters and the convoy safe; we had not a grain of rice left when it made its first appearance; and but for the supply you sent, God knows what the consequence might have been, for our Sepoys began to grow very troublesome, and I wonder not at it, considering the fatigue they undergo.

(*Signed*) JOSEPH SMITH, Commander-in-Chief.

Considerable discontent was aroused among the troops on account of the terms of surrender, as they were thereby deprived of the prize-money to which they considered themselves entitled, and in the following year, before the despatch of a force against the Marawars of Ramnad (an expedition in which the 4th Battalion was not engaged), the Nawab found it necessary to divide a sum of Rupees 5,10,000 among the troops, in which presumably all those who had been employed against Tanjore participated, and to promise that in future prize-money would be granted in the customary manner.

1772.

In August 1772, General Smith resigned the command-in-chief, and was succeeded by Colonel Sir Robert Fletcher, but the latter gave so much trouble that in January 1773, he was ordered to take command of the garrison at Trichinopoly. He then pleaded his privilege as a Member of Parliament and demanded to be sent back to England, to which request the Government gladly acceded, and General Smith once more assumed command.

1773.

Further Operations Against Tanjore.

The death of Madu Rao on the 18th November 1772 seemed to offer opportunities, both to Haidar Ali and Mahomed Ali, of taking advantage of the dissensions which were certain to arise among the Mahrattas with regard to the succession to his throne, and Mahomed Ali accordingly urged the Madras Government to assist him once more in an attack on Tanjore, the pretext put forward being the non-payment of arrears of tribute. To this the Government agreed, and, on the 6th July 1773, a force which included the 4th and six other Carnatic Battalions, was assembled at Trichinopoly under General Smith.

After the necessary preliminary arrangements had been made, which on this occasion included an agreement with the Nawab as to the amount of prize-money to be paid to the troops, the army marched on the 31st July, and encamped near the Sugar-Loaf rock. Marching again on the 2nd August, Ginjipatti was reached on the 4th, and Vallam on the 5th. On the night of the 5th, the enemy's camp was surprised by the European Grenadiers, and the enemy dispersed. On the 6th August, while General Smith was reconnoitring the ground round Tanjore, the enemy, who were encamped to the north of the fort, sent out a party of cavalry which was routed by Captain Rumley with considerable loss, and on the 7th, the investment was complete.

Ground was broken on the 20th August, and on the 24th, the enemy made a vigorous sortie, which was repulsed with loss. On the 27th, the first batteries opened fire, and the construction of others was commenced. On the 11th September, the enemy marched out to attack a post on the eastern side, but were driven back. By the 17th* September, there was a practicable breach, on which day at about one o'clock in the afternoon, the place was surprised, and carried by storm by four companies of British Grenadiers and six battalions of Sepoys without the loss of a single man, although there was a garrison of at least 20,000 men in the fort.

The following account is given of the surrender of the Raja:—

"When the assaulting party had entered the fort, Colonel Cosby, who was Adjutant-General to General Smith during the siege, was deputed by the General to treat with the Raja who, with a chosen body of men, had, on the breach being carried, returned into his palace, and appeared determined to defend himself in that position to the last. Colonel Cosby, with only an interpreter, was admitted to his presence, after passing through several intricate passages filled with men who, it seems, had devoted themselves to die with their chief, and which their gloomy countenances strongly indicated they would have done. He found him in a small chamber, surrounded by a few of the most confidential of his people. The interview was solemn and impressive, but it

---

* Neill says that the assault took place on the 16th September but all the other authorities agree in giving the 17th.

took not long to convince the Rajah of the imprudence of further resistance; and when Colonel Cosby assured him he was fully authorised to promise, not only that his life should be protected by the English, but that also every delicacy and respect should be observed towards himself, the females, and rest of his family, and reminded him of General Smith's well-known honourable character, he, after a heavy sigh or two, asked Colonel Cosby if he would swear to that effect by the sword he then held in his hand, and that he was properly authorised to give him protection. The reply being in the affirmative, he arose, said he was satisfied, and gave orders to his people to lay down their arms, as he relied on the honour of the English, and proper guards were immediately appointed by Colonel Cosby for the protection of the palace."

The losses during the siege amounted to 6 officers, 16 Europeans, and 29 sepoys killed; and 14 officers, 50 Europeans, and 74 sepoys wounded, while 4 officers died—from what cause is not stated. The total thus amounted to 193.

The army shortly afterwards returned to Trichinopoly, while the Nawab's troops proceeded against Nagore, which was given up by the Dutch without resistance.

The following resolution was issued by the Court of Proprietors on the 19th May 1774:—

"Resolved that the thanks of this Court be given to Brigadier-General Joseph Smith for his long, faithful and meritorious services to this Company in the government of their forces on the Coast of Coromandel, and more especially for his late able conduct in the reduction of Tanjore, in which service the officers and troops under his command have manifested the most exemplary discipline and resolution."

1774-1775.

The regiment appears (from the *Madras Army List*) to have been stationed at Vellore in 1774.

Warren Hastings, who had been Governor of Bengal since 1772, became first Governor-General of India in 1774, and held the appointment till 1785.

On the 23rd November 1774, Robert, Lord Clive, Baron of Plassey, died by his own hand in the 50th year of his age. His career is a history in itself and it is impossible to give even a sketch of it here. Philippart closes his account of this gallant soldier's services in the following words:—

'So long as the English nation retains a footing in India, the memory of this great man, who laid the foundation of British glory in that Peninsula, must be held in veneration by every English and native inhabitant. The Indian army must ever hold in grateful remembrance his noble gift of £30,000 for the benefit of the wounded officers and soldiers, now become a fund of such immense importance for such beneficial application. This memoir cannot be more appropriately closed than by repeating the words of the great Lord Chatham, who emphatically designated Lord Clive 'a heaven-born General, who without being versed in military affairs, had surpassed all the officers of his time.'"

In December 1774, Haidar Ali made attempts to renew the treaty of 1769 with the Madras Government, but as the latter had to refer all the correspondence to the Government at Calcutta, the negotiations were so protracted that Haidar gave them up in disgust, and never subsequently made any attempt to reopen them.

In October 1775, General Joseph Smith resigned the service, and Brigadier-General Sir Robert Fletcher again became Commander-in-Chief on the 14th. The Commander-in-Chief in Bengal was Lieutenant-General John Clavering. The Court of Directors, who strongly disapproved of the delivery of Tanjore to Mahomed Ali, recalled Mr. Wynch who, as Governor, had been responsible for that action, and in December, Lord Pigot arrived from England to take his place.

1776-1777.

On the 11th April 1776, Lord Pigot carried out the orders regarding Tanjore received from the Court of Directors, and replaced the Raja on his throne. Mahomed Ali, objecting strongly to this proceeding, succeeded in bribing certain of the Members of Council, and a fraudulent claim was brought forward against the revenues of Tanjore.

The dissensions which ensued culminated, on the 24th August, in the arrest of the unfortunate Governor, in which Sir Robert Fletcher, the Commander-in-Chief, took a leading part. On assuming power, the Council, with a view to keeping the garrison of Fort St. George (where the 4th Battalion appears to have been stationed) quiet, promised to give the troops a donation which, however, had not been paid by December, as in that month the Commanding Officers, among whom we find Captain Edington, who was acting as Adjutant-General with the rank of Lieutenant-Colonel and Commanding the 4th Battalion, wrote to point out the fact.

It was not till a considerable time had elapsed that the Court of Directors ordered the restoration of the Governor and the dismissal of the remainder of the Council, and in the meantime Lord Pigot had died on the 10th May 1777.

Sir Robert Fletcher had also died, at Mauritius, in December 1776 and in April 1777, he was succeeded as Commander-in-Chief by Brigadier-General Stuart, but the latter was suspended on the 31st August, on account of his share in the arrest of Lord Pigot, and was succeeded in turn by Colonel Ross Lang.

General Stuart was not tried by Court-Martial until 1780, when he was acquitted, and Captain Edington (4th Battalion) and the other officers who had taken part were consequently also acquitted.

1778.

Siege and Capture of Pondicherry.

In June 1778, news having arrived in India that war with the French was inevitable, preparations were at once commenced so that, immediately on the arrival of news that war had been declared, an advance might be made against Pondicherry and the other French settlements on the Coast, which had been restored to France by the Treaty of Paris on the 10th February 1763.

A strong force was accordingly assembled, which included eleven complete Carnatic Battalions, and the Grenadier companies of ten others, including that of the 4th Battalion, which were formed into four Grenadier Battalions. On the 30th July, Colonel Braithwaite was ordered to march from Wandiwash towards Pondicherry. On the 3rd August, Major-General Hector Munro who, with the new Governor, Sir Thomas Rumbold, had arrived from England in February as Commander-in-Chief, took command of the army.

On the 8th August, the army encamped on the Red Hills, within four miles of Pondicherry, and summoned the French Governor to surrender on the following day. Reinforcements arrived on the 20th August and on the 21st, possession was taken of the Bound Hedge. On the 31st, the place was reconnoitred, and a battery commenced, which was completed on the 4th September, when further batteries were begun. Meanwhile the British had proved successful in a naval action with the French squadron on the 10th August*, and on the 21st, the British squadron, under Sir Edward Vernon, anchored in the roads.

On the 18th September, fire was opened from the batteries, the fort replying vigorously, and by the 24th, a breach was beginning to appear. Work was greatly delayed by heavy rain and want of tools, and the garrison, under M. Bellecombe, displayed the greatest bravery and devotion, but by the 15th October, it was decided that an assault could be attempted. This intention was, however, frustrated by an inrush of water. An attack was nevertheless made on the ravelin, which did considerable damage to the enemy.

By the 16th, they were again ready to assault, but at eleven o'clock in the morning, M. Bellecombe sent out a flag of truce, and agreed to deliver up the place on the 19th. The French officers were permitted to return to France, the General, who had been wounded, not leaving Madras until May 1779.

Throughout the siege, the utmost gallantry was displayed on both sides, and the losses were consequently heavy. The French lost 322 Europeans and 146 Sepoys and *Topasses* killed and wounded, while the British casualties amounted to 67 Europeans and 155 Sepoys killed, and 193 Europeans and 491 Sepoys wounded— a total of 906. (These are Vibart's figures, Wilson giving a total of 820).

I do not know with which Grenadier Battalion the company of the 4th was serving, but the total losses of the Grenadier Battalions were one Lieutenant, one Havildar and 14 Sepoys killed; and one Captain, one Lieutenant, 2 Ensigns, 2 Sergeants, 3 Subadars, 2 Jemadars, 5 Havildars, 5 Naicks and 92 Sepoys wounded.

After the surrender, Colonel Baillie was placed in command of the garrison, and the fortifications were completely destroyed by December 1779.

For their services on this occasion, Sir Thomas Rumbold was rewarded with a Baronetcy and Sir Hector Munro was granted the Knighthood of the Bath.

---

* Wilson says that this action took place on the 10th August; Wilks gives the 2nd August.

The mention above of the term *Topasses* may require some explanation. The author of the *History of Ayder Ali Khan* (whom James Bristow calls " M. le Maitre de la Tour"), writing in 1784, says:—

" The Topasses are black Christians, who call themselves Portuguese, and have the names of the first families in Portugal; but who, to all appearance, are descended from slaves, born and brought up in the houses of the Portuguese, who treat very favourably, and with great humanity, those slaves whom they call Creanza de Caza, or Children of the House. The Europeans have never been able to form good troops out of these people; which arises, no doubt, from the contemptuous manner they treat them with: instead of which, Ayder has always put them on an equality with the Sepoys, and even preferred them to his other troops......In consequence of this treatment, they may be regarded as Ayder's best troops, and those he can most rely on."

Orme is perhaps more explanatory, if less complimentary:—

" The Christians who call themselves Portuguese always formed part of a garrison: they are little superior in courage to the lower castes of Indians, and greatly inferior to the higher castes, as well as the Northern Moors of Indostan; but because they learn the manual exercise and the duties of a parade with sufficient readiness, and are clad like Europeans, they are incorporated into the companies of European troops. From wearing a hat, these pretended Portuguese obtained among the natives of India the name of *Topasses*; by which name the Europeans likewise distinguish them."

In December 1778, Lieutenant-General Sir Eyre Coote, K.B., arrived in Madras on his way to Bengal as Commander-in Chief and, having reviewed the troops in Madras on the 1st January 1779, issued the following order:—

" Lieutenant-General Sir Eyre Coote, on his return to the Command of India, felt himself particularly happy in the recollection that he should have the honour once more of leading those troops whose military firmness and intrepidity he has been an eyewitness of in so many instances during former wars. But on his arrival here he begs leave to address the Army on this establishment with the overflowings of a heart replete with gratitude to them as an Englishman, as King's and Company's officers, for the essential services they have so lately rendered the English nation, its allies and most particularly their masters, the Honourable East India Company. The Service they have been employed on during the siege of Pondicherry, required leaders of approved military abilities, and soldiers in the highest sense of the word, and as such, the Army on the Coromandel Coast have signalised themselves to all the world."

1779.

The Expedition to Mahé.

Early in the year, it was decided to send an expedition against Mahé, now the last of the French possessions in India, and accordingly a force was assembled under the command of Lieutenant-Colonel Braithwaite, which consisted of two battalions of European infantry, the 3rd (Captain Walker), 4th (Captain Fraser) and 20th (Captain Muirhead) Carnatic Battalions, three companies of Artillery, and some Engineers and Pioneers. Philippart says that the 4th were commanded by Captain Muirhead on this expedition, but I believe this to be wrong.

The force arrived at Anjengo on the 28th February, having, it is believed, marched from Trichinopoly through Madura and the Arriangow pass into Travancore, and losing some 50 sepoys on the way by death and desertion. This appears to have been the first sea voyage undertaken by the regiment and the European troops with this expedition were the first to enter Travancore. The embarkation took place on the 2nd March and, on the 14th, Colonel Braithwaite arrived at Mahé and on the 15th, a battery was commenced, to reduce the fort of Komachi which had been formed by scarping a high chalk hill and consisted of upper and lower forts, accessible only by long rope ladders, which the defenders drew up after them.

Haidar Ali, for whom this was only the port whence he could obtain supplies from without, sent troops to assist the French in the defence and Monsieur Picot, the Governor, declared his intention to defend the place, so work was carried on, the French firing a few guns from Fort St. George and Chimban without effect.

The battery would have been ready on the 20th March but on the 19th, to the great astonishment of Colonel Braithwaite, M. Picot sent out proposals to surrender, and accordingly the place was given up at 2 p.m. on that day, thus falling into the hands of the English without their firing a shot. The cause of the surrender is said to have been the discontent of the Nayars with Haidar's Government; had this not been the case, the place was considered almost impregnable, all the forts being almost inaccessible. Haidar Ali was greatly enraged at its capture.

The fortifications were all destroyed, and eight companies of the 4th Battalion were sent round by sea to Madras, together with eight companies of the 3rd Battalion, while the remainder of the force was sent to Tellicherry, and of them we shall hear further.

On the 23rd April 1779, the following order was issued by Government, thanking the troops employed at Mahé for their services:—

"The Honorable the President and Select Committee take this method of expressing their entire satisfaction in the conduct of the officers and troops employed on the expedition to Mahé and of returning their thanks to them. The Honorable the President and Select Committee having with much pleasure received information of the very chearful and soldierlike manner in which the 3rd, 4th and 20th Battalions of sepoys (commanded by Captains Fraser, Muirhead and Walker) embarked at Anjengo for the service of the expedition to Mahé, think it proper to express the highest approbation of the zeal and good conduct shown on this occasion, which reflects great honor on the said battalions and the European Officers belonging to them. The President and Select Committee desire that the Commanding Officers of the said three battalions will particularly explain to the black officers and sepoys the sense which the Committee entertain of their behaviour, and the attachment they have shown to the Company's service."

1779—1780.
The Tellicherry Detachment.

It had been the intention of Government to send to Guzerat the troops employed in the expedition to Mahé in order to join the force under General Goddard, but meanwhile they received an urgent appeal for assistance from Tellicherry, against which place a large body of Nayars was advancing, at the instigation of Haidar. The detachment accordingly moved to Tellicherry early in December, and Colonel Braithwaite shortly afterwards departed, leaving Major John Cotgrave in command.

The detachment at Tellicherry consisted of about 100 Europeans, the 20th Carnatic Battalion, and the Grenadier Companies of the 3rd and 4th Carnatic Battalions (4 Subalterns, 4 Sergeants, 8 Native Officers, 297 Non-Commissioned Officers and men).

At daybreak on the 5th May 1779, a determined attack was made by a large body of Nayars, estimated at about 1,000 men, and some of them managed to force their way into the Fort, but after very severe fighting the garrison succeeded in clearing out the enemy with a loss of 217 men killed and wounded.

For over a year the Madras troops were detained at Tellicherry and throughout that time there was continuous fighting. On the 14th September, Lieutenant Campbell with about 100 sepoys made a sally and drove the enemy into the river, drowning over 300 of them. The total loss of the enemy on this occasion amounted to 550, while the British casualties were one Ensign and three Sergeants killed and 90 sepoys killed and wounded. A further sally on the 14th October cost the enemy another 400 killed and wounded, and Major Cotgrave, in a letter to Government in August 1780, in which he estimates the strength of Haidar's force at about 10,000 men with 30 guns worked by Europeans, states that he believes that up to that date at least 2,000 of Sardar Khan's (Haidar's general) men had been destroyed. He goes on to say:—

"I hope the Bombay gentlemen will speedily send troops to relieve us. If they do not, I fear we shall lose many by desertion, as the sepoys are very anxious to return to their families. The fatigues they have undergone are almost incredible; they are constantly on duty, and the only relief that can be contrived is removing them from one post to another."

The Mutiny of the Grenadier Company. That Major Cotgrave's fears were not without foundation was shortly proved to be the case as, in December, the two Grenadier companies, one of the 4th and one of the 3rd Battalion, mutinied owing to their prolonged detention on the Malabar Coast in violation of repeated promises, which was aggravated by their fears for their families in the Carnatic, then being overrun and laid waste by Haidar Ali. Major Cotgrave's report of this regrettable incident, dated the 14th of that month, was as follows:—

"Two Grenadier companies (one of the 4th, the other of the 3rd Battalion) on being ordered to parade for the usual guards in the lines, declared they would no longer serve the English company, ran to their arms, and surrounded the European officers (having knocked down with the butts of their firelocks, the black officers who endeavoured to oppose them.)

They recited all the hardships they had undergone here since their arrival, said they were cheated out of their double batta, that they were deceived, and the promises made them broke of being sent back to the coast; first after the capture of Mahé, and afterwards in the promises made them of being relieved in five or six months from Bombay;

that their families were killed or dispersed through the Carnatic, and starving since Hyder had entered it. No arguments or persuasions of the officers could make them return to their duty, and had I not, on the first intimation of the affair, marched with the detachment of marines, and drawn them up opposite to them with a field piece, I do not know to what extremities they would have gone. A drum-head court-martial sentenced one to be blown off from a gun, and two others to receive 1,000 lashes each, who were the principal ringleaders, and this was instantly put in execution in presence of all the troops........"

The Commander-in-Chief, Sir Eyre Coote, did not hear of this event till March 1781, but as soon as the news reached him he urged the Bombay Government to make immediate arrangements for the relief of the detachment, and in a letter to the Madras Government he stated:—

"It is much to be lamented that at so critical a period we should have been so circumstanced as not to have been at liberty to act up to those promises so repeatedly and publickly pledged to the Sepoys under Major Cotgrave."

This remonstrance was effective, and the detachment was shortly afterwards relieved and sent round by sea to Cuddalore.

1780.
The Campaign Against Haidar Ali.

When, in 1779, the British began to operate against the French possessions in India, they were warned by Haidar Ali that if they attacked the French he would retaliate on the Carnatic, and accordingly, as has been seen, he gave assistance to the French in the defence of Mahé. With a view to averting the threatened retaliation, the feeble Councillors of Madras sent missions to Haidar in July 1779, and again early in 1780, but the latter refused to be conciliated and the second envoy was refused an audience and was informed that Haidar had lost all faith in the promises of the British.

Early in 1780, Haidar assembled his huge army opposite the pass of Chengam, which leads into the Carnatic by Tiruvannamalai. This army, one of the most formidable ever assembled by any native prince in India, consisted of some 600 French troops under Colonel Lally* (a relative of the great Lally); 14,000 of his best stable horse; 12,000 Silladar horse; 2,000 Savenore horse; 15,000 regular infantry, trained in the European manner; 12,000 select and veteran peons; 18,000 peons selected from the garrison; 10,000 tributary Poligars; 2,000 rocket men; 5,000 well-equipped Pioneers; and 100 guns—making a total of about 90,000 Cavalry and infantry and 100 guns, many of the corps being commanded by experienced French officers. Innes Munro states that this immense force, when in camp near Conjeeveram, covered a space of 7 miles long and 3 miles broad.

---

* It is related of him that, about 1778, he was disposed to take service with Haidar Ali who stipulated to pay him 5,000 rupees a month for a certain number of men. Lally, not being able to bring the full number, received only 2,000 rupees as his first month's pay. "He demanded an audience, talked loud, and gasconaded.—'Be quiet,' said Hyder, 'and be grateful for getting so much; you have not fulfilled your stipulation, and I have overpaid you in proportion to your numbers: I do not give an officer 5,000 rupees a month for the beauty of his single nose.'"

On the 20th July, Haidar entered the Carnatic, and laid waste a wide stretch of country round Fort St. George, extending from Pulicat on the north almost as far as Pondicherry, and devastated a similar strip round Vellore. On July 22nd, a detachment plundered Porto Novo, and on the evening of the 24th, a body of horse appeared at St. Thomas' Mount and looted St. Thomé.

The troops at this time were dispersed all over the country, being stationed at Poonamallee, Nellore, Trichinopoly, Pondicherry, Tanjore, Guntur and Masulipatam, and Innes Munro remarks that though the strength of the army was supposed to be some 30,000 men, no more than 4,000 could be collected for any emergency within a month's time.

The Madras Council, unready as ever, in spite of its knowledge of Haidar's intentions, was at last roused from its lethargy by this near approach of danger, and ordered Colonel Harper's Corps—subsequently commanded by Colonel Baillie—to move south from Guntur by way of Kalahasti and Tirupati. Colonel Braithwaite's force, which was at Pondicherry, was ordered to march northwards to Chingleput and thence to Madras, and setting out on the 12th August, duly arrived at the Mount on the 24th. A select corps from Trichinopoly under Colonel Cosby was at first ordered to act on the enemy's line of communications, but was subsequently directed to join the main army. Small parties were also sent to assist the Nawab's garrisons in Arcot, Warriapollam,* Ginjee and Wandiwash, that despatched to the last mentioned fort, under Lieutenant Flint, obtaining admittance with some difficulty on the 11th August, where it was besieged by a larger force on the following day, but continued to hold out with the utmost bravery until relieved on the 24th January 1781—a period of 167 days.

Haidar invested Arcot on the 21st August, but moved thence on the 29th, on learning that the British army, under the command of the Commander-in-Chief Sir Hector Munro,† had marched from Madras on the 26th. The Governor, Mr. Whitehill, wished to retain Munro in Madras to preserve his majority on the Council, but Lord Macleod, commanding the 73rd Highlanders at Poonamallee, upon whom as next in command the leadership of the army should devolve, objected to the assembly of the army at Conjeeveram while Haidar was overrunning the whole country, and refused to take command unless the army were concentrated near Madras, so the Commander-in-Chief himself had to carry out the plan which he had originated.

Although, fortunately for itself, the 4th Battalion did not take part in the operations of the ill-fated Colonel Baillie, it is yet of some interest to give an account of the disastrous battle of Perumbakkam or Pullalur, owing to the association of Colonel Baillie with the regiment, which he commanded for so long during

---

* Possibly Oddapalayam.

† Munro served as a Major in various parts of India with H. M. 89th Regiment, and was in command at the battle of Buxar in 1764. He returned to England shortly after the campaign of 1781, rose to the rank of General, and commanded in Scotland for some years before his death.

its earliest days. Besides, although a digression, and apart from its regimental interest, some account of these operations is necessary for the proper understanding of the events which come afterwards.

Colonel Baillie's Disaster. On the 24th August 1780, Colonel Baillie arrived at a place six miles south of Gummidipundi, within 28 miles of Munro's camp at St. Thomas' Mount and somewhat nearer Madras, and the junction of the two forces could easily have been effected on the 25th. The Commander-in-Chief, however, ordered Baillie to march on Conjeeveram, where the army from Madras (5,209 strong) arrived on the 29th. Meanwhile Haidar had detached a force of 11,000 men, with guns, under Tippu Sultan, to intercept Baillie, who was delayed by floods in the river Korttalaiyar, near Vengal, from the 25th August till the 4th September. Baillie's force consisted of 207 Europeans, 2,606 sepoys, six 6-pounders, and four 3-pounders. On the morning of the 6th, Tippu's army appeared and Baillie took up a position near Perumbakkam, 14 miles from Munro's camp, losing on that day 100 men killed and wounded by the enemy's guns. On the same evening he wrote to Munro for assistance, while Tippu, who had lost heavily, sent to ask for reinforcements from Haidar. The latter had, on the 6th, interposed his army between Munro and the road by which Baillie was expected, but Munro made no move to frustrate his intention, and did nothing on the 6th, 7th and 8th, in spite of the fact that the sound of firing, which showed that Baillie was engaged, was distinctly audible. On the 8th, Baillie's letter was received, and the flank companies of the army—only 1,007 men—under Colonel Fletcher, were sent to Baillie's assistance, and succeeded in eluding Haidar, joining Baillie on the 29th, and bringing his force up to a strength of 3,720 men. On the same night they started to march for Conjeeveram, while Haidar, perceiving that it was the intention of Munro to remain where he was, quietly moved off in the darkness to Perumbakkam.

Baillie had scarcely moved from the latter place when he encountered the enemy, and after some desultory fighting, came to the unaccountable resolution of halting where he was for the night, in spite of Colonel Fletcher's protests, his reason, as given to Captain Baird, being that "he was determined to halt till daylight that he might have an opportunity of looking about him." He was at this time within 9 miles of Munro, and, had he only continued his advance, must have effected a junction with that force, as Haidar was between two fires.

At daylight on the 10th September, the march was recommenced with the enemy in sight, who opened a distant fire, and Baillie again halted, although another ¾ mile would have given him a strong post in the village of Pullalur. Ten companies of sepoy Grenadiers were now sent forward under Captains Rumley and Gowdie to attack the enemy's guns, which they carried, but were forced to retreat hastily by the arrival of Haidar's army. Baillie, who was dismounted, had now by running about and overfatigue become incapable of cool thought, and no effort was made in the interval which ensued after the appearance of Haidar to occupy either the village or a fairly strong position along a bank and ditch close by.

The remainder of the action may be described in a few words. The wretched troops—in the open, and exposed to a cross-fire from 50 guns—made a brave resistance until their ammunition was exhausted, an event which was hastened by the explosion of two tumbrils, and then, formed into a square by their now severely wounded commander, received and repulsed no fewer than 13 different attacks of the enemy's horse, but a final desperate effort of the latter threw the sepoys into irremediable confusion, and the little force was practically annihilated.

Writing on the subject of this disaster, the anonymous author of the *Life of Sir David Baird* states:—

"The various descriptions of this memorable and most unequal contest all agree in confirming the belief that, vast as was the disparity between the contending armies, and although Haidar had upwards of 70 pieces of cannon in the field, the day would have been won by the English if the fortune of war had not been so decidedly against them. The enemy were repeatedly and continually repulsed, their infantry gave way, while their cavalry were falling in all directions and, it is said, Hyder was only prevented from retreating by the persuasions of Colonel Lally, who represented to him that retiring would bring him in contact with Sir H. Munro, who was in his rear ...."

Innes Munro says that

'History cannot produce an instance, for fortitude, cool intrepidity, and desperate resolution, to equal the exploits of this heroic band."

Of 86 officers engaged, 36 were killed, 34 wounded and taken, and 16 taken unwounded. Colonel Baillie and the other prisoners were removed to the dungeons of Seringapatam, where the former died on the 13th November 1782: his tomb may still be seen in Seringapatam not far from Tippu's summer palace, on the walls of which the Sultan caused to be portrayed a very striking representation of his triumph.

It is of interest to note that amongst those wounded and captured were Lieutenants Bowser and Turing of the 1st Madras European regiment, of whom the former subsequently became Colonel of the 4th Battalion and for a short time was Commander-in-Chief of the Madras Army, while a note on the numerous Turings will be found elsewhere in these records.

To return to the main army, Sir Hector Munro, discovering in the morning that Haidar had disappeared, had marched towards Perumbakkam, and was within 2 miles of that place while Colonel Baillie's force was being annihilated, but remained inactive in spite of the entreaties of some of his officers. On hearing of the disaster, he hastened back to Conjeeveram and, abandoning his heavy guns and stores, commenced his retreat to Chingleput on the 11th September. On the same day Haidar moved back to his former camp at Muttavakkam where, finding that his troops, who had suffered heavy losses, were by no means anxious to attack Munro's army, he contented himself with detaching a force to annoy it on the march.

Munro reached Chingleput on the 12th where he was joined by Colonel Cosby's detachment from the south which, after a gallant but vain attempt to take Chittapet* on the 7th, had marched on Conjeeveram, but had been diverted to Chingleput by timely news of Baillie's disaster. On the 13th, Munro, leaving his sick at Chingleput, marched to St. Thomas' Mount, where he arrived on the following day and on the 15th, moved to a more secure position at "Marmalong"† with a river to his front—Haidar being still in his camp 40 miles away. During this retreat the army lost upwards of 500 killed and wounded, mostly sepoys, of whom the rearguard consisted.

Speaking of these men, Innes Munro says:

" Many of Colonel Baillie's sepoys fought hard in General Munro's army next day, which was no small mark of their loyalty and courage..........After everything that can be adduced against them, it must be acknowledged that the Company's sepoys are good troops, and exceedingly well officered."

The only hope of the Madras Government now rested on the aged but indomitable Commander-in-Chief in India, Sir Eyre Coote, who arrived in Madras with reinforcements on the 5th November, and took over sole direction of the war. He brought with him orders for the suspension of the Governor, Mr. Whitehill, who was succeeded by Mr. Smith.

Haidar meanwhile had returned to Arcot on the 19th September, and that place capitulated soon after, mainly owing to the treachery of Mahomed Ali's Governor.

Encounter near Madras. Early in December 1780, the 4th Battalion formed part of a small force detached by Sir Eyre Coote from Madras to dislodge a strong force under one of Haidar Ali's best generals, "Lawlah" by name, who had posted himself some 30 miles to the north of Madras, and was consequently cutting off all supplies from that direction. The detachment consisted of three battalions of infantry, a regiment of cavalry and some light guns, and was commanded by Lieutenant-Colonel Cosby. Philippart, in his notice of the services of the latter officer, says:

" This service was performed with such secrecy and skill, that every one of the enemy's videttes were taken; and had not a delay been occasioned by being obliged to wait the fall of the tide of a river that lay in the road, few of the enemy, it is supposed, could have escaped, it being intended to surprise them before daylight; but as the dawn broke when within a short distance, Colonel Cosby's approach was prematurely descried, and the enemy had more time for preparation than was intended them. They, however, were soon defeated, and fled in confusion, leaving their camp, some horses, arms, and a quantity of provisions, cattle, etc., etc., to the captors; and Colonel Cosby returned to headquarters in the course of twenty-four hours, having in that time marched sixty miles, bringing in with him, besides what he had taken from the enemy, a further supply of provisions, collected on his route."

---

* Probably Settupatti.

† This must have been "Mambalam" which is just across the River Adyar opposite St. Thomas' Mount.

On the return of the detachment, Colonel Cosby received the following letter from Sir Eyre Coote:—

December 14, 1780.

"My dear Colonel,

I am sorry for your disappointment: however, you have done more than could have been expected after the unfortunate detention you met with. You do very well to refresh your men at Motoo Kistna's Choultry. I march to-morrow to the Mount.

"Lieut.-Col. Cosby."

(Signed) EYRE COOTE,
Commander-in-Chief.

1781.

Sir Eyre Coote's Campaign against Haidar Ali.

At the commencement of the year 1781, Haidar was engaged in the siege of Ambur, Vellore, Wandiwash, Perumukkal and Chingleput, of which Ambur capitulated to Tippu on the 13th January.

Sir E. Coote, who had assembled, at the Mount, early in the month, his army, which consisted of 1,600 Europeans, 800 Nawab's horse, 10 Battalions of Sepoys each 500 strong and including the 4th Battalion, and 62 guns, began his march on 17th January, leaving General Stuart in command in Madras, and relieved Chingleput on the 19th, crossing the River Palar on the same day.

On the 20th, a force under Captain Davis was detached to Karunguli which, so Coote had been informed, the enemy were evacuating. The information was discovered to be erroneous, but Captain Davis succeeded in capturing the fort on the 21st, after hard fighting, mainly owing to the gallantry of Captain Moorhouse, who blew open the gates.

On the 24th January, Wandiwash was relieved, just in time, as only one day's ammunition remained to the garrison which, though only consisting of two British officers and 2½ companies, had, owing to the heroic efforts of Lieutenant Flint, maintained a stout defence against Haidar's principal officer, Mir Sahib, with a powerful train of artillery, 11,000 foot and 22,000 horse, since the 12th August 1780.

A French fleet under M. D'Orvé, which appeared before Madras on the 25th, caused Coote to retrace his steps as far as the heights above Karunguli, but, hearing from General Stuart that nothing was to be feared from a landing of the French, he returned and relieved Perumukkal, which had been gallantly defended by Lieutenant Bishop with only one company, on the 3rd February, and thence moved towards Pondicherry with a view to destroying the boats at that place, arriving there on the 5th February.

Haidar had meanwhile moved to Conjeeveram on learning that the British Army was retiring on Madras but, hearing that they were now continuing their march to the south, followed them in the direction of Cuddalore. This move compelled Coote, then at Pondicherry, to march to cover Cuddalore, the two armies moving parallel to one another. On arrival at Cuddalore on the 8th February, Coote found himself in a desperate position, being without supplies and unable to bring Haidar to an action, while the latter laid waste all the surrounding country. Had the French fleet properly performed the duty of intercepting supplies by sea, on which the British army entirely depended, the latter must either have capitulated or have been dispersed, but with incomprehensible folly the fleet moved off to the eastward and Coote was rapidly reprovisioned from Madras and Nagore. Haidar then left a containing force before Cuddalore and marched with his main body to the north of the Coleroon, where he kept his army supplied from the resources of Tanjore, which unfortunate province now lay at his mercy. The detachment at Nagore (two battalions under Captain Lamotte) was withdrawn from that place by sea and joined Coote, but brought no advantage to the latter, as his only chance of relief lay in bringing the enemy to an action, and this he was unable to do. On its evacuation by the British garrison, Nagore was at once occupied by Lally.

The army remained stationary in the neighbourhood of Cuddalore from the 8th February to the 16th June, suffering great privation. During this period only two events occurred to relieve the monotony. The first of these was the assault of the fort at Tiruvadi, which lies about 16 miles west of Fort St. David, and was taken in April by a detachment under the personal command of Coote, which included the 4th Battalion. The second event was a fruitless attempt to relieve Tiyaga-durgam, which fell, on the 7th June, on the exhaustion of its ammunition.

The Repulse at Chillambaram. On the 16th June, Coote moved southwards with a view to making an attempt upon the fortified pagoda at Chillambaram, which Haidar had strengthened as a depot for provisions, and at noon on the 8th, he crossed the river Vellar. For an account of what occurred on this occasion I cannot do better than give a verbatim extract from Colonel Wilks' history:

> Finding that the enemy was nowhere near it in considerable force, and being greatly misinformed regarding its garrison, which was reported to be but a few irregulars and actually consisted of nearly 3,000 men, partly regulars, and the remainder the distinguished peons of Chittledroog under Jehan Khan, an officer of reputation, he (Coote) determined in pursuance of this defective information, to attempt carrying it on the same night by a coup de main. Four battalions of Sepoys* with two twelve-pounders, four six-pounders, and two howitzers, moved under his own immediate direction at dusk; they carried the pettah or town without difficulty and pushed on with rapidity to a second line of defence, which surrounded the place at a distance of about 100 yards: the gate of this line of works was forced by a twelve-pounder, and the troops advanced under a heavy fire, with the greatest spirit, to the body of the place, the entrance into which was protected by the usual Indian apparatus of winding traverses, and three successive gates, built up behind with a few feet of masonry to prevent their being blown open. The first gate was forced after some difficulty, and the outer area between the first and second being as usual inadequately flanked or commanded, the troops succeeded in forcing the second gate also; but for the area between the second and third gates, commanded by the rampart of the body of the place, and lined with thatched huts, where a portion of the garrison usually resided, a better preparation was arranged.

---

* Wilson says the 4th and 9th Battalions and the Trichinopoly Detachment.

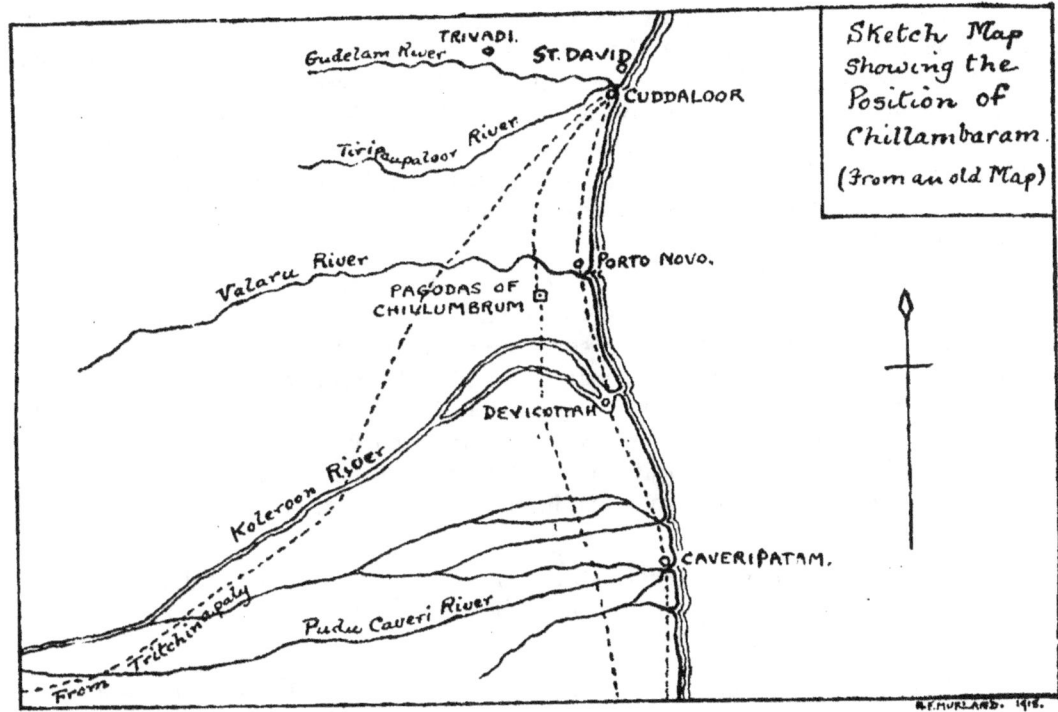

Exclusively of the ordinary means of defence, bundles of straw had been placed on the ramparts in reserve, with vessels of oil ready to moisten them and increase the combustion: a few lighted port-fires, dropped down on the straw roofs, gave a commencement to the flame, and the bundles of oiled straw successively thrown down, converted into a mass of flame nearly the whole area to be passed; as a farther defence, if even the third gate should be forced, a select body of Chittledroog spearmen were placed in reserve on each side of the interior of the gate. But the retreat of the assailants rendered this reserve unnecessary; nothing could prevail on the Sepoys to rally, and the officers and artillerymen, compelled to abandon one gun, drew off the remainder with great difficulty and serious loss. The small amount of the European troops, and a desire of reserving them for greater emergencies, had prevented their employment in this enterprise; but on thus being foiled, Sir Eyre Coote ordered up the Grenadiers of the army, with the intention of resuming the assaults; but before their arrival, being better informed of the actual means of defence possessed by the garrison, he drew off the whole in the course of the night, carrying with him a small supply of grain which had been found in the pettah; and after the lapse of four days recrossed the river and encamped near the village of Porto Novo."

Another account says:—

" On arriving at the main street, which led to the pagoda, the detachment was warmly saluted by showers of ball from wall-pieces, etc., that scoured the street; however, a party with two twelve-pounders dashed through, and firing one of the guns against the gate, so shattered it, that the garrison called for quarter; but some of the English being overheard declaring that their ammunition was expended, the enemy returned to the works, and drove them from the gateway with considerable loss."

It may be noted that the British losses on this occasion amounted to 8 officers and 250 rank and file killed and wounded, in addition to the twelve-pounder abandoned to the enemy as related above.

On the 24th June, Admiral Sir Edward Hughes arrived from Madras with the news that Lord Macartney had assumed the Government, and that he had been ordered to attack the Dutch possessions. It was at first proposed that a descent should be made on Negapatam, aided by a detachment from the army, but the risks of this proposal caused its speedy rejection, and it was decided that a further and combined attack should be made on Chillambaram, a decision which had no sooner been arrived at than the news was brought to Coote that Haidar Ali with his whole army was within a few miles.

The Battle of Porto Novo, July 1st, 1781. The intelligence which Haidar had received of the repulse of the British army at Chillambaram, which had no doubt lost nothing in the telling, decided him to move at once and complete the defeat of his enemy, and accordingly he made a forced march of 100 miles in 2½ days from Srirangam in the Tanjore country and, interposing his army between the British and Cuddalore, commenced to fortify a position within three miles of the British camp, while his cavalry covered the whole country round and prevented Coote from obtaining any information as to his strength or dispositions.

Sir Eyre Coote now requested Sir E. Hughes to cover Cuddalore with the fleet while he moved forward to try his fortune in a battle, the result of which must mean triumph or annihilation.

At seven o'clock on the 1st July, the British army left its camp and was formed up in two lines facing almost due north. The first line, under Major-General Sir Hector Munro, consisted of the 73rd Regiment, and the Madras and Bengal European Regiments; the 2nd, 4th, 9th, 14th and 15th Carnatic Battalions and the Trichinopoly Detachment; one European troop and two native regiments of cavalry; and thirty pieces of cannon. The second line, commanded by Major-General Stuart, was composed of the 16th, 17th, 20th, and 18th Carnatic Battalions and twenty-six field pieces. The baggage guard comprised the 21st Carnatic Battalion, two regiments of cavalry, 300 Mahratta horse and six guns.

The ground consisted of sand-hills intersected by deep nullahs and the enemy had placed a battery on every hillock. The direction of the road to Cuddalore pointed N. N. W., having on its left the termination of a lagoon. The plain was covered by large bodies of cavalry, with this lagoon in rear of their right centre, and Haidar's select cavalry with some light artillery was drawn up behind the lagoon, facing north, in readiness to attack the flank of the British army when it had passed the lagoon and was engaged with the masked batteries to its front.

Sir Eyre Coote who, it must be remembered, was ignorant of the whereabouts and nature of the enemy's position, reconnoitred to the front of his little army—which had been weakened by the necessity of detailing a baggage guard, which was moving between his right and the sea—and, discovering the enemy's works after his force had advanced about a mile and a half, spent an hour in carefully examining them. The line taken up by the enemy extended from commanding ground on the right to the sandhills near the shore on the left, and was strengthened with great skill by front and flanking batteries.

During Coote's reconnaissance the army was subjected to an incessant cannonade both from the front and from behind the lagoon on the left, to which the British guns were forbidden to reply. At nine o'clock, the General had come to a decision and, without any preliminary movement which could advise the enemy of his intention, rapidly marched to the right in column to the east of the range of sandhills, which ran along the coast some 1,100 yards from the sea and which covered the greater part of this manœuvre, until he reached an opening in the sandhills where a road was found which had been constructed by Haidar for the movement of his guns.

A commanding hill, which Haidar had omitted to guard, was occupied and the first line, clearing the passage through the sandhills, and driving back a strong corps of the enemy, deployed in battle order facing west, and waited under a heavy fire until the sandhill behind was in possession of the guns of the second line, when it moved rapidly forward, a long thick hedge covering its right, and a battalion in column with some guns its left.

Meanwhile Haidar's artillery had been withdrawn to a new line at right angles to its former position, and opened a tremendous cannonade, in spite of which the British army advanced steadily, making skilful use of every advantage of ground, and, successfully repelling a general charge of cavalry made diagonally upon the angle of the left by Kiram Sahib, by its superior fire and steadiness forced the enemy's line at 4 o'clock, and compelled it to a precipitate retreat.

While the first line was thus advancing, the second was attacked in a most determined manner by a large force of infantry, supported by cavalry and guns, and a severe struggle ensued in which the second line eventually triumphed, after repulsing three fierce attacks.

Munro states that the enemy came on with such resolution at this point that Captain Moorhouse of the artillery actually melted a brass six-pounder by the rapidity of his discharges of grape. Becoming impatient at this stubborn resistance Haidar ordered a desperate charge of the whole cavalry on both lines, which was repulsed, the defeat of that portion which attacked the second line being assisted by the flanking fire of a small schooner—the *Intelligence*—close in shore, while its repulse by the 1st line has already been mentioned.

Haidar now saw that all was lost, and ordered a general retreat, which his army lost no time in carrying out. The victory could not, unfortunately, be made decisive, owing to the want of cavalry and the exhaustion of the army.

On this brilliant day, a British force, only numbering 7,878 men with 55 guns and 598 gunners, overthrew an army of which it seems to have been impossible to arrive at the exact numbers. According to Coote's despatches, the enemy numbered 620 Europeans, 1,100 Topasses, 23 battalions of Sepoys, some 18,000 strong, 40,000 cavalry and 120,000 irregulars, with 47 guns. Innes Munro thinks the whole number was about 100,000 and Wilks says 80,000.

The casualties on the British side, owing to Coote's brilliant manoeuvring, only amounted to 306 killed and wounded, while a moderate computation fixes the losses in Haidar's densely-packed masses at 10,000 killed and wounded, Innes Munro stating that there were at least 4,000 dead.

The British army after the action halted near the village of Muttupalaiyam.

The following extract is from Coote's account of the battle, dated the 6th July :—

"The behaviour of the whole army on this most interesting day was uniformly steady and worthy of the highest commendation........In short every individual of our little army seemed to feel the critical situation of our national concerns........The only difficulty was to restrain the order of the troops within prudential bounds. Eager to advance, it became particularly necessary to guard against accidental disorder, situated as we were with multitudes of Cavalry against us on the watch to take advantage of hurried or confused movements........The spirited behaviour of our Sepoy Corps did them the greatest credit. No Europeans could be steadier; they were emulous of being foremost on every service it was necessary to undertake."

Captain Robson, in his *Life of Hyder Ally*, says :—

"Thus ended this glorious battle, which day should be a jubilee to all European nations, who have any possessions in India; they may consider it as that on which their fate in India totally depended. Had that day been lost, I verily believe we should have been deprived of all our possessions in that country."

While Haidar was operating to the south, Tippu Sultan had captured Tayaga-durgam, and was ordered to resume the siege of Wandiwash, which place he accordingly invested on the 27th June. A reinforcement from Bengal under the command of Colonel Pearse was now at Nellore on its way to Madras and, partly to cover it, partly on account of the news from Wandiwash, Coote moved north, drawing his supplies from the fleet. On the way he offered battle to Haidar which was, however, declined and the latter moved westwards.

Coote, quitting the sea-coast, then proceeded towards Perumukkal and Karunguli. At the latter place he learnt that Tippu had raised the siege of Wandiwash on the 18th July, deterred from attempting to storm it by the readiness of the garrison and the moral effect of the battle of Porto Novo. The British army then moved towards St. Thomas' Mount by way of Chingleput to join the detachment from Bengal. Tippu on leaving Wandiwash had made preparations to ambuscade this detachment on its way from Nellore to Madras but, eluding him by taking a little-frequented route along the sea-shore, it arrived safely in the neighbourhood of Pulicat, where it was joined by Coote on the 3rd August.

Returning to St. Thomas' Mount, the army was, on the 8th August, formed into brigades, five in number, and the 4th Carnatic Battalion was placed in the 5th Brigade, with the 15th and 20th Carnatic and 26th Bengal Battalions, under the command of Lieutenant-Colonel Brown of the Madras Establishment.

Having now united his forces, Coote decided to turn his attention to Tirupasur,* a fortress situated 33 miles to the west on a road leading to Arcot and Vellore. Marching *via* Poonamallee, which was held by the British, he reached his objective on the 19th August, and found that the place had been considerably strengthened and was garrisoned by 1,500 men. On the 22nd, when a breach had been made and the troops were ready for the assault, a flag of truce was sent out offering to surrender on terms which were at once rejected, and the garrison was given a quarter of an hour within which to surrender unconditionally. A moment afterwards it was discovered that Haidar's whole army was rapidly approaching and without an instant's delay the troops were given orders to storm but, being met by a flag of truce with a declaration of surrender, ascended the breach without opposition and Haidar, on seeing what had occurred, withdrew after refusing to agree to an exchange of prisoners.

Tirupasur.

A convoy sent to Poonamallee, on the 25th August, for fresh supplies having returned with a sufficiency of rice for a few days, Coote marched on the following day to endeavour to bring Haidar to an action. Haidar had meanwhile occupied the same encampment at Muttavakkam from which he had confronted Sir Hector Munro in the preceding year, and decided to offer battle on the same auspicious ground on which he had defeated Colonel Baillie. On the 26th, Coote reached Perumbakkam, where large bodies of cavalry to the south-west indicated that the enemy was at last prepared to fight.

The Battle of Pullalur† August 27, 1781.

On the 27th August, the army moved forward at daybreak, and at 9 a.m. the advanced guard, consisting of the 8th Battalion with two regiments of cavalry and Coote's Guard, under the command of Lieutenant-Colonel Brown, marching nearly due west, had reached the spot where Baillie had spent the night of the 9th September 1780, and the enemy's army came in view.

The British army was formed in two lines, the first, commanded by General Munro, comprising the 1st (Crawford), 2nd (Edmondson) and 3rd (Pearse) Brigades, while the second, under the command of General Stuart, consisted of the 4th (Owen) and 5th (Captain Davies) Brigades, the 4th Battalion, as already mentioned, forming part of the last-named. The total effective strength was some 11,000, while Coote's estimate of the enemy's forces was over 150,000 with 80 guns.

A very high wind was blowing and thick clouds of dust rendered indistinct all objects at a distance, but a small tope on a slight rise with a watercourse to its front and right, which was observed about 100 yards in front of the left of the advanced guard, appeared to be a position of importance, and was at once occupied by the 8th Bn. of sepoys (Captain Walker) with guns.

---

* Tirupasur was important as being the key to the "Pollams", or hilly country, governed by many petty chieftains, tributaries to the Nawab of the Carnatic, from whom were derived considerable supplies for the army.

† This has also been called the battle of Tracollom—I do not know why, but it may possibly be from the village of Tirukallikadu, near Little Conjeeveram.

The first line was now formed in battle order, facing what appeared to be the chief mass of the enemy's force to the south-west, the second line being destined to support the first and reinforce the battalion at the tope. This operation, rendered slow by the broken nature of the ground, which was intersected by nullahs and in places covered with thick jungle, had scarcely been carried out when a heavy cannonade from the jungle and a village on the right was found nearly to enfilade the first line, and it became necessary to change front and throw back the right. A jungle was interposed between the position of the first line and this division of the enemy, which was commanded by Tippu Sahib, and a cannonade was opened until it could be discovered whether this jungle were passable. Being found penetrable, the army slowly moved through in columns and, arrived on the other side, formed up facing west, where a commanding bank enable their artillery to silence that of the enemy, which appeared to move south to join the main army.

Meanwhile the tope first occupied on the left was subjected to a hot fire from the enemy's guns, and was reinforced by the whole of the second line, with the exception of two battalions, one of which was the 4th, which were sent to join the 24th Bengal Regiment with the baggage, as it had now been discovered that the main force of the enemy was directed against this point. The enemy's position was one of great strength, the line extending along a fortified bank and watercourse, with its left resting on the pagoda and village of Pullalur, and its right on another village, behind which vast numbers of troops were massed.

Things were not looking well for the British at this point, the Circar battalion which had been sent forward by Colonel Owen to take a village from which the enemy were annoying the left flank of the troops in the tope, being beaten back in disgraceful confusion, but the veteran 20th Battalion under Captain Muirhead repaired the disaster by driving the enemy out with the greatest precision and steadiness. A fierce cannonade now commenced, but it was found that the enemy were in such strength that they threatened to outflank Owen's troops. The latter having reported this to Sir Eyre Coote, Colonel Pearse was ordered to reinforce the left with the 3rd Brigade, and accordingly left the first line and, marching to the left, took up a position in extension of Owen's line, with the 9th Battalion thrown back on his left flank to keep off the enemy's large bodies of horse. While this movement was being carried out the remainder of the first line, consisting of the 1st and 2nd Brigades was ordered to file off to the left and re-form along the avenue to Vellore, facing south, with its right opposite the village of Pullalur.

The post at the tope was now some 1,400 yards diagonally in front of the left of the first line, and formed a support to the right of the second line, which extended along its front nearly opposite the enemy's right.

The 2nd Brigade under Major Edmondson, which formed the right of the first line, now advanced directly against the village of Pullalur, supported by the 1st (European) Brigade under Colonel Crawford, and, meeting with but little resistance as Haidar had already withdrawn his guns from this point, quickly drove the enemy out and with their 6 pounders caused considerable loss among Haidar's retreating bodies of infantry, but owing to the difficulties of the ground were unable to cut them off as Coote intended.

To return to the left, Colonel Pearse had been joined by the 4th Battalion from the baggage at 3 o'clock, and at 5 o'clock Coote himself proceeded to the left to see what were the best means of co-ordinating the movement of his two lines which were now widely separated. He decided to push forward his left and the success of the 2nd Brigade against Pullalur at the same time was the signal for the whole of the second line, with the exception of three battalions kept in reserve at the tope, to advance and force the enemy's right, and just at sunset the line attained an eminence from which the retreating enemy could be cannonaded. The British army was now in possession of the enemy's ground, which was the sole advantage gained by this dubious victory, which at one period had every appearance of being likely to prove a disaster.

The nature of the ground prevented heavy losses, the British having only 28 Europeans and 105 sepoys killed, 25 Europeans and 207 sepoys wounded, and 58 sepoys missing. Among the six officers killed were Colonel Brown and Captain Hislop, and of seven wounded Major-General Stuart had the misfortune to lose a leg at the beginning of the action, being hit by the same shot which took off one of Colonel Brown's legs. Owing to the enemy's practice of carrying off their killed and wounded it was impossible to ascertain their losses, but they are estimated to have lost about 2,000. On the day after the battle Sir Eyre Coote issued the following order:—

> The Commander-in-Chief takes the earliest opportunity of returning his thanks to the whole army he has the honour to command, for their very steady and gallant conduct throughout the action of yesterday, and which alone ensured the success of the operations of the day. He desires that this order may be particularly explained to the black troops, whose behaviour on all occasions gives the greatest satisfaction. The spirited conduct of our troops must strike the enemy with that awe and respect for our arms, which cannot fail to be of essential service to our national cause, and, it is hoped, will eventually be the means of shortening the confinement and suffering of our brother soldiers in the enemy's miserable prisons. The Commander-in-Chief takes this opportunity also of mentioning that he will set forth to His Majesty and the Company the very essential services this army has rendered........"

The 28th August was employed in attending to the wounded and in burying not only the dead of the preceding day, but also the remains of Baillie's detachment, and on the 29th, the army returned to Tirupasur, the men having absolutely no food left, while the followers had been without food for two days.

Sir Eyre Coote now proceeded to Madras to confer with Government, and there he tendered his resignation, being unwilling to serve longer in command of an army which was unable to move for lack of provisions, but he was persuaded by Lord Macartney to make one more effort, and accordingly rejoined the army.

On the 21st September, he moved two marches from Tirupasur to Tiruttani, and on the 23rd, captured the small fort of Polur, where he found a small store of grain, but his main reliance for food rested now, as ever, upon the skill of his searchers for subterranean stores. At Polur he received a report from Colonel Ross Lang, then besieged in Vellore, of the desperate state of the garrison of that place and the necessity of an early surrender unless he were speedily relieved, and he also received information that Haidar was strengthening a position some ten or twelve miles off to obstruct his march towards Vellore.

The army had only some two days' supplies, but Coote decided that a determined effort must be made and, throwing his heavy guns and baggage into Polur marched seven miles towards Sholinghur on the evening of the 26th. A heavy night's rain rendered the tents too heavy to be moved next morning, a circumstance of which Haidar was duly apprised and which induced him to announce to his army that there would be no movement that day and to send off his cattle to graze and many of his troops to forage for grain at several miles distance.

The Battle of Sholinghur, September 27th, 1781.

On the morning of the 27th, Sir Eyre Coote went forward to reconnoitre the country to his front and, ascending an eminence, perceived a long ridge of rocks which ran out into the plain from the Sholinghur Hills and which was occupied by the enemy. Desiring to examine further, he ordered up the second Brigade, which dislodged the enemy, and now saw Haidar's whole army some three miles to the south, with large bodies a mile in front, and an advanced corps of cavalry encamped near the ridge, which moved off on the appearance of the Brigade with some loss from the fire of an 18-pounder.

Orders were at once sent to Colonel James Crawford, next in command, for the army to advance as rapidly as possible, the baggage being left in charge of two battalions with four guns at a suitable spot near the hills. Advancing over the ridge, the army was formed in two lines, with the centre of the first line opposite the main body of the enemy, drawn up some 2 miles off, with its right on a small rock, and its left on a grove and eminence. The second line formed an extension on its left, in echelon of battalions, which was necessary on account of large bodies of cavalry on the flank.

The ground between the opposing forces was comparatively open, but irregular ridges and groups of rocks afforded good cover to both armies.

Haidar's main body was drawn up behind the crest of a low ridge, its front covered by swampy rice fields, his guns being posted at intervals along the ridge, and in advanced positions on some of the groups of rocks. His left was commanded by Tippu Sultan, and on his right were the Grenadiers under Lally, while he commanded the centre in person. Besides the main body, detached forces exceeding the British army in strength were descried moving towards both flanks, and large masses of cavalry were collected at various points in readiness to charge. Haidar had been completely surprised, having thought that the advance of the Brigade was merely a reconnaissance, and that Coote would not move forward until the following day. Under the circumstances he now intended to act on the defensive until the confusion caused by the surprise had been remedied.

The day was already well advanced when the British army moved forward. The 2nd Brigade, commanded by Colonel Edmonston, which had been ordered to file off to the right, had gone much further than Coote had intended, and caused a wide interval between itself and the remainder of the army. Perceiving this error, Haidar at once opened a severe cannonade along the whole front, undeterred by which Coote ordered the whole line to advance and to close up the interval on the march. Wilks says that at this stage the British army looked like two diminutive corps almost surrounded by large armies.

According to Innes Munro, the advance of the 2nd Brigade round the large tank on their left flank was unobserved by the enemy and came as a complete surprise, throwing them into considerable confusion. As the line advanced, several temporary openings were caused by the necessity of defiling to pass the groups of rocks, an opportunity which was seized by two principal masses of the enemy's cavalry, who charged these points with the greatest determination which they had hitherto been known to exhibit. Each mass as it reached the opening wheeled to right and left to double up the flanks of the infantry, but found no flanks, the act of defiling having provided the necessary protection by leaving two lines at an obtuse angle which received the masses of cavalry with a crossfire. One such mass* galloped right through between the 18th and 21st Carnatic Battalions of Colonel Owen's Brigade, suffering heavy losses, and was followed up by the fire of the rear rank of the line, turned about for the purpose, while the other was directly repulsed with still heavier loss. It was on this occasion that the 21st battalion, later the 80th Carnatic Infantry, captured the standard, for which they were, up to the time of their disbandment after the Great War, allowed an extra Jemadar. These charges, though repulsed with loss, had given time for Haidar to withdraw his guns, all of which were sent off except one six-pounder, which was captured.

The 2nd Brigade of the first line now gained the left flank of the enemy's position, whence they brought their guns to bear with considerable effect on the retreating columns.

Meanwhile the second line, notably the 17th Carnatic Battalion and 13th Bengal Regiment, had been warding off the attacks of Tippu's horse on the left flank, which was at one time nearly turned, and eventually drove off the enemy with loss, who retreated at about the same time as the main body.

An attempt on the baggage guard by a large force of cavalry and infantry with 12 guns having also failed, the British were now left masters of the field, and the whole army encamped on the ground previously occupied by the enemy.

---

* "The last effort was made by a body of about 1,000 horse. They had solemnly vowed upon the Koran to take the first opportunity of breaking through the English line, and had that day been completely intoxicated with bang and opium in order to excite a false courage for the execution of their desperate enterprise. They charged the 13th Bengal and 17th, 18th and 21st Madras, who gave them one volley at 50 yards and another when they went through, which caused them to pay a bloody price for their temerity."

The trophies of the day were three cavalry standards and one gun, which Sir Eyre Coote said he would willingly have exchanged, together with the credit of victory, for five days' rice. The strength of the British army in this battle was 11,500, of which 1,500 were Europeans, and the losses did not exceed 100 killed and wounded. Haidar's whole army, estimated by Coote at 150,000 men with 70 guns, was present on the field, and the Mysoreans admit that they were surprised, and that their losses probably exceeded 5,000. After the battle Haidar retreated to Kaveripakkam.

The part played by the 4th Battalion in this important victory cannot, unfortunately, be discovered, the army having been re-brigaded after the battle of Pullalur, and no record of the alterations then made are now traceable. "*Sholinghur*" was added to the honours of the regiment in the year 1889.

After the battle of Sholinghur, the army being in its usual desperate situation for want of supplies, Coote decided that he must keep moving through the Chittoor Palaiyams in search of grain and accordingly marched on the 28th September, traversed the pass of Sholinghur and arrived at Attamancheri on the 2nd October, where he received assistance from Bomarazu, Chief of Karvetnagar, one of the principal Poligar chiefs of North Arcot.

On hearing that the Poligars were assisting Coote, Haidar sent a force of 6,000 men to plunder the country, but Coote, on receiving news of this, marched with a detachment consisting of 3 battalions of infantry and all the available cavalry, under the immediate command of Major Edmondson, on the 14th October. In the Chittoor Palaiyams he succeeded in surprising and completely dispersing the enemy with the loss of all their supplies and 40 horses, and returned to Attamancheri after an absence of 38 hours, of which 32 had been spent in the saddle, a wonderful performance for a man of his years.

At this time Coote declared, in a report to Government, that never since he had been a soldier, which was then forty years, had he seen such distress in any army as then prevailed in his.

The Action near Virakanellur, 23rd October 1781. The necessity of obtaining further supplies prevented any further operations for some time. Sir Eyre Coote, induced by the urgency of the relief of Vellore, sent a detachment under Colonel Owen, consisting of a party of cavalry, a few artillerymen, the Grenadier company of the Bengal European Regiment, the 24th Bengal, and 4th, 8th, 14th and 21st Carnatic Battalions with their guns, some twenty miles in advance, partly with the object of protecting the Poligars, who were endeavouring to assist the garrison of Vellore, and partly in order to intercept some of the grain convoys intended for the enemy, which usually came from Chittoor through the pass of Devalampetta.

This detachment, encamping some distance in front of the Pass, which is near Virakanellur, some twelve miles north-east of Chittoor, was, at daybreak on the 23rd, suddenly attacked on all sides by Haidar in person with nearly the whole of his regular infantry and field guns, and all his select cavalry, who made the greatest efforts to effect the destruction of the small force before it could reach the Pass or be relieved by Coote.

Colonel Owen at once ordered the tents and baggage to be set on fire, and retreated towards the Pass in order to rejoin the main army, which was little more than a mile distant.

Although hotly pressed by the enemy on both flanks and in rear, the troops fought with undaunted courage, but unfortunately just as they were entering the Pass, the 8th Battalion was broken by a sudden onslaught of the enemy, their commandant, Captain Walker, killed, and their gun captured. On hearing this, however, Captain Moore with the Grenadier Company and the 21st Battalion, who were the next troops in rear, rushed back and, forcing his way with the bayonet through the dense masses of the enemy, laid 150 of them dead on the spot, and brought back the gun in triumph. The whole detachment being now within the defile, and showing no signs of giving way, Haidar gave up the pursuit, greatly mortified at his failure to destroy such a small force, which he had made certain of being able to annihilate before Coote could come to its rescue. The success of the retreat to the pass was largely due to the artillery under Captain Moorhouse, who took up a series of skilfully selected positions to cover the infantry.

In this action the 4th Battalion had nine officers present, including Lieutenant Dawes in command.

After reaching the Pass, the detachment encamped at the village of Matawudi near Pallipat, where it was joined by the main army, and a party was sent to bury the dead which, with the wounded, numbered 300, besides 17 European and native officers. The losses of the enemy, as computed by themselves, amounted to no less than 3,000.

1781.
The First Relief of Vellore.

On the 26th October 1781, Coote moved to Pallipat, from which place he sent a detachment to Tirupasur with his sick and wounded. On its return this detachment not only brought further supplies of money from the Presidency but also intercepted, on its way to Haidar's camp, a convoy of 700 bullocks. A lucky discovery of a large quantity of hidden grain near Pallipat now enabled Coote to move to the assistance of Colonel Lang in Vellore and, marching on the 1st, he relieved that garrison on the 3rd November, which had been holding out with the greatest heroism for 16 months, by supplying it with six weeks' rice. On his approach, Haidar, still suffering from the discouragement occasioned by his failure at Virakanellur, retired to the opposite side of the River Palar.

A few days after the relief of Vellore, Coote marched off again towards the Palaiyams in order to look for supplies for the army, taking Colonel Lang and the European Grenadiers with him, and leaving Captain John Cuppage in command of the garrison.

His first objective was the fort of Chittoor, which he had been informed was a depot for the enemy's supplies, and there the army arrived on the 6th November. After a gallant defence, the place fell on the 11th,* when the rampart had been breached, but it was then found that there were no supplies there whatever.

On the 15th November, news was received that Captain Temple had been attacked by Haidar at Pallipat, and had withdrawn to the hills, leaving his guns and baggage. On the 16th, Coote marched on Pallipat, the enemy making a show of disputing the passage of the river Ponniar, and encamped at the Pass of Devalampetta. On the 17th, he descended the Pass and halted at Pallipat, where he was joined by Temple.

The monsoon was now approaching and it became necessary for Coote to return to a part of the country where supplies were more readily accessible, a decision which was hastened by news of the investment of Tirupasur by Tippu, a report which was confirmed by the sound of firing in that direction. Marching on the 19th November, on which day the rains broke, he found the last branch of the Palar just fordable, and camped near Tirupasur on the 21st, after a forced march, and relieved the place.

Sir Hector Munro, with a force of 4,000 men, had meanwhile captured Negapatam, which had a garrison of 8,000 men, and thus forced Haidar's troops to evacuate the country round Negapatam and Nagore. The British had, consequently, now a larger area from which to draw supplies.

The last event of the year was the loss of Chittoor, which Haidar retook on or about the 26th December, and, violating as usual the terms of capitulation, sent the officers of the garrison to Seringapatam and the men to Bednur. It is noteworthy that the loss of this place seems to have been fully expected as Innes Munro records that, before leaving it, Coote's officers left letters for their friends in prison at Seringapatam to be delivered by the officers of the garrison when Haidar should have recaptured the place!

1782.

The Second Relief of Vellore.

On the 2nd January, in which month Mahomed Ali's brother, Abdul Wahab Khan, surrendered the almost impregnable fort of Chendragiri to Haidar, Coote, although his state of health gave grounds for the greatest anxiety, once more took the field on receipt of news from Vellore that that place was again *in extremis*. The importance of Vellore to the British at this time consisted in its being the only key to the passes leading to the enemy's country remaining in their possession.

---

* Wilks says the 11th November, while Wilson, probably on the authority of the author of *Memoirs of the War in Asia*, gives the 10th.

On the 5th January, when the army was near Tirupasur, the General had a fit of apoplexy but in spite of entreaties from Madras not to endanger "a life so valuable to the State," was sufficiently recovered next morning to continue the march. A short extract from Colonel Wilks, written on this occasion, will serve to show the extraordinary hold which Coote had on the hearts of the sepoys of his army.

> "For nearly two hours, during which little hope was entertained of his recovery, the despondency painted on every countenance, and particularly on those of the native troops, whose attachment and confidence exceeded the bounds of human veneration, and who could with difficulty be restrained from transgressing the limits of decorum to satisfy their anxiety, presented altogether a scene of mournful interest."

Battles of the Swamp

On the 6th January, it is recorded that the army halted at a village called "Edinburg," which greatly affected the Scottish soldiers. On the 9th January, as the army was about to cross the dry bed of the River Ponniar, the enemy appeared in force on the opposite bank, but was deterred from making any attempt by the skilful arrangements of Coote, who had selected the Sholinghur road in order to have the protection of the Palaiyam hills.

On the following day, however, when the army had marched about five miles and was entering a swamp of ricefields bordering on a large tank near Mahimandalam Durgam, Haidar's army appeared in two strong columns on the left and rear. Posting a brigade to watch each column, and disregarding the incessant cannonade of the enemy, Coote successfully passed the whole of his convoy over the swamp, and encamped within four miles of Vellore on the same evening, having lost 3 subalterns and some 70 men killed and wounded in the skirmishes with the enemy. On the next day—the 11th January—he relieved Vellore, and supplied it with provisions for three or four months.

On the 13th January, the return to Madras was commenced. Haidar, exasperated by his failure to stop the convoy on the 10th, had made arrangements to attack the army again at the same place. Three sluices were cut in the bund of the tank, and the morass was flooded with water, and, being trampled over by the cavalry, was rendered almost impassable for infantry. On a position on rising ground within cannon-shot of the morass, Haidar had placed several large batteries of 24-pounders, besides all his field-guns, and drew up his whole army under cover of the brushwood.

As soon as the European brigade was struggling in the centre of the swamp, the order to fire was given, and a cannonade was opened from over 50 guns. The troops, however, showed the greatest steadiness, and without in the least falling into confusion, pushed rapidly forward and formed up on the other side in order of battle, whereupon Haidar seeing that his plan had failed, drew off, and returned to Arcot.

On this occasion the British losses amounted to 1 Captain, 1 Subaltern, and 44 men killed and wounded.

On the 16th January, Haidar again appeared, and made a show of offering battle on the ground on which the Battle of Sholinghur had been fought, but after ten hours' vain manœuvring, the army pursued its march to Tiruttani, and arrived at Tirupasur without further incident. On the 20th January it reached Poonamallee.

On the 18th February 1782, a severe disaster was sustained at Annagudi, the Southern Detachment under Colonel Braithwaite being defeated by Tippu Sultan and forced to surrender after 26 hours of desperate fighting. Braithwaite's force consisted of 100 Europeans, 1,500 Sepoys and 300 cavalry, while Haidar had Lally's Corps, 400 strong, 10,000 picked horse, and 10,000 infantry.

About the 10th March, Haidar's army was strengthened by the addition of some 3,000 French troops, including a regiment of Africans. Nothing further occurred until the 8th April, when Cuddalore was forced to capitulate to the enemy. This place had been left but slenderly garrisoned, Sir Eyre Coote having counted on the fleet to guard it, whereas the fleet had gone off to Trincomallee, and the garrison surrendered without a shot being fired—Munro says by orders from the Presidency.

On the 11th May, Haider and the French suddenly appeared before Perumukkal, on receipt of which news Coote at once marched to its relief, but, delayed by torrents of rain, was too late, and the place, which was only garrisoned by a company, capitulated on the 16th, the united forces of the enemy then marching on Wandiwash. Coming to the determination that by a successful action alone could the state of affairs be brought to wear a brighter aspect, Coote marched to Wandiwash when the enemy had been before that place for four days. Haidar withdrew towards Pondicherry and the British army followed, coming in sight of the enemy on his second day's march, who were drawn up in a strong position near Killiyanur, some 14 miles north-west of Pondicherry, on which Coote did not dare to risk an attack. In order to draw the enemy away from this position, Coote now changed his route and, marching to the west, camped before the fort of Chitapat.* This had the desired effect and Haidar hastened to its relief, leaving the French behind. On hearing that Haidar had moved, Coote marched towards Arni, which was one of Haidar's most important depots, and the latter after sending forward Tippu by forced marches with orders to reinforce the garrison of Arni, followed on the 31st.

The Battle of Arni, June 2nd, 1782. At about 8 o'clock on the 2nd June, when Coote had arrived within three miles of Arni, the enemy's advanced guard came up with Coote's rearguard, which was commanded by Lieutenant-Colonel Elphinstone, and at once opened a severe cannonade. Coote at once faced about the army, and formed it up in line, with a brigade of infantry, and the cavalry, under Lieutenant-Colonel Owen, formed up to protect the baggage in rear, while the guns replied to the enemy's fire.

---

* Now called Settupatti.

As soon as the line was formed, it advanced upon the enemy, but the latter did not await the onset and retreated, while maintaining their cannonade. Owing to the necessity of guarding the baggage, the pursuit of the enemy could not be followed up until Owen's brigade had closed up, when a further advance was made. The enemy then withdrew across the Cheyar River, but while they were crossing, a bold dash by Captain James Lindsay led to the capture of one gun and eleven ammunition tumbrils, which ended the action. Wilks speaks of this day as:—

"A day of severe fatigue and varied cannonade rather than of battle, and a succession of skilful manœuvres to combine with the essential protection of the baggage the means of closing with the enemy, were performed by the troops with a degree of confident steadiness and alacrity which were deemed to surpass all that their veteran Commander had before witnessed in their conduct."

The casualties of the day amounted only to 74 killed and wounded, of whom seventeen, mostly of the 78th Regiment, died of fatigue. In this battle Mir Saleh, the Native Commandant of the 4th, was killed, and the following order, issued after the battle, is of great interest:—

"The Commander-in-Chief very much laments the loss of Meer Saleh, Commandant of the 4th Battalion, killed yesterday, as a brave and faithful soldier of the company: he is pleased to promote his eldest son, Tippoo Saib, to be Jemadar, and his second son Mahomed Saib to be Havildar in the 4th Battalion.

Innes Munro gives a fuller account of the manner of his death, as follows:—

"It is but justice to mention that in this action fell Meer Sally, black commandant of the fourth battalion of Madras sepoys, whose attachment to the company, and whose bravery and experience in military affairs, were universally respected and admired. This valuable officer fell a sacrifice to that spirit of predestination which universally prevails amongst Mahomedans. He was requested to stand out of the way of a random shot that was coming directly towads his battalion, which he scornfully refused to do, saying 'Let God's will be done,' and he was instantly killed General Coote testified his good opinion of this brave man, immediately appointing his brother who was an inferior Officer in the same corps, to succeed him in his command."

On June 3rd, Coote made some show of besieging Arni, but as the place had been strengthened by Tippu during the action on the preceding day, he gave up the idea, and on the 14th, moved in a south-westerly direction against the enemy. Haidar retreated before him, and he consequently returned to Arni. On the 6th June, Haidar moved eastward and Coote again took up the pursuit on that and the following day, halting on the 8th near Nedungal, where he sustained a reverse in the loss of his grand guard, consisting of 166 men, 54 horses and 2 guns, which was completely cut up owing to a ruse of the enemy and the rashness of its commander. The army next proceeded to Wandiwash, where it remained for four days and replenished its supplies, and arrived at the Mount on the 20th June, having lost between five and six hundred men.

While Haidar's attention was engaged by the events in the neighbourhood of Arni, Vellore was once again successfully relieved on the 14th June by Ensign Byrne with no greater a force than 100 irregular Sepoys, though the detachment was unfortunately captured on its return by a force under Tippu and Lally. Coote himself deposited a further supply of seven months' rice in Vellore on the 5th August, returning to Madras on the 20th.

In the same month it was decided to make an attempt to recover Cuddalore, and the army marched once more on the 26th August, reaching the Red Hills near Pondicherry on the 4th September, but owing to the failure of the plan for keeping the army supplied by sea, the expedition had to be given up.

Sir Eyre Coote's health now gave way and he handed over the command of the army to Major-General James Stuart (the officer who had lost a leg at Pullalur) and proceeded to Bengal, sailing from Madras on the 28th September. General Stuart marched the army back to Madras, where it was cantoned for the remainder of the year.

The melancholy state of affairs in Madras in 1782 is thus summed up by Philippart:—

"For some years previous Hyder Ally had carried on a successful war against the Company, and had collected almost the entire revenue of the Carnatic. The whole country was overrun by his cavalry and, with the exception of Velore, Wandiwash, Carrangooly, and a few places on the sea coast, every fort was occupied by detachments from his army. The Company's finances were at the lowest ebb, and their credit exhausted. The Madras army was paid and fed from Bengal. The calamities of war were at this time made more terrible by the effects of a dreadful famine, which depopulated the Carnatic. The streets of the Fort, of the Black Town and the Esplanade of Madras, were covered with starved wretches, many of whom were dead and others dying. The vultures, the Paria dogs, jackals and crows, were often seen eating the bodies before life was extinct. The general distress and calamity was aggravated by the destruction of a fleet of grain vessels, which had anchored in the roads with a supply of food. The inhabitants were in a moment deprived of the gleam of hope which this near approach of relief had inspired. On the 15th October, in the night-time, a monsoon gale set in, and almost all the ships in the roads were driven on shore and wrecked. The loss of the rice-ships at this late season was an irreparable misfortune. The famine increased; and it was estimated that, in consequence of this accident, upwards of ten thousand inhabitants perished.... At this time Sir Eyre Coote's army was in a deplorable condition; its pay and batta in arrear six months. As nothing could be purchased, rice and provisions were issued to the troops. The officers were generally in great distress."

Death of Haidar Ali. On the 7th December 1782, Haidar Ali died of carbuncle at Narasingarayanapet, near Chittoor, and was succeeded by his son, Tippu Sultan, who, on receipt of the intelligence, hastened from Malabar, and joined his army at Chakmagalur, in South Arcot, on the 9th January 1783. (Wilks gives the 9th—Wilson says the 2nd).

It may be of interest to give a very brief account of the early history of this remarkable man. He was the son of an officer of native infantry, who was killed in some obscure quarrel between two native states. His early youth was passed in miserable circumstances, and he received no education whatever. In 1749, he joined the Mysore army and rose rapidly, until eventually he was strong enough to turn against his master, and practically made himself ruler of Mysore. In 1751-52, he visited Pondicherry and conceived a great admiration for the French, subsequently modelling his army on the European pattern.

His career of conquest commenced with the subjugation of the Baramahal in 1766, and he then took Sera from the Mahrattas, thus extending his frontiers almost to the Kistna. He then turned upon Bednore, and finally conquered practically the whole Malabar Coast. Prior to the war of 1767, he had once met one of Coote's detachments in 1760, when he was assisting Lally, and had completely defeated it.

His later career may be traced in these pages, and affords one of the most remarkable instances in history of a man rising, by sheer force of character, from a lowly position till he dominated the whole of South India.

Wilks, in his *Sketches of the South of India*, has written a brilliant study of his character, from which I give the following short extract:—

> "In common with all sovereigns who have risen from obscurity to a throne, Hyder waded through crimes to his object; but they never exceeded the removal of real impediments, and he never achieved through blood what fraud was capable of effecting. He fixed his steadfast view upon the end, and considered simply the efficiency, and never the moral tendency of the means............... His European prisoners were in irons, because they were otherwise deemed unmanageable; they were scantily fed, because that was economical; there was little distinction of rank, because that would have been expensive; but, beyond these simply interested views, there was, by his authority, no wanton severity; there was no compassion, but there was no resentment; it was a political expenditure for a political purpose, and there was no passion, good or bad, to disturb the balance of the account............Everything was weighed in the balance of utility, and no grain of human feeling, no breath of virtue or of vice, was permitted to incline the beam. There was one solitary example of feelings incident to our nature; affection for an unworthy son, whom he nominated to be his successor, while uniformly, earnestly, and broadly predicting, that this son would lose the empire which he himself had gained."

1783.

General Stuart's Operations.

On the 5th January 1783, the army was formed into two lines, the first consisting of three brigades, under Colonel Reinbold, 15th Hanoverians, and the second comprising the 4th and 5th Brigades, under Colonel Pearse, Bengal Artillery. The 4th Carnatic Battalion was in the 5th Brigade, which was commanded by Lieutenant-Colonel Elphinstone, 73rd Regiment.

Major-General Stuart, though urged continually by the Governor, Lord Macartney,* to take advantage of Haidar's death and move against the Mysore army before it should have been joined by Tippu, did not move southwards till the 4th February.

It had been decided to demolish the forts at Wandiwash and Karunguli, as their occupation was of no advantage and difficulties were continually experienced in keeping them provisioned. Karunguli was reached on the 6th February, and thence the army proceeded to Wandiwash. Near the latter place the camp of the united forces of Tippu and the French was observed, and General Stuart moved against them as far as Nedungal, where the two armies were only separated by a branch of the River Palar. A few shots were exchanged, but the enemy declined the proffered battle, and the army withdrew to Wandiwash and thence to Poonamallee, which was reached on the 23rd February.

A large part of the following month was spent in re-provisioning Vellore, which, according to Innes Munro, the army heartily wished might share the same fate as Wandiwash and Karunguli, owing to the fatigue and hardships occasioned by the frequent expeditions made for its relief. This operation was carried out without interruption from Tippu, who was hastily marching to his own dominions on account of the news of the capture of Bednore by General Matthews with the Bombay army.

On the 21st April, having arranged for the co-operation of the fleet under Sir Edward Hughes, General Stuart, with an army 14,490 strong, of whom 2,945 were Europeans, commenced his march to recover Cuddalore from the French. So dilatory were his movements that it was not until the 7th June that the General found himself in position before Cuddalore, a distance of 126 miles from his starting point.

Death of Sir Eyre Coote. The Army had been anxiously expecting the arrival of its Commander-in-Chief, Sir Eyre Coote, who had sailed from Bengal, and who arrived in Madras on the 24th April, but was again taken ill. His illness had been aggravated by the anxiety he had suffered on the voyage, his vessel having been pursued by French men-of-war for forty-eight hours and, on the 28th April, he died, to the great grief of the whole army, more especially the native regiments.

His character as a General is thus summed up by Fortescue:—

"It was no fault of Coote that he could not give as good an account of Hyder Ali as Smith, the fact being that whenever he moved outside Madras he entered a country which, owing to Hyder's devastations, was as truly a wilderness, except in the matter of water, as the Sahara itself..........He fought actions for the revictualling and relief of his

---

* Lord Macartney, who belonged to a Co. Antrim family, became "President and Governor of Fort St. George" on the 23rd June 1781, and first "Governor of Madras" in February 1785.

garrisons and his operations are therefore little worth study apart from his tactics in the actual field of battle. There, however, he seems to have been one of the greatest masters of his own or any other time. The man was never so dangerous as when within range of cannon shot. If there was a weak point in an enemy's position, Coote hit it unerringly, and would contrive to draw his enemy out of his stronghold and to fight him on his own ground. He could handle ten thousand men with the ease and precision of a Sergeant drilling a squad in the barrack-yard; and thus, in spite of the terrible encumbrance of followers and baggage, he would advance with perfect confidence into the midst of cavalry that outnumbered him by six to one, with his infantry and artillery only."

Coote was born in 1726, and after serving for some time in Germany and Scotland, went to India in 1754, as a subaltern in Aldercron's Regiment. He accompanied Clive to Calcutta, and held a command at the battle of Plassey. In 1759, he was appointed Lieutenant-Colonel of the 84th Regiment. In 1764, he was presented with a diamond-hilted sword by the Company, and in 1771, he was promoted to Major-General.

His body was taken to England, and buried at Rockburne, in Hampshire, where his monument bears the following epitaph by Mr. Banks, M.P.:—

"This monument is erected by the East India Company, as a testimonial of the military talents of Lieutenant-General Sir Eyre Coote, K. B., Commander-in-Chief of the British Forces in India; who, by the success of his arms, in the years 1760 and 1761, expelled the French from the Coast of Coromandel; in 1781 and 1782 he again took the field in the Carnatic, in opposition to the united strength of the French and Hyder Ally; and in several engagements defeated the numerous forces of the latter; but death interrupted his career of glory, on the 28th day of April 1783, in the 58th year of his age."

Fullarton says that his death is supposed to have prevented much bloodshed in the settlement, as Coote was sent to the Coast with full authority to rescind the assignment of the Nawab's territory to the Company, and to restore him to the management of his own country, and this the Government was determined to resist—"at a time too when the country belonged more properly to Hyder and the French than to either party."

1783.
Operations Round Cuddalore.

Before giving a short resume of General Stuart's operations at Cuddalore, it may be stated that, although the 4th Carnatic Battalion was present on this occasion, it suffered no casualties and does not appear to have been actively engaged.

From the 7th June, when it arrived before Cuddalore, to the 13th, the army was occupied in landing stores, this time being spent by M. Bussy in strengthening the defences. An attack was made on the outer lines of defence on the 13th, but the main attack was repulsed with heavy loss, the firing being in General Stuart's opinion the heaviest he ever beheld; the British, however, succeeded in retaining their hold on a redoubt in the French lines. The name of the Coast Army was upheld on this occasion by the 20th Battalion, which divided the honours of the day with the 101st Europeans. Wilks says that the British casualties amounted to 1,050, and those of the French to 450, while the British captured thirteen guns; Munro, writing at the time, says the British lost 1,020, and the French 846; while Wilson puts the British losses at 944. The French withdrew within the walls on the same night, taking their heavy guns with them.

On the 17th June, the British fleet was driven off by the French squadron under Admiral Suffrein, who landed 3,600 men to assist Bussy, and on the 25th, the latter made a vigorous sortie, which was, however, unsuccessful, the French suffering heavy losses. It is of interest to note that one of the French prisoners taken on this occasion was a young Sergeant Bernadotte, afterwards one of Napoleon's Marshals and King of Sweden, and in this connection Wilks relates the following anecdote:—

"Among the wounded prisoners was a young French Sergeant, who so particularly attracted the notice of Colonel Wangenheim, Commandant of the Hanoverian troops in the English service, by his interesting appearance and manners, that he ordered the young man to be conveyed to his own tents, where he was treated with attention and kindness until his recovery and release. Many years afterwards, when the French army, under Bernadotte, entered Hanover, General Wangenheim, among others, attended the levee of the conqueror. 'You have served a great deal,' said Bernadotte, on his being presented, ' and, as I understand, in India'?—' I have served there '—' At Cuddalore?' —' I was there '—' Have you any recollection of a wounded sergeant, whom you took under your protection in the course of that service?' The circumstance was not immediately present to the General's mind, but on recollection he resumed, 'I do indeed remember the circumstance, and a very fine young man he was; I have entirely lost sight of him ever since, but it would give me pleasure to hear of his welfare'—'That young Sergeant,' said Bernadotte, 'was the person who now has the honour to address you ; who is happy in the public opportunity of acknowledging the obligation, and will omit no means within his power of testifying his gratitude to General Wangenheim."

The British army, weakened as it was by casualties and sickness, was now overmatched by the French, strengthened by the reinforcements from the fleet, and it may be considered fortunate that the arrival of news of the conclusion of peace brought these operations to an end, hostilities finally ceasing on the 2nd July.

The war with Tippu was continued, and Colonel Fullarton carried out some successful operations till the 11th March 1784, when a treaty of peace was concluded at Mangalore, under circumstances of the utmost indignity to the British deputies.

It should not be forgotten that, during these campaigns of 1780—1783, the troops throughout suffered the greatest hardships, and the following extracts will show under what difficult circumstances the sepoys of the Carnatic battalions maintained their honourable record.

Colonel Wilson says :—

"It is worthy of remark that while the British soldiers were always paid up-to-date, or nearly so, the native army, serving alien masters, was kept constantly in arrears for several consecutive years, notwithstanding which, and the extreme severity of the service, it steadily resisted, with few exceptions, the numerous offers conveyed by the emissaries of Hyder and Tippoo. Such fidelity under similar circumstances, is without parallel in the military history of any nation."

Innes Munro, who served alongside the Carnatic troops throughout these campaigns, writing in 1789, says :—

" Enough cannot be said of the fidelity and generous conduct of the Company's black officers and sepoys during the whole series of these unparalleled sufferings. Every cruel mode that could be suggested by the enemy was adopted to force them into their service, but the brave sepoys were satisfied to suffer every hardship and indignity rather than forfeit their allegiance to the Company. Numbers of the black officers were barbarously murdered for their inflexibility, while others, with the sepoys, were set to hard labour upon the most scanty portion of food; but all was ineffectual to shake their fidelity. The attachment of the sepoys was equally conspicuous in their kind attentions to some of the Europeans who happened to be confined in the same prison with them, they having frequently bought meat for them, in the bazaar, with the hard-earned pittance which they daily received; observing that, though the black people could do without it, they well knew that it was impossible for Europeans to exist without meat. They also had the kindness, during the journey towards the Carnatic after their release, voluntarily to carry the knapsacks of those poor European soldiers, who, from weakness, were overcome with fatigue."

1784.

In October of this year, the distinction between " Carnatic " and " Circar " Battalions was abolished, and the battalion was re-named the 4th Madras Battalion.

Part I.

CHAPTER III.

THE 4th MADRAS BATTALION.

October 1784—12th July 1796.

1785—1787.

In April 1785, nearly 1,200 Europeans and about 3,000 Sepoys, largely of the Bombay establishment, who had been confined in fortresses in various parts of the country, were handed over at Hoskote, and taken to Vellore on the 25th. A few of these (Ensigns Corner, Forbes and Innes) appear to have served with the 4th in later years.

On the 29th May 1785, Lieutenant-General Sir John Dalling, *Bart.*, assumed command of the army, in place of Lieutenant-General Ross Lang, but resigned in September. General Robert Sloper was now Commander-in-Chief in Bengal.

On the 23rd August 1785, the infantry of the Madras Army was formed into six brigades. The 4th Madras Battalion, as it was now called, was posted to the 3rd Brigade, commanded by Colonel Nixon, with the 3rd European Regiment, and the 12th and 21st Madras Battalions.

In February 1786, the 4th Battalion was stationed in the new cantonment at Wallajahbad, forming part of the 2nd Brigade, under Lieutenant-Colonel Keating, with the 5th, 9th, 15th, 21st and 25th Battalions, and remained there throughout the year.

The Marquess Cornwallis became Governor-General of India in 1786, and remained in office till 1793.

In April 1786, Major-General Sir Archibald Campbell became Governor and Commander-in-Chief at Madras, in succession to Lord Macartney. He had been sent out to India, as a Colonel and Chief Engineer, in 1768, to improve the fortifications in Bengal, Madras and Bombay. This was not the officer of that name who served under Cornwallis in Mysore and later at Seringapatam, in the Peninsula, and in the Burma War of 1824.

Sir A. Campbell only retained his appointment till the 7th February 1788, and Mr. John Holland acted in his place for six days, when he handed over to his brother, Mr. Edward Holland.

1788.
Expedition to the Kalahasti Zemindari.

Early in July 1788, a detachment composed of the 4th and 8th Battalions with four guns, under the command of Captain Dunwoody of the 8th Battalion, was sent into the Kalahasti Zemindari on service.

The fort at Panmore* was taken by storm just before daybreak on the 20th July, with a loss of 20 men killed and wounded. The forts at Virur† and

---

* This must have been Pamur, a Village in Kanigiri Taluk of Nellore District, which formerly belonged to the Kalahasti Estate, and which has the ruins of a fort.

† Virur is a village quite close to Pamur, also with a ruined fort in the neighbourhood.

Sitarampur* were evacuated immediately afterwards and the service successfully completed, for which Captain Dunwoody and the detachment received the thanks of Government.

No record has so far been discovered of what part the 4th Battalion took in this expedition, nor is it known what casualties, if any, they suffered.

1788.

Expedition to Guntur.

The Nizam having refused to carry out his agreement to hand over the district of Guntur to the British, Lieutenant-Colonel James Edington was placed in command of a force some 3,000 strong, which was assembled at the end of August 1788, in order to compel the Nizam to fulfil his engagement.

The 4th Madras Battalion, 7 officers and 496 men, formed part of this force.

The Nizam, however, submitted before Colonel Edington arrived and, in September, Ongole and the forts of Inakonda,† Bellamkonda,‡ and Timirikottai§ were occupied without resistance by the 4th, 8th and 12th Madras Battalions, which remained in occupation on the withdrawal of the troops a few months afterwards.

Further details of this expedition are still required, as it is not known which fort the 4th Battalion was sent to occupy.

The Resident at Haidarabad at this time was Lieutenant-Colonel Sir John Kennaway, *Bart.* (1788-94.)

1789.

The 4th Battalion was presumably left in occupation of one of the forts in the Ceded Districts ‖ throughout 1789. It is not known when they left the Ceded Districts in order to join the force which was assembled at Wallajahbad in February 1790.

---

* Sitarampur was a fort mounting two cannon and 50 "Jinjalls" at the base of the Sivadurgam in Chittoor district, which was not fortified, though a few buildings stood upon its summit. All these fortress in the Kalahasti Zamindari were destroyed by the British and only the ruins now remain.

† "Inakonda" is now written *Vinukonda*, and is in Guntur District.

‡ *Bellamkonda* is in the Sattanapalli Taluk of Guntur District.

§ Timirikottai is Timmeracode, in the Palnad, 38 miles N. of Vinukonda.

‖ The term "Ceded Districts" is commonly applied to the northern districts of the Madras Presidency. They comprised the present districts of Bellary, Cuddapah, Kurnool, and the Palnad. They obtained their name by being ceded to the East India Company by the Nizam in 1800, to supply revenue for the maintenance of the Hyderabad Subsidiary Force, at that time under the command of Colonel Arthur Wellesley.

1790.
Renewal of the War against Tippu Sultan.

On the 29th August 1788, and again on the 23rd September and in November, Lord Cornwallis urged upon the Government of Madras the necessity of taking instant steps to attack Tippu Sultan, who was then before the Travancore Lines, and there is no doubt that, had the Government of Madras been equal to the emergency an army might have fallen on Tippu's rear at the end of December, before he had succeeded in capturing the lines.

Lord Cornwallis had just determined to proceed in person to Madras when news of the appointment of Major-General Medows to be Governor and Commander-in-Chief of that Presidency (he having handed over the Government of Bombay to General Robert Abercromby, a brother of the better-known Sir Ralph Abercromby), decided him to remain in Bengal and direct operations from there.

General Medows' Operations. It was not until the 20th February that General Medows arrived in Madras but preparations were at once actively commenced to put the army in a state of efficiency. A force was assembled at Wallajahbad in February which marched for Trichinopoly on the 29th March. This force was joined by that of Colonel Nixon, bringing the army up to a strength of about 15,000 and on the 24th May, the General, who had embarked for the south on the 17th, took over command, making his first march on the 26th. Before commencing operations the army was arranged in brigades, and divided into two wings, the 4th Madras Battalion forming part of the 3rd Native Brigade, with the 9th and 23rd Madras Battalions, under Major Cuppage of the Madras Army, this Brigade being in the right wing commanded by Colonel Nixon, Madras Army.

The intention of the General was to reduce Palghat and the forts of Coimbatore and to ascend by the pass of Coimbatore, while the force under Colonel Maxwell, consisting mainly of the reinforcement expected from Bengal, was to advance direct into the Baramahal.

Colonel Maxwell's force was to have been commanded by Colonel Kelly, but the latter was killed in September.*

---

* Colonel Kelly was killed in a duel in a field near Arni by Lieutenant-Colonel Urban Vigors on the 29th September, 1790, and was buried in Arni fort, where his adversary erected a monument 65 feet high to his memory "as a mark of respect for a gallant soldier." This duel was caused by Colonel Vigors having spoken of Colonel Kelly, on his appointment to the command, as "an old woman" to his wife, who passed on the remark to Mrs. Kelly, and the latter insisted on her husband demanding "satisfaction," with the above result. Colonel Wilson says that Vigors was only a Captain (commanding the 21st Bn.) when the duel took place.

Owing to commissariat troubles, the army only occupied the frontier posts of Karur on the 15th June,* and remained there till the 2nd July, when, continuing the march, the weak fort of Aravakurichi surrendered on the 6th July, and Dharapuram on the 10th, both without resistance. After a further halt the advance was resumed on the 17th, a brigade being left behind to cover some expected convoys, and the army arrived in the neighbourhood of Coimbatore on the 21st, where it was anticipated that Tippu's army would be met, though the latter was at that time actually over the ghauts on his way to Seringapatam.

A detached force was at once sent off under Colonel Stuart to prepare for the siege of Palghat, but was compelled to return owing to the heavy rains, and was then despatched in the opposite direction to reduce the fort of Dindigul, another detachment, under Colonel Oldham, being sent to capture Erode.

Meanwhile the cavalry of the main army under Colonel Floyd† had been kept continuously employed in skirmishing with a large body of irregular horse under Sayyid Sahib, which had been left behind by Tippu to harass the British army and which was now, to the great indignation of Tippu, driven across the river Bhavani and forced to ascend the ghauts by the Gajalhatti pass.

Dindigul capitulated to Colonel Stuart on the 22nd August after an assault, led by Captain Thomas Bowser, had been repulsed with loss on the previous day, and the detachment was ordered to proceed to Palghat, which also surrendered after some resistance on the 22nd September, Colonel Stuart then returning to Coimbatore, leaving a garrison in the fort with six months' provisions.

Colonel Oldham had in the meantime reduced Erode on the 6th August, and rejoined the main army, with which things were going anything but well. A chain of depots extending from Tanjore and Trichinopoly through Karur, Erode and Satyamangalam was in the hands of the British and seemed to offer a good line of supply for an army ascending the pass of Gajalhatti, an operation which General Medows hoped to carry out in October, but none of these places was strong for defence and the army was badly situated, being broken up into three divisions, one under Colonel Floyd (2,800 men and eleven guns) sixty miles in advance, the main body at Coimbatore, and Colonel Stuart thirty miles to the rear at Palghat.

Early in September, Tippu commenced to descend the ghauts by the pass of Danayakankota, a fact which Colonel Floyd reported to General Medows, but that

---

* The dates given throughout this campaign are Vibart's.

† This officer, afterwards General Sir John Floyd, *Bart.*, began his military career in 1760, when, at the early age of twelve, he went to Germany with Elliot's Light Dragoons, and had his horse shot under him at the battle of Emsdorff. He remained with Elliot's Dragoons for 20 years, and went to India in 1782 as Lieutenant-Colonel of the 23rd (afterwards the 19th) Dragoons. He became a full General on the 1st January 1812, and died in 1817.

officer, disbelieving the report, ordered Floyd to remain in his advanced position. Tippu crossed the Bhavani on the 12th September and on the 13th Floyd came in contact with him near Satyamangalam and, after heavy fighting throughout the day, commenced to retreat on the 14th. Tippu at once took up the pursuit, but was repulsed at Cheyur, and the division succeeded in effecting a junction with the main army at Veladi on the 15th. The united forces advanced towards Cheyur on the 18th September and camped near that place on the 20th, but returned to Coimbatore on the 23rd, where they were joined by Colonel Stuart's division from Palghat.

Pursuit of Tippu. Tippu had meanwhile withdrawn to the north of the river and, on the 20th September, General Medows marched in pursuit round by the Bhavani to the Kaveri and Erode, which the enemy had occupied and abandoned, the garrison having retired on Karur. From Erode Tippu, followed by the British army, marched southwards, apparently to intercept a large convoy under Major Younger which was expected from Karur. It eluded him, however, and succeeded in joining the army at Kadimudi on the Kaveri on the 7th October. Tippu then doubled back on Coimbatore but, hearing that that place had been reinforced, proceeded to Dharapuram, which capitulated to him on the 8th October.

General Medows, seeing that it was necessary to strengthen Coimbatore before marching further, returned there and, having carried out his object, and Karur and Dindigul also being put in a better state of defence, again marched to seek the enemy at Erode, but on approaching that place on the 29th October, he discovered that Tippu, who had received information of the invasion of the Baramahal, had marched northwards. About a quarter of the enemy's army had, however, been left under Kammar-ud-din to watch General Medows, who, believing that Tippu had gone towards Maxwell, began to cross the Kaveri at Erode on the 8th November, and on the 10th arrived in the Baramahal.

Maxwell, with the so-called Centre Army, 9,500 strong, consisting largely of Bengal troops, had entered the Baramahal on the 24th October and, after reconnoitring Krishnagiri on the 1st November, esablished his headquarters near Kaveripatnam on the 9th. On the 11th his cavalry were driven back with considerable loss by the advanced parties of Tippu's army, and the whole force of the enemy appeared on the 12th, and spent this and the two succeeding days in manœuvring with a view to attacking Maxwell to advantage, but without result.

On the 15th November, on which date Maxwell nearly succeeded in surprising Tippu at Settamaranahalli, General Medows' army appeared from the south and, on the 17th, effected a junction with Maxwell's force at Pulahalli, 12 miles south of Kaveripatnam, Tippu withdrawing to the west, towards the pass of Palakodu. On the 18th, both armies marched towards the pass of Toppur, some 20 miles distant, and the British army arrived at the pass just as Tippu's army was entering it. Incredible as it may appear, however, General Medows refused to allow Colonel Stuart, who commanded the right wing, to push forward and attack the enemy entangled in the pass until the remainder of the army had come up, by which time the enemy had escaped, and the British army encamped for the night at the head of the pass after a tedious march of twenty miles which had given them no advantage, except that Tippu was separated from his heavy baggage.

On the junction of the two forces, the army was re-brigaded, and the 4th Madras Battalion was now in the 7th Brigade (Lieutenant-Colonel Dupont) of the right wing under Colonel Stuart.

Tippu now headed for Karur and, announcing that he would cross the Kaveri below that place, marched along the north bank to Trichinopoly where he made various demonstrations without other result than the devastation of Srirangam. On the 27th November, General Medows arrived opposite Karur and, believing that Tippu had crossed to the south, sent a force under Colonel Oldham across the river to reinforce various places. The General now proposed, as the best means of diverting Tippu from the low countries, to march up the ghauts, but news from Trichinopoly compelled him to march to that weak and extensive depot, where he arrived on the 14th December.

Orders were now received to return to Madras, where Lord Cornwallis had arrived on the 13th December, and the march was accordingly commenced on the 30th.

On leaving Trichinopoly, Tippu had proceeded to Tayaga-durgam, which was commanded by that excellent officer Captain Flint, the defender of Wandiwash, but two attempts were beaten off with loss, and he repaired to Tiruvannamalai which he took, and thence to Perumukkal which also fell. He then encamped near Pondicherry.

The British army followed Tippu's route as far as Tiruvannamalai, and thence moved to Arni, where the heavy stores and guns were left under Colonel Musgrave, and the remainder of the army proceeded by Conjeeveram to Vellakottai, 18 miles from Madras, where it arrived on the 27th January 1791, thus bringing to an end this most unsatisfactory campaign.

1791.
Lord Cornwallis' Campaign against Tippu Sultan.

On assuming command of the Grand Army at Vellakottai on the 29th January, Lord Cornwallis decided to abandon the southern line of advance on Mysore on account of the distance which the adoption of that route interposed between the army and Fort St. George, its principal source of supplies, and the danger of trusting to the long and weak chain of posts along that line. He determined, therefore, to commence his operations from Ambur, with Vellore as a strong intermediate depot.

The advance was commenced on the 5th February, and on the 11th the army was concentrated near Vellore. Tippu, believing that the British army was heading so as to ascend the passes near Ambur or those of the Baramahal, hastened from Pondicherry by the passes of Chengam and Palakodu to intercept the enemy, but Cornwallis, manœuvring a battalion towards Ambur so as to maintain the deception, marched northwards and, turning to the west, ascended the pass of Mugali, and attained the table-land of Mysore without firing a shot.

Kolar was occupied on the 28th February, and Hoskote on the 2nd March, the garrisons of both places acting in a strange fashion by refusing to surrender but offering no resistance. On the 4th March, Tippu's cavalry appeared, but was so badly handled that it was practically disregarded. On the following morning the Mysore army made a demonstration in force but Cornwallis, drawing up his army in battle formation, continued to move in the direction of Bangalore, the army breaking into column on the flank and rear when the baggage had passed, so that Tippu was obliged to content himself with a distant cannonade. On the same evening, 5th March, the army took up its ground before Bangalore.

On the 6th March, Cornwallis moved his camp to stronger ground and, in the afternoon, sent out Colonel Floyd with the cavalry and a brigade of infantry to cover a reconnaissance to the south-west. As this force was preparing to return, a body of about 1,000 Mysorean horse appeared from the west. Tippu, when he heard of the British movement, had sent this force to protect the flank of his baggage and army which was being moved, under cover of the undulating ground, to a position to the west of Bangalore.

Siege of Bangalore. Colonel Floyd at once drove back the enemy's horse and unexpectedly discovered the rear of the enemy's infantry and guns mixed up with the heavy baggage and, though strict orders had been given against any active engagement, the opportunity proved irresistible and a charge was ordered. This being pursued too far, the cavalry was compelled to retreat in disorder, covered by Major Gowdie, who advanced with the infantry and guns. The casualties amounted to 71 men and Floyd himself was wounded, while 271 horses were lost, which were more difficult to replace than the men.

Tippu now moved his camp six miles further west to Kengeri, leaving Bahadur Khan with a garrison of 8,000 men to defend the fort, and a garrison of 2,000 regular infantry and 5,000 peons for the defence of the petta. After a careful examination Lord Cornwallis decided to commence the siege from the north-east, where his camp was already established. The fort was of great strength and possessed two gates, the Mysore gate and the Delhi gate, the latter of which faced the petta, on the north of the fort. The petta had several gates and was surrounded by a rampart and ditch, with a space between nearly 100 yards wide planted with impenetrable thorns, in which, however, there was a gap opposite the fort.

On the 7th March, one of the gates of the petta was successfully stormed under a heavy fire, but owing to its extent it was not possible to occupy the whole place. Tippu, who was furious on hearing this news, ordered the bulk of his infantry into the petta to recover it at all costs, but this movement was anticipated by Cornwallis who reinforced the petta, and after protracted fighting the enemy were driven out with a loss of 2,000 men, the casualties on the English side amounting to 131. In the storming of the petta the only Madras troops engaged were the Pioneers, the honours on this occasion resting with H. M. 36th and 24th Regiments and the Bengal Native Infantry. The death of Lieutenant-Colonel Moorhouse of the Madras Artillery, an incident which has been depicted by Home, occurred during the fighting for the petta.

The siege of the fort was now commenced, and was carried on under unusual circumstances. History affords no other example of the siege of a place of strength which was not only not invested, but was constantly supplied with fresh troops, while the besieging army was continually threatened by the whole of the enemy's large force.* The infantry, we are told, wore their accoutrements and the cavalry was kept saddled up all night throughout the entire period.

It is recorded in the private diary of Bell, Commissary of Stores to the army, who was present at the siege, that, having enquired of an Irish sub-conductor, who came from the trenches for ammunition, what prospect there was of completing the breach, the latter replied: "Breach or no breach, depend upon it they will get in. Sure it is open at the top!"

On the night of the 21st March, at 11 p.m., the assault was made upon the breach which had been made in the curtain to the left of the gateway and, after an obstinate struggle, was completely successful, the British thus making themselves masters of the place with a loss to the enemy of nearly 1,500 in killed alone, including the Killadar, while their own losses amounted to 226. It has not yet been discovered which of the Madras battalions were engaged on this occasion, when they suffered a loss of 32 killed and 35 wounded. The total casualties of the army throughout the siege were 431 killed and wounded, but the hospitals were crowded with sick, largely owing to deficient supplies.

On the 22nd March, Cornwallis moved south-west of the fort and, after repairing it, marched northwards en route to Devanhalli. Tippu moved at the same time on Dodballapur, and the two armies crossed each other on the march, Tippu retreating, with the loss of one gun, to the north-west, in the direction of Sivaganga. Devanhalli and Chikballapur surrendered to Cornwallis, but the latter place was subsequently retaken and each man of the garrison suffered amputation of a leg and an arm. Cornwallis marched north for seventy miles and then halted for eight days. Resuming his northern route, on the 12th April, he was joined at Kotapalli by a corps of irregular cavalry, some 10,000 strong, sent by Nizam Ali, a horde which proved to be worse than useless and only served to consume forage and supplies without conferring any

Advance on Seringapatam.

---

*The cirumstances attending the siege of Delhi, during the Mutiny, were somewhat similar.

advantage in return. After the junction had been effected, the united forces moved to Venkatagirikota to pick up a convoy escorted by 4,000 men. Tippu attempted to cut off this convoy, but his attempt was frustrated and the British army returned to Bangalore on the 28th April.

Tippu at length took up a position near the present town of Closepet on the main road to Seringapatam *via* Chennapatna, supported by the forts of Ramgiri and Savangiri. Cornwallis, hoping to turn this position and avoid the stretch of country which had been completely devastated by the Mysore army, decided to advance on Seringapatam by the Kankanhalli road, but found that the whole country had been deprived not only of its cattle and grain but even of its inhabitants, who had been removed to Sivasamudram.

He advanced, however, on the 3rd May, having withdrawn the garrison of Bangalore and replaced it by a detachment from each Corps, the whole commanded by Colonel Oldham. On the 13th May, the army reached Arakere, nine miles east of Seringapatam, by which time the Bombay army under General Sir Robert Abercromby had ascended through Coorg and was in possession of Periyapatna, forty miles to the west of Seringapatam.

Battle before Seringapatam, 15th May 1791. On arrival at Arakere, Lord Cornwallis found a large body of the enemy in a strong position some six miles to his front with their right resting on the river Kaveri and their left along a rugged and apparently inaccesible mountain. This was at first thought to be merely a detachment, but intelligence was received during the night that the whole of the Mysore army was drawn up in front, strengthened by batteries on high ground above and by a swampy ravine below. The fact that the British advance was limited to a frontage of less than a mile by the river on their left and steep hills on their right had had no small effect in inducing Tippu at last to chance a general action.

Cornwallis now found that the ridge of hills on his right was practicable and that, by descending the other side and crossing the continuation of the swamp which lay before the enemy's position, the end of the range of mountains which formed the enemy's position could be ascended at a point where the main road from Chennapatna crossed the ridge; and he decided to attempt by a night march to turn the enemy's left flank and cut off his retreat to the fort and island of Seringapatam.

Orders were accordingly given for the cavalry, six European, and twelve Native infantry regiments (including the 4th Madras Battalion), and some guns, to march at 11 p.m., while the remainder of the army was left under Colonel Duff to protect the camp and heavy baggage. A severe thunderstorm and the intense darkness of the night unfortunately caused the force to lose its way, and compelled the abandonment of the original plan, but Cornwallis decided that it would nevertheless be more advantageous to attack the enemy on his left flank, and accordingly descended the heights to the east of the ravine, a movement which was quite unexpected by the enemy.

In the rear of Tippu's position was the high hill of Karighat, his position being on a lower branch of this hill, of which a more direct continuation extended northwards and formed a strong rocky ridge two or three miles to his left, at right angles with the British column descending the east hill to cross the ravine which lay along his front.

A large body of cavalry and infantry with 8 guns was sent to seize this ridge and, anticipating the British column, which was also heading for this ridge, at that point, opened fire from its guns. The British column now occupied a slight ridge some 500 yards from that occupied by the enemy which, being covered with rocks, afforded some shelter and support, and faced a powerful corps of Tippu's whose main body on the left had changed front and was preparing to advance in line. To oppose this a change of formation was necessary, and part of the column was ordered to form at right angles to the left flank, during which movement it was charged by Tippu's horse, but repulsed it with loss.

The smaller front of the English, consisting of five battalions under Colonel Maxwell, was now ordered to attack the rocky ridge, which was carried out under a heavy fire with such rapidity that not only were the enemy's infantry routed but three guns were captured. The remainder of the line then advanced upon the main body of the enemy and the action became general. The Mysorean infantry retreated before the British lines, but in good order and covering the withdrawal of their guns, the retreat becoming more rapid as Colonel Maxwell began to make his presence felt on the flank. Colonel Floyd with the British cavalry now charged the rearguard and almost destroyed it, but was checked before a position on some broken ground and drew off, but Nizam Ali's cavalry were massed before the left flank of the advancing infantry and, refusing to move for some time (the result of preconcerted treachery), checked the whole line, thus allowing Tippu's guns and infantry to get away.

The British army occupied their ground for the night having lost 81 men killed and 339 wounded during the day, Tippu's loss amounting to some 2,000. It has not yet been discovered what were the casualties of the 4th Battalion. This battle is sometimes called the Battle of the Black Rocks.

The army halted till the 18th May, when Cornwallis marched to Kannambadi, some eight miles beyond Seringapatam, with a view to effecting a junction with the Bombay army under General Abercromby, but the army was now suffering such distress from want of supplies and the cattle were so nearly approaching starvation that Cornwallis, after examining the east, west and north faces of the fortress, saw that it was impossible to move his heavy guns and stores from where they were and on the 21st May he sent orders to Abercromby to withdraw, the pre-arranged plan of co-operation between the two armies being now impracticable.

On the 22nd May, he destroyed the whole of his battering train and heavy baggage and, in the most wretched state from hunger and exposure, the army commenced the return march to Bangalore on the 26th May, taking a more northerly route, than either of the two previously mentioned. On the same day near Melkote, advanced parties of Mahratta cavalry were encountered, the forerunners of two Mahratta armies under Parsaram Bhao and Hari Pant which, accompanied by Captain Little's Bombay detachment, had now arrived just too late to be of any use, except as regards the supplies in the bazaars which always followed them on their marauding expeditions. On the 19th June, the hill fort of Huliyurdurgam was reached, which surrendered and was dismantled, and the united armies proceeded slowly on their way to Bangalore, which was reached on the 11th July 1791. Throughout the march from Kannambadi to Bangalore the 4th Battalion was employed under Captain Alexander Read,* head of the Intelligence Department, in collecting supplies for the army, and on the 23rd June repulsed a body of horse which had attacked the convoy of Brinjaras at Venkatagiri-Kota.

Return to Bangalore.

On the 15th July 1791, Lord Cornwallis, now well supplied by the exertions of Captain Read, with whom the 4th Madras Battalion was still serving, marched to reduce the various forts covering the road from the Carnatic which ascended the ghauts into Mysore by the pass of Palakodu, the only open and easy ascent of the three main passes.† On the same day, Major Gowdie, who had been sent on in advance with the 7th Brigade, reached Hosur, whence the enemy, taken by surprise, fled with precipitation. Gowdie was next ordered to Rayakota, and appeared before that place on the 19th July, and carried the lower fort by storm on the following day, the upper fort surrendering on the 22nd. About the same time the forts of Anchetti-durgam, Nilagiri, Ratnagiri, Hude-durgam, and Chandraya-durgam all either surrendered at once, or were taken after slight resistance. On the 29th July, the army returned to the neighbourhood of Hosur to cover a convoy from Ambur which arrived on the 10th August.

The next operation to be undertaken was the reduction of the hill forts in the district of Chikballapur to the north-east of Bangalore which endangered the line of communications with the Nizam's army. Major Gowdie was sent on this service also, reinforced by the detachments under Captain Read, consisting of the 4th and part of the 3rd and 15th Madras Battalions. The two forces effected a junction, on the 14th September, near Rahmanghar, a strong fort, which was at once summoned to surrender. The Killadar refusing, batteries were constructed on the 17th, and after a few rounds had been fired the Killadar gave in and delivered up the place. On the 18th, Captain Read was sent against Ambaji-durgam and Chillamkottai, two forts near Rahmanghar, both of which surrendered on the first summons.

---

*Captain Read, as a subaltern, had been A. D. C. to the ill-fated Colonel Baillie, and subsequently became the first Collector of Salem District.

†Vide note on the Mysore passes at the end of this Chapter.

Major Gowdie was now ordered to proceed to the attack of Nandidrug, an immensely strong fort commanded by Lutuf Ali Beg,* which was situated on the top of a mountain 1,700 ft. high, and absolutely inaccessible on three sides, ranking in point of strength after Savandrug, Chittaldrug, and Krishnagiri. His force, consisting of 8 guns, 6 mortars, 1 regiment of Europeans, and 6 battalions of sepoys, of which the 4th Battalion was one, arrived before the place on the 22nd September, and the petta was stormed on the same day. On the 23rd, Kammar-ud-din arrived in the neighbourhood of the fort and the Gowdie took post near Chikballapur, but after a careful examination of the northern face of the drug he moved into position before the west face on the 29th.

<small>Siege and Storming of Nandidrug.</small>

With infinite labour a road was cut to the top of a hill adjoining the mountain from which it was expected that a battery would be able to breach the place, but unfortunately it was found on completion of the work that the hill was too far off, and thus all the toil of the troops was wasted. No alternative was left but to attempt to work up the rugged face of the mountain to within breaching distance of the fort, and it was decided that this attempt should be made. "The exertions required to make a road on the face of this mountain surpassed whatever had been known in any former siege in India," and but for the assistance of elephants the guns could not have been taken up at all. This arduous work lasted a fortnight, the troops engaged on it being all the time under fire from the cannon and "ginjalls" of the fort. When the batteries were completed, two breaches were made, one at the re-entering angle of the outwork, the other in the curtain of the outer wall, but the inner wall, being 80 yards off, could not be reached. Major Gowdie then summoned the Bakshi to surrender, but he refused to do so, nor did he take advantage of the offer to send out the women and unarmed inhabitants.

On the 17th October, Lord Cornwallis detached the flank companies of the 36th and 71st regiments to lead the assault, which was to be under the personal command of General Medows. On the 18th, Cornwallis moved the army to within 4 miles of the place (with a view to intimidating the Killadar), and ordered that the batteries should continue to fire until nightfall, and that the assault should be made when the moon rose.

---

* Lutuf Ali Beg was one of Tippu's best officers. He conducted the siege of Onore in 1783, which was gallantly defended for seven months by Captain Torriano. Philippart tells the following story in connection with this siege:—

"On this day, an old woman was detected in the character of a spy. On examination, she confessed her errand, and that she had been in the garrison two days. Her directions were to stay much longer, and make what observations she could, particularly to learn whether the Commanding Officer had survived the bad wound it was understood he had received, on the 1st of the month, at the breach. She was immediately turned out of the fort, having been desired by Captain Torriano to give his compliments to Lutoph Ally Beg, and that on any future occasion, when he chose to employ a lady in so honourable an office, if he would send a younger one, she should be fully enabled to inform him, amongst other particulars, of the real state of his health and spirits."

The plan decided upon was to storm the breaches, and attempt to escalade the inner wall: should the latter fail, it was thought that lodgment could be made between the outer and inner walls, and that thence the inner wall could be regularly attacked.

Before daybreak on the 18th, the flank companies were assembled in the advance parallel, about one hundred yards from the breaches, so as to be in readiness for the assault. The flank companies of the 36th and 71st, under Captain Robertson, were ordered to advance on the breach in the curtain, the light companies under Captain Hart the breach in the outwork, and the flank companies of the 4th European Regiment* under Captain Gabriel Doveton (4th Madras Battalion) were to follow with ladders for escalading the inner wall.

On the word being given, the troops rushed forward to the assault, and were almost immediately discovered by the enemy. The fort was illuminated with blue lights and a heavy fire of cannon, musketry, and rockets opened. The fire was fortunately ill-directed, but some damage was caused by large stones which the garrison rolled down on their assailants. However, the storming party succeeded in mounting the breaches and pursued the enemy so hotly that the latter had no time to secure properly the gate of the inner wall, and this having been forced with some difficulty, the troops penetrated into the body of the place. A large number of the garrison escaped over a low part of the wall, but the slaughter which must have ensued was largely prevented by the exertions of Captain Robertson, the loss of the garrison not exceeding forty men. The flank companies had 2 men killed and 28 wounded, and the total casualties of the British during the siege amounted to 40 Europeans and 80 sepoys. Captain Read was severely wounded during the construction of the approaches.

Thus Nandidrug, defended by seventeen pieces of cannon, well-garrisoned, and strengthened by additional works fell to the British army in three weeks, though it had taken Haidar Ali three years of tedious blockade to wrest it from the Mahrattas.

The conduct of the Artillery employed against the fortress was entrusted to Major Edward Montagu, of the Bengal Artillery, although he was the youngest artillery officer with the army.

---

* There appears to be some divergence of opinion as to whether these were the flank companies of the 4th European Regiment or of the 4th Madras Battalion. The anonymous author of the "*Life of Sir David Baird*" says the 4th Native Infantry, but this is probably wrong as the remainder of his account is copied practically verbatim from Dirom, from whom Wilson, who says the 4th European Regiment also certainly took his facts. It is curious, however, that these companies should have been commanded by an officer who is known to have been the Commanding Officer of the 4th Madras Battalion shortly afterwards.

The following is an extract from the General Orders by Lord Cornwallis:—

"Lord Cornwallis having been witness of the extraordinary obstacles, both of nature and art which were opposed to the detachment of the army that attacked Nundydroog, he cannot too highly applaud the firmness and exertions which were manifested by all ranks, in carrying on the operations of the siege; or the valour and discipline which was displayed by the flank companies of H. M.'s 36th and 71st Regiments, those of the Madras 4th European battalion, the 13th Bengal battalion of Native Infantry, and of the 3rd, 4th, 10th, 13th, and 27th battalions of Madras Native Infantry, that were employed in the assault of last night, and which by overcoming all difficulties, effected the reduction of that important fort..."

In March 1841, the Madras European Regiment, which subsequently became the 102nd Foot and afterwards the 1st Royal Dublin Fusiliers, was granted the honour of "*Nundy-droog.*" It is not clear why the other regiments who were present were not granted a similar distinction.

It may be of interest to note here that, in 1810, General Gowdie had Lieutenant Andrew Walker of the 1st-4th as his Aide-de-Camp.

After the fall of Nandidrug, the very strong fort of Kammaldrug surrendered on the first summons, while the fort of Pennagaram fell to Colonel Maxwell on the 31st October, and Garamkonda, which was being invested by Nizam Ali, was at last taken on the 7th November. On the 3rd November, Lieutenant Chalmers,* who had defended Coimbatore for 28 days against tremendous odds, surrendered to Kammarud-din on terms, which were, however, violated, and the wretched garrison was sent to the dungeons of Seringapatam.

Before an advance could be made on the latter stronghold, it was necessary to reduce a few forts which still remained in the hands of the enemy. Savandrug was accordingly besieged on the 10th December and, though of immense strength, was taken by storm on the 21st, with a casualty list of only one private soldier wounded, the garrison having been seized by a sudden panic.

The 4th Madras Battalion took no active part in this operation, being with Captain Read's detachment, which was engaged in watching the southern road from Kankanhalli to prevent any relief from that side.

---

* This officer was released from captivity in 1792. When Tippu Sultan attempted to negotiate for peace with Cornwallis, the latter at once said that he was unable to negotiate with a person who not only disregarded treaties, but directly violated articles of capitulation. He added, "Send hither the garrison of Coimbetoor, and then we will listen to what you have to say." (*Philippart.*)

Chalmers survived to become Major-General Sir John Chalmers, K.C.B., and died in 1819.

1792.

Renewal of the Campaign against Tippu Sultan.

On the 25th January, Lord Cornwallis concentrated his army near Savandrug for the advance on Seringapatam, but in this campaign the 4th Madras Battalion took no part, being left behind to garrison Bangalore till the 19th March.

The siege of Seringapatam being well advanced, Tippu sued for peace, and preliminaries were signed on the 24th February, and ratified on the 19th March, by which Tippu undertook to pay an indemnity, and gave up one half of his dominions to the allies. Calicut, Dindigul, Sankaridurgam, the Baramahal, Coorg, and many other places were consequently ceded to the British.

General Medows and Lord Cornwallis both gave up their shares of prize-money for the campaigns of 1790-92 to the army, the latter thus relinquishing a sum of £47,244, and the former £14,997. General Medows, I may note, was so mortified by the failure of his part of the attack on Seringapatam on the 6th February, that he attempted to commit suicide, by shooting himself in the stomach. He was held in great esteem, both by Cornwallis and the army.

On the conclusion of the campaign, six months' batta was given to all the officers and men who had taken part in it. In July 1794, the thanks of both Houses of Parliament to the troops employed during the war with Tippu were published to the army and, in the following month, those of the Court of Proprietors of the East India Company.

On the declaration of peace, the administration of, and command of the troops, in the Baramahal, was entrusted to Captain A. Read, and the 4th Madras Battalion, under Captain James Turing, was placed in occupation of Pennagaram.

In June 1792, there was a detachment of the battalion, about 130 strong, at Tirupattur, and one of 50 at Virabhadradurgam.

Sir Charles Oakeley, *Bart.*, became Governor of Madras in 1792, after acting as Second in Council to General Medows from October 1790.

1793—1796.

During 1793, the battalion, forming part of the 3rd Brigade under Lieutenant-Colonel Dugald Campbell, remained at Pennagaram, with small detachments at other places, and was consequently not employed in the operations against, and capture of, Pondicherry, in August.

On the 13th July 1793, the Commanding Officer, Captain James Turing, died, and was buried in a field on the glacis of the fort at Pennagaram, where his tomb forms the only remaining indication of military occupancy. Captain Gabriel Doveton was appointed as his successor, but did not immediately take up the appointment, and the battalion was left under the command of Lieutenant William MacGregor.

Sir John Shore, *Bart.* (afterwards Lord Teignmouth), became Governor-General of India in 1793, and held the appointment till 1798, and in 1794, Lord Hobart was appointed Governor of Madras.

Throughout 1794, the battalion remained at Pennagaram, with detachments at Virabhadradurgam* (Lieutenant MacRae), Tirupattur, Chendrayadurgam† and Solapaddi‡.

In February 1794, the sons of Tippu Sultan were sent back to Seringapatam in charge of Captain Gabriel Doveton, a Grenadier Company of the 4th Battalion, with a troop of cavalry, forming the escort from the frontier of Mysore to the Capital. Lieutenant J. H. Symons accompanied Captain Doveton on this occasion.

In 1795, the battalion was stationed at Rayakota, as part of the 5th Brigade, with detachments at Virabhadradurgam (Lieutenant MacRae), Chendrayadurgam, (Lieutenant MacGregor) and Kangundi § (Lieutenant Grant).

Mahomed Ali, Nawab Walajah of the Carnatic, died on the 13th October 1795, and was succeeded by his eldest son, Umdat-ul-Umara. The latter was the first native of India to become a Freemason.

On the re-organisation of the Madras Army in July 1796, the 4th Madras Battalion, together with the right wing of the 25th Madras Battalion, became the 1st Battalion of the 4th Regiment of Madras Native Infantry, with the 15th Madras Battalion, and the left wing of the 25th Madras Battalion, as its 2nd Battalion.

---

* East of the Palakodu-Rayakota road, commanding the entrance to the Palakodu Pass.

† Five miles S. W. of Rayakota. Very little now remains of this fort. The plain below the hill is still known as *Bailwan*, meaning a parade ground. The site was discovered with difficulty by the Tahsildar of Krishnagiri in 1915.

‡ At the junction of the Toppur and Kaveri rivers.

§ About eight miles east of Kuppam (M. and S. M. Railway Station). The seat of a Poligar and now a Zemindari.

A Note
On the Passes from Mysore into the Carnatic.

For the better understanding of the problem which faced the Commander of a force operating against Mysore from the Carnatic, the following list of the principal passes between the two countries will be found useful:—

(1) *The Mugali Pass*, which was considered to be too far to the north, and not sufficiently connected with posts, but was used by Cornwallis in 1791. The following note explains how Cornwallis was able to make use of it:—

"During the peace, before operations commenced against Tippu in 1790, Captain (afterwards Major-General) Beatson made a thorough exploration of the whole face of the Carnatic from the River Godavari to Cape Comorin. He made a particular study of the passes leading from Travancore and from the Carnatic into Mysore, and after the war commenced in 1790, accompanied only by a single company of Sepoys, made a rapid advance from Arni into the enemy's country, and minutely examined the passes of Cuddapanatum, Pedanaigdurgam and Muglee. His intimate knowledge of the latter enabled him to lead Cornwallis' army through it in February 1791, which so completely deceived Tippu, who thought the pass was impracticable that though the latter made forced marches from Royakota, he was not able to gain touch with the British army till the latter was within ten miles of Bangalore.

(2) *The Peddanayakandurgam Pass*, between Ambur and Venkatagiri-Kota, which is very steep and difficult to ascend.

(3) *The Palakodu Pass*, by which the Mysore Army had always invaded the Carnatic. It is the only open and easy ascent. The road passes through open country for 28 miles to Hosur; thence it descends gradually amongst the hills between Mysore and the Baramahal, defended by various hill forts to Kaveripatnam in the middle of the valley.

From Kaveripatnam many roads branch to the east, forming passes into the Carnatic, of which the three principal are :—

(a) *The Ambur Pass*, defended by the hill fort of Ambur, in the Carnatic.

(b) *The Chengam Pass*, in the Baramahal, whence unprotected roads lead to Tiruvannamalai, Ginji and Arni, *via* Kalasapakkam.

(c) *The Atur Pass*, also in the Baramahal, defended by the fort of Atur, and leading by Tayagadurgam to Pondicherry. This was used by the French to communicate with Mysore.

It will be seen from the above note how necessary it was for Cornwallis, before advancing on Seringapatam, to make sure of his communications with the Carnatic by capturing the forts which commanded the pass of Palakodu.

Part I.

CHAPTER IV.

THE 1st BATTALION 4th REGIMENT OF MADRAS NATIVE INFANTRY.

13th July 1796—5th May 1824.

1797-1798.

The 1st Battalion 4th Regiment Madras Native Infantry remained at Rayakota, under Major Gabriel Doveton, during 1797 and 1798 with detachments at Salem (300 men under Captain Innes), Virabhadra-durgam (Lieutenant Brown), Chendraya-durgam (Lieutenant Cormick), and Kangundi (Lieutenant Symons).

In 1798, Lord Clive became Governor of Madras, and the Marquess Wellesley, Governor-General of India, holding the appointment till 1805, while Lieutenant-General Sir Alured Clarke, K. B., became Commander-in-Chief in India.

1799.
Final War against Tippu Sultan.

Since the treaty of Seringapatam in March 1792, the hatred entertained by Tippu Sultan for the British had become intensified from year to year, and his sole object was to compass their expulsion from the Peninsula. Accordingly he opened communications with Zemān Shah, the ruler of Afghanistan, with a view to obtaining his co-operation in a simultaneous attack on the British and at the same time engaged in intrigues with the Mahrattas and was in active correspondence with the French.

The discovery of these intrigues decided the Government of Madras that the time had come when steps must be taken to put an end to this formidable power, established in such close proximity to, and ever awaiting a favourable opportunity to fall upon, the Carnatic, and accordingly the Madras Army was assembled at Vellore in January under Lieutenant-General Harris* where it was joined on the 18th by the Nizam's Contingent from Haidarabad, which brought it up to a strength of about 40,000 men†. The Bombay Army 6,420 strong, under Lieutenant-General James Stuart, marched from Cannanore on the 21st February, to co-operate in the attack on the Mysore capital.

With the movements of these armies, the former of which commenced its march on the 28th February, we have, unfortunately, little to do, the flank companies of the 1st-4th having been detached from the main army at Kelamangalam on the 9th March, to form part of a force (5,400 strong) under Lieutenant-Colonel A. Read, whose duties were to protect the frontier of the Baramahal, to

---

* Lord Harris joined the Royal Artillery as a Cadet in 1759 and, in 1765, transferred to the 5th Foot. He served in America from 1774 to 1778, and was present at many battles, including Bunker's Hill. He accompanied Sir W. Medows to India in 1780, as his Secretary, and fought in all the campaigns in Mysore. He became a full General in 1812, and received the G.C.B., and in 1815, was elevated to the peerage.

† is noteworthy that the number of followers with this force was 120,000, but this number was exceeded in the Mahratta War of 1817, when the Marquis of Hastings had a fighting force of 110,000 men, accompanied by no less than 500,000 camp followers.

collect supplies, and ultimately to co-operate with a force under Colonel Brown, which had been assembled near Trichinopoly and was about to march on Seringapatam via Karur, Erode, and Kaveripuram.

It will be as well, however, to give a short outline of the movements of the main army. Selecting the road by Anekal, Talghatpuram, and Kankanhalli, which had been chosen by Lord Cornwallis for his advance in 1791, General Harris reached the neighbourhood of Bangalore on the 14th March, and on the 21st of that month the army was assembled at Kankanhalli.

On the following day, news was received from General Stuart of Tippu's repulse with heavy loss at Sidasir* (Siddheshwara) on the 6th March, and on the 26th General Harris himself inflicted a defeat on the Mysore Army at Malavalli. The siege of Seringapatam was opened on the 8th April, the Bombay Army arriving on the 16th. By the 3rd May, the breach was considered practicable and on the following afternoon, at about 1-30 p. m., the assault was delivered by a storming party under Major-General Baird, which met with triumphant success. Tippu Sultan himself was killed, and prize was taken to the value of over ninety-one lakhs of rupees.

Tippu Sultan. Thus perished Tippu Sultan, commonly known as the "Tiger of Mysore" from the ferocity of his character. He was in the habit of declaring that he would rather live two days as a tiger than 200 years as a sheep. He had a great hatred of the British, which he vented on the unfortunate prisoners who fell into his hands. To give an instance of his brutality, he ordered, during Lord Cornwallis' advance on Seringapatam in 1791, the decapitation by the village chuckler, of two prisoners confined at Hosur—Captain Hamilton of the Engineers and a midshipman. The sentence was carried out by the chuckler, and anyone who knows what a chuckler's knife is will realize the gruesome barbarity involved in such an execution.

Also, during the siege of Seringapatam he had some grenadiers of the 33rd Regiment put to death, some by having nails driven into their heads; while others had their necks broken by Chettys, who were kept to display feats of strength.

Tippu was born in 1753, and is described as being of low stature, corpulent, with high shoulders, and a short thick neck; but his hands and feet were remarkably small. His complexion was rather dark, his eyes large and prominent, with small arched eyebrows and an aquiline nose. He had an appearance of sternness in his countenance, which distinguished him above the common order of his people. Though brave and intelligent, he was far from being the equal of his father in the field. The tiger constituted the symbol of his State, appearing on his flag, his throne, and his private cipher; while a number of live tigers were found chained in the courtyard of his palace, and had to be destroyed after the fall of Seringapatam.

---

* The troops in this battle were continuously engaged from daylight till five in the afternoon, and it is recorded by an officer who was present that several of the muskets of men in his regiment melted, and burst in the muzzle and touch-holes from the heat of firing.

To return to Colonel Read's detachment, with which we are more immediately concerned; from Kelamangalam the force marched to Rayakota, and proceeded to capture the forts on the frontier. Sulagiri was stormed with slight loss on the 24th March, and Peddanayakandurgam was surrendered on the 30th. On the 22nd April, the fort at Kaveripuram fell and, as Colonel Brown had not yet arrived, Read continued his march on the 23rd. He did not reach Maratahalli at the head of the pass till the 27th, and it was the 6th May before he got the supplies through the pass. The delay can readily be understood when we learn that the convoy consisted of 33,000 Brinjari bullocks, 4,358 pack-cattle with rice, etc., 2,560 slaughter cattle, and 21,900 sheep, besides other supplies.

On the 6th May, Colonel Read was joined by Colonel Floyd (who had been sent from Seringapatam to meet the detachments) and Colonel Brown at Kandahalli; and on the 7th, the whole 14,000 men, including 6,000 Nizam's cavalry, assembled at Anur and moved forward to Seringapatam, where they arrived safely on the 13th May—ten days too late to take part in the storming of the fortress.

The casualties of the 1st 4th in this campaign appear only to have amounted to 3 men killed and 14 wounded.

On the 17th May 1799, Colonel Read was detached to occupy Savandrug, Gopaldrug, Bangalore, Nandidrug and various other places in Mysore.

In June 1799, after the settlement of Mysore, the sons of Tippu Sultan were sent to the fortress of Vellore, which was placed under the command of Lieutenant-Colonel Doveton, "an officer in all respects qualified for the charge," who conducted them from Rayakota to Vellore on the 12th July. A note on some of the Dovetons who served in Madras will be found elsewhere in these records.

During the campaign of 1799, the remainder of the 1st 4th Battalion was in all probability still garrisoning the forts in the Baramahal.

1800.

In the beginning of 1800, a strong detachment under Colonel Stevenson was to have been sent into Malabar and Wynad against the Pychy Raja, of whom we shall hear again,* but it did not move until late in the year. The operations were not concluded until May 1801, and for this reason we may assume that the 4th Madras Native Infantry was not engaged, as it is known that on the 1st January 1801 it was garrisoning Fort St. George.

On the 26th January 1800, Major-General George Harris resigned command of the Madras Army, and was succeeded by Major-General Braithwaite of the Company's Service.

---

* See 1805—the Rising in Wynad.

1801.

The Insurrection in Tinnevelly and Madura.

From the time when he became Nawab of the Carnatic, in 1749, Mahomed Ali had had difficulty in maintaining his authority over the Poligars, or minor Rajahs, in Tinnevelly and Madura, and from 1753 to 1763 they were only kept in subjection by the energy and ability of Mahomed Yusuf. At that time there were thirty-two Poligars in Tinnevelly, those on the eastern side having a following of Nayakans and those on the western side of Marawans, of whom Orme says:—

> "Their arms are lances and pikes, bows and arrows, rockets and matchlocks; but whether with or without other weapons every man constantly wears a sword and shield. In battle the different arms move in distinct bodies, but the lance-men are rated the most eminent and lead all attacks. This weapon is eighteen feet long: they tie under the point a tuft of scarlet horse-hair, and when they attack horse add a small bell.
>
> Without previous exercise they assemble in a deep column, pressing close together, and advance at a long steady step, in some degree of time, their lances inclining forward but aloft, of which the elasticity and vibration, with the jingle and dazzle, scare the cavalry, and their approach is scarcely less formidable to infantry not disciplined with fire-arms."

After the capture of Madura from Mahomed Yusuf in 1763, the Poligars remained quiet for some time, but in 1783, led by Kattaboma Nayakan, Poligar of Panjalamkurichi, and encouraged by the Dutch, they broke out in rebellion again. An expedition under Colonel Fullarton, however, soon subdued them, and Tinnevelly remained comparatively peaceful until 1798, when Kattaboma Nayakan once more caused disturbance. As all the available troops were at this time required for the war against Tippu Sultan, no steps were taken until after the fall of Seringapatam in 1799, when an expedition was sent under Major Bannerman, who was completely successful in subduing the Poligars, Kattaboma Nayakan, who had fled to the Tondiman Rajah,* being given up and hanged at Kaitar, and the fort at Panjalamkurichi levelled to the ground.

On the 2nd February 1801, the troops in Tinnevelly were in cantonments at Sankaranayanar Koil, about 30 miles north west of Palamcottah, and the officers were all dining in Palamcottah with Major Colin Macaulay† who was in command of the province of Tinnevelly, when news was brought to them that the Poligar prisoners, who had been in confinement since the quelling of the previous revolt by Major Bannerman in 1799, had escaped from the fort in Palamcottah, and fled to Panjalamkurichi.

---

* Now the Rajah of Pudukotta.

† Welsh says he was Resident of Travancore, but I think he obtained this appointment at a later date.

The principal prisoners were two brothers of the late Poligar of Panjalamkurichi, the elder bearing the same name, Kattaboma Nayakan, while the younger, though dumb, was almost worshipped by the people of the country.* A near relation of the family, named Sivatayya, who had escaped in 1799, was the leader of the conspiracy to effect their freedom. On their arrival at Panjalamkurichi, they occupied the Walanadu hill near that place with a force of at least 4,000 armed men.

Major Macaulay at once assembled all the available troops, only some 900 strong, and marched to Kaitar on the 3rd February. He arrived at Panjalamkurichi on the 9th February, when it was found that the fort, which had been completely destroyed by Major Bannerman, had been rebuilt and was as strong as ever. The garrison was about 1,500 strong, but the people of the surrounding country rapidly assembled, until there was a force of between 4,000 and 5,000 men, and Major Macaulay was forced to retreat to Palamcottah on the 10th February, Captain Vesey with the 1st-3rd Regiment repulsing a night attack made by the enemy.

Application was at once made to Government for reinforcements, but instead of waiting for these, Major Macaulay made several attempts on the enemy, all of which were unsuccessful. On the 27th February, a small detachment was sent to take Kadalgudi, but the Poligars heard of this and reinforced the garrison with 2,000 men, with the result that the detachment, after a gallant fight, had to retreat with a loss of 3 killed and 18 wounded. On the 3rd March, the force moved to Kaitar (21 miles) and remained there to await the reinforcements. Several of the smaller forts were taken by the Poligars, who also captured Tuticorin, but the Srivaikundam Pagoda, 15 miles from Palamcottah, held out until relieved by Major Sheppard on the 16th March, when the garrison was withdrawn.

On the 27th March, the reinforcements arrived, bringing the force up to a strength of about 2,800 men. At the beginning of this year the headquarters of

---

* Welsh says:—" I cannot close this account of horrors without a few words in memory of one of the most extraordinary mortals I ever knew; a near relation of Catabomia Naig, who was both deaf and dumb, was well known by the English under the appellation of Dumby or the Dumb Brother; by the Mussulmans, as Mookah; and by the Hindoos, as Oomee; all having the like signification. He was a tall, slender lad, of a very sickly appearance, yet possessing that energy of mind, which, in troubled times, always gains pre-eminence; whilst, in his case, the very defect which would have impeded another, proved a powerful auxiliary in the minds of ignorant and superstitious idolaters. The Oomee was adored; his slightest sign was an oracle, and every man flew to execute whatever he commanded. No council assembled at which he did not preside; no daring adventure was undertaken which he did not lead. His method of representing the English was extremely simple; he collected a few little pieces of straw, arranged them on the palm of his left hand to represent the English force; then, with other signs, for the time, etc., he drew the other hand across and swept them off, with a whizzing sound from his mouth, which was the signal for attack; and he was generally the foremost in executing those plans, for our annihilation. Whatever undisciplined valour could effect, was sure to be achieved wherever he appeared; though poor Oomee was at last doomed to grace a gallows, in reward for the most disinterested and purest patriotism."

the 1st 4th Regiment was in camp at Mamadore, with 500 men in garrison at Fort St. George and it was probably the latter who formed the five companies of the 1st 4th under Captain Nagle, sent to reinforce Major Macaulay.

On this occasion Captain Nagle received the following letter:—

"Sir,

I am directed by Major-General Bridges to signify to you, that the celerity in the movement of the detachment under your command from Madras to Trichinopoly, is considered by the Officer Commanding the army in Chief as a strong proof of your zeal and activity, and which he shall keep in his remembrance.

(Signed) MONTAGUE COSBY, M.B.

Headquarters, Trichinopoly, March 22nd, 1801."

The force marched on the 29th March 1801, and on the 30th a body of Poligar pikemen appeared, near "Pashenthelly"* which was almost annihilated by the cavalry under Lieutenant James Grant, who killed four men with his own hand.

Repulse at Panjalamkurichi.
Panjalamkurichi was reached on the 31st March. The fort was found to consist of an irregular oblong about 500 feet long and 300 feet broad, and was surrounded by mud walls 12 feet high, while a thick hedge of thorns encircled the whole. Major Macaulay decided to attack the bastion at the north western angle, and by about 3 p.m. his guns had made what appeared to be a practicable breach. The storming party, of which the grenadier company of the 1st 4th formed part, then advanced to the assault, covered by the fire of the remainder of the force, which had been disposed on the flanks. Under a heavy fire they succeeded in crossing the hedge, and reached the top of the breach, but further than this they could not get, every man who showed himself being instantly killed or disabled, and they were forced to retire with considerable loss, the total casualties amounting to 4 officers and 49 men killed, and 13 officers and 254 men wounded. Colonel Welsh, who was present, says that only 46 out of 120 Europeans in the storming party were unhurt.

The casualties of the 1st 4th comprised Lieutenant Mangnall and 8 men killed; and Lieutenant Clapham (in groin), Subadar Burhan Sahib of the Grenadier Company (left arm), Subadar Ahmed Khan of the Light Company (neck), and 33 rank and file wounded.

In his report Major Macaulay said:—

"Notwithstanding the intrepid firmness of the assaulting party, the daring and desperate resistance of the enemy made it utterly impossible to enter the place, all those who attempted it being instantly piked or shot. Perceiving at length the impossibility of succeeding, I was reduced to the painful necessity of ordering the troops to retire. Our loss is very severe. The whole behaved with the greatest animation and ardour."

After this repulse, Major Macaulay took up a position about 1,500 paces from the fort, and there awaited further reinforcements, continually harassed by the enemy, the whole country being now up in arms.

---

* This must have been Payanthella, about 5 miles north-west of Panjalamkurichi.

On the 21st May 1801, Lieutenant-Colonel P. Agnew, the Adjutant-General, superseded Major Macaulay in the command, and additional troops arrived on the following day. On the night of the 22nd, breaching batteries were constructed, and on the morning of the 23rd, fire was opened on the south-west bastion and wall. A practicable breach having been made in the bastion, and the wall nearly demolished, the assault was made at about one o'clock on the afternoon of the 24th. The advance was for some time checked by the hedge, and when the breach was reached the storming party was met with such a vigorous resistance that it was only after a severe struggle, which lasted twenty minutes, and the death of nearly all the defenders of the bastion, that an entrance was effected. On the fall of the bastion, the remainder of the garrison to the number of 3,000, rushed out of the opposite side of the fort in a compact body, and were pursued and dispersed by the cavalry, who accounted for large numbers of them, their losses being estimated at about 1,000 men.

Storming of Panjalamkurichi.

Colonel Welsh states that 4 officers and 43 men were killed, and 5 officers and 172 men wounded. Sixteen of the 1st 4th were wounded, including two officers, Lieutenants Birch and Fraser, of whom the latter died on the 26th May.

On the capture of the fort a reason was found for the ill-success of the previous attempt in March, as the bastions were hollow and afforded no footing for the assaulting party, while the defenders, standing below armed with pikes 18 to 20 feet long, could reach the attackers without exposing themselves in the least. Besides, the breach was so narrow that only a few men could ascend at one time.

It should be noted that in these operations Colonel Agnew was assisted by a body of one thousand Poligars of Ettiyapuram, who were hereditary enemies of the Panjalamkurichi Poligars. Colonel Welsh's account of the death of one of these appears to be of sufficient interest to be quoted here :—

"Not having done our Eteapoor allies sufficient justice, considering the share they took in the whole service, I shall conclude this part of my narrative with the death of one of their chiefs. Mortally wounded, he desired that his body might immediately be carried to Major Macaulay, who was at the time surrounded by his English officers. The old man, who was placed upright in a chair, then said, with a firm voice, "I have come to show the English how a Poligar can die." He twisted his whiskers with both hands as he spoke, and in that attitude expired."

The fort of Panjalamkurichi no longer exists, the site being now a cultivated field in the neighbourhood of Otapidaram, where the remains of those who fell in the two assaults were buried.

After their defeat, the rebels, including the Poligar and his dumb brother, fled to Sivaganga in Madura district, where they were received with open arms by the Poligar.

On the 26th May 1801, Colonel Agnew marched towards Ramnad, and was considerably harassed on the way. The force reached Nagalapuram on the 28th, and Tiruppuvanam on the 2nd June. On the 7th June, an attack was made by the Poligars near Tirupuchetti, where Captain Nagle of the 1st 4th was in command of the picquets, and the force lost Major Gray and 16 men killed, and 4 Lieutenants and 34 men wounded. Again on the 10th June, between Manamadura and Patinur a loss was sustained of 10 Europeans and 86 Natives killed and wounded, mainly owing to the carelessness of the officer commanding the rearguard, who failed to take up a proper position to cover the passage of the river Vaigai.

On the 11th June, the force marched 11 miles to Paramagudi, and on the 12th, 12 miles to Sattirakudi. Ramnad was reached on the 14th, and a halt was made for six days. On the 22nd June, Colonel Agnew arrived at Komarri, 20 miles from Ramnad, near the east bank of the Palamari river, and left a garrison there, returning to Madura, owing to the difficulty of keeping himself supplied, on the 4th July.

The 24th July found the force at Trikatiyanur, where they waited to be joined by another force under Lieutenant-Colonel James Innes, which was operating from Dindigul. The junction was effected on the following day after considerable fighting, the casualties amounting to 21 killed and wounded.

Welsh remarks on this day's fighting :—

"The enemy this day used rockets against us for the first time; and I saw a poor Sepoy burned to death, with one sticking fast in his chest, from which he could not extract it nor extinguish the flame."

The combined force marched to Ukur on the 28th July, the enemy making an attempt on the rearguard, but they were repulsed with considerable loss. Seruvelli was reached on the 29th, the force having been fired on throughout the day, with a loss of 36 killed and wounded.

From the 31st July to the 1st September, the force was occupied in endeavouring to pierce the dense jungle between Seruvelli and Kalayarkoil, an attempt which had eventually to be abandoned, and on the 2nd September, Colonel Agnew marched to Ukur, where he established his headquarters.

The insurrection was finally quelled early in October by the capture of Kalayarkoil, an operation in which the 1st 4th Regiment was not employed, having, with the 2nd 3rd, proceeded, on the 14th September, to join the field force coming from Madura. The regiment was sent back to Madura early in October, to escort the heavy guns, stores and elephants to that place, and whilst there Captain Nagle received the following order from Colonel Agnew:

"*Oct. 12, 1801*.—The flight of a large body of rebels toward the Vierapatchy hills renders it expedient to reinforce Lieutenant-Colonel Innis's detachment, now on its march to Dindigul: You will therefore proceed and join that officer."

On the 18th October, the rebels were dislodged from their strongholds in the hills, and on the following day Colonel Innis ordered Captain Nagle to proceed to the Dindigul valley, to preserve that district from depredations and to apprehend or destroy any fugitive rebels he might encounter. The detachment captured the chief of the remaining Poligars who were still in arms and lodged him in Dindigul.

Shortly afterwards the leaders of the outbreak were captured in the jungle. Kattaboma Nayakan; Chinna Marathai, the Poligar of Seruvelli; and his brother, Vellai Marathai were hanged, while Dalavoi Pillai, and Duraisami, son of Chinna Marathai, were transported for life. The bulk of their property was handed over to the Poligars of Ettiyapuram and Maniyachi, who had taken the side of the Government.

Altogether these operations cost the army between 800 and 900 killed and wounded, including 14 officers killed, and 26 wounded.

After the suppression of the rebellion, a General Order was issued by Government, of which the following is an extract:—

"The whole course of operations connected with that service has been distinguished by a spirit of animated bravery and persevering exertion which has merited the warmest approbation of the Governor-in-Council, and his Lordship in Council, in bestowing on the officers and troops the applause due to their conduct, reflects with the greatest satisfaction on the advantages which have been derived to the public interests by the suppression of a confederacy which threatened the most injurious consequences to the tranquility of the British possessions."

1801.

Assumption of the Carnatic. On the capture of Seringapatam in 1799, it was discovered from the state papers taken there that the Nawab, Umdat-ul-Umara, who had succeeded his father Mahomed Ali in 1795, had been conspiring with Tippu Sultan against the British government. It was decided, therefore, that the British should assume the direct government of the Carnatic, and on the 31st July 1801, Umdat-ul-Umara having meanwhile died, his brother, Azim-ud-Daulah handed over the whole of his authority over the Carnatic, receiving an allowance of one-fifth of the estimated revenue.

On the 1st August 1801, Lieutenant-General John Stuart became Commander-in-Chief of the Madras Army, and in this year Lieutenant-General Gerard (afterwards Viscount) Lake became Commander-in-Chief in India.

On the 22nd September 1801, a Volunteer Battalion was raised for service in the Moluccas, then in the hands of the Dutch, the 1st 4th being one of the regiments from which men were selected.

Captain Joseph Walker of the 1st 4th was placed in command of a detachment of the Madras European Regiment which formed part of the expedition sent to Ternate, and on the withdrawal of the troops, was left in command with a small garrison, which no doubt included many men of his own regiment.

1802.

On the 1st January 1802, the headquarters of the 1st 4th were at " Yelay "* and 561 men were in garrison at Fort St. George, but, according to Philippart, the corps was shortly afterwards moved to Vellore, where it was reviewed by Sir T. Dallas, then in command of the garrison. " Notwithstanding that five companies of the battalion had been separated from the other five, and employed for nearly a year in constant service against the Poligars, Sir T. Dallas was pleased to express, in garrison orders, his entire approbation of the discipline and appearance of the corps, and reported the same to headquarters."

On the 11th October, a body of 400 Nayars attacked the fort of Panamaratta Kota† in the Wynad, which was occupied by a party of the 1st 4th Bombay Infantry. The officer in command of this regiment, whose headquarters were at Pulingal, only nine miles off, remained inactive, but General Wellesley sent the 1st 8th Madras Infantry and 200 Mysore Horse to their assistance from Seringapatam.

A detachment composed of the 33rd Regiment and the 1st 4th Madras Infantry was also ordered to march to the Wynad, but the 1st 8th operated with such success against the Nayars, that the advance of this detachment was stopped.

In November 1802, the regiment was once more ordered on field service, with directions to march to Bangalore.

1803.
The Mahratta War.

The Mahrattas had first become an organised nation in the seventeenth century under the rule of Sivaji. On the latter's death, the Government passed from the feeble hands of his successors, the Rajas of Satara, into those of the astute Brahmin ministers, the Peshwas, who had their seat at Poona. The Mahratta Confederacy was then formed, of the Peshwa (Baji Rao) at Poona; Holkar at Indore; the Gaekwar of Baroda; Daulat Rao Sindhia of Gwalior; and the Raja of Berar, who was Chief of Nagpur, and also bore the title of Bhonsla.

Confusion on the occasion of the succession to the Peshwa's *masnad* resulted in Daulat Rao Sindhia gaining the ascendancy at Poona, and as that chief was ambitious of becoming the head of the Mahratta Empire and possessed the largest corps of infantry under foreign adventurers, this constituted a direct menace both to the British and to their ally the Nizam of Haidarabad.

---

* I have not been able to trace this place. It was, apparently, in the neighbourhood of Madras.

† This means " Palmyra Tree Fort." This place was formerly known as Panortacottah, and is also known as Panamaram.

In 1800, the British, who had already disbanded the Nizam's French Corps at Haidarabad, took the Nizam under their protection by a general defensive treaty. It was obvious that the consequence of this must eventually be a struggle with the Mahrattas.

War now broke out between Sindhia and Holkar, and after considerable success on the part of the former for some two years, he and the Peshwa were defeated by Holkar in a battle under the walls of Poona on the 25th October 1802. The Peshwa fled to Bassein, where he landed on the 6th December, and there concluded a treaty with the British, under the terms of which he agreed to exclude foreign adventurers from his service, to have a permanent Subsidiary Force established in his dominions, and to co-operate with the British in return for their protection.

The convulsed state of the Mahratta Empire made it necessary for the Marquis Wellesley, who had arrived in India as Governor-General in 1798, to take steps for the protection of the British possessions and to support the defensive alliance concluded with the Peshwa.

Plan of Campaign. It was consequently decided to group all the available troops in convenient stations so as to be able to act against the Mahrattas in three columns; one from Oude under Lord Lake; one towards Cuttack; and one from North-West Mysore and the Nizam's Dominions.

The last-mentioned force consisted of 20,000 men under Lieutenant-General John Stuart, and the Haidarabad Subsidiary Force about 9,000 strong under Colonel Stevenson. In January 1803, the 1st Battalion 4th Regiment of Madras Native Infantry, under the command of Major Joseph G. Hill, was in camp near Bangalore, with 1,010 men, and formed part of the force under General Stuart which assembled at Harihar on the 6th March. On the arrival of Major-General the Hon. Arthur Wellesley, General Stuart's force was divided, the former being given a division about 10,600 strong, and a plan was decided upon, namely that General Wellesley was to move forward, effect a junction with Colonel Stevenson, and strike at Poona, whilst the remaining troops, which included the 1st 4th, were to form a reserve near Mudgal.

Wellesley Advances. Before dealing further with the 1st 4th, which was to remain in Harihar for some time longer, we shall follow the movements of General Wellesley during the earlier part of 1803. He left Harihar on the 9th March, crossed the Tungabhadra river on the 12th, and, by the 21st, was in the neighbourhood of Dharwar. On the 3rd April, he reached Miraj and, on the 15th of that month, he interviewed Colonel Stevenson, whose force was encamped at the confluence of the Bhima and Nira rivers at Sarhatti. Wellesley reinforced Stevenson with one brigade, and gave him orders to move up the Bhima near its junction with the Mulamuta, towards Poona. On the 19th April, Wellesley was within one march of the Bhor ghat, where he heard that it was Holkar's intention to burn Poona before abandoning it, so with the cavalry and one battalion of infantry he pushed forward, covering 60 miles in 32 hours, and entered the city on the 20th. The remainder of the force arrived on the 22nd, having marched about 350 miles in 38 days, and Wellesley moved into camp 10 miles outside Poona. On the 7th May, the Peshwa arrived from Bassein and, on the 13th, entered Poona in state.

On the 29th July, Wellesley reported to General Lake that the situation of the various forces was as follows:—The Maharajah Holkar had withdrawn north of the Tapti and, owing to his enmity with Sindhia, refused to join the other chiefs; Sindhia was at Jalgaon, in rear of the Ajanta pass, near the Nizam's frontier, with 18,000 horse, 11 battalions of infantry, and 150 guns; the Raja of Berar was with him and had 20,000 horse, 6,000 infantry and 40 guns; Sindhia had an advanced corps of horse in the Ajanta hills.

Wellesley was at Sangwi on the river Sina, about 20 miles north-east of Ahmednagar; Colonel Murray was in Poona with two battalions of Native Infantry; the Nizam was at Aurangabad with the Subsidiary Force; and Stevenson was watching the Ajanta hills.

In case of hostilities, Wellesley's plan was to attack Ahmednagar, thus securing his communications with Poona and Bombay, to keep the Nizam to guard the frontier, and with Stevenson to attack the enemy's forces. Meanwhile the corps in Guzarat was to attack Broach.

On the 6th August 1803, Wellesley was at Walki, about 10 miles south of Ahmednagar,

Declaration of War. where he had arrived after experiencing great difficulties with his transport. Colonel Collins,* British Resident with Sindhia, had left the Mahratta camp on the 3rd August and, on the 6th, Wellesley ordered operations to commence against Broach. On the 7th, war was formally declared against Sindhia and

---

* *Colonel Collins.*—An officer who accompanied Wellesley to an interview with Colonel Collins at Aurangabad on the 29th August, has left an account of that extraordinary man, which is too good to be omitted:—

"On reaching the tent of the Resident we were unexpectedly received with a salute of artillery, for such was the state maintained by this representative of John Company (known in Bengal by the nickname of King Collins), that he had a brigade of field pieces, worked by native artillerymen, attached to his escort. In front of a noble suite of tents, which might have served for the Great Moghul, we were received by an insignificant little, old-looking man, dressed in an old-fashioned military coat, white breeches, sky-blue silk stockings, and large glaring buckles to his shoes, having his highly-powdered wig, from which depended a pig-tail of no ordinary dimensions, surmounted by a small round black silk hat, ornamented by a single black ostrich feather, looking not altogether unlike a monkey dressed up for Bartholomew Fair. There was, however, a fire in his small black eye, shooting out from beneath a large, shaggy, pent-house brow, which more than counterbalanced the ridicule that his appearance naturally excited. After the usual compliments, the principals retired into an inner tent, where matters not to be entrusted to vulgar ears were discussed. But the last words uttered by the little man, as they came forth from the tent, I well recollect. 'I tell you General, as to their cavalry, you may ride over them wherever you meet them; but their infantry and guns will astonish you.' As, in riding homewards we amused ourselves, the General among the rest, in cutting jokes at the expense of 'little King Collins,' we little thought how true his words would prove."

Berar and, on the 8th, Wellesley, with 8,903 men, commenced the siege of Ahmednagar, which fell on the 11th August. The rapid capture of this immensely strong fortress had a great moral effect, one of the Mahratta chiefs in the British camp writing to his friends in Poona that:—

"These English are a strange people, and their General is a wonderful man; they came here in the morning, looked at the *pettah* wall, walked over it, killed all the garrison, and returned to breakfast! What can withstand them?"

Immediately afterwards, Wellesley's infantry set out for Aurangabad, the crossing of the Godavari taking a week, and were joined by Wellesley at Aurangabad on the 29th August, on which day Broach was taken. Meanwhile, on the 24th August, a large body of Mahratta horse had managed to cross the Ajanta ghat, in the absence of Stevenson, whose force (7,920 strong) had gone east to the Badauli ghat, and on the 25th they occupied Jalna and were said to be moving on Haidarabad.

In order to counteract this move, Wellesley marched on the 30th August, Stevenson then being at Jafarabad, and reached Rackisbhone on the Godavari on the 3rd September. The enemy had then moved on Amba, but on Stevenson retaking Jalna on the 2nd, they moved off to Partur where, hearing that Sindhia's army had crossed the Ajanta ghat, they retired northwards, arriving near the ghats on the 14th. Wellesley had meanwhile moved on the 6th to Kurka, east of Rackisbhone, six miles north of the Godavari, and remained there till the 11th, when he marched north-west to Hadgaon, 20 miles north of the Godavari. Here, on the 18th September, he was at last joined by Major Hill with the 1st 4th Madras Native Infantry, and we must now retrace our steps and follow as far as possible the movements of the 1st 4th up to that date.

The first intimation so far discovered that the 1st 4th had left Harihar is derived from **The 1st 4th March North.** *the Duke of Wellington's Despatches,* and it is proposed to trace their movements by means of a series of extracts from the letters written by Sir Arthur Wellesley at the time. The regiment was escorting an important convoy of supplies and money and, as we shall see, Wellesley waited for them before marching to attack the Mahrattas. On the 11th August, he wrote to Major Hill to say that Major Dallas had left 1,400 loads of rice behind at the village of Moorum and ordered him to take as many as he could on his spare bullocks, if Lieutenant Griffiths, who had the same orders, had not removed all of them.

On the 17th August, he wrote to Colonel Stevenson :—

"I shall order Major Hill's battalion, which is coming with supplies from Kistna to Kurdlah, to march upon Moongy Puttun: this will give security to everything there. They will not be at Moongy Puttun for a fortnight, at soonest."

On the 18th August, he wrote to Lieutenant-Colonel Close*:—

"I have received from Hyderabad bad accounts of Major Hill: he had lost one-third of his bullocks before he had even begun to cross the Kistna."

On the 19th August, he wrote to Lieutenant-General Stuart:—

"I have heard from the Resident at Hyderabad, that Major Hill had not crossed the Kistna on the 6th and had lost one-third of his bullocks by the effects of the rain............ This rain appears to have been universal."

In a letter to General Stuart, dated the 24th August, we find that Major Hill did not expect to march from the Kistna till the 13th.

Another letter to General Stuart, dated the 28th, says:—

"Major Dallas's corps is in fine order, and I intend to keep it in the field; and I believe I shall do the like with Major Hill's..........I do not think of sending any corps to Poonah till Major Hill shall join."

On the 30th August, Wellesley wrote to Major Hill that Berar and Sindhia had entered the Nizam's territories and were said to be moving towards the Godavari; that Lieutenant Griffiths, in advance of him, had been ordered to take post at Kurdlah or some other strong village, and maintain himself there till Hill should join him; and that he should advance on "Moongy Puttun" on the Godavari, unless he found the enemy too strong for him, and there await further orders.

On the 31st, he wrote to Colonel Stevenson:—

"I cannot permanently move to the eastward at present, for several reasons: one of the most pressing is that I am obliged to look out for a battalion marching from the Kistna with bullocks, treasure, etc."

On the 4th September, he informed Colonel Close that Major Hill was near Toljapur, and that he had lost many cattle.

On the 6th, he told Major Malcolm† that Griffiths and Hill were getting on well, and would be in safety at Dharur in a few days.

On the 7th, he wrote to Colonel Stevenson:—

"If you are sufficiently strong, I am desirous to remain in this quarter, to cover the advance of Major Hill, with money and a large convoy of bullocks, and to check the operations of the enemy towards Hyderabad."

And again, on the 8th September, to General Stuart:—

"I want only to be joined by Major Hill's and Lieutenant Griffiths' Companies. These, I hope are at no great distance from the fort at Dharore, to which I have ordered them."

---

*Lieutenant-Colonel (afterward General Sir) Barry Close was British Resident at Seringapatam.

†Major (afterwards Sir John) Malcolm was Political Officer with the Nizam at Haidarabad.

On the 10th, Wellesley sent Major Hill a route to proceed to Ramusgaum Senta, and ordered him to send messages daily. He informed him that Ramusgaum was only 3 coss (*i.e.*, 6 miles) from his (Wellesley's) camp which, as already noted, was then at Kurka.

On the 13th September, he wrote to Colonel Stevenson :—

"I expect to be immediately joined by Major Hill, with money; and when that shall arrive, I do not care how far I go to the northward."

On the 14th, he ordered Lieutenant Barrett, who was in charge of the boats at Rackisbhone, to send three boats to Ramusgaum Senta for the use of Major Hill's detachment should the river become impassable for men or cattle.

On the 15th, he informed General Stuart that he had heard that the enemy were bringing their infantry up the ghaut, and he was waiting only for Major Hill to move upon them.

On the 16th September, he wrote to Major Kirkpatrick, the British Resident at Haidarabad :—

"I have received a letter from Major Hill, by which I learn that the Killadar of Dharore would not allow him to encamp in the neighbourhood of that fort, so as to derive any protection from it for his convoy."

He goes on to say that he has written to the Killadar ordering him to give British troops every assistance, and asks that it may be represented to the "Soubahdar" —meaning the Nizam. On the 16th, he repeated his orders of the 14th to Lieutenant Barrett, and on the 18th he reported to Major Malcolm that Major Hill had arrived, and had brought 2,400 bullocks, adding, in a letter to General Stuart dated the 19th, that of 2,405 bullocks 2,277 were serviceable.

This brings us up to where we left Wellesley, at Hidgaum, and from a letter to Colonel Stevenson, dated the 19th, we learn his intentions :—

"Major Hill is arrived with my money, etc., and I intend to make a movement to the northward to-morrow. I shall encamp at Golah Paugree on the Doodna. I shall continue my march to the northward on the following day; but I cannot yet say if I shall pass to the eastward or westward of Jaulna."

He continues by ordering Stevenson to move upon the enemy on the 21st, and push them towards Ajanta, whilst Wellesley marches towards the eastern passes of Badauli and Lakanwarra by Jafarabad.

On the 21st September, Wellesley had conferred with Stevenson at Badnapur, a report having been received that the Mahrattas were occupying a position between Bokardhan and Jafarabad, and it was arranged to march in that direction by two routes, reunite their forces on the 23rd, and attack the Mahrattas on the 24th. The two armies, therefore, separated, but Wellesley, having arrived at Nalni, in the neighbourhood of Assaye, on the 23rd heard from his Madrassi Scouts, on whom he depended for definite information, that the Mahrattas were about to retire, and resolved to attack them with his own force without waiting for Stevenson.

We find another letter, dated 23rd "Camp near Assye," to the O.C. 1st Bn. 4th Regiment N.I., in which the O.C. is ordered:—

"To proceed to Sailgaon, distant 10 coss in the direction of Jafferabad, with 500 Mysore Cavalry, to escort 1,000 bullocks from there at daybreak on the 24th."

It was fortunate for the regiment that the army in the meantime fell in with the enemy as, had they not been encountered till the following morning, the 1st 4th might have been absent, and thus have lost the chance of taking part in one of the greatest battles in history.

There are innumerable accounts of this decisive victory, but of all these by far the best and most complete appears to be that written by Thomas Carter in his *"Medals of the British Army and How they were Won,"* and accordingly the whole description has been abstracted *en bloc,* and will be followed by Wellesley's own opinion of the battle, as revealed in numerous letters and reports. As this account is somewhat long, the principle elsewhere adopted of printing quotations in smaller type has been departed from, as it is very tiring to the eyes to read such small print.

The Battle of Assaye 23rd September 1803.

"On the 21st September, Major-General the Hon. Arthur Wellesley had a conference with Colonel Stevenson, and a plan was concerted to attack the enemy's army with the divisions under their command on the 24th. This intention was not carried out, as circumstances occurred which determined the former to attack without waiting for the junction of the troops.

"On the 23rd September, while on the march, it was discovered that the enemy was much nearer than was imagined; whereupon Major-General Wellesley immediately determined to move in advance to reconnoitre them, and if convenient bring them to action. He ordered the cavalry to mount, and went on with them for this purpose; the infantry, except the rear battalion (1st 2nd N.I.), received directions to follow by the right. The 2nd 12th to join the left brigade to equalize the two; the 1st 2nd to cover the baggage on the ground marked for the camp, and to be joined by the rear-guard on its arrival, and the four brass light 12-pounders of the park to be sent to the heads of the line.

"These dispositions did not occasion ten minutes' halt to the column of infantry, but the cavalry, moving in front with the Major-General, came first in sight of the enemy's position, from a rising ground to the left of the road, and within cannon-shot of the right of their encampment, which lay along one of the banks of the river Kaitna,*

---

* The correct name of this stream is the Kelna. Wellesley wrote "Kailna" which was misprinted "Kaitna."

a stream of no magnitude, but with steep sides and a very deep channel, so as not to be passable except in particular places, mostly near villages. Along their rear ran a similar stream, (the Jooee nullah), which fell into the Kaitna half a mile beyond their left. Scindiah's irregular cavalry* formed their right, and the Berar troops their left. These were composed of 17 battalions, amounting to about 10,500 men, formed into three brigades, each of which had a corps of cavalry of better kind than the rest, and a body of skilled marksmen; and the artillery amounted to about 102 pieces, or perhaps a few more.

"The infantry were dressed, armed and accoutred like the Sepoys; they were remarkably fine bodies of men, and in a high state of discipline. Although the English Officers had left them, there was a number of French and other European Officers both with the infantry and artillery. The guns were served by Golandaze, exactly like those of the Bengal service, which had been some time before disbanded, and were probably the same men. It was soon, however, found that they were extremely well-trained, and that their fire was both as quick and as well directed as could be produced by the Company's artillerymen. What the total number of the enemy was cannot be ascertained, or even, guessed at with any degree of accuracy, but it is certainly calculated very low at 30,000 men, including the light troops who were out on a plundering excursion (and were those which had marched in the morning) but they returned towards the close of the action. In the field were the two Rajahs, attended by their principal ministers; and, it being the day of the Dusserah feast, the Hindoos, of which their force was chiefly composed, had religious prejudices to make them fight with spirit, and to hope for victory. The force of Major-General Wellesley's army in action was nearly 4,700 men of whom about 1,500 were Europeans, including artillery with 26 field pieces, of which only 4 twelve and 8 six-pounders were fired during the action; the remainder being the guns of the cavalry and the second line, could not be used.

"On the Major-General's approaching the enemy for the purpose of reconnoitring, they commenced a cannonade, the first gun of which was fired at 1-20 p.m. and killed one of his escort. He then resolved to attack their left, in order to turn it, and ordered the infantry column to march in that direction, while some of his staff looked out for a ford, to enable his troops to cross the Kaitna and execute this movement. All this march being performed considerably within the reach of the enemy's canonade, the fire increased fast, and by the time the head of the column reached the ford, about a short half-mile beyond their left flank, it was tremendously heavy, and had already destroyed numbers. During this movement, the first line of the enemy's infantry changed their front to the left, and formed with their left on Assye, or Assaye, a village on the Jooee, near the left of their second line, which did not change position, the right of their first line resting on the Kaitna, where the left had been. They brought up many guns from their reserve, and the second line to the first.

---

* The cavalry was estimated to number 30,000 (Vibart).

"Being obliged to cross the ford in one column by sections, the British were long exposed to the cannonade. The first line formed nearly parallel to that of the enemy, at about 500 yards distance, having marched down the alignment to its ground. The second line rather outflanked the first to the right, as did the third (composed of the cavalry) the second. The left of the first line was opposite the right of the enemy's. During this formation their artillery fired round shot with great precision and rapidity, the same shot often striking three lines. It was answered by the guns of the first line of the British with great spirit and coolness, but the number of gun bullocks killed soon put the advance of the artillery (except by men) out of the question.

The British lines were formed from right to left as follows:—

First Line. Pickets, 4 twelve-pounders, one battalion of the 8th, and one of the 10th N.I., and the 78th Regiment.

Second Line. 74th Regiment, 2nd Bn. 12th, and 1st Bn. 4th N.I.

Third Line. 4th N. Cavalry, 19th Light Dragoons, 5th and 7th N. Cavalry.

"Orders were then given for each battalion to attach a company to protect and assist the guns during the advance; this was immediately afterwards countermanded, but the order did not reach the 78th, consequently the eighth company, commanded by Lieutenant Cameron, remained attached to them. Major-General the Hon. Arthur Wellesley then named the picket as the battalion of direction, and ordered that the line should advance as quickly as possible, consistent with order, and charge with the bayonet, without firing a shot. At 2-45 the word was given for the line to advance, and was received by Europeans and Natives with a cheer. Almost immediately, however, it was discovered that the battalion of direction was not moving forward as intended, and the first line received the word to halt. This was a critical moment; the troops had reached the ridge of a little swell in the ground that had somewhat sheltered them, particularly on the left, and the enemy, supposing them staggered by the fire, redoubled their efforts, firing a number of chain shot with great effect. Dreading the consequences of this check to the ardour of the troops, the Major-General rode up to one of the Native corps of the first line, and, taking off his hat, cheered them on in their own language, repeating the words "to march." Again the soldiers received the order with loud cheers, and the three left battalions of the first line, followed by the *1st Battalion of the 4th,* advanced in quick time, and with the greatest coolness, order and determination upon their opponents. On coming within about 150 yards, the 78th withdrew its advanced centre Sergeant, and the men were cautioned to be ready to charge. Soon after the battalion opposed to them fired a volley, and about the same time some Europeans were observed to mount their horses and ride off. The 78th instantly ported arms, cheered, and redoubled its pace, when the enemy's infantry, deserted by their officers, broke and ran. The 78th pushed on and fired, the front rank to the charge, overtaking and bayonetting a few individuals. But Scindiah's gunners held firm by their guns; many were bayonetted in the act of loading, priming, or pointing, and none quitted them until the bayonet was at the breast.

"Almost at the same instant the first battalion of the 10th closed with the enemy, and in the most gallant style. The smoke and the dust (which, aided by a brisk wind in the faces of the British, was very great) prevented them from seeing any further to the right.

"The 78th now halted for an instant to complete the files and restore exact order, and then moved forward on the enemy's second line, making a complete wheel to the right, whose pivot was the right of the army, near the village of Assaye.

"In consequence of the pickets having failed to advance, the 74th pushed up, in doing which they were very much cut down by grape, and at length charged by cavalry headed by Scindiah in person. They suffered severely (as did the pickets and the 2nd Bn. 12th N.I.) and the remains were saved by the memorable charge of the cavalry, commanded by Lieutenant-Colonel Maxwell. This part of the British line, however, though it broke the enemy's first line, did not gain much ground; and the foe still continued in possession of several guns about the village of Assye, from which they flanked the British line when arrived opposite their second.

"Several of the enemy also coming up from the beds of the river and other ways, attacked and killed a large proportion of the artillerymen, amongst whom were 4 officers. They also regained possession of many of the guns of their first line, which had been taken and passed, and from them opened a fire of grape on the British rear. The guns, with the escort of the 78th Highlanders, before mentioned, escaped, and joined the regiment when halted opposite the enemy's second line.

"The British infantry was now in one line, the 78th Regiment still on the left of the whole, and as it had the longest sweep to make in the wheel, it came up last. When the dust cleared a body of the enemy's best cavalry was seen in front of the left flank, purposing to turn it, on which the left wing of the 78th Regiment was thrown back at a small angle, and preparations were made for opening the two guns, which at that moment came up.

"It is impossible to praise too highly the behaviour of the infantry at this critical moment. Deprived of the assistance of their artillery, the enemy's second line being untouched and perfectly fresh in their front, firing steadily upon them, flanked by round shot from the right, grape pouring on the rear, and cavalry threatening the left. Not a word was heard or a shot fired, all waiting the orders of the general with the composure of a field day, amidst a scene of slaughter scarcely to be equalled. This, however, was not of long duration. The British cavalry came up and drove off the body that threatened the left, who did not wait to be charged, when Major-General Wellesley ordered the principal part of the line to attack the front, while the 78th and 7th N. Cavalry moved to the rear, and charged the guns which were firing from thence. The enemy's second line immediately retired; one brigade in perfect order, so much so that it repulsed a gallant charge of the 19th Dragoons, at the head of which Colonel Maxwell was killed.

"After being obliged to change front two or three times under the fire of grape, the 78th succeeded in clearing the guns in the rear. The enemy's light troops, that had been out, now came on the ground, and were ordered to be attacked by the Mysore horse, which they did not wait for, and the firing entirely ceased. About 4-30 p.m., the enemy had set fire to all their tumbrils, which blew up in succession, many of them some time later; and the corps which had retired in good order appears soon to have lost it, for they threw their guns into the river, four of which were afterwards found, exclusive of 98 left on the field of battle.

"Thus terminated the battle of Assye, or Assaye, the first victory gained by the Iron Duke in which he commanded in chief, and one of the most decisive as well as the most desperate at this period ever fought in India. The British loss was very great; of Europeans killed and wounded, including artillery and officers, there were upwards of 600 and the natives were estimated at about 900. The 74th, 78th and 19th Light Dragoons received honorary colours..........Scindiah's first minister,* who was considered the principal instigator of the war, and his principal French officer, Colonel Dorson, were killed, with about 1,200 men, and 3,000 wounded; such, at least, was understood afterwards to be their calculation, but as their army was so much dispersed it must have been an approximation. Their troops retired about ten miles along the Jooee, unpursued by the victors, and halted there about two hours, when they moved again towards Adjanta, proceeding down that ghaut into Candeish, at which time, from the reports of the people of the place, they had no guns, nor any body of men that looked like a regular battalion.

At sunset the British collected about the village of Assye, and lay on their arms all night, except the cavalry, which, after resting some hours, were sent back to assist in escorting the baggage; and about 10 a.m., on the 24th, the troops were encamped on the left bank of the Kaitna, on the ground the column had moved over previous to crossing the ford into the field of battle. That evening at sunset the cavalry and one battalion of N. I. of Colonel Stevenson's division arrived, and the next morning (25th) the remainder of his force, which a day or two afterwards were ordered to follow the enemy into Candeish, and to possess themselves of the city of Berhampore and the hill fort of Asseerghur."

An officer, who was present when the British army advanced to cross the stream, wrote as follows:—

"I was particularly struck at this time with the beauty of the line formed by our cavalry, and with the steady movement of the column of infantry, so unlike the usual order of march......Not a whisper was heard through the ranks; our nerves were wound up to the proper pitch, and everyone seemed to know and feel that here was no alternative but death or victory."

Another account gives the following further particulars:—

"The General, after the line had been formed for attack, placed himself at the head of his troops, waving his hat and encouraging the native battalions in their own language. Beside him rode Mountstuart Elphinstone and Gokhale, a brave Mahratta chieftain

---

* Jadun Singh.

who was killed fourteen years later in the combat of Ashti, fighting against us, and Wellesley's orderly dragoon had his head taken off by a cannon-ball, the body was kept in its seat by the valise and holsters, and it was some time before the terrified charger could rid itself of its ghastly burden.

The troops of the Madras Army fought well. After the battle a staff officer saw a number of Mahomedans of the 8th Regiment assembled for a funeral. He asked them whom they were about to inter. They mentioned the names of five commissioned and non-commissioned officers of a very distinguished family of the corps. 'We are going to put these brothers into one grave,' said one of the party. The officer, who had been well acquainted with the individuals who had been slain, expressed his regret and was about to offer some consolation to the survivors, but he was stopped by one of the men, 'There is no occasion,' he said, 'for such feelings or expressions; these men were soldiers; the Government they served will protect their children, who will soon fill the ranks they lately occupied'. Such was the fine feeling in the old Company's Army."

On the morning after the battle, the following General Order was issued:—

"Major-General Wellesley returns his thanks to the troops for their conduct in the action of yesterday, the result of which is so honourable to them, and likely to be so advantageous to the public interest.

The actual casualties of the British in the battle were, 23 officers killed and 30 wounded; 198 Europeans killed and 442 wounded; 428 Sepoys killed, 1,138 wounded, and 18 missing—a grand total of 2,277.

Among the killed was Captain Mackay, 4th Madras Cavalry, Commissary of Cattle in the Army. He had been positively refused permission by the General to lead his squadron into action, but instead of remaining with the baggage, he risked his commission and lost his life.

Amongst the troops which fought on the side of Sindhia were those of that interesting person the Begum Sumroo or Sombre, who was so called from her first husband, Walter Reinhard, otherwise known as Sombre, the perpetrator of the massacre of Europeans at Patna in 1763. She was a Musalman of remarkable beauty and force of character, and later joined the Roman Catholic Church. She organised a force under European military adventurers, and on Sombre's death, in 1778, she married another Frenchman, called Le Vassoult, who committed suicide in 1795. After his death her troops were placed under the command of Colonel Saleur, who commanded them at Assaye. The Begum submitted to General Lake in 1803, and died in 1836*. The pick

---

* Among other deeds recorded of this amiable lady, she had two slave girls, who set fire to her houses at Agra, buried alive in a pit dug in front of her tent.

The Marquis of Hastings, who met her in 1814, writes of her:—

"The Begum dined with us. As she is a Christian, none of our dishes came amiss to her; and good Madeira wine is peculiarly acceptable to her palate. She has the remains of a fine face, with a fairer complexion than is frequent among the natives, and peculiarly intelligent eyes. Her head, I think, must always have been out of proportion to her body, for it is large, and she is short beyond what one can ascribe to sinking from age."

of Sindhia's infantry at Assaye were commanded by Colonel Pohlman* another adventurer.

In this battle the 1st 4th, 755 strong, was as we have seen, on the left of the second line, but moved forward to the attack with the first line. It suffered considerable losses, the casualties being Lieutenant Maver, one subadar, one havildar, and 24 rank and file killed; and one sergeant, one subadar, six havildars and 82 rank and file wounded; besides one man missing. The following, so far can be discovered, is a list of the British Officers present with the regiment at this time:—

The 1st 4th at Assaye.

Major Joseph G. Hill, Commanding; Lieutenant G. A. Muat, Adjutant; Captains James Nagle, James Wilson and James Ceville; Lieutenants William Clapham, George Birch, W.M.D. Robertson, L.S. Smith, George Moore, John Dalziel and Robert Maver; Assistant-Surgeon Foljambe. As regards the Commanding Officer of the regiment during the battle, a curious point arises. It will be noticed that up to the day of the battle and also afterwards, Major Hill is shown by Major-General Wellesley's letters to have been in command. However, in a notice of the career of Lieutenant-Colonel James Nagle given in *Philippart's East India Military Calendar,* it is stated that he commanded the 4th in the battle of Assaye, and that for his services in this battle he was granted an addition to his arms, with the motto *"On with you."* In the absence of contemporary records, it is impossible to say definitely which officer was in command, but in view of what is said above, it appears probable that on the 23rd September, from sickness or some other cause, Major Hill was deprived of the honour of leading his regiment into action.

For its participation in the battle of Assaye the regiment bears—not the least amongst its honours—the Elephant and *"Assaye,"* and the 23rd September is celebrated annually as the regimental day *par excellence.*

In his report, dated the 24th September, to his brother the Governor-General, the Marquis Wellesley (afterwards Lord Mornington), Wellesley says:—

Wellesley on the Battle of Assaye.

"I cannot write in too strong terms of the conduct of the troops; they advanced in the best order and with the greatest steadiness, under a most destructive fire, against a body of infantry far superior in number, who appeared determined to contend with them to the last, and who were driven from their guns only by the bayonet; and, notwithstanding the numbers of the enemy's cavalry, and the demonstrations they made of an intention to charge, they were kept at a distance by our infantry."

Writing to General Stuart on the 24th, he says:—

"The fire from their cannon was the hottest that has been known in this country.

---

* "Colonel Pohlman was a German, who was in chief command of all Sindhia's regular troops. From his declining to act against the British at the battle of Assaye, he was taken into the Company's pay, with the regiments that accompanied him. The Colonel was an exceedingly cheerful and entertaining character. He lived in the style of an Indian Prince; had his Seraglio, and always travelled on an elephant, attended by his whole bodyguard of Moguls, all dressed alike in purple robes, and who marched in file, in the same order as the British Cavalry."

On the 26th, he wrote to Major Malcolm :—

"We have got more than 90 guns, 70 of which are the finest brass ordnance I have ever seen..... The bay horse was shot under me, and Diomed was piked...........Will you let me have the grey Arab?"

Writing again to the same on the 28th, he says :—

"The Bheels in the ghaut have cut up vast numbers of them. Colonel Stevenson is gone after them...................Their infantry is the best I have ever seen in India, excepting our own; and they and their equipments far surpass Tippoo's. I assure you that their fire was so heavy, that I much doubted at one time whether I should be able to prevail upon our troops to advance; and all agree that the battle was the fiercest that has ever been seen in India. Our troops behaved admirably; the Sepoys astonished me."

On the 29th, he wrote to General Stuart :—

"We have got 76 brass guns, and have burst 26 iron, making in all 102...............I really believe it was one of the most furious battles that has ever been fought in this country............We have taken seven stands of colours........................I shall have to send 700 men to the hospital, which I must establish at Adjuntee, upon the extreme frontier."

In a letter to Colonel Stevenson, dated the 12th October, he said :—

"I acknowledge that I should not like to see again such a loss as I sustained on the 23rd September, even if attended by such a gain."

Regarding Colonel Orrock, who, by leading the picquets and the 74th Regiment in the wrong direction, caused them such heavy losses, he wrote :—

"I do not wish to cast any reflection upon the officer who led the picquets. I lament the consequences of his mistake, but I must acknowledge that it was not possible for a man to lead a body into a hotter fire than he did the picquets on that day against Assaye."

On the 30th October, a General Order by the Governor-General was published at Fort William, of which the following is an extract :—

The Governor-General's Order.

"The Governor-General in Council has this day received from Major-General the Hon. A. Wellesley official report of the signal and splendid victory obtained by the troops under the personal command of that distinguished officer, on the 23rd September, at Assye in the Deccan, over the combined armies of Dowlat Row Scindiah and the Rajah of Berar. At the close of a campaign of the most brilliant success and glory in every quarter of India, this transcendent victory demands a testimony of public honour, equal to any which the justice of the British Government in India has ever conferred on the conduct of our officers and troops in the most distinguished period of our military history............

The Governor-General in Council signifies his warmest applause of the exemplary order and steadiness with which the troops advanced, under a most destructive fire, against a body of the enemy's infantry considerably superior in number, and determined to oppose a vigorous resistance to our attack. The numerous infantry of the enemy were driven from their powerful artillery at the point of the bayonet, with an alacrity and resolution truly worthy of British Soldiers; and the firmness and discipline manifested by our brave infantry, in repelling the great body of the enemy's cavalry, merit the highest commendation.....................

H. E. in Council directs Major-General the Hon. A. Wellesley to signify to all the officers and troops employed on this glorious occasion, and especially to Lieutenant-Colonel Harness and to Lieutenant-Colonel Wallace, who commanded brigades, and to the officers of the staff, the high sense entertained by the Governor-General in Council of their eminent and honourable Services...................

In testimony of the high honor acquired by the army under the personal command of Major-General the Hon. A. Wellesley, at the battle of Assye, the Governor-General in Council is pleased to order, that honorary colours, with a device properly suited to commemorate that signal and splendid victory be presented to the corps of cavalry and infantry employed on that glorious occasion......................."

When these records of the regiment were first issued, I wrote about these honorary colours as follows :—

"As regards the last paragraph extracted from this order, the honorary colours were only presented to the troops of the Royal Army engaged in the battle. No record has been discovered to show why a similar honour was not extended to the Company's troops, and we can only presume that the Directors of the Company did not feel themselves called upon, in a period of trouble and financial anxiety, to go to the necessary expense."

Since then, evidence has been forthcoming to show that these colours were actually issued to the Company's regiments, and as a result of further enquiries made in an endeavour to trace the circumstances under which the 1st 4th colour was lost, authority has now been given for its replacement.

Movements after Assaye. After the battle of Assaye, Wellesley appears to have remained in camp till the 5th October 1803, when he marched north and arrived at Ajanta on the 8th. Here, however, he heard that Sindhia and Berar had moved southwards, and accordingly he fell back on Pulmari, one march from Aurangabad, remaining there from the 11th till the 15th October. On the 16th, Stevenson occupied Barhanpur, and on the same date the enemy were said to have marched north again, on hearing of Wellesley's move to the south. Wellesley accordingly followed them and reached Ajanta once more on the 18th, remaining in that neighbourhood until the 25th October. Meanwhile Stevenson, who had opened the siege of the fortress of Asirgarh on the 17th October, took the petta on the 18th, and the fort itself on the 21st.

A second raid to the south by the Mahrattas again compelled Wellesley to move from Ajanta on Aurangabad, where he arrived on the 29th October. On the 2nd November, he started in pursuit of the enemy and crossed the Payan Ganga river on the 19th. On the 23rd, an armistice was concluded with Sindhia alone, on condition that the latter kept his army in Berar, 40 miles to east of Ellichpur but Sindhia failed to observe this condition and once more joined forces with the Bhonsla. On the 28th November, Wellesley effected a junction with Stevenson at Patholi, and on the following day they came in sight of the combined armies of Sindhia and Berar.

The Battle of Argaum, 29th November 1803.

From a tower in Patholi, Wellesley perceived a confused mass which he concluded to be the Mahratta armies on the march, but as his troops had had a hot and trying march, he decided not to pursue the enemy at once. When, however, he went forward to put out piquets and select the ground for an encampment, he found a long line of cavalry, infantry and artillery drawn up in regular order on the plains of Argaum, immediately in front of the village of that name, about 6 miles from his proposed camping-ground at Patholi. Although it was late in the day, he at once determined to attack.

The enemy's infantry and guns were in the left of their centre, with a body of cavalry on their left. Sindhia's army, consisting of one very heavy body of cavalry, was on the right, having on its right a body of Pindaris and other light troops. Their line was more than five miles in length, with the village of Argaum in rear, and in front a plain, which was, however, intersected by many nullahs.

Wellesley formed up his army in two lines, the infantry in the first, the cavalry in the second and supporting the right. The Haidarabad and Mysore Cavalry supported the left. The line was almost parallel to that of the enemy, with the right rather advanced in order to press upon the enemy's left. Some little time elapsed before the lines could be formed, owing to a part of the infantry which led the column having got into some confusion when the enemy opened their cannonade.

When formed, the whole line advanced at about 4-30 p.m., in the greatest order. A fierce attack was made upon the 74th and 78th Regiments by a large body of the enemy, supposed to be Persians* who were destroyed to a man, and Sindhia's cavalry charged the 1st 6th M.N.I., which was on the left of the line, but were repulsed with a loss of 600 killed and wounded. Elsewhere, the whole of the enemy retired in the utmost disorder before the steady advance of the British line, leaving behind them 38 pieces of cannon and all their ammunition. Twenty or thirty standards were also captured.

The British cavalry then took up the pursuit and followed the disorganized enemy for several miles, destroying great numbers of them, and capturing several elephants and camels, with a considerable quantity of baggage. Had there been one hour more of daylight, not a man would have escaped.

The total casualties in this important victory amounted to 3 Captains and 6 Subalterns wounded; 15 Europeans killed and 151 wounded; 31 sepoys killed, 148 wounded and 5 missing. The casualties of the 1st 4th were one European wounded and one missing; three Native officers killed, and 29 sepoys wounded. It was impossible to discover what the losses of the enemy were, but they must have been very great. The cavalry alone are estimated to have accounted for 3,000 in the pursuit.

---

* They were really Arabs.

Colonel Stevenson was so weak from illness that during the battle he directed his division from the back of an elephant. As Wellesley says that the troops conducted themselves with their usual bravery, we may assume that the 1st 4th played as gallant a part in this engagement as at Assaye.

On the 30th November, Wellesley published the following General Order:—

"Major-General Wellesley congratulates the troops upon the success of yesterday, which he has every reason to hope was effected without very great loss. The Major-General's thanks are due, upon this occasion, to all the troops for the perseverance with which they went through the fatigues of the day, and for the steadiness they displayed during the action............

The Paymaster of each division will pay 200 rupees to each Corps of cavalry and infantry in their respective divisions as a zeafet."

From Wellesley's correspondence, we discover that the confusion to which reference has been made was due to one of those sudden and often unaccountable accesses of panic to which, on occasion, even the best of troops are subject. Writing on the 2nd December, he says:—

"What do you think of nearly three entire battalions, who behaved so admirably in the battle of Assye, being broken and running off, when the cannonade commenced at Argaum, which was not to be compared to that at Assye?............The troops were under arms, and I was on horseback, from 6 in the morning till 12 at night."

Again, in a letter to General Stuart, dated the 3rd December, he says:—

"You will have been surprised to have seen that part of our Native Infantry got into confusion. The fact was that the 1st 10th, and 2nd 12th, and the Native part of the picquets, broke and ran off, as soon as the cannonade commenced, although it was from a great distance and not to be compared with that of Assye...............However, those of them whom I was able to collect and form again behaved steadily afterwards."

After the battle of Argaum, Wellesley and Stevenson marched to Ellichpur, where they arrived on the 5th December 1803. Here a halt was made on the 6th, in order to establish a hospital, and the march was resumed on the following day, the two divisions moving by different routes.

On the 9th December, they arrived before the strong fort of Gawilgarh, which crowned **Siege of Gawilgarh.** one of the highest peaks of the Satpura Range, and which Wellesley intended to reduce. Batteries were opened on the 12th December, and on the 13th they opened fire on the walls. By the night of the 14th, the breaches were found to be practicable and, on the 15th, the fort was stormed with the greatest gallantry by Colonel Stevenson's division.

The 1st 4th consequently took no part in the actual assault, though we find from the detail of working parties that the regiment anticipated the duties of its future career as a Pioneer regiment by doing much laborious work in connection with the siege. The difficulties of this work may be illustrated by an extract from Colonel Welsh:—

"We had been one night working very hard at a battery half-way up the hill, and afterwards cleared a road up to it, but no power we possessed could move our iron battering guns above a few hundred yards from the bottom, so steep and rugged was the ascent.

" I was just relieved from working by a fresh party, and enjoying a few moment's rest on some clean straw, when the officer commanding the working party came up to Colonel Wallace, and reported that it was impossible to get the heavy guns up to the battery. The Colonel who was Brigadier of the Trenches, exclaimed :—'*Impossible! hoot mon! it must be done; I've got the order in my pocket!*' With such a spirit animating the force it is not surprising that even obstacles which appeared insuperable were overcome."

The following is an extract from an order by General Wellesley, dated Deogaon, Thursday, 15th December 1903 :—

"Major-General Wellesley has great pleasure in congratulating the troops under his command upon the brilliant success of this day. In the course of this short but laborious siege, Major-General Wellesley has with pleasure observed in all a most anxious and zealous desire to forward the service, the most steady perseverance in the performance of laborious services which would be thought impracticable by other troops, and that gallantry which they have shown so frequently during the campaign, and which has carried them with honour through so many difficulties."

The success of this siege practically brought the campaign to a close. Peace was concluded with the Raja of Berar at Deogaon on the 17th December 1803, and on the 23rd the treaty was ratified. On that day the army was inspected by Amrut Rao, brother of the Peshwa, who was so pleased with the appearance of the troops that we are told he presented a "*ziafat*" of 300 rupees to each corps. On the 30th December, a similar treaty was concluded with Daulat Rao Sindhia at Anjangaon.

Note.—At the time of this campaign, the troops were armed with the musket, which was decisive at 80 yards, and effective at 160 yards. Well-trained troops could fire 2 to 3 rounds per minute. Artillery fire was decisive at 400 yards and effective at 700 to 800 yards. During the campaign the Native troops were only allowed one tent per company.

1804.

Munkaisir, 5th February 1804. The campaign against the Mahratta chiefs having terminated successfully, Wellesley determined to cross the Godavari and disperse the numerous gangs of freebooters, composed of the disbanded fragments of the Mahratta armies, who were ravaging the country principally on the borders of the Nizam's dominions. On the 2nd February 1804, Wellesley, then at Nimgaum, about 30 miles south-east of Ahmednagar, issued orders for a force composed of all the cavalry, the 74th Regiment, the 1st 8th M.N.I., and 100 men from each of the other battalions of Native Infantry (formed into a corps under the command of Captain Nagle of the 1st 4th M.N.I.), to march under his personal command against a party of these bandits, who consisted mainly of the former Arab garrison of Ahmednagar, and were said to be in the neighbourhood of Munkaisir, near Barsi.

The march was begun on the morning of the 4th February, and the force arrived at Sailgaon, near Purandar, after a march of 20 miles, only to learn that the enemy had broken up their camp at Vayarag and were 24 miles distant. Wellesley, however, marched again at night, with a view to attacking them at daylight on the 5th, but unfortunately the road was very bad and he did not reach Munkaisir till 9 a.m. Meanwhile, his allies (as Wellesley says, "like true Mahrattas,") had given the enemy warning, and when he arrived they had already begun to move off. However, a brisk pursuit was maintained and the result of the day's work was the complete defeat of a numerous and formidable body, who were the terror of the country, were daily increasing in numbers, and had already defeated a body of the Nizam's troops. The loss on the British side was trifling, amounting only to 1 cavalryman killed and 3 wounded.

On the 6th February, the following General Order, was issued:—

"Major-General Wellesley thanks the troops for the persevering activity with which they underwent the fatigues of the march on the 4th and 5th instant............The advance of the infantry under Major Swinton was very proper, and in the best order."

In later years Wellesley, when Duke of Wellington, frequently referred to this march as the greatest he ever made, and in his letters from Munkaisir he does full justice to the extraordinary effort made by the infantry who, as he informed General Stuart on the 5th, were up with the cavalry when he advanced to the attack. He remarks in one letter that he had made some "dreadful marches to the southward after the freebooters" and, writing to Colonel Murray on the 7th February, he says:—

"I marched on the morning of the 4th, 20 miles; at night 24 miles, and arrived here (Munkaisir) at 9 o'clock on the morning of the 5th. The whole was over by 12 o'clock on the 5th. I think that by that time the troops had marched 60 miles, from 6 in the morning of the 4th, in which time they halted 10 hours, from 12 at noon to 10 at night of the 4th.............I think we now begin to beat the Mahrattas in the celerity of our movements."

In a letter to Major Malcolm on the same date, he says,—

"The exertion made by the troops is the greatest I ever witnessed."

On the 27th February, Wellesley returned to Poona. The proposal to present him with a gold vase (subsequently changed to a service of plate), value 2,000 guineas, on the 4th March, was signed, amongst others, by Lieutenant-Colonel J. Hill, and the officers, 1st Bn. 4th Regiment M.N.I. Wellesley was also presented with a sword valued at 1,000 guineas at Calcutta.

While I have been unable to trace the complete record of the regiment in 1804, the following extract from a biographical notice of Major Charles Armstrong, by Philippart, seems to show that they were employed on yet another expedition, though the exact date is not given:—

"In 1804, he marched in command of his regiment (1st 16th M. N. I.), which with the flank companies of one of the King's regiments and the 4th N. I., under the command of Colonel Moneypenny of H. M. Service, proceeded against the Chittoor, Vincataghery and Bumrauze Poligars, who had risen in arms against the civil authorities. This force was afterwards joined by the 5th and 19th regiments N. I., and 4th regiment Native cavalry. The service which lasted but a few months only, was exceedingly fatiguing."

If the above refers to the 1st 4th, the probabilities are that it took place towards the end of the year, after the regiment's return to the south.

As early as January 1804, Wellesley had remarked on the hardships suffered by the officers during the campaign of 1803, observing in one letter:—

"I am convinced there is not one officer with the Army, who has not been obliged to live at an expense far exceeding his pay, since the troops crossed the Kistna............ I am desirous that the officers should be relieved at an early period from the distress which I know they suffer at present."

Some compensation was afforded them on the 12th April, by an order of the Governor-General's granting 6 months' full batta to all officers who had served in the campaign.

The 1st 4th appear to have been in Poona in April, and in June the troops were inspected by General Wellesley, who issued the following order, dated the 9th:—

"Major-General Wellesley takes this opportunity of expressing his satisfaction upon finding the Corps of Native Infantry in such good order, upon the inspection which he has made of them, and he will not fail to report their state to H. E. the Commander-in-Chief."

In June 1804, the 1st 4th were presented with new colours at Poona, and on the 18th of that month Wellesley decided to send them back to the Carnatic.

The 1st 4th return to the Carnatic. Accordingly, on the 24th June, Lieutenant-Colonel Hill of the 1st 4th was directed to march with the 19th Dragoons, 4th Native Cavalry, six 6-pounders, the 1st 10th M.N.I., the Pioneers less 5 companies, and his own regiment Wellesley giving him, among others, the following instructions:—

"As soon as the troops, departments, etc., shall be prepared to move, you will march to the southward, by a route which is enclosed...... In passing Meritch or any other fortress, you will avoid approaching it so closely, or encamping so near it as to occasion any alarm...... You will march upon the Tappal Road......... There are boats upon all the rivers to transport the troops."

The 1st 4th marched by Erur on the Kistna, Gurgiri on the Gatprabha, Sangili on the Malprabha, Deogiri on the Warda, and Harihar, and were expected to arrive at the Kistna on the 12th or 13th July.

In a letter to Colonel Hill, dated the 30th June, the Deputy Adjutant-General says that he has received the Colonel's letters, and that the General does not approve of his application for Brigadier's allowances, or for a Brigade-Major and Brigade Quartermaster, and will not allow any of them. Further, that he is surprised at his asking for them.

On the 2nd July, he instructs Colonel Hill to look out carefully for tappall peons, and to pay for everything en route, and in another letter of the same date he mentions that Colonel Hill has reported on the miserably weak state of his cattle.

On the 6th July, he instructed Colonel Hill:—

"To send one battalion across the Kistna first, to proceed by itself across the Gutpurba, and Malpoorba, and halt near Sungoly. Then one regiment of cavalry, then the other regiment, then artillery unattached to corps, then last battalion of infantry, until all are re-assembled near Sungoly."

The last mention to be found of the 1st 4th on their southward march is dated the 18th July 1804, in which Colonel Hill is informed that the Killadar of Misserycotta has refused to deliver up his fort to the Peshwa's government. Hill is sent a letter calling on the Killadar to deliver up the fort, and is ordered to give him half an hour to do it. If it were not given up, he was to attack at once, and if it were evacuated he was to let the Killadar go and hand over the fort to the Peshwa's representative. Misserycotta was a mud fort of some extent but no strength, 12 miles south of Hubli, and had a garrison of 200 peons. Hill was recommended to attack in several places, particularly the gateway; to surround the fort with cavalry; and fire with cannon on it from all sides. No trace can be found of the result of these recommendations, nor whether the fort was attacked, or surrendered, and the next reference we have to the 1st 4th finds them established in Seringapatam.

The men of the regiment were probably luckier than those of the 4th Cavalry who, on their arrival at Arcot in December 1804, saw their families for the first time since they marched to Seringapatam with the Grand Army in 1799.

On the 26th June 1804, Major-General Wellesley had resigned the military and political powers vested in him by the Governor-General, and before proceeding to Fort William, *viâ* Seringapatam, he issued an order to the Army, dated the 24th June, of which the following is an extract:—

Complimentary Order.

" Upon the occasion of quitting the army in consequence of the orders of the Governor-General, Major-General Wellesley once more returns his thanks to the officers and troops for their uniform good conduct since he has had the honor of commanding them. In the space of little more than a year those in this quarter in particular..........and those which are under orders to march to the Southward, have been tried in every mode in which it is possible to try troops, and have uniformly manifested that patience under fatigues, and severity of climate, that activity and perseverance in labor, and bravery and discipline in action, which are the characteristic qualities of the best soldiers; their success, and the honor which the troops have acquired are proportionate to the good qualities which they have displayed."

Wellesley eventually became Prince of Waterloo, Duke of Wellington, Duque da Vittoria, Marquez de Torres Vedras, Marquis of Douro, Earl of Wellington, Earl of Mornington, Conde de Vimeiro, Viscount Wellesley, Viscount Talavera, Baron Mornington, K.G., K.T., K.P., G.C.B., and Knight of the highest grades of foreign orders too numerous to mention.

On the 10th November 1804, the troops received the thanks of the House of Commons, and those of the Court of Directors and General Court of Proprietors of the East India Company.

On the 17th October 1804, Major-General Sir J. F. Cradock (afterwards Lord Howden), became Commander-in-Chief in Madras.

1805.
The Rising in the Wynad.

A short account will be given of events in Malabar prior to the employment of the 1st 4th Regiment in that province in 1805.

In May 1790, the Madras Government had come to an agreement with several of the Malabar Rajas to consider them as allies of the Honourable Company, if they would give assistance against Tippu Sultan. The terms of the agreement were somewhat vague, and this led to trouble in 1792, when it was desired to make a settlement after the Mysore War.

The chief cause of the trouble was Kerala Varma Raja, the Raja of Kottayam in North Malabar, commonly called the Palassi or Pychy Raja, who was greatly venerated by the people, particularly by the Nayars of the Wynad. An agreement was made with him in 1794, but this was broken by him in the following year, and an attempt to capture him, made in April 1796, was unsuccessful. He was, however, pardoned later in the year.

In 1797, he was found to be negotiating with Tippu Sultan and in January of that year a party of his followers attacked a British detachment, killing Captain Bowman and many men. The Bombay Government at once undertook operations against him, but after some desultory fighting he was once more pardoned and granted an annual allowance of Rs. 8,000.

In September 1798, it was decided that the Wynad belonged to Tippu Sultan, but it was ceded to the Company after the fall of Seringapatam in 1799 and, from the 1st July 1800, the whole of Malabar was transferred from the Bombay to the Madras Government.

In 1801, Colonel Arthur Wellesley marched through the country, and the Pychy Raja was driven into the jungles of the Wynad, but during the two following years there was a general rising throughout the whole province, which was largely due to the mismanagement of Major Macleod, the Principal Collector. This rising commenced with the massacre of the garrison at Panamarattakota in the Wynad.

By 1803, the number of troops in Malabar had risen to over 8,000, and a further reinforcement was sent in 1804, which occupied Wynad. In September 1804, a party of the irregular police known as *Kolkars* just missed capturing the Pychy Raja, for whom a reward of 3,000 pagodas (about £1,200) had been offered in June. An indication of the nature of the climate of the Wynad in the rains is given by the fact that of 1,300 of these Kolkars who were in the Wynad in September, only 170 were fit for duty by the 17th October.

In January 1805, the 1st 4th Regiment was stationed at Seringapatam with a detachment of 74 men in garrison in Mysore. No information has been discovered as to when they proceeded to Malabar, but in November 1805 we find at least a part, and probably the whole, of the regiment in Panamarattakota, under the command of Lieutenant-Colonel Hill. It may be presumed that they marched to the Wynad through Nanjangud, as there is a road leading from Mysore through the Wynad down to the West Coast.

Some time during this year—but whether before or after the operations against the Pychy Raja is not yet accurately determined—an expedition was sent out under the command of Colonel Hill to capture one of the proscribed rebels, Karveryallay Kannan, for whom a reward of 300 pagodas had been offered on the 16th June 1804. Having heard that the rebel was only one coss distant from his camp Colonel Hill divided his force into three parts, one under himself, one under Lieutenant Blakiston (Madras Pioneers)* and the third under Lieutenant Walker (1st 4th).

The rebel was taken by surprise, but managed to escape in the darkness: his wife and four children were, however, secured. The only casualties were 5 men of the 1st 4th, and 4 of the Police Corps, wounded by arrows.

Pursuit and Death of the Pychy Raja. On the 1st November 1805, Mr. Baber, the Sub-Collector, was put in charge of the Wynad, and proceeded to Panamarattakota, where he asked for a lightly-equipped detachment of 200 men from Colonel Hill, in order to pursue the Pychy Raja and his rebel following.

This detachment, with Colonel Hill and three other officers, and 200 Kolkars, accompanied Mr. Baber to Pulpalli, but the whole country was found to have been deserted by the inhabitants. Eventually, however, the people were induced to come in, though throughout the time spent by the detachment at Pulpalli there were skirmishes with parties of the rebels, many of whom were shot, and others taken prisoner. Mr. Baber then set to work to try and induce the people of Pulpalli to give information which would lead to the apprehension of the Pychy Raja, and at last on the 30th November three men brought in information that the Pychy Raja and nearly all the other rebel leaders were on the opposite side of the Kangura river, a short distance into Mysore.

Mr. Baber at once marched with a detachment consisting of Captain Clapham with 50 men of the 1st 4th, and 100 Kolkars, and at length reached the Kangura river. After proceeding about a mile and a half into Mysore territory, the rebels were discovered, and the 15 hour march was brought to an end by a sharp fight, by which the rebels were dispersed, leaving many dead on the ground.

To continue the narrative in Mr. Baber's own words:—

'It was only on my return from the pursuit that I learnt that the Rajah was amongst the *first* who had fallen. It fell to the lot of one of my cutcherry servants, Canara Menon, to

---

*Now the Queen Victoria's Own Madras Sappers and Miners.

arrest the flight of the Rajah, which he did at the hazard of his life (the Rajah having put his musket to his breast) and it is worthy of mention that this extraordinary personage, though in the moment of death, called out in the most dignified and commanding manner to the Menon, 'not to approach and defile his person'................

There was no other property discovered, but a gold Cuttarum or knife and a waist-chain—the former I have now in my possession, the latter I presented to Captain Clapham........

Thus terminated the career of a man who has been enabled to persevere in hostilities against the Company for nearly nine years, during which many thousand valuable lives have been sacrificed and sums of money beyond all calculation expended."

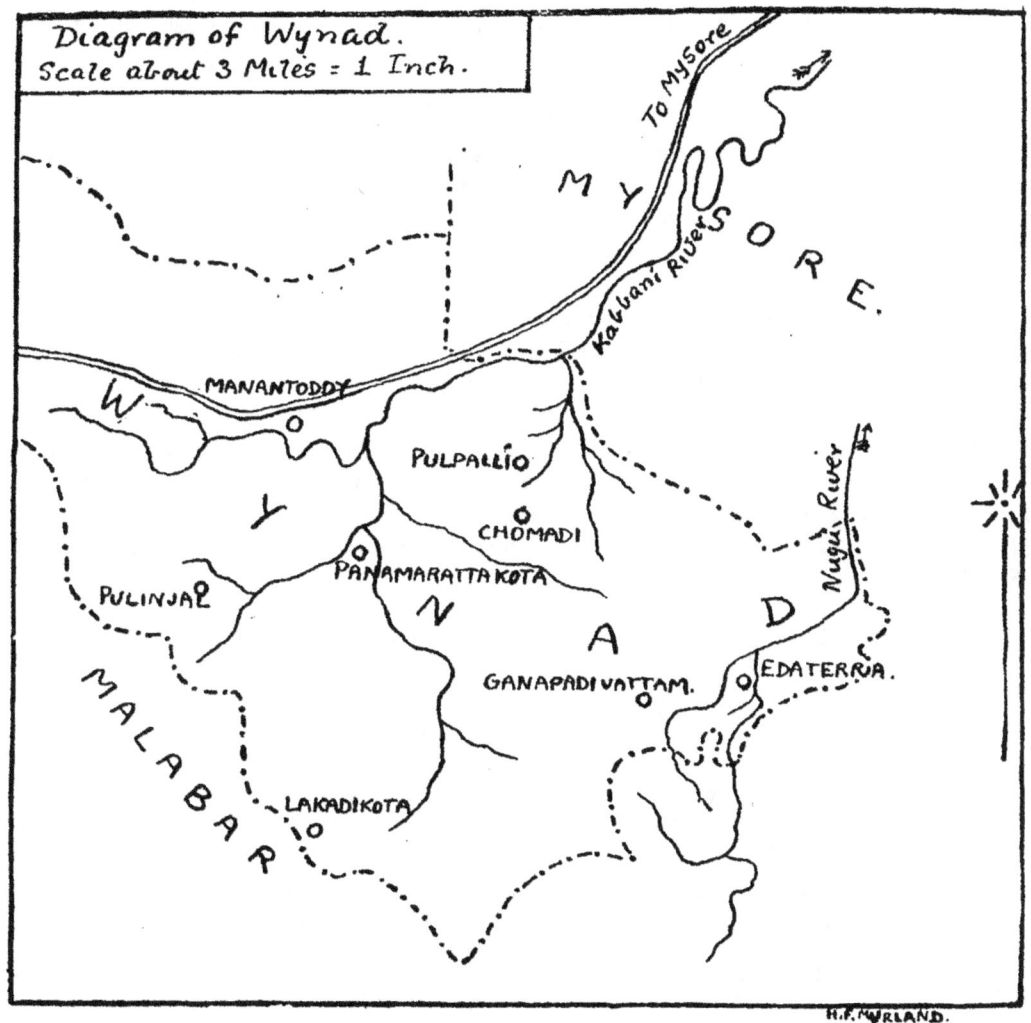

Although more than a century has passed, it is noteworthy that the memory of Kerala Varma Raja is still cherished by the people of the Wynad as the *Saktan Raja*. (*Saktan* meaning powerful, or great).

Mr. Baber received the thanks of Government for his services, and a donation of 2,500 pagodas (£1,000).

Throughout the whole of this service in the densely-wooded and mountainous Wynad, the troops suffered greatly from want of proper shelter, provisions and medical aid.

Lord William Bentinck was Governor of Madras at this time, and the Marquess Cornwallis came out to India once more, for a second tour as Governor-General, but died, and was succeeded by Sir George Barlow, who held the appointment till 1807.

1806—1807.

In January 1806, the 1st 4th was still at Panamarattakota in the Wynad, with detachments at Edaterra, Lakadikota, Pulinjal, Chomadi and Benotta, but, by January 1807, it had moved to Palamcotta, where it remained until the outbreak of the Travancore War.

On the 10th July 1806, there was a serious outbreak of mutiny by the 2nd 23rd M.N.I. and part of the 1st M.N.I., at Vellore, where the family of Tippu Sultan had been interned. The outbreak was supposed to have been caused by the introduction of a new pattern of turban, which was ordered, on the 14th November 1805, by Lieutenant-General Sir J. F. Cradock, the Commander-in-Chief, but, beyond all doubt, the rising was instigated by the Mysore Princes and their followers, as is made clear in the following extracts from letters* written by Colonel A. Cuppage, Commanding at Nundydroog, to Colonel Barry Close, then Resident at Poona. The first letter is dated the 30th July 1806:—

"One thing is established, that the 1st were equally in the secret with the 23rd, and all at the instance of the Princes. That the principal leader, a Native Officer, who was saved, I hear, and now in irons, was to have had three lakhs of rupees as his portion, and every Private twenty rupees a month for life, if they had succeeded; by the accompanying page of evidence you will perceive a Havildar was to have had eight pagodas. He is one of three Havildars and thirty-five Privates taken up at Trichinopoly, with whom were found McKeras' silver bowl, tea-pot and several other articles of value, they were besides well supplied with cash. Notwithstanding the evidence of the man, it is pretty clear, the murder of the Europeans was a primary object. The first thing they did was to bring two six-pounders, one to bear with round on the European barracks (the men who got to the cavalier were fortunately sleeping outside) and the other on the Main Guard with grape, whilst the Europeans were asleep; these guns were entirely served by the men of the 1st then on duty, the men of the 23rd being young hands and griffins. Poor Armstrong, it would appear, was sleeping in his pallinqueen near the gate without the fort, where he was first badly wounded by a fire from the works, and Moormen came afterwards and put him to death.

---

* Copies of these letters, which were in the possession of the late Mr. C. W. E. Cotton, I. C. S., were kindly sent to me by Mr. F. J. Richards, I. C. S.

Much stress is laid by some on the new Turband (what there is in it, to object to, I cannot tell you, never having seen it, but the orders for it are rescinded) as exciting the men to the step they took, but these two particular Corps had never been required to wear it, as I understand, and here, where it had never been seen, I discovered some days since, that the Moormen of these four companies (for the other castes did not take a part in their cabals) allowed themselves such freedom of speech as evinced to me that this description were ready to take a part in a similar performance to that exhibited at Vellore, if an object or opportunity presented itself for imitation, and the other paper I enclose you shows that it is not altogether confined to the Mysore men of which these Companies are mostly composed; however, secured as the Princes are, and probably to be removed to a distance from their adherents altogether, not much, I conceive, is to be apprehended............"

The second letter is dated the 4th August 1806:—

"I have just had the following from Vellore of the 2nd:—It appears by the confession of a Subedar and a Jemadar under sentence, the two I before mentioned to you, that the conspiracy was to have been extensive—letters were written and ready to be despatched to all the Polligars in the vicinity who formerly were in a state of rebellion and to all the Moors, friends to the house of Hyder in Mysore, by which the Princes expected to have had 10,000 men under their command in a very few days. Vellore was to be retained, and all they asked the sepoys was to keep it for eight days, by which time they expected abundance of support. The Moormen in the Pettah were all in their pay and interest and they were to have acted a very important part, by which none of us could possibly have escaped, but as if by the interposition of Divine Providence, the plan was prematurely carried into execution by the drunkenness of a Jemadar, who insisted on beginning on Thursday morning, the 10th July 1806, when the time settled was to have been on the Monday following, by which circumstance the people of the Pettah were prevented from co-operating. Another fortunate thing was that the sepoys began plundering, by which they were dispersed and could not be got together in a sufficient body to enable the Princes to escape. All the Native Commissioned and Non-Commissioned were in the secret excepting a very few, and 300 men in Forbes' had previously taken the oath. They held meetings in the Pettah, but the 23rd were not let into the secret till near the time of action. There was nothing before this new turban came out; discontent began to prevail which was blown up by the Palace and their emissaries —but what is wonderful that no one should ever reveal the secret except one Sepoy, who was put in irons as a madman by Forbes, at the instigation of the Native Officers, who said that he was bringing a bad name on the Corps and that they were all willing to wear the turban. This completely develops the mystery to those who were sceptical before as to the real cause..........You will have heard of the improprieties at Hyderabad, which from dates clearly evinces that they were to have acted in concert with the people of Vellore......"

Nearly all the unfortunate officers of the garrison were murdered, and the situation was only saved by the prompt action of the gallant Colonel Gillespie (afterwards Sir Robert Rollo Gillespie, K. C. B., who was killed during the Nepal War of 1814), who was stationed at Arcot with the 19th Light Dragoons, and who, on receipt of the news, collected about a troop of his regiment, and fought his way into Vellore. It is related that, on his appearance, a Sergeant Brodie, who had served with him at St. Domingo,

"Instantly recognised him, and, turning to his drooping comrades, exclaimed, 'If Colonel Gillespie be alive, he is now at the head of the 19th Dragoons, and God Almighty has sent him from the West Indies, to save our lives in the East!'"

The obnoxious order introducing the new turban was cancelled on the 17th July 1806, and the seven senior Mysore Princes were forthwith sent to Bengal by sea in *H. M. S. Culloden,* while in May 1807, the junior Princes and families reached Calcutta by land, after a march of five months from Vellore.

On the 17th September 1807, Lieutenant-General H. MacDowall became Commander-in-Chief in Madras, and in the same year Lord Minto, P.C., became Governor-General, holding the appointment till 1813. Lieutenant-General Sir George Hewlett became Commander-in-Chief in India, also in 1807.

1808—1809.
The Travancore War.

Towards the end of 1808, the subsidy payable by the Raja of Travancore having fallen into arrears, the Resident, Lieutenant-Colonel Macaulay, insisted on the dismissal of the Dewan, Paliathu Menon, who thereupon inaugurated a conspiracy with the object of turning the British out of Travancore.

On the 28th December 1808, at midnight, an attack was made on the house of Colonel Macaulay at Cochin by about a thousand Nayars, headed by the Dewan's confidential friend Pulpanabha Pillai, and aided by the minister of the Raja of Cochin. With the assistance of a Portuguese Clerk, Colonel Macaulay managed to conceal himself, and the attacking party, while they plundered the house, did not succeed in finding him. Fortunately a vessel with troops on board appeared in the morning, and the Nayars withdrew, enabling the Resident to make his escape.

About the same time a vessel with 31 privates and a surgeon, belonging to the 12th Regiment, put into Alleppey. The men were decoyed on shore, tied in couples back to back, and, with stones tied round their necks, were thrown into the backwater. This massacre was perpetrated by the Dewan's brother.

At this time the subsidiary force in Quilon, which included the 1st Battalion 4th Regiment, was under the command of Lieutenant-Colonel Chalmers, to whom news was brought on the 29th December that large numbers of armed men had assembled round the Dewan's house. He at once ordered the troops to be ready to attack them, and a short time afterwards received information that a large body of Nayars was about to march on Quilon from Parur, a village on the coast some ten miles to the south. Captain Clapham, with five companies of the 1st 4th and one gun, was immediately despatched to occupy some heights near the Dewan's house, and to remain there during the night. On approaching the heights, Captain Clapham found that a small hill on the right of the road was already held by the insurgents, whose numbers were increasing every moment, and he had scarcely time to load when he was attacked by a strong body in column. He reserved his fire until the enemy had come within ten paces, and then delivered a volley. The fire was returned, but after several attempts the enemy were forced to retire.

On the following morning, Captain Clapham was joined by Major Galbraith Hamilton with two companies of the 2nd 13th, and the Dewan's house was taken, together with six 4 pounders. Immediately afterwards the Travancore troops were reported to be crossing the bar at Ivicka, some five miles to the north, so Major Hamilton was given orders to push on to Anjuricha to intercept their advance. On his way he met and dispersed several small parties of Nayars.

On arrival at the bar, it was found that a considerable body of the Nayars, whose total force amounted to about 4,000 men, had already crossed and were drawn up to cover the landing of the remainder, so Major Hamilton at once attacked them and drove them into the river with great loss. Finding, however, that the enemy were getting round his flanks in boats, he withdrew and in the afternoon, on reports being received of the advance of 10,000 men from Parur, Colonel Chalmers moved the troops into the ruined fort. On the next morning, finding that there would be no immediate attack, he encamped near the Cantonment which he entrenched to the best of his power.

At first, in spite of the attempt made on the life of the Resident, the Government of Madras thought of conciliatory measures, but on hearing of the attack on the troops at Quilon, negotiations were abandoned, and troops were ordered to advance on Travancore from various directions. Lieutenant-Colonel Arthur St. Leger, Madras Cavalry, was to advance from the east; Lieutenant-Colonel Cuppage from the north; and Colonel Wilkinson, who was in command of a detachment in the southern districts, was to reinforce the army in Travancore if found necessary.

In January 1809, Colonel Chalmers had under his command at Quilon H. M.'s 12th Regiment, and the 1st 4th, 1st 2nd, 2nd 13th and 2nd 18th Regiments of Madras Native Infantry, with four guns. The number of the enemy had risen to about 30,000 with 18 guns.

The Battle of Quilon. On the 15th January 1809, information was received that the enemy was advancing in force from several directions, and Colonel Chalmers ordered his troops out to meet them in two columns. The whole force was encamped to the east of the bazars, parallel to the sea-shore and at a distance of about a mile from it, facing north-east. They thus practically commanded all the roads from the south and east. The right wing, under the command of Lieutenant-Colonel Picton, was composed of 4½ Companies of the 12th, the 2nd 13th N.I., and the 1st 4th N.I., (on the extreme right) with 2 guns, Colonel Chalmers himself commanded the left wing which comprised 4¼ companies of the 12th, the 1st 2nd N.I., the 2nd 18th N.I., and 2 guns.

The enemy advanced in three large bodies, the first from the south-east, on the road from Ithkeri; the second from the east, on the road from Ralianur; and the third from the north.

The right wing advanced to its front, and while 4½ companies of H.M. 12th, and 8 companies of the 2nd 13th N.I., with the two guns, wheeled to their left and attacked the second, or eastern, body of the enemy in flank, the 1st 4th turned to their right and advanced to the attack of the first, or south-eastern party. The left wing, with two guns, changed front to their left and prepared to attack the third body. They were not permitted to do this without considerable annoyance from the fire of the second body; in fact, so greatly were they hampered by this fire that they had frequently to face to the right-about.

The 1st 4th, which was commanded by Captain David Newall,* attacked and dispersed the body of Nayars to which they were opposed, killing a number of them, and capturing four guns, while their own casualties were slight, being only Captain Newall and 12 men wounded. The remainder of the right wing, after a good deal of fighting, defeated the force opposed to them, captured two guns, and pursued the enemy along the road to Karyerikota.

The left wing, being relieved of the fire of the eastern body, advanced to the attack of the northern body, routed them, and captured five guns. The 4½ companies of the 12th Regiment, belonging to the left wing, pursued the enemy for a short distance in an easterly direction, but at this time a Carnatic battalion serving with the enemy appeared with three guns from the Old Bazars and threatened to attack them in rear. The left wing thereupon reformed, facing north, and advanced against the Carnatic battalion, which it dispersed with the loss of its three guns. The Nayars retreated by the road to Karyerikota, with the exception of the Carnatic battalion, which fled northwards by the Aurka road. The engagement lasted five hours and resulted in the total defeat of the enemy with heavy loss and the capture of 14 guns.

The following is an extract from an order issued subsequently by the Governor in Council:—

"From the extent of the combined force which was opposed to the British troops, this signal victory reflects the highest honor on their discipline and valour: and the Governor in Council has great satisfaction in expressing his strongest approbation of their meritorious conduct.................Lieutenant-Colonel Chalmers is requested to convey the thanks of the Governor in Council to...........Captain Newall........ with the other officers and troops of the detachment who bravely signalised themselves on this occasion."

Philippart refers to this battle as follows:—

"Captain Newall commanded the 1st battalion 4th regiment in action with the troops of the Rajah of Travancore on the 15th January 1809. The 1st battalion 4th regiment formed a part of the brigade under Colonel Picton of H. M'.s 12th Foot, and during the action was detached from the brigade, to attack the advance of four battalions of Travancore troops, who were advancing with four six-pounders, for the purpose of turning the right of the British line. Capt. Newall, with the battalion under his command, charged the enemy's battalions, completely routed them, and captured all their guns. On this occasion Capt. Newall received a severe wound in the arm. He was honoured with the thanks of Colonel Chalmers, the officer commanding the Division, and of the Honorable the Governor in Council of Madras, in general orders."

---

* This Captain Newall, when a Lieutenant-Colonel in the 2nd 4th, was appointed Resident in Travancore in 1824.

On the 31st January 1809, the cantonments were again attacked by the Nayars with a similar result, the enemy suffering very heavy losses. Meanwhile Lieutenant-Colonel St. Leger moved from Trichinopoly and, marching by way of Palamcotta, reached the Arambuli Lines on the 3rd February and captured that stronghold, the fall of which had a great effect on the masses of Nayars concentrated near Quilon. Marching inland, a large body of the enemy was completely routed on the 17th February, and by the 2nd March the force was within three miles of Trivandrum.

On the 19th February, Colonel Chalmers received a reinforcement and decided to attack the enemy's position at Killianur which was protected by batteries and occupied by about 5,000 men. The 1st 4th formed part of the first brigade, under Colonel Picton, which was ordered to turn the left of the position, while the second brigade, commanded by Lieutenant-Colonel Stuart, attacked in front. Both attacks were made with the greatest gallantry, and were completely successful, the enemy abandoning seven guns in their flight.

Action at Killianur

A General Order was published on the 3rd March 1809, of which the following is an extract:—

"The Honorable the Governor in Council............requests that Lieutenant-Colonel Chalmers will convey to Lieutenant-Colonel Picton, to the Hon. Lieutenant-Colonel Stuart, and to the officers and men who served under them, the public thanks of the Honorable the Governor in Council for their meritorious exertions on this occasion."

On the 26th February, Colonel Chalmers marched from Quilon in order to effect a junction with Colonel St. Leger, and encamped twelve miles north of Trivandrum.

At the same time Lieutenant-Colonel Cuppage, who had entered Travancore by the northern frontier without much opposition, advanced and took up the strong position of Parur, a few miles south of Quilon, while the troops under Colonel Wilkinson occupied the passes of Shencotta and Achinkoil. On the 3rd March, the Resident arrived and the Raja submitted, agreeing to pay the expenses of the war. On the 15th March, a new Dewan was publicly proclaimed minister.

Paliathu Menon fled, and when tracked down in a temple at Phagwadi, committed suicide. His brother and six of his friends were taken to Quilon and hanged, and this act of justice terminated the war.

1809.
The Officers' Mutiny.

It would not appear right to pass over without notice one of the most extraordinary outbreaks recorded in the history of any army, and at the same time it appears desirable to show, in a short account of the mutiny of the officers of the Madras Army, that this blot on their honourable history was only incurred under the greatest provocation, and was directly caused by the stupidity and want of discretion of those in authority.

The officers of the Madras Army had been discontented for a considerable time, their principal grievances being, firstly, that their allowances were much smaller than those of the officers of the Bengal Army and, secondly, that nearly all appointments on the Staff and to the command of districts had been given to officers of the Royal Army. These grievances were aggravated by the discontinuance of certain allowances in July 1807, and the abolition of the tent contract in May 1808. The latter was particularly hard on Commanding Officers, as it was done in time of peace, when they looked to recouping themselves for the heavy expenses incurred during the long campaigns of 1803-6.

A memorial of these grievances was submitted on the 23rd January 1809, and recommended to Government by the Commander-in-Chief. In reply, the Court of Directors upheld the discontinuance of allowances but admitted and censured the large number of appointments given to officers of the Royal Army. The matter would probably then have been dropped, had not the Quartermaster-General's report, marked private and confidential, which had been given by the Governor, Sir George Barlow, to Colonel Capper, the Adjutant-General, come to be circulated in some unauthorised manner to Commanding Officers.

The result was that, on the 25th September 1808, five Commandants of Cavalry, and twenty-three of Infantry charged Lieutenant-Colonel John Munro, the Quartermaster-General, with having made false and infamous insinuations tending to injure their characters as officers and gentleman, and Colonel Munro was placed in arrest by Lieutenant-General Hay Macdowall, the Commander-in-Chief, but not till the 20th January 1809. The following circumstance appears to have some connection with the delay and subsequent sudden action. On the 15th January, Government informed the Commander-in-Chief that they proposed to employ Major Blacker, the D. Q. M. G. on special duty in Travancore. General Macdowall replied that he thought the selection should have been left to him, and that he considered Captain Macdowall more suitable for the appointment. On the 16th, Government refused to accept this nomination, and on the 20th, Colonel Munro was placed in arrest and his Deputy was consequently unable to proceed to Travancore.

Colonel Munro appealed to Government, but General Macdowall refused to forward the appeal, so Munro sent it in direct. Government then requested the Commander-in-Chief to release Munro, but he declined to do so without a positive order, which was given on the 26th January, and obeyed.

On the 30th January, General Macdowall, who had announced his intention of resigning, sailed from Madras to Negapatam, but left an order, dated the 28th, in which Colonel Munro was severely reprimanded for having appealed to the civil power. Government directed that this order should be expunged from the public records and anticipated General Macdowall's resignation by dismissing him. At the same time Colonel Capper, the Adjutant-General, and Major Boles, the Deputy Adjutant-General were suspended for giving currency to an order of such an offensive character. Major-General Gowdie (Madras Army) who, as next senior, succeeded as Commander-in-Chief, intimated to Major Boles that he would be reinstated if he expressed regret for his conduct, but this he refused to do.

On the 20th February, the Supreme Government condemned the conduct of General Macdowall and assured Sir G. Barlow of their support. Major Boles, who was in difficulties owing to the loss of his allowances, now asked for permission to proceed to England, but was refused on very trivial grounds, the truth being that the Governor wished to gain the ear of the Court of Directors first.

The summary punishment of Colonel Capper and Major Boles aroused great excitement and indignation in the army, and several addresses were sent to the latter informing him that his brother officers intended to organise a fund for his support, some of which made use of rather indiscreet language. It may be noted that Colonel Capper and General Macdowall were both lost at sea on their way to England in March. (*The former belonged to the 1st 4th—vide List of Officers*).

Early in February, a memorial was secretly prepared for transmission to the Supreme Government, pointing out the grievances of the officers of the army. This memorial was almost entirely confined to the officers in Travancore and the Southern Division, and the intention of forwarding it was abandoned about the middle of March. Unfortunately a copy came into the hands of Sir George Barlow who, on the 1st May, published in General Orders a long list of officers suspended, dismissed or removed from their commands, and this merely on the strength of private information, without trial, and without giving the officers in question an opportunity of offering any defence.

From this time the great majority of the officers placed themselves in opposition to Government and in many places speedily passed into actual mutiny. With the events which occurred in those places we are not concerned here.

Towards the end of July, Government decided to test the feelings of the army by calling upon all European officers to sign the following declaration:—

"We the undersigned officers of the Honourable Company's Service do, in the most solemn manner, declare upon our word of honor as British Officers, that we will obey the orders, and support the authority of the Governor in Council of Fort St. George, agreeably to the tenor of the Commissions which we hold from that Government."

The 1st 4th was at this time at Quilon where, on the 9th July, orders given to the three battalions there to march from Travancore, were disobeyed on the ground that Government intended to separate them and place them under the control of H. M.'s Regiments. Piquets of 100 men under European officers were regularly detailed from each Native battalion to guard against surprise.

On the 7th August 1809, the Honourable Colonel Stuart, Commanding at Quilon, addressed the following letter to the Chief Secretary to Government at Madras:—

"It is with extreme regret that I am obliged to report, for the information of the Honourable the Governor in Council, that the two corps at this place, viz., 2nd and 1st battalions of the 4th regiment, which had been under marching-orders for some time past, and only waited for the necessary camp equipage and pay, have now refused to move.

The late measures of Government, as carried into effect at the presidency and Trichinopoly, have created a most violent ferment among the corps here. At those places where the European force was so far superior in number to the native, the measure probably was, executed without difficulty; but here, where there are seven battalions of sepoys, and a company and a half of artillery, to our one regiment, * I found it totally impossible to carry the business to the same length, particularly as any tumult among our own corps would certainly bring the people of Travancore upon us.

It is in vain, therefore, for me, with the small force I can depend upon, to attempt to stem the torrent here by any acts of violence.

Most sincerely and anxiously do I wish that the present tumult may subside without fatal consequences; which, if the present violent measures are continued, I much fear will not be the case. If blood is once spilt in the cause, there is no knowing where it may end; and the probable consequence will be that India will be lost for ever. So many officers of the army have gone to such lengths, that, unless a general amnesty is granted, tranquillity can never be restored.

The Honourable the Governor in Council will not, I trust, impute to me any other motives for having thus given my opinion. I am actuated solely by anxiety for the public good and the benefit of my country; and I think it my duty, holding the responsible situation I now do, to express my sentiments at so awful a period.

Where there are any prospects of success it might be right to persevere; but, where every day's experience proves that the more coercive the measures adopted, the more violent the consequences, a different and more conciliatory line of conduct ought to be adopted.

I have the honour, etc."

The following address was presented to Colonel Stuart on the 7th August by the officers of the Company's Service at Quilon:—

"Things of importance, when required to be told at a juncture like the present, admit of no preamble, we, therefore, proceed to inform you, that authentic information having been received of the determination of government to exert every resource, under every circumstance, and at all risks, to stifle the voice of the army, which has merely been calling aloud for justice, under the assumed designation of quelling a dangerous insurrection and mutiny, a shadow of which we are convinced never existed, it becomes to us a bounden duty, not only to deny a fact, thus unwisely, as well as unjustly asserted, but to exert every active measure within our power to prevent the operation of an assumption so palpably destructive in its tendency.

The orders of government, appointing certain officers of his majesty's service to do duty with the native corps of the honourable company's army, which were circulated at this station yesterday, and which are so diametrically opposite to the spirit of the regulations for the guidance of the army, together with the very alarming communications respecting threatened proceedings in different parts of the Madras establishment, which

---

* His Majesty's 19th Regiment.

> have from day to day been received from Travancore, combined with the late measures of government, calling on their officers for a pledge of allegiance, beyond the sacred obligation of their commissions, have all conspired to excite such a degree of alarm in our minds, which it is impossible to describe.
>
> We feel that a new order of things is intended, and perceive in the change nothing less than a subversion, by force, of the constitution, established by the united wisdom of the British legislature for the government and preservation of our country's empire in the East.
>
> The dispersion of the honourable company's troops, and in particular instances their aggregation under the control of a superior European force of his majesty's service, plainly confess the object in view: considering that the success of this system of dividing, in order to destroy, must inevitably be attended by consequences as shocking to individuals as ruinous to the state, and firmly believing that the object (if legitimate) is attainable by measures of a very different complexion, we feel ourselves compelled to state to you, that we see a strict propriety of urging, that the execution of the order for separating the force under your immediate command at this place should be postponed until the determination of government be known, on the address forwarded by you, on the night of the 4th instant, by which time we are sanguine in the hope that affairs will bear a more favourable aspect.
>
> We have, etc., etc."
>
> (Signed by 50 officers).

About the 16th August, the declaration was tendered to the officers of the 1st 4th, 1st 2nd and 2nd 9th, but all refused to sign except four, amongst whom were the Commandants of the 1st 4th and 2nd 9th. On the 22nd August, the officers of the 4th were prevailed upon to submit. Altogether only a very small minority consented to sign but, with a few exceptions, all the most distinguished officers signed.

On the 11th September 1809, Lord Minto, the Governor-General, arrived in Madras and, on the 25th, a general amnesty was published, with a few exceptions. All the officers who had been suspended were permitted to rejoin their corps on the 30th, on signing the declaration. A number of the excepted officers were subsequently cashiered by Court-Martial, some of them having elected to be dismissed rather than be tried by Colonel Wilkinson, a strong adherent of the Governor's but with a very few exceptions all the officers were subsequently restored.

With regard to Sir George Barlow, who did not vacate his appointment till the 21st May 1813, Sydney Smith writes as follows :—

> "...................that a civilian, a gentleman accustomed only to the details of commerce should begin his government, over a settlement with which he was utterly unacquainted, by telling one of the bravest set of officers in the world, that, for six years past, they had been, in the basest manner, sacrificing their duty to their interest, does appear to us an instance of indiscretion which, if frequently repeated, would soon supersede the necessity of any further discussion upon Indian affairs."

The testimony borne by Lord Mornington and the Duke of Wellington to the discipline of the Madras Army will be found in another place.

1810—1813.

At the beginning of 1810, the 1st 4th Regiment was in camp at Trivandrum, but later in the year it marched to Bangalore to form part of the garrison, and remained there throughout 1811.

On the 10th April 1810, Lieutenant-General George Hewitt became Commander-in-Chief, and was succeeded by Major-General Sir S. Auchmuty on the 27th September 1810.

Colonel Welsh, who was in Bangalore in 1811, gives us some interesting pictures of life in Mysore at that time, of which the following is a brief extract:—

"On the 14th October, the Rajah honoured the races with his presence, and both ladies and gentlemen were separately introduced to him by Mr. Cole [the Resident], when each received an apathetic shake of his cold paw........He came in a beautiful English carriage, drawn by four dun horses, and accompanied by a body of pike-men clad in green. On the evening of the 15th he held a durbar or levee, in his Palace in the fort, when he received ladies and gentlemen there in the same cool manner; and after keeping us sitting in dull silence for an hour, dismissed us all, with attar and betel. To make up for this, however, he sent us a fine royal tiger to be hunted on the race-course. Mr. Cole, always the leader, speared him four times, though scarcely drawing blood; after which Lieutenant Aubrey pinned him to the ground, the pike entering the loose skin of his jowl while he lay crouching under a small paddy bank; Captain Pepper struck him next, and provoked him to rise and wrench the first spear out; he then staggered a short distance, and took to a small tank, where several spears were flung at him, and one thrown by Pepper pierced his ribs and actually drowned him. Mr. Cole, being well mounted, and a capital spear-man, was the only person who, for a long time, dared to face him; and, weakened as he was, it was no easy job to destroy him. A small rough dog belonging to Lieutenant Mercer never quitted the tiger till he was drowned, when a Sepoy volunteered to dive and bring him out, and actually did so.

"The next day a couple of royal tigers were sent, when Mr. Cole killed the first single-handed, though a large and active one. The second, being a more knowing brute, immediately gave chase to Major Russell, of our cavalry, who was nearly overtaken by him, when two black men ran in his way, one of whom he killed with a single bite, and then retreated under the new race stand. Into this place a woman and child had crept for safety, and as he came in at one end, and laid hold of her cloth, she wisely left it with him, and retreated with her infant uninjured. As we could not contrive to lure him out again, I pistolled him, by breaking his back, and then dismounting, we killed him with our spears. Whilst we were undecided, however, as to his back being fairly broken, he seized a square stone lying in front of him, and actually broke several of his teeth upon it.

"On the 6th November, the Rajah sent each lady in the Cantonment two fine shawls, and to each Native Corps five hundred pagodas as a present. The Europeans also got one thousand pagodas each regiment, which was an acknowledgment to the ladies for their visit, and to the troops for several parades and extra duties, to do him honour."

In 1812, the 1st 4th Regiment moved from Bangalore to Bellary, and remained there throughout 1813.

On the 21st May 1813, Lieutenant-General the Hon. J. Abercromby, Governor of Madras, became Commander-in-Chief, and in the same year General the Earl of Moira, K.G., P.C., (afterwards Marquess of Hastings) became Governor-General, remaining in office till 1823.

1814—1815.

Disturbances in the Northern Districts.

As regards the services of the regiment for the next seven years, I must confess that, with the materials at my disposal, I have not been able to trace accurately what part it took in quelling the numerous outbreaks which occurred in the Northern Districts during that period, so I have been compelled to confine myself to giving merely a rough sketch of these disturbances. Reference to the military records at Fort St. George would no doubt supply the information still required.

On the 1st January 1814, the regiment was in camp near Kurnool, and on the 1st July following, they were moved to Samalkot ("Samulcottah") and Rajahmundry, in Godavari district, where they remained till 1817.

Mohiri. The cause of this move was doubtless the unsettled and threatening state of this part of the country, and more particularly of the district which had formerly constituted the Mohiri Zemindari. There had originally been a Rajah of Mohiri, but the last representative, Narayana Deo, was murdered by his brothers in 1786, and the Zemindari lapsed to Government. With a view, however, to conciliating the inhabitants of the country, Government, in 1786, recalled the Rani from Chikati, where she had taken refuge after the murder of her husband, and confirmed her in the possession of the Zemindari. In 1810, as the revenue had fallen into arrears, the Zemindari was attached and sold by public auction.

Parlakimedi. The district remained quiet up to 1814, when disturbances began to arise, not only in Mohiri, but also in the large Zemindaris of Parlakimedi, Chinnakimedi and Peddakimedi. The first mentioned of these was under the Court of Wards, the Zemindar, Raja Jagannath Gajapati Narayana Deo, being a minor, and the manager of the estate, Padmanabha Deo had, by 1813, become so unpopular with the Bissoyis (tributary hill chiefs), and with the people of the country in general, that something very like an insurrection broke out, the insurgents burning and plundering several villages.

As a result of this, Government decided to put down the disturbances by force, and the Magistrate, Mr. Woodcock, and the Collector, Mr. Spottiswoode, were sent to Kimedi to enquire into the complaints made by the Bissoyis against the Manager, while Colonel Fletcher was appointed to command the troops in Ganjam. While negotiations were proceeding with the insurgents, there were no further acts of aggression, and consequently the Magistrate decided not to employ the troops at all. Padmanabha Deo was removed from his post as Manager, and there was a lull in the disturbances which, however, soon began to break out again. I believe that the only regiment employed on this occasion was the 3rd N.I., but I have no definite details.

In 1814, in another part of the District, the Raja of Goomsur, Dhanunjaya Bhanj, who appears to have been a monster of cruelty, was committing all kinds of atrocities, and was accused of the murder of his own mother by his father, Strikara Bhanj. As the Raja adopted a hostile attitude to Government, his Zamindari was declared to be forfeited, by a proclamation, dated the 21st May 1815.

Goomsur.

The Raja showing no signs of yielding, the troops under Colonel Fletcher were marched from Aska into Goomsur. I do not think the 1st 4th were in Goomsur on this occasion. Colonel Fletcher occupied the fort of Kallada without opposition on the 20th May, but the Zamindar escaped, and, after a forced march of 19 hours, the pursuit had to be abandoned. Dhanunjaya Bhanj, however, shortly afterwards gave himself up to the Collector, and the troops returned to Cantonments in June 1815.

When brought to trial, Dhanunjaya Bhanj was acquitted, the evidence against him being considered insufficient, and in 1832 he was actually reinstated as Raja of Goomsur. Colonel Fletcher was tried by court-martial for plundering the Zemindar's property, Government remarking that under any circumstances it could not be claimed as prize, but should have been preserved with a view to its regular confiscation or as the case might be.

In August 1815, a most dreadful outbreak of epidemic fever broke out in Ganjam, reducing the population of the town from 30,000 to 6,000 inhabitants, and rapidly spreading through the district. In consequence, the troops and the headquarters of the Collector were transferred to Berhampur in November.

On the 25th May 1814, Lieutenant-General Sir Thomas Hislop succeeded General Abercromby as Commander-in-Chief in Madras, and the Right Hon. Hugh Elliot became Governor of Madras, holding the appointment till 1820.

1816.

The Pindaris.

At the beginning of 1816, the 1st 4th M.N.I. was stationed at Samalkot, with detachments at Cocanada, Rajahmundry and "Piddahpore," which may have been either Pithapuram or Peddapuram, both of which places are in the neighbourhood of Samalkot.

At the end of the year there was an irruption of Pindaris into the Ganjam district, and as there is a possibility that the 1st 4th was employed on this occasion, it may be as well to give such particulars of this raid as are available.

From 1794, when the Pindari leaders, who were an off-shoot of the Mahratta armies, first obtained assignments of land from Sindhia, till about 1800, there were two principal leaders, Hiru and Buran, who raised their standards annually, during the Dassara, in the Narbadha Valley. About 1800, both died, Hiru leaving two sons, Dost Muhammad and Wasal Muhammad, of whom the former died shortly afterwards, leaving the latter as sole head of the band. (It may be noted here that each separate association of Pindaris under one leader was called a *darra;* the forays on which they set forth were called *labhars;* and the leader was termed the *Labharia.*)

The band which broke into Ganjam was some 4,000 to 5,000 strong, and consisted almost entirely of men from Wasal Muhammad's *darra*. It crossed the British frontier, from the Jeypur side, about the middle of December 1816, and marched on Kimedi, to which place Lieutenant Tweedle, who was on the frontier with a company of Madras Native Infantry, retired as the *labhar* advanced. Emboldened by this, the Pindaris attacked the town, and succeeded in burning and plundering part of it on the night of the 19th December, although Major Oliver was there with three companies of infantry. Having ascertained that their camp was only two miles distant, this officer determined to surprise it before morning, and met with complete success, occasioning considerable loss to the *labhar,* notwithstanding the smallness of his force and his utter lack of cavalry.

In the course of the following morning the whole band moved off, taking the direct road to Ganjam, before which station they appeared on the 25th. They hastily plundered part of the town, and retired through Goomsur. Lieutenant Borthwick instantly commenced a most active pursuit, and on the 27th he fell in with a party of about 1,000 in the neighbourhood of Boirani, of whom he destroyed 20 men and 50 horses. Not satisfied with this success, he resolved to beat up the Pindari camp, rightly judging that, as the Pindaris knew the British troops to consist of infantry only, their camp would not be far off. Leaving a Jemadar's party to pursue a direct road, he himself, with 50 men of his company, took a circuitous route, so as to fall upon the enemy from the opposite quarter. His success was brilliant, and, soon after, the Pindaris disappeared from the district. Their destination was supposed to be the rich temple of Jagannath (Puri), but before reaching that place they appear to have turned off to the west and vanished in the direction of their own country.

1817—1818.
Disturbances in Mohiri.

From 1817 to 1821, the 1st 4th were still stationed in the Northern Division, with detachments at Samalkot, Injaram, Peddapuram, Rajahmundry, Aska and Berhampur, and during that time they were constantly employed against the unsettled tribes in the hills.

In October 1816, Padmanabha Deo, who had retired to his estate at Tekkali, once more

Parla-kimedi. began to stir up rebellion, and at the beginning of 1817, one Gudipati Lachanna commenced the disturbances by burning Nagarikatakam and five other villages in the Karakavalasa estate. Mr. Spottiswoode, the Collector, promptly entered the Zemindari, with four companies of Sepoys from Vizianagram (regiment not traced, but probably not the 1st 4th), and found the passes stockaded, but the presence of the troops seems to have temporarily prevented further outrages. No military operations were, however, attempted, and the troops were subsequently withdrawn, but not before Durga Raz, the grandson of a former Zemindar, who was directly concerned in the disturbances, had been caught and hanged.

Goomsur. Part of the regiment seems to have been employed in Goomsur at the beginning of 1817, as a regimental return, dated the 1st January 1817, show 275 men as absent "on Field Service at Goomsur," but no particulars of their services on this occasion are forthcoming.

Mohiri. The management of the Mohiri estate, which had been secured in 1810 by Bandam Chalamaya, the Katcherri shroff, was in the meantime most unsatisfactory. With the permission of Government, Mr. Spottiswoode had undertaken the management of the taluk on the 14th November 1816, at the request of the Bandam family. The Collector received a commission of 1½ *per cent*, for managing the taluk, and thus appears to have become the servant of his own shroff. Maja Deo, one of the murderers of Narayana Deo in 1786, was still alive, living at Chicacole, and the taluk peons had a grievance upon being dispossessed of their inam lands.

A body of peons, headed by one Sarsungi Mahrata, formed a retreat at Sirhut in the Mohiri hills, not far from Berhampur, and betook themselves to a course of outrageous plunder. On the 8th March 1817, Sarsungi Mahrata entered the town of Berhampur by night with his adherents, and burnt and plundered nearly the whole of it, threatening to return on the following night to complete the work of destruction. Efforts were made to capture him, but in vain, as the Bandam family was unpopular and Mahrata professed the cause of the ancient Zemindari.

Disturbances continued in Mohiri throughout the whole of 1818. Troops were stationed at Ichapur and Berhampur to protect the country, and peons and rangers were employed to guard the villages from Mahrata's ravages. On the 9th February 1818, it was decided to raise a corps for this purpose, which was called the Ganjam Hill Rangers, and Captain James Jobson of the 1st 4th was selected to command it. The whole province appears to have aided and abetted the insurgents to the full extent of their power, and in spite of a reward of Rs. 10,000 offered for the capture of Sarsungi Mahrata, he still continued at large, and people were mutilated, murdered and robbed, or carried up to the hills, where they were kept until they paid ransom.

Mahrata had been driven into Kimedi towards the end of 1817, but early in 1818, he returned to Mohiri, and, about the end of May, a detachment which included a party of the 1st 4th, which was then in camp at Aska, was sent out to endeavour to capture him, but without success. This force was commanded by Captain Jobson of the 1st 4th.

Sorokota. On the 3rd June, a party of the regiment under the command of Lieutenant Van Heythusen attacked a post on a hill near "Surcottah" (Sorokota, in Berhampur Taluk), and with the assistance of a detachment of the 2nd 4th, which arrived during the engagement, succeeded in driving the insurgents out, but Mahrata once more effected his escape. Seven men of the 1st 4th were wounded on this occasion.

On the same day, Captain Jobson died from fatigue and exposure, and besides him, Mr. Mason, the Assistant Collector, five other officers, and 300 men, died either from this cause or from fever, as a result of the hardships suffered during these operations. Mahrata was eventually captured, but instead of being hanged as a rebel, he was sent to Gooty as a state prisoner.

1819—1820.

On the 1st January 1819, regimental headquarters was at Aska, while 325 men were on field service in Goomsur, where there was still a good deal of disturbance. Strikara Bhanj, the ex-Zemindar, had escaped from custody at Berhampur in 1818, and returned to Goomsur, where he was soon at the head of a party, and virtually recovered possession of his Zemindari. There is no record of any troops having been actively employed against him, and eventually, on the 3rd May 1819, Government formally reinstated him in his Zemindari. The disturbances in the Northern Districts were constantly renewed, and were not finally quelled until 1836, after much fighting in which the 4th M.N.I. took no part, being then stationed elsewhere.

The regiment remained stationed at Berhampur and Aska throughout 1820.

1821.

The 1st 4th was still at Berhampur and Aska at the beginning of 1821, and on the 1st January of that year had a detachment of 191 men on field service in Parlakimedi, where there had been a further outbreak of burning and plundering in September 1818. There is no record, however, of any active employment of the troops, though the Zemindari continued in a disturbed state for many years afterwards.

On the 15th June 1821, Lieutenant-General Sir A. Campbell, *Bart.*, K.C.B., became Commander-in-Chief in Madras. This officer had been created a Baronet for his services at the battle of Talavera, where he commanded the fourth Division.

1822—1823.

From the 26th August 1821 to the 15th January 1822, the 1st 4th M.N.I., which had now left the turbulent district of Ganjam, was at Nagpur, where it doubtless formed part of the Madras Subsidiary Force which was relieved by the Bengal Army in 1822.

On the occasion of this relief, the following complimentary letter was written to Colonel Scott, then commanding the Force, by the Resident, and was published to the Army in an order by the Governor-in-Council, dated 15th February 1822.

"The period of the service of the Madras troops in this quarter has been distinguished by events and transactions of no common importance, and it is unnecessary for me to report what the public records will testify, both with regard to their exploits and to the commendation they have uniformly received from the Supreme Government.

As being more immediately within my province, it is a pleasing duty to me to offer my testimony to the constant good conduct, and strict discipline of the force, both European and Native, whether stationary or marching within the territories under my superintendence. I can assert with perfect conviction that during the whole time of their service, now a period of five years and upwards, not a complaint of any consequence has been made of their irregularity or maltreatment of the natives of the country, and this alone is sufficient to stamp the high character of the troops in general, and in particular reflect a degree of credit on yourself and the Officers of the force to which no panegyric can add.

In conclusion, I cannot refrain from offering to you personally the expression of the high satisfaction which I have derived from all our intercourse whether public or private. Our earlier connection in the public service was distinguished by a crisis of peculiar danger to the British interests in this quarter which will never be forgotten for the brilliancy of the actions it gave rise to, so honorable to yourself and the troops under you, and I owe it to you to say that the cordiality of your co-operation, on all occasions, and the spirit of accommodation and friendliness which you have maintained throughout our long public correspondence, have essentially contributed, with the bravery and discipline of the troops, and the judgment and activity of the different officers employed, to the establishment of the present order and tranquillity subsisting in every part of these territories."

On the 22nd February 1822, the regiment arrived at Secunderabad, which was destined to be its station for the next five years.

In 1823, on the departure of the Marquess of Hastings, Mr. John Adam acted as Governor-General till the arrival of Lord Amherst, P.C., who remained in office till 1828. Lieutenant-General the Hon. Sir Edward Paget, G.C.B., became Commander-in-Chief in India in 1823.

1824.

On the 6th May 1824, the double battalion system was abolished, and the 1st Battalion 4th Regiment of Madras Native Infantry, still serving at Secunderabad, was re-named the 4th Regiment of Madras Native Infantry, while the 2nd Battalion of the 4th reverted to its former number, and became the 15th Regiment of Madras Native Infantry (afterwards the 75th Carnatic Infantry).

Part I.

CHAPTER V.

THE 4th REGIMENT OF MADRAS NATIVE INFANTRY.

6th May 1824—12th JUNE 1883.

1824—1826.

On becoming the 4th Regiment of Madras Native Infantry, on the 6th May 1824, the battalion remained in garrison at Secunderabad till 1827.

The Commander-in-Chief, Sir A. Campbell, died on the 11th December 1824 and, pending the arrival of his successor, Lieutenant-General Sir Thomas Bowser, who had been Colonel of the 4th, acted as Commander-in-Chief.

On the 3rd March 1826, Lieutenant-General Sir G. T. Walker, G.C.B., took over from General Bowser.

The farewell order published by the latter on the 26th January, of which the following is an extract, furnishes a good illustration of the flowery periods of a past generation :—

> "It is with feelings of attachment and regret, cheered by the pride of honourable recollections, that Lieutenant-General Bowser for the last time addresses the Army of Fort St. George. The ties of more than half a century, during which the Lieutenant-General has had the honour of being associated in the interests of the officers and soldiers of that army, must necessarily be strong, and in offering them the tribute of his sincere admiration, and the gage of his perfect regard and esteem, he can temper the painful feeling of permanent separation, by the knowledge and recollection alone, that this gallant and distinguished army is at the very Zenith of its glory and its reputation and that the same army which aided the exploits of a Coote, and witnessed the dawn of a Wellington's Career, should, at this epoch, be proving itself equally zealous, devoted and efficient.........and that valour which had hitherto been almost limited to the narrow confines of a country, has proved itself of general application wherever required or directed. With the proud consciousness of having shared the dangers and honours of such an army, and being the oldest soldier serving in India, Lieutenant-General Bowser now bids his comrades a last, a heartfelt, and an affectionate farewell............"

General Viscount Combermere, G.C.B., G.C.H., became Commander-in-Chief in India in 1825.

1827—1833.

In 1827, the 4th M.N.I. was moved to the south, and arrived at Palaveram on the 23rd February 1827, where it remained until the 8th January 1831. It then marched to Vellore, which was reached on the 17th January, and was stationed there till the 21st September 1833. Its next station was Bangalore, where it arrived on the 5th October and remained until called upon to take part in the Coorg War of 1834.

On the 11th May 1831, Lieutenant-General, Sir R. W. O'Callaghan, K.C.B., became Commander-in-Chief in Madras, and on the 15th October 1833, General Lord William Cavendish Bentinck, G.C.B., G.C.H.,* relieved General Sir Edward Barners, G.C.B., as Commander-in-Chief in India, as well as assuming his appointment as Governor-General. The Governor of Madras at this time was Sir Frederick Adam, K.C.B.

---

* This was the Guelphic Order of Hanover, now extinct.

1834.

The Coorg War.

In January 1833, the Government of Madras remonstrated against the tyrannical Government of Chikka Vira Raja of Coorg, who had been ruler of that country since 1820. The Raja replied to Mr. Casamajor, the Resident of Mysore, who was sent to confer with him, that Coorg was an independent country, and that he would do as he pleased.

Mr. Graeme, the Resident of Nagpur, who was then residing at Bangalore for the benefit of his health, was next sent to the Raja who, however, confined two of his agents, namely Dara Set, a Parsi merchant of Tellicherry, and Kalpatti Karunakara Menon, the Head Sheristadar of Malabar District, who is described as "an old and faithful servant of the Company." These he refused to give up until he was handed over certain of his relatives who had fled to Mysore in September 1832, and claimed the protection of the British Government.

The Raja, who was undoubtedly subject to violent fits of insanity, then wrote insolent letters to the Governor of Madras, and to the Governor-General and, having highly inflated ideas of his own power and importance, resolved on war.

A force, 6,000 strong, was therefore organised to depose him, and this, owing to the bad roads and difficulties of supply, was divided into four columns, which were to converge on Mercara.

The force was placed under the command of Colonel Lindsay, C.B., H.M. 39th Foot, and Colonel J. S. Fraser accompanied him in the capacity of Political Agent of the Governor-General for Coorg Affairs.

The Eastern Column. The Eastern Column, which was commanded by Colonel Lindsay himself, is that with which we are chiefly concerned, as the 4th M.N.I., which was then stationed at Bangalore, served with it. The other troops were: one Company Foot Artillery with three light and two heavy howitzers, two mortars, and one 6-pounder; 400 men of H.M. 39th Regiment; the 35th, 36th and 48th M.N.I.; the Rifle Company of the 5th N.I.; and 300 Sappers and Miners.

On the 2nd April 1834, this force marched from Bettadapura upon Sulekote, and reached the river Kaveri opposite Hebbal, where a barrier had been thrown up on the Coorg side, consisting of a loopholed wall of mud and stone. Colonel Fraser, the Political Agent, attempted to cross, carrying a white handkerchief, but was fired on. Two howitzers then opened with grape and, under cover of this, the advance guard, with Colonels Lindsay and Fraser, crossed, and the enemy gave way, retiring on Ramasami Kanawe. The strong position at the fortified pagoda near that place was carried in about a quarter of an hour.

The Coorg force consisted of about 100 Mussulmans, of whom about 60 were armed with matchlocks and the remainder with swords; a very few Coorgs, provided with firearms, and having also the management of the "jinjals"; and about 50 ryots armed with bows and arrows—the whole commanded by a Coorg Karyagar.

A breastwork and barrier near Haringi, six or seven miles west of Ramasami Kanawe, was also taken, at the cost of a few men wounded, the enemy, who were 350 in number, mostly Coorgs, losing 6 killed.

On the 4th April, the force only advanced five miles, on account of the difficulty of the road, obstructed as it was by large felled trees, and at 4 p.m., on that day, a flag of truce, sent by the Raja, came into camp, accompanied by one of his four Dewans, Lakshmi Narayana, and by another person, Muhammad Taker Khan, who called himself the Raja's friend, and four of their attendants; after which no further resistance was offered.

Of the two preliminary conditions for an armistice, one had been complied with, as Kalpatti Karunakara Menon had been delivered by the Raja to the British camp, but the Raja himself had not surrendered.

On the 5th April, another Dewan, Apparanda Bopu, with a party of 400 Coorgs, went to meet Colonel Fraser, surrendered to him, and offered to conduct the Company's troops to the capital.

Occupation of Mercara. At 4 p.m., on the 6th April, they entered the Fort of Mercara; the Raja's flag, which was flying on one of the bastions, was lowered, and the British colours hoisted in its stead under a salute of 21 guns. A company of H. M. 39th Regiment remained within the Fort, and the remainder of the troops encamped on the heights around.

Vira Raja, at the commencement of the war, had removed to his palace at Nalknad, a place almost inaccessible to the army. He had taken with him his women, his band, his treasures, and what remained of the families of the Coorg Rajas. Had he taken his place at the head of his Coorgs, and directed the defence, great loss would undoubtedly have been caused to the invading troops in a country so thickly forested, and so well provided with natural obstacles. Incited, however, partly by hope that a reconciliation was still possible, and partly by fear that he might lose all, he sent orders forbidding the Coorgs to encounter the Company's troops, and hence the slight resistance met with by the latter.

No record has been found as yet of the casualties of the 4th M.N.I., but particulars as regards their strength in the field, and their share in the captured booty, will be found in Part II of these records.

We now turn to the progress of the other columns.

The Northern Column, under Colonel G. Waugh, and consisting of one brigade of 6-pounder guns from Bellary; headquarters and 300 rank and file, H. M. 55th Regiment; the 9th M.N.I., 31st M.L.I, and the Rifle Company of the 24th M.N.I.; with 200 Sappers and Miners,—left Hoskote on the 1st April, and marched to Sanivarsante. It then crossed the Hemavati river and, after some fighting at that place and at Mudravalli, drove the enemy out of Codlipet.

The Northern Column.

On the 2nd April, it came on the strong stockade in the Buck pass, which was held by the Coorgs, commanded by Madanta Appachu, a fine old Coorg of tall stature and martial bearing who, after the British accession became Head Sheristadar, and a most loyal and devoted servant of Government till his death in 1876.

The troops attacked the stockade, under the command of the Field Officer of the day, Major Bird, 31st Light Infantry, but in spite of every attempt, lasting four hours and a half, were repulsed. A misdirected flank movement of H. M. 55th Regiment, under Colonel Mill, was equally unsuccessful. Colonel Mill was shot dead, as were Ensigns Robertson, 9th N.I., and Babington, 31st L.I. Major Bird decided to withdraw the column, and with little additional loss, brought it under cover, but on account of the heavy list of wounded, and to find a convenient camping place, retreated several miles. In this unfortunate affair about 48 were killed and 118 wounded.

The Western Column, under Colonel David Foulis, consisted of half a company of Golandauze with four 6-pounder guns; headquarters and 300 rank and file, H. M. 48th Regiment; 20th and 32nd M.N.I.; and 200 Sappers and Miners.

The Western Column.

This column left Cannanore on the 31st March, to force the Heggala Ghat and occupy Virarajendrapet. On the 2nd April, two companies were repulsed at the crossing of the Stony river, and Lieutenant Erskine of H. M. 48th was killed, but on the 3rd, the force fought its way up the pass, and on the following day cleared the ghat and occupied Heggala, with a loss of one officer and 12 men killed, and 36 wounded.

On the 13th April, a detachment, under Major Tweedie, took possession of the palace at Nalknad and, leaving a detachment under Colonel Brock at Virarajendrapet, the main body marched on Mercara, and encamped near the Muddaramudi river, seven miles south of Mercara. Colonel Stewart's force joined this column at Virarajendrapet, and then proceeded to open the Sidapur pass into Mysore.

A sub-division of the Eastern Column, under Colonel Stewart, advanced from Periyapatna, on the 2nd April, towards the Kaveri, opposite Rangasamudra, where the enemy was stationed in considerable force but, being plied with a few cannon shot, retired across country, leaving six men dead.

The Eastern Auxiliary Column.

Colonel Stewart crossed the Kaveri at Kondangiri and proceeded to Virarajendrapet, as already stated, to co-operate with the Western Column.

The Western Auxiliary Column. A Western Auxiliary Column, under Lieutenant-Colonel George Jackson advanced from Kumbla, on the coast, to Sulya, and took the enemy's stockade on the 29th March. On the 1st April, a reconnoitring party, sent out towards Mallur and Bellare, was driven in with loss, and Colonel Jackson retreated on Kumbla but, being much harassed by the enemy, was forced to turn off to Kasaragod, which he reached on the 6th, having lost 2 officers and 30 men killed, and 36 men wounded.

Colonel Jackson was so much overcome by the failure of his expedition that he himself applied for a Court-Martial to enquire into the cause of his failure, and in the result, was completely exonerated from blame. The fault lay with the authorities who sent him on a hopeless task, his troops only consisting of 150 rank and file of H.M. 48th Foot; 400 rank and file of the 40th M.N.I.; 50 Sappers and Miners, who never joined, but remained at Cannanore; and not a single gun. The Brigade-Major of this column was Captain McCleverty, H.M. 48th Regiment, who was afterwards Commander-in-Chief in Madras.

Surrender of the Raja. Meanwhile, Colonel Fraser had offered favourable treatment to the Raja if he would surrender, and the latter, after a vain attempt to gain fifteen days' time, entered Mercara Fort, at noon on the 10th April, accompanied by his unarmed attendants and women, and gave himself up, but before leaving Nalknad, the remainder of the royal family was inhumanly butchered by his orders, as was also the Dewan Kunta Basava.

The ex-Raja was sent off from Mercara, with an escort of the 35th and 48th N.I., commanded by Colonel Stewart, and was handed over to the Commissioner of Mysore on the 12th May 1834. Thence he was sent to Vellore, and finally to Benares, where he drew a monthly pension of Rs. 6,000 from the Coorg revenues. In 1852, he was permitted to visit England where, in 1862, he died, and was buried in Kensal Green cemetery, thus bringing to an end the line of the Rajas of Haleri.

His favourite daughter, Gauramma, was baptised on the 30th June 1852, Queen Victoria standing sponsor through the Archbishop of Canterbury, and was christened Victoria Gauramma. She married an English officer—unhappily—and died on the 1st April 1864. Her husband and child disappeared mysteriously, and were never heard of afterwards. Seven sons were born to the Raja, one at Mercara, and the remainder at Vellore and Benares, but the family has ceased to have any connection with Coorg, and I have no information as to what eventually became of their descendants.

1835.

On its return from Coorg the 4th M.N.I. continued to be stationed in Bangalore, with a detachment of 44 men in Rayakota. With regard to this Rayakota detachment, the following tradition, recorded by Dykes, who wrote in 1850, is distinctly amusing:—

"At Salem there are a few old veterans and at Rayacottah some fifty sepoys from one of the regiments stationed at Bangalore. The detachment from Bangalore is to take charge of the strong hill fort of Rayacottah, which they perform after a somewhat amusing fashion. Guard is kept from sunrise to sunset on the lone rock that towers some thousand feet above the broken ground around its base; but with the twilight the heavy gates are closed and locked, and the redcoated Sepoys are to be seen hastening down the winding path that leads from the battlement—crowned precipice to their humble cottages below. They say that there is a subterraneous passage near the massive gateway; and a story is told of the place, that may be given here as strongly illustrating one of the great holds which the British Government possesses on the fidelity of the native army. Down this mysterious chasm some five or six adventurous Sepoys had once rashly wandered in search of treasures said to be hidden there. They never came back, and their troubled spirits were nightly heard wailing around the rock. In those days the castle was guarded at all hours; and each night, as the clock struck twelve, the sentry at the gate heard a wild and unearthly voice asking three times over '*Where is my family?*' The boldest of the garrison were afraid, and three successive nights none durst answer; but at last one more courageous than the rest, when the sad question was once more put, '*Where is my family?*' loudly replied, '*In Raya Vellore, in Raya Vellore, drawing a pension, drawing a pension;*' and then, say the Sepoys the ghosts went down to their long home, glad, and for ever."

On the 21st August 1835, General Sir Henry Fane, G.C.B., became Commander-in-Chief in India, and in this year Lord William Bentinck departed, Sir Thomas Metcalfe acting as Governor-General, until the arrival of Lord Auckland, G.C.B., P.C., in the following year, the latter retaining office till 1842.

In October 1835, Lieutenant-General Sir R. W. O'Callaghan, K.C.B., inspected the troops at Bangalore, and subsequently issued the following General Order:—

'· The Commander-in-Chief has derived much gratification from his Inspection of the Troops at Bangalore, and has noticed with great satisfaction the clean and soldier-like appearance of the men and their steadiness under Arms as evidencing their efficient state of discipline. His Excellency particularly observed the excellent order of the Horse Artillery under Captain Seton—His Majesty's 13th Light Dragoons under Lieutenant-Colonel Brunton—His Majesty's 39th Regiment under Major Poole, and the 4th and 12th Regiments of Native Infanty."

1836.

The 4th M.N.I. remained in Bangalore till the 17th December 1836, when it marched to Cannanore, arriving there on the 9th January 1837.

On the 11th October 1836, Lieutenant-General Sir Peregrine Maitland, K.C.B., became Commander-in-Chief in Madras.

1837.

The Insurrection in Canara.

At the close of the Coorg War, the districts of Amara-Sulya, Puttur and Bantwala, which had been ceded to Coorg in 1799, were re-transferred to South Canara and, in 1837, discontent arose owing to the Collector of Mangalore demanding cash payments, whereas under the Coorg Rajas, assessment had been paid in kind.

Some malcontents succeeded in raising a disturbance, and made a successful attack, at Puttur, on the Collector and two companies of Sepoys who had advanced from Mangalore to meet them. The Collector and his troops were compelled to return to the coast, harassed on their flanks by increasing bands of raiders, one of which succeeded in reaching Mangalore, where the jail was opened and the Kutcherry burnt.

One of the ex-Dewans of Coorg, a Brahman, named Lakshmi Narayana, displeased with the ascendancy of his Coorg brother-Dewans, attempted to plan a simultaneous rising in Coorg, but this was speedily suppressed by the activity of the Superintendent, Captain Le Hardy, and the loyalty of Dewan Bopu and the general body of Coorgs.

On the 5th April 1837, a force, which included one hundred men of the 4th M.N.I. from Cannanore, was despatched under Colonel Green of the 4th to the relief of Mangalore, where, however, the garrison was having no real difficulty in holding its own. The raiders were soon dispersed, and the Cannanore detachment rejoined head-quarters on the suppression of the rebellion in May.

1838.

In 1838, the regiment was stationed at Cannanore, with a detachment of 81 men at Tellicherry, and remained there until early in 1840. The provinces of Malabar and Canara were then commanded by Major-General James Allan, C.B.

On the 21st December 1838, Lieutenant-General Sir Jasper Nicolls, K. C. B., who subsequently became Commander-in-Chief in India, took over the appointment of Commander-in-Chief in Madras, and issued the following General Order:—

"On assuming the command which was announced in the General Order of Government of yesterday, Lieutenant-General Sir Jasper Nicolls assures the Army of Fort St. George that he highly appreciates the distinction and honor thus conferred upon him.

The series of difficulties nobly overcome, and of victories gallantly achieved by it during the past century, proclaim the high qualities of the Madras Army, and must ever distinguish it in the pages of Indian history.

To uphold its honor, and ensure its efficiency, will be the Lieutenant-General's duty, it will also be his pride; and he confidently relies on the zealous co-operation of all ranks in the attainment of these most important objects.

The greatest security on the essential points is afforded by the flattering encomiums conferred upon the army by Lieutenant-General Sir Peregrine Maitland, from whose able and zealous exertions in the command, his successor confidently anticipates great and permanent advantages, both to the service and to himself."

The retiring Commander-in-Chief's order was as follows:—

"It affords Sir Peregrine Maitland much gratification, in resigning his command, to record the high opinion he entertains of the Madras Army, and his approbation of the general conduct of all ranks in the service—European and Native,—and it is a source of sincere satisfaction to the Lieutenant-General to know that in his Successor, Lieutenant-General Sir Jasper Nicolls, K.C.B., an officer so well known to the Indian Army, the Native Troops especially will find a chief, by whom they may feel assured their merits will be duly appreciated, and their interests thoroughly understood.

Sir Peregrine Maitland requests the General and Field Officers, and General Staff will accept his cordial acknowledgments for the able and zealous support they have at all times afforded him, and he desires to offer to the Army his sincerest wishes for its continued prosperity and honor."

1839.

The regiment was still stationed at Cannanore throughout 1839. On the 15th October of that year, Lieutenant-Colonel Dyce, who had served with the 4th for very many years, was selected to command the 2nd Madras European Regiment, then being formed at Arni.

From the 5th October 1839, Major-General Sir Hugh Gough, K.C.B., acted as Commander-in-Chief in Madras, in place of Sir Jasper Nicolls who, prior to his departure, issued the following order:—

"His Excellency the Commander-in-Chief being about to embark for Bengal, and probably to loosen the intimate communication which he has enjoyed with the Army of Madras, during his short command of it, is anxious to express the high satisfaction which that intercourse has given him.

His Excellency felt a pride in finding himself placed in authority over an Army which had produced, or supported so many eminent men—but he was and is confident, that similar ability, zeal, and energy are ready at this moment to rise into action when called for by difficulty or danger.

The Commander-in-Chief returns his best thanks to Officers Commanding Divisions and Forces for their steady attention to their various duties and for their maintenance of discipline.

Sir J. Nicolls will ever be anxious to hear that this Army continues to maintain its proud position amongst the Forces of our Gracious Sovereign in India—and with every hearty good wish for its honor and welfare, he bids it farewell!"

1840—1842.

On the 9th January 1840, the regiment moved to Bellary, where it remained until the 6th February 1842, when it marched to Madras, arriving on the 17th March 1842. On the 5th April 1842, orders were issued for the regiment to proceed to Moulmein, in relief of the 14th M.N.I., which was proceeding on service to China, but this order must subsequently have been cancelled.

On the 1st August 1840, Lieutenant-General Sir S. Whittingham, K.C.B., became Commander-in-Chief in Madras, but died on the 19th January 1841. Major-General J. Allan, C.B., and Major-General Robert Henry Dick, K.C.B., K.C.H.,—the latter a Pensinsula and Waterloo veteran, who fell at the battle of Sobraon on the 10th February 1846—acted for some time, and on the 24th September 1842, the Command-in-Chief was assumed by the Governor, Lieutenant-General the Marquis of Tweeddale, K.T., C.B.

Lord Ellenborough, P.C., had assumed the appointment of Governor-General on the 28th February 1842.

On the conclusion of the war with China by a treaty signed at Nankin, on the 29th August 1842, both the Governor-General and the Governor of Madras bore strong testimony to the gallantry of the Madras regiments employed in that campaign. In an order published by Lord Tweeddale on the 10th March 1843, issuing to the army a despatch received from Lieutenant-General Sir Hugh Gough, *Bart.*, G.C.B., Commanding the troops in China, he says:—

"It gives the Commander-in-Chief of the Madras Army the greatest satisfaction, to have this opportunity of adding to its records the marked approbation of the gallantry, good conduct and patience of its Officers and Soldiers, in dangers and difficulties, as now pronounced by the high authority of the Lieutenant-General.

Devotedness to the service, and attachment to their officers, have always marked the character of the Madras Sepoys. Their perseverance and gallantry before the enemy have secured for them the confidence of the British European Soldiers who fight side by side with them in assaulting a breach or who support them under fire when exposed to the attacks of the enemy.

It is the mutual confidence that exists beween the British Soldier and the Native Sepoy that makes them so formidable in the field of battle."

In this connection, the following extract from a General Order (No. 1235 of 1874), which sets forth the services of Brevet Lieutenant-Colonel James Hadfield, is given as an illustration of the conduct of the Madras troops in China:—

"He accompanied the 37th Madras Native Infantry to China in the first war in 1840: was present at the taking of Cheunpee; and at the storming of the forts of the Bocca Tigris in the Canton river; present at the action of the 25th May, 1841 before Canton, and engaged in the affair of the 30th May, when a large body of Chinese endeavoured to relieve the city. On this occasion, during a tremendous thunderstorm, the company of the 37th Regiment, Madras Native Infantry, which he commanded, was cut off from the rest of the force, and surrounded by several thousands of Chinese troops; but notwithstanding the rain prevented the sepoys from discharging their muskets, yet they repulsed every attack made upon them, until an hour or two after dusk, when they were extricated from their perilous position by a detachment of Royal Marines armed with percussion fire arms.

For this affair he was mentioned in despatches; received the brevet rank of Major and appointed Honorary A.-D.-C. to the Viceroy, Lord Ellenborough. Likewise, every native officer, non-commissioned officer and private belonging to his company were (*sic*) admitted to the advantages of the Order of Merit, and when Parliament voted their thanks to the army and navy engaged in this war, special mention was made of his gallant conduct and of that of his company by the Duke of Wellington in the House of Lords and by Lord Stanley in the House of Commons."

1843—1844.

On the 11th April 1843, the regiment left Madras on foreign service, and was stationed at Singapore till the 1st April in the following year:—

On the 9th May, 1844, it arrived at Hong-Kong, and was stationed there, with a detachment at Kowlung, till the 27th May 1845. A return, dated the 1st January 1845, shows that the headquarters of the regiment was at "Koolungsor," with about 500 men at Victoria, Hong-Kong.

The Land Forces in China were at this time commanded by Major-General George D'Aguilar, C.B.

In July 1844, Sir Henry (afterwards Viscount) Hardinge, G.C.B., became Governor-General, General Sir Hugh Gough, G.C.B., having meanwhile become Commander-in-Chief in India.

1845—1847.

In 1845, the 4th M.N.I. returned from service in China, and arrived at Vellore on the 20th August, where it remained till the 16th December 1847. In the latter year they had a detachment of 47 men at Arcot.

Major Burton, writing about 1908, says:—

"Fifty years ago the ditch at Vellore, which was full of water, contained a number of crocodiles. There was then a garrison order forbidding the killing of these reptiles, but the British subalterns—always bent on sport—used to catch them surreptitiously by an arrangement of hooks, baited with a goose, or used to shoot them when they came to the surface, a pariah dog, soundly beaten on the bank, serving as a dinner-bell to the hungry monsters. It is even said that no less a person than the Brigadier had been seen looking on at the sport from a place of concealment, although it was indulged in contrary to his orders. It is also related that when the gun was fired nightly after "Last Post," the crocodiles all sank to the bottom of the moat, probably owing to the noise and concussion, and soldiers wishing to break out of barracks were in the habit of taking advantage of this to swim across in safety, and so escape for the night, returning in the same manner when the morning gun was fired at reveille.

1848—1851.

Leaving Vellore on the 16th December 1847, the regiment marched to Harihar, where it arrived on the 22nd January 1848, and there it was stationed until the 9th October 1851.

In January 1848, the Earl of Dalhousie, P.C., assumed office as Governor-General. On the 23rd February 1848, Major-General Sir E. K. Williams, K.C.B., K.C.T. and S.,* became acting Commander-in-Chief in Madras, and the Honourable Henry Dickenson, Esq., became Governor. The outgoing Commander-in-Chief issued the following order, on his departure from Madras:—

"Lieutenant-General the Marquis of Tweeddale takes leave of the Madras Army with feelings which must lead him ever to retain the deepest interest in its welfare.

The anticipations with which His Lordship assumed Command have been most fully realized. He has found the Madras Army all that his knowledge of its history from the days of Clive and Coote, and England's illustrious Duke, had taught him to expect—and it is to him a most gratifying duty thus to place on record his conviction that he leaves it in a state of discipline and order, firmly based upon the most soldier-like and loyal principles; reflecting the highest honor upon all, both Natives and Europeans.

---

* Knight Commander of the Tower and Sword. This appears to have been a Portuguese order, but I have no further information about it.

His Lordship offers to the several General and Commanding Officers and to the Officers of the General Staff his cordial acknowledgments for the zealous and able support which they have uniformly afforded him—and he offers to all ranks his hearty good wishes for their continued prosperity and success."

On the 13th March 1848, Lieutenant-General Sir George Henry Frederick Berkeley, K.C.B., became Commander-in-Chief, and on the 7th April, Major-General the Right Honourable Sir Henry Pottinger, Bart., G.C.B., became Governor.

In 1849, General Sir Charles J. Napier, G.C.B., became Commander-in-Chief in India, being succeeded, on the 6th December 1850, by General Sir William Maynard Gomm, K.C.B., and on the 29th September 1851, Lieutenant-General Sir Richard Armstrong, C.B., K.C.T. and S., became Commander-in-Chief in Madras.

1852—1854.

The regiment left Harihar on the 9th October 1851, and marched into Coorg, arriving at Mercara on the 14th November, where it remained until the 17th December 1854. In 1853, a detachment of two companies was at Puttur, but I do not know if this was a permanent arrangement or not.

On the 27th October 1853, Lieutenant-General William Staveley, C.B., succeeded Sir Richard Armstrong as Commander-in-Chief, the latter, on his departure, issuing an order, of which the following is an extract:—

"Lieutenant-General Sir Richard Armstrong, K.C B., K.T. and S., having, consequent on failing health, tendered his resignation, Lieutenant-General William Staveley, C.B., has been nominated to succeed him in a Command which Sir Richard Armstrong has had the honor to exercise, with pride and gratification, for upwards of two years.

Since His Excellency assumed Command of the Army, many of all arms, European and Native, have with alacrity embarked for service in Burmah; where they have on all occasions evinced how fully they are embued with that courage and fidelity by which the long-established character of the Madras Army has been sustained........

The Lieutenant-General in thus bidding farewell to the Madras Army as its Commander-in-Chief, feels impelled to express his anxious and sincere wishes for the welfare and happiness of all who stand in its ranks. Sir Richard Armstrong can never lose sight of its merits, as herein recorded, and is firmly persuaded that by a continuance of its present good conduct and discipline, the Army will not only add to its already well-known honor and renown, but establish further claims to the consideration of the Government and of the Honorable Court of Directors.

On the death of General Staveley, on the 5th April 1854, Major-General W. H. Sewell, C.B., acted until the 23rd September 1854, when the office was assumed by Lieutenant-General the Hon. George Anson, afterwards Commander-in-Chief in India.

1855—1856.

The regiment arrived at Trichinopoly, from Mercara, on the 26th January 1855, and remained there until the 26th November 1856. In April 1856, there were detachments at Kumbakonam, Tranquebar, Tanjore and Negapatam. Its next station was Palamcottah, where it arrived on the 13th December, and remained until the 11th April following.

General the Hon. George Anson having become Commander-in-Chief in India, Major-General M. Beresford acted in Madras till the 10th June 1856, when Lieutenant-General Patrick Grant, C.B. (shortly afterwards, K.C.B.), assumed command at Fort St. George and retained the appointment till the 26th February 1861. He acted as Commander-in-Chief in India from June 1857 (Major-General Marcus Beresford acting for him at Madras), when General Anson died, until Lord Clyde arrived to take over the command. A short extract from his farewell order, on leaving Madras, may be given here:—

"The Services in the Field of the Troops of this Presidency employed in the suppression of the Rebellion and Mutiny are now matter of history, and the glowing terms in which they have been recognized must endure for ever, an imperishable record of the achievements of these noble Soldiers.

In the foremost rank, and in high distinction second to none engaged in that arduous struggle stand the Madras Fusiliers who fought under Neill, Havelock and Outram; while it never can be forgotten that, to their immortal honor, the Native Troops of the Madras Army have been, in the memorable words of the Earl of Ellenborough, 'faithful found among the faithless.'

These are facts of which every Soldier, European and Native, from the Private to the General, may justly feel proud; and it will ever be to me a source of the highest gratification that during the most critical and eventful period of British Rule in India, it has been my good fortune to have been at the head of an Army so distinguished for all the best qualities of faithful, brave and loyal Soldiers........"

Sir Patrick Grant could not, of course, have known how short is the memory of the Government of India, nor could he have foreseen that within half a century not one battalion of Madras Infantry would remain in the service.

The Right Hon. Charles John, Viscount Canning, P.C., became Governor-General on the 1st March 1856.

1857—1860.

In 1857, the regiment was once more ordered on foreign service and, embarking presumably at Madras, reached Rangoon on the 3rd May. For the greater part of its stay in Burma it appears to have been stationed at Thayetmyo, but a return, dated July 1859, states that regimental headquarters was at "Meaday," with a detachment of 157 men at Prome, while the regiment is stated to be under orders for Cuddapah—a fate which, however, it was destined to escape.

Foreign Service in Burma.

It remained in Burma until the 17th May 1860, and thus had no opportunity of taking part in the suppression of the great Mutiny of the Bengal Army in 1857-58. Reference has already been made to the gallant deeds and loyalty of the Madras Army during the Mutiny.

On the death of General the Hon. George Anson in 1857, Lieutenant-General Sir Colin Campbell, G.C.B. (afterwards Lord Clyde), had become Commander-in-Chief in India, and was succeeded by General Sir Hugh H. Rose, G.C.B. (afterwards Lord Strathnairn), in 1860.

On the 1st November 1858, the Hon. East India Company was abolished, and the direct Government of India was assumed by H. M. Queen Victoria, with Earl Canning as First Viceroy of India.

On the 5th November, the Governor-General issued to the Army a resolution by the General Court of the East India Company, expressing their thanks to the servants and officers of the Company of every rank and in every capacity, and stated that:—

"The Governor-General is satisfied that, amongst all, there is but one common feeling of acknowledgement of the just, considerate, and liberal treatment, which has ever characterised the Great Company which has now ceased to govern the British Territories in India."

In March 1859, Sir Charles Edward Trevelyan, K.C.B., succeeded Lord Harris as Governor of Madras.

1861—1865.

For the best part of another twenty years, the regiment remained in the Presidency without seeing any active service. I have quoted elsewhere (Part II—1857) the remarks of General Burton on the scandalous manner in which Madras regiments were kept in the background until Sir Neville Chamberlain felt impelled to protest, but I may add that in this respect matters have remained unchanged. The Government of Madras, which has never displayed the slightest interest in its own regiments, has witnessed, without protest or comment, the gradual disbandment of the whole of the Madras Infantry and, while it was known to every soldier that one or two of these regiments fell short of the general standard of the Army, the cause of this was equally well known. The men have *always* been good soldiers, but no regiment can suffer from a succession of officers, found unfit for service in more favoured corps, without losing its former efficiency. There is nothing, however, more difficult to contend with than prejudice, especially when based on ignorance.

On the 28th May 1860, the regiment reached Madras, where it remained until the 13th January 1865, when it marched to Secunderabad.

From the 27th February till the 26th December 1861, Major-General R. Budd (a former Commanding Officer of the 4th), acted as Commander-in-Chief in Madras, being succeeded by Lieutenant-General Sir James Hope Grant, G.C.B., who, on assuming the command, issued the following order:—

"Lieutenant-General Sir James Hope Grant, G. C. B., this day assumes the Command-in-Chief of Her Majesty's Madras Army.

He enters on the exercise of his duties with pride and satisfaction. He cannot but appreciate the honor of having been selected for the Command of an Army so greatly distinguished for its fidelity and good discipline during some of the more eventful periods of British rule in India. A portion of the Madras Army has already served under Sir Hope Grant's orders, both in Bengal during the Mutiny, and in the late War in China. Those Services were performed to his entire satisfaction. From Divisional and other Commanders, Sir Hope Grant feels assured he will receive the like judicious support, and from all other ranks a continuance of that orderly conduct, which on every suitable occasion have called forth the high commendations of his predecessors in Command."

On the 18th February 1861, Sir William Thomas Denison, K.C.B., became Governor of Madras and, in 1862, the Earl of Elgin and Kincardine, K.T., G.C.B., P.C., became Governor-General, and remained in office till the 12th January 1864, when he was succeeded by Sir John Laird Mair Lawrence, *Bart.*, G.C.B., K.S.I., (afterwards Lord Lawrence). On the 25th May 1865, Lieutenant-General Sir John Gaspard LeMarchant, G.C.M.G., K.C.B., who had previously been Governor and Commander-in-Chief of Malta, became Commander-in-Chief of the Madras Army. In the same year, General Sir W. Rose Mansfield, K.C.B. (afterwards Lord Sandhurst), became Commander-in-Chief in India.

1866—1874.

The regiment arrived at Secunderabad on the 13th March 1865, and remained there until the 17th February 1871, when it marched to Bellary, by Wings, and arrived there on the 15th March 1871. The Right Wing left Bellary on the 19th December 1874 and reached Palaveram on the 27th January 1875, while the Left Wing, leaving Bellary on the 26th December 1874, arrived on the 3rd February 1875.

On the 8th November 1867, Lieutenant-General W. McCleverty succeeded to the command-in-chief in Madras, and was in turn succeeded, on the 22nd May 1871, by Lieutenant-General (afterwards Field-Marshal) Sir Frederick Paul Haines, K.C.B.

The Abyssinian Campaign took place in 1867-68, the only Madras troops employed being some companies of the Q.V.O. Sappers and Miners. The only officer of the regiment who saw service on this campaign was Ensign J. E. Porteous.

In 1869, the Earl of Mayo, K.P., became Viceroy, but was assassinated in the Andaman Islands on the 8th February 1872. Pending the arrival of his successor, the Earl of Northbrook, P.C., Lord Napier of Merchistoun, the Governor of Madras, acted as Viceroy, his place being taken (from February to May 1872) by Sir Alexander John Arbuthnot, K.C.S.I., Madras Civil Service. In May 1872, Lord Hobart became Governor of Madras.

General Lord Napier of Magdala, G.C.B., G.C.S.I., was appointed Commander-in-Chief in India in 1870 and, in that capacity, visited Madras in January 1874.

1875—1878.

On the 24th March 1875, the Headquarters and Left Wing of the regiment left Palaveram to proceed on foreign service, and disembarked at Rangoon on the 7th April, relieving the Wing of the 39th Madras Infantry, and remaining there till the 26th March 1877, when they were transferred to Moulmein, which was their station from the 28th March 1877 till the 27th March 1878.

Foreign Service in Burma.

The Right Wing of the regiment left Palaveram on the 26th February 1876, and disembarked at Rangoon on the 2nd March, where it remained till the 11th February 1877. On the 25th February 1877, it reached Tounghoo, which was its station until the 10th February 1878.

The regiment once more found itself reassembled at Bangalore in 1878, the Headquarters and Left Wing arriving there on the 6th April, and the Right Wing on the following day. Here it remained till called upon to take part in the Afghan War.

In 1875, the Duke of Buckingham and Chandos, P.C., became Governor of Madras.

On the 2nd May 1876, Lieutenant-General (afterwards Field Marshal) Sir Neville B. Chamberlain, G.C.B., became Commander-in-Chief in Madras. In the same year the Earl of Lytton, G.C.B., became Viceroy, and General Sir Frederick Paul Haines, K.C.B., became Commander-in-Chief in India.

1879—1880.
The Afghan War.

On the 3rd September 1879, the murder of Sir Louis Cavignari and other members of the British Mission to Kabul caused hostilities to be renewed against the Afghans.

For this campaign the Madras Army was ordered to furnish three regiments of Native Infantry, and three companies of Sappers and Miners, the regiments selected being the 1st, 4th and 15th Madras Infantry, the latter, it will be remembered, being the former second battalion of the 4th in the days of two battalion regiments. Colonel W. A. Gib of the Madras Staff Corps was selected to command this force and was appointed Brigadier-General.

The 4th regiment of Madras Native Infantry, 609 strong, left Bangalore on the 8th October 1879, under the command of Lieutenant-Colonel G. C. Hodding and with the following British Officers, namely: Majors Godson, Barnet and Blenkinsop, Captain Porteous, and Lieutenants Passy and Wilmot. It proceeded by rail to Jhelum, whence it marched to Ali Musjid by way of Peshawar and Shergai, and on arrival there was placed in the 2nd Division, commanded by Major-General R. O. Bright, C.B.

At Ali Musjid it remained until January 1880, without anything of special interest occurring, the principal duties performed being the garrisoning of small forts and pickets in the vicinity.

On the 14th January 1880, the Mohmands, having risen, threatened to attack Dakka. A body of 5,000 of these tribesmen crossed the Kabul River and appeared near Kam Dakka, and another of about 3,000 occupied the Gara Heights, three miles south-east of Dakka Fort.

Dakka, January 1880.

General Ross, then commanding the Reserve Division, decided that the troops in Dakka, 650 strong, under Colonel Boisragon, 30th Punjab Infantry, should attack the Mohmands on the Gara Heights, while a force under Brigadier-General J. Doran, C.B., should move northwards from Landi Kotal, via the Anjiri Kandao and Shilman Ghakhe Passes, upon Kam Dakka, thus intercepting the enemy's retreat.

The Landi Kotal force, which included 200 men of the 4th M. N. I., under Colonel Hodding, marched from the old fort on the Loargai plateau at 4-30 a.m., on the 15th January. Owing to the darkness of the night the advance was extremely slow, and the head of the column only arrived on the Anjiri Kandao at 7-40 a.m. At 8-45 a.m. the descent was commenced, the troops moving in single file along a mere goat track. Many baggage animals were lost over the precipices, and the rearguard took 67 hours to cover a distance of only 17 miles.

At the foot of the Torsappar, General Doran received information that the enemy were occupying the Shilman Ghakhe in force, and a halt was accordingly made to let the mountain guns come up. At 10-30 a.m. the advance was resumed and at about 11-30 Colonel Boisragon's guns were heard. It was nearly 1 o'clock when the gorge of the Shilman Ghakhe came in sight. In the pass, some opposition was offered by the enemy, but was speedily overcome, and by 2-30 p.m., the enemy were also driven from the heights north of the Shilman Ghakhe, and the pass cleared.

In the meantime, General Doran was informed by heliograph that the Gara Heights were taken, and that the Dakka force (which had attacked too soon to enable the Landi Kotal force to co-operate effectively) was between them and the Kabul river. At 2-45 p.m., dense masses of flying enemy were seen moving down the right bank of the river and across the mouth of the nullah running from the Shilman Ghakhe to the Kabul river. So, after waiting in vain for the baggage for some time, General Doran commenced to descend about 3-20 p.m. The mouth of the nullah was not reached till nearly 5 p.m., when some damage was inflicted on the enemy. At 6-20 p.m., the force joined Colonel Boisragon's detachment at Kam Dakka. The baggage was ordered to remain for the right at Arbul but none of it got so far that night or even the next.

The Official History says:—

"Very great difficulty was experienced by Colonel G. S. Hodding, Commanding 4th Madras Infantry, who was in charge of the baggage with 200 of his regiment, in getting the animals over the extremely difficult road. The almost impossible nature of the path beyond the Anjiri Kandao caused an immense block of animals at that place, and the confusion was increased by a false alarm causing a panic among the mule drivers and followers in which some loads were lost, and many drivers deserted."

The night of the 15th was spent on the Anjiri Kandao, without water, and on the next day, in spite of the exertions of Colonel Hodding and his officers, they only covered 4 miles. On the 17th, they struggled over the Shilman Ghakhe and with the assistance of 100 men of the 31st Punjab Infantry, who came out to meet them, reached Kam Dakka during the night.

Meanwhile General Doran had decided, on the 16th January, to pursue the Mohmands across the river, and skin rafts were accordingly constructed by the Madras Sappers, on which 600 men and the Sappers, under Colonel Boisragon, crossed the river before nightfall and occupied the village of Rena, which was destroyed early next morning. The force then re-crossed the river and marched back to Dakka.

General Doran's column returned to Landi Kotal on the 18th January, by the Gara Pass and Haft Chah, the baggage being sent round by Dakka.

Vibart says of this expedition :—

"Three hundred of the 4th M. N. I. under Col. Hodding had formed the baggage-guard, and had a very hard and uninteresting time of it. 300 of the 1st M. N. I. formed the rearguard of the column. Both regiments were deservedly complimented—the 4th for getting the baggage over a very difficult country, and the 1st for its marching power."

The following is a short extract from the orders issued by the General Officer Commanding :—

"The Detachment 4th M. N. I. under the command of Lieutenant-Colonel Hodding was entrusted with the unpleasant duties of rearguard. So onerous and difficult in this case were those duties that it was only by dint of the most incessant exertions by night as well as by day that the rearguard was enabled to rejoin the column at Kam-Dakka after an absence of nearly three days."

The other officers of the regiment present on this expedition were Captain Porteous, Lieutenant Passy, and Surgeon Dill.

On the night of the 26th March 1880, a determined attack was made by Khugianis and Shinwaris on Fort Battye, a very weak post, held by only 100 of the 4th Madras Native Infantry and 50 Sowars of the 4th Bengal Cavalry, commanded by Major E. B. Blenkinsop, 4th M.N.I., but fortunately reinforced for the moment by 150 of the 31st Punjab Infantry under Lieutenant F. C. C. Angelo, who were passing through.

Fort Battye, March 1880.

The attack began at 11-30 p.m., with a sudden rush of the enemy from the road up to the south wall of the fort. The garrison turned out immediately, but not before the enemy, having established themselves under the cover of the wall, poured in a heavy fire, coupled with showers of stones, into the camp. Lieutenant Angelo and three men were killed, and Subadar-Major Sher Singh and several others severely hurt, though fortunately most of the Afghan bullets flew high.

At the same time another party of the enemy rushed the transport lines, and there killed several men. It was not long, however, before the native infantry, gaining the walls, drove the enemy back, while the cavalry detachment opened fire from the north and west faces of the fort whenever opportunity offered.

Finding that their assault had failed, the Afghans soon began to retreat, and in a short time they were scattered in all directions over the hills. Several prisoners were captured the next morning by mounted patrols from the fort, and from other reports it appeared that the tribesmen numbered some 1,200, of whom, according to their own account, 25 were killed and 40 wounded. One Havildar (Ghouse Khan), one sepoy and one follower of the 4th were killed, and several were wounded.

Major Blenkinsop heliographed to Safed Sang for reinforcements, which were sent up. He pointed out the weakness of the fort and recommended a stronger permanent garrison. The wall of the fort on the south side, against which the principal attack was made, was so low that nearly the whole of the east face could be enfiladed by an enemy posted behind rocks 100 or 150 yards distant on the plain. The transport lines on the east face of the fort were also a constant source of weakness, as the space was filled with carts and animals, under cover of which the enemy were able to come up close and fire.

Elachipur. Some time in March 1880, the date not being exactly known, the 4th M.N.I. took part in an expedition to Elachipur against the brother of the late Khan of Lalpura, but owing to the enemy having dispersed, the troops returned to Jalalabad without firing a shot.

The officers who accompanied the regiment on this expedition were: Colonels Hodding and Barnett; Captain Porteous; Lieutenants Passy and Eardley-Wilmot, and Surgeon Dill.

The Waziri Country. As a punishment for the attack made on Fort Battye, a fine of 5,000 rupees was imposed on the villages in the Waziri country. They, however, declined to pay; and an expedition, consisting of troops from Jalalabad and Gandamak, including the 4th M.N.I., was sent into their country on the 4th April. On the 5th, an envoy from the Waziris came into camp, but left without consenting to pay, and the force consequently commenced to work up to the neighbouring forts and villages, meeting with no resistance to speak of. A number of towers were blown up during the advance.

On the 6th April, a messenger came in from the enemy with 3,500 rupees and a promise to pay the remainder, so the force returned to camp. On the 7th, the balance of the money demanded was paid, and the force returned to Gandamak and Rozabad.

Besud, May 1880.

In May 1880, the Mulla Khalil having preached a jehad in Kunar, had occupied Besud and Goshta with a large number of Safis.

On the 9th May, the 4th M.N.I. were ordered from Rozabad to Jalalabad, and on the 14th, General Doran sent 200 rifles of the 1st and 4th M. N. I. under Major G. Tyndall, 1st M.N.I., across the river in rafts, to occupy the foot of Pir Muhammad Khan.

On the 18th May, General Doran received orders to attack the enemy on the following day, and, it being his intention to take them by surprise, he marched from Dabela Kala at 4-30 a.m., with 75 sabres, 2 guns, and 542 rifles, including 92 of the 4th M.N.I. under Captain Porteous. At 6 a.m. he came in view of the enemy, about 2,000 strong, from a hill about one mile east of Beninga.

An attack was made, the detachment of the 4th M. N. I. forming the general reserve, and after some fighting the enemy were driven back, pursued with some success by the cavalry, and took refuge in the fort, where they were overpowered.

The force marched back to Dabela Kala at 10 a.m.

On the 21st May, Azimulla Khan Kala, a strong fort on the northern side of the Paikot pass, was destroyed, and on the 22nd a similar fate befell the fort of Banaras Khan. On the evening of the 22nd, the force commenced to re-cross the river, which was now a torrent 400 yards wide, to Jalalabad, an operation which lasted till the 24th and to the difficulty of which the following Brigade Order by Brigadier-General J. Doran bears witness:—

'Brigadier-General J. Doran wishes to convey his warmest thanks to the troops employed during the recent operations in Besud. In those few days every attribute of good soldiers was called for and displayed. The endurance of the troops was tested by severe marching and exposure under the fiercest sun. Their discipline was perfect, their steadiness was proved by the ascertained effect of their fire, their gallantry where opportunity afforded was conspicuous and seen by all. The passage of the Cabul river with the very scanty appliances available was in itself a feat of which the troops may well be proud................

The Brigadier-General believes that no record of such a feat can be found in our Military History. The troops will hereafter learn that Brigadier-General Doran has become witness in his despatches to their excellent services in no measured terms. He is confident that no page in the history of this campaign will bear higher testimony to the sterling value of our troops than that which tells of the operations in Besud in May 1880. Brigadier-General Doran desires that this order may be entered in the records of every corps concerned."

Minor Expeditions.

After his defeat by General Doran, the Mulla Khalil was said to have gone to Kama and, on the 2nd June 1880, an expedition, which included 100 rifles of the 4th M. N. I. from Jalalabad, under Major J. Godson, assembled at Girdikats. On the 3rd, the river was crossed by two ferries, and on the 5th, the inhabitants of the district came into camp and tendered their submission. The objects of the expedition having been gained, the troops re-crossed the river on the 6th and 7th June, and marched back to the respective stations.

On the 26th June, the 4th M. N. I. left Jalalabad for Safed Sung (Gandamak) and from that time until the 17th August was engaged in occupying that place and intermediate stations, besides taking part in the expeditions to Kailagu, Waziri, and Pachiri, of which no details appear to have been recorded.

Close of the Campaign. On the 17th August 1880, the 4th M. N. I. left Safed Sung on its final march to India, and, after a few days' halt at Hassan Abdul and other places, owing to the prevalence of cholera, reached Bangalore on the 19th October, 1880, after an absence of one year and eleven days.

Although unfortunate in having no opportunity of taking part in any general action during the campaign, the 4th, as will have been seen, did a great amount of useful work with minor expeditions, and thoroughly earned the addition to its honours of "*Afghanistan 1879-80.*"

It is to be regretted that there is no more precise record of its doings, nor has any casualty list been discovered, the only fact known in that respect being that Major Godson, 2 Havildars, and 2 Sepoys died of fatigue and exposure.

1881.

Throughout this year, the regiment was stationed at Bangalore, with one very picturesque break in the monotony of garrison life, when it was called upon to take part in the installation of the young Maharaja of Mysore. Leaving Bangalore on the 14th March, it arrived at Mysore on the 24th, and remained till the 28th, returning to Bangalore on the 4th April.

In 1880, the Marquess of Ripon, K.G., P.C., became Viceroy. Major-General W. Payn acted as Commander-in-Chief in Madras from the 3rd February till the 8th November 1881, when he was relieved by Lieutenant-General (afterwards Field Marshal) Sir Frederick Sleigh Roberts, V.C., K.C.B., C.I.E. In 1881, General Sir Donald M. Stewart, G.C.B., C.I.E., became Commander-in-Chief in India.

1882.

The Egyptian Expeditionary Force.

The 4th Madras Native Infantry which, on the 1st January 1882, was in Bangalore with a small detachment of 20 men at Hosur, was selected to form part of the Indian contingent which proceeded to Egypt in August 1882.

In Reserve at Aden. The Left Wing, with Colonel R. Griffith, officiating Commandant, Major R. M. Clerk, Lieutenants Passy, Stevens, Burrows and Holloway, embarked at Madras on the *S. S. Asia* on August 18th, and did not arrive at Aden until the 8th September, having, we are informed, "been delayed by adverse currents," though the time taken for the voyage might well lead one to suppose that they were on one of the old "wind-jammers."

The right wing, with Major Barnett and Captain Porteous, embarked at Madras on the *S. S. Chupra* on the 25th August and arrived at Aden on the 11th September, having thus a slightly more rapid voyage than the left wing.

Both, however, being too late to take part in the campaign, the regiment remained at Aden as a reserve, greatly to the disappointment of both officers and men, until the 24th September, when, the war being over, it embarked under Major Barnett for Madras on the *S. S. Clan MacDonald*, arriving at Madras on the 7th, and at Bangalore on the 11th October 1882.

Colonel Hodding, the Commandant, joined at Aden on the arrival of the regiment and left for Europe on the 24th September. Major Blenkinsop also joined at Aden and returned to India with the regiment. Colonel Griffith was appointed Commandant at Suez, and Major Mildmay Clerk became Baggage-Master at Ismailia and subsequently D. A. Q. M. G. and Railway Transport Officer, for his performance of which duties he was favourably mentioned by Major-General Macpherson.

1883.

The year 1883 marks an important change in the status of the 4th M.N.I., and brings to a close its long and honourable record as an Infantry Regiment. On the 13th June 1883, the 4th Regiment of Madras Native Infantry was changed into a Pioneer battalion, with the title of the 4th Regiment of Madras Native Infantry (Pioneers). The incongruity of labelling a regiment as both "Infantry" and "Pioneers" was removed at a later date.

The desire to become a Pioneer regiment appears to have arisen in the regiment as far back as 1879, in Afghanistan, where it had a great deal of what was really Pioneer work to do, and where it frequently came in contact with the 32nd Sikh Pioneers. This resulted in application being made to the Commander-in-Chief in Madras—Lieutenant-General Sir Neville Chamberlain—and, with his cordial support, the suggestion was forwarded to the Commander-in-Chief in India. It was not till 1882 that approval and sanction came from the Secretary of State for India and in the following year, when Lieutenant-General Sir F. S. Roberts, V.C., was Commander-in-Chief in Madras, both the 4th M.N.I., and 1st M.N.I., became Pioneer Regiments.

Part I.

CHAPTER VI.

THE 4th REGIMENT OF MADRAS NATIVE INFANTRY (PIONEERS).

13th June 1883—1885.

THE 4th REGIMENT OF MADRAS INFANTRY (PIONEERS).

1885—1901.

THE 4th MADRAS PIONEERS.

1901—2nd October 1903.

1883.

When, on the 13th June 1883, the 4th M.N.I., was converted into a Pioneer battalion, it was still stationed in Bangalore, and was there given its first experience, as a Pioneer Regiment, of Pioneer work.

On the 28th November, the regiment marched to Krishnarajapuram to prepare a site for a Camp of Exercise, returning to Bangalore on the 8th December and remaining there till the end of the year.

1884—1885.

From the 3rd to the 25th January 1884, the 4th Pioneers were at a Camp of Exercise at Krishnarajapuram, and during this year they were busily employed on Pioneer work, constructing the Agram entrenchments at Bangalore.

On the 5th October 1884, the regiment left Bangalore under orders for work on the Harnai railway. Karachi was reached on the 13th October, and here a halt was made till the 22nd November, owing to the prevalence of cholera further up the line. Leaving Karachi on the 22nd November, work was started on the 24th in the Nari Gorge, where the regiment remained till the 20th December. From the 25th December 1884 to the 7th April 1885, they were at Sunari; and from the 17th April till the 23rd November 1885, they worked in the Bhostan-Peshin valley with the 23rd and 32nd Sikh Pioneers.

Harnai Railway.

From the 29th November 1885 till the 4th January 1886, work was carried on at Pungah, and on the 7th January they reached a notoriously unhealthy spot called Dalojal. Up till now the health of the men had been remarkably good, but at Dalojal there was so much serious sickness that it was decided that the regiment should return to the Madras Presidency, and accordingly they left Harnai on the 6th February 1886, and reached Trichinopoly on the 26th of the same month.

Fuller details of the work done by the regiment are given in the section dealing with Pioneer work.

In 1884, the Earl of Dufferin, K.P., G.C.B., G.C.M.G., P.C., became Viceroy of India, and was succeeded by the Marquis of Lansdowne, G.C.M.G., in 1888.

In 1885 the title of the regiment was again changed, and they became the 4th Regiment of Madras Infantry (Pioneers).

In 1885, General Sir Frederick S. Roberts, V.C., G.C.B., C.I.E. (afterwards Earl Roberts of Kandahar, Waterford and Pretoria) became Commander-in-Chief in India

1886—1888.

After their arrival at Trichinopoly on the 26th February 1886, the regiment was engaged in completing the lines of the 30th Madras Infantry. On the 11th December 1886, the Left Wing of the Regiment (321 strong) proceeded to Madras on garrison duty, returning to Trichinopoly on the 17th January 1887.

The Right Wing proceeded to Bangalore on garrison duty on the 1st March 1887, returning to Trichinopoly on the 30th of the same month.

1889.
The Lushai Expedition.

In 1888, a Lieutenant Stewart was murdered by the Lushais, while surveying. It was decided, therefore, to send a punitive force, to avenge the murder, in the open season of 1888-89.

The 4th Madras Pioneers received orders to send a detachment to join the Lushai Expeditionary Force, and accordingly this party, composed as shown in the margin, left Trichinopoly on the 3rd January 1889, and proceeded to Lushai in the Chittagong Hill Tracts.

Capt. G. B. Stevens, Comdg.
Lieut. C. T. Swan.
" G. V. Holmes.
Surg. F. C. Pereira.
Subr. Mahomed Akbar.
" Sangili.
Jemr. Muthusami.
" Abdur Rahim.
" Munisami.
1 Hospital Assistant.
200 N. C. O.s and men.
27 Followers.

There they were employed from the 28th January till the 20th April 1889, during the whole of which time they were hard at work, making roads, and on the construction of a fort at Lunglet. During this period they only had one day's holiday. On the 15th March a picked party of 20 rifles, under Lieutenant G. V. Holmes, was sent with a punitive column to Howsata's village, which was shelled and occupied on the 22nd March.

Not a single man of the detachment was lost, and the health of the men was generally good, and in spite of their being underfed owing to the rice ration having been reduced to 1½ lbs. from 2 lbs. (which it had always been before), they worked willingly and well, and upheld the reputation of the regiment.

The following is a copy of the farewell order by Colonel U. W. Tregear, Commanding Lushai Expeditionary Force, dated Camp Lunglet, 9th April 1889:—

"Captain G. B. Stevens, and Officers, 4th Madras Pioneers, on the eve of your departure for your Presidency, I am anxious to address a few words to you and the Native Commissioned and Non-Commissioned Officers of your detachment. You joined the force on the 28th January last, and since then, have been continuously employed, and I can bear testimony to the hard and excellent work performed by your men. The cheerful spirit which has at all times been shown by all ranks reflects great credit upon your corps, and when making my final report on this expedition I shall have much pleasure in bringing the good service of your detachment to the favourable notice of His Excellency the Commander-in-Chief."

The detachment returned to Trichinopoly on the 9th May 1889.

The following is an extract from the General Order by the Government of India, dated 5th July 1889:

Field Operations—Lushai.

No. 592. The Governor-General in Council is pleased to direct the publication, for general information, of the subjoined correspondence relating to the operations recently carried out by the Lushai Expeditionary Force, under the command of Colonel U. W. Tregear, 9th Bengal Infantry.

From Major-General E. H. H. Collen, Secretary to the Government of India, Military Department, to the Adjutant-General in India (166-L, dated Simla, the 1st July 1889):—

"In acknowledging the receipt of your letter No. 2631-A, dated the 19th ultimo, with Colonel Tregear's Report of the Operations of the Lushai Expeditionary Force, I am to say that the Government of India concur in the opinion expressed by the Commander-in-Chief, that the objects of the expedition have been accomplished; and I am to request that, under His Excellency's orders, an expression of the acknowledgments of the Governor-General-in-Council may be conveyed to Colonel Tregear and the officers and men under his command, for the excellent manner in which the operations have been carried out.

2. Colonel Tregear's report will be published in an early Gazette."

From Major-General W. K. Elles, C. B., Adjutant-General in India, to the Secretary to the Government of India, Military Department (No. 2631-A, dated Simla, the 19th June 1889):—

"In continuation of this office letter No. 1039-A., dated the 10th April 1889, forwarding Colonel Tregear's report on the punitive expedition conducted by him to Howsata's village, I have the honour, by direction of the Commander-in-Chief, to submit for the information of the Government of India, a further report from Colonel Tregear of the operations in detail of the Expeditionary Force under his command up to the date of its return to India.

2. The objects of the expedition were:—
   (i) To construct a road from Demagiri in the direction of the Shendu country.
   (ii) To punish Howsata and Jahoota for the murder of the late Lieut. Stewart.
   (iii) To establish an advanced post to be garrisoned during the rains.

3. From the present report, together with that submitted on the 10th April last, it will be seen that these objects have been fully effected. Dense bamboo jungle, and the hilly nature of the country passed through offered considerable difficulties, but nevertheless a road of easy gradient, practicable for laden elephants, has been constructed, and of a width and description, which, it is hoped, will ensure its resisting, in a great measure, the action of the rains. Howsata's village has been destroyed, and Lieutenant Stewart's gun recovered from the Chief's grave. Finally an advanced post has been established at Lunglet, 41 miles from Demagiri, and garrisoned by the Frontier Police.

4. This season's operations, which commenced on the 11th January, were brought to a close on the 5th May, when the last of the troops sailed from Chittagong for Calcutta.

5. In the absence of opposition, the expedition must, in great measure, be regarded more in the nature of a *pioneering* one, although the punitive measures undertaken were fully effected in the destruction of the villages of Howsata and Jahoota, and will, it is hoped, serve as a deterrent against the commission of further raids by the offending tribes in future.

6. Colonel Tregear is to be congratulated on the satisfactory manner in which he has carried out the work which devolved upon him as Commander of the force, and the Commander-in-Chief would also bring to the notice of the Government of India the conduct of officers, regimental, staff, and departmental, all of whom without exception, appear to have done good work. The behaviour of the troops was excellent, and the difficult and trying marches which fell to them were accomplished with commendable cheerfulness."

For his services on this expedition Captain G. B. Stevens was mentioned in despatches.

1889.

On the 3rd October 1889, a detachment, 270 strong, under Major E. G. Blenkinsop, **Periyar Project.** left Trichinopoly to work on the Periyar Project and rejoined the regiment at Bangalore in 1890. Further particulars are given in the section devoted to Pioneer work.

1890.

On the 6th January 1890, the Headquarters of the regiment left Trichinopoly, and moved to Bangalore, where they were joined by the detachment from the Periyar in the following March.

While in Bangalore, work was carried on to complete the South Lines at Agram.

1890—1891.
Operations in the Chin Hills.

In the open season of 1888-89, at the same time as Colonel Tregear's force proceeded **Previous Expeditions.** against the Lushais, another force under General Faunce was sent against the Siyins, who had a number of Burmese prisoners. All the villages of the Siyins were destroyed, and a post was established at Fort White.

In the open season of 1889-90, another expedition, under General Symons started from Kan, established a post at Haka, and visited Falam. This force was met at Haka by another from Bengal, which had advanced from Lunglet under General Tregear.

In 1890, Mr. Wetherell, a political officer, was murdered by the Thettas, and from the generally disturbed state of the tribes in the Chin Hills it was evident that a further series of expeditions would have to be made in the ensuing open season. As these expeditions necessitated a great amount of road-making, it was decided that Pioneers should be employed, and the reputation of the 4th as Pioneers being now well established, orders were given for a Wing of that regiment to proceed to Burma.

Accordingly, on the 20th November 1890, the Right Wing, under the command of Captain G. B. Stevens, and composed as shown in the margin, left Bangalore for service in the Chin Hills. Two companies, under Lieutenant Churchill, with Lieutenant Holmes, proceeded to the post at Fort White, and the remaining two companies and Wing Headquarters to Haka.

Capt. G. B. Stevens, *Comdg.*
Lieut. F. Churchill.
  „ G. V. Holmes.
  „ R. F. Rainey.
Surg. M. J. Kelawala
Subr. Ramasami.
  „ Mahomed Salar.
  „ Abdul Sattar Khan. (*died at Madras en route.*)
  „ Abdur Rahim.
Jemr. Munisami.
  „ Abdul Sharif.
  „ Abdul Aziz.
1st Grade Hospl. Asst. Nagappa Pillai.
400 N.C.O.s, Rank & File, and Followers.
(Lieutenant A. Mears, joined subsequently).

Here, in addition to sending out parties with punitive columns, of which fuller details are given hereafter, an immense amount of Pioneer work was completed.

Between January and March 1891, the two detachments, working from Haka and Fort White respectively, constructed a road uniting the two posts, the two sections meeting at Falam, while the Fort White companies also cut a road through the jungle to Tiddim, and built a post there.

It had been intended that the Wing should return to India at the end of the open season, when their roadmaking had been completed, but, owing to the disastrous outbreak in Manipur, and the fear of a general rising of the Chins, it was decided that they should be kept on as a reinforcement to the garrisons of the Chin Hills.

On the commencement of the rains, therefore, the Headquarter companies concentrated at Haka, sending a detachment of 50 rifles, under Lieutenant Rainey, to Rowvan, while the other two companies were split up between Fort White and the posts on the road into the Kale valley.

In spite of the rains a great deal of work was carried out, the more important works of the Haka detachment being two posts, each for a garrison of 50 rifles, at Bwelet and Yokwa, while the *chef-d'oeuvre* of the Fort White companies was a pukka stone Telegraph Office and Treasury. Further details of the work performed will be found in the section on Pioneer work.

1891.

The following are fuller details of the parties who accompanied the various columns sent out in the open season:—

Thetta Column. In February 1891, a column under Colonel Mainwaring, 39th Garhwalis, consisting of 200 rifles, marched to Thetta village via Gangaw, and were joined en route by 50 Pioneers under Lieutenant R. F. Rainey. Steps were taken to punish the Thettas for the murder of Mr. Wetherell, and the column then made an expedition into the Baungshe country, advancing as far as Shurkwa, without meeting much resistance.

In February 1891, a column under Captain Rundall, 2nd 4th Gurkhas, consisting of 150 Gurkhas, 150 39th Garhwalis, and 50 Pioneers under Lieutenant G. V. Holmes, with two mountain guns, was actively employed against the Kanhaws. The column was most successful, the whole Kanhaw tribe surrendering after their principal village had been captured and destroyed. There was only one casualty on our side, a Havildar of the 2nd 4th Gurkhas being killed, while the enemy sustained a loss of 12 killed and many wounded.

Kanhaw Column.

In March 1891, two columns were sent out, one from Fort White, commanded by Captain Rundall, of the same composition as the Kanhaw column, with Lieutenant F. Churchill commanding the detachment of 4th Pioneers; and the other from Haka, under Colonel Mainwaring, similarly constituted, and with Lieutenant R. F. Rainey commanding the Pioneer detachment.

Tashon Column.

These two columns marched simultaneously, by the road cut by the 4th Pioneers, to Falam village, in order to enforce the surrender of the Tashon tribe. Effecting a junction at Falam, the force remained out for about a fortnight, meeting with no opposition, and having no casualties.

Jemadar Abdullah Khan, with 25 rifles 4th Pioneers, accompanied Colonel Mainwaring's column in April 1891, when he proceeded to the relief of Lieutenant Mocatta and his column, who had been attacked at Tlang-Tlang village. Lieutenant Mocatta's column was hampered with 17 wounded men, and had had to burn their dead on the march, and, had it not been for the arrival of the relief column, the whole detachment might have been lost.

Tlang-Tlang Column.

The following is an extract from the report by Captain F. Rundall, commanding North Chin Hills, (No. 274, dated Fort White, 23rd March 1891) :—

"..........*4th Madras Pioneers.*—I was much struck by the smartness, good discipline, and efficiency of this regiment. I have seen the men under fire and I have seen them toiling at the severe labour of road-making in these difficult hills, and I found that whatever work was allotted to them, it was done courageously, smartly and well, in a manner which elicited well-merited praise from everyone. The men and officers have, by the nature of their work, been obliged to endure more exposure and severe toil that any of the other troops, but they have maintained throughout their energy, cheerfulness, and good discipline. Should I ever be again engaged on work similar to than lately entrusted to me, I trust that I may have the good fortune to have the 4th Madras, Pioneers as my comrades."

The following is an extract from the Report by Major-General R. C. Stewart, C.B., A.D.C., commanding Burma District (No. 9-D, dated 3rd June 1891) :—

" No one who has failed to visit these mountains can appreciate the difficulties the troops have to contend with on these expeditions, and the hardships, privations and exposure which must be suffered by both officers and men. In addition to this, there is the anxiety attending the knowledge that at any moment troops or convoys may be subject to ambuscade, and that in action we have to deal with an almost invisible enemy, who knows every inch of the country and who is cunning enough to take every possible advantage of the regularity of our own movements and of the presence of a baggage train which has to be protected.

19. There has been no period since Upper Burma was annexed during which the troops have been more harassed, or more repeatedly employed on field operations, than during the past season in the Chin Hills........

23. The wing of the 4th Madras Pioneers has done most excellent work, which is testified to both by Colonel Mainwaring and Captain Rundall. I do not think that praise in higher terms than those employed by Captain Rundall could be accorded to any regiment, and it is the greatest possible pleasure to me to submit it to the Commander-in-Chief, Madras Army............

28. Of the other officers who are mentioned by General Graham, I think the special thanks of Government, and suitable recognition of their services, may be accorded to Captain Stevens and Captain Churchill, 4th Madras Pioneers."

The following is an extract from the letter by Lieutenant-General the Hon. J. C. Dormer, K.C.B., Commander-in-Chief, Madras Army, to the Adjutant-General in India forwarding the above report (No. W. 2158, dated Ootacamund, 1st July 1891) :—

"It will, I feel sure, afford His Excellency much pleasure to learn that the troops generally did good service notwithstanding the great difficulties caused by the nature of the country and its unhealthiness, and I cordially join with Major-General Stewart in his approval of the manner in which the 4th Pioneers and the 39th Gurhwalis acquitted themselves."

1891—1892.

Operations in the Chin Hills.

In order to bring all the tribes in the Chin Hills under proper control, it was decided to organise a fresh series of expeditions in the open season of 1891-92, and the value of the wing of the 4th Pioneers having been proved in the previous season, it was decided that the whole regiment should now be employed.

Accordingly, on the 1st November 1891, the Left Wing and Headquarters of the regiment, under the command of Lieutenant-Colonel J. E. Porteous, and composed as shown in the margin, left Bangalore and embarking at Madras on the *I. M. S. Clive*, arrived in Rangoon on the 7th November, 1891.

Lieut.-Col. J. E. Porteous, *Commdt.*
Capt. F. L. Holloway, *Wing Comdr.*
Lieut. C. R. Keate, *Adjutant.*
„ C. T. Swan, *Qr. Mr.*
Surg.-Major Reporter.
Subr.-Major Sungili.
„ Peddannah.
„ Mir Abbas.
Jemr. Munisami.
„ Suliman Sharif, *Nat. Adjt.*
„ Sriramulu.
„ Ramasami.
1st. Gr. Hospl. Asst. Jacob.
N.C.O's. and men, 364.
Followers 49, Horses 2.

Meanwhile, the Right Wing concentrated at Fort White under Captain G. B. Stevens, the two companies which had been at Haka under Captain F. Churchill moving to Fort White at the end of 1891.

The Left Wing and Headquarters left Rangoon on the 8th November and proceeded by rail to Prome, where they embarked on the *I. M. S. Irawaddy* and two flats on the 9th, and arrived at Pakkoku on the 14th, halting en route at Thayetmyo, Minhla and Pagan.

On the 20th November 1891, they marched from Pakkoku, repairing the roads and bridges en route, their route being as follows:—

Kanhla	6 Miles	20th Nov. 1891.
Tibbuja	15 ,,	21st ,,
Pyinchaung	12 ,,	22nd ,,
Pauk	15 ,,	25th ,,
Chaungu	7 ,,	27th ,,
Yebyu	11 ,,	28th ,,
Yedu	7 ,,	29th ,,
Amyaban	11 ,,	30th ,,
Thilin	13 ,,	2nd Dec.
Shwekandaing	12 ,,	3rd ,,
Morle	16 ,,	4th ,,
Minywa	7 ,,	5th ,,
Gangaw	12½ ,,	7th ,,
Myinza	8½ ,,	9th ,,
Kan	13 ,,	10th ,,

Or 166 miles in 21 days.

At Minywa Captain E. L. Holloway, with Jemadar Sulaiman Sharif, and 50 rank and file, was left behind to join the Baungshe Column. It is proposed to deal with the movements of the various columns separately hereafter, and meanwhile to continue the record of the movements of the Left Wing of the regiment.

Halting at Kan for a week, for want of transport and rations, they set out again for Haka on the 17th December, their route being:—

Longlet	12 Miles	17th Dec. 1891.
Chaungwa	12 ,,	18th ,,
Rowvan	16 ,,	19th ,,
Yokwa	10 ,,	22nd ,,
Bwelet	10 ,,	23rd ,,
Haka	12 ,,	24th ,,

Or 72 miles in 8 days.

On arrival of Headquarters at Haka, Surgeon Kelawala resumed medical charge of the regiment from Surgeon D. Graves, who had relieved Surgeon Reporter on the 9th November.

On the 11th January 1892, Headquarters and the Left Wing moved into No. 3 Camp on the Haka-Sihang Road, having completed a mule-track as far as this camp, a distance of 71 miles.

On the 25th January 1892, they moved to No. 3 camp (10 miles from Haka) to which a good mule-track with bridges had been completed. At this camp Lieutenant C. L. Keate left on the 28th January 1892, having been appointed Wing Commander, 31st Burma Regiment. On the same date, Lieutenant C. T. Swan left, in command of a detachment consisting of Subadar Mir Abbas and 25 rifles, to join the Tlang-Tlang column.

On the 1st February, the Wing moved another 3¼ miles to No. 4 camp, where Captain F. Churchill joined and took over the duties of Adjutant. On the 16th February, the Wing moved to No. 5 camp, 4 miles further on. From here another detachment of 50 rifles, under Subadar-Major Sungili, left to join the Tashon Column, Lieutenant C. T. Swan taking command of them at Haka.

On the 27th February, No. 6 camp, another 1¾ miles, was reached, where Captain E. L. Holloway rejoined from the Baungshe Column.

On the 29th February, the Wing moved another 11 miles to No. 7 camp, sending a detachment to No. 8 camp, 2 miles away.

On the 11th March, another 4¼ miles brought the Wing to No. 9 camp; No. 10 (5 miles) was reached on the 1st April; and the 11th and last camp was occupied on the 14th April. This camp was about 31 miles along the Haka-Falam road, and here the men from the Tashon Column, under Lieutenant Swan, rejoined the Wing on the 18th April, while 200 men of the Right Wing, under Lieutenant Holmes, joined on the following day.

On the 20th April 1892, the regiment left this camp, and set out for Kalewa, their route being :—

    Nippinchaung   .. 22nd April 1892.
    Kanchaung   .. 25th   ,,
    Sihang   .. 27th   ,,
    Indin   .. 28th   ,,
    Kalemyo   .. 29th   ,,
    Kalewa   .. 3rd May 1892.

On the 5th May 1892, the regiment embarked on the river steamer *Amyen* for Pakkoku, arriving there on the 7th and, embarking again on the *I.M.S. Privateer* on the 11th May, Myingyan was reached on the same day.

On the 19th May, Headquarters embarked on the *I.M.S. Pagan,* and arrived at Mandalay on the following day, the regiment marching into the cholera camp at Amarapura on the 29th May.

On the 10th June, the regiment proceeded by rail to Rangoon, where they embarked on the *I.M.S. Dalhousie* on the 12th, and reached Madras on the 18th, leaving Madras two days later, and arriving at Bangalore on the 21st June 1892.

At Rangoon, a detachment of 2 Native Officers, 1 Hospital Assistant, and 174 Rank and file, under Lieutenant A. Mears, was left behind, the accommodation on the *Dalhousie* being insufficient. This detachment rejoined regimental Headquarters at Bangalore on the 2nd July 1892.

1892.

In addition to the large amount of work carried out by both Wings of the regiment during 1891-92, particulars of which are given in the section on Pioneer work, the following are details of the parties who accompanied the various punitive columns sent out to overawe the Chins:—

On the 25th December 1891, a column, under the command of Major Gunning, K. R. R., composed of 100 men of the King's Royal Rifles; 100 men of the 2nd Burma Battalion and 2 guns, No. 8 Mountain Battery; and accompanied by Captain E. L. Holloway, Jemadar Sulaiman Sharif, and 50 men of the 4th Madras Pioneers, marched to explore the country of the Baungshe tribes south of Haka, and to deal with the tribes themselves.

Baungshe Column.

The following is from a report on the operations of these columns by Brigadier-General A. P. Palmer, dated Myingyan, 23rd May, 1892:—

"The column left Minywa on the 25th December and marched on Shurkwa, found that place an inconvenient centre, so established a post at Lotaw, whence Lungo and other villages to the South were visited. No opposition was met with, but the troops had some very severe marching crossing the deep malarious valleys of the outer hills, and suffering much from sickness.

A garrison, composed of 100 men of the 2nd Burma Battalion, and 20 men of the 4th Madras Pioneers, was left at Lotaw, and the column returned to Haka and was broken up on the 30th January, 1892.

The Lotaw detachment, when marching to Haka, was attacked at Shurkwa on the 29th March, and forced to inflict a severe punishment on the villagers, with the loss of one man killed and one wounded.

On the 5th February 1892, a column under the command of Major A. G. F. Browne, D. S. O., 39th Garhwal Rifles, composed of 100 of the King's Royal Rifles; 150 men, 39th Garhwal Rifles; and 2 guns, No. 8 Mountain Battery; and accompanied by Lieutenant C. T. Swan, with Subadar Mir Abbas and 25 men of the 4th Madras Pioneers, marched to punish the Tlang-Tlang tribes, who had risen in April 1891, and attacked a party escorting Lieutenant Mocatta, the Political Officer, who was proceeding to meet the Political Officer of South Lushai at Tao.

Tlang-Tlang Column.

Brigadier-General A. P. Palmer's report says:—

"The column marched from Haka on the 5th February, towards Munlipi and Hurian Kan, established a post at Lao Var, met Captain Shakespear from Fort Tregear on the 14th, punished the villages concerned in the attack on Lieutenant Mocatta and other outrages, and returned to Haka unopposed with 104 guns taken or surrendered as fines."

The following is an extract from Major Browne's report, dated Haka, 5th March 1892:—

"It only remains for me to tender my cordial thanks to all officers, non-commissioned officers, and men who worked under me, and notably to officers commanding corps and departments, as below:

*   *   *   *   *   *

Lieutenant C. T. Swan, 4th Madras Pioneers.

*   *   *   *   *   *

On the 10th March 1892, two columns, called the Tashon and Newengal columns respectively, set out to establish a post at Falam, and to bring under control the Tashon tribe and others in the neighbourhood. The Tashon column started from Haka under the command of Major Howlet, 2nd Burma Battalion, and consisted of 100 men of the King's Royal Rifles; 150 men of the 2nd Burma Battalion; 2 guns, No. 8 Mountain Battery; and 50 men of the 4th Madras Pioneers, under Lieutenant C. T. Swan, who was accompanied by Subadar-Major Sungili. The Newengal column started from Fort White, under the command of Captain Hugh Rose, 1-3rd Gurkhas, and consisted of 150 men of the King's Royal Rifles; 150 men of the 39th Garhwal Rifles; 2 guns, No. 8 Mountain Battery; and 50 men of the 4th Madras Pioneers under Lieutenant A. Mears, who was accompanied by Jemadar Abdullah Khan.

Tashon Newengal Columns.

The following is an extract from Brigadier-General Palmer's report:—

"Newengal and Tashon.

11. We now come to the most important part of the operations from a military point of view, and that which in the opinion of both Political Officers was most likely to be productive of fighting, namely, the subjugation of the Tashons.

To effect this, the Tashon Column under Major Howlet, 2nd Burma Battalion, and the Newengal Column under Captain Rose, 1-3rd Gurkhas, left Haka and Fort White respectively on the 10th March. Falam was occupied without resistance on the 13th and the columns started out again, the Newengal on the 16th, and Tashon on the 20th, to visit the Newengal Country to the North-West, and the Yahao villages to the West, the post of Falam having been meanwhile made over to 150 men of the Garhwal Rifles from Haka.

The Tashon column, after a peaceful expedition, returned to Falam on the 2nd April, and Haka on the 6th April, on which day it was broken up."

On the 3rd January 1892, a column under the command of Captain G. B. Stevens, 4th Madras Pioneers, and composed of 50 men of the King's Royal Rifles; 100 men of the 1st Burma Rifles; 2 guns, No. 8 Mountain Battery; and 50 men of the 4th Madras Pioneers, under Lieutenant G. V. Holmes and Subadar Abdur Rahim, left Fort White with orders to visit the Kanhaws and other tribes to the north of them, and to open up communication with Manipur. Lieutenant Holmes acted as Staff Officer to Captain Stevens, in addition to commanding the detachment of Pioneers.

Kanhaw Column.

The following are extracts from Brigadier-General Palmer's report:—

"Kanhaw.

10. Meanwhile the Kanhaw column, commanded by Captain Stevens, 4th Madras Pioneers, having left Fort White on the 3rd January, marched North to Lenacot, where a post was established, visited the Tornlong tribes, despatched a flying column to Manipur, mapped out a large extent of unsurveyed country, and parted with guns and cooly corps on February 22nd, they having to join the Newengal column.

Captain Stevens then visited the eastern slopes of the Letha range, opening a road to Yazagyo, and returned to Tiddim on March 20th, having completed the original programme of work. The column then, however, proceeded to visit the northern Newengal villages and finally returned to Fort White and was broken up on April 16th. No active opposition was met with."

"Botong Affair.

14. During the absence of Newengal-Lushai Column, an attack was threatened on the Botong post by the Chins of Halai and Shampi, aided by certain Yahaos and Newengals.

This disturbance was promptly dealt with by Captain Stevens, 4th M. P., who marched out from Fort White with 35 King's Royal Rifles, 40 4th Madras Pioneers, and 55 1st Burma Rifles, to the Manipur River and, in conjunction with the troops of Botong garrison under Lieutenant Henegan, punished the offending villages.

Botong garrison was then withdrawn across the river on the 9th May, being no longer needed as a base for the Newengal-Lushai Column. Mobingyi was also evacuated on the 16th May, no shots being fired by the Chins during this withdrawal."

"20..........The march of the Kanhaw Column to Manipur and its descent later over the Letha range into the Kubo valley, together with the successful movement of the Newengal-Lushai Column from Fort White to Daokhoma and Lungleh, will probably have permanent and far-reaching effects.

trust, therefore, that the Major-General will agree with me in considering that this record reflects the greatest credit on the troops, who have endured hardships and privations in an inhospitable and rugged country, and on the commanders of columns, who, by their attention to detail and readiness of resource, made such results possible.

I would especially call attention to the long record of work set forth in Captain Stevens' full and interesting report of the Kanhaw Column, which traversed over 600 miles from first to last and opened out much hitherto unknown country.

* * * * * *

"25. I trust that the services of Officers Commanding Columns will be suitably acknowledged, all having shown that they could be thoroughly trusted in independent positions to carry out difficult and arduous undertakings.

The services of Captain G. B. Stevens, 4th Madras Pioneers, appear specially deserving of recognition. This officer has served in the Chin Hills in command of the Right Wing of his regiment during the last two seasons, during which much excellent work has been done by his men on the roads and building posts, and he has moreover commanded the North Chin Hills since December 1891. The manner in which he conducted the extensive movements of the Kanhaw Column deserves high commendation; and he likewise showed his ability as a commander in the field by the way in which, after arranging for the withdrawal of the Botong post, he planned and carried out the punitive expedition against the village of Haili, bringing the operations to such a satisfactory close that the withdrawal to the East of the Manipur River was effected without a shot being fired into our column. Captain Stevens appears to be an officer whom it would be to the advantage of Government to push on in the service, as he has shown not only that he can carry out instructions in a most satisfactory and creditable manner, but that he can be trusted in an emergency to take the initiative and act with judgment on his own responsibility."

Newengal Lushai Column. In March 1892, a column, under the command of Captain Hugh Rose, 1-3rd Gurkhas, and composed of 100 men of the King's Royal Rifles; 150 men of the 39th Garhwal Rifles; 1 gun, No. 8 Mountain Battery; and 47 men of the 4th Madras Pioneers under Jemadar Abdullah Khan, set out to visit the tribes in Newengal and Lushai.

The following are extracts from Brigadier-General Palmer's report:—

"Newengal-Lushai.

12. The Newengal Column proceeded to its ration depot at Mobingyi and thence marched *via* Botong to Nikwe, where a heavy fine was inflicted. It then returned to Botong, where it arrived on the 8th April; there, being ordered to retrace its steps and march on Daokhoma to aid in the suppression of the Lushai rebellion, it started again on the 21st on a very arduous march, to appreciate which it must be remembered that heavy rain had set in and that the course of the column lay due west, while all the ranges of hills and streams in this part of the country run North and South, the valleys being divided by narrow ranges, whose elevation averages from 3,500 to 4,000 feet above that of the watercourses.

13. A post was left at Botong, west of Manipur River as a supporting point to the column, should it have to fall back, and another at Mobingyi, east of Manipur River, whence heliographic communication could be kept up with Fort White and Botong.

The column reached Lalbuta on 30th April, Daokhoma on 2nd May, Vansanga on 9th May, and Lungleh on 13th. Hardly any opposition was met with, so the only punishment which could be inflicted on the Lushais consisted in burning their villages and destroying their live-stock and stores of grain. Owing to heavy rain aggravating the natural difficulties of the march, a very heavy mortality occurred among the mules."

* * * * * *

25. The enterprising march from Fort White to Lushai of the column under Captain Rose has proved to the tribes our ability to penetrate their country in any direction and must have had the best effect. The endurance displayed by the troops and their triumph over all the obstacles encountered have already received the commendation of His Excellency the Commander-in-Chief in India, and I trust the services of this small force may receive recognition in the advancement of its Commander, Captain Rose, 1st 3rd Gurkhas."

The following is an extract from Regimental Orders, dated *I.M.S. Pagan*, 19th May 1892, by Lieutenant-Colonel J. E. Porteous, Commanding:—

The following speech made by Brigadier-General Palmer, Commanding Myingyan District, is published for information:—

"Colonel Porteous, Officers, Non-Commissioned Officers and men of the 4th Pioneers, I have been in the District for a short time only, so I am sorry I am unable to speak much of you. I have heard that the 4th Pioneers have been the best friends of the 23rd Punjab Pioneers. Any General would be proud of having two such regiments under his command. You have been very useful in opening up lines of communication in the Chin Hills. The work done specially by the Right Wing for the last year and a half has been known very creditably in this District. The Pioneers did good service in the Kanhaw Column. Their gallant act under Captain G. B. Stevens in rendering timely assistance to the Lushai Column by some of the men swimming across a river, rebuilding a dismantled bridge, and expelling the rebel Chins, reflects great credit on this Corps. The leading man of the distinguished party which swam the river shall be noted when I receive full reports. I wish to congratulate Captain Stevens and his men on their recent gallant deed when I see them here. I will report very favourably on their good behaviour. I shall strongly recommend Captain Stevens for some recognition of his services and if he receives no reward it will not be my fault. I am glad to say, Colonel Porteous, you have kept up the reputation of the old Coast Army by having your Corps in such an excellent condition. I am sorry that you suffered from rain on your return, but as you will shortly go to your station, the men will forget all such little troubles when they see their families.

Colonel Porteous, I wish you and your regiment good-bye and good luck."

The following is an extract from the report (dated 31st July 1892) on these operations, sent by Lieutenant-General the Hon. J. C. Dormer, K. C. B., Commander-in-Chief, Madras Army, to the Adjutant-General in India:—

"I have the honour to forward herewith two reports received from Major-General R. C. Stewart, C. B., Commanding the Burmah District, together with the reports from officers who commanded columns during the past season (1891-92) in the Chin Hills and on the North-Eastern frontier of Burmah.

2. I would express my concurrence with the opinion held by Major-General Stewart as to the excellent work done by the various columns and the soldierlike spirit displayed by all ranks of the troops engaged.

4. The object aimed at by the several columns seems to have been most satisfactorily attained—a result due not only to the spirit, energy and endurance of the troops employed, but also to the ability and forethought with which all was arranged and carried out by General Stewart, whose valuable services I would again bring to His Excellency's notice.

5. I would also endorse the recommendations made by Major-General Stewart as to officers whose services he has specially brought to notice, and express my hope that these may meet with due recognition."

The following are extracts from the report (No. 179-D, dated Rangoon, 6th June, 1892) on these operations by Major-General R. C. Stewart, C. B., Commanding the Burma District:—

".........Indeed I may say that more has been done, for, in addition to that plan of operations which was at first prepared, the Kanhaw Column has marched from Fort White to Manipur, and the Newengal Column has penetrated from the Northern Chin Hills to the Lushai Country, returning by Chittagong and Rangoon. I need not remark on the original operations of the Kanhaw and Newengal Columns, for full information will be found in the reports which are enclosed, as well as in the Summary of the G.O.C. the Myingyan District, and when the maps and reports of the Intelligence Officers who accompanied the Columns are completed, it will, I trust, be found that much information of unknown tribes and countries has been obtained and many blanks in the map accurately filled in; but I would wish to express my satisfaction with the officers who controlled and successfully carried out the march of the Kanhaw Column from Tiddim to Manipur, and that still more arduous march from Botong to Daokhoma, Lungleh, and through the Lushai Country to Chittagong.

4. As regards the former operation, it is remarkable to remember that in the beginning of 1891 nothing was known of the country North of Fort White beyond the limit of the operations of Brigadier-General Faunce's Column in 1889, and that now the country of the Tornlongs on the North-West, Haitsi and Lopa on the North-East to Yazagyo in the Kubo Valley have been penetrated and the country mapped, while northwards a column has marched unopposed, *via* Tiddim, Tungyang and Lenacot, into the valley of Manipur and the town of Imphal...................

I need refer no further here to the march of this column into the Lushai country. It is detailed in full in Captain Rose's report; but I wish to express my admiration of the determination displayed by all ranks in overcoming the difficulties, and of the fortitude with which they endured the hardships of the road—hardships which must have been of no mean order if it is right to judge by the appearance of men of the column when they landed in Rangoon.

6. I must here make special mention of the Botong affair. When the Newengal column moved out to Nikwe towards Lushai, I left a post of 100 men 10th (Burmah) Madras Infantry at the former place partly as a reserve to the column in case it required assistance, and partly to hold open the communications with Fort White and to prevent attack on the rear of the column. This post was subsequently attacked, and when Captain G. B. Stevens, 4th Madras Infantry (Pioneers) moved out from Fort White to the assistance of Lieutenant J. Henegan, 10th Madras Infantry, he was attacked when endeavouring to cross the Nankatha river. Captain Stevens graphically describes the affair in his report and brings to notice the gallantry of the Pioneers* who swam across the river and repaired the bridge, and I trust these men will meet with the reward they deserve.

The Baungshe, Tlang-Tlang and Tashon columns, which have operated in the Southern Hills, have been invariably successful, and the reports which are enclosed show a record of hard work and successful arrangement in the face of considerable difficulties, which reflects the highest credit on the commanders. It is much to be regretted that the sickness in the Baungshe column was so severe, and it would certainly have been better to have timed the departure of this column to a later date. It is remarkable that throughout these operations there has been no open resistance on the part of the tribes, and not a single instance has occurred of individuals being attacked on the road, which during former years was so common.

* * * * *

"The 4th Madras Infantry (Pioneers) have earned a name for themselves of which they may well be proud. At the work of pioneers they are excellent, and in willingness, powers of marching and general endurance cannot be beaten; they have always shown a fine spirit in the field, and are a brilliant example of what a regiment can be made by its officers.

8. I wish to bring to notice of the Commander-in-Chief for special reward the names of Captain G. B. Stevens, 4th M. I. (Pioneers) and Captain Rose, 39th Bengal Infantry.

The former has served for two seasons in the Chin Hills. He is of untiring energy; on this occasion he has superintended the whole of the Pioneer work in the Northern Hills; he has commanded the Kanhaw Column with success, as well as the column which marched to Imphal; to himself, I consider, is mainly due the excellent spirit in the 4th Madras Infantry (Pioneers)......................

I also beg to bring to notice the particularly good services rendered by the following Native Officers.............Subadar Abdur Rahim, 4th Madras Infantry (Pioneers), has done excellent work under Captain Stevens. He has unfailing energy and resource.

---

*These men were Privates No. 2432 Mullary and No. 2517 Munisawmy. Each was awarded the 3rd Class of the Order of Merit, " For conspicuous gallantry in action at the passage of the Manipur River on the 4th May, 1892, in having unarmed and under the fire of a party of Chins swum across the river carrying with them a cradle for the repair of a bridge, by which the detachment to which they belonged was enabled to cross and disperse the enemy."

Pte. Mullary's Order of Merit now hangs in the Officers' Mess.

In the Botong affair he superintended the building of the raft by which the garrison was brought in safety across the Manipur River, and he has displayed an admirable coolness under fire at a critical moment.

Jemadar Abdullah Khan was in sole command of the detachment of the 4th Madras Infantry (Pioneers) which accompanied the Newengal column to Lushai. This party under this Jemadar, the first on the move and the last into camp each day, did pioneer work for the column on the march from Botong to Vansanga and Lungleh, which has been described to me as admirable, and this officer's conduct in particular as splendid. His control over his men and his energy stamp him as an officer of merit.

I recommend these officers for special recognition."

For his services during these operations Captain G. B. Stevens was awarded a Brevet-Majority, while Subadar Abdur Rahim and Jemadar Abdullah Khan were admitted to the 2nd Class of the Order of British India, with the title of *Bahadur*.

1892—1894.

On the 22nd June 1892, the regiment found itself once again in cantonments at Bangalore.

In January 1893, they commenced work on the North Lines at Badarhalli, which were completed during their stay in Bangalore. On the 10th November 1894, the regiment moved to Trichinopoly, arriving there on the 1st December following. It may be of interest to give the route by which they marched:—

1. Hebbagod	12 miles	7 furlongs.
2. Oosoor	12 „	6 „
3. Udanhally	12 „	1 „
4. Royakotah (cross a ghat)	9 „	4 „
5. Mahaindramangalam	8 „	2 „
6. Palagod	8 „	1 „
7. Sogatur	12 „	0 „
8. Admankota (cross a ghat)	5 „	4 „
9. Topur	11 „	6 „
10. Pujarputti	8 „	3 „
11. Tharamungalam	10 „	4 „
12. Atyamputti	14 „	0 „
13. Munchowoti	14 „	0 „
14. Namakuldroog	13 „	5 „
15. Vauliputti	8 „	10 „
16. Totiam	12 „	4 „
17. Musiri	9 „	7 „
18. Salliyatti	14 „	0 „
19. Puttur Bridge	11 „	0 „

In 1893, General Sir George S. White, V.C., G.C.I.E., K.C.B., became Commander-in-Chief in India. In 1894, the Earl of Elgin, P.C., succeeded the Marquis of Lansdowne as Governor-General of India.

1895—1896.

On the 12th September 1895, four companies of the regiment, now stationed at Trichinopoly, proceeded, under Captain F. Churchill, to Paliyanpatti, in Tanjore district, to dig ballast for the South Indian Railway Company. This detachment rejoined on the 25th September.

Floods at Trichinopoly. From the 31st July to the 3rd August 1896, the regiment was employed, at the request of the Collector of Trichinoply, during the heavy floods of the Kaveri, in stopping breaches on the Kodamurti—Woriur road and, from the 1st to the 7th August, at Melur, on the island of Srirangam, to close a breach made by the Kaveri in the flood-bank on the island.

The thanks of the Board of Revenue were recorded in a Resolution (No. 2268, Rev.) in December, 1896.

Negapatam. On the 24th October 1896, in accordance with G. A. O. No. 1 of 23rd October 1896, a detachment of 350 rifles, under Captain F. Churchill, proceeded to Negapatam to quell the riots caused by the men in the South Indian Railway Workshops. On the 30th October, Captain Churchill returned to Trichinopoly with three companies, leaving G. Company at Negapatam, under 2nd Lieutenant Geddes, in case of emergency. On the 18th November, 2nd Lieutenant Geddes was relieved by Lieutenant Swan, and on the 21st November, the latter was relieved by Captain Churchill, who returned to Trichinopoly with the detachment on the 23rd December, 1896.

1897—1898.

Ootacamund Lake Reclamation. In June 1897, the Government of India sanctioned the employment of the 4th Madras Pioneers on the Ootacamund Lake Reclamation project, on the understanding that there would be no expense to the State. Accordingly, the regiment proceeded to Ootacamund, under the command of Major G. B. Stevens, in seven detachments, travelling by rail to Mettupaliyam, thence in trucks on the ghat railway (then in process of construction) as far as Kullar, and completing the journey by road.

A depot was left at Trichinopoly under the command of Captain F. Churchill.

As the work done at Ootacamund has been made the subject of a full report by Lieutenant-Colonel G. B. Stevens (31st March 1899) it is unnecessary to give any details here. (*Vide Pioneer Work Section*).

By the 10th October 1898, the whole regiment was back in Trichinopoly, the return from Ootacamund being made in four detachments.

The Executive Engineer, Mr. Somers-Eve, reported on the work of the regiment in most flattering terms, and the Government of Madras expressed its satisfaction with the result of their efforts.

On the 7th March 1898, a detachment of 69 rank and file, under 2nd Lieutenant J. A. Keble, left the depot at Trichinopoly, and proceeded to Ali Musjid to join the 21st Madras Pioneers, then forming part of the Tirah Expeditionary Force. The detachment rejoined the depot at Trichinopoly on the 22nd April 1898, on the conclusion of hostilities.

Draft to Tirah.

In 1898, General Sir William S. A. Lockhart, G.C.B., K.C.S.I., became Commander-in-Chief in India.

1899.

On the 12th June 1899, the regiment, still stationed in Trichinopoly, detached two companies, under Captain F. Churchill, to Madura and Aruppukota, in aid of the civil power in connection with the serious riots which had broken out in Tinnevelly. Captain Churchill was relieved by 2nd Lieutenant Mackie on the 4th August 1899, when one company returned to Trichinopoly and the remainder of the detachment rejoined on the 29th November.

Tinnevelly Riots.

On the 19th November 1899, during the War in South Africa, a detachment of one Company, under 2nd Lieutenant Mackie, proceeded to Rameshwaram and the island of Pamban, on special service, in order to guard the end of the telegraph cable there. The detachment rejoined the regiment on the 27th January 1900.

Pamban.

In 1899, Lord Curzon of Kedleston, P.C., became Governor-General, and held office till 1905, with a short break in 1904, when Lord Ampthill, Governor of Madras, acted as Governor-General.

1900.

On the 21st, 27th and 29th June 1900, drafts of a total strength of 2 Native Officers and 75 Rank and File left Trichinopoly to join the 1st Madras Pioneers at Bangalore, the latter regiment embarking at Calcutta on the 10th and 17th July as part of the China Expeditionary Force.

Drafts to China.

4 N.C.O.'s and 4 Ward Orderlies left Trichinopoly, on the 8th August, for Wellington, to join the 61st Native Field Hospital, which embarked for China at Calcutta in four sections; the last on the 5th September 1900.

The drafts returned from China and disembarked at Madras on the 10th July 1901, rejoining the regiment at Trichinopoly on the 13th July 1901.

On the 13th November 1900, a detachment of 80 Rank and file, under Subadar Harichandra Rao, proceeded to Trivandrum to furnish the Resident's escort.

In 1900, General Sir A. Power Palmer, K.C.B., became Commander-in-Chief in India.

1901.

In this year the title of the regiment was again altered, and it became the 4th Madras Pioneers.

From March to June 1901, the regiment was employed in constructing a camp for Boer prisoners of war at Trichinopoly.

On the 1st May 1901, Subadar Harichandra Rao's detachment at Trivandrum was relieved by another of the same strength under Subadar Abdul Aziz, which was withdrawn on the 12th December 1901.

On the 25th July 1901, a detachment of three companies, under Lieutenant R. Mackie, with Lieutenant R. J. Malet, 6 Native Officers, and 305 Rank and File, proceeded to Bangalore, for garrison duty, and employment as butt-markers and register-keepers at the South India Rifle Association meeting. Headquarters, and the remaining five companies of the regiment, under Major E. L. Holloway, followed on the 4th December. With the arrival of Subadar Abdulla Khan, *Sirdar Bahadur*, with the Trivandrum detachment on the 27th December 1901, the regiment was once more re-assembled in Bangalore.

1902—1903.

On the 22nd November 1902, owing to an outbreak of fever and plague, the regiment was compelled to vacate its lines at Badarhalli, and proceeded to camp at Dasarhalli, where it remained until the 9th February 1903.

In 1902, General Viscount Kitchener of Khartoum and the Vaal, G.C.B., O.M., G.C.M.G., became Commander-in-Chief in India.

In May 1903, a detachment of 300 men proceeded to Bellary, under Captain C. R. Scott-Elliot, for work in connection with the Bellary-Rayadrug Feeder Line.

By India Army Order No. 181, dated the 2nd October 1903, the title of the regiment was altered to "64th Pioneers," in conformity with H. E. the Commander-in-Chief's (Lord Kitchener's) scheme for the numbering of the regiments of the whole Indian Army consecutively. By this change the regiment lost its old number, of which it was so deservedly proud, whilst retaining its precedence as the fourth in seniority of the Indian Army. In view of this seniority, it is evident that the sequence of numbers should have commenced with the Madras Army, and the method of re-numbering, as adopted, roused considerable feeling.

Part I.

CHAPTER VII.

THE 64th PIONEERS.
2nd October 1903—30th November 1921.

THE 2nd BATTALION, 1st MADRAS PIONEERS.
1st December 1922—31st March 1929.

THE 2nd BATTALION, MADRAS PIONEERS.
1st April 1929—31st December 1930.

1903—1907.

The regiment remained in garrison at Bangalore until the 19th December 1904, when it marched to Ootacamund, in the Nilgiri Hills, for employment on the construction of the railway from Coonoor to Ootacamund.

On arrival at Mysore, the officers, British and Indian, were entertained by H. H. the Maharaja, and when the regiment crossed the Mysore frontier, a telegram was received from H. H., expressing regret at its departure, and hopes of its early return to the State. Throughout the march, every assistance was given by the Mysore State Officials.

The final day's march was up the Segur Ghat, a very steep climb which put a great strain on the transport bullocks four of which had to be yoked to each cart.

The regiment remained at Ootacamund from the 1st January 1905 till the 1st October 1907, and full details of its work will be found in Part V of these records.

In 1905, the Earl of Minto, P.C., G.C.M.G., became Viceroy of India.

1907—1912.

On the 4th October 1907, the regiment arrived at Belgaum, leaving a detachment, under Captain S. B. Watson, at Ootacamund, which rejoined headquarters on the 30th March 1908. The regimental depot had already been at Belgaum for some time.

During its stay in Belgaum, the regiment was employed for some two years in re-building its own lines, and in 1910, a detachment was sent to Aurungabad, under Major J. A. Bliss, to re-build the lines of the Poona Horse.

On the 15th March 1912, the regiment entrained for Secunderabad, where it remained in garrison till the 10th November 1913. Here a considerable amount of Pioneer work was carried out, details of which, and of the work at Belgaum, will be found in Part V.

In 1909, General Sir O'Moore Creagh, V.C., G.C.B., became Commander-in-Chief in India and, in the following year, Baron Hardinge of Penshurst, P.C., G.C.B., G.C.M.G., G.C.V.O., I.S.O., became Viceroy.

1913.

At the beginning of this year, the regiment was still at Secunderabad. One Double Company (Captain Malet's) took part in Divisional manoeuvres, held early in January, under the direction of Lieutenant-General Sir John Nixon, Commanding the Southern Army.

On the 28th January, the regiment was inspected by Brigadier-General Rodwell who also inspected it again on the 4th November, prior to its departure for Burma. On the 18th April, Major T. B. Skinner left to take command of one of the battalions of the Nayar Brigade.

On the 20th October, the regiment was inspected by Major-General Phayre, Commanding the 9th (Secunderabad) Division.

On the 22nd September, the regiment was warned to be in readiness to move to Burma early in November, having been lent to the Government of Burma for road making in the Hkamti Long District, beyond rail head at Myitkyina, and on the 23rd October orders were received for the regiment to embark at Madras on the 13th November.

On the 30th October, H. E. the Viceroy, Lord Hardinge, accompanied by H. H. the Nizam of Hyderabad, reviewed the troops in garrison at Secunderabad, and held a reception at the Residency in the evening, when all the officers were presented.

On the 6th November, Lieutenant-Colonel Swan left for Maymyo in order to make arrangements with the Government of Burma as to the work to be carried out, and, on the 11th the regiment, on relief scale, left Secunderabad in two special troop trains. A list of the officers who accompanied the regiment will be found in the Part dealing with Pioneer Work. Madras was reached, *via* Bezwada, on the 13th, where the regiment at once embarked on the *R. I. M. S. Northbrook,* and arrived in Rangoon river on the 17th. On the 18th November, the regiment disembarked, and on the following day entrained for Mandalay, where it arrived on the 20th, when Lieutenant-Colonel Swan resumed command. On the 22nd November the regiment was inspected by Major-General Pilcher, C.B., Commanding the Burma Division, and four days later entrained for Myitkyina at Field Service strength, leaving behind a depot, with Major J. A. Bliss, M.V.O., in command, Jemadar Muttuvelu, the recruits and the band.

<small>**The 64th move to Burma.**</small>

Myitkyina was reached on the 27th November, and on the 3rd December the regiment marched out to commence the work, of which full particulars will be found elsewhere.

1914.

In April 1914, the regiment returned from work on the Putao Road, and was busily employed in constructing lines at Myitkyina in which to pass the rains.

As soon as the weather permitted, the double companies commenced their annual courses of training and musketry.

On the declaration of war against Germany on the 4th August 1914, the fact that the regiment was employed on special work in Burma deprived it of the opportunity of early employment on field service with any of the Expeditionary Forces sent from India to France, Mesopotamia, East Africa, China or Egypt, and it was destined to remain in Burma for the next two years. On the 4th August, the British Officers on leave in England were Lieutenant-Colonel Swan, Major Watson, and Captain Malet. Of these, only Major Watson was allowed to remain in

<small>**Outbreak of War.**</small>

England, and after some time spent in training men for the New Army, he eventually proceeded to France to join the 107th Pioneers. Colonel Swan and Captain Malet were sent back to India with the other officers of the Indian Army, on the *S. S. Dongola,* and rejoined the regiment in Burma in September.

At the same time, Captain Marsden and Lieutenant Burne were on their way to Japan on a North German Lloyd ship which landed its passengers at Manila, and these two officers did not rejoin the regiment until the 9th October, after a devious journey *via* Hong-Kong, Singapore, Calcutta and Rangoon.

By November, the annual training of the regiment was practically completed, and on the 9th of that month it was inspected by Major-General Raitt, Commanding the Burma Division, with the exception of No. 4 Double Company, which had already left Myitkyina to recommence work on the road. Full particulars of the work done during the remainder of this year will be found in Part V.

In 1914, General Sir Beauchamp Duff, G.C.B., K.C.S.I., K.C.V.O., C.I.E., A.D.C., became Commander-in-Chief in India.

1915.

The Kachin Rising.

Early in December 1914, there were persistent rumours that the Kachins were meditating a rebellion; and an attack on Myitkyina, which had once before in its history been raided and partially burned by the Kachins, was anticipated on the 4th of that month, with the result that measures had to be taken to protect the station, the regiment supplying picquets for the more important points, such as the railway station and the Treasury, and putting out outposts on the northern side. Nothing happened, however, and it was not until the opening of the New Year that there were any signs of an outbreak.

On the 2nd January 1915, a party of Kachins stole some buffaloes in the neighbourhood of the Military Police Post at Kamaing, at the entrance to the Hukawng Valley, the garrison of which is found by the Myitkyina Battalion. A party of six Gurkhas, sent out to recover the buffaloes, was captured by the Kachins at Ichi, north-east of Kamaing, whereupon a stronger party, with Mr. Baker as Political Officer, was sent out, but found some 300 Kachins in a strongly stockaded position, and was forced to retire, with a loss of one man killed, and another wounded. This slight success, no doubt greatly magnified by the Kachins, was sufficient to set the whole Hukawng Valley ablaze, and it was realised that the situation was serious. Accordingly, two strong columns of Military Police, with guns, were sent out from Myitkyina to subdue the Kachins in the Hukawng Valley, which they ultimately succeeded in doing.

Rising at Kamaing.

The real instigators of this rising were four Shans—Nga Po Thaik, Nga Kyi, Nga Ni, and Nga Se Bon—from Katha, who commenced a tour of the villages in the Hukawng Valley. Now the inhabitants of Lower Burma, and the Shans, dread the Kachins, and it is evident that these four men would not have entered upon what, to them, must have seemed a most perilous enterprise, unless they had been given some powerful inducement, and it seems probable that in this case, as in so many others, the motive force was German money.

Causes of the Rising.

Be that as it may, the leader, Nga Po Thaik, succeeded in gaining considerable influence amongst the Kachins. He claimed to possess magical powers, and said that he could produce fire from his mouth to destroy his enemies, and that so long as he was with the Kachins, no harm could come to them. He asserted that in one of his previous lives he had been King of Ceylon, and drew attention to his broad forehead, which showed that he had spent another part of his existence in the form of an elephant, all of which was readily believed by the Kachins. The result was that they decided on a rising, and their resolve was strengthened by a rumour that all the Military Police had been taken away for the war in Europe.

Having thus succeeded in causing a rebellion in the Hukawng Valley on the west, the Shans next moved to the east, in order to foment disturbances in the Mali Valley. On the main ridge of tangled hills which overlooks the Mali Hka, there was a large village called Wawang, some 15 miles from Shingboi, where a Kachin of unusual size and strength, named Pawlum Kron Li, had usurped the functions of *Agyiwa* or head-man, and had established a personal reign of terror throughout that part of the country; and in this village the Shans established themselves.

Trouble in the Mali Valley.

Their great desire was to induce the Kachins of Nmaizin Long, on the other side of the Mali Hka, whose prowess was greatly respected by the other Kachins, to cross the river and, after wiping out the Military Police posts at Laza and Nsop Zup, and dealing with the parties of Pioneers working on the road, to make a descent on Myitkyina. Messengers were accordingly sent across to the principal *Agyiwas* of Nmaizin Long, with presents of meat, to invite their co-operation, but their reply was that the senders should first do something to show that they were really in earnest, and that the trans-Mali Kachins would join them after they had made the first attack.

The principal difficulty of the Kachins has always been the scarcity of grain and supplies in general, and the lack of means of transport, the result being that when a large number of them is concentrated in one place, they very soon run short of food, and have to disperse to their several villages to replenish their supplies.

Consequently, the Kachins at Wawang decided that their first attempt should be made on the P.W.D. ration store at Shingboi, near which there was only one company of Pioneers encamped. The Kachin has such a good opinion of himself that the latter was no doubt considered only a trifling obstacle, and they hoped that, having possessed themselves of the large quantity of rice and atta known to be in the store, they would be joined by the trans-Mali Kachins, and proceed to overrun the whole country.

The attitude of the Kachins in general, in the country lying between the Mali Hka and the Hukawng Valley, was by no means unfriendly, but they stated, quite candidly, that if the Nmaizin Long men came across the river, they would be compelled to join them, as otherwise their own heads would be endangered, and their villages burnt.

The first intimation of impending trouble was received on the 23rd January 1915, when a Kachin came in to Shingboi and gave information that a large number of men had assembled at Wawang, and had announced an intention of making an attack on the ration store on the following night, which was the ninth of the Kachin month, and considered auspicious; and that, should anything occur to prevent this attack, it would take place on either the 17th or the 19th. Captain Murland, who happened to be at Shingboi, telephoned the news to Laza and Nsop Zup, and it was passed on to Myitkyina by telegraph.

No attack was made on the 24th January, but as there seemed to be no doubt that an outbreak was impending, orders were sent from Myitkyina on the 27th that Mr. Lowis, the Executive Engineer, who was given the powers of a first-class magistrate, should proceed at once to Wawang, with Major Bliss and 100 men of No. 1, Double Company (then at work some miles to the south-west of Shingboi), and clear up the situation.

Attack on Wawang. Accordingly, on the night of the 27th January, No. 1 Double Company, which had marched to Shingboi during the day, set out for Wawang. Major Bliss was in command, and he was accompanied by Captain Marsden, who had just arrived from Myitkyina, and by Mr. Lowis, who had the track leading to Wawang reconnoitred during the day.

The intention was to reach Wawang before daylight, and it was hoped to take the Kachins by surprise. The leading party was followed, some hours later by the mules carrying its rations, water and blankets, escorted by a party of men of G. Company, under Jemadar Gopalsami.

The track was a most difficult one, through dense jungle and over steep hills, and in some places followed the rocky bed of a stream overhung by bamboos. It was a very dark night and, as the men had to march in single file, it may be imagined by anyone who knows how slow night-marching can be, even on good roads, and the miseries of those forming the tail of such a column, that the pace was not very rapid.

Just before dawn, the column reached a *taungya* clearing, when two shots were fired—presumably by one or two men posted in the clearing to give warning of anyone approaching—but nothing further occurred till the foot of the steep hill, on which Wawang stands, was reached, just at daybreak, when the head of the column was greeted by a volley fired from the jungle at close range, which, however, did no damage.

At this point a cleft bamboo was found in the pathway, with a small piece of paper, on which was written, in Shan, a bombastic warning to the effect that the council was sitting and that anyone who disturbed it would do so at his peril. The dense jungle made it impossible to see anything and, as the column deployed and proceeded to advance up the hill, the only sign that there was an enemy was the frequent shots, fired in many cases by men concealed in trees.

At length the outskirts of the village were reached, after a stiff climb, and it was found that a stockade had been built to obstruct the way, from behind which some of the bolder Kachins continued to fire. The stockade was rushed, Major Bliss himself shooting dead the last man to leave it, who turned out to be no other than Pawlum Kron Li. The village was now entered and set on fire, and the enemy seemed to have completely disappeared.

Two Havildars and one Private had been wounded during the advance, and it was decided that the column should retrace its steps, to get medical attention for the wounded men, and to obtain water and rations, which were badly needed as the men were very much exhausted.

The column accordingly marched back to Shingboi; only one shot was fired at them on the return journey, when a volley fired into the jungle luckily killed the Kachin who had fired the shot, and who turned out to be the head-man of another village.

A column was now formed at Myitkyina, and was sent up to Shingboi with orders to visit Wawang and the surrounding villages, to inflict punishment on the Kachins, and to endeavour to capture the Shans, who were now known to have been the ring-leaders. This column was under the command of Lieutenant-Colonel C. T. Swan, 64th Pioneers, with Lieutenant F. O. N. Burne as his Staff Officer, and accompanied by Major W. T. Abbey, Deputy Commissioner, Myitkyina District. It consisted of a Mountain Battery; 2 Companies, Border Regiment (T.F.); and 2 Companies, 1/10th Gurkha Rifles. A party of No. 2 Double Company under Captain E. Marsden acted as escort to the guns, and was kept hard at work making the narrow zigzag tracks over the hills passable for the large mules of the battery.

The column set out for Wawang on the 6th February, and in the course of a few days, the whole country had returned to its normal peaceful condition.

The four Shans were eventually brought in by the Kachins. When the attack on Wawang commenced, they had fled into the jungle, but the Kachins had no intention of letting them escape, so they were caught, and eventually handed over to the Deputy Commissioner. Their promise that so long as they were present, no harm could come to the Kachins had proved to be their undoing. They were tried by the Sessions Judge at Mandalay in September 1915, sentenced to death and hanged, their only defence being that they had travelled to the Kachin hills in search of drugs, and had nothing to do with the rebellion.

For their share in these operations, Lieutenant-Colonel Swan received the thanks of Government, and Major Bliss and Captain Marsden were "mentioned in despatches," while two non-commissioned officers—Havildar Rahmon Sharif and Lance-Naik Khader Beg—were awarded the Indian Distinguished Service medal.

The following is an extract from the *Pioneer*, dated 12th December 1915:—

"In the report on the North-Eastern Frontier for the year which ended with the 30th June last, some particulars are given of the Kachin rising in the Mogaung and Kamaing subdivisions of the Myitkyina District, Upper Burma. Rumours had been spread that owing to the war, the Government were short of troops, and the headman of Thama, with the Shan Pretender and three followers from the Katha District, tried to bring about a general rising of the tribes. Some of them readily joined in, and the trouble seemed likely to spread. A detachment of 100 men of the 64th Pioneers, with whom was Mr. F.C. Lowis, Executive Engineer in charge of the Myitkyina-Putao Road, was attacked by the people of Wawang on the 29th January. The village was at once stormed, though the Kachins offered stout resistance, retiring from one point of vantage to another on the very steep and thickly wooded road, and making a final stand at a hastily built stockade, from which they were driven at the point of the bayonet. Two headmen were killed on this occasion. A Moveable Column was afterwards formed and the disaffected tracts were visited, most prompt measures being taken to stamp out the rising. Various detachments went rapidly from point to point and complete success was gained. The Shan Pretender and his followers fled across the border but were captured and brought in by trans-frontier villagers. Three Kachin leaders were arrested and sentenced to transportation for life. The punishment inflicted upon the Kachins was severe enough to check all further disaffection, and the strong personal influence exerted by various Civil Officers kept many of the headmen from foolishly committing themselves."

The following is the report on operations carried out by the column under Lieutenant-Colonel C. T. Swan, between the 9th and 16th February 1914, as submitted to Government:—

This Column, composed of troops as shown in the margin and accompanied by Major W.B.T. Abbey, Political Officer, assembled at Shingboi on the 8th February, and went into camp on that day at the Daru Hka river. On the morning of the 9th February, the column set out for a camping ground near the Tamang Hka, and went into bivouac there at 1 P.M. having met with no opposition *en route*. The track was extremely steep and slippery, and the party of the 64th was kept busily employed in improving it, to enable the mules of the Mountain Battery to negotiate it. On the following morning, the column advanced on Wawang Village, now only 3 miles distant, and after the Mountain Battery had fired 35 shells at Sabawnang's house, a prominent mark on the Wawang ridge, the infantry advanced to the attack, and occupied the village without opposition at 12-30 P.M. Sabawnang's house was burnt, and a search carried out in the neighbouring jungle produced two guns, the column then going into bivouac.

Staff:—
   Lieut.-Col. C. T. Swan, *Commanding*.
   Lieut. F. O. N. Burne, *Staff Officer*.
   Capt. E. Marsden, *Transport Officer*.
   Major S.R. Godkin, I.M.S., *S.M.O.*

Troops:—
   1 section 22nd Derajat Mountain Battery.
       (Major K. D. Field).
   1st Battalion 10th Gurkha Rifles.
       (Major F. E. Coningham)
   64th Pioneers. (one I.O. and 25 Rifles)
       (Capt. E. Marsden)
   Burma Military Police, 18 Sowars M.I. and 9 Infantry (Kachins)
   Army Bearer Corps. (6 men)

On the morning of the 11th February, Mr. F.C. Lowis, C.I.E., with Capt. H. R. Williams and 50 rifles 1/10th G. R. left camp to visit Wara village. Enquiries were made at various villages *en route*, but nothing of interest was discovered, and the party returned to Wawang. On the same morning, Major W.B.T. Abbey, with Major F. E. Coningham, Lieut. B. R. Mullaly, and 50 rifles 1/10th G. R. set out to visit the Hkashang villages of Tingsa Bum and Dukrau. No opposition was met with, and, having burnt the house of a Dukrau Kachin who had fought at Wawang on the 29th January, the party returned to Wawang on the same day.

On the 12th February, the column remained in bivouac at Wawang, while the Civil Officers continued their enquiries, and communication was established with Laza by helio. On the 13th, Major Abbey, with Lieut. B. R. Mullaly and 50 rifles 1/10th G. R. carried out a reconnaissance along the track to Waship Zup and the Nidgjaw Ferry, no opposition being met with.

On the 14th February, the column remained at Wawang, and on the following day set out to return to the Daru Hka, leaving behind Lieut. B. R. Mullaly, I.G.O. and 50 rifles 1/10th G. R. who were to accompany Mr. Hertz, C.I.E., Deputy Commissioner of Putao, on a tour. A depot, consisting of one Gurkha Officer and 25 rifles 1/10th G. R., with 8 Sowars, B.M.P. had been left in camp at the Daru Hka to guard surplus ammunition and stores, and the column arrived here on the afternoon of the 15th. On the march, news was received that the four Shans, who had caused the trouble at Wawang, had been brought in by friendly Kachins from Nkraun village, across the Mali Hka, and handed over to Mr. Hertz at Wawang.

On the 16th February, the column was broken up, Major Coningham with some 150 rifles 1/10th G. R., remaining in camp at the Daru Hka, in readiness to accompany Major Abbey on a tour to Imbroying. This party, which met with no resistance, took a few prisoners, and returned to Myitkyina on the 1st March.

1915—1916.

On its return to Mandalay from Myitkyina on the 15th June 1915, the regiment was required to find a detachment to take charge of the camp for Turkish prisoners of war from Mesopotamia, which had been formed at Thayetmyo, and accordingly Nos. 2 and 4 Double Companies, with Captain Mackie and Lieutenant Hare, were sent there.

The following is an extract from a speech delivered by the Lieutenant-Governor of Burma, Sir Harcourt Butler, at a parade held at Mandalay on the 25th August 1915:

> "I desire to take this opportunity of saying farewell to all the troops of the Mandalay Garrison—to the 91st Punjabis, the last in Burma of the Burma Regiments which were formed from the Military Police, and did such excellent work in the stirring times that followed the annexation; to the Burma Sappers and Miners who have proved that a Burman can be made a soldier; to the 64th Pioneers, who have done most useful work on the Myitkyina-Putao Road, amidst great difficulties and the worst of climatic conditions, and to whom I am also indebted for their aid in suppressing the Kachin rebellion; to the Military Police, who have shown their loyalty by volunteering for war service, and of whom nearly 3,000 have left Burma for the front; and, last but not least, to the Borders, the Territorials, who with great self-denial consented to relieve regular troops in the East in the time of a great war. I hope they will soon obtain the desire of their hearts and take their proper place at the front.
>
> To one and all of the Mandalay Garrison I wish the best of good fortune."

On the 30th November 1915, Nos. 1 and 3 Double Companies, under Major J. A. Bliss, M.V.O., with two other British Officers, 6 Indian Officers, 218 rank and file, and 8 followers, moved to Bhamo on relief scale, to relieve two companies of the 80th Carnatic Infantry, pending the arrival of another unit to garrison Bhamo.

On the 5th January 1916, the regiment was inspected at Mandalay by Major-General H. A. Raitt, C. B., Commanding the Burma Division and, two days later, paraded for inspection by the Lieutenant-Governor, Sir Harcourt Butler. A guard of honour was furnished by the regiment at Government House, on the 4th January, which was commanded by Subadar Sayyid Munawar, and consisted of 2 Jemadars and 100 rank and file.

In April 1916, Lord Chelmsford, P.C., G.C.M.G., G.M.S.I., G.M.I.E., G.B.E., became Viceroy, and General Sir Charles Carmichael Monro, G.C.B., G.C.M.G., G.C.S.I., became Commander-in-Chief in India.

1916.
The Campaign in Mesopotamia.

On the 22nd January 1916, telegraphic orders were received for the regiment to mobilise for service overseas. In honour of the selection of the regiment for field service, the Commandant remitted all punishments then being carried out.

On the 3rd February 1916, the regiment entrained for Rangoon, on relief scale, having received orders to proceed to Jhansi for mobilisation, owing to the difficulty of mobilising at Mandalay with part of the regiment on detachment at Thayetmyo.

On the same date, the following telegram was received from Major-General Raitt, C.B., Commanding Burma Division:—

"Very much regret that it is impossible for me to see your battalion off to-morrow. I wish them every good luck, and congratulate them on their good fortune in being selected to go to the Front, where I am sure they will hold to the great reputation of the regiment. Burma owes them much for the services they rendered in the North."

At Rangoon, the Thayetmyo detachment rejoined headquarters, and on the 8th February 1916, the regiment embarked for Calcutta.

On the 16th February 1916, the regiment arrived at Jhansi, where it went into camp, and was there rejoined by Captain Murland and Lieutenant Hemsley, the former from recruiting duty, and the latter from employment as A.D.C. to the G.O.C., 9th (Secunderabad) Division. On completing its mobilisation, it entrained for Bombay on the 19th February, leaving a depot at Jhansi under Lieutenant Hare, with 2nd Lieutenant Elliot, I.A.R.O. The depot remained at Jhansi till the 25th February, when it moved to Bangalore, arriving there on the 29th February.

On the 21st February, the regiment embarked for Basra, on the *H. T. Edavana*, at Bombay, with the following British Officers:—Lieutenant-Colonel C. T. Swan (Commandant); Majors J. A. Bliss, M.V.O. (No. 1 D.C.) and R. Mackie (No. 4 D.C.); Captains T. B. Skinner (No. 2 D.C.); H. F. Murland (No. 3 D.C.);

and Hemsley (M.G. Officer); Lieutenants F. O. N. Burne (Adjutant) and D. G. S. Urmson (Quartermaster); 2nd Lieutenants D. Aylward (I.A.R.O.), H.G.T. Rossel, M. Slade and S. Smith (I.A.R.O.); Major S. R. Godkin, I.M.S. (M.O.).

Captain R. J. Malet was still employed as Brigade-Major, Presidency Brigade; Captain H. St. G. Harvey-Kelly was commanding the Shwebo Battalion, Burma Military Police; and Captain M. Castle Smith was Instructor at the School of Musketry, Pachmarhi.

The following Indian Officers accompanied the regiment:—Subadar-Major Krishnaswami; Subadars Sayyid Munawar, Anantadri Nayudu, Narayanasami (I), Durugayya, Narayanasami (II), Musa Raza Khan, and Viraraghavulu; Jemadars David, Krishnamurti, Shamsuddin, Abdul Aziz, Gnanaprakasam, Puniyakoti, Muhammad Abdul Karim, Shanmugam, and M. Anthony.

64th Arrive at Basra. On the 28th February, the regiment arrived at Basra, having been delayed somewhat at the bar of the Shatt al Arab, where a number of transports were waiting. The bar at this time only allowed the passage of vessels drawing 11 feet, except at high tides, when vessels of from 17 to 22 feet could enter. Owing to a sudden fall of rain, which rendered the ground impassable for transport, the regiment was unable to disembark till the 1st March, when it had its first experience of Mesopotamian mud in marching to camp at Maqil. On the 3rd March, a further move was made to Makina Masus (which the British troops aptly named "Muck in the Marshes"), on the outskirts of the town.

Basra was very crowded, as the various units which afterwards formed the 14th (Indian) Division, of which it was understood the regiment was to form a part, and those of the 13th (British) Division of Kitchener's Army, which had been re-formed in Egypt after taking part in the Gallipoli campaign, were arriving daily, and concentrating at Makina Masus. The officers of the regiment had brought with them to Basra their Burmese ponies, which from their small size caused much amusement to the men of the 13th Division.

The regiment was fairly fortunate in the time of its arrival, so far as the temperature was concerned, which in Mesopotamia is extremely variable, ranging from 23º to 127º or more. While October and November are reasonably cool, and from December to February it is distinctly cold, especially at night, the weather in March and April is unsettled and, besides occasional rain and hail, sandstorms, sometimes lasting for several days, are apt to commence. From May to September, the heat is excessive, and is greatly accentuated by the tree-less plains of which all lower Mesopotamia consists.

Summary of the Campaign. Before dealing with the movements of the regiment, it will be as well to give a short résumé of the operations which had already taken place, prior to its arrival. Space forbids any account of the causes which led to war with Turkey, but the act which finally caused a breach was the bombardment by the *Goeben* and *Breslau* of the Russian ports on the Black Sea, on the 29th October 1914, and a State of War was declared from the 31st.

In the meantime, precautionary measures had been taken, in the event of war becoming inevitable and, on the 16th October, the 16th Brigade, of the 6th (Poona) Division, under Brigadier-General W. S. Delamain, had been sent up the Persian Gulf, from Bombay, so as to be in readiness to protect the pipe-line at Abadan, whence oil from the Persian oil-fields was obtained for the Royal Navy. This brigade landed at Fao on the 6th November and, on the 13th, Lieutenant-General Sir A. A. Barrett arrived and took over command, the remainder of the 6th Division following shortly after. Basra was occupied on the 23rd November, after some resistance by the Turks, and Qurna was taken on the 9th December.

Basra.

On the 9th April 1915, General Sir J. E. Nixon took over the command from General Barrett, whose health had failed, and the force became an Army Corps. On the 14th April, Major-General C. J. Melliss defeated the Turks and Arabs in the hard-fought battle of Shaiba, which put an end to Turkish hopes of recovering Basra by an advance down the Euphrates, and on the 15th May, Major-General G. F. Gorringe, by a victory at Ahwaz, drove the Turks back from Arabistan and the pipe-line. On the 3rd June, after a most daring advance up the Tigris, Amara was occupied by Major-General C. V. F. Townshend.

Shaiba and Ahwaz.

Once more it became necessary to turn to the western flank, where the Turks were assembling in force and, on the 25th July, General Gorringe gained another victory, after much hard fighting and, overcoming incredible difficulties caused by the flooded nature of the country, occupied Nasiriya.

Nasiriya.

The question as to whether Kut al Amara should be occupied, and the still more important question of an advance on Baghdad had for long engaged the attention of the authorities in England and in India, and sanction for an advance as far as Kut was now accorded to General Nixon. By the 11th September, the whole of the 6th Division had been assembled at Ali Gharbi and, on the 28th, General Townshend was again victorious and, after severe fighting, drove the Turks northwards out of Kut.

Kut al Amara.

General Nixon now decided that he was strong enough to push on to Baghdad, and for this purpose, proposed to concentrate his force at Aziziya. General Townshend, however, was of opinion that two Divisions would be required to take Baghdad, and General Sir E. Barrow, the Military Adviser at the India Office, was opposed to any further advance. General Nixon was informed that no reinforcement could be expected from the War Office and, on the 5th October, the Viceroy (Lord Hardinge) wired to him to stop any further forward movement. On the 23rd October, however, after much discussion, the Cabinet gave permission for an advance and, on the 26th, General Nixon issued orders for this to commence on the 14th November.

Advance on Baghdad.

Ctesiphon. General Townshend accordingly advanced, and occupied Zor on the 19th. His splendid Division was beginning to show signs of the strain put upon it and, unknown to the British, the Turks had been strongly reinforced by fresh troops of better quality than those which had hitherto opposed the 6th Division. On the 22nd November, Townshend launched his attack on the strong position at Ctesiphon, but though his troops gallantly stormed the first line of entrenchments and, continuing the action for two more days, gained a tactical victory, they were not strong enough to press on further and, on the 25th November, were forced to withdraw to Lajj. Their casualties during the three days' battle had been over 4,300, while the Turks sustained a loss of 6,000 (excluding desertions) and 1,200 taken prisoner.

Retreat to Kut. The retreat was continued to Aziziya on the 28th and, on the 1st December, the two Turkish Army Corps, now in pursuit, were checked at Umm at Tubal, but Townshend had to abandon the damaged gunboats *Firefly* and *Comet*. Kut al Amara was reached on the 3rd, after 12 days' continuous marching and fighting, with very little food, water or sleep. The sufferings of the wounded had been terrible.

Here it was eventually decided to remain until sufficient forces had been assembled to drive back the Turks, and Kut was completely invested, the garrison consisting of 11,607 troops and 3,500 followers, with a civil population of some 6,000.

Attempts to relieve Kut. Orders had meanwhile been given for General Nixon to be reinforced from France and Egypt and, on the 12th December, Lieutenant-General Sir F. J. Aylmer arrived at Amara to take command of the Tigris Corps which was to be formed for the relief of Kut, and to consist of the 3rd (Lahore) and 7th (Meerut) Divisions, with the 6th Cavalry Brigade, which Townshend had sent back to Ali Gharbi before the Turks closed in on Kut. These reinforcements had been arriving but slowly and, by the 3rd January 1916, when it was decided that General Aylmer should advance to relieve Kut, his force only consisted of the Cavalry Brigade and the 7th Division (Major-General Sir G. Younghusband), about 13,000 strong. Although more troops had arrived at Basra, the shortage of river transport, which had hampered the operations throughout, made it impossible to send them up and at the same time keep General Aylmer supplied. Belated efforts had been made to send more river steamers from India but many of these had been lost—out of 24 stern-wheelers sent between November and February, 17 sank *en route*. The Turkish force was estimated at 22,000, with 2,000 Arabs.

Shaikh Saad. On the 4th January 1916, General Younghusband advanced against the Turks but, on the 6th, was checked at Shaikh Saad. On the 7th, General Aylmer arrived, with about two more brigades and, after a stubborn battle, occupied Shaikh Saad. The British casualties were 3,700, and the Turkish losses 4,000, including 650 prisoners.

Wadi. On the 13th January, a further battle was fought on the river Wadi, with a loss to the British of 1,600, and to the Turks of 2,000, and the latter withdrew to the Hanna position. Halil Bey had now succeeded Nur-ud-Din in command of the Turkish Army. On the 14th, Major-General Keary arrived with part of the 3rd Division and, on the 19th, General Nixon, who had for long been in very bad health, handed over command at Basra to Lieutenant-General Sir Percy H. Lake.

Hanna. Heavy rain and floods in the Tigris from the middle of January rendered movement almost impossible but, on the 21st January, General Aylmer made a determined attack on the Hanna position, which was, however, repulsed with a loss of 2,740 men, the Turks losing 2,000. There was now a lull in the operations, pending the arrival of further reinforcements. On the 7th February, the 13th (British) Division was ordered from Egypt to Mesopotamia, and troops to form another (14th) Indian Division from India. From the 10th February, operations in Mesopotamia were brought under the control of the Imperial General Staff, at the War Office.

Dujaila Redoubt. On the 6th March, General Aylmer issued orders for the capture of the Dujaila Redoubt, with the intention of turning the Turkish right, and occupying the whole of the Es Sinn position. The troops got into position by a night march on the 7th and, reaching their position of assembly at 6-45 a.m., on the 8th completely surprised the Turks, and the 26th Punjabis could have marched straight into the Turkish trenches. General Kemball, however, refused to allow any advance till his preparations were complete. At 8 a.m., General Christian (36th Brigade) and Colonel Campbell (9th Brigade) begged to be allowed to advance and at last received permission. The 8th (Colonel Dunsford) and 37th (General Fowler) Brigades actually reached the redoubt, but were bombed out and, after a day of hard fighting and many misunderstandings owing to the difficulties of communication, General Kemball was forced to withdraw to the Tigris on the 9th March. His casualties were 3,474, and the Turks lost 1,280.

General Aylmer was now superseded by General Gorringe in command of the Tigris Corps, and heavy floods in the Tigris stopped any further attempt at advance for the time being. On the 10th March, General Keary sent General Egerton forward, who captured Thorny Nala, and on the 16th, followed this up by driving the Turks out of Mason's Mounds. By the 24th March, the 13th Division was nearly all at Shaik Saad, and General Gorringe now had a force of some 30,000 men, with 127 guns, while the Turkish strength was approximately 20,000. Before turning again to the movements of the 64th, the following extract is given from the Official History of the Campaign:—

> "The *moral* of officers and men remained excellent, but they felt keenly the continued lack of success; and, though their fine discipline prevented the open expression of their views there is evidence to show that there was a considerable feeling among officers and men that the gallantry of the force had been greatly handicapped. Though there were some doubts, as there must always be in unsuccessful operations, regarding the tactical ability and direction of their commanders, what were more generally resented were the absence or inadequacy of up-to-date military armament and equipment, the shortage of all transport, the limited scale and variety of rations, the lack of what are often

termed 'comforts' and the still imperfect medical arrangements. Nevertheless, the evidence of non-combatants present at this time is a striking tribute to the spirit which animated the whole of the fighting force in their monotonous and uncomfortable existence. It must be remembered that in Mesopotamia there was little relaxation for officers and men during their short periods of rest from trench warfare—no comparatively pleasant billets to fall back to, few amusements, no regular periods of short leave at home or in civilised parts, and often increased discomfort if they fell ill or were wounded."

Meanwhile the 64th, which, as already noted, had arrived at Makina Masus on the 3rd March and, from the 6th, was employed daily in improving the existing roads and constructing new ones in the suburbs of Basra—an occupation which was found most irksome, as all ranks were anxiously awaiting orders to move up river.

On the 8th March, half No. 3 Double Company, under Captain Murland, embarked for Filai Filah, north of Amara, for work on a serious breach in the bank of the Tigris. The remainder of the Double Company, with 2nd Lieutenant Aylward, followed on the 16th March.

On the 16th, the regiment received orders to move up the Tigris and accordingly embarked on the 18th in two parties. Orders were issued before moving for officers' swords to be returned to the Indian Base Depot at Basra. The first party, on the *S. S. Shurur,* consisted of Major Bliss, M.V.O., Captains Skinner and Hemsley, and 2nd Lieutenants Rossel and Slade, with No. 1 Double Company, half No. 2 Double Company, Signallers and Machine Gun Section. The second party, on the *S.S.P. 11,* consisted of Lieutenant-Colonel Swan, Major Mackie, Lieutenants Burne and Urmson, 2nd Lieutenant S. Smith, and Major Godkin, I.M.S., with No. 4 Double Company and half No. 2 Double Company. (The regiment was still organised in Double Companies, and the new Company and Platoon organisation was not adopted till November).

The river being in full flood, the heavily-laden river steamers made poor headway, not doing more than 2½ to 3 knots an hour. When tying up at night, piquets were posted, but below Shaikh Saad the Arabs were by this time overawed by the sight of so much shipping, and the constant flow of troops proceeding to the front. The weather was mainly cold and wet, and the space on board much constricted, so all were glad when the ten days of slow progress came to an end. On the way up the river, Captain Skinner's syce was drowned by throwing a bucket overboard with a rope attached to it—a common form of accident at this time on the Tigris.

On the 28th March, the regiment arrived at Wadi, where the ships tied up for the night, in expectation of disembarking next day, and subsequent employment in the trenches. During the night, however, orders were received from Corps Headquarters to disembark at dawn on the right bank, and march back to Shaikh Saad, where the regiment was to come under the orders of the G.O.C. Defences.

During the march, the regiment passed several piquets in contact with the Turks, and roving bands of Arabs, and desultory firing was taking place. Everyone was stiff, as the result of the hot sun and ten days' enforced inactivity. Colonel Watson, then commanding the 107th Pioneers, joined the regiment for part of the march, and gave it the benefit of his experiences.

On the 3rd April, work was commenced on a redoubt about two miles west of the camp; on the 14th, work began on the road from Shaikh Saad to Ora; and from the 20th to the end of the month, the regiment was employed in improving and strengthening the river bund. On the 1st May, the following message was received from the Brigade-Major to the G.O.C. Defences, L. of C. :—

"G. O. C. wishes to express his great appreciation of the way you have rendered the road from Orah here passable for guns and vehicles. Please inform all concerned."

During the early days at Shaikh Saad, the 13th Division began to arrive, in preparation for the big attack on the Hanna position, and the regiment consequently met the men of Kitchener's Army for the first time, making great friends with the 9th Worcesters, who were in the adjoining camp. After the departure of the 13th Division, the troops at Shaikh Saad only consisted of the 14th Hussars, 4th Devons, a detachment of the 1st Brahmins, and one battery R.H.A. Nearly the whole of the corps being on the left bank of the river, detachments of Turks began to feel their way in towards Shaikh Saad, and bands of marauding Arabs became very active at night. In addition to the work carried out by day, up to the middle of April the regiment took its share of piquets in the outpost line at night, and there were constant alarms. No enemy attacks in any force were, however, made, and after the battle of Bait Isa on the 15th April, the Arabs and patrolling Turks ceased to appear.

On the 1st May, the regiment marched to Gomorrah to meet the 6th Cavalry Brigade and assist the guns and transport over bad places on the road. On the 4th May, orders were issued for all winter clothing to be returned to store and, from that date, the regiment was detailed to find garrisons of one Havildar and 12 men each for two of the blockhouses in the defence line. On the 5th May, work was commenced on two more redoubts and, from the 10th, No. 2 Double Company and all the available carpenters were sent daily to work on the new aerodrome.

On the 11th May, No. 1 Double Company, with Major Bliss and Captain Rossel, left Shaikh Saad for Ora, where work was begun on the Ora Canal control sluice, and on deepening the canal bed. The latter work was completed as far as one mile south-west of Sodom on the 14th, when a temporary road from Sodom to Said Hashim was begun. This road was completed to within a quarter of a mile of Said Hashim on the 16th and, on the same day, the banks of the Ora cut were revetted, and its channel deepened.

No. 1 Double Company.

On the 17th May, No. 1 Double Company marched to Sodom, accompanied by a covering party of one Indian Officer and 40 rifles, 45th Rattray's Sikhs (who rejoined their own unit at Ora on the 29th). At Sodom, No. 4 Double Company, with Major Mackie, 2nd Lieutenant S. Smith and Captain Glover, who was attached from the 34th Sikh Pioneers, joined the detachment.

To return to No. 3 Double Company, of which, as we have seen, the first party left Basra on the 18th March—Captain Murland was given orders at Amara by General Austin, G.O.C. Defences, and proceeded to Filai Filah on the 12th March. Being a small party, it had been ordered to camp in the post, which was garrisoned by a company of the 20th Punjabis and was on the right bank of the river, so that, the breach being on the left bank, the river had to be crossed daily. The only boats available being two *bellums*, brought from Amara, and the river being in flood, it took the company 4 hours to cross the first day, but the men rapidly improved and using their shovels as paddles, the time taken to cross was eventually reduced to 2 hours. On the 25th March, the remainder of the Double Company, which had had to march from Amara arrived, bringing a *mahela*. By the 29th March, a retaining bund had been completed, and orders were received for the Double Company to retrace its steps to Amara and repair all breaches in the river bank. These were very numerous, as the river still continued very high in flood, and interfered greatly with reinforcements marching up the river.

No. 3 Double Company.

The Double Company consequently had a great deal of work to do, and had great difficulty in getting rations, and it was not till the 3rd May that a camp was reached near Amara, where orders were received to rejoin the regiment at Shaikh Saad. The return march was commenced on the 5th May, and the Double Company rejoined regimental headquarters on the 14th.

We must now turn again to the front line, where much had happened. On the 19th April, Field Marshal Von der Goltz, who had been military adviser to the Turks, died of typhus at Baghdad, and Halil Pasha was thereafter in command of the Sixth Army. General Gorringe, with the approval of Sir Percy Lake, had decided to attack the Turks on the left bank, where they held the Hanna, Fallahiya and Sannaiyat positions, but heavy rain and floods in the river delayed his plans. However, all was ready by the 4th April and, on the 5th, the 13th Division (Major-General F. S. Maude) attacked the Hanna position which, though of great strength and consisting of 5 lines, with a depth of 1½ miles, it was found that the Turks had evacuated. The Division pressed on, but was held up in front of the Fallahiya position which, however, was taken by the 38th and 39th Brigades in the evening, at a cost of 1,860 casualties.

Hanna and Fallahiya.

Early in the morning of the 6th April, the 7th Division, which had relieved the 13th, advanced on the left of the Sannaiyat position, but the position of the enemy's trenches was not accurately known, so the attack was not made till after daylight and was stopped by heavy fire. The troops dug themselves in, but were driven out by floods from the marshes, and withdrew, having suffered 1,168 casualties. On the 7th, General Younghusband again moved forward and dug in about 800 yards from the trenches, advancing another 300 yards in the evening. On the night of the 8th April, the 13th Division, which was 7,000 strong (the 7th Division now having only 3,250 effectives) took over the trenches, and assaulted the position on the morning of

Sannaiyat.

the 9th. The leading troops got into the first line, but the attack was thrown into confusion by a sudden panic among the troops following, and the Division, with over 1,800 casualties, was driven back and took up a line 400 yards from the trenches.

On the 10th April, Sir Percy Lake decided that any further attack must be made on the right bank of the Tigris. General Keary (3rd Division) was to have advanced on the 12th, but was stopped by heavy rain. At dawn on the 15th, the 7th and 9th Brigades captured Twin Pimples, and arrived within 600 to 900 yards of the Bait Isa position, which they took on the 17th. General Gorringe ordered the 13th Division to relieve the 3rd Division and attack the Chahela trenches on the following day, but in the night the Turks counter-attacked with 12 battalions. The brunt of this counter-attack fell upon the 9th Brigade, which was driven in and carried away part of the 7th Brigade, but the remainder of the latter, and the 8th Brigade (General Edwardes), which repulsed five attacks, held their ground, and the Turks were forced to retreat, with a loss of 4,000 to 5,000 men. The British casualties were 1,600.

Bait Isa.

It was now considered that a further attempt on the Sannaiyat position, assisted by fire from the right bank, offered the only chance of getting through to Kut in time, as General Townshend reported that he was practically at the end of his resources. Accordingly, on the 22nd April, the 7th Division once more attacked, captured the two front lines of trenches with the greatest gallantry, and reached the third line, but was eventually driven back, with a casualty list of 1,283. They were beaten by the weather rather than by the enemy.

Sannaiyat.

With the failure of this attack, all hope of reaching the besieged garrison in time had practically vanished but, on the night of the 24th April, a last desperate attempt was made to send provisions to Kut, the *S. S. Julnar*, with 200 tons of supplies, making a gallant effort to break through. Though riddled by fire, she reached Maqasis, but struck a cable and grounded, and was forced to surrender. Lieutenant Firman, R. N., her Commander, was killed, and Lieutenant-Commander Cowley, R.N.V.R. (of the Lynch Steamer *Mejidieh*), and five of the twelve naval ratings who formed the crew, were wounded. All were decorated, Firman and Cowley being awarded the V. C. Cowley, whose wonderful local knowledge, and 33 years' experience of the Tigris, had been of the greatest value to the military authorities, was undoubtedly put to death by the Turks afterwards—to their everlasting disgrace.

All was now over and, on the 25th, Lord Kitchener (Secretary of State for War) authorised Sir Percy Lake to open negotiations for the surrender of Kut. On the 26th, Townshend sent a message to Halil Pasha and, after ineffectual efforts to get better terms, Kut capitulated on the 29th. The casualties during the siege had been 3,776, and there were 1,450 sick and wounded, of whom 1,136 were exchanged, and another 345 three months later. Nearly 12,000 men went into captivity, of whom over 4,000 died, owing to their abominable treatment by the Turks. The operations for the relief had cost 40,000 casualties.

Surrender of Kut.

The fall of Kut was a severe blow to all ranks in Mesopotamia. The Official History says:—

"It was indeed a sad ending, and one that all ranks of Tigris Corps felt most deeply, to their long and weary struggle against adversity in nature and misfortune in combat. In the course of nearly four months' operations, their losses had amounted to over 23,000 officers and men. On the 25th April their effective rifle strength, including drafts and a few replacements which had gradually reached them, totalled 23,450, *viz.*, 13th Division 6,600, 3rd Division 5,900, 7th Division 5,200, 35th Brigade 2,800, 36th Brigade 1,570, 37th Brigade 1,380. Of these formations, the 7th Division, which had been with the Corps from the commencement of the relief operations, had only been out of contact with the enemy for three days. Of their battalions the 2nd Black Watch had at the end of April only 48 left of their original 842 and many of these 48 had been wounded; the 6th Jats had 50 remaining out of 825; the 125th Rifles 88 out of 848; and the 1st Seaforth Highlanders 102 out of 962; while other battalions had suffered almost as much. The total casualties of the 28th Brigade during this period numbered 3,731; and in all units the losses in officers had been exceptionally heavy."

On the 2nd May, the following message was received by the G.O.C., Tigris Corps from H. M. the King Emperor:—

"Although your brave troops have not had the satisfaction of relieving their beleagured comrades in Kut, they have under the able leadership of yourself and subordinate commanders fought with great gallantry and determination under most trying conditions. The achievement of relief was denied you by floods and bad weather and not by the enemy whom you have resolutely pressed back. I have watched your efforts with admiration and am satisfied that you have done all that was humanly possible and will continue to do so in future encounters with the enemy.— George R. I."

The Sodom Detachment. The 64th had meanwhile been hard at work behind the lines. Taking first the detachment at Sodom, this remained out from the 18th May till the 27th June, rejoining regimental headquarters on the 28th, and during this period the following work was carried out.

On the 18th May, the ruins of Sodom were demolished; from the 18th to the 22nd, the centre line for a light railway was laid out to Said Hashim and towards Shaikh Saad and, between the 23rd and 27th, the railway bank was completed as far as Said Hashim. Between the 19th and 24th, the water-control cut at Sodom, and between the 27th and the 1st June, the sluice gate at Sodom, were completed. Between the 29th May and the 3rd June, work was done on the Sodom—Shaikh Saad railway bank, and between the 27th May and the 4th June, the road-bridge at Sodom was completed. Between the 31st May and the 14th June, Sodom Post was constructed and wired in, and between the 5th and 20th June, work was done on the motor and cart roads to Said Hashim. Between the 21st and 23rd June, the railway bank from the Said Hashim end was ballasted, and from the 24th to the 27th, the railway bank was prolonged across the Gomorrah cut towards Shaikh Saad.

Other miscellaneous works done were:—Clearing the channel to the sweet water canal; clearing channels for irrigation; deepening the entrance to the canal at Ora; work on the canal to Ora to prevent wastage of water, and deepening the canal bed;

sinking a well at Sodom; laying out a railway diversion near Said Hashim; and road work towards Shaikh Saad. During the 49 days from the 11th May to the 28th June, the men had holidays on three days only.

On the 1st June 1916, regimental headquarters was at Gomorrah. On the 6th June, orders were issued laying down a close season for all game up to the 8th August. The Tigris Corps was at this time encamped on the regular breeding-grounds of the sandgrouse, and no one who has not seen them can believe what incredible numbers of these birds there were—huge flights which literally darkened the sky when on their evening flight to the river for water. The standard diet at this time being bully beef and Delhi biscuits, shooting was, of course, very much for the pot, and it is believed that the regimental record was over 30 birds at one shot.

<small>Regimental Headquarters.</small>

On the 19th June, the 64th came under the orders of the 3rd Indian Army Corps, now under the command of General Maude, and on that date received the following message from Corps Headquarters:—

"From to-morrow the 64th Pioneers will be employed on railway construction under direction of Captain Berkeley, I. A. R. O. Work on formation level is to commence to-morrow, if not already begun. Track laying to begin on following day. Camp will be moved as railway progresses. Supplies and water to be brought to camp by rail. From this date 64th Pioneers come under Corps orders which will issue direct from Chief Engineer to O. C. 64th Pioneers. Progress report will be wired daily to Chief Engineer, stating what mile bank and track have reached respectively. Pillars marking miles from Shaikh Saad will be erected. Blockhouses will be completed and wired in as track is laid, and numbered from Shaikh Saad."

In accordance with these orders, the regiment was employed almost continuously on railway work between Shaikh Saad and Es Sinn, and thence on to Imam al Mansur, till the 12th December, and for a short time only during this period were all the companies concentrated at regimental headquarters.

Between the 1st and 20th June, miscellaneous work performed included the construction and wiring of a post on the left bank of the Tigris north of Shaikh Saad; work on the motor and cart roads to Said Hashim; the demolition of some old wells in Shaikh Saad; the rebuilding of the pier at the aerodrome; and the ramping of the Gomorrah water-cut for wheeled traffic.

On the 1st June, the first consignment of railway material arrived on the *S. S. Mosul*, and the next few days were occupied in unloading and collecting material at the site of the goods yard, south of the Ordnance and Supply and Transport Advanced Base Depots. From the 8th, selected Indian ranks were set to work under Captain W. S. C. Glover for instruction, and railway work began in earnest from the 21st.

In addition to the construction and maintenance of more than half the main line permanent way from Shaikh Saad to Sinn (most of the remainder being done by the 34th Sikh Pioneers), and the construction of the terminus at Shaikh Saad, sidings were laid to the Ordnance and S. and T. Depots and to the Engineer Field Park; blockhouses were constructed and wired up to blockhouse No. 14, and wiring was also done between blockhouses Nos. 1 to 5, and between blockhouse No. 1 and redoubt F. In addition, the extension from Sinn to Imam al Mansur was completed, together with blockhouses.

At this time, beyond finding occasional guards and garrisons for posts in the outpost line, the regiment had little to do in the nature of infantry work.

On the 24th June, a search party of one N.C.O. and 6 men, with a *drabi*, was sent out from regimental headquarters at Gomorrah to look for a sepoy who had been sent in to regimental headquarters from Sodom, on a mule, and had not returned. The *drabi* was taken as a guide, as he said that he had seen the mule that the missing man was riding lying dead near the camp. The party was attacked by a band of 60 mounted Arabs, who rode them down and killed three sepoys and the *drabi*, wounded one sepoy, and released the others after stripping them. This occurred in full view of the camp, but no one realised at first what was happening. The cavalry turned out, but were too late to catch the Arabs. The bodies of the killed were recovered on the 25th, and buried, but no trace was ever found of the man on whose account the search party had been sent out.

In July, the daily temperature rose as high as 127 degrees, and there were many dust storms, which seriously hampered the work. One of these lasted for two whole days, during which no work was possible. Work at railhead was also held up for several days in July and August, owing to shortage of material, which also made it necessary, later on in September, to dismantle several sidings previously constructed at Shaikh Saad, which had subsequently to be re-laid.

On the 4th July, Lieutenant-Colonel Swan became seriously ill and was admitted to hospital, and Lieutenant-Colonel J. A. Bliss, M.V.O., assumed command. On the 17th July, Major Mackie and Captain Burne were also admitted to hospital and were subsequently evacuated to India, as was Colonel Swan, who eventually proceeded to England. The medical arrangements were still very defective, and the shortage of river transport caused great difficulty in evacuating the sick. In addition to many thousands treated locally, nearly 11,000 officers and men were invalided out of the country in June, over 12,000 in July, and 11,000 in August.

On the 7th August, No. 2 Double Company (Captain Skinner) moved by rail to Twin Canals to carry on the line from there and to make a loop line at the station. On the 16th September, No. 4 Double Company marched to Corps Headquarters at Mason's Mounds, where it was employed on guard duties and making camp sanitary arrangements. On the 5th October, it marched to Sinn where, under orders of the C.R.E., 14th Division, it dug trenches for the storage of ammunition at the Ordnance Depot. It resumed railway work on the 9th, and worked towards Twin Canals and, on the 14th, moved to a camp near blockhouse No. 50, in the 8th Brigade Area near Sinn Abtar.

On the 1st October, No. 2 Double Company marched from Twin Canals to Sannaiyat, where it came under the orders of Headquarters, 7th Division, and worked on the construction of reserve line trenches, pending the arrival of the 121st Pioneers. On the 16th October, it moved to camp alongside No. 4 Double Company.

On the 7th and 8th October, regimental headquarters, with Nos. 1 and 2 Double Companies, moved to the Shaikh Saad defended area and, on the 23rd, No. 1 Double Company, with the draft from the 32nd Pioneers, and Nos. 2 and 4 Double Companies, moved by rail to Sinn, for work on the railway extension to Imam al Mansur.

Reorganisation. Owing to the failure to recruit Madrasi Musalmans since the outbreak of the war, the Double Company of this class had become greatly under strength and in October it was found necessary to bring it up to strength with Hindus. On the 19th October, 2nd Lieutenant V. Curle arrived with a draft of about 135 men from the 32nd Sikh Pioneers, and was followed by 2nd Lieutenant Banister, on the 2nd November, with a further 50 Sikhs. The chief difficulty in keeping the regiment up to strength lay in the impossibility of getting men back who had once gone down the river. They were found very useful, and it was difficult to trace their whereabouts. Twenty N.C.O's. and men who arrived from Amara on the 24th September were the first to return since early in April and, on the 8th December, a draft of nearly 100 men reached Shaikh Saad, who had disembarked at Basra in August and had been commandeered by the Road Pioneer Company.

On the 15th November, orders were received to amalgamate the existing four Double Companies into three, and make a separate double company of the Sikhs. This was carried into effect on the 12th December, when Nos. 1 and 4 Double Companies were amalgamated and became No. 1 Company, with Nos. 1 and 2 Platoons composed of Musalmans and Christians, and Nos. 3 and 4 of Paraiyans, Nos. 2 and 3 Companies were Tamils, and No. 4 Company, Sikhs. From now on (*i.e.*, 12th December) the term "Company" was substituted for "Double Company."

On the 14th November, the 34th Sikh Pioneers were taken off railway work, and No. 2 Double Company moved to Twin Canals, and No. 4 to blockhouse No. 42 for work on the permanent way. On the 30th November, No. 2 moved again to Sodom, where it completed a new motor road from Shaikh Saad to within three-quarters of a mile of Twin Canals.

On the 15th November, Captain Hemsley was appointed G.S.O. 3, 3rd Corps, and, on the 23rd, Captain Burne rejoined the regiment from India.

On the 11th December, regimental headquarters and No. 3 Double Company moved to Twin Canals and thence to Sinn on the 12th, camping at Three Ball Bridge with No. 1 Double Company and the Sikh draft. On the same day, No. 4 Double Company arrived, followed by No. 2 Double Company on the 13th.

Early in December, the regimental machine guns had been handed over to Ordnance and 8 Lewis guns taken over in exchange. With the exception of 2nd Lieutenants Banister and Fraser, who had just done a five days' course at Sinn, no one in the battalion knew anything about the gun.

The regiment had now finished with railway work for the time being, and General Lubbock, Director of Railways, expressed his appreciation of their services in a letter, dated the 20th December 1916, as follows:—

"I forward a copy of a letter received from Berkeley, and have to add my own thanks for the excellent work done by your battalion. I hope, if you have not got more interesting work on hand, we shall be able to get you to build the extensions which seem imminent."

The letter from Captain A. M. Berkeley, in charge of Military Light Railways, read as follows:—

"In parting with the 64th Pioneers, I feel it is only due to Colonel Bliss and his officers and men to write and tell you how very sorry I am to lose the regiment. They have built more than half of the line, besides the terminus at Shaikh Saad, and have worked excellently. The officers have taken the greatest interest in the work, which they have picked up very well, and their supervision has been of the greatest assistance. The Indian Officers and the men also displayed a very intelligent interest in whatever work they were put on to, and I trust that when the railway comes to be extended to Kut, I shall be so fortunate as to get this regiment back for the work."

These hopes were, unfortunately, destined to be fulfilled, the regiment, as will be seen hereafter, being taken away from much "more interesting work" to carry forward the railway extension.

Having dealt with the activities of the regiment up to the 12th December, I must now give a short account of happenings elsewhere since the fall of Kut.

The British were no longer under the necessity of taking risks, and the Turks were in no condition to resume the offensive, besides which, the advance of the Russians, under General Baratoff, towards Baghdad had commenced. Sir Percy Lake was ordered to maintain himself in a position as far forward as possible, but not to risk further heavy losses. On the 20th May, it was found that the Turks had withdrawn most of their troops on the right bank, and General Keary occupied the Dujaila-Maqasis line and, in June, entrenched an advanced position at Imam al Mansur. The Turks still held the Sannaiyat position in strength, where the 7th Division had sapped up to within about 90 yards of the front line. At the end of June, the 13th Division was withdrawn to Shaikh Saad, and the 14th Division took over the front line on the right bank, with the 3rd Division in reserve.

On the 11th July, General Maude relieved General Gorringe in command of the Tigris Corps, Brigadier-General Cayley succeeding him in command of the 13th Division, and Major-General Cobbe took command of the 7th Division, and Brigadier-General Crocker the 6th Cavalry Brigade. General Brooking was commanding the 15th Division at Nasiriya.

The hardships suffered by the troops in Mesopotamia had by now begun to attract attention at home. The Official History says:—

"During the intense heat of June, sickness and disease levied from the Tigris Corps a very heavy toll. The scorching heat, against which tents were but scant protection, increased in intensity as the days passed without any signs of the usual *Shamal;* there was no escape by day from the dust and heat (most of the flies had died from the heat), and little relief by night, when it was comparatively cool, from the sandflies and other flying pests; and added to these, the tedious monotony of existence in the desert, with little to occupy the mind beyond the daily military routine, contributed greatly to the discomfort of the healthy and the sufferings of the sick............The revelations that had been made in regard to hardships and sufferings of our men in Mesopotamia and criticisms on the conduct of the operations there had led to the appointment in August by H. M. Government of a Commission to enquire into the matter; and it was decided to recall the Commander-in-Chief in India to London to give evidence before it; General Sir Charles Monro being selected to replace Sir Beauchamp Duff in India."

In August, the War Committee decided to appoint a younger officer to the command in Mesopotamia, and Sir Percy Lake was relieved by Major-General Maude, whose place was taken by Major-General A. S. Cobbe. The 13th Division and two cavalry regiments were withdrawn to Amara, and the 7th Cavalry Brigade arrived at Basra.

The Russian attempt to advance on Baghdad had proved a failure. On the 7th May, General Baratoff had occupied Qasr-i-Shirin and, on the 20th, a Russian patrol of two officers and about 100 men had reached Ali Gharbi, after a 200 mile march, and returned, after an interview with Sir Percy Lake who, by command of H.M. the King, decorated the officers with the Military Cross "in recognition of this exploit, and of this the first meeting of British and Russian troops, as allies in the field, for one hundred years." On the 1st June, Baratoff attacked Khaniquin, but the Turks had been reinforced and he was repulsed, and retired on Karind. On the 1st July, he withdrew from Kermanshah, which was occupied by the Turks, who reached Hamadan on the 10th August, Baratoff retiring on Kazvin.

The Russians.

From September till December, Maude, now a Lieutenant-General, was occupied in improving the health and training of the troops, perfecting his line of communications, and amassing reserves of supplies, ammunition and stores. Conditions of life at the front had been enormously improved. On the 10th October, General Sir Charles Monro arrived at Basra and made a tour of inspection, reporting to the War Office that he was quite satisfied with the progress being made.

The Force was re-organised in two Corps of two divisions each, the 1st Indian Army Corps (Lieutenant-General Cobbe) comprising the 3rd (General Keary) and 7th (General Fane) Divisions, while the 3rd Indian Army Corps (General Marshall) comprised the 13th (General Cayley) and 14th (General Egerton) Divisions. The total combatant strength was over 100,000 and the striking force at the front about 50,000.

There had been little activity on the Tigris front and, on the Euphrates line, General Brooking had defeated the Arabs in the neighbourhood of Nasiriya on the 11th September.

By the beginning of December everything was in readiness for an advance on the line of the Hai.

From the 23rd January 1917, companies in the regiment were lettered instead of numbered, so from this point onwards in the narrative, No. 1 becomes A; No. 2, B; No. 3, C; and No. 4, D Company.

1916—1917.
General Maude's Offensive.

On the 10th December 1916, General Maude issued an operation order announcing his intention of pushing forward the left of his force to secure an entrenched position on the Hai. From the 12th December, most of the Army troops came under Corps orders, and the 64th Pioneers, with No. 2 Bridging Train (1st Sappers and Miners), was attached to the 13th Division (3rd Corps), which had arrived from Amara, and was concentrating in the 3rd Corps Area. On the 13th, the artillery of both Corps was to bombard the Sannaiyat position on the left bank of the Tigris, and the 1st Corps was to act so as to give the impression that an attack on Sannaiyat was intended. On the same night, the Cavalry Division was to move from Arab Village and bivouac south of Sinn Abtar. On the 14th, the Cavalry Division was to move east of the Dujaila Redoubt, to secure the passage of the Hai at Basrujiya, south of Atab, clear the enemy from the Hai, south of Kala Haji Fahan, and operate towards the Shumran bridge. The air force were to raid and destroy the Shumran bridge. The 1st Corps was to bombard the Sannaiyat position from 3-30 to 3-40 a.m., and from 6 to 6-30 a.m., and be prepared to assault the front line trenches if necessary. The 3rd Corps was to secure and entrench a line from the Dujaila depression to S. 7, east of Besouia, on the Hai, and thence, on the south of that river, to one mile N. W. of Basrujiya, and the Hai was to be bridged. The old line of Turkish trenches from the Dujaila Redoubt to the Hai was also to be held, while the remainder of the Corps was to pivot on its right and clear the left bank of the Hai, south of Kala Haji Fahan, of hostile troops.

Advance on the Hai.

On the 13th December, the 64th marched with the 13th Division to Imam al Mansur, and during the early hours of the 14th, the advance to and across the Hai was carried out without opposition. The orders to the 64th were "to improve the track from Imam al Mansur to the bridge and to the ford near S. 3, and to supply working parties to assist No. 2 Bridging Train in the construction of two bridges at Atab." On the 14th, regimental headquarters moved to Atab, and the regiment worked on the ramps to the bridges, and on the improvement of the road, from the 14th to the 16th.

The Air Force had failed to hit the Shumran bridge on the 14th, but during the night it was successfully bombed whilst being towed in sections upstream and it was not till the 17th that the Turks were able to re-construct it on the west of the Shumran peninsula. The cavalry advanced to Kala Haji Fahan, but were checked by fire about half a mile from the Shumran bridge. The 39th Brigade (13th Division) advanced to about 1½ miles north-west of Besouia.

On the 15th, the Turks were found to be holding the Khudaira bend and the Hai Salient in strength. Some 300 Arabs advanced against the Atab bridgehead during the morning, but were driven off. The 13th and 14th Divisions advanced to a line Maqasis-Kala Haji Fahan-Umm as Saad Ford. The total casualties on the 14th and 15th were 398.

On the 16th December, the 1st Corps took over the line Maqasis-Pentagon, and the 3rd Corps crossed the Hai and took up a line from Kala Haji Fahan to the Atab bridgehead. The casualties for the day were 68.

On the 17th, regimental headquarters moved some two miles upstream from Atab, and the regiment worked on ramps for four pontoon bridges, B and D companies about 2 miles west of Atab, and A and C Companies half a mile south of Kala Haji Fahan. On this day the regiment reverted from the 3rd Corps to Army Troops, and came under the orders of General Headquarters. The 1st Corps now took over the line from Pentagon to the east of the Hai Salient, and the 3rd Corps extended its line further westwards from Kala Haji Fahan. During the 18th, there was little action of consequence. The regiment continued work on the bridge ramps, and also strengthened the river bund, and filled in water channels running outwards from the wire, which gave the Arabs a means of ingress.

On the 19th, Major-General Rimington, C.B., the Engineer-in-Chief, gave instructions for the work to be performed by the regiment on the scheme for the second line of defence, which curved westwards from Calf's Head and round to the Hai, S. E. of Atab.

"The front-line defences consist of short lengths of trenches about 50 yards long, and wired at intervals of 300 to 400 yards. The 64th Pioneers are ordered to construct:—
- (a) A second line, consisting of similar lines of trenches opposite the intervals and about 200 yards in rear.
- (b) A third line, to consist of strong posts for 100 rifles, 200 to 300 yards in rear of the second line, and about 800 yards apart.

The strong posts are to be constructed first, and wired. Machine-gun emplacements are required in all three lines. Eventually, reserve trenches at the rate of one battalion per mile are to be constructed 300 to 400 yards behind the third line, and the whole joined up by communication trenches."

Work accordingly began on the 19th, and continued till the 22nd.

On the 20th, a column under General Crocker was sent to the Husaini bend of the Tigris, about 6 miles west of Shumran, and Captain Witts, with the Bridging Train, made a very gallant attempt to effect a crossing of the river, but the attempt was abandoned, with some 54 casualties. It is not clear what General Maude's intentions were in attempting this crossing, but probably he wished to force the Turks to disperse their forces further. From now till the beginning of January, the troops were mainly engaged in consolidating their positions, and pushing forward the advanced trenches facing the Khudaira bend and the Hai Salient.

On the 22nd December, the regiment received orders to leave its work on the second line defences, and march to Imam al Mansur for the construction of the railway extension to Atab. Work on the railway embankment was started on the same afternoon. On the 24th December, the 3rd Labour Corps was attached to the regiment for employment in carrying material, and work was carried on without interruption till the 26th. From the 26th, the work was interrupted by want of material at railhead, and by heavy rain, but by the 29th, the line was completed to within one mile of Atab.

In addition to the railway construction, B and D Companies did some work on the second line defences at Calf's Head and, on the 26th and 27th, a party from A Company constructed gun-pits for anti-aircraft guns in the Dujaila Depression near Imam al Mansur.

The heavy rain had by now damaged the railway considerably. Also, the effect of the water on the soil was to turn it into slime which got on to the rails, and made it impossible for locomotives to move. Consequently, on the 30th December, A Company was moved to Sinn, to carry out repairs to the line and, on the next day, regimental headquarters and C and D Companies followed. B Company was left at Imam al Mansur and, except for a few days in January, was detached from the regiment till the 28th February, 1917.

On the 1st January, the regiment, less B Company, was concentrated at Sinn, and work began on the railway yard in the station and on the permanent way eastwards. Assistance was given by a detachment of the 3rd Labour Corps, and the work of repairing the line continued steadily till the 28th January. On the 3rd January, A Company moved to Twin Canals and, on the 9th, C Company to S.P. 4.

On the 13th, under orders from the Engineer-in-Chief, D Company moved to Atab, for work on the defences east of the Hai. The work consisted of wiring lunettes, strong points and communication trenches.

On the 15th, the regiment, less B Company, was distributed as follows :—Regimental headquarters at Three Ball bridge, Sinn; A Company, Twin Canals; C Company, S.P. 4; D Company, Atab. On the 21st, the regiment witnessed, from Sinn, the first real barrage it had seen, during the course of an attack by the 13th Division. Munitions were now sufficiently plentiful to enable this very necessary preliminary to a present-day attack to be carried out, and it was cheering to know that it had been rendered possible by all the hard work which the regiment, and other Pioneer units, had put in on the railway, resulting in a regular service of supply and munitions trains. On the 22nd, C Company moved to railhead, near Atab. On the 28th, orders were received for the regiment, less B Company, to concentrate at Atab for work under the 3rd Corps.

We must now turn once more to the position in the front line trenches. The heavy rain at the end of December had rendered all operations impossible. As described in the Official History:—

> "The whole area became deep in mud, camels and motor lorries were immobilised, carts carried less and stuck frequently, pack mules had to make fewer or slower journeys and even the railway trains, carrying half loads, took double the usual time over their journeys, the engines being frequently held up by the mud on the rails, left in some cases by infantry crossing the line."

Khudaira Bend. From the end of December, the 8th and 9th Brigades (3rd Division) had been steadily pushing forward trenches in front of the Khudaira Bend position and, on the 9th January, these brigades assaulted and captured the front line of trenches. Severe fighting followed, and the British casualties were nearly 700; the Turkish losses were heavy, and they withdrew to the second line trenches. On the 11th, the 9th Brigade attempted to drive the Turks out of the bend, but the latter appear to have been reinforced and the brigade was checked. A series of short advances, with much hard fighting, lasted from now on till the 18th, when the Turks evacuated their trenches and withdrew across the river. The 3rd Division had 1,639 casualties in the eleven days' fighting, and the enemy suffered severe losses.

The Hai Salient. On the 11th January, the 3rd Corps advanced some 400 yards at the Hai Salient and consolidated its trenches. The Hai itself was now a considerable stream, some fourteen feet deep. On the 25th January, the 39th and 40th Brigades (13th Division) assaulted the front line and succeeded in gaining a footing, there, but the 39th was subsequently driven back by a counter-attack. The casualties of the day were 1,135. On the 26th, the 36th Brigade (14th Division), supported by the 35th Brigade, made good the ground lost by the 39th Brigade. On the 27th January, the 36th Brigade captured three lines of trench; on the 28th, the 13th Division occupied the whole of the Turkish first and second line trenches east of the Hai, and, on the west, the 14th Division consolidated its gains. General Marshall now decided to concentrate on driving the Turks back on the west of the Hai, and the 29th, 30th and 31st January were occupied in consolidating his lines and preparing for an assault.

64th joins 14th Division. On the 28th January, the regiment (less B Company) had received orders to concentrate at Atab for work under the 3rd Corps and, on the 29th, headquarters and D Company reached a point (Q. 13) 1½ miles south-west of Kala Haji Fahan, where they were joined by A and C Companies on the 30th, when the regiment received orders from Colonel Ogilvie, C.R.E., 14th Division, for work that night. From now onwards, till after the crossing of the Tigris at the Shumran Bend, the regiment, less B Company, was employed unremittingly and, as a general rule, at night, on the construction of defences and communications, for the most part to the west of the Hai. Much of the work was performed under fire and up to the 23rd February the regiment suffered the following casualties:—Killed; Subadar Musa Raza Khan and 4

Indian other ranks; Wounded, Captain H. F. Murland and 28 Indian other ranks. In addition one man was wounded by a premature burst from a 60-pounder battery in position in rear of the regiment.

The bivouac of the regiment at "Q. 13" was situated in a deep nala, just beyond range of the enemy's heavy guns. The entrances to the complicated trench systems of the 13th and 14th Divisions lay on a line about half a mile to the north, so the regiment was well placed for the work required. It usually marched at 6 p.m., and, as a general rule, two companies were employed each night, and the approach to the work was made in artillery formation, so as to minimise or avoid casualties.

Towards the middle of the month, when working nearer the Tigris and in forward trenches, bayonets were fixed, in anticipation of interference by the Turks. They, however, were not particularly enterprising by night and, though they kept up a constant and heavy fire from guns, rifles and machine-guns, they did not as a rule undertake raids.

The weather during this period was frequently wet and on one occasion the nala at Q. 13 was badly flooded, water rising to a depth of three to four feet in the tents. The Sikh Company, which was not in camp at the time, was unable to salve its belongings and the men, on their return, were much upset to find everything buried in mud and water.

On the 1st February, the 38th and 40th Brigades of the 13th Division assaulted and captured the last line but one of the enemy defences east of the Hai. The operations on the west were not so successful, the 36th and 45th Sikhs of the 37th Brigade being driven out of the Turkish trenches, after a gallant resistance, while the 35th Brigade on their left was checked by heavy hostile fire. Attempts to retake the trenches were a failure, owing to congestion by the wounded in the trenches. Out of a total of 17 British and 30 Indian officers and 1,180 other ranks in the 36th and 45th Sikhs, 16 British and 28 Indian officers and 988 other ranks had become casualties. The total casualties on the 1st amounted to 1,273. On the 3rd, the 1|2nd Gurkhas and 1|4th Devonshires of the 37th Brigade captured the trenches from which the 36th and 45th had been driven back, with 728 casualties. On the 4th, it was found that the Turks had withdrawn from their trenches along the Hai and appeared to be holding a line from the Liquorice Factory, opposite Kut, across to the south of the Shumran bend. The total British casualties from the 13th December to the 3rd February amounted to 8,524, those of the Turks being well over 10,000.

The Dahra Bend. On the 9th February, the 38th Brigade captured a portion of the Turkish line west of the Liquorice Factory, and to the west the 39th Brigade drove back some Turkish detachments. From this date till the 16th, the 64th Pioneers was attached to the 13th Division.

The following is a copy of a telegram, dated 7th February 1917, from the G.O.C., 3rd Corps to the G.O.C., 14th Division:—

"Advanced G. H. Q. wires 6th February—Army Commander has received following message from Chief London to which suitable reply is being sent:—'I am directed by War Cabinet to convey to you and ranks of the force under your command their appreciation and congratulations on the successes achieved during the last few weeks on the Tigris. With much satisfaction they have received your report that great credit for these results is due to Lieutenant-Generals Marshall and Cobbe and to their subordinate Commanders, and that the determination and fighting spirit of the troops has been superb'."

On the 10th February, the 35th Brigade took the Liquorice Factory, and on the 11th the Turks withdrew from their advanced positions on the west, and by the evening of that day they were completely enclosed in the Dahra bend. On the 11th, the 35th Brigade captured a strong point which still further circumscribed the Turkish position.

On the 15th February, the 13th Division, supported on its right by the 14th Division successfully assaulted the enemy's centre, the 40th Brigade leading, and a further fine assault by the 35th Brigade broke down the Turkish resistance, except in the north-west corner of the Dahra bend, which was finally cleared of the enemy on the morning of the 16th. Nearly 2,000 Turks were captured, besides a quantity of ammunition and stores, and 2,500 rifles.

On the 16th February, the 64th rejoined the 14th Division, receiving the following message from the G.Os.C., 13th Division and 40th Brigade:—

"Corps wire that you are transferred to the 14th Division from 6 p.m. to-night. G. O. C. Division and 40th Brigade wish to thank you and all ranks for the invaluable work you have done for us."

On the 15th February, General Maude had issued an Order of the Day, of which the following is an extract:—

"After a period of severe and strenuous fighting, extending with only short pauses over a period of two months, I wish to express to the Navy, to Lieutenant-Generals Marshall and Cobbe, to the divisional and Brigade Commanders, to the Staffs, including my own, and to all ranks of the fighting troops, my warmest thanks for their splendid work, and my congratulations on their brilliant successes. To the regimental officers, non-commissioned officers and men, a special word is due for their matchless heroism and fighting spirit, and for their grit and determination so fully in accord with the best traditions of British and Indian regiments. Whilst regretting deeply the casualties necessarily incurred in the attainment of our object, the series of stinging blows dealt to the enemy, his severe losses which are out of all proportion to the size of his force, and his obviously falling spirits afford ample proof to all ranks that their sacrifices have not been in vain……………..……To each and every member of the navy and army, and to those who, though not belonging to either of the services, have helped to bring about the results achieved, I tender my warmest thanks for their whole-hearted and magnificent support. The end is not yet, but with such absolute co-operation and vigour animating all, continuance of our success is assured."

On the 18th February, the following message was received by the regiment from the 14th Division:—

"3rd Corps wires following message from Commander-in-Chief, India, has been received by Army Commander:—'Please accept on behalf of myself and all ranks of the Army in India most hearty congratulations for yourself and all ranks serving under your command on the brilliant success achieved. I hope wounded all doing well'."

Sannaiyat. From the 15th to the 17th February, there was heavy rain, resulting in high floods in the Tigris. On the 16th February, the 21st Brigade of the 7th Division assaulted the Sannaiyat position, and successfully occupied the second line of trenches, but was shelled out again by the Turks. The Tigris continued to rise till the 21st, when it showed signs of falling, and it was decided to attempt a crossing on the 23rd. On the 22nd, General Peebles' 19th Brigade, of the 7th Division, captured part of the two front lines of the Sannaiyat position, and established itself securely, the 28th Brigade occupying the remainder of these lines in the evening. The casualties for the day were 1,332. On the same day, a party from the 3rd Division made a successful raid across the river at Maqasis.

Battle of the Shumran Crossing. For the crossing of the Tigris on the 23rd, General Egerton's 14th Division had the honour of being selected, and the 37th Brigade (Brigadier-General O. W. Carey) was detailed to form the covering party. The bridging of the river was to be carried out by Captain Witts, R. E., and the ferrying arrangements by Major Pemberton, R.E. (12th Company, Q.V.O. Sappers and Miners). The approaches to the river were to be carefully prepared by night, and the 2nd Norfolks, 1/2nd Gurkhas and 2/9th Gurkhas were detailed to cross by the ferries, which were rowed by volunteers from the 2nd Norfolks, 1/4th Hampshires, 71st, 72nd and 88th Companies, R.E., 12th, 13th and 15th Companies, Sappers and Miners, and 128th Pioneers. When the left bank of the Tigris had been made good, the Bridging Train was to come up and throw a bridge across.

At dusk on the evening of the 22nd, the whole Division was fallen in, in readiness for the night advance to Shumran. It was disconcerting to see "Fritz" (an enemy aeroplane) make an appearance overhead at about 6 p.m., but as the troops were stationary and the light failing, he apparently observed nothing. The tasks allotted to the regiment were:—

(i) Improvement of communications approaching the bridgehead, to enable the Bridging Train to come up.

(ii) Improvement of lateral communications along the river front.

The operation of the 14th Division came as a complete surprise to the Turks, and the first parties succeeded in crossing, at about 6 a.m., before the enemy could develop a really serious fire. The regiment arrived at the river in the early morning, by which time the Norfolks and Gurkhas were making good progress on the left bank. Lines of Norfolks could be seen doubling forward, and the ferries were returning filled with captured Turks.

The regiment set to work and carried on all day, under a heavy but fortunately ill-aimed artillery fire. In spite of the river being in flood, the Bridging Train carried out its task most admirably, under unremitting but badly directed artillery fire from the enemy. By 4-30 p.m., the bridge, 295 yards long, was ready for traffic, and a position had been established on the left bank, the casualties amounting to 350, mainly amongst the men who rowed the pontoons across. I can find no record of what the casualties of the regiment were on this day, but the fire was distinctly "hot" at times. In the evening, while marching back, Jemadar P. Narayanasami's platoon was observed to disappear entirely in the smoke and dust of a Turkish "coal box," but the men were quite undisturbed.

The 7th Division co-operated during the day by capturing the third line, and the greater part of the fourth line, of the Sannaiyat position. It was indeed a memorable day, and the turning-point in the Mesopotamian campaign.

That night, the regiment bivouacked on the right bank and, early next morning, saw the whole fleet of naval gunboats making up stream to play its part in the pursuit of the Turks. The 14th Division continued its advance in the Shumran peninsula on the 24th, and the Air Force reported that the Turks were in full retreat towards Baghdad. The Turkish rearguard fought well, and foiled the efforts of the Cavalry Division to outflank them. The losses of the 14th Division amounted to about 1,100.

The following messages were received by the regiment from the G.O.C., 14th Division:—

"*23rd February.* General Marshall wires hearty congratulations to you and all troops concerned on most successful crossing.

"*24th February.* (From General Egerton). Please convey to all ranks my thanks for, and admiration of, their magnificent performance yesterday and to-day.

"*25th February.* Army Commander wires to 3rd Corps:—'Many congratulations to you and 14th Division on brilliant fighting and important captures to-day. He hopes you and cavalry will add to latter to-morrow substantially'."

During the 24th, the 1st Corps passed through the Sannaiyat and Suwada positions with little opposition, and Kut was found to be deserted early the following morning, when General Maude commenced a vigorous pursuit of the retreating enemy, of whom 4,500 had already been captured.

On the 25th February, the regiment was ordered to concentrate near 14th Division headquarters and, on the same day, was withdrawn from the 3rd corps, and became Army troops, which was a great disappointment, as it was now detailed for work in the neighbourhood of Kut and was thus deprived of more active opportunities with the pursuing army.

B Company. I must now turn to B Company (Major Skinner), which, during these events, had been detached from the regiment. It had been left at Imam al Mansur to work, with the 2|119th Infantry, on the construction of a series of blockhouses to the Hai and, by the 2nd January, fourteen of these blockhouses had been completed.

A new alignment was then given, and the position of three blockhouses had to be altered and, on the 4th, another alignment was given, and four more blockhouses made. Again, on the 6th, a final alignment was selected, necessitating the construction of three more blockhouses. A redoubt was also dug.

On the 10th January, the company moved to Sinn for the repair of roads near the Supply Depot, and the D.D.S. and T. wrote as follows to the O.C., 64th Pioneers, on the 2nd February :—

> "I wish to thank you for the most excellent road laid round the depot at Sinn by your regiment. The late rains seem to have improved it, if anything, and this in spite of the heavy traffic it has borne. I had intended writing in before, but particularly noticed it to-day when getting into it from the Imam road."

On the 15th January, the company moved to Calf's Head, for work on the second line defences, which comprised the construction and wiring of a redoubt with machine-gun emplacements, digging communication trenches, and wiring lunettes and redoubts. On the 6th February, the company moved again, to the neighbourhood of Besouia, and worked till the 20th on the construction of a bridgehead position such of the Hai, which included digging and wiring lunettes, strong posts and redoubts. Between the 21st and 24th, the company was employed in making a bund between the Cavalry Division camp and Atab, as the river was in flood and rising. It finally left Besouia on the 28th February and rejoined regimental headquarters.

On the 25th February, the regiment, under orders of the Engineer-in-Chief, moved to a camp on the left bank of the Tigris on the western side of the Shumran peninsula. Here it worked from the 27th February till the 13th March, improving and strengthening the bund along the bank of the Tigris in the Shumran peninsula and as far as the east of the Khudaira bend. This was considered essential so as to secure a dry area during the floods and to establish a dry line of communications on the left bank.

64th moves to Baghdad. On the 13th March, the regiment was ordered to march to Baghdad, which was reached on the 20th—104 miles in seven days, during which only seven men went sick. The stages were as follows :—14th, Imam Mahdi (16 miles); 15th, Shidhaif Ash Sharqiya (17 miles); 16th, Aziziya (18 miles); 17th, Zor (17 miles); 18th, Ctesiphon (16 miles); 19th, 2½ miles north of Diyala (13 miles); 20th, ¼ mile from Advanced Base Headquarters (7 miles).

Pursuit of the Turks. Before dealing with the subsequent movements of the regiment, a short account must be given of the advance of the Army on Baghdad. On the 25th February, the Turkish rearguard succeeded in holding off the 13th Division and the Cavalry Division near Imam Mahdi. On the 26th, the Turks were far ahead of our troops, but the Navy took up the pursuit and inflicted much damage, recapturing the *Firefly,* and taking several other vessels. This action had the effect of completely demoralising the Turks. The Cavalry Division reached Aziziya on the 27th, and a halt had now to be called for a few days to enable supplies to be arranged for.

On the 5th March, the Cavalry, renewing the advance, were held up by some 2,500 Turks entrenched at Lajj, and sustained some loss, but the Turks retired during the night, and took up a position on the Diyala river. Here the 38th Brigade found them, on the 7th March, in considerable strength. An attempt to cross the Diyala in pontoons after dark failed, and in a further attempt made on the following night only a small party of the 6th Loyal North Lancashire Regiment, led by Captain O. A. Reid, succeeded in crossing. This party repulsed continuous attacks by the Turks throughout the night. On the 9th, the 7th Division (General Fane) was checked at the Tel Aswad position on the right bank of the Tigris, but during the night the 13th Division effected a crossing of the Diyala, and relieved Captain Reid's party, which had again beaten off an attack by a Turkish battalion during the day, inflicting over 100 casualties on them. Captain Reid was awarded a well-earned V. C.

On the 10th March, the Turks withdrew from the Tel Aswad and Umm at Tubul position and evacuated Baghdad that night, retreating to the north. On the 11th, General Thomson, with the 35th Brigade, occupied the city.

With the subsequent operations of General Maude's divisions in the neighbourhood of Baghdad we are not immediately concerned. General Cobbe, with the 7th Division, advanced to Mushahida on the 14th March, Falluja was occupied on the 18th and, on the 23rd, General Keary occupied Shahraban. By the 29th March, Maude had succeeded in driving the two Turkish army corps apart, one towards Kifri, and the other towards Samarra, which was taken by the British on the 24th April, after severe fighting at Istabulat.

In the meantime, the results of the revolution in Russia were becoming apparent, and there was no longer any hope of a Russian advance on Mosul from the Caucasus and Persia.

1917.
Baghdad.

As we have seen, the regiment reached Baghdad on the 20th March and from that date **The Kharr Bund.** was placed under the orders of the Chief Engineer, 1st Corps, for work on the construction of the Kharr Bund. Shortly after the British occupation of Baghdad on the 11th March, the Turks cut the Sakhlawiya dam on the river Euphrates. This dam was of great depth and, the Euphrates being on a considerably higher level than the Tigris, the result of breaching it was to divert about a third of the waters of the Euphrates along the Sakhlawiya canal in the direction of Baghdad and the country south of the city. It was also expected that the country over which ran the first eleven miles of the Decauville railway from Baghdad to Mufraz on the Euphrates would be submerged.

On the 27th March, water from the Euphrates began to appear in the Masudiya canal in front of the bund but, by the 30th, the latter was completed.

The regiment was now withdrawn from the 1st Corps and placed under the orders of the Engineer-in-Chief for the construction of a division on the Decauville railway, for which a new alignment had been reconnoitred by Major Berkeley, the Assistant Director of Railways. Work began on the 30th, and D Company (Captain Urmson) went into camp at Abu Khunta, about 8 miles south of regimental headquarters, to take up the first eleven miles of the existing line and return it to headquarters for use on the new alignment. Frames were made up in the regimental workshops, and A (Lieutenant Curle), B (Lieutenant Stonehewer), and C (Captain Aylward) Companies prepared the new embankment and commenced linking up.

<small>Baghdad-Mufraz Railway.</small>

The removal of the old line was completed by the 13th April, and work on the railway continued till the 25th, on which date, but for the floods from the Euphrates, trains would have commenced to run. Much delay was caused by the lack of tools and material. From the 10th to the 21st April, D Company was employed in collecting material and rolling-stock from Sindiya, and sending it down to Baghdad. No expansion-pieces were available, with the result that the heat, which was so intense that the men had to use sand bags to protect their hands from the rails, caused parts of the line to become crooked. It therefore became necessary, during the latter half of April, to re-adjust the line already laid.

On the 8th and 9th April, two platoons of B Company made a ramp at Rotah pontoon bridge near the Baghdad customs house.

Serious trouble from the Euphrates floods began on the 21st April, when a part of the line was breached about a mile from the Iron Bridge, by the action of the water scouring through an old culvert in the embankment. Under the direction of Colonel Stack, C.R.E. of the 3rd Division, a bund was made by lowering rails perpendicularly into the water, sliding sheets of corrugated iron over them, and piling earth quickly in front.

<small>The Baghdad Bunds.</small>

On the 25th April, a bund holding back some miles of flood water from the Euphrates at Umm Mosahr was breached, and all traffic was stopped by the flooding of the railway line and the road to Falluja. Colonel Stack again took charge, and the work of closing the breach was undertaken by the regiment, which moved to Umm Mosahr, assisted for part of the time by three sections of No. 20 Company, Sappers and Miners, the 4th Labour Corps, and about 70 local Arabs. This work continued till the 21st May, and a detailed note will be found in Part V of these records.

Less serious breaches occurred at Amariya and Nukhta, which were closed by A Company between the 30th April and 20th May.

Two platoons of B Company were attached to the 15th Division from the 21st to 30th April for work on roads and water supply at the Divisional Headquarters camp.

On the 22nd May, A and D Companies were detailed to repair and improve the Decauville railway, which had been damaged by the floods. Two level crossings and nine culverts were put in, and the line was lifted and packed in places where it had sunk. A station building and some new sidings were constructed at Mufraz. This detachment also did some work on the Baghdad-Mufraz road, and constructed a few culverts.

Hinaidi-Baquba Railway. On the 18th May, orders had been received from General Headquarters for two Companies to report at Hinaidi the same evening for work on the Hinaidi-Baquba Railway from the following day, and, in accordance with these orders, B and C Companies moved to Hinaidi. A report on their work will be found in Part V.

Baghdad-Samarra Railway. On the 17th June, orders were received for regimental headquarters and D Company to move to Kadhimain, about seven miles north-west of Baghdad, to relieve the 32nd Sikh Pioneers on the Baghdad-Samarra railway. They reached Kadhimain on the 20th, while A Company remained to work on the Decauville railway. The regiment was now distributed as follows:—

R. H. Q. and D Company	Kadhimain.
B and C Companies	Hinaidi.
A Company	Mufraz.

Regimental headquarters and D Company remained at Kadhimain, making up the slope of the railway embankment, till the 5th July, when they moved to the Iron Bridge, two miles south-west of Baghdad. Here some work was done on water-cuts on the left bank of the Masudiya canal, and some road work was also carried out to the west of the Iron Bridge.

On the 4th July, A Company moved from Mufraz to Umm Mosahr and, after repairing the Nukhta and Mahmudiya roads, rejoined headquarters on the 18th. On the 19th, D Company moved to Falluja for road and railway work. Between that date and the 9th August, regimental headquarters and A Company were engaged in infantry training which, owing to the great urgency of work, had hitherto been impossible. During this period the only other work performed was on the 27th July, when repairs were carried out on the bank of the Masudiya canal.

River Diyala Bund. On the 9th August, General Headquarters issued orders for regimental headquarters and A Company to move to Diyala for work under the Engineer-in-Chief. The move was made by road, *via* Hinaidi, and Diyala was reached on the 13th, where camp was pitched at the confluence of the Diyala and Tigris. Great difficulty was at first experienced in getting Arab labour and it was not until the arrival of an interpreter on the 18th, who was sent out to look for labour, that any headway could be made in this respect, but, by the 25th, three Arab contractors had been brought in and eventually competition became so keen that the rate per donkey load of brushwood fell from Re. 1-4-0 to Annas 12. D Company rejoined from Falluja on the 11th September, and the work on the bund was completed by the 18th. Some notes on the work will be found in Part V.

It will be remembered that D Company left regimental headquarters on the 19th July, marching to Sakhlawiya, where it arrived on the 22nd, *via* Nukhta and Falluja. Between the 23rd July and the 1st September, this Company carried out repairs to the Sakhlawiya-Falluja road, and constructed roads between Bustan and Seriya post, and between Bustan and the mouth of the Sakhlawiya canal. (*Vide* notes in Part V). The Company, which had been split up into detachments to enable the working parties to be near their work, was concentrated again at Falluja on the 2nd September and, after some work on the Falluja defences on the 4th and 5th, proceeded to Baghdad, *via* Nukhta, where it arrived on the 7th, and rejoined regimental headquarters at the Diyala on the 11th.

D Company at Falluja.

On the 18th September, regimental headquarters and A and D Companies were placed at the disposal of the Deputy Director of Works for the construction of a bund from the north end of the work just completed to the east bank of Baghdad City, the work to be started from the Baghdad end. On the 27th, therefore, headquarters and D Company moved to Karadah and camped in the 52nd Brigade area about 600 yards from the Tigris north-east of the Diyala-Baghdad road, A Company following on the 28th. Work began on the following day, and continued till the 15th October, the greater part of which consisted of laying out work for, and supervising the work of, the 3rd Arab Labour Corps. Meanwhile orders were received on the 10th October for regimental headquarters, with A and D Companies, less one section, to proceed to Nukhta in relief of the 48th Pioneers, for work on the Baghdad-Falluja railway. One section was to be left at Karadah to continue supervision of the Arab labour on the bund. The following letter of appreciation of this section's work was received from the officer in charge of Bunds :—

Baghdad-Diyala Bund.

"Jemadar Darmalingam and the detachment of your regiment left here on the bund work left for the Advanced Base Rest Camp yesterday, *en route* to rejoin you. They have been of the greatest assistance in getting the revetment started and a good stretch of it done, and have shown the 12th Labour Corps men how to do it. The latter are now carrying on properly by themselves, thanks to the good start your men gave them. The contractors rather flooded us out at first, so the men had sometimes to work rather long hours, which they did most willingly and well."

The 12th Labour Corps had arrived on the 11th, to take over the work and, on the 17th, headquarters, with the two Companies, marched to Khan Police Post *via* Umm Mosahr and Nukhta.

We must now turn to B and C Companies, which had arrived at Hinaidi on the 18th May. Work was begun on the railway to Baquba on the 21st, and consisted at first of earthwork and work in the station yard, but other labour was shortly afterwards sent for yard work and the preparation of material. The detachment supplied linking, packing and levelling parties, while a Labour Corps completed the earth-work. A detachment of about 200 men of the 2/6th Gurkha Rifles assisted during the linking by carrying frames, and unloading trucks. The whole distance of 35½ miles, 2 feet 6 inches gauge, was linked in 34 working days. It was found that, when construction trains were punctual and material good and sufficient, 1½ miles of line could be laid in a day. A report on the work will be found in Part V,

Hinaidi-Baquba Railway.

On the 6th August, orders were received for the detachment to proceed to Baquba for work under the 14th Division of the 3rd Corps. C Company therefore marched to Baquba on the 8th, and B Company on the 11th August.

Road-work at Baquba. Between the 12th and 15th August, the detachment was employed on road-work in the vicinity of Baquba. This included an approach to a new bridge over the Diyala at Shiftat, and a new road from the old Diyala bridge to a camp north-east of the town. The roads to and from the Shiftat bridge were improved, and some small bridges made, and Subadar Nanjappa, with a party from B Company, made a 30 foot trestle bridge over a canal. Between the 16th and 18th August, 2¼ miles of the 20 foot road from Baquba to Buhriz, along the west side of the Khorassan canal, were completed. The following letter was received, on the 24th, from Head-quarters, 14th Division:—

"The G. O. C. wishes to thank Colonel Ogilvie and all ranks of the 2nd Q. V. O. Sappers and Miners, 64th and 128th Pioneers, the former for planning, the latter for supervising and carrying out recent improvements effected in our communications over the Diyala, and in the approaches to and from camps, which have involved continuous hard work.

General Egerton has particularly noticed the speed and thoroughness of the work done, and he wishes all ranks informed that he appreciates their special efforts."

Baquba-Shahraban Railway. From the 18th August, the detachment was employed on the extension of the Hinaidi-Baquba railway to Shahraban. Work was done first on a diversion to a temporary bridge over the Diyala, east of the permanent bridge and, from the 10th September till the 23rd October, on the earthwork of the track up to, and at, Shahraban. The work was heavy, being in hard baked clay, in which the engineer in charge expected the men to do 200 cubic feet *per diem*, which was impossible. An entry in the War Diary reads:—"As tasks are already 80 to 100 cubic feet in hard baked clay, with a lead of 7 to 15 feet, and a lift of 3 feet, the men cannot do more: Captain Bevan of the railway admitted that he had asked for 600 men for the work we are to do with 310."

Shahraban-Table Mountain Railway. From the 25th October till the 28th November, the detachment was employed on the extension of the railway from Shahraban to Table Mountain in the Jabal Hamrin, a distance of 8¼ miles. The survey for the line was carried out by Captain Aylward, M.C., of the 64th, and the linking was done by the detachment. The earthwork was begun by the detachment but, orders having been issued for the work to be completed urgently, infantry working parties and Arab labour were afterwards sent, whose work was supervised by the Pioneers. Notes on this work will be found in Part V.

On the 27th November, orders were received for the detachment to return to regimental headquarters. The move was carried out *via* Shiftat and Khirr Railway Depot, and the detachment rejoined headquarters on the 3rd December, for work on the **Falluja railway.**

The following letter, dated 11th December 1917, was addressed by Major Burn, R.E., Baquba Road, to the Assistant Director of Railways, Kut:—

"I beg to bring to your notice with a view to suitable recognition the excellent work done by the detachment of the 64th Pioneers under Colonel Watson on the extension from Shahraban to Table Mountain. The detachment surveyed the line, completed the earthwork, which was heavy, supervised the Infantry working parties, constructed the bridges, which involved considerable difficulties, linked the line, and packed and boxed it. The line was eight miles long and involved much heavier work than we have found hitherto; they completed the whole work in fifteen days and considering their working strength was under 400 and their only assistance was 300 Infantry part of the time, I consider that they are entitled to great credit for the amount of work done and the skill with which it was done. I have already verbally expressed my appreciation to General Lubbock and to the Quartermaster-General and hope that in this case some adequate recognition will be awarded."

The Assistant Director of Railways, Kut, wrote as follows (dated 26th December) to the Director of Railways, Baghdad:—

"I forward you herewith a copy of Major Burn's appreciation of the work done by the detachment of the 64th Pioneers under Colonel Watson on the Shahraban-Table Mountain extension.

I fully support Major Burn's desire that their work should be adequately recognized, and it is with much pleasure I do so."

From the Director of Railways, Baghdad, to General Headquarters, Baghdad, dated 5th January 1918:—

"Copies of reports received from the Assistant Director of Railways, Kut, and Major Burn are forwarded herewith for information.

I concur in the opinions expressed."

From Major-General R. Stuart Wortley, D.Q.M.G., General Headquarters, to the Officer Commanding, 64th Pioneers, dated 13th January 1918:—

"I am directed to convey the appreciation of the General Officer Commanding-in-Chief of the good work done by the battalion under your command on the Shahraban-Table Mountain extension."

Baghdad-Falluja Railway. Turning again to regimental headquarters at Khan Police Post, near Nukhta, A and D Companies started work on the 4 feet 8½ inches standard railway line to Falluja on the 20th October. To begin with, the men did tasks of 120 cubic feet *per diem*, but by the 18th December, when the main track reached Falluja Station, they were completing tasks of 150 cubic feet, most of the soil being very hard. An infantry working party attached to B Company in December averaged 40 to 50 cubic feet per man daily.

The first supply train from Baghdad reached Falluja on the 21st December, on which date an opening ceremony was held by General (afterwards Sir Harry) Brooking, Commanding the 15th Division, who was formerly Commandant of the 61st (K.G.O.) Pioneers and is now Colonel of Corps Headquarters, Madras Pioneers (formerly the 81st Pioneers).

The Regiment continued work on the various sidings, platforms, ramps, etc., at Falluja Station till the 31st December.

It should not be forgotten that the hot weather of this year (1917) had been the most trying on record. Candler, in his *"The Long Road to Baghdad,"* says:—

"According to the Baghdadis it was the hottest season in the memory of man. Most things were too hot to touch. The rim of a tumbler burnt one's hand in a tent. The dust and sand burnt the soles of one's feet through one's boots. Even the hardy Arab and Kurd made such an outcry that one had to water the ground where they worked."

Sir Stanley Maude, who had been consolidating his position round Baghdad so as to prepare for a possible Turco-German offensive for the recovery of the city and, as we have seen, been busily engaged in improving his communications by extending the railways, had decided in July to occupy Dhibban and drive the Turks out of Ramadi. Dhibban was taken without difficulty, but an attack on Ramadi by the 7th Brigade on the 11th July failed............ Little further of importance occurred till the 29th September, when General Brooking, with the 15th Division, after a brilliant action, captured Ramadi, took 3,456 Turkish prisoners, and accounted for practically the whole enemy force on the Euphrates. On the 28th, General Norton, with the 7th Cavalry Brigade, occupied Mandali, and in October, General Marshall's 3rd Corps occupied the Jabal Hamrin. In November, Tikrit was taken by General Cobbe's 1st Corps.

On the 18th November, Sir Stanley Maude died of cholera at Baghdad, and was succeeded by Lieutenant-General Sir W. R. Marshall, Lieutenant-General Sir R. G. Egerton taking command of the 3rd Corps, and Major-General Thomson the 14th Division.

On the 4th December, the 7th Division left Mesopotamia for Egypt, the new 17th Division taking its place in the 1st Corps.

1918.

Falluja, Baghdad and Samarra.

Orders were now received for the regiment to work on the extension of the standard gauge railway from Falluja to Dhibban on the Euphrates. This involved some very heavy earthwork, especially at the canal north of Sakhlawiya. An entry in the War Diary, dated 1st January, reads:—

Falluja-Dhibban Railway.

"The extension is approximately 11 miles; in it there are long stretches of bank 3 feet to 4 feet high. The canal north of Sakhlawiya involves 2½ lakhs of cubic feet of earth over some 250 feet, the bank here running to 23 feet in height."

From the 22nd January, the regiment was assisted by parties of men from the 6th Jats and 97th Infantry. Platelaying began on the 1st February, and the extension to Dhibban, a length of 11 miles 50 yards, was completed by the 18th, the time taken being actually 62 hours, excluding the time taken to construct the bridge at Sakhlawiya, with an average strength of 510 men. Casualties due to the work were one death and 5 minor injuries. The first supply train ran through on the 18th. Some further notes on this work will be found in Part V.

On the 12th February, orders were received from the Assistant Director of Railways that the regiment was to be ready to move by companies for work on the Hilla Section of the standard gauge railway. B Company, therefore, moved from Dhibban to Khirr railway depot on the 16th, followed by headquarters and C Company on the 23rd. A Company rejoined headquarters on the 27th after constructing some platforms at Dhibban Station.

General Headquarters had sanctioned the retention of D Company (Major Skinner) temporarily by the 15th Division for urgent work at Dhibban, and this company worked there, from the 23rd February till the 22nd March, on roads, ramps and piers, besides constructing and linking a hospital siding on the railway. On the 23rd March, it moved to Falluja and, after some work on the railway and an embankment in the Inland Water Transport yard, arrived at Khirr on the 28th March.

On the 22nd February, B Company (Brevet Lieutenant-Colonel Watson) commenced **Baghdad-Hilla Railway.** the earthwork of the track, and each company settled down to work as it arrived. Regimental headquarters remained at Khirr, whence it was easiest to administer the companies, till the 19th March, when it moved *via* Mahmudiya to Khan Haswah, remaining there till the 30th. The companies moved independently as the work dictated, the long distances between sources of water often making it necessary for them to encamp far from their work.

By the 31st March, the whole regiment, except No. 9 Platoon, under Captain Curle, which was left at Mahmudiya for work on the bridges, was concentrated at Khirr and ready to start platelaying on the 1st April. Tasks performed by the men averaged from 135 to 158 cubic feet of earth daily, varying according to the distance the companies had to march to work, which was sometimes as much as four miles. In addition to the regiment, a great deal of Arab labour was employed, but the Arabs would only work near their own villages.

The linking of the main line began on the 1st April, and was completed on the 25th May. Out of the total mileage of 56 miles 1,440 yards from Baghdad South to Hilla 55½ miles were completed by the regiment. The greatest length linked on any one day was 11,304 feet (over 2 miles) in 6½ hours by 670 men. The average distance linked daily from the 3rd to 6th April was 9,144 feet by 658 men in 5 to 5½ hours, and, from the 17th to 21st April, 8,845 feet by 670 men in 4 hours 7 minutes each day. These figures are given to show what can be expected from skilled men under favourable conditions. The work was very hard, and it was found that the men ate all their food at the midday meal and had nothing left on return to camp in the evening, so an extra ration of 4 oz. of rice per man daily was sanctioned by General Headquarters. The platelaying, which was in charge of Captain D. Aylward, was done by A, B and C Companies, while D Company continued on earthwork, and No. 9 Platoon on bridge work.

The movements of the regiment during this period were :—8th April, Awairij; 14th, Mahmudiya; 24th, Khan Haswa; 1st May, Khan Nasiriya; 7th, Mahawil; 19th, Nil Canal; 26th, Hilla.

On the 19th May, Major Skinner, with 4 Indian Officers and 203 other ranks, (Sikhs) left the regiment to join the new 1/155th Pioneers, then being raised by Brevet Lieutenant-Colonel S. B. Watson of the 64th.

Samarra-Tikrit Railway. The regiment was now ordered to Samarra, where it arrived on the 16th June, for work on the standard gauge extension to Tikrit. Earthwork was commenced on the 18th, and platelaying on the 19th, the intention being that the regiment should lay and pack half a mile of line daily but, being now only 490 strong, owing to the departure of the Sikh Company, this was found to be impossible. On the 21st June, the arrival of a draft increased the strength to about 600 men and, with other labour available to do the packing, an average length of about 5,400 feet of line was then completed daily.

The delay was caused by the constant late arrival of the construction train, which resulted in the men being kept on work till afternoon, and caused a great increase in the sick list owing to the tremendous heat. Early in August, however, orders were given for work to cease at 10 a.m., irrespective of how much had been done.

The total length of line linked was 33 miles 220 yards and, in addition, a station yard was constructed at Tikrit.

On the 30th August, C Company (Captain Curle) proceeded to Hawaislat near Al Ajik for work on the line, and a small party under Lieutenant Cornwell left for Hilla, to work under Captain Bowen of the Railways. C Company was employed on miscellaneous work, including improvements to bridges and rejoined the regiment on the 29th September. The party from B Company, under Lieutenant Cornwell, remained on detachment in the neighbourhood of Hilla till the 30th September, its work including laying out the Hilla-Jarboyia extension and constructing a track for motor traffic, besides carrying a 15 feet span bridge over the Mashamiya Canal.

1918-1919.
Quraitu.

Hinaidi-Quraitu Railway Towards the end of September 1918, the regiment was ordered to proceed to Haush Quru for work on the Kardarra-Khaniqin extension of the Hinaidi metre-gauge line, and on a hill road from Haush Quru to Qasr-i-Shirin, moving by rail from Samarra to Baghdad, thence to Hinaidi by river, and on to

Haush Quru by road, *via* Ruz, Jasan and Khaniqin. A Company (Captain Aylward) had already been sent off on the 26th August, to start work on the railway bridge over the Huluwan river.

The regiment reached Haush Quru on the 5th October, and began the work on the 7th, which continued till the middle of May 1919.

A Company. A Company arrived at the Huluwan river on the 3rd September, and remained at the camp near the bridge site on the north bank till the 17th January 1919, most of this period being spent on the concrete bridge over the river. Constant trouble was experienced in sinking the wells, owing to the difficulty of keeping the water out, the pumps supplied being quite inadequate. The men were constantly at work in the icy cold water, and, to avoid the consequent incidence of fever, a ration of rum was issued to each man as soon as he came out of the water. To add to the difficulties, each heavy fall of rain, especially in November, caused a corresponding rise of the river, and resort was had to various expedients so as to get the men across the river in all weathers. By the 15th January, work on the bridge was practically completed.

A Company, with the assistance of two platoons from D Company from the 19th November, also constructed the bridges and culverts for the railway from Huluwan to Baba Mahmud, and re-made the road bridges on the Baba Mahmud road. The two platoons of D Company returned to regimental headquarters on the 19th January while, on the 17th, A Company left the Huluwan river and arrived at Haush Quru, by half companies, on the 1st and 18th March, putting in the railway bridges and culverts *en route*.

The company was now split into two detachments, Nos. 1 and 2 Platoons moving, on the 6th April, to the neighbourhood of Ahmad (on the Haush Quru-Qasr-i-Shirin road), where they made the road passable for motor traffic, and then moved to railhead at Quraitu, while Nos. 3 and 4 Platoons camped 3 miles north of Haush Quru. At Quraitu, the detachment worked on the station yard, the work including a cutting through a hill which, when completed, was 38 feet wide at the top and 18 feet at ground level, the sides being sloped at $\frac{1}{2}$ in 1. Its strength was increased by the arrival of leave details belonging to all the Companies and, from the 2nd May, it was divided into three parties, each of about 50 men, who worked day and night in reliefs of 6 hours. The amount of rock blasted and removed increased from an average of 1,300 cubic feet in an ordinary working day, with an average of 49 men daily, to an average of 3,366 cubic feet in 24 hours, with a lead of 30 feet.

Nos. 3 and 4 Platoons meanwhile worked on the road between Haush Quru and Ali Agha, and also on railway bridges and culverts till the 13th May 1919, when the whole Company concentrated at Quraitu. During October and November, some 48 men of A Company were attached to Nos. 12 and 13 Companies, Sappers and Miners, at Khaniqin.

We must now turn to regimental headquarters and the other Companies, which, as we have seen, reached Haush Quru some six weeks after A Company had arrived at the Huluwan river. B and C Companies started work on the track formation at once, and met with rock which required blasting, so B Company was left at Haush Quru while, on the 3rd November, regimental headquarters moved on to Quraitu and C Company to Abadi-Aziz-Khan. B Company rejoined headquarters on the 26th November. B and D Companies remained with headquarters till the work was completed, constructing many culverts and small bridges, besides a bridge at Ali Agha. The average daily task varied from 40 to 120 cubic feet, owing to difficulties with rock.

<small>R. H. Q. and B, C and D Companies.</small>

Meanwhile, C Company, during November, improved the service road from Abadi-Aziz-Khan towards Ibrahim Kalantar, and commenced work on the railway track, and on the concrete railway bridge over the Quraitu river. Till the 19th May 1919, when it rejoined headquarters, it worked on the above bridge and on two other concrete bridges, one called the "Quraitu Valley" bridge, and the other a railway bridge over the Ab-i-Kizil river, besides carrying out some work at Quraitu station. As at the Huluwan river, this company was caused much trouble by the rain which fell intermittently during the winter months.

<small>C Company.</small>

With the operations carried out by General Marshall in the meantime we are not concerned. Considerable fighting had taken place, culminating in the battle of Sharqat (28th-30th October 1918), where General Cobbe completely defeated the Turks and captured over 11,000 prisoners. The British army advanced on Mosul, but the Turks sued for peace, and an armistice was signed at Lemnos on the 30th October, hostilities coming to an end at noon on the 31st.

<small>Armistice.</small>

In January 1919, the regiment was informed that it had been detailed to form part of the Army of Occupation.

Throughout the service of the regiment in Mesopotamia, both officers and men had been indebted to the generosity of the ladies of Calcutta who, by almost every mail, sent them large consignments of parcels containing every imaginable form of "comfort," and it is only fitting that I should here record how greatly all ranks appreciated their thoughtful kindness.

1919—1921.
Persia.

On the 18th April 1919, the regiment received orders from Headquarters, Persian Line of Communications, to march from Quraitu to Kermanshah, but did not leave Quraitu till the 19th May. The marches were as follows:—19th, Ibrahim Kalantar *via* Qasr-i-Shirin (12 miles); 20th, Sar-i-Pul (13 miles); 21st, Pai-Taq (13 miles); 23rd, Sar-i-Mil (15 miles); 24th, Karind (8 miles); 25th, Harunabad (22 miles); 26th, Hassanabad (12 miles); 27th, Maidasht.

Pai-Taq is at the foot of the steep Taq-i-Girreh Pass, and the 22nd was spent in adjusting transport loads to under 8 maunds *per* cart, with the result that the transport ascended the Pass with little effort. The latter half of the march to Harunabad was particularly hot and trying, and Lieutenant-Colonel Lakin, commanding the Persian Line of Communications, who met the regiment here, complimented the Commanding Officer on the manner in which the regiment had finished the march. On arrival at Maidasht, the regiment was ordered to halt for a week's infantry training, in order to regain its mobility after the constant Pioneer work on which it had hitherto been engaged.

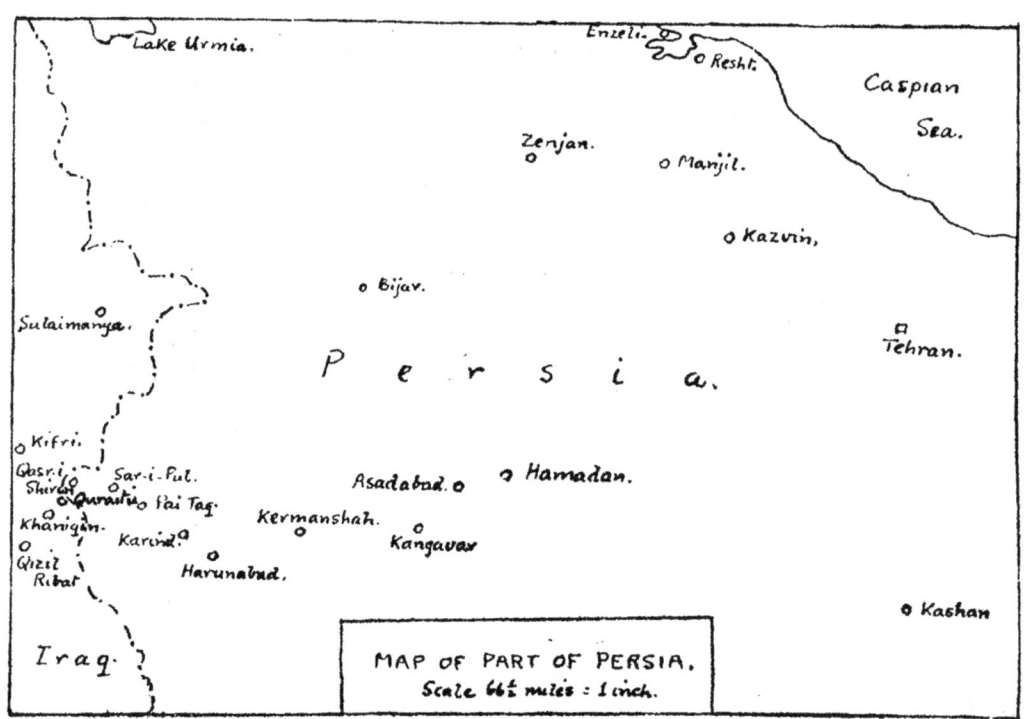

A brief description of the country in which the regiment now found itself may be of interest. North-West Persia consists of an upland, averaging about 5,000 feet in altitude, traversed by many mountain ranges which often attain an altitude of 10,000 to 12,000 feet. The country is for the most part barren and rocky, except in the valleys and along the village streams, where plantations of trees, vineyards, and orchards of luscious fruit flourish. The climate is dry and pleasant in the summer, and the temperature seldom rises above 95° in the shade, but the winters are rigorous and, though they vary considerably, the country is frequently snowbound between November and April.

B Company (Captain Burne) was left at Karind, and camped on the high ground north of the Kermanshah road, about one mile east of Karind. Here it was employed, till the 5th June, in constructing huts, with water and sanitary arrangements, at the Rest, Leave and Mechanical Transport Camps at Karind. On the 6th June, it set out for Kara Su *via* Harunabad, Hassanabad and Maidasht, rejoining headquarters on the 9th.

The regiment had meanwhile moved camp, on the 4th, to Tueh Latif, three miles east of Maidasht, where it worked on the road through the Tueh Latif Pass, and, on the 6th, marched 12 miles to Kara Su bridge, a few miles from Kermanshah. Here a range was built, and company training and musketry were carried out till the 23rd. On the 14th, A, B and C Companies repaired the road from Kara Su bridge to Taq-i-Bustan, a distance of six miles, the object of the work being to make the road fit for lorry traffic from the Leave Camp.

On the 23rd June, the regiment was inspected by the Officer Commanding Persian Line of Communications and, on the 24th, set out for Asadabad, the marches being as follows:—24th, Bisitun (20 miles); 25th, Sahneh (17 miles); 26th, Kangavar (19 miles); 27th, Asadabad (23 miles).

Kermanshah-Hamadan Road.
As the regiment had been ordered to work on the Kermanshah-Hamadan road, D Company (Lieutenant Mills) was left at Pul Shekna, and B Company at Deh-Buzan, 12 and 6 miles respectively from Asadabad. At the latter place huts were available for about 200 men, besides guards and stores, and here regimental headquarters remained, while work was proceeding on the road.

The work consisted of widening the road from 12 to 18 feet by adding metal and a 3-foot berm on either side while, in addition, the soling of much of the existing road had to be taken up and re-laid and certain portions re-aligned, soled and metalled. Masonry bridges were built at Asadabad and Tajiabad Bala. Gangs of Persian coolies assisted in the collection of metalling and rolling it in, but were very irregular in their attendance, and the work was also greatly hampered by passive obstruction by the local notables in regard to the supply of water until towards the end of July, when the assistance of Prince Saifulla Mirza was enlisted, who brought about some improvement. The leading man in the neighbourhood of Tajiabad Bala, where C Company (Lieutenant Daldy) was working, objected even to the removal of stones from the ground, but changed his attitude after a personal interview with the Company Commander.

During this period, officers and men gradually began to know the Persian people. They are not a virile race, and are crafty and fond of intrigue, but are, however, sociable and cultured, and most hospitable. The greater part of the country folk consists of Kurds, a fine-looking and hardy race, but, in spite of an imposing appearance, which is enhanced by the tall hats they wear, which add considerably to their stature, they are really lacking in stamina and pluck, and have neither the personal bravery nor fighting qualities of the Arab or the Pathan of the North-West Frontier of India.

A Company (Captain Monypenny) meanwhile remained with headquarters at Asadabad, B Company being at Deh Buzan, with a platoon, under a Havildar, on detachment for part of the time near Mandirabad. C Company left headquarters on the 9th July, and moved about four miles to the Shah Pass, with No. 12 Platoon on detachment in the Asadabad Pass. On the 25th August, it moved to Tajiabad Bala. D Company remained at Pul Shekna, with a platoon at Rahmatabad for part of the time.

Kermanshah. Towards the end of August, information was received that the regiment would spend the winter at Kermanshah. Work on the road was completed in October and, on the 7th of that month, D Company moved to Kara Su bridge, and took over the guards there and at the Leave Camp. Headquarters left Asadabad on the 9th, leaving A Company at that place, and marched to Kangavar, where it was joined by B Company from Deh Buzan, and continued the march to Kermanshah *via* Bisitun and Kara Su bridge, where D Company rejoined. These two Companies were employed on guards and fatigues at the Leave Camp, and carried out Company training till the 31st October, when they moved to Kara Su bridge.

Garrison Duties. A and C Companies, in the meantime, continued to work on the road and bridges till the 27th October, and joined forces at Asadabad on the 28th. By the 5th November, they were distributed in posts as detailed below, relieving the infantry garrisons hitherto furnished by the 122nd Rajputana Infantry:—

A Company. Nos. 1 and 2 Platoons   Siahbid.
               No. 3 Platoon   Maidasht.
               No. 4 Platoon   Hassanabad.

C Company. Nos. 9 and 10 Platoons   Hajjiabad.
               Nos. 11 and 12 Platoons   Sahneh.

The regiment remained distributed as above till April 1920, the men being employed on hutting and road-work, in addition to the normal routine duties. An arrangement was made with the C.R.E. whereby road and other work required by him was carried out in the mornings, while the afternoons were devoted to company training and musketry.

During the winter months, snow fell occasionally, and there was frost at night, but the men stood the cold very well. In March 1920, information was received that **the regiment, which had hitherto** been employed on No. 2 Section, Line of Communication Defences, was to proceed up the line and take over No. 3 Section, and that the garrison at Kara Su would be relieved by the 2/26th Punjabis.

Move to Hamadan. On the 1st April, therefore, regimental headquarters, with B Company, one platoon of A Company, and two platoons of D Company, marched to Bisitun, picking up Nos. 9 and 10 Platoons of C Company at Hajjiabad. Three platoons of A Company, and two of D Company, were left for garrison duties on No. 2 Section of the Defences. On the 2nd April, regimental headquarters set out for

Hamadan, the marches being as follows:—2nd, Sahneh (17 miles); 3rd, Kangavar (19 miles); 4th Asadabad (23 miles); 5th, halted to adjust the loads of the transport carts preparatory to ascending the Asadabad Pass, which rises 2,500 feet in 5 miles; 6th, Kangi Khan (16 miles); 7th, Hamadan (17 miles).

No. 12 Platoon (C Company) was taken from Sahneh Post and left at Yangi Khan Post under Jemadar Munisami, and No. 11 Platoon remained at Sahneh under Subadar Gopalasami, while Nos. 9 and 10 Platoons were left at Kangavar, with Major H. Harvey-Kelly as Post Commandant.

On arrival at Hamadan, the regiment relieved a detachment of the 83rd Wallajahbad Light Infantry, which was on duty there, and sent one platoon of D Company on detachment to Manian (67 miles) and another platoon to Ab-i-Garm (97 miles). The detachment which had been left for duty with No. 2 Section of the Defences rejoined headquarters on the 17th April, with the exception of No. 15 Platoon (D Company), which remained at Kermanshah for Pioneer work.

By the middle of April, therefore, regimental headquarters was at Hamadan, with detachments at Kangavar, Sahneh, Yangi Khan, Manian, Ab-i-Garm and Kermanshah.

Defence schemes were prepared and, so far as routine duties and fatigues permitted, the regiment settled down to carrying out all branches of training. In May, confirmation was received of the news that Enzeli had been occupied by the Bolsheviks and, during May and June, camps were prepared for the reception of Russian refugees.

On the 30th May, a guard of honour was provided at Hamadan for the Shah of Persia, who received the Commandant and other officers of the regiment on the following day at Shivrin.

"Blisscol." In June 1920, orders were received that the 64th, less two companies, was to form part of a new column of Norperforce, which was to be concentrated at Zenjan. The column was to be under the command of Lieutenant-Colonel J. A. Bliss, M.V.O., D.S.O., 64th Pioneers, and to be known as Blisscol. Headquarters, with A and B Companies, was ordered to march on the 13th June, and meanwhile the whole of C Company, with the platoon from Kermanshah, was concentrated at Hamadan, the posts which it had hitherto garrisoned being taken over by the 2/26th Punjabis.

On the 9th June, a party was sent out under Captain T. A. Kemble (64th), to reconnoitre the direct route to Zenjan. This party returned on the 14th, and reported that the road was impracticable for wheeled transport, and that about five months' work would be required to make it practicable. On the 14th, regimental headquarters arrived at Rawan, 32 miles from Hamadan, having halted the previous night at Ilandashi, and here orders were received to stand fast and carry out field training for seven days from the 21st. On the 30th June, therefore, the regiment returned to Hamadan. Infantry training was continued in July and, on the 3rd, the regiment made a demonstration march through Hamadan bazaar. Pioneer work carried out during the month included the repair of 2½ miles of road from Hamadan to Faqira, and Nos. 5 and 6 Platoons constructed some culverts at Tajiabad between the 14th July and the 30th August. Headquarters remained at Hamadan till the middle of April 1921, carrying on training, besides finding guards and duties, and providing escorts for convoys proceeding down the line.

In August 1920, information was received that a state of war existed in Mesopotamia, **The Arab Rebellion.** and that the line between Baquba and Qizil Ribat had been cut by Arabs. The Officer Commanding Persian Line of Communications now became responsible for the whole line from Kazvin to Baquba and, as a result, the regiment was ordered to take over the posts at Asadabad, Kangavar and Sahneh from the 2/26th Punjabis. A Company accordingly left Hamadan on the 16th August to take over these posts. In addition, orders were received to send a detachment as reinforcements to Quraitu and, on the 2nd September, Lieutenant L. S. Hamilton, with one Indian officer and four Lewis gun sections (21 men) left Hamadan.

The regiment was also ordered to send all men due for demobilisation and re-engaged men to rail-head at Quraitu for railway work, and a party of 110 men was accordingly despatched on the 26th August, followed later by a smaller party from the detachments at Manian and Ab-i-Garm. This party, increased by a number of men who were on their way to India on leave, was detained, much to the men's disappointment, at Quraitu or the neighbouring posts till March or April 1921, eventually rejoining at Baghdad or Basra, when the regiment was on its way back to India. One of the posts on the railway, garrisoned by a detachment from this party, was attacked by *budmashes,* and the N.C.O. in charge, Havildar Arunachalam, who went out of his post and captured some of the enemy, was afterwards awarded the I.D.S.M. and promoted for his conduct on that occasion. Another small party of the regiment, under Subadar Gopalasami, which was detached at a small station on the Euphrates line towards Nasiriya during the rebellion, had a sharp engagement with the rebels.

In Persia also, as in Mesopotamia, this was a time of political crisis and inter-tribal warfare, and great efforts were being made by the British political officers in Persia, to prevent the Kurdish tribes on the Perso-Mesopotamian border from throwing in their lot with the Arabs. These efforts were so successful that certain tribes were encouraged to support the British.

As regards the inter-tribal disputes, the British naturally maintained an entirely neutral attitude. The methods of fighting, it must be said, were amusing. The fights, which were of rare occurrence, were conducted amidst a perfect uproar, with much galloping to and fro, but directly one single casualty on either side occurred, it was customary for both parties to withdraw immediately! On one occasion, two tribal factions staged a battle at Maidasht on either side of the camp of the British railway survey party, which happened to be working in that locality. The chief engineer made both sides honorary members of his camp for the occasion, and each hostile leader came and took tea with him in turn!

On the 19th December 1920, the detachment at Sahneh was relieved by the 2/26th Punjabis, and a platoon of A Company was sent to Hamadan. On the 13th January 1921, the detachment at Ab-i-Garm was relieved by a platoon of the York and Lancaster Regiment and went down the line to garrison the posts at Ameria, Rawan and Ilandashi. With these exceptions, no changes were made in the distribution of the regiment till it left Hamadan. The weather during the winter months was very severe. At Hamadan, which is at an altitude of 6,000 feet, there was deep snow from November to March, and every precaution was taken to keep the men fit and to prevent frost-bite. Sentries wore leather coats under their greatcoats, also two pairs of socks and fur-lined boots, and were made to oil their feet and patrol their beats briskly. They were relieved every hour and given hot coffee on coming off duty. The men were encouraged to take plenty of physical exercise and stood the cold very well, the health of the regiment remaining excellent throughout. The heavy falls of snow gave much work in keeping the roads clear, and snow had to be regularly cleared from the flat mud roofs of the huts, which required constant repair. The men at the various posts were in great demand for starting motor cars which declined to move on account of the cold. Miscellaneous Pioneer work was also carried out, such as clearing the ground for, and marking out, an aerodrome, and constructing ablution rooms and a magazine for artillery ammunition in the Kaleh Konah.

Garrison Duties.

Owing to the rebellion, and the length of the line of communications, during the period from August 1920 to March 1921, the battalion was dispersed in detachments from Quraitu to Hamadan and Ab-i-Garm, with escorts sometimes travelling as far as Kazvin, a total distance of 450 miles by a motor road which was frequently blocked by snow or floods. In addition various details were detained at Basra or Baghdad. Letters from regimental headquarters to the depot at Bangalore frequently took a month to arrive.

In March 1921, information was received that the regiment was to return to India, and orders were subsequently issued for the regiment to march on the 15th April. The detachments at Manian, Ameria, Rawan and Ilandashi rejoined on the 11th, on relief by the 122nd Infantry, which also took over from headquarters at Hamadan. The move began on the 15th, marches being as follows:—

Return to India.

15th, Yangi Khan (17 miles); 16th, Asadabad (15 miles); 17th, Kangavar (23 miles); 18th, halted at Kangavar; 19th, Sahneh (19 miles); 20th, Bisitun (17 miles); 21st, Kermanshah (23 miles).

Whilst awaiting further orders at Kermanshah, a detachment repaired the bridge at Bisitun on the 25th April and, on the 27th, A Company, with 4 additional

Lewis guns, under Major Harvey-Kelly, was sent as escort to mechanical transport proceeding from Quraitu to Baghdad.

On the 2nd May, the regiment left Kermanshah, the marches being as follows:— 2nd, Maidasht; 3rd, Hassanabad; 4th, Harunabad; 5th, Karind; 6th, Sar-i-Mil (5,000 feet); 7th, Pai Taq; 8th, halted at Pai Taq; 9th, Sar-i-Pul; 10th, Quraitu. Here, on the 12th, a train loaded with transport was derailed, 5 men being slightly injured and 4 mules killed. The train was put back on the rails on the 13th and, on the 14th and 15th, the regiment left Quraitu in six trains.

On the 16th May, the regiment arrived at Hinaidi, near Baghdad, and, on the 18th, was inspected by General Sir Aylmer Haldane, K.C.B., D.S.O., General Officer Commanding-in-Chief, who made the following speech, thanking the regiment for its services in Mesopotamia and Persia:—

"Lieutenant-Colonel Watson and all ranks of the 64th Pioneers, after an absence of about eight years, you are about to return to India, and you will return home with a very satisfactory record of good work. You arrived in Mesopotamia early in 1916 and, besides sharing in the fighting and taking part in the capture of Kut, did much useful work on railways and road construction.

Before I took command of the forces here, you had been sent to Persia, and it is greatly to your credit and the good spirit and discipline of the battalion that you passed through the trials of two exceptionally severe winters, which were borne extremely well and with the loss of very few of your numbers through sickness. This is all the more creditable as you come from Southern India and are quite unaccustomed to cold; and it shows what a good battalion can accomplish.

There have been many changes in India since you left that country, and I notice when I read the papers that agitators who do not regard the true welfare and happiness of their country, are still trying to make the soldiers of the Indian Army discontented, and shake their allegiance. I may mention to you that, in the six campaigns in which I have served, the Indian Army has taken part, and I am proud to have been associated with them; and I feel confident, from what I know of them, that under all circumstances they will always maintain their great reputation for bravery and loyalty to the King-Emperor.

I wish you all good luck and happiness on leaving my command, and I am sorry to lose so good a battalion."

The regiment left for Kut by rail on the same day, where it embarked on a river steamer, and arrived at Maqil, near Basra, on the 21st May. It was employed on guard duties round Basra till the 8th June, when it embarked on the British India S. S. *Cooeyanna*. On the 16th June, it reached Bombay, and arrived at Bangalore on the 19th, thus ending a tour of 6½ years' service overseas in Burma, Mesopotamia and Persia.

On the arrival of the regiment at Bombay, the following message was received from Lieutenant-General Delamain, Adjutant-General in India:—

"On your return to India from field service overseas, His Excellency the Commander-in-Chief extends to you and all ranks under your command his heartiest welcome, and congratulates all on the gallantry and devotion with which they have maintained the high tradition of the Army."

The Commander-in-Chief in India was now General Lord Henry Seymour Rawlinson of Trent, G.C.B., G.C.V.O., K.C.M.G., G.C.S.I., A.D.C.

I may add here an extract from a letter addressed by Lieutenant-Colonel C. R. Scott-Elliot, Commandant, 1/61st (K.G.O.) Pioneers, to the O.C. Depot, 64th Pioneers:—

"I wish to put on record my appreciation of the services of the draft which you supplied to this regiment for service on the North-West Frontier in 1919-20. They gave me every assistance and in spite of very trying conditions in the hot weather, combined with a cholera scare, they carried out their duties cheerfully without any complaint.

I was especially pleased with the way they speedily adapted themselves to the customs of this Regiment, and their steady behaviour on night duty in the picquet line, by not returning the fire of snipers or allowing their imaginations to run loose, was especially gratifying."

I cannot do better than close this, the period which included the Great War, by quoting the following message from His Majesty the King-Emperor to the Indian Army and Imperial Service troops, delivered by H. R. H. the Duke of Connaught at Delhi in February 1921:—

" The Great War from which our Empire has emerged victorious involved the most powerful nations of the earth and spread over vast seas and continents. From the crowded record here and there certain features stand clearly out, arresting the attention and admiration of the world to-day and claiming with confidence the verdict of posterity. In this honourable company the Indian Army has an assured place.

Scattered far and wide under alien skies, in adversity and in triumph, the Indian troops played their part with stout and gallant hearts. True to their traditions, they answered the Empire's call with soldierly discipline and fortitude, and staunch in the loyalty they have ever displayed to the throne and person of their King-Emperor, they made this cause their own and willingly laid down their lives for their Sovereign.

Gratitude for loyalty such as this lies deep in my heart and is beyond the power of words. They did their duty."

1921.

The Moplah Rebellion.

On arrival at Bangalore, arrangements were made to send off as many officers and men as possible on their well-earned special war-leave, and the process of reorganising the regiment into a Headquarter Wing and three Companies was begun.

In the middle of this reorganisation, with the temporary confusion thereby entailed, the regiment was called upon to find a company for service in Malabar, where the Khilafatist agitation amongst the Moplahs had by now come to a head. Towards the end of August, regimental headquarters received orders to hold A Company in readiness to move to Malabar at short notice to assist in quelling the disturbances,

Officers and men were recalled, and orders to entrain were received on the 24th August, on which date a detachment about 110 strong, with two Lewis guns, under the command of Major T. B. Skinner, left Bangalore for Podanur.

With so many men absent on leave, it was not found possible to send a complete Company, so a composite Company of three platoons, each platoon composed of details from one of the three Companies, was formed. No. 1 Platoon was composed of men of A Company, No. 2 of B Company, and No. 3 of C Company.

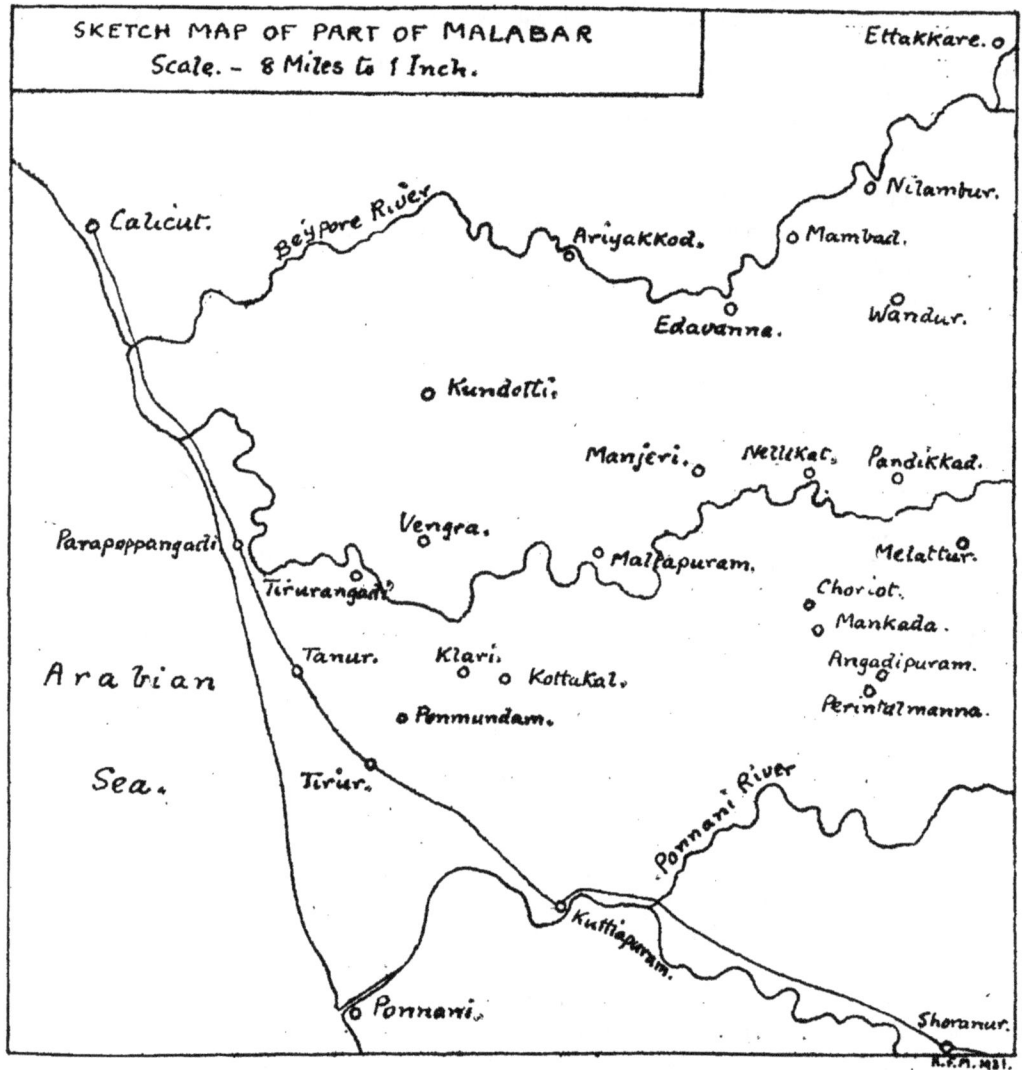

The number of British Officers—three—was specified by Bangalore Area Headquarters, and this number had to be maintained for the whole period of the detachment's service in Malabar. Area Headquarters further decided that the detachment should proceed as infantry, and were not to take their Pioneer equipment. The result of this was that their Pioneer equipment had subsequently to be sent down to the detachment by regimental headquarters.

On arrival at Podanur, on the 25th August, the O. C. detachment received orders to proceed to rail-head with all speed, and repair the railway line. Owing to congestion on the line ahead, the detachment was unable to reach rail-head at Kuttiapuram till the 26th August; here the construction train was found ready and, accompanied by the Chief Engineer, the detachment proceeded to repair the damage done by the rebels, who had removed keys and damaged bridges everywhere.

By the 27th August, the line had been completed through to Tirur, where the detachment joined up with the repair party from Calicut. Detachment headquarters remained at Tirur till the 4th September, a demonstration march round the town being carried out on the 29th August. On the 30th August, a party of 6 Moplahs was captured, who were looting houses round the Kacheri. On the 31st, one platoon of the detachment patrolled the line in an armoured train as far as Feroke, but without incident.

On the 1st September, the detachment was ordered to go by rail to Parapoppangadi, and from there to clear up the situation round Tirurangadi, for which place a moveable column had left on the 29th August. On arrival at Parapoppangadi, a runner was met, with a message to say that the enemy had all either been killed, or had surrendered; the detachment, therefore, returned to Tirur, where it was shortly afterwards reinforced by two platoons of the Leinster Regiment, and ordered to round up a mob of Moplahs at Tanur. On arrival there, the mob was found to have dispersed, but nine prisoners were taken, including a known leader. On the following day, the detachment, with two platoons of the Leinsters and some police, was again sent to Tanur and arrested 82 "wanted" rebels.

On the 4th September, the detachment was sent by river up to Ponnani and, with this place as a centre, proceeded to round up Moplahs wanted by the police. Accompanied by police, for purposes of identification, visits were made during the next few days to Pallipuram, Velliakkad, Purattur, Muttur and Edapall, and 202 arrests were made. Twelve captures were also made at Ponnani, including well-known Khilafatist agitators. On the 7th September, Lieutenant S. A. Bowden arrived to relieve Captain Sydney Smith and, on the 10th, the detachment returned to Tirur.

On the 11th, 14th and 15th, escorts were provided for convoys proceeding to Mallapuram, and on the 11th, two platoons, with the Lewis guns, were sent, under the command of Captain Ford, to patrol the line in the vicinity of Olavakkad, in consequence of information received that 1,000 Moplahs intended to sack Palghat. The inhabitants of Olavakkad were found panic-stricken and delighted to see the troops, but though the train patrolled the line to Palghat during the night, no sign was seen of the Moplahs, who were now supposed to be marching on Angadipuram. The train consequently returned to Tirur on the morning of the 13th. Many alarmist reports of this nature were received from the panic-stricken Hindus during the early part of the rebellion.

On the 13th September, Major T. B. Skinner was appointed Staff Officer to the O. C. Malabar Troops, and handed over command to Captain Ford, while on the 15th, Captain T. J. Barnes joined the detachment. On the 16th, the detachment was ordered to Mallapuram and, from the 17th, was split up into three separate parties, viz.:—A Company Platoon (Captain Ford) proceeding to Manjeri; B Company Platoon (Captain Barnes) to Wandur; and C Company Platoon (Lieutenant Bowden) to Pandikkad.

As these three detachments were independent of each other for practically the whole time they remained in Malabar, it will be best to follow the doings of each one separately. Broadly speaking, they were at first employed on Infantry duties, such as assisting in the defence of posts and road protection, and later, as Pioneers, with the chief object of keeping road communications clear.

In order to facilitate the administration of the detachment, permission was sought, after the men had returned from leave, to relieve the men of B and C Companies in Malabar by men of A Company, and so have a properly constituted Company on service, instead of a mixed detachment. This permission was eventually given, and from about the middle of November, the detachment was composed entirely of A Company men, with a proper company organisation. To prevent confusion, therefore, the A, B and C Company Platoons will now be referred to as Nos. 1, 2 and 3 Platoons respectively.

No. 1 Platoon.

This platoon took over Manjeri Post from the Dorsetshire Regiment on the 17th September. The people in the neighbourhood were in a state of panic and, during the day, a terrified villager came to the Post, saying that the Moplahs were attacking Hindus near-by. A party was turned out at once to investigate, and found that the cause of the alarm was a cow which had fallen down a well! There were, however, numbers of rebels in the vicinity, a party of 150, with guns and knives, being reported two miles south-west of Manjeri.

On the 18th, firing was heard to the west of the Post, and the police reported that a column had gone out from Mallapuram to engage the enemy. Captain Ford, therefore, took out 20 rifles, with the object of cutting off any Moplahs, who might be retiring south. Unfortunately, no enemy were encountered, and the party returned, after burning a house which the police said was a Moplah meeting-place. On return, a wounded Indian Officer of the 83rd Wallajahbad Light Infantry was found at the Post, who said that lorries with men of his regiment had been ambushed.

On the following day, four lorries with men of the 83rd W.L.I. passed through the Post, but returned on finding the whole country-side shouting and assembling. Frightened Hindus came flying in from the vicinity, saying that the Moplahs had assembled half a mile from Manjeri, and were going to attack the Post, but no attack materialised, though more shouting was heard during the night. Three enemy spies were caught on the 20th September, on which day a small party of the Dorsets arrived to strengthen the Post, followed by two machine guns on the 25th. On the 22nd, a band of 200 rebels came within two miles of Manjeri, and threatened to burn a Hindu carpenter's house, but they were turned back by a Moplah woman who said that, if they carried out their threat, the troops would burn the Moplah houses.

On the 27th September, the detachment turned out to act as "stops" along the Manjeri-Mallapuram road, to prevent rebels, who were being attacked by three columns operating from different directions, from breaking away eastwards. The detachment returned with 8 prisoners, but did not get any target to fire at. There had been no opportunity to train the men in this form of warfare since the return of the regiment from Mesopotamia, and there is little doubt that they showed themselves too freely on the skyline. They were seen several times by Moplah women, who doubtless gave the rebels warning to keep away.

On the 3rd and 6th October, parties from the detachment assisted the Dorsets to piquet the Edavanna road for the protection of motor convoys, but no enemy was met. On the 7th, the detachment was ordered at very short notice to Mallapuram, and thence, *via* Perintalmanna to Mankada, to protect the Raja of that place. No incident occurred here and, on relief by the Dorsets, the detachment proceeded, on the 13th, to Mannarakkad, *via* Perintalmanna, at which place the usual report was received of an impending attack, which did not materialise.

On the 16th October, news was received that the rebels had broken two bridges four miles west of the Post. Coolies to assist in the repairs were collected with difficulty, and the detachment marched out to the site; on arrival, it was found that the girders of two 30 feet spans had been thrown down, and that repair was impossible without more appliances. The detachment, therefore, improved the ford and ramped the approaches. On the 18th, the approaches to Choriot bridge, four miles south-east of Mannarakkad, were improved by making a corduroy track of young teak trees and sleepers; and on the following day, another bridge, four miles north-west of Mannarakkad, on the Melattur road, which had been broken by the rebels, was repaired.

During the remainder of October, the detachment was employed on garrison duties, and nothing of interest occurred.

On the 5th November, Lieutenant S. A. Bowden took over command of the platoon from Captain Ford and, on the 6th, the Choriot bridge collapsed, the detachment working at a new one from the 7th to the 11th. No wire or spikes being available for trestles, two crib-piers were put up instead, and a corduroy track of betel-nut trees was laid over the river bed between the two temporary bridges at Choriot.

On the 12th, repairs were carried out to some small bridges between Mannarakkad and Choriot, and on the 13th, work was done on the road and bridge in the Palghat Pass. On the following day, the detachment took part, with the 83rd W.L.I., in a "round-up" of rebels and, during the rest of the month, worked on the Post defences. Minor repairs to Choriot bridge were carried out on the 30th.

During December, the detachment was employed on routine duties, and there is nothing further to record, except that, on the 7th, the track to Potassheri was made fit to take A. T. Carts.

No. 2 Platoon.

This platoon halted at Wandur on the 18th September, and moved to Mambad on the following day. The bridge over the river on the south side of the village had been wrecked by the rebels, and was at once repaired by the platoon, which then made arrangements for the proper defence of the Post.

On the 21st September, information was received that the rebels had an outpost on the bridge two miles north of Mambad. Captain Barnes moved out with some 20 rifles before dawn, with the object of destroying the enemy party, boots and socks being removed to ensure silent movement. A sentry in front of the Post, however, gave the rebels warning, and they dispersed into the jungle. The sentry and another man were captured. Captain Barnes then reconnoitred the road to Nilambur and, finding that trees had been felled across it and barricades erected, wired the information to Headquarters. Another attempt to destroy the enemy was made in the evening, but without success, though another sentry was captured. The rebels were undoubtedly kept well-informed of the movements of the garrison, some of the Hindu population being hand-in-glove with them.

On the 22nd, arrests of wanted men were made, including several Khilafatist agitators. On the 23rd, which was a Friday, the villagers who were mostly Moplahs, talked of rising as one man after the mid-day prayer and attacking the Post, but no attack occurred.

Ambush near Nilambur. On the 24th September, orders were received from the O. C. Dorsetshire Regiment at Wandur for the platoon to meet and join up with his column two miles north of Mambad, and take part in the operation against Nilambur. On arrival at the *rendez-vous*, the platoon pushed on, and cleared away the obstructions on the road. Captain Barnes then went ahead with his men, and two platoons of the Dorsets, under Lieutenant Spencer. When within three-quarters of a mile of Nilambur, an enemy ambush was encountered, at a place where there was jungle and thick undergrowth on both sides of the road. The following is Captain Barnes' report:—

"It was difficult to know where the bullets were coming from—some of them were using muzzle-loaders and powder, and we managed to silence these without any trouble. Being guided by the smoke, we traversed the hedge with Lewis guns, and a sniper was put up in a tree, who managed to get some as they retired. I climbed a tree with a Lewis gun, traversing to and fro as they retreated. It is difficult to say how many were hit, as they fell in the undergrowth. We were still being troubled by the firing from the hedge, so Lieutenant Spencer and I decided that the only way to deal with them was to get at them with the bayonet. So he took some men round one way, and I the other. When I came across the place where the snipers had concealed themselves, I could not see them, but they evidently had a clear view, for one fired at me (I was about two yards away), and hit me in the wrist and hip. I fired four bullets from my revolver into the bush, and came back on the road, and directed Lewis gun fire on this spot; several bombs were also thrown over; this had some effect. By now the guns had come up, and Colonel Herbert ordered two shrapnel shells to be fired through the undergrowth. The fight lasted from half to three-quarters of an hour resulting in one killed and seven wounded on our side, and from 20 to 30 of the enemy killed."

Nilambur was reached without further fighting, and Captain Barnes, who received a mention in despatches for his gallantry on this occasion, was evacuated to Bangalore on the following day. Rebels were heard in the jungle near the Post on the night of the 24th/25th, but no attack was made.

The platoon, under Jemadar Balaraman, now moved to Edavanna where, under the Staff Captain's instructions, it was billeted at the dak bungalow. Captain L. S. Hamilton arrived to take command on the 29th September and, the platoon being at Edavanna for the purpose of controlling the river traffic, selected a new camp site on the river bank, and, with the help of local labour, made posts covering the river and the Mambad-Edavanna road.

On the 1st October, small hostile parties on the surrounding hills were dispersed by fire and, on the 2nd, Captain Hamilton took a fighting patrol down the road and through the jungle between Mambad and Edavanna, but encountered no rebels. Three platoons of the Dorsets arrived on the 3rd and, between the 6th and 15th, the platoon helped to piquet the Manjeri and Wandur roads for the protection of convoys.

On the 18th October, a platoon of the Chin-Kachin Battalion took over the Post, and the detachment proceeded to Manjeri the next day. It took part in a round-up of Moplahs on the 20th, acting as escort to a pack-gun, which it dragged into position. Captain Hamilton took a party in lorries to fetch in some of the Leinsters and Dorsets who were marching down the road from Edavanna and, after his return to the gun, the platoon's Lewis gun obtained some hits on a small hostile party.

On the 21st, the platoon moved *via* Mallapuram to Kottakal and, on the 22nd, the day on which this place was reached, a Moplah sentry group, on a hill overlooking the road, was successfully outflanked, two of the enemy being killed. A Moplah spy, who was brought in and handed over by the police on the 23rd, was shot while trying to escape. On this day, No. 2 Platoon was joined by No. 3, and the two were employed together, till the end of the month, on road work, and in constructing a blockhouse at Kottakal bridge, the latter work taking two days to complete.

On the 31st October, Captain Slade relieved Captain Ford, taking charge of the whole 64th detachment, and immediate command of No. 2 Platoon, while Lieutenant Bowden took command of No. 1 Platoon, and Captain Hamilton of No. 3. On the 31st, Captains Slade and Hamilton, with Captain Sullivan, R.A.M.C., and Lieutenant Dundas, of the Leinsters, and one sepoy, went to Klari and searched for hostile Moplahs, taking one prisoner. On the 1st November, No. 3 Platoon, under Captain Hamilton, was sent to Manjeri, leaving No. 2 Platoon at Kottakal.

On the same day, whilst at work on the road, the working party was informed by a Hindu that a band of ten to fifteen Moplahs had just tried to molest him 200 yards north of the road through Kottakal bazaar. Captain Slade and Lieutenant Bowden immediately set off with six men and, searching about, found the Moplahs running away across the fields. They opened fire, killed four rebels, and took one prisoner.

On the 2nd November, the detachment took over the duty of road protection from the Leinsters, who were engaged in active operations. On the 3rd and 4th, in addition to work on the road, the Platoon provided a night guard at Kottakal bridge. On the 5th, while a small party worked on the approach to the bridge east of Kottakal, Captain Slade, with a Lewis gun section, and accompanied by Lieutenant Dundas and a section of the Leinsters, marched to Kuttiapuram to search for Moplahs reported to have been concerned in a dacoity there on the 4th, and to deal with hostile gangs encountered *en route*. A mile and a half out from Kottakal, a band of 30 to 40 strong was seen on a hill to the west, and was dispersed by fire at close range; casualties not known. On arrival at Kuttiapuram, the house of a well-known dacoit was searched, but the owner escaped. After return to camp, two bands, each about 30 to 40 strong, were dispersed by fire.

On the 6th November, the platoon again took over road protection from the Leinsters, who were co-operating with the 83rd W.L.I. in a "drive." That afternoon, a report reached the Post that a band of 10 to 15 rebels was giving trouble on the Tirur-Kottakal road, five miles from Tirur. An officer of the Suffolk Regiment went out by car with an escort provided by the detachment; the gang was encountered on the return journey, was fired on, and sustained two casualties. On the 7th, a telegram reached the Post, warning the troops to expect an attack that night from a band of about 500 rebels from Vengra; defences were improved, and extra precautions taken, but no attack took place. By the 10th, work on the road in this locality was finished, and the next day, the detachment again provided the road protection, as the Leinsters were out on operations.

Orders were now received for the platoon to go to Ponmundam, whither it marched on the 12th, and camped on a hill 400 yards east of milestone $12\frac{1}{2}$ on the Mallapuram-Tirur road. The 13th was spent in putting the camp in a state of defence, and most of that night was spent standing-to, as hostile bands, numbering some 300 to 500 were in the vicinity, holding meetings and making much noise. Fire was opened eventually on the nearest gathering, which then dispersed.

Assisted by local labour, the platoon was employed on work on the Mallapuram-Tirur road till the 20th November. The local labour was not satisfactory, as the usual road coolies are Moplahs, and the Hindu refugees, who took their place, were not accustomed to the work. While at Ponmundam, Subadar-Major Sayyid Ali, late 2/73rd Infantry, and 31 other local Moplahs, petitioned to be allowed to return to their homes and normal pursuits, and were sent under escort to Kottakal.

On the 20th, the detachment was warned for work on the Wandur-Kallikkavu road and, leaving Ponmundam on the 21st, arrived at Wandur on the 23rd. Here the detachment was joined by No. 3 Platoon from Pandikkad. Work on the road continued till the 30th, by which date the road was clear to Kallikkavu. Escorts for the working party were found by the Kachins from Wandur. The bazaar at this place was sacked by Moplahs on the night of the 24th/25th. They fired some houses and murdered some Hindus, but did not attack the Post.

On the 27th December, the detachment (Nos. 2 and 3 Platoons) moved camp to Modho Malai, and to Kallikkavu on the 1st December. The two platoons remained together till the 9th December, working on the defences and construction of huts at Kallikkavu, clearing the roads to Karuvarakundu and Nilambur, and repairing culverts, originally reconstructed by the 64th, along the Kallikkavu-Wandur road. The materials available in the first instance for these culverts were not sufficiently durable.

On the 5th December, the working party, with its Chin escort, encountered two hostile ambushes on the Nilambur road. One Chin was wounded, and the enemy casualties were not known. On the 9th, No. 3 Platoon left for Pandikkad. No. 2 Platoon remained at Kallikkavu, to complete the work on the Wandur road and, on the 14th, marched to Nilambur, clearing the road *en route*. The platoon now worked in conjunction with a platoon of No. 9 Company, Q. V. O. Sappers and Miners, clearing the road to Ettakkare, and thence towards Madghani. Camp was moved to Ettakkare on the 15th December.

No. 3 Platoon.

On the 17th September, this platoon arrived at Pandikkad, under the command of Lieutenant S. A. Bowden and, on the day after its arrival, was warned to look out for fugitives of Khun Haji's band, who were being attacked at Nilambur by the Wandur Column on that day. The enemy was not encountered, and a report that this notorious rebel was coming to loot the Post on the 19th was not fulfilled. Except for acting as escort to the Sappers repairing the Melattur bridge on the 22nd, and helping in the repair on the 23rd, the platoon had nothing to do during the rest of the month, beyond garrisoning the Post in co-operation with a detachment of the Dorsets.

A fighting patrol, which was taken on the 26th to a place where the Dorsets had been ambushed a few days previously, when attacking Nemnini Hill along the Wandur road, did not encounter any rebels. On the 1st and 5th October, the detachment patrolled the neighbouring hills without meeting the enemy, and a fighting patrol taken down the Melattur road on the 6th had no better fortune. On the 15th

October, the rebels destroyed the Nellikat bridge—a column went out after them, on the following day, from Manjeri, and the Pandikkad garrison was given an opportunity of firing on the rebels as they retreated before the column.

On the 22nd October, on relief by the 2/8th Gurkha Rifles, the platoon proceeded to Kottakal *via* Mallapuram and, as already related, worked in conjunction with No. 2 Platoon, till the end of the month. On the 1st November, the platoon, now under the command of Captain Hamilton, was sent to Manjeri, to clear the Ariyakkod road of obstructions. Captain Hamilton went out to reconnoitre the road on the day of his arrival at Manjeri, and had great difficulty in salving the car, which got ditched. Work on the road began on the 3rd, and on this day the platoon accounted for six men of an enemy outpost. The road was cleared by the 5th, when an order was received to improve the surface of the road, and camp was moved to the 8th milestone.

The road was made fit for Ford vans and light lorries by the 13th November, the date fixed by Force Headquarters, only after much hard work; a great effort was made on the 12th, when the platoon left camp at 6 a.m., marched 6 miles to work, worked all day, and marched 6 miles back, arriving in camp at 5 p.m.

On the 13th November, a small party cleared away an obstruction on the Kundotti road, and on the following day the platoon returned to Manjeri. On arrival, the O. C. detachment was informed of the heavy attack made by the rebels on Pandikkad Post that morning, and was ordered to re-build the Post. The detachment marched there on the following day, and began work at once, completing it by the 20th. The original perimeter wall of the Post was only one brick thick, and the rebels had actually pushed it over when they charged against it. The new wall, breast-high, and some 600 yards long, was made two bricks thick. The Post was then wired, and a *chevaux-de frise*, 5 feet wide, of split and pointed bamboo stakes, was erected between the wire and the wall. Five machine-gun posts were also constructed. After clearing away some obstructions on the Mellatur road on the 22nd, the platoon joined No. 2 Platoon at Wandur on the following day.

As already narrated, the two platoons remained united till the 9th December, when No. 3 Platoon returned to Pandikkad, in order to make the road to Karuvarakundu fit for motor vehicles. On completing this work, it moved to Tirurangadi *via* Mallapuram and, camping at the 10th milestone on the 14th December, worked on this road.

The whole detachment was concentrated again towards the end of December, and arrived at Bangalore on the 29th. Captain Urmson, who had been employed as Brigade-Major to the troops in Malabar, rejoined the regiment on the 31st December. Captain Kemble had been employed as Base Commandant during the operations.

A telegram was received from Major-General J. T. Burnett-Stuart, C.B., C.M.G., D.S.O., Commanding the Madras District, thanking the detachment for their good work in Malabar.

1921—1923.

The regiment remained in garrison at Bangalore till September 1923. On Christmas Day, 1921, orders were received for a detachment to be sent to Bellary, to guard some thousands of Moplah prisoners confined in camp at that place. A detachment of about 200 men, under the command of Major M. Castle Smith, accordingly left Bangalore for Bellary on the 26th December 1921, and did not rejoin regimental headquarters till the 3rd November 1922.

A detachment under Subadar Narayanasami I, *Bahadur,* was sent to Rajankunti, on the 17th October 1921, to make trenches, etc., for an Artillery Practice Camp, returning on the 15th December.

In 1921, the Earl of Reading, P.C., G.C.B., G.M.S.I., G.M.I.E., G.C.V.O., became Viceroy of India.

On the 1st December 1922, the title of the battalion underwent yet another change, and it now became the "2nd Battalion, 1st Madras Pioneers."

1923-1924.
Waziristan.

During the spring of 1922, the regiment was warned that it might be required in the autumn for road-work in Waziristan. Orders to entrain were actually received but were cancelled on the same day. On the 25th August 1923, orders were received for the battalion to proceed to Waziristan for urgent work, the probable duration of which would be four months.

The advanced party left Bangalore on the 6th September, followed by the battalion three days later, a depot being left at Bangalore, while the furlough men were not recalled. The following officers accompanied the regiment:—

British Officers.	Subadars.	Jemadars.
Brevet Lieut.-Colonel A. E. S. Fennell.	Narayanasami, *Bahadur,* Subadar-Major.	Arogyasami, I. D.S. M.
Major H. St. G. H. Harvey-Kelly.	Dharmalingam.	Ramannah.
Major T. B. Skinner.	P. Narayanasami, I. D. S. M.	Balasundaram.
Captain H. H. R. Deane.	Balaraman.	Govindasami.
Captain S. A. Bowden.	Balagurusami, I. D. S. M.	Arunachalam, I. D. S. M.
Lieut. R. F. Worthington.		Kadirvelu.
		Muhd. Jaffar Hussain, I. A. E. C.
		Ramasami.

The battalion reached Khirgi on the 17th September and, by the 20th, was distributed as follows:—Regimental Headquarters, Headquarter Wing and A and C Companies at Sorarogha; 2 platoons of B Company at Jandola; B Company, less 2 platoons, at Kotkai.

On the 21st September, the battalion began work on the maintenance of the Jandola-Razmak circular road. The work consisted chiefly of putting in side-drains and culverts, and dry stone-walling. The detachment at Kotkai worked for part of the time at a tunnel, about a mile north-west of the camp. The object of this tunnel was to prevent the road, which at this point followed the Inzar Algad, from being washed away during the spate season.

Jandola-Razmak Road.

At Kotkai, the detachment also made some piquet posts on the hills on the left bank of the Tank Zam, for occupation by the troops during the withdrawal from this line. Part of the duties of the Kotkai and Jandola detachments was to keep the river crossings passable for mechanical transport. The detachment at Jandola was increased by two platoons of C Company on the 24th September.

The battalion, less detachments, moved to Kotkai on the 10th November, and continued work on the road and on the tunnel. On the 2nd December, it moved to Jandola. During the whole of this period, in addition to the road work, which was continuous, Sundays being the only days off work, the battalion was responsible for the defence of its own portion of the camp perimeter.

While at Jandola, the regiment was warned for work on the road through the Shahur Tangi, and proceeded to Chagmalai, at the junction of the Shahur and Mastung rivers, in two echelons, on the 7th and 9th December. The battalion formed part of the 9th Infantry Brigade, which was divided up for the purpose of the work into two portions, one at Chagmalai, and the other at Spli Toi, at the upper end of the Tangi.

Shahur Tangi Road.

The first few days were spent in building the camp defences; on the 14th, the battalion constructed Eden piquet and the mule track leading to it, and, on the 15th, C Company was employed building Castle piquet, in conjunction with a party of the 3rd/9th Jats. B Company began work on the road on the 15th, and the whole battalion on the 17th, between chains 112 and 131, on the right bank of the river. A good deal of blasting was necessary in several places.

Work continued steadily till the end of January 1924, when it was stopped pending a decision regarding the necessity of realigning a portion of the road. Originally the road, after crossing the Mastung and Shahur rivers opposite Chagmalai, followed the left bank of the Shahur for a certain distance, then crossed to the other bank. Two bridges would thus have been necessary, and would have taken a long time to build. To save time and money, it was decided to cut out the two bridges and follow the left bank of the river.

The battalion, therefore, was put on to work on the left bank from the 8th February 1924 and, as the rock strata followed the slope of the hill on this bank, the work was found to be much easier.

On the 14th February, C Company was moved to Spli Toi to work on blocks Nos. 23 and 24, and was followed by B Company on the 15th March, for work on the last 15 chains of Block No. 24. These companies worked as far as Haidari Kach.

During the whole time that the battalion was at work on the Shahur road, it took its share of perimeter defence. To begin with, this entailed some 13 sentries nightly, which, under the circumstances, put a heavy strain on the men in addition to quarter-guard duties. The battalion length of perimeter was, however, reduced by about half, on the arrival at Chagmalai of the 2/3rd Sikh Pioneers.

B and C Companies returned to Chagmalai on the 12th April, and the battalion, having completed its share of the work, left Chagmalai *en route* for Bangalore on the 14th. Entraining at Khirgi on the 17th, it reached Bangalore on the 24th April 1924.

The health of the battalion remained good throughout its stay in Waziristan. The winter is severe, the wind being particularly trying in the early morning. The camps on the Razmak-Jandola road had been in existence for some years, and the troops were made very fairly comfortable in them, but this was not the case at Chagmalai. The incidence of fever was most severe at Kotkai, which seemed to produce a particularly virulent form.

While in Waziristan, the regiment had one Pioneer wounded, while one Havildar was killed and one Pioneer injured by an explosion while blasting. One Lance-Naik, one Pioneer and one Follower died of disease.

A copy of the report submitted by the Commandant to the Colonel on the Staff, R. E. and Pioneers, will be found in Part V.

The following letter, dated the 19th April 1924, was received by the Commandant from Major-General T. G. Matheson, Commanding Waziristan District:—

"Now that you are leaving the District, I wish to say good-bye to you and all ranks of the battalion under your command, and to thank you for the very good work you have done in Waziristan.

You have been employed in two large projects of road construction in Waziristan which are without parallel on the North-West Frontier—the Jandola-Sorarogha-Razmak Circular road, and the Jandola-Sarwekai road through the Shahur Tangi.

In both these projects, the road had to be pushed through within a specified and limited period. I had to ask the troops to make a special effort to complete their tasks, and with great success have you responded to the call.

I wish to thank all ranks of your Battalion for their most notable work.

I wish you all good-bye and good luck for the future."

The following telegram, dated the 2nd May 1924, was received from General Sir W. R. Birdwood, General Officer Commanding-in-Chief, Northern Command:—

"Very sorry to be losing unit from Northern Command. Good wishes to all ranks on your arrival at Bangalore."

1924-1925.

On the 4th June 1924, the regiment received orders to proceed on relief to Mandalay during the ensuing cold weather, and accordingly entrained, on the 31st December 1924, for Madras, where it embarked for Rangoon on the *S. S. Erinpura* on the 2nd January 1925. Lieutenant-Colonel Fennell had proceeded to England on leave, and did not rejoin till February. The following officers accompanied the battalion to Burma:—

British Officers.	Subadars.	Jemadars.
Major H. F. Murland, *Commanding.*	Thambusami, I.D.S.M. *Subadar-Major.*	Ramannah.
„ F. O. N. Burne, M.C.	Dharmalingam.	Munisami.
Captain T. J. Barnes.	Sauriyanayagam.	Govindasami.
„ A. H. Baker, *Adjutant.*	Gnanaprakasam.	Arunachalam.
„ S. A. Bowden, *Quartermaster.*	Balaraman.	Sangili.
Lieutenant S. S. Mallannah.	Balasundaram.	Kadirvelu.
	Arogyasami, I.D.S.M.	Ramasami.
		Ramachandra Rao.
		Muhd. Jaffar Hussain, I.A.E.C.

On arrival at Rangoon, on the 5th January, the battalion was transferred to the *B. G. S. Irrawaddy* and two large barges, one on either side of the steamer, and proceeded up river on the same day. As there had been some trouble in Burma, owing to a campaign against paying taxes, orders were received for the battalion to land and march through various places, as shown in the following itinerary:—

6th January		Dedayai.
7th	„	Yandoon.
8th	„	Henzada.
9th	„	Myanaung.
10th	„	Prome, where the battalion marched through the town early the following morning, and was entertained by U Me, C.I.E., the Deputy Commissioner.
11th	„	Thayetmyo, where the battalion again landed.
12th	„	Minhla.
13th	„	Yenangyaung, where the battalion landed and marched up to the oilfield.
14th	„	Pagan.
15th	„	Pakokku, where the battalion marched through the bazaar and civil lines.
16th	„	Pannyo.
17th	„	Myinmu.
18th	„	Mandalay.

On the 2nd February, the battalion was inspected by Major-General Tytler, Commanding Burma District, and spent the remainder of the year in garrison in Fort Dufferin.

On the 31st March 1925, Lord Rawlinson died, and was succeeded as Commander-in-Chief temporarily by General Sir Claud W. Jacob, K.C.B., K.C.S.I., K.C.M.G. (formerly of the Hazara Pioneers) until the arrival of Field-Marshal Sir W. R. Birdwood, *Bart.*, G.C.B., G.C.M.G., K.C.S.I., C.I.E., D.S.O.

The Earl of Lytton, P.C., G.C.I.E., Governor of Bengal, acted as Viceroy for some months in 1925, during the absence of Earl Reading in England.

1926-1927.

Putao Road. Towards the end of this year, the regiment left Mandalay in two parties for contract work on the Putao road, a depot being left at Mandalay. The first party consisted of A and B Companies, which left Mandalay on the 30th October, and arrived at Myitkyina on the following day. The second party, consisting of Battalion Headquarters, the Headquarter Wing and C Company, left Mandalay on the 11th November, and reached Myitkyina on the 12th. The movements of the various detachments into which the regiment was split up, are detailed below:—

Headquarters, Headquarter Wing and Sumpra Bum Detachment.

Left Myitkyina and marched to Alam (12½ miles) on the 15th November; Chingran Hka (9 miles), on the 16th; Weshi (12 miles), on the 17th; Nsop Zup (9 miles), on the 18th; Njip Zup (8 miles), on the 19th. From Njip Zup, the Sumpra Bum Detachment, consisting of Subadar Balasundaram, 55 Indian other ranks and 5 followers, set out for Sumpra Bum (130 miles).

Battalion Headquarters remained at Njip Zup till the 23rd February 1927, when it moved to Tiang Zup, remaining there till the 5th April, and arriving at Myitkyina on the 10th April, where it entrained for Mandalay on the 17th, and arrived on the 18th April 1927. The Sumpra Bum detachment rejoined Headquarters at Myitkyina on the 14th April.

A Company.

Marched to Tiang Zup, where it remained till the 21st February 1927, when it moved on to Ooty Camp. It returned to Myitkyina on the 15th April and entrained for Mandalay with Battalion Headquarters on the 17th April.

B Company.

Marched to Supkaga, where it remained till the 18th February 1927, when it moved to Hill camp, remaining there till the 25th March. It entrained at Myitkyina on the 8th April, and reached Mandalay on the 9th.

C Company.

Left Myitkyina on the 14th November 1926 for Njip Zup, where it remained till the 20th February 1927. It then moved to Pub Camp, leaving there on the 31st March, and entraining, with B Company, on the 8th April 1927.

Full particulars of the work carried out on this contract will be found in Part V of these records.

In 1926, Lord Irwin, P.C., G.M.S.I., G.M.I.E., succeeded Earl Reading as Viceroy of India.

1928.

Towards the end of 1927, arrangements were made for the regiment to take up further Pioneer work, this time in the Hukawng Valley, and accordingly an advance party, consisting of Jemadar Arogyasami and 20 rank and file, left Mandalay for Mogaung on the 4th December 1927.

Hukawng Valley Road.

On the 11th December, A and B Companies left Mandalay, and a second party, consisting of the Headquarter Wing and C Company, entrained on the 21st December. A depot was left at Mandalay. The following were the movements of the various detachments:—

Battalion Headquarters and Headquarter Wing.

Arrived at Mogaung on the 22nd December 1927; marched to Sawn Hka, on the 23rd; Kamaing, on the 24th; Pakhren Bum (9 miles) on the 25th, and remained there till the 20th March 1928, when it moved to Hkause Chaung. On the 22nd March, Groups 2 and 3 moved to Mataing Hka; on the 6th April, Group 3 moved to Pakhren Bum; on the 9th April, Group 2 moved to Sasing Hka; again on the 18th to Hkause Chang, and on the 22nd to Pakhren Bum. The whole detachment returned to Kamaing on the 26th April, reached Mogaung on the 28th, and entrained for Mandalay on the 30th.

A Company.

Marched from Mogaung to Pakhren Bum and reached Horeb Camp on the 4th January 1928, remaining there, and at Pimple Camp, on work till the 26th April 1928, when it reached Kamaing and rejoined Headquarters.

B Company.

Also marched to Pakhren Bum, and one platoon reached Horeb Camp on the 26th January 1928, while three platoons arrived at Bison Camp on the 8th February. On the 27th February, the whole company moved to Sasing Hka, remaining there till the 18th April, and arriving at Mandalay on the 24th April 1928.

C Company.

Accompanied Headquarters to Kamaing on the 24th December, and from there branched off at Maubin for Mataing Hka, where it arrived, *via* Pungchen, on the 26th. On the 10th January 1928, two platoons moved to Elephant Camp and, on the 23rd March, on to Hwelon Hka, where they were joined by the remainder of the Company on the 24th. It left on the 18th April, and arrived at Mandalay, with B Company, on the 24th April 1928.

Full particulars of the work done will be found in Part V of these records.

Return to India. On the 29th November, the battalion set out to return to India. Entraining at Mandalay, in two trains, it embarked at Rangoon on the *S. S. Ethiopia* on the 30th November, and reached Madras on the 3rd December. Leaving Madras on the same night, it arrived at Bangalore on the 4th December 1928.

1929-1930.

The regiment now resumed garrison duties in Bangalore, and was soon busily engaged in the task of re-organisation, the new scheme for forming Pioneer battalions into Corps of Pioneers coming into force with effect from the 1st April 1929. By this scheme, the battalion once again changed its title, becoming the "2nd Battalion, Madras Pioneers."

Bangalore Water Supply Scheme. In October 1930, an opportunity for Pioneer work presented itself, in connection with the scheme to form a large reservoir by building a dam across the Arkavati river, about 20 miles from Bangalore, in order to supply water to the city.

No. 4 Company marched out, with Captain Baker and Lieutenant Anis, on the 3rd October 1930, and returned on the 5th January 1931.

No. 5 Company, with Captain Murcott and Lieutenant Wallawalker, marched out on the 25th October, and returned on the 6th and 8th December 1930.

No. 6 Company, with Lieutenants Shrinagesh and Mehtab Singh, marched out on the 6th, 8th and 10th December, and returned on the 24th January 1931.

In 1930, General Sir Philip W. Chetwoode, *Bart.*, G.C.B., K.C.M.G., D.S.O., A.D.C., became Commander-in-Chief in India.

Part II.

ORDERS AND CHANGES AFFECTING THE REGIMENT.

1759—1930.

Note.

This part of the Records comprises the principal orders relating to changes in the pay and establishment of the Regiment during the course of its history, but, in addition, a great number of notes has been added, with the object of depicting the life of the Regiment at various periods. The reading of a succession of Army Orders presents a somewhat dreary prospect, but it is hoped that with the additional notes and references, the observant eye will be able to form a picture of Army Service in India, more particularly in the early days, and that this part of the Records will be found to be by no means the least interesting.

1759.

When, in September 1759, the 5th Battalion of Coast Sepoys came into being —though it must be remembered that the majority of the men of which it was composed had been serving in the Company's military forces for many years previously—it consisted of 9 companies, each company consisting of "1 Subadar; 2 Jemadars; 6 Havildars; 6 Naigues; 1 Trumpeter; 2 Tom-Toms; 2 Colourmen; 1 Vakeel; 1 Puckall; and 93 Private Sepoys. Total, 115."

"Two Subalterns, three Serjeant-Majors, and one Black Commandant (who is to be under the orders of the Commissioned Officers) to be appointed to the care of each battalion..........Two linguists, and five armourers to be included in the establishment of each battalion. The linguists to receive each the pay of two private Sepoys. Each armourer the pay of one. Thus in the Sepoys' roll one man per company must be entered on the roll as contingent men, whose pay will defray the above mentioned expense........It is proposed that the battalions should be clothed, numbered, and distinguished also by their colours. The following are the distinctions proposed.—......*No. 5. Fifth Battalion.* Clothing red; Facings red; Colours red. The Grenadier Company with a White Cross."

Two battalions were allotted to Trichinopoly; two to Madras; one to Chingleput; and two to Conjeeveram. As we find the 5th Battalion stationed at Trichinopoly shortly after it was raised, we may surmise that it was one of the two battalions assigned to that place.

The following is a further extract from the recommendations for the organisation of the new battalions, which were submitted by a committee composed of Colonel Stringer Lawrence and Messrs. Charles Bourchier and John Pybus:—

Courts-Martial.—Regimental Courts-Martial may be composed of one Subidar, two Jemidars, two Havildars, one Naig and one Colorman; and as much as possible to be chose out of different companies to the Prisoner.

General Courts-martial to be composed of three Subidars, three Jemidars, two Havildars, two Naigs, two Colormen, and one private Sepoy. Subidars and Jemidars to be tried by four Subidars and three Jemidars. Havildars and Naigs, as in our service like Serjeants and Corporals to be tried as private men........ ....

Colormen.—As the Colormen are commonly chose out in the company from the best and bravest men in it, so they are the first to succeed to the vacancies of officers, which may happen in the company. For that reason they are distinguished by being permitted to sit on Courts-martial.

Grenadiers.—In General it is recommended to the officers as much as possible to take notice of those men who in any way distinguish themselves. Taking down their names and putting them in the Grenadier Company, that in time those companies be composed of real brave good men. And now and then promotions of officers may be made out of those companies for encouragement when it can be done without prejudice to any remarkable merit in the Colormen, who are first to succeed......"

As regards the pay of the various ranks; that of the Captains (of whom there were three appointed to supervise generally) was fixed at Rs. 2,000 *per annum*, while the unfortunate subaltern only received Rs. 300 *per annum*. The Indian ranks received, monthly, Subadars, Rs. 60; Jemadars, Rs. 16; Havildars, Rs. 10; Naigues, Rs. 8; and Sepoys, Rs. 6. The Native Commandant, in addition to his pay as Subadar, drew Rs. 54 *per mensem* as extra allowance. Subadars were allowed batta at the rate of Fanams 8 *per diem;* Jemadars, Fanams 4; Havildars, Naigues and Sepoys, Fanams 2. (There were 12 Fanams to the Rupee). European Serjeants when commanding companies of sepoys were granted an extra allowance of Rs. 20 *per mensem*.

1760.

From the original formation of the regiment, up to the year 1813, it was kept up to strength by recruits from the Carnatic; principally from about Vellore, Trichinopoly, Madura and the Baramahal.

Orme remarks on the improved efficiency of the sepoys shortly after their formation into battalions, as follows:—

"Colonel Coote by constantly exposing his own person with the sepoys, has brought them to sustain dangerous services from which the Europeans were preserved."

1761.

In July 1761, Government reduced the strength of each company from 115 to 100, and at the same time increased the number of battalions from six to seven, the total number of Native Infantry then amounting to 6,300 of all ranks.

Each battalion was now composed of nine companies, and officered by two European Subalterns, three Serjeants, and one Native Commandant. Another battalion was raised in August, on account of the operations against Nellore and Vellore, and a ninth battalion in September, though in authorising this the Governor took occasion to remark to Colonel Caillaud, who was then Commander-in-Chief of the Forces, "that Mr. Lally made the Siege of Fort St. George, and Colonel Lawrence invested Seringham, with a less number of Sepoys than are now with the Army"— which provoked an indignant reply from the recipient.

About the same time, two bell tents for each company, and leather coverings for the locks of the muskets were sanctioned in consequence of the following representation from Colonel Caillaud:—

"The great demand for arms among the seapoys proceeds in part from their having no kind of shelter for them in the field excepting what they receive from pieces of wax cloth wrapped round their locks, the consumption of which is very great, and must be attended by expense; to obviate this, I think if the sepoys were allowed two bell tents a company, and leather coverings for their locks that the expense of such stores in the end would be saved by the number of arms which would be preserved by it; allowing the expense to be even something more, the advantage of keeping their arms dry and fit for service is an object worth consideration."

Early in November, Major-General Stringer Lawrence returned from England and resumed command of the Coast Army. His first duty was to issue a stringent order regarding the serious abuses which had crept into the army, and he required a monthly return to be submitted by every Commanding Officer, accounting for every man under his command. The principal abuse seems to have been that whenever a man died, or in some other way became a casualty, it was not reported, and the Commanding Officer continued to draw pay for him; one Major Alesieu, Commanding at Wandiwash, going so far as to inform the Garrison Paymaster that "he would, by his authority as commandant, flog any Conicopoly that shall offer to take any account of casualties"—a rather old-fashioned way of dealing with the Military Accounts Department.

1762.

On the 13th July 1762, when the expedition was about to sail to Manilla, sepoys were for the first time allowed to make family payments, the following being an extract from the order:—

"It is therefore agreed that they be advanced four months' pay, and to encourage them the more readily to enter on this service, it is resolved that each sepoy and lascar that enters voluntarily, shall have one month's batta also advanced to them, and that such of them, as are desirous of it, may have any part of their pay delivered to their families during their absence, who are to give in their names, that a list of them may be delivered to the Deputy Governor and Council appointed to proceed with the expedition, who are to be directed to stop such a part of their pay at Manilla as they may have desired to be received here by their families."

On the 26th July 1762, the following orders were issued regarding vacancies in the native ranks:—

"For the more regularly compleating, and raising the Sepoy Companies or promoting the officers belonging to them, it is ordered that the Sepoy Companies shall be compleated as often as the Governor and Council shall judge necessary, but never without a particular order.

When on service in the field the Commanding Officer may compleat the Sepoy Companies whenever he shall think necessary, and appoint officers to any vacancies, but the Commanding Officers in Garrison shall always acquaint the Commander-in-Chief with all vacancies of officers, pointing out those who are best qualified to succeed, and await his confirmation.

The next in rank and seniority shall always succeed, provided there be no material objections; all objections to the next in rank shall be represented.

Whenever any sepoys are ordered to be raised, vacancies of officers filled up, or the companies compleated; they shall be presented by the officers of sepoys to the Commanding Officer in the field, or in garrison, and when approved of by him, the Paymaster shall enter their names in his rolls, and their pay shall commence from the first day, of the month, provided their names were inserted on that day, and not otherwise.

All men unfit for the duty of sepoys shall be discharged the service, the Commanding Officer shall give a list of such monthly, if any there be, to the Sepoy Paymaster that they may be discharged from the rolls, and every Commanding Officer of Sepoys as well as all Commanding Officers in the field, or in garrison, are strictly to attend to this part of their duty."

1763.

On the 14th November 1763, Mr. (Afterwards Sir) Robert Palk succeeded Mr. George Pigot as Governor, and held the appointment till 1767, dying at the age of 81 in 1798. He started life in the Church, and was Chaplain to Admiral Boscawen at the siege of Pondicherry. He subsequently acted as Paymaster and Commissary with the forces in the field, and was employed by the Governor as an intermediary between Colonel Lawrence and Mr. Saunders—"with the real view of softening and managing Colonel Lawrence's warm and sudden temper." He married a sister of Henry Vansittart and, on leaving India in 1769, was made a Baronet and entered Parliament.

In December 1763, Major Preston, Commanding the Army before Madura, represented to the Commander-in-Chief that the Native battalions were not sufficiently officered, and that each ought to have one Captain, two Subalterns, and nine Serjeants permanently posted to it. He further stated that the European officers then doing duty with the sepoys were heartily tired of their situation, and recommended that every officer in the European Infantry should take his tour. Government did not, at that time, sanction any increase in the number of European officers, but contented themselves by replying as follows:—

> "With respect to the hardships which Major Preston complains the sepoy officers labour under the Board allow that to discipline the sepoys is a fatigueing service, and should therefore be given to the youngest and most active officers, who must at the same time consider that the preferment they get by means of the sepoys, and the gratuity they receive while they continue with them, should be looked upon as a very sufficient recompense for the extraordinary pains, and trouble attending that service."

On the 27th December 1763, it was decided that each Native officer should receive a commission, and that Commandants should be charged a fee of five pagodas; Subadars, three pagodas; and Jemadars, one pagoda. It appears, however that this decision was not carried out till 1766.

1765.

In November 1765, the Army was re-organised and it was decided that the establishment of sepoys should consist of 10 battalions, to be stationed as follows:—

"At Madras and its dependencies,	2 battalions.
At Vellore and its dependencies, Arcot, Sautghur, Cuddapahnattam	1 battalion.
At Chingleput, Permacoil, Ginjee and Wandiwash	½ battalion.
At Cuddalore, Wodiarpolliam and Arrialoor	½ battalion.
At Trichinopoly and the outposts	2 battalions.
For Madura and Palamcotta	2 battalions.
For Masulipatam and the North	2 battalions."

Each battalion was to be officered by one Captain, one Lieutenant, and one Ensign.

In December 1765, this establishment was again found to be insufficient and an extra battalion was raised for the Carnatic, and two for service in the Northern Circars.

At the same time eight independent companies were raised for garrison duty at Thiaghur, Arcot, Wandiwash, Permacoil, Ginjee, Chingleput, and Cuddalore.

1766.

On the 1st January 1766, new Military Regulations came into force, from which the following particulars are extracted:—

Each battalion was to consist of ten companies, of which two were to be called Grenadier companies, and to be distinguished by their colours. Their pay was to be as follows:—

	Rank.	Nett Pay of Each per Month.	Stoppages for Clothing Monthly for each.	Full Pay of each as issued.	Batta when in the Field per Day.
1	Subadar	16 0 0	1 0 0	17 0 0	0 6 0
2	Jemadars	4 21 0	0 21 0	5 0 0	0 3 0
6	Havildars	2 31 40	0 10 40	3 0 0	0 1 30
6	Naigues	2 7 0	0 7 0	2 14 0	0 1 30
2	Colourmen	1 24 0	0 5 40	1 29 40	0 1 30
2	Tom-Toms	1 24 0	0 5 40	1 29 40	0 1 30
1	Vakeel	1 24 0	0 5 40	1 29 40	0 1 30
1	Puckall	1 24 0	0 5 40	1 29 40	0 1 30
78	Sepoys	1 24 0	0 5 40	1 29 40	0 1 30
100					

The above table represents pagodas, fanams and cash. Pagodas 17 appear to have been equivalent to Rupees 59-8-0, so that each pagoda was worth three rupees eight annas. In addition to his pay as a Subadar, each Native Commandant received an allowance of Rs. 52-8 as Commandant. The Serjeants-Major received nett pay of 9 pagodas each *per mensem*.

One Captain, two Subaltern officers, five Serjeants-Major, and one Native Commandant, who was to be under the orders of the Commissioned Officers were appointed to the care of each battalion.

One of the Havildars of each company was to act as Adjutant to his company and, provided he did the work (which presumably corresponded to the work now done by the Orderly Havildars) satisfactorily, was to be first considered for promotion to Jemadar. In the same way, one of the Jemadars was to act as Adjutant to the battalion "with the same hopes of promotion, and it will be a great recommendation if they understand English."

The Captains were to receive 500 pagodas each in lieu of off-reckonings and the Subalterns were each given 10 pagodas a month extra, while it was required of them "that they should provide themselves with good Linguists, at their own expense."

"When the sepoys are in the field, each company will be provided with two Bell tents at the public expense, but the sepoys must provide themselves with one large Markee to each company; in the field also each company is to have six mamootys, and two hand hatchets, or bill hooks, which the Subadar is carefully to preserve, or he will be made to pay for those that are lost. To carry the tents and tools, each company will be allowed two bullocks, and for carrying water, one Puckall or two Bhesties."

As regards recruiting, sepoys were to be chosen, if possible, out of the following castes, viz.—"Rajpoot, Musselmen, Comawar, Rachwar, Yelmawar, and Buckserry." Of these the *Comawars* and *Yelmawars* are now represented by the Kamma, Kapu, Reddi, and Velama castes; these were originally soldiers by profession, but are now mainly agriculturists and traders. They appear to have followed the Vijayanagar army south, and settled in Madura and Tinnevelly districts under the Nayak Governors.

The *Rachwars* are now represented by the Rajus or Razus, who mostly live in the neighbourhood of Rajapalaiyam. They are probably military descendants of the Kapu, and Kamma and Velama castes. They claim to be Kshatriyas and at their weddings worship a sword.

The *Buckserrys* I had identified as the Bakkas, a sub-caste of Balija, some of whom, descended from the Balija or Nayak Kings of Madura, Tanjore and Vijayanagar, claim to be Kshatriyas, but Colonel Wilson states that the term was originally applied to men enlisted at or near, Buxar—"Buxarries". Orme, it may be noted, in his account of the defence of Calcutta against Surajah Dowlah in 1756, refers to "Buxerries, or Indian matchlock men."

It was laid down that "in all promotions some regard should be had to length of service, and consequently seniority, and in particular to the candidate speaking English."

Also that "it is highly necessary that Serjeants of Sepoys should be men of exemplary diligence, knowledge and sobriety, and it would be of great use if they endeavoured to attain a knowledge of the country languages, such as Moors, Malabars, or Gentoe" (*i.e.* Hindustani, Tamil, or Telegu.)

In April 1766, an order was added to these Military Regulations, that in the event of their being wounded or invalided, provided that they had behaved well, Jemadars would receive a monthly allowance of 2½ pagodas; Havildars and Naigues, 1 pagoda 29 fanams 40 cash; and Private Sepoys, 1 pagoda.

1767.

About February 1767, on the recommendation of General Caillaud, a Field Officer was appointed to command the whole corps of sepoys, and directed to join Colonel Smith, the following reasons being given for the appointment:—

"Government Consulations, Fort St. George, 5th February 1767. Having judged it necessary to appoint a Field Officer at the head of the sepoys, we have pitched upon you for this service, not doubting but your care and attention will be exerted to the utmost to promote good order, and discipline among them; without which our best endeavours to render this corps of that use which is expected of them, will be ineffectual. And here we cannot help observing to you that notwithstanding the regulations established we have too much reason to suspect that money is lent to the sepoys by officers and others, and that considerations are given for the recommendation of Sepoy Officers for promotion. We do therefore direct that you use every possible means to put a stop to such pernicious practices by acquainting the officers, and others, that whoever is found guilty thereof, will most certainly meet with our severest resentment.

(Signed) CHARLES BOUCHIER,
"*and Council*"

To Lieutenant-Colonel TOD.

About the same time it was ordered that tom-toms and trumpets should be discontinued in the Native Infantry as soon as a sufficient number of men could be taught the different beats on the drum as practised in the European battalions.

About March 1767, Government sanctioned the appointment of a Native Doctor to each sepoy battalion on the pay of a Havildar.

In July 1767, it was resolved to attach light field pieces to the Native Infantry, the following order being issued on the subject:—

"A number of short brass three-pounder guns being sent out this year and which we may imagine may be very usefully employed, by attaching two to each battalion of sepoys, it is agreed that those that are mounted be sent to camp, and Colonel Smith is to be directed to appoint them to such of the battalions as he shall judge proper, and two men are to be selected out of each company to work them, whose pay, on account of this extraordinary duty, is to be increased to two pagodas per month including stoppages. An European gunner, and a lascar may also be appointed to each gun, if necessary."

1768.

Some reference to the dress of officers of this period is to be found in the entertaining, if somewhat scandalous, *Memoirs of William Hickey*. Hickey was sent out to Madras as a cadet in 1768 and, before sailing, was given at the India House, a printed list of necessaries he should take with him, the official at the India House informing him at the same time

"that I must recollect in addition to take a few yards of scarlet, blue, green and yellow cloths, in order to make up regimentals according to the Corps to which I should be attached, the Infantry wearing scarlet, but with different facings of blue, yellow or green, the Artillery like His Majesty's blue with scarlet facings, and the Engineers scarlet faced with black velvet."

Hickey continues :—

"I then went to my father's tailor, Anthony Marcelis, of Suffolk Street, Charing Cross, to order regimentals, but not knowing to what Corps I should be appointed, I conceived the best thing I could do would be to have a suit of each description, which I directed accordingly. Upon my way from Marcelis I met in the street a dashing fellow in a scarlet frock, with black waistcoat, breeches and stockings, which in my eyes appeared remarkably smart. I therefore returned instantly to the tailor to bespeak a similar dress, as I was then in mourning for my mother.

Marcelis suggested an improvement, which was to have the coat lined with back silk, and black buttons and button holes, which not only looked better than the plain red, but was more appropriate as military mourning.

Mr. Walter Taylor, a very old friend of my father's, presented me with a beautiful cut and thrust steel sword, desiring me to cut off half a dozen rich fellows' heads with it, and so return a Nabob myself to England. In three days after I received this sword, I burst forth a *martial* buck of the first stamp, and not a little vain was I of the figure I made. I seldom appeared two successive days in the same dress; my intimates beheld me with astonishment, observing I was going abroad in a splendid style. Some of brother Joseph's acquaintances enquired what the devil regiment I had got into, for that they met me in half a dozen different uniforms in as many days............

The first time I appeared in my scarlet and black, I committed a sad solecism in dress by wearing my military sword. Of this error I was unconscious until told of it by a young man who perfectly understood the etiquette of dress, and he said I was very wrong, that the sword should be black, with a sword loveknot of black. Of course I lost no time in equipping myself 'comme il faut.' My father made no complaint of my having such a variety of clothes, but much as to the cut of them. Making double-breasted coats for such a climate as the East Indies he pronounced preposterous and absurd yet in this he was mistaken. Officers in India dress precisely the same (in point of coat at least) as in Europe, and although certainly absurd in such extreme heat, actually button the lapel close up to the throat."

The only change which appears to have been made in the interior economy of the native army in this year appears to have been that recruits were allowed pay from the date of enlistment. Hitherto, men enlisted between the 1st and 15th of the month commenced to draw pay from the 15th; but if enlisted between the 15th and the end of the month they were not entitled to pay until the 1st of the succeeding month.

1769.

After the conclusion of the treaty with Haidar Ali in April 1769, the Nawab of the Carnatic, who up to that time had consented to be debited with the cost of ten battalions of sepoys, professed his inability to pay for more than 7,000 men. The Native Infantry then in the service consisted of nineteen battalions, and fifteen independent companies. Although Government considered that the existing force was no more than sufficient, they were obliged to meet the Nawab's wishes as far as possible, and did so by disbanding the 11th battalion, and by reducing the strength of the others to 763 men of all ranks, as follows:—

	Subadars.	Jemadars.	Havildars.	Naigues.	Drummers.	Fifers.	Colourmen.	Puckalies.	Sepoys.
1st and 2nd Grenadier Companies ..	2	4	10	10	2	2	2	2	120
Commandant's Company	1	2	5	5	1	1	1	1	60
7 Battalion Companies	7	14	35	35	7	..	7	7	420
Total ..	10	20	50	50	10	3	10	10	600

At the same time Government informed the Nawab that he must garrison Arcot, Satghar, Ginjee, Wandiwash, Tiruvannamalai, and Chittapet with his own troops, and allotted their own battalions as follows:—

1st and 3rd battalions.	Conjevaram.
17th ,,	Madras.
5th, 6th, 14th and 16th battalions.	*Vellore and Ambur.*
4th, 7th, and 8th battalions.	Trichinopoly.
9th and 10th ,,	Madura and Palmcottah.
15th ,,	Ongole and Palnad.
2nd, 14th, 13th, 18th and 19th battalions.	Northern Circars.
Eight independent Companies.	Masulipatam.
Four ,, ,,	Cuddalore.
One ,, ,,	Tayaghar.
One ,, ,,	Perumukkal.
One ,, ,,	Chingleput (?)

On the 16th June 1769, changes were made in the designations and numbers of the Native battalions. Those in the south were called *"Carnatic Battalions"* and numbered from 1 to 13, the three kept up for the defence of the Company's Jaghir (1st, 3rd and 17th) coming first. Those serving in the North were called *"Circar Battalions"* and were numbered from 1 to 5 successively.

The 5th Battalion of Coast Sepoys consequently now became the 5th Carnatic Battalion.

During 1769, the employment of vakeels with the Native battalions having been discovered to be a source of great abuses, they were dismissed, and their places taken by conicopolies or writers, acting under the immediate orders of the Paymasters. A head writer and an assistant were allowed for each battalion on 6 and 4 pagodas each, respectively, in garrison, or 10 and 6 pagodas in the field.

The pay of the European Serjeants was considered too high, and was accordingly reduced, the Serjeant-Major and Quartermaster-Serjeant alone drawing 9 pagodas each *per mensem,* while the other three drew 7 pagodas each.

About the same time it was ordered that when two or more battalions were serving together, the senior officer should appoint a Subaltern to act as Adjutant to the whole.

In August 1769, it was ordered that all the Sepoys should have blue facings, that the turbands and cummerbunds should also be blue, and that the drawers should be bordered with blue.

In the early days, great variation in dress was permitted and Lieutenant (afterwards Lieutenant-General Sir Henry) Cosby claimed the distinction, in 1765, of being the first officer on the Coast of Coromandel to persuade the Sepoys to submit to a uniformity of dress.

Whilst on the subject of uniform, I may note here that the first mention of uniform for the troops on the Coast was in December 1672, when it occurred to the Company that by displaying the garrison of Fort St. George uniformly clad in woollen coats, the native Princes might be induced to follow the example, and so stimulate the trade in woollen cloth.

From the Company to Fort St. George.

" It being found here in Europe very necessary and convenient for the Soldiers to have coates of one collour, not only for the handsome representacon of them in their exercise but for the greater awe to the adversary, besides the encouragement to themselves, wee have thought requisite that our Soldiers with you should bee put into the like habitt........

And this example probably may begett a vent of our cloth, if the practize will take with the Princes of the Country to put their Regiments and Companies into cloth coates of severall collors....."

The reply from Fort St. George pointed out an objection :—

From Fort St. George to the Company.

"The bestowing of coates upon your Souldiers would be very creditable, and so we understand it is already in practise at Bombayn; but the proportion of the English being so small in respect to the Portuges and Mestizos, unless we gave the same to all it would rather shew our weakness than our strength........"

"Mestizo" was a word from the Portuguese, meaning a person of mixed descent, an Eurasian.

In 1679, uniforms made from red cloth, for which there was no sale, were issued to the garrison, the cost being recovered from the men's pay.

On the 4th September 1769, it was ordered that in future no one under the rank of Jemadar should be appointed to sit on Courts-martial, thus doing away with the panchayat-like composition of the old Courts-martial.

About the end of the year, the officers commanding sepoy battalions asked that they might be allowed to pay their own men instead of this being done by the Paymasters, but Government declined to make any alteration in the existing regulations.

1770.

In February 1770, an Invaliding Committee, composed of the Commander-in-Chief, the Commandant of Fort St. George, and the Town-Major was appointed to select sepoys for the invalid list.

On the 12th March 1770, the following order was issued directing that Regimental Registers should be kept, similar to the Long Roll of the present day :—

" The Board observing that the vacancies in the sepoy battalions are chiefly caused by desertion, to prevent which as much as possible, it is ordered that a book be kept for each battalion in which shall be entered the name, and description of every sepoy, setting forth his age, caste, the district and village he came from, and where his family or relations reside, and that the battalions be drawn out, and informed that desertions shall in future be punished with death, agreeable to the Articles of War, which it is resolved to get translated into the country languages, and it is also ordered that a reward of five pagodas be given for apprehending every sepoy deserter."

On the 14th May 1770, Lieutenant-Colonel Lang, Commanding at Trichinopoly, having brought to notice the difficulty of managing native servants, Government issued an order that, after proper enquiry, a native servant might be punished according to the nature of his offence.

In May 1770, acting on the recommendation of General Smith, Government ordered that Officers Commanding battalions should not stop more than four, or at most five, rupees from any sepoy. At the same time the scale and cost of the articles to be provided at the expense of the men was laid down as follows:—

	Rupees.	Fanams.	Cash.
"1 blue turband	1	6	0
1 blue sash	0	8	0
2 pairs of drawers	1	2	0
1 white jacket	0	8	0
	4	0	0

"General Smith further acquaints the Board that he does not imagine that the above will be sufficient for a whole year to enable the sepoys to appear in a soldier-like manner, but that he does not see how any further stoppages can be made without distressing them beyond what they can bear."

It may be noted that the nett pay of a sepoy was one pagoda and 24 fanams, or Rupees 5 annas 8; a rupee being valued at 12 fanams.

In this year an enquiry was held into the causes of the numerous desertions in the "Madras Battalion," commanded by Captain M'Kain, and it was ascertained that some men had been flogged by his order without any trial, and that he had been in the habit of employing non-commissioned officers, as well as sepoys on his own private business. He was court-martialled, and found guilty on the latter charge, the sentence being suspension for two months, but as regards the charge of flogging without trial the Court observed that:—

"The same is not contrary to the established usage of the army, nor does it appear that the prisoner made a wanton or cruel abuse of that custom."

The sentence was confirmed, but the practice of inflicting corporal punishment without trial was thenceforth expressly prohibited on pain of dismissal from the service, except in cases where an immediate example might be necessary and when a like punishment might justifiably be inflicted on a soldier of the European Corps.

On the 28th May 1770, the following order was issued regarding the acquirement of Hindustani by officers of sepoys:—

"Every Indian officer of the sepoy corps is, or ought to be acquainted with the Moorish language, which is the general language of Hindustan, and the best sepoys will be found to understand it. Every officer commanding sepoys ought to be able to converse in that language, and this should be deemed an essential indispensible qualification for such a command."

In August 1770, the Native battalions were formed into three brigades, two for service in the Carnatic, and one for the Northern Circars. At the same time the 3rd or "Madras Battalion" was broken up, and the others, from the 4th to the 13th inclusive, were moved up one number, the 5th Carnatic Battalion being in consequence now designated the 4th Carnatic Battalion. The Coast army was, therefore composed as follows:—

First Brigade.

3rd Carnatic Battalion.	Captain Povery.
4th ,, ,,	,, *Baillie.*
6th ,, ,,	,, Cowper.
7th ,, ,,	,, Cook.
8th ,, ,,	,, Brown.
9th ,, ,,	,, Nixon.

Second Brigade.

1st Carnatic Battalion.	Captain Hopkins,
2nd ,, ,,	,, Harper.
5th ,, ,,	,, Cosby.
10th ,, ,,	,, Bruce.
11th ,, ,,	,, Fletcher.
12th ,, ,,	,, Evans.

Third Brigade.

1st Circar Battalion.	Captain Bellingham.
2nd ,, ,,	,, Madge.
3rd ,, ,,	,, Bowman.
4th ,, ,,	,, Casemore.
5th ,, ,,	,, Collins.
6th ,, ,,	,, Marchand.

At the same time the establishment of the European officers for a battalion of Sepoys was fixed at 1 Captain, 5 Lieutenants and 5 Ensigns, in consideration of which augmentation the additional allowances heretofore drawn by the Subalterns and Staff Serjeants were reduced.

On the 31st December 1770, an order was published directing that the stoppage from sepoys "on account of slops" should not exceed; from a Havildar, 7 fanams; from a Naigue, 5 fanams 12 cash; from a sepoy, 4 fanams. The slops in question were to be provided as follows:—

Turband	Three in two years.
Sash	One *per annum*.
Drawers	Two pairs *per annum*.
Under-jacket	Two *per annum*.

These stoppages were to made by the Paymaster, and the "slops" were not to be provided by officers commanding battalions, but by an agent appointed by government for the purpose.

1771.

In this year Josias Du Pre was President of Fort St. George.

In May 1771, Government desired to carry out an order which directed that an European Serjeant should be posted to every company of sepoys, but it was found that the number required could not be withdrawn from the European regiments without detriment to their efficiency; nevertheless, it was determind that the Native battalions should be completed with Serjeants, provided that capable men could be obtained.

During the early part of 1771, the Native battalions were inspected by Brigadier-General Smith, who reported on them as follows:—

" The sepoys also are much improved, and to all appearance, will be more so. A spirit of emulation amongst the several battalions seems evidently to prevail, which will be the certain means of bringing them to the greatest regularity."

He went on to point out that their great defect lay in their careless manner of firing, and impressed upon Government the absolute necessity of granting a regular allowance, both of blunt and ball cartridges, to enable the men to practice, and he concluded with the remark that—

In the King's Service every regiment is allowed a certain quantity of powder, lead, and cartridge paper annually for exercising, and no troops require it so much as sepoys."

The result of this representation was that Government decided to permit battalion commanders to submit indents for whatever ammunition might be necessary for exercising the sepoys.

The highest Staff appointment on the Coast at this time was that of Brigade-Major.

1773.

In June 1773, an European officer was appointed to each battalion, as Adjutant, and in order to meet the expense of this addition the ten Colormen were struck off the rolls, and a sum equivalent to the aggregate amount of their pay was assigned as an allowance to the Adjutant.

On the 17th June, the following order was issued regarding Adjutants:—

It is likewise resolved that the officers appointed Adjutants in the Sepoy battalions keep copie of all the monthly returns and the proceedings of Courts-martial, likewise an exact Roster of both the European and Black officers, and it is recommended to them in the strongest manner to be particularly careful to discharge their duty with alertness and spirit, and seriously consider that an Adjutancy is the most eligible appointment young officers can enjoy, being the most conducive, of all others, towards rendering them masters of their profession."

In the year 1773, the appointment of Adjutant-General was instituted for the first time in India, when Major Henry Cosby was given that designation, with the rank of Lieutenant-Colonel.

1774.

In April 1774, a company of Guides was raised from the several Native battalions in the Carnatic, and placed under the command of Lieutenant Geils of the Artillery, for the purpose of preparing a survey of the Carnatic. This company was reduced in December 1775.

1776.

In January 1776, copies of the Articles of War in Tamil were issued to officers in command of Native battalions, with orders to have them publicly read once every two months, both to their respective battalions, and to all detachments therefrom.

In March, an order was issued to the effect that two-thirds of the Subalterns posted to a battalion of sepoys must always be present with it.

In December, Government decided to reduce the number of sepoys in each battalion to 650, and to form the surplus men into six extra battalions, four for the Carnatic, and two for the Northern Circars. The complement of European Commissioned and Non-Commissioned officers for the Native battalions was fixed as follows:—

Carnatic Battalions.	*Circar Battalions.*
1 Captain.	1 Captain.
4 Lieutenants.	3 Lieutenants.
6 Ensigns.	4 Ensigns.
10 Serjeants.	10 Serjeants.

The result of this order was that the following battalions were added to the strength of the Coast Army:—

13th Carnatic Battalion.	Captain Hugh Robert Alcock, *Commanding.*
	Lieutenant Richard Anderson, *Adjutant.*
14th Carnatic Battalion.	Captain Donald Campbell, *Commanding.*
	Ensign Joseph Little, *Adjutant.*
15th Carnatic Battalion.	Captain John Davis, *Commanding.*
	Lieutenant John Cuppage, *Adjutant.*
16th Carnatic Battalion.	Captain Thomas Lane, *Commanding.*
	Ensign James Richardson, *Adjutant.*
7th Circar Battalion.	Captain Thomas Bridges, *Commanding.*
	Ensign James Mackay, *Adjutant.*
8th Circar Battalion.	Captain Thomas Rowles, *Commanding.*
	Lieutenant George Wahab, *Adjutant.*

The 4th Carnatic Battalion sent a draft to the 13th Battalion on this occasion.

1777.

On the 17th January 1777, two battalion companies were added to each of the sixteen Carnatic battalions, and the Grenadier companies of each battalion were increased by one Jemadar, one Havildar, one Naigue, and twenty-five Privates.

In spite of the additions ordered in the previous year, there do not appear to have been more than 7 Subalterns and 7 Serjeants serving with any battalion in 1777.

At this period the drill establishment must have been very strong, as on the 27th January the sum of eight pagodas *per mensem,* granted as an extra allowance to the Drill Instructors, was ordered to be distributed as follows:—Drill Serjeant, 2 pagodas; two Drill Havildars, 3 pagodas; three Drill Naigues, 3 pagodas.

On the 23rd April, Government gave orders for five additional battalions to be raised, and the 17th, 18th, 19th, 20th and 21st Battalions were accordingly formed. The 4th Carnatic Battalion sent a draft to the 17th, which was being raised at Fort St. George. The 19th Battalion was raised at Cuddalore by Captain Joseph Bilcliffe, who became Colonel of the 4th Battalion many years afterwards.

In July 1777, the following orders were issued regarding arms, colours, and dress :—

"All the European Officers of Sepoys and the Black Officers attached to the grenadier company, also the Black Commandants, are in future to use fuzils, the other Black Officers to have Spontoons. All the colors of the sepoy corps on this establishment to be uniform, distinguishing only the number of the battalion, with the word 'Carnatic' or 'Circar.'

The hats of all the officers through the army are to be plain, cocked with gold looping; hat string and tassel as at present.

Besides the full frock, the officers of sepoys are to have jackets with caps, in the manner of Captain Alcock's battalion, with a small silver plate in front, distinguishing the number of the battalion, and whether 'Carnatic' or Circar.' The uniform, hats and breeches of all the officers to be the same as at present."

The *spontoon* was a kind of half-pike, formerly borne by officers of infantry and used for signalling orders. The *fusil* was a light musket or firelock, and hence the word Fusilier, meaning an infantry man who bore firearms, as distinguished from a pikeman or archer.

1778.

In 1778, it seems that Subalterns were still very scarce. Mr. William Petrie, Resident of Karical, writing from that place at about the time when the army was encamped before Pondicherry, brought to notice the circumstance that two companies of the 12th battalion, which composed the garrison, were officered by two boys, the senior of whom was under 15 years of age; in consequence of which Mr. Petrie was under the necessity of seeing to everything himself, even to the posting of the guards.

The regulations of the Company, which made the military subordinate to the civil officer, was one of the principal causes of the enmity between civil and military, which produced so many unfortunate incidents. Colonel Fullarton says :—

"By the regulations alluded to, the Commandant of a garrison or province came under the detail command of the civil chief. The chief received reports and paroles, kept the keys of the garrison, and had direction of stores, magazines and defences in the fort. Hence it happened during the late war (1781-83) that the command was not delegated to the military officer until the enemy were in motion against the place. Then it was only so delegated that the chief might provide for his own safety and throw the odium of surrender on the Commander. Thus, instead of a regular military control, a systematic animosity prevailed............These irritations were too frequently increased by military vehemence on the one hand, and by assumptions of the civil service on the other. As the natives of India have little respect for any but the military character, the civil servants, in order to acquire confidence, have usually assumed a superiority over the military."

In June 1778, eight Carnatic battalions were warned for service against Pondicherry. The Grenadier companies of these battalions, and those of the remaining thirteen battalions (of which the 4th was one), were formed into four Grenadier battalions. To supply the place of these companies, the officers commanding the thirteen Carnatic battalions not under marching orders, and those commanding the eight Circar battalions were authorised to raise 20 men for each battalion company, a total increase of 3,360 men.

In December 1778, Lieutenant-Colonel Thomas Burrows succeeded Lieutenant-Colonel Cosby as Adjutant-General.

1779.

When, in July 1779, an independent corps of five companies was raised for service in Guntur District, Ensigns Francis Capper and John Munro, 4th Carnatic Battalion, were posted to it.

At this period an European regiment, when on the march from station to station, was always accompanied by two or more companies of sepoys for the purpose of escorting the baggage, and performing such duties as involved more than ordinary exposure.

1780.

Sepoys had formerly to furnish their own tents, but in October 1780 Government decided to furnish tents from the public stores free of charge, and at the same time ordered that no stoppages should be made on account of slops or half-mounting, but that sepoys should be allowed to provide their own.

In October 1780, Commandants were deprived of the right of exercising their discretion in recommending officers for promotion, and were directed invariably to recommend the officers next in rank for the vacancy.

The following extract from Arbuthnot's *Life of Sir Thomas Munro* is of interest :—

"The pay of an infantry cadet in Madras in 1780 was only £3 a month, with the result that the subalterns of that time lived in a state of most miserable poverty. Sir T. Munro says that he was three years in India before he was master of any other pillow than a book or a cartridge-pouch and his bed consisted of a piece of canvas stuck on four cross sticks."

Writing from Poonamallee in March 1780, Captain Innes Munro gives the following description of the uniforms worn by the sepoys at that time :—

"Their uniforms have a very military appearance, consisting of a red light infantry jacket, a white waist-coat, and a blue turban placed in a soldier-like manner upon the head, edged round with tape of the same colour with the facings, and having a tassel at the lower corner. The sepoy has a long blue sash lightly girded round his loins the end of which, passing between his legs, is fastened behind. He wears a pair of white drawers, tightly fitted, which only come half down his thigh, and being coloured at the lower end with a blue dye, appear as if scalloped all round; a pair of sandals upon his feet, white cross-belts, a firelock and bayonet, complete the sepoy's dress..................

The dress of the black officers is much the same as described above; with this difference only that their coats are made of scarlet cloth with tinsel epaulets, light drawers all the way down to their ankles, and a large crooked scimitar by their sides."

The following is given as the Money Table in 1780, but it must soon after have changed considerably, if Colonel Wilson's calculations are correct:—

$$6 \text{ Cash} = 1 \text{ Fanam} = 2d. \text{ sterling.}$$
$$12 \text{ Fanams} = 1 \text{ Rupee} = 2s. \text{ sterling.}$$
$$4 \text{ Rupees} = 1 \text{ Star Pagoda} = 8s. \text{ sterling.}$$

The cash was a fictitious coin.

The original value of the pagoda was $7s. 6d. = 45$ fanams.

Whilst on the subject of coins, the following information may be of interest.

The original pagoda was the Golconda pagoda, which was a copy of the old Vijayanagar pagoda. In 1670—80 the following is given as the coinage in use:—

Madras.   80 Cash = 1 Fanam.
36 Fanams = 1 Pagoda. (8s. 4d.)
Reals of Eight were worth 5s., and Rupees were worth 2s. 3½d. There was a copper coin called a "*Doodoe,*" worth 10 cash.

Pulicat.   24 Cash = 1 Fanam.
24 Fanams = 1 Pagoda. (8s. 6d.)

Golconda.   12 Fanams = 1 Pagoda. (12s.)

Porto-Novo.
Tranquebar.   } 18 Fanams = 1 Pagoda. (6s.)

With such a mixed coinage in circulation it is little wonder that the sepoys constantly complained of being defrauded when they drew their pay.

In 1730, M. M. Pagodas (so-called as they had an "M" stamped on either side of the Hindu deity) were introduced, but were a failure as the Nawab's Treasury would not accept them. These were succeeded (*circa* 1740) by the Star Pagoda, which had a star on the reverse.

In 1790, the following is given as the rate of exchange:—

Gold.	Calcutta Mohurs	23¼	per	100	Star	Pagodas.
	Madras Pagodas, new	92	,,	,,	,,	,,
	Porto-Novos	117½	,,	,,	,,	,,
	Porto-Novos, old	116¼	,,	,,	,,	,,
Silver.	Madras Rupees	361	,,	,,	,,	,,
	Pondicherry Rupees	354	,,	,,	,,	,,
	Sicca Rupees	355	,,	,,	,,	,,
	Bombay Rupees	355	,,	,,	,,	,,

1781.

In January 1781, Government promised a gratuity equal to two months' pay to men of the Carnatic battalions ordered by sea to the Northern Circars, Calcutta, or Bombay.

Captain Thomas Madge, commanding a battalion of infantry in the Circars, writes to Sir Robert Palk concerning a relation of the latter's that he was taking him on detachment duty:—

> "Which I thought more for his interest than if he had remained at Ellore, as the morals of most of the officers left in the Circars were such as would not have improved his."

1783.

On the 5th November 1783, the grade of Captain-Lieutenant was reintroduced, and the establishment of European officers in each battalion fixed at 1 Captain, 1 Captain-Lieutenant, 2 Lieutenants and 7 Ensigns. The Captain-Lieutenants were to have the rank of Captain in the army and were not eligible for either of the regimental staff appointments, this latter regulation being on account of a petition from the infantry subalterns which showed that infantry Lieutenants of 13 years' service frequently found themselves commanded by Captain-Lieutenants of Artillery with 4 or 5 years' service, and also "in consideration of the gallant and meritorious services of the subalterns with the army in the late trying campaigns."

1784.

On the 12th July 1784, owing to the scarcity of Non-Commissioned Officers with the European infantry the number of Serjeants with each sepoy battalion was limited to three, *viz.*—Serjeant-Major, Quartermaster-Serjeant, and Drill Serjeant.

In the same month the following order was published:—

> The Commander-in-Chief having been applied to to fix the line of duty to be observed by Captain-Lieutenants of the Sepoy Corps, he is pleased to direct that whenever three or more companies (not exceeding five) are detached from a battalion; and the Captain Commanding, with the colours and staff, does not go, the Captain-Lieutenant shall be appointed to command, and should the battalion at any time be divided into more than two parts, the division second in importance and strength shall be the right of the Captain-Lieutenant. With respect to the interference of the Captain-Lieutenant in the interior management and discipline of the battalion, he can have no right further than in common with the other officers, whose duty makes it incumbent on them to give every exertion in their power to promote the spirit and discipline of the corps, and fulfilling the orders of the Commanding Officers."

In October 1784, the establishment of the army was revised, that of the Native Infantry being fixed at 35 battalions of 9 companies each, one of which was to be composed of Grenadiers. The following was the strength ordered for each battalion:— 1 Captain, 1 Captain-Lieutenant, 2 Lieutenants, 6 Ensigns, 3 servants, 1 Native Commandant, 8 Subadars, 9 Jemadars, 36 Havildars, 36 Naigues, 495 Sepoys, 9 Drummers, 5 Fifers and 9 Puckallies. The usual allowances for the European Adjutant, the Native Commandant, and the Non-Commissioned staff were provided for.

At the same time the distinction between the Carnatic and Circar battalions was abolished, and it was ordered that all should be known by the general denomination of Madras battalions.

Great discontent was aroused throughout the army by an order of Government directing the cessation of full batta from the 1st October 1784, and of all batta whatsoever from the 1st January 1785. Numerous memorials were submitted pointing out that prices had risen 120 *per cent* higher in 1784, than they had been in 1776, and that the pay of the army was on the average twelve months in arrears. Government consequently restored half-batta on the 22nd December 1784, under the name of *"temporary allowance"*, the term *"half-batta"* being subsequently reintroduced in June 1792.

1785.

In January 1785, it was decided to institute a regular system of periodical reliefs, as the continuance of sepoy battalions in the same district for a length of time had been followed by inconvenient results, especially in the case of the Circar battalions, who lost greatly by desertions when ordered to the South.

In February 1785, it was ordered that a register should be kept in every Native corps in which the age, length of service, description, and character of every man should be regularly entered.

On the 23rd August 1785, the establishment was reduced to 21 battalions of 10 companies each. The strength of a company was increased from 55 to 68 Privates and 5 Havildars and 5 Naigues allowed to each. At the same time the appointment of Native Commandant was abolished as unnecessary, because:—

"There are but few instances where they have been of much service, but frequent ones where they have done mischief........When they are clever men, their influence over the Native Officers and Sepoys becomes dangerous, and when they are not so they can be of no use."

The Commandants then serving were given the option of remaining as Subadars or retiring on a pension. Further, the great disparity between the pay of Subadars and Jemadars was removed by decreasing the pay of a Subadar from 17 to 13 pagodas (Rs. 45-8-0) and by increasing that of a Jemadar from 5 to 7 pagodas (Rs. 24-8-0) *per mensem*. An allowance for a Native Adjutant was provided by ordering a stoppage of Re. 1 monthly from each Subadar, and one for a Havildar-Major by stopping As. 8 from each Jemadar. Havildars and Naigues employed as drill instructors were deprived of their allowances, and given to understand that their services would be rewarded by promotion.

It was also directed that the Native Infantry should be formed into six brigades, to four of which an European regiment was to be attached, but this was carried out in only one instance, namely in the new cantonment at Wallajahbad where the following troops were assembled in February:—His Majesty's 23rd Light Dragoons, the 36th, 52nd and 73rd Regiments of Foot, 400 Hanoverians, 2 Companies of Artillery, and the 4th, 5th, 8th and 9th Battalions of Sepoys.

On the 22nd October 1785, Recruit Boys were introduced by the following order:

"The Honourable Company having been pleased to allow one son of each sepoy who has been killed, or died in the service, to receive the pay of his deceased father; the Commissary of Musters is therefore to allow two boys, the sons of sepoys so killed or dead, to be inserted in the muster-roll of each company, amounting altogether, with the effectives to the fixed establishment, and a remark is to be made opposite to the name of each boy, so that he may not be mistaken for an effective; but when arrived at the age of puberty, such boy, if able-bodied, must enlist, or be struck off the roll."

About the end of 1785, a native doctor was attached to each battalion, his pay consisting of about Rs. 25, stopped from the native ranks, and Rs. 9. (the pay of a sepoy) from Government.

1786.

On the 24th April 1786, honorary medals were directed to be given "to such of the sepoys as had resisted the many endeavours used to seduce them from the British Service, as a reward for their firmness, fidelity and attachment," but it would appear that these were never issued.

On the 20th May 1786, the establishment was raised from 21 battalions to 28. The 4th Battalion sent a draft to the new 24th on its being raised in Madras. The number of companies was reduced from 13 to 9, two of which were to be grenadier companies. The number of subalterns was fixed at 8, exclusive of one allowed as Adjutant. The establishment now consisted of:—1 Captain, 4 Lieutenants, 4 Ensigns, 8 Sergeants, 8 Subadars, 8 Jemadars, 32 Havildars, 32 Naigues, 544 Privates, 8 Drummers, 8 Fifers, 8 Puckallies. The staff consisted of an Adjutant, Assistant Surgeon, and Black Doctor; extra allowance being made for a Sergeant-Major, Quartermaster-Sergeant, Drill Havildar, Drill Naigue, and Drum and Fife Major, in addition to the pay of their rank.

Shortly afterwards the native troops were brigaded in five brigades, the 2nd of which was complete at Wallajahbad under Lieutenant-Colonel Keating, and comprised the 4th, 5th, 9th, 15th, 21st and 25th Battalions.

In December 1786 it was decided that colours should be supplied gratis—hitherto they had been paid for out of stoppages.

1787.

On the 10th March 1787, it was ordered that the army should be divided into four divisions—East, West, North, South. Of these the East and West divisions were placed under the immediate orders of the Commander-in-Chief and included the 2nd, 3rd and 5th brigades.

On the 24th May 1787, it was resolved that no native soldier should be recommended for the invalid or pension list unless he had been wounded, or had served 23 years, and that no man, European or Native, should be admitted on the invalid establishment unless fit for garrison duty. The rates of pension, published at the same time, were:—Commandant, 14 pagodas; Subadar, 6 pagodas; Jemadar, 3 pagodas, 10 fanams, 40 cash; Havildar, 1 pag. 29 fan. 40 cash; Naigue, 1 pag. 20 fan.; Drummers, 2 pag.; Sepoys and Puckallies, 1 pag.

The Native Commandants having been abolished in 1785, this item would appear to be unnecessary.

In September 1787, the Standing Orders for Native Infantry were revised, and came into force on the 1st November 1787. The establishment of recruit boys was changed to 40 per battalion, exclusive of the regular number of sepoys. They were to be admissible at the age of 11, if healthy and well-limbed, and to be transferred to the ranks as soon as they became fit. Their pay while recruit boys was fixed at 33 fanams (Rs. 2-12) *per mensem*. In the case of a vacancy in the commissioned ranks, a recommendation roll was to be submitted to the Commander-in-Chief, and if the senior had been passed over, the reasons were to be stated in the roll. The Drill-Havildar and 7 senior Havildars, Drill-Naigue and 7 senior Naigues, and 2 Privates from each company, who were to be called *"Confidential Men,"* were to be considered first for promotion, the Commandant having the power to strike any N.C.O. or man off the list.

On the 21st February 1787, the ship *"Rose"* sailed from London, and reached Madras on the 2nd June 1787—101 days—which was a record up to that date.

To show the unfortunate position of officers of the Coast Army at this time, the following remarks by Colonel Fullarton, written about 1787, are of interest:—

"During the late war many officers were obliged to sell their furniture and wearing apparel, in order to procure a scanty subsistence; while others could not possibly find means of appearing as became their station. If a pittance of their arrears was to be advanced, it often came attended with circumstances so singularly disreputable that nothing short of penury could justify the offer or acceptance; if in Company's bonds, they were hardly negotiable; if in Bengal bills, the holders of them lost thirty, forty or fifty per cent; and if the payment took place in an out-garrison, the discretion or caprice of the paymaster alone determined the mode of payment. Needy officers, at the mercy of such a superior, have frequently submitted to receive a month's arrears in rice, teas, wines, or other merchandize."

1789.

In September 1789, the number of subalterns was reduced from 9 to 8, an order having been issued that the Adjutant was to be included in the establishment.

1790.

Early in 1790, the establishment was raised by two companies. Each Native Officer promoted in consequence was to supply the following number of recruits before his promotion was confirmed:—Jemadars promoted Subadars, 38; Havildars promoted Jemadars, 18; Naigues promoted Havildars, 12. Half-a-pagoda per man was allowed to Native Officers to defray recruiting expenses.

In May 1790, the establishment of recruit boys was raised from 40 to 50.

In this year the Governor and Council resolved that traffic in the sale or purchase of slaves be prohibited by public proclamation. A reward of 30 pagodas was offered for the discovery of every offender, with an additional 10 pagodas for every slave released in consequence.

1792.

In June 1792 the two additional companies raised at the commencement of the Mysore War were reduced.

In November 1792, the establishment of subalterns was fixed at 7 Lieutenants and 2 Ensigns, inclusive of the Adjutant, with a view to preventing any variation in the number of each grade.

On the 28th December 1792, it was ordered that the pay of battalions should be drawn and disbursed by Commandants. Hitherto it had been issued by civilian paymasters who made a profit on the exchange of pagodas for fanams.

The services of the native troops during the campaigns against Tippu Sultan, in 1791-92, were rewarded by the issue of a medal, bearing on the obverse the figure of a native officer holding a flag, and on the reverse, *"For Services in Mysore A. D. 1791—1792."*

1794.

Recruiting for the Coast Army was not at this time exclusively confined to the Madras Presidency as, in 1794 and 1795, Captain White of the 2nd Bengal European Regiment (afterwards Major-General Sir Henry White, K.C.B.) was actively employed in raising a large body of recruits in the provinces under the Presidency of Bengal for the corps on the Madras establishment.

1796.

On the 12th April 1796, Major Gabriel Doveton, then commanding the regiment, sent a party of one Havildar, one Naigue and three Privates to Arcot and Vellore on recruiting duty.

On the 12th and 13th July 1796, orders were published completely reorganising the army. The establishment of Native Infantry was fixed at 11 regiments, each composed of two battalions of 8 companies each.

The 4th Regt. consisted of :—
{ 1st Battn. 4th, and Right Wing, 25th Battn.
{ 2nd Battn., 15th Battn., and Left Wing, 25th Battn.

The Colonel was allowed a company in each battalion, and the Lieutenant-Colonels and Majors each one company in their respective battalions. The establishment of a regiment was fixed at:—1 Colonel, 2 Lieutenant-Colonels, 2 Majors, 7 Captains, 1 Captain-Lieutenant, 22 Lieutenants, 10 Ensigns, 20 Subadars, 20 Jemadars, 100 Havildars, 100 Naigues, 40 Drummers and Fifers, 1,800 Privates, 160 Recruit boys, 20 Puckallies. The Staff consisted of:—2 Adjutants, 1 Paymaster, 1 Surgeon, 2 Assistant-Surgeons, 2 Sergeant-Majors, 2 Quartermaster-Sergeants, 2 Native Adjutants, 2 Native Doctors, 2 Drum Majors, 2 Fife Majors, 2 Drill Havildars, 2 Drill Naigues.

The period of furlough for British Officers was fixed at 3 years, and subalterns were to be 10 years in India before they became entitled to furlough. The rates of pay were also laid down as follows:—

	In Garrison or Cantonments.			In the Field.		
	Pag.	Fan.	Cash.	Pag.	Fan.	Cash.
General Officer on the Staff	1031	10	40	1218	31	40
Colonel, not a G. O. on the Staff	328	5	20	328	5	20
Lieutenant-Colonel	168	31	40	303	21	0
Major	126	23	50	229	36	60
Captain	76	36	60	126	0	0
Captain-Lieutenant	58	5	20	107	10	40
Lieutenant	45	0	0	77	31	40
Ensign	32	34	10	60	36	60
Adjutant, non-effective	21	10	40	27	10	40
Quartermaster, do.	17	21	0	23	21	0
Surgeon, as Captain	76	36	60	126	0	0
Assistant-Surgeon, as Lieutenant	45	0	0	77	31	40

On the 7th October 1796, a recruiting party, consisting of one Havildar, one Naigue and two Privates was sent to Nellore; one Private to Tiruvannamalai; and two Privates to Palamaner.

The following extract from the despatches of the Duke of Wellington is of interest:—

"At Madras it is not the practice to remove officers from one corps to another, excepting when absolutely necessary, and the army is in very high order: in Bengal, from circumstances which I shall mention hereafter, they are moved when and where they please, and there is no army that lays claim to the title of *disciplined* that is in such a bad state. The conduct of the Coast Army will illustrate another part of this subject. Although their rise is not regimental, the officers are permanently posted to corps; and notwithstanding that their grievances were heavier than those suffered by the officers in Bengal, there was not the same violence of complaint, nor any reason to fear for the consequences of discontent. The grievances were not less felt than in Bengal; but as they were regularly organized, and each corps commanded by an officer whose credit depended upon its state of discipline and who was responsible for its allegiance, the complaints were never so loud; the army never acted in one body as in Bengal. To their credit it may be said, that if it had been necessary, they would have gone to Bengal, and quelled a mutiny for the redress of grievances in the success, of which they were more interested than those who mutinied."

Colonel Fullarton (1787) remarks of the Bengal Army:—

"If we trust to our Military on the Bengal establishment for protection against these alarming enormities, we shall find that entire corps have existed on paper who, exclusive of the Commandant and Staff, never had any existence but on paper; and it will farther appear that those Sepoys who have a real existence are neither well disciplined nor regularly paid."

1797.

On the 21st January 1797, it is recorded that by order of Major Read a "Surgeon's Mate" was sent to Salem on recruiting duty for the 1st 4th M. N. I. This Surgeon's Mate appears to have been one Samuel McMorris.

On the 15th March 1797, a uniform turband and cummerbund to be made of blue cloth were prescribed for the use of Native battalions, to be introduced from the 1st May following.

In the same month pay was ordered to be drawn upon separate abstracts for each company, instead of upon one general abstract for each corps.

On the 5th April 1797, an order was issued providing for the periodical inspection and review of the corps composing the army, a practice which appears to have fallen into abeyance.

In April 1797, Lord Mornington, the Governor-General, called at Madras on his way to Calcutta, and wrote to Lord Clive—who was to succeed Lord Hobart as Governor of Madras—as follows:—

"With respect to the military establishment at Fort St. George, I have the satisfaction to declare to your Lordship that I do not believe there exists in any part of the world an army more distinguished for its high state of discipline, or for the activity, gallantry and skill of its officers, than that which will be under your immediate direction."

1798.

In 1798, General Harris reported that the recruits of the Southern Countries, though inferior in caste, size and appearance to those of the Northern Countries, were "found to stand the pressure of military hardships with much fortitude and to manifest, at all times, a firm adherence to the service."

On the raising of two extra battalions on the 12th October 1798, the 1st 4th sent a draft, under Captain George Martin to the 2nd Extra Battalion (28th Madras Infantry), composed of 1 Subadar, 1 Jemadar, 5 Havildars, 5 Naigues, 2 Drummers, and 100 Privates.

1800.

Regimental rise was introduced in the infantry regiments of the Madras Army in January 1800, one year after its introduction in the cavalry.

On the 1st January 1800, the 1st 4th sent a draft to the 2nd 16th (Dyce's 32nd Madras Infantry), then being raised at Madura.

On the 25th June 1800, the Regimental Adjutants and Quartermasters were abolished, being considered unnecessary as each battalion had an Adjutant and Quartermaster.

In July 1800, the 1st 4th sent a draft to the 2nd 19th (Macgregor's 38th Madras Infantry), then being raised at Ellore.

On the 11th July 1800, it having been pointed out to Government that the troops suffered greatly owing to the inadequacy of their pay, the monthly rates of pay of the native ranks were revised as follows, with effect from the 1st July 1800:—

Native Officers. Subadars who have served 10 years in the rank, 20 star-pagodas;* 6 years, 15 pagodas; under 6, 12 pagodas (the old rate). Jemadars, 7 pagodas. Native Adjutants in future to be selected from Jemadars. Batta to remain as before.

Rank and File. Havildars, 3 pagodas. Naigues, 2 pagodas 21 fanams. Sepoys and Native Doctors, 2 pagodas. Sepoy boys, 1 pagoda.

Batta of Havildars, Naigues and Sepoys, 1 fanam *per diem* or 1 seer rice when rice may be issued from public stores. Pay and batta of Drummers, Fifers, Puckallies and Bhesties to remain as before. No batta for boys.

The above rates to be clear and exclusive of all stoppages for clothing, which was provided for, as before, by issues of cash from the public treasury. The above rates to be the same every month, irrespective of the number of days in the month.

1801.

On the 21st February 1801, a company of the 1st 4th, under Lieutenant William Clapham, was sent on command, "to join a light company of H. M.'s 74th Regiment," but it is not stated for what purpose, though it may only have been to assist them on the march. (*See note on this subject, 1779*).

On the 20th August 1801, a new code of general orders and regulations was issued, of which the following extract regarding orderlies is noteworthy:—

"The attachment of orderly soldiers of officers being solely for the performance of duties purely military, the disgraceful practice of employing Native soldiers in carrying articles of table consumption! in running by the side of palankins! in supplying the place of domestics, and horse-keepers behind carriages and bandies! and in following close at the heels of mounted horses, is to be discontinued, and no orderly soldier, except on urgent occasion, is to exceed the regulated military pace in the execution of his duty."

After the mutiny at Vellore in 1806, the wisdom of the above order, and of a similar one regarding recruit boys, was called in question as tending to destroy the

---

* I find that at this time a sum of 90 pagodas was equivalent to 315 rupees. The pagoda was consequently still worth Rs. 3-8.

intimate association between officer and sepoy, and the latter order was rescinded on the 22nd August, the Commander-in-Chief remarking:—

"His Excellency has been induced to adopt this decision from the conviction that the advantage gained by the restriction of the boys to duties purely military has not balanced the injury the service has sustained by the loss of the facility to the acquirement of a common language and knowledge of customs, which their former attachment to the junior officers produced."

On the 22nd September 1801, it was resolved to raise a new Volunteer Corps to serve in the Moluccas for three years, and the detachment of the 1st 4th at Fort St. George was one of the corps from which men were permitted to volunteer. The new corps embarked at Madras on the 16th October 1801, and on its return, in October 1804, became the 2nd 20th (40th Madras Infantry).

1802.

At this time the monthly allowance of a regiment for hutting and camp equipage was 272 pagodas (Rs. 952). From this sum the regiment was to be kept in constant readiness for service, with the proper complement of tents, cattle and followers, and carriage supplied for regimental stores, in addition to supplying hutting accommodation for the men.

1803.

In January 1803, cummerbunds were discontinued as part of the issue of clothing.

On the 28th January 1803, when the establishment of Pioneers* was augmented and they were formed into two battalions, Captain Davis of the 4th was appointed to the first battalion of that Corps.

1804.

On the 17th February 1804, it was ordered that no officer should be recommended as Adjutant unless he knew sufficient Hindostanee to be able to explain his orders to the men in that language.

In September 1804, it was ordered that the half-pay of his rank should be allowed to the nearest heir of every native officer and soldier who had died in battle or in consequence of wounds received during the late war against the Mahratta confederates. If the deceased officers and soldiers had left sons, this was to be continued for 12 years only, but where the families of the deceased consisted only of women and aged persons, the provision was to be continued during the life of the nearest heir of the family.

1805.

On the 14th November 1805, the notorious order regarding turbands was issued, viz:—

"Lieutenant-General Sir J. F. Cradock has established a turband for the native commissioned officers, non-commissioned officers, and rank and file of regiments of Native Infantry..
......The turband so established shall be considered to be the uniform of the above

---

* Now Queen Victoria's Own Madras Sappers and Miners.

mentioned corps, and shall be worn as such to the exclusion of every other that may heretofore have been authorised. Sealed patterns of the turband will be furnished to corps, and the Commander-in-Chief forbids any deviation whatever from those patterns as established for Grenadiers, Light Infantry, and battalion companies, either in their fashion or trimmings, or in their dimensions or weight."

1806.

On the 1st January 1806, the stoppages formerly made on account of the supply of medical aid and country medicines were discontinued, and native dressers, 2 per battalion, were ordered to be received on the strength of the corps to which they were attached, and to be paid at the rate of 10 pagodas *per mensem*.

On the 30th June 1806, an allowance of 35 pagodas *per mensem* when marching or in the field, and 18 pagodas when in garrison or cantonments, was granted to each battalion in which an officers' mess was maintained.

Early in 1806, new regulations for the army, prepared by Major Pierce, Deputy Adjutant-General, were introduced, including the following:—

"It is ordered by the Regulation that a native soldier shall not mark his face to denote his caste, or wear earrings when dressed in his uniform, and it is further directed that at all parades, and upon all duties, every soldier of the battalion shall be clean shaved on the chin. It is directed also that uniformity shall, as far as it is practicable, be preserved in regard to the quantity and shape of the hair on the upper lip."

The new turbands were issued in April, May and June 1806, and the mutiny at Vellore broke out in May, the regiments concerned being the 2nd 23rd (46th M.I.) 1st 1st (1st M.I.), and 2nd 4th (5th M.I.). The 1st and 23rd regiments were struck off the strength of the army from 31st December 1806, and their places supplied by two battalions each, numbered respectively 24th and 25th. These two regiments were restored to their original positions in the army in consideration of the gallantry displayed by the 1st 24th at the Battle of Seetabuldee near Nagpore on the 26th and 27th November 1817.

The obnoxious orders regarding dress were cancelled on the 17th July 1806, and on the 24th September, all unauthorised alterations in dress or interference with national observances, were strictly prohibited.

On the 22nd August 1806, the Commander-in-Chief announced his determination not to recommend any officer for appointment to the Staff, unless duly qualified in the native languages.

On the 24th September 1806 an order was issued stating that the pattern of turband introduced on the 15th March 1797 was to continue in use. Leather cockades and plumes were forbidden, and stocks abolished. The fullest permission was given to the native troops to wear their marks of caste at all times and in any manner they thought proper, and the same liberty granted them in respect of the hair on the upper lip, and "the wearing of joys and ornaments peculiar to different families and castes."

On the revision of the invalid establishment in November 1806, an invalid company was attached to each battalion to carry out recruiting, and one of these was stationed at Vellore to recruit for the 1st 4th.

1807.

On the 13th May 1807, a new scale of pensions was introduced, *viz*:—

Subadar, 1st class, 10 pagodas; 2nd class, 7 pagodas 21 fanams; 3rd class, 6 pagodas; Jemadar, 3 pagodas 21 fanams; Havildar, 1 pagoda 29 fanams 40 cash; Naigue, 1 pagoda 21 fanams; Sepoy, Puckally and Bheestie, 1 pagoda; Drummer or Fifer, 2 pagodas.

Considerable feeling existed at this time between the officers of the King's army and those of the Hon. Company, the latter being frequently passed over for important commands in favour of the former. The following extract from a letter written by an officer from Trichinopoly in August 1807 affords an amusing illustration of the attitude of one of the King's officers:—

"Hence the arrogance of a reply to a lieutenant-colonel, of 25 years standing, who commanded a corps of Sepoys, and asked a King's colonel (commanding the station) leave for his Sepoys to attend an annual Hindoo festival; urging, when this was denied, that it had been an *invariable custom* to grant the leave, for the 25 years he had been in the service.—'Then', replied the commandant (who was not three years old when the lieutenant-colonel entered the army), 'I, Theodosius Pompadore Mount-Razor, colonel commanding the **** do now abolish, and put a stop to the said custom, in its 26th year!' turning upon his heel, on finishing the sentence."

1808.

In May 1808, the tent contract (*vide 1802*) was abolished, and it was determined that the establishment of camp equipage, lascars, and carriage for camp equipage and regimental stores should be permanently maintained at the public expense. Hutting allowance was then fixed at the following rates:—

For each Subadar, Rs. 24; Jemadar, Rs. 12; Havildar, Rs. 4; Naigue, Rs. 3; Private, Rs. 2.

In this year the facings of the 1st 4th M. N. I. were *orange,* and the lace was *silver*.

A General Order, dated the 6th July 1808, announced the issue of a medal for SERINGAPATAM. This medal was issued in gold, silver-gilt, silver, copper-bronze, and pure-grain tin. There is no record as to whether the men of the 4th Battalion received these medals or not. That they were not originally intended to be worn is shown by the fact that permission to wear them (with an orange ribbon) was given by a General Order in 1851. (*q.v.*)

1809.

In June 1809, the establishment of privates on the strength of native battalions was reduced from 900 to 800.

An account of the mutiny of officers, which took place in this year, has been given elsewhere. (*vide* Part I).

1810.

In October 1810, the following were admitted to the benefit of the Hutting Regulations:—Drum-Majors, Rs. 4; Vakeels and Dressers, Rs. 3; Drummers, Fifers, Puckallies and Bheesties, Rs. 2.

On the 2nd November 1810, a reward of 500 pagodas for proficiency in Hindostanee was introduced. All cadets who arrived in Madras after the 1st May 1809 were eligible, but the examination had to be passed within three years from the time of landing in the country.

In 1810, the Court of Directors of the Hon. East India Company, owing to the exorbitant charges made by ship's captains for a passage to India fixed the following maximum rates for those travelling at their own expense:—

	£
For Generals and Members of Council	250
For Colonels and Senior Merchants	200
For Majors and Junior Merchants	150
For Captains and Factors	125
For Subalterns and Writers	110
For Cadets	95

If, however, a cadet was prepared to join the mess of the Third Officer, £55 was the maximum charge payable.

In comparing the above rates with those of to-day, it is necessary to bear in mind that they included wines, messing, etc., for a period of five or six months. While however, the ship was in port, the passengers were expected to live on shore at their own expense.

1811.

In a return, dated 1st January 1811, of the 1st 4th M.N.I., two Courts-Martial are shown to have been held during the period covered by the return. In one, Quarter-Master-Serjeant G. Himbler was tried for "Insolence—Disobedience of orders—and for being drunk," and was sentenced to be reduced and receive 300 lashes; while in the other, Private Moothoo Verah was found guilty of theft, and was sentenced to 700 lashes and to be afterwards drummed out.

European soldiers serving in India at this time led no easy life. Up to the beginning of the 19th century, breaches of military discipline amongst them were punished by transportation to one or other of the penal settlements, and some light is thrown on the estimation with which service in India was regarded, by a report written by the Governor of the Calcutta jail in 1814, in which he states that,

"There is no record of an European convict trying to escape from the jail, as the prospect of going to New South Wales is more desirable than military service in this climate."

On the 15th January 1811, the provision for the families of native soldiers killed, or dying on foreign service was extended to the families of public followers.

On the 30th September 1811, a new pattern knapsack was introduced, and also a havresack, principally for the carriage of rice. The following is the list of necessaries to be carried in the knapsack:—3 white jackets; 3 pairs drawers; 2 pairs knee bands; 2 handkerchiefs; 2 duputtahs; 2 loongies; 1 flat dish; 2 basins; emery, blacking, whiting or heel-ball, and pipe-clay. Watch-coat and carpet to be strapped to the knapsack. A jumbo to be slung from the sepoy's right shoulder.

This knapsack must have been of no ordinary dimensions.

1812.

On the 22nd January 1812, pantaloons were permitted to be worn instead of short drawers, and on the 4th February this was made compulsory. The full-dress pantaloons were to be white, and each man was to have two pairs, besides coloured pantaloons "of striped sousee or other suitable cloth." A uniform pattern of sandal was introduced at the same time.

About the end of 1812, it was ordered that Havildars should in future be armed with halberts and swords slung in frog belts, except Havildars of light companies, who were to carry fusils and small fusil cartouch-boxes.

From the 1st October 1812, the establishment of battalions was reduced to 780 privates.

1813.

On the 23rd February 1813, the establishment of recruit and pension boys was revised, a battalion of infantry having 30 of the former and 40 of the latter, totalling 70. Recruit boys were not to be under 11 years old, to be healthy and well-grown, and were to be discharged at the age of 18, if unfit for transfer to the ranks. Pension boys were to be admissible at any age under 11 and if unfit for transfer at 14, were to be discharged.

On the 10th August 1813, two native dressers were allowed to each battalion: one first dresser at 10 pagodas, and one second dresser at 7 pagodas *per mensem*.

Although the Governor-General in Council had, on the 30th October 1803, directed that honorary colours, with an appropriate device, should be presented to every regiment or battalion engaged at the battle of Assaye, no steps were taken to carry out the order at Madras until October 1811, when the Commander-in-Chief moved the Government to adopt the device of the Elephant, as borne by His Majesty's regiments which had been present on that occasion. Government approved of the recommendation, and ordered the preparation of the requisite number of badges, silver for the Native Officers, and copper for the other ranks. These badges, however, do not appear to have been issued till May 1813, when 179 were issued in silver, and 7,269 in copper.

1814.

On the 22nd July 1814, regulations were published regarding the issue of family certificates, and the department was placed under an officer designated the "Superintendent of Family Payments."

Between the years 1814 and 1821, while the 1st Battalion 4th Regiment M. N. I. was stationed in the Northern Division, a great number of men, chiefly Bengalis, was enlisted at Jaggannat (Puri), Berhampur and Samalkot.

1816.

In April 1816, the allowances of Adjutants were fixed at Rs. 132 *per mensem*, consisting of staff pay Rs. 62; writer and stationery, Rs. 40; horse allowance, Rs. 30.

On the 25th May 1816, the payment of military pensions was transferred to the Superintendent of Family Payments.

Officers of the Company's service had not hitherto been admitted to the dignity of Knight Grand Cross of the Order of the Bath, but the distinction was bestowed on Major-General Sir David Ochterlony, the conqueror of Nepal, in December 1816. The Marquess of Hastings, then Governor-General and Commander-in-Chief, in investing Sir David with the insignia in April 1818, remarked *inter alia*:—

"You are to receive the honourable badge with which I am commissioned to invest you, as a recognition of your admirable zeal, and of the advantages secured by that zeal to your country's interest. Such a public acknowledgment of your professional merit would alone be sufficient matter of pride; yet I have to congratulte you on what must be still more touching to your feelings. You have obliterated a distinction painful for the officers of the Honourable Company; and you have opened the door for your brothers in arms to a reward, which their recent display of exalted spirit and invincible intrepidity proves could not be more deservedly extended to the officers of any army on earth."

1817.

On the 10th February 1817, two-poled tents were substituted for the old single-poled tents.

On the 7th May 1817, the establishment of privates was fixed at 900, but this order was cancelled in the following August.

1818.

On the 9th February 1818, when four battalions of hill rangers were raised, Captain James Jobson of the 4th was recommended for the command of the 2nd or Ganjam Battalion of Hill Rangers. These battalions were, however, found unsatisfactory, and were reduced in February 1819.

In July 1818, the Court of Directors ordered a subaltern officer to be appointed as Interpreter and Quartermaster in each native battalion, with staff salary equal to the Adjutant's, *viz*—Staff pay, Arcot rupees 62, moonshee and stationery, Rs. 40; a horse, Rs. 30. Total, Rs. 132. This officer, in addition to the duties of Quartermaster, was to act as Interpreter to all Courts-Martial.

In August 1818, the average number of British Officers present with their battalion was, 1 Field officer with each battalion; 1 Captain to 5 companies; 3 Subalterns to 5 companies.

On the 24th August 1818, officers commanding battalions, who set aside a senior when selecting for promotion, were ordered to state clearly and fully their reasons in writing.

On the 10th October 1918, one Native Officer and three Non-Commissioned Officers were ordered to be sent from each native battalion to Poonamallee to be instructed in the new infantry sword exercise.

1819.

On the 13th January 1819, when six extra battalions were raised, Captain Baker of the 4th was appointed to raise the fifth of these battalions at Bangalore. All six were reduced on the 30th November 1821.

On the 2nd February 1819, the rank of Subadar-Major was introduced into the native army, with the sanction of the Court of Directors. The selection was to be made by the Commander-in-Chief, and mere seniority was to have no claim to consideration. Brevet pay, at Rs. 25 *per mensem*, was added to the ordinary allowance of a Subadar of a company. The number of Subadar-Majors was limited for the time being to 58—1 for the Body-Guard, 8 for the Cavalry, 2 for the Artillery, and 46 for the Infantry.

The grade of Colour-Havildar was introduced at the same time, with the additional pay of Rs. 2 *per mensem.*

On the 17th February 1819, the issue of woollen trowsers in lieu of jackets was sanctioned at the rate of one jacket or one pair of trowsers in each year.

On the 14th December 1819, an order, dated the 30th October, was published ordering the formation of regimental and general military bazaars, and giving regulations for their management.

On a motion of thanks, in the House of Commons, to the Marquess of Hastings and to the Army in India, on the 4th March 1819, by the then President of the Board of Control (the Right Hon. George Canning), Lord Morpeth paid the following compliment to the Indian Army:—

"He thought the Indian or Native part of that army, whose operations had been so warmly extolled, had vied with British soldiers in coolness and deliberation; but there was one circumstance, in regard on many of our officers in India, which had always struck him with peculiar force,—to all the qualifications, of soldiers, they united all the accomplishments of scholars. This was exemplified by their scientific labours; they had performed the measurement of mountains, for the purpose of discovering the difference in altitude between those of the old continent and their competitors in the new; they had traced the courses of the Ganges and the Indus, amid the fatigues of war. Many of these very officers had been the companions of the early victories of Sir Arthur Wellesley, and maintain their former glory."

1820.

On the 15th January 1820, it was proposed to assimilate the facings of all the regiments in the army, but no alteration was made.

1821.

On the 5th October 1821, revised rules were published regarding pensions to heirs of men losing their lives on foreign service or in battle in India.

1822.

In September 1822, pensioners were granted the privilege of living wherever they wished, and if there were no military officer at the place selected, the civil authorities were ordered to undertake the duty of mustering and paying them.

1823.

In February 1823, Officers Commanding were forbidden to entertain any man under 5 feet 5 inches in height or above 20 years of age.

Sir John Philippart, writing in 1823, makes the following observations on the men of the Madras Army at this period:—

"There cannot be men more suited, from their frame and disposition, for the duty of light cavalry, than those of which the Madras corps is composed. They are, generally speaking, from five feet five inches to five feet ten inches in height, of light but active make. Their strength is preserved and improved by moderation in their diet, and by exercises common to the military tribe, and which are calculated to increase the muscular force.

The Native infantry of Madras is generally composed of Mahomedans and Hindoos of good cast: at its first establishment none were enlisted but men of high military tribes. In the progress of time a considerable change took place, and natives of every description were enrolled in the service. Though some corps, that were almost entirely formed of the lowest and most despicable races of men, obtained considerable reputation, it was feared that encouragement might produce disgust, and particularly when they gained, as they frequently did, the rank of officers. Orders were in consequence given to recruit from none but the most respectable classes of society; and many consider the regular and orderly behaviour of these men as one of the benefits which have resulted from this system.

The infantry Sepoy of Madras is rather a small man, but he is of an active make, and capable of undergoing great fatigue upon a very slender diet. We find no man arrive at greater precision in all his military exercises; his moderation, his sobriety, his patience, give him a steadiness that is almost unknown to Europeans: but although there exists in this body of men a fitness to attain mechanical perfection as soldiers, there are no men whose mind it is of more consequence to study. The most marked general feature of the character of the natives of India, is a proneness to obedience, accompanied by a great susceptibility of good or bad usage; and there are few in that country who are more embued with these feelings than the Madras Sepoy."

1824.

On the 6th May 1824, it was ordered that the 25 regiments of two battalions each, which were then on the establishment, should be formed into 50 separate regiments. The officers were to be posted alternately, *i.e.*, the odd numbers of each rank to the 1st and the even numbers to the 2nd battalions of their present regiments, when the several regiments on the new formation were to be numbered in the order in which they were first raised. The establishment of officers to each regiment was fixed at 1 Colonel, 1 Lieutenant-Colonel, 1 Major, 5 Captains, 10 Lieutenants, 5 Ensigns. The 1st Battalion 4th Regiment consequently became the 4th Regiment, and its 2nd battalion became the 15th Regiment.

On the 6th August 1824, the establishment of regiments then on foreign service was increased to 900 privates, with an additional Havildar and Naigue *per* company, and the strength of the remaining regiments was increased to 800.

1825.

In January 1825, the establishment of regiments not on foreign service was increased to 850, which was further increased to 900 on the 13th September 1825.

1826.

In January 1826 the establishment was again increased to 950.

On the 25th August 1826, it was ordered that the strength of a regiment of native infantry should be fixed at 800 rank and file except the 1st, 32nd and 36th, which were on active service, 960 strong.

With the bringing of the 1st and 2nd Extra Regiments on the strength, on the 15th September 1826, as the 51st and 52nd Regiments of Native Infantry, the Madras Army attained its maximum strength.

1827.

From the arrival of the 4th M. N. I. at Palavaram in 1827 up to the year 1838, no recruiting parties were sent out, a sufficient number of eligible recruits having been procured from among the men's relations in the lines. These, together with the Boy establishment, sufficed to fill up all vacancies, which, from the remarkably healthy state of the corps during this period, were inconsiderable.

1828.

A return of Courts-Martial, dated the 1st January 1828, shows a case in which a sepoy was tried on the following charges:—

" 1st, For mutinous conduct in having on the afternoon of the 29th October 1827 presented and snapped a musket loaded with Ball Cartridge at Jemidar Coopah of the 4th Regt. N. I. he being in the execution of his duty.

2nd, For having subsequently to his presenting and snapping his musket as aforesaid, said ' You are my enemy and I shall kill you some time or other ' or words to that effect.

3rd, For making away with one round of Ball Cartridge, the property of the Honorable Company."

The sepoy was sentenced "to be shot to death with Musketry," and the sentence was duly carried into execution on the 24th December 1827.

In February 1828, the establishment of privates was reduced to 720.

On the 11th April 1828, girdles were issued to all Havildars. There is no information to show of what material they were made, nor how they were worn.

By an order of the Commander-in-Chief, dated the 17th December 1828, the red linen trousers worn by the Native ranks were discontinued and black trousers substituted.

1829.

In January 1829, the use of Regimental Colours at festivals was forbidden.

In this year the number of companies in each native battalion was reduced from 10 to 8, each to consist of 80 men, while at the same time a reduction was also made of 2 Lieutenants and 1 Ensign.

1830.

In September 1830, new standing orders dealing with interior economy were issued.

1831.

By an order, dated the 20th December 1831, fuzils were issued to the Havildars in lieu of pikes.

Some time in 1831, the regimental lace was changed from *silver* to *gold*. The facings remained *orange* as they had been at least since 1808.

1833.

On the 10th October 1833, a Havildar of the 5th Native Infantry at Palaveram shot Lieutenant-Colonel J. M. Coombs of the 10th N. I., commanding the station, on a parade of all the troops. He was sentenced to be hanged in the presence of all the troops in the garrison, and his body was ordered to be hung in chains in the cantonment.

1834.

In August 1834, it was ordered that Native Officers' commissions should be signed and issued in the same manner as those of European Officers, and promotions should not be notified in General Orders by the Commander-in-Chief as heretofore.

There seems to have been a great variety of rupees in currency at this period. A regimental return states that the cash chest was examined on the 30th December 1834, and was found to contain:—

" Raja Roopees		326 0 0
Soorat Roopees		71 0 0
Madras Roopees		78 6 11
		475 6 11 "

The escort of the British Resident in Mysore was a separate Corps up to the 2nd September 1834, when it was broken up and the personnel transferred to regiments of Native Infantry.

On the 19th September 1834, the Wynaad Rangers, which I think was a corps raised for service in the Coorg War, was broken up.

1835.

In January 1835, instructions were issued for the drill of officers with swords. This drill included the command "Port Swords," which is no longer in use.

In February 1835, the Governor-General-in-Council issued an order abolishing the practice of punishing soldiers of the Native Army by the cat o'nine tails or rattan, and directing that sentences of dismissal from the service should be imposed instead. I find, however, that corporal punishment had been re-introduced by January 1846, but have not been able to trace the order.

In July 1835, the following order was issued:—

"Instances having occurred of applications on the part of subaltern officers proceeding to Europe on Medical Certificate, for a second grant of passage money in cases of the loss of the ships on which they had taken their passage, the Governor-General-in-Council desires it may be clearly understood that such applications are wholly inadmissible; and Subaltern Officers are reminded that they may always secure themselves from such loss at a trifling expense by ensuring their passage."

The following circular, issued from the Horse Guards in 1829, was published to the Army in November 1835:—

"I. The General Commanding in Chief considers it necessary to call the attention of the General Officers in Command, and through them of the Commanding Officers of Regiments, to the necessity of prohibiting, most strictly, the practice which has crept, more or less, into some Regiments of Infantry, and especially among the Officers, of suffering the Mustachio, or the Beard on their chin, to grow.

II. The practice has never obtained by competent authority, in any Regiment of Infantry, and it ought never to have obtained by sufferance."

In publishing the above circular, H.E. the Commander-in-Chief directed that "Hair was not to be worn on the face or neck below the line of the mouth and bottom of the ear."

In this order we see the genesis of the mutton-chop whisker.

On the 24th September 1835, Lord Auckland, G. C. B., was appointed Governor-General of India and Governor of Bengal, and took the oaths at Fort St. George on the 4th March 1836.

The following list shows the garrisons in the Madras Presidency in November 1835:—

Presidency Division.	Fort. St. George.	*Centre Division.*	Arcot.
	St. Thomas' Mount.		Arnee.
	Palaveram.		Vellore.
	Poonamallee.		Tripassore.
	Wallajahbad.		Chittoor.
			Nellore.
Northern Division.	Masulipatam.		Ongole.
	Ellore.		Cuddalore.
	Samulcottah.		
	Vizagapatam.	*Mysore Division.*	French Rocks.
	Berhampore.		Bangalore.
	Vizianagram.		Hurryhur.
	Chicacole.		Nundidroog.
	Aska.		
	Rajahmundry.	*Malabar and Canara.*	Cannanore.
	Condapilly.		Tellicherry.
			Calicut.
Southern Division.	Trichinopoly.		Mangalore.
	Palamcottah.		Onore.
	Dindigul.		Sedashigur.
	Madura.		Manantoddy.
	Negapatam.		
	Palgautchery.	*Ceded Districts.*	Bellary.
	Quilon.		Gooty.
	Trivandrum.		Cuddapah.
	Ootacamund.		Cumbum.

Hyderabad Subsidiary Force.   Secunderabad.

Nagpore Subsidiary Force.   Kamptee.

1836.

On the 26th July 1836, orders were issued forbidding troops to take part in processions.

On the 19th August 1836, a warrant was issued for the distribution of the booty captured during the operations in Coorg, amounting in value to Rupees 14,96,735. The Government of India admitted the claim of Captain R. Campbell, 4th N.I., to a share in the booty, and rejected the claim of Lieutenant H. Colbeck. The 4th N.I., was entitled to participate in the distribution as follows:—2 Captains at 120 shares each; 6 Lieutenants, 1 Assistant-Surgeon and 3 Ensigns at 60 shares each; 5 Subadars at 7 shares each; 1 Second Apothecary, 1 Regimental Serjeant-Major, 1 Quartermaster-Serjeant and 8 Jemadars at 3 shares each; 34 Havildar-

Majors and Havildars, and 1 Second Tindal at 1 share each; 32 Naigues, 13 Drummers, 509 Privates, 8 Puckallies, 17 Regimental Lascars, 20 Tent Lascars, 1 Native Second Dresser and 1 Native Medical Pupil at two-thirds of a share each; a total of 664 individuals, entitled to 1,343 2/3 shares. The Brigadier-Commanding drew one-sixteenth of the whole amount, or Rs. 95,168-8-7, and the amounts drawn by other ranks were as follows:—

Captains	Rs.	5,585 11 9
Subalterns, etc.	Rs.	2,792 13 11
Subadars	Rs.	325 13 4
Jemadars, etc.	Rs.	139 10 4
Havildars, etc.	Rs.	46 8 9
Privates, etc.	Rs.	31 0 6

At a Court-Martial held at Cannanore in August 1836, a sepoy of the 51st N. I. was sentenced to be hanged for having shot and killed a Havildar of the same regiment. It was ordered that his body should be suspended in an iron cage in some conspicuous spot in, or near, the cantonment of Cannanore.

From the 31st August 1836, Vakeels of all corps in the Presidency were discontinued.

On the 2nd September 1836, it was ordered that the practice of closing the envelopes of official letters with paste or gum, instead of wax or wafers, should cease, as causing inconvenience and frequently injuring the enclosure!

In October 1836, regimental Quartermasters were relieved from the duty of examining the regimental abstracts and from attending at the pay office to receive the amount, Company officers being thenceforth made responsible for all matters concerning the pay of their men.

On the 28th November 1836, the attention of officers was called to the existing orders regarding dress. Except when taking exercise in the morning, before nine o'clock, officers were prohibited from appearing in public otherwise dressed than in the uniform of their rank and, whether in Dress or Undress, the costume was required to be *complete and unmixed*. It was added that these orders were not intended to apply to officers when engaged in field sports, cricket or similar amusements.

1837.

On the 2nd May 1837, good conduct pay was granted at the rate of Re. 1 *per mensem* after 16 years' service, and another Re. 1 after 20 years' service.

At the same time the following Orders were instituted:—

The Order of British India.—This Order was to be given to Native Officers for long and honourable service. The first class was to consist of 100 Subadars with the title of *Sardar Bahadur,* and an allowance of Rs. 2 *per diem* each, in addition to their regimental allowances and retiring pensions. The second class was to consist of 100 Native Commissioned Officers with the title of *Bahadur*, and an allowance of Re. 1 *per diem* each, in addition to their usual allowances and pensions.

Three-sixths of these appointments were allotted to Bengal, two-sixths to Madras, and one-sixth to Bombay.

Sixty-seven officers were admitted to the Order with effect from the 1st May 1837, but no officer of the 4th was included in the original list.

The Indian Order of Merit.—This Order was to be awarded for distinguished service in action. Every Native Officer or N. C. O. obtaining admission to this Order was to receive:—

In the 3rd class, 1/3 of his full pay in addition to his pay or pension.

In the 2nd class, 2/3 ,, ,, ,, ,,

In the 1st class, Double pay or full pay in addition to his ordinary pension.

A despatch from the Court of Directors at the same time issued new regulations for pay and pensions, as follows:—

	Pay including half-batta.	Extra batta when marching in the Field.	Pension, after 15 years.	When disabled by wounds or for very long service, not less than 40 years.
Subadar, 1st class	70-	14-3-3	25-	40-
,, 2nd class	52-8	14-3-3	25-	40-
,, 3rd class	42-	14-3-3	25-	40-
Jemadar	24-8	7-8-	12-	20-
Havildar	14-	5-	7-	12-
Naigue	12-	5-	7-	12-
Drummer	11-	5-	4-	7-
Private	7-	1-8-	4-	7-

These new regulations meant a considerable reduction and occasioned much discontent.

On the 15th November 1837, the Court of Directors decided that officers of the Civil, Military, and Marine Services, when residing in England, should be permitted to draw their pay quarterly, instead of half-yearly.

1838.

On the 3rd January 1838, a sepoy of the 14th N. I., who had shot dead the Subadar-Major of his regiment, was sentenced to be blown from a gun, and the sentence was duly carried out at Vizianagram.

On the 1st May 1838, the benefit of medical aid, in Garrison and in the Field, was extended to all classes of followers, whether permanently or temporarily employed.

On the same date, Officers Commanding regiments of which the light companies had not yet been provided with the double sighted Light Infantry Musket, were directed to indent for the number required, in exchange for the ordinary Muskets then in use.

In July 1838, the 2nd Native Veteran Battalion was reduced, and the whole of the native veterans formed into one Corps, designated "The Madras Native Veterans."

On the 3rd September 1838, the allotment of "Shotted Cartridges" for Native Infantry of the line on Field Service was fixed at 48 rounds per man and 5 flints, of which 24 rounds were carried in the pouch. Within the frontier, on the line of march or escort duty, 12 rounds per man of shotted ammunition, and 2 flints, were to be carried in the pouch.

On the 6th September 1838, sanction was given for an increase of 10 Privates per Company.

At this time there was in the Presidency a department for the suppression of Thuggee, with a General Superintendent-in-Charge. A separate jail for Thugs was maintained at Palmanair.

1839.

In March 1839, a further increase of 10 Privates, 1 Havildar and 1 Naigue per Company was sanctioned, and, on the 17th August, a ninth Company was ordered to be raised in each battalion, while on the 22nd August an additional Lance-Naigue was authorised for each Company.

Owing to this augmentation, the 4th M. N. I., then stationed at Cannanore, detached recruiting parties to the Northern Circars, Vellore and Madura, which rejoined in December 1840, when the regiment was up to strength.

In March 1839, a new scale of allowances was fixed for the regimental staff:—

	Staff Pay.	Office Allowance.	Horse Allowance.	Office Tent.	Total.
Adjutant, Native Infantry	92-7-0	40-0-0	30-0-0	30-0-0	Rs. 192-7-0
Quartermaster and Interpreter, Native Infantry	62-0-0	40-0-0	30-0-0	—	„ 132-0-0

The allowance of Rs. 24 *per mensem* granted to Adjutants for carriage of regimental books was discontinued, and it was ordered that only the *bona-fide* expenses for this purpose should be drawn when actually marching.

On the 2nd July 1839, the Governor-in-Council was pleased to declare that, on occasions of public rejoicing, when the Troops were entitled to "dry batta," it should be issued to them, at certain large stations which were named, on the same day for the celebration of which it was granted, while in other stations it should be included in the abstracts for the following month.

This "dry batta" was apparently what was afterwards termed "sweetmeat money."

On the 13th July 1839, the Commander-in-Chief announced that no further appointments of Adjutant or Quartermaster would be made unless the officers had passed the prescribed examination in the Hindostanee language.

On the same date, Infantry Regiments of the Line (European and Native) having Bands, were permitted to employ one Serjeant or Havildar and fourteen Privates, as Musicians, instead of one Serjeant or Havildar and ten Privates as previously.

On the 6th August 1839, owing to the increase of establishment, regiments were allowed four, instead of three, private two-poled Tents per Company.

On the 21st September 1839, new Recruiting Regulations were issued, one being to the effect that if any officer enlisted an objectionable recruit, he should be charged with any expense incurred on account of that recruit. Amongst the more obvious causes for which a recruit should be rejected was specified:—

"Clause V. Weak or disordered intellect. This will be best ascertained by addressing a few questions to the recruit."

On the 21st December 1839, sanction was accorded for the introduction of a tin lamp for all station and regimental guard-rooms, in place of the earthen chatty hitherto in use. It was expected, as a consequence of this improvement, that "the Walls and Floors will be no longer soiled and dirtied."

1840.

In February 1840, "Puckallies" were introduced in place of "Bheesties."

In September 1840, one Lieutenant and one Ensign were added to the establishment.

Lieutenant-General Burton writes of the Madras Army at this time as follows:—

"In 1840, the time of which I am writing, the Madras Army was full officered, and was in a state of good discipline and efficiency.........The men are not tall, but there is no want of activity and of strength in proportion to their size. They are mostly well featured, but dark in complexion; they are always ready to work with spade and pickaxe, an excellent trait which the Bengal Sepoys do not so commonly possess; they are good marchers, frugal feeders and possess, in short, many good qualities on active service. They have few caste prejudices, and when properly led are fully as reliable as their more showy brethren of the other presidencies.

As regards the clothing of the Sepoy at this time, he writes:—

"The dress and equipment of the native army was in a most antiquated style. The muskets were flint and steel; the men wore bobtail coatees, barred in front with white tape, and on their heads a marvellous structure called a turband. This turband, of which I sent a specimen to the Nagpore Museum in 1875, was a kind of shako, spreading out at top, built of bamboo basket-work, perfectly stiff and hard (it must have been, in Eastern phrase, a very "grandfather of headaches"!), covered with blue cloth, and with a narrow brass rim, over all which was an outer removable cover of black varnished linen for *undress*. At the apex was a brass affair as big as, and shaped like, the half of a small orange, on which projected two ribs, very like two little boats keel upwards, also of brass.

It was a tradition that the use of this arrangement was as a musket rest when lying down to fire, the turband being then placed on the ground in front of the fighting-man! However this may be, it had its other uses, seeing that it served as a kind of extra pocket or travelling bag for its wearer……………………… I must not forget that in full dress a broad pipeclayed tape band, with an equally well pipeclayed rosette, something like a double dahlia, was carried diagonally along the right side of the fabric, on the top edge of which the rosette was perched as a finish to the whole concern.

The knapsack, weighing, when filled, about 14 or 15 pounds (to the best of my recollection) was also a wonderful equipment. The great point was, that it should be perfectly square in itself, and should sit perfectly square, also, on the Sepoy's back. After an "Inspection of necessaries" parade the knapsacks were repacked (and the process timed with watches) on parade, and the sound of fists driving the articles into their proper space and place was like the beating of innumerable carpets! The pack was suspended under the shoulders by two leathern straps, which came under the armpits, and had a connecting strap across the chest; the whole contrivance being admirably adopted to cut the man under the arms, to constrict his chest-play, and to impede his breathing……………………I may as well also note the way in which the men, in those old days, were shod. The whole native army wore sandals of a very unserviceable pattern, kept on the foot by only a broad strap over the instep, and a thin toe ring, a cord, as it were, of leather, passing round the big-toe. Not only did this toe-ring cause terrible galls—so much so that many men were usually excused wearing sandals on account of sores thus occasioned, and many others wore a bit of rag wrapped round their toes—but likewise it was most difficult to keep the sandals on when the men had to run, as at light drill, etc. After a company had pelted in at the double from covering the front of the regiment at extended order, the parade ground would be dotted with the black sandals very much as if a flight of crows had settled down on it."

1841.

To show how much cheaper was the cost of living in India seventy years ago, I quote from General Burton, who says:—

"In 1841 Samulcottah was one of the cheapest stations in the Presidency. The vetch called *coolthee* used in South India for feeding horses, was sold at ninety seers, that is, one hundred and eighty pounds, for a rupee. It cost me just a rupee a month to feed my pony! The price of tobacco was likewise astonishingly low. Lunka cheroots, made at Samulcottah, were sold at a rupee and a half per thousand. Now, in 1888, the price is from twelve to twenty rupees per thousand, according to size, and I am not sure that they are not even dearer than this; at all events, I am well within the mark."

In 1841, permission was given to detach a small recruiting party to Vellore.

In March of this year, the Madras European Regiment was granted, among others, the following honours:—

"*Nundy-droog;*" which it assisted to capture in 1791, and for which His Lordship in Council is pleased to permit it also to bear a royal tiger on the colours and appointments.

"*Pondicherry*"; the corps having been employed at the sieges and reduction in 1761, 1778 and 1793.

It is to be regretted that H. E. the Governor-General-in-Council did not recognise in a similar manner the services of the Native battalions employed on these occasions.

1842.

On the 18th February 1842, the establishment was increased by the raising of a tenth company, and the addition of a tenth Lieutenant. This necessitated greater activity in recruiting, and accordingly the party at Vellore was strengthened, and two other parties sent out, one of which proceeded to Madura and the other to Mysore.

General Burton writes of the musketry course, as carried out in the forties, as follows:—

"The musketry course, or 'ball-firing' as it was then called, was a simple affair. Neither officers nor men were bothered with theoretical instruction or tall talk about trajectories, etc., and position drill, etc., which now make life a burden. The recruit was taught to hold his musket straight, to aim over a sand-bag tripod, and then to burn priming and black cartidge, as a preparation for his firing with ball at from fifty to a hundred and fifty yards. The squad of recruits, on returning from their first day's ball firing, came in triumph with their muskets decorated with flowers, and after the whole course was finished, were formally sworn in under the colours, and were brought on the roster for duty.

The ball practice was, altogether, a terrible farce. The targets were coarse cotton cloth stretched on an iron frame and whitewashed, and with circles for 'centre' and 'bull's-eye' painted in black. An orderly-boy was placed in a pit in front of each target to mark the hits; the signal for bull's-eye being a waving of the flag instead of showing it perpendicularly.

In my zeal as a young officer I proclaimed a reward of a rupee for every bull's-eye in my company (the light), and this reward bore fruit in an unpleasant way. A certain havildar, by no means renowned for good shooting, made a bull's-eye at every practice; and on mentioning my surprise at this to the native officers they screwed up their faces in a way which showed that there was something to be explained. It turned out that the orderly-boy in the pit was a son of the havildar, and that a peculiar cry was given by a confederate boy on the wing of the butt when the father came to fire. The consequence, if a hit at all, was an inevitable bull's-eye."

On the 24th June 1842, the Court of Directors approved of the continuance of his pay, without allowances, to an officer undergoing the penalty of imprisonment under the sentence of a Court-Martial.

In October 1842, the Commander-in-Chief expressed his regret that it should have been necessary in no less than twenty-one regiments to appoint an officer from another regiment to act as Quartermaster and Interpreter, and hoped that there would soon be an improvement in that respect.

It may be of interest to note that at this time European deserters who were brought to trial by Court-Martial, and found guilty, were sentenced to be marked "D" on the left side, in addition to a term of imprisonment.

This practice was still carried out in 1863, and at a Court-Martial held at Cannanore in 1864, a Private Soldier who had used insubordinate language to an officer and had struck a N. C. O. was sentenced to penal servitude for seven years, to be discharged with ignominy, "and further to be marked with the letters 'B.C.' in the usual manner."

The Commander-in-Chief, however, decided that the marking should not be carried into effect.

I do not know the meaning of the letters "B.C.", but presume that they were meant to signify "Bad Character."

1843.

On the 27th January 1843, the establishment was reduced by 10 Privates per company, and on the 28th of the following month a further reduction was made of one Havildar and one Naigue per company, the establishment of the battalion now consisting of 50 Havildars, 50 Naigues and 900 Privates.

In February 1843, the establishment maintained for the reception of cadets on their first arrival from England was moved from Fort St. George to Palaveram.

In September 1843, the attention of Commanding Officers was drawn to an order published in 1839 by which the number of Lance-Naigues allotted to corps was fixed at 4 per Company in regiments of Light Infantry, and 3 per company in regiments of Native Infantry, each Flank and Rifle Company of the latter being allowed 4, but in March 1844 the number of the latter was increased to 5.

1844.

The following was the composition of the regiment as given in a return, dated the 1st January 1844:—

Caste.	Indian Officers.	Havildars	Naigues.	Lance-Naigues.	Drummers.	Privates.
Christians	—	1	1	—	7	—
Mussulmans	10	28	24	17	—	301
Brahmins and Rajputs	2	5	5	2	—	36
Mahrattas	1	—	1	—	—	15
Telegus (Gentoo)	4	15	16	10	—	320
Tamils	1	8	9	7	—	180
Other Castes	1	—	2	—	—	51
Indo-Britons	—	1	—	—	11	11
Total	19	58	58	36	18	914

In March 1844, the Court of Directors directed that no Subaltern officer should thereafter be given charge of a troop or company until he should have passed a prescribed examination in the Hindostanee language.

On the 5th April 1844, a revised system of Sword Exercise was introduced.

In November 1844, the distances at which ball practice was to be carried out were fixed as follows:—

Muskets and Fusils. 96 120 142 180, and 240 paces.

Rifles. 120 142 180 240 and 300 paces.

The Commander-in-Chief remarked that the main object in all Infantry practice should be to teach the men when in line to fire straight to their front so that their shots might take full effect upon the enemy's ranks at 100 paces. The only ball practice carried out by the regiment in this year was at 96 paces, when an average was obtained of 1 hit to $2\frac{3}{4}$ rounds fired. The results for regiments which fired at 240 paces were very poor, in one case only 1 hit to $27\frac{3}{4}$ rounds fired. In 1845, the regiment fired at 120 paces and obtained the same average as in 1844.

On the 31st December 1844, a General Order was issued regarding Rifle Companies. The Rifle Company was to take the left of the Regiment on all occasions, and not to be detailed for minor posts in Garrison or Cantonment, when it could be avoided, but to be placed on honorary or principal guards, where the men would be in a collected state and under their own Non-Commissioned Officers. Their drill was to be carried out as in Rifle Regiments. The only regiments with a proportion of rifles at this time appear to have been the 1st, 5th, 16th, 24th, 26th, 36th, 38th and 49th Native Infantry.

The name of the recipient was not engraved on any medal before September 1844.

1845.

On the 4th February 1845, a sixth Captain was allowed for each regiment.

On the 21st February 1845, officers' messes were established, by order of the Governor in Council:—

"The Court of Directors having repeatedly expressed their desire that Regimental Messes should be established in the various corps of the Indian Army, and that officers of all ranks should become permanent Members of them, attending regularly or occasionally, according to their domestic conditions and in furtherance of this important object, an allowance is granted by Government in aid of their attendant expenses."

Rates of donation were not to exceed one month's pay proper, and rates of subscription were not to exceed $1\frac{1}{2}$ *per cent.* monthly on pay and garrison allowances.

From the arrival of the 4th M.N.I. at Vellore in 1845 up to the year 1869, no recruiting parties were detached. During this period recruiting was carried on at regimental headquarters, chiefly from relatives of the men.

In this year the issue of percussion smooth-bore muskets, in supersession of flint-locks, was commenced.

Although it does not affect the services of the 4th, the following General Order (No. 156 of 1845) cannot fail to be of interest to all ranks of the Madras Army:—

Fort St. George, 15th August 1845.

" The Most Noble the Governor in Council directs the publication of the sub-joined despatch from the Honourable the Court of Directors.

Letter, dated 2nd July 1845. No. 57.

We forward copy of a Letter from the Lord Provost and Chief Magistrate of the City of Perth with its accompanying Medal, which the Inhabitants of Perth are desirous should be presented to Kolapa, Sepoy of the 16th Madras Native Infantry, as a mark of their sense of his gallantry in protecting and carrying off the body of the late Lieutenant Alexander P. Campbell, 2nd Bombay Native Infantry, who was killed in action in December last. We have great satisfaction in forwarding this medal, which you will convey to the sepoy for whom it is intended.

The Chairman of the Board of Directors of the Hon'ble East India Company.

Perth, 12th June 1845.

SIR,

On the occasion when the Lieutenant Alexander P. Campbell, 2nd Bombay L. I., was killed on the 31st December last, near Sassedroog, his body was protected, and ultimately carried off thro' the gallantry of a Sepoy of the 16th Madras N. I., of the name of Kolapa.

The Inhabitants of Perth feel a strong desire to express their sense of the gallantry of this Sepoy in having protected the body of their Townsman at the risk of his own life, and in order to do so they have had prepared a Medal, which I now transmit, and which they are desirous of being allowed to present to him.

Independent altogether of the meritorious conduct of this individual on the occasion when Lieutenant Campbell was killed, I should hope that this mark of respect to him might have no injurious effect on the Native Soldiers generally, and I beg on behalf of the Inhabitants of Perth, respectfully to request that you will be pleased to allow the Medal to be presented to one for whose conduct they entertain so much respect and to whom they are so anxious to be allowed to express their feelings by presenting this Testimonial.

I have the honour to be, Sir, your most humble and obedient servant
(*Signed*) C. G. SIDEY,
Lord Provost and Chief Magistrate of the City of Perth.

The Commander-in-Chief is requested to cause the Medal to be delivered to Private Kolapa of the 16th Regiment, with authority to wear the same with his Military uniform."

1846.

On the 25th August 1846, Drummers and Fifers were admitted to Good Conduct Pay, at the rate of one rupee a month after 16 years', and an additional rupee after 20 years' service, with effect from the 1st September 1846.

At this time officers who were removed from one station to another were allowed a period not exceeding one month for preparation, and a further period for travelling to join, calculated at the rate of 10 miles a day, with a halt for every Sunday.

New regulations for Hutting Money were issued on the 5th December 1846. This allowance was granted on every final change of station, and also to men transferred to another corps (not at their own request), to newly-enlisted men on joining regimental headquarters, and to men invalided. The allowance could not be drawn at stations where the troops were in receipt of batta. The rates were:—

Subadar	Rupees 24	*Trumpet, Farrier, Bugle, Drum and Fife Major.*	Rupees 4.
Jemadar	,, 12	*Naigue and Native Dresser*	,, 3.
Havildar	,, 4	*Trumpeter, Farrier, Bugler, Drummer, Fifer, Private, Gun Lascar, Puckally, and Bheastie*	Rupees 2.

The subaltern's quarters in the forties are thus depicted in the pages of *the Delhi Sketch Book*:—

> "The room contains a solitary chair,
> A broken couch from which protrudes the hair,
> A ruined lamp, a picture of "Old Nick",
> A Shovel, tongs, and candle stick,
> A few books ranged upon the table,
> With whips and bridles (better in the stable).
> Some "odds and ends", valueless and small,
> A trunk containing very near his all."

1847.

On the 11th February 1847, the establishment was still further reduced to 700 Privates.

1848.

In this year a case occurred of pension being claimed fraudulently, and on enquiry it was discovered that pensions had been paid in no less than 82 cases to persons supposed to be still alive, but who had been dead for periods varying from a few months to ten years.

On the 30th June 1848, an order was issued limiting the number of servants of all descriptions for whom passage would be provided at the public expense, for officers proceeding on the Peninsular and Oriental Steam Company's Steamers, as follows:—General Officers, six; Colonels, five; Lieutenant-Colonels, four; Majors, three; Captains and Regimental Staff Officers, two; Subalterns, Warrant Officers and Native Officers, one.

I have not so far been able to discover when Courts of Requests were instituted, but certain regulations connected with them were published for the information and guidance of the Army in October 1848. There were both European and Native Courts and the former, consisting of five, and in no instance of less than three, Commissioned Officers, were authorised to adjudicate on actions for debt and all personal actions against Officers, provided that the amount of the claim did not exceed rupees four hundred. The Native Courts consisted of either three European, or three Native, Commissioned Officers, in the latter case with an European Officer of not less than five years' standing, to superintend and record the proceedings. They were authorised to deal with similar claims against Native ranks not exceeding rupees two hundred in amount, but were not permitted to determine any dispute relating to caste, or concerning any right to real property. These Military Courts were convened monthly, in each Cantonment, provided that there were any cases to be dealt with.

1849.

The Thursday holiday allowed to the troops in India was instituted in 1849 by the Commander-in-Chief in India, Sir Charles Napier, the reason probably being that Sunday was not really a holiday for British Troops, who had to turn out for church parade.

New regulations for the establishment and maintenance of Bands of Music were issued on the 26th September 1849. Each officer was to pay a donation of 30 days' net pay of regimental rank on appointment, and a monthly subscription of two days' net pay of regimental rank. The band establishment was fixed at one Havildar per regiment, and 2 Privates per Company, who were to be "effective to the Service as Soldiers; to be perfectly drilled; and liable to serve in the ranks in any emergency." The Bands of Cavalry Regiments were to be dressed in clothing of the same colour as worn by their respective corps, while Bands of Infantry were to be dressed in white with the regimental facings.

On the 26th November 1849, certain stations, hitherto attached to the Bengal Presidency, were handed over as follows:—

To be permanently occupied by troops of the Madras Army.	Cuttack, Saugor, Hussingabad, Jubbulpore, Nagode, Nursingpore, Mhow.
To be permanently occupied by troops of the Bombay Army.	Neemuch. Nusseerabad.

At the same time the stations of Nowgong, Jhansi, Oraee, Bandah, Humeerpoor and Calpee were transferred from the Saugor Division to the Cawnpore Division.

In consequence of the above change, Cuttack was included in the Northern Division, and the remaining stations formed a new Saugor Division of the Madras Army.

1850.

General Burton writes as follows regarding the introduction of boots in lieu of sandals :—

"About 1850, boots became popular—that is, in the eyes of the British Officers, for the men, being good conservatives, disliked all changes, and had rather have kept to the old sandals. Nor, indeed, was the boot a blessing, for, as the Sepoy could not afford to wear socks, it so befell that his feet were more damaged with the boot than they had been with the sandal.

It was not an uncommon thing to find five or six men in a company with bare feet on parade, having been "excused boots" by the doctor. On the line of march it was far worse, and half the regiment went bootless and barefoot during one part or other of a march between one station and another."

In this connection it may be remarked that though in these modern days the sepoy does wear socks, men "excused boots" on parade are not altogether unknown. It naturally takes some time for the feet of a recruit, who has gone barefoot all his life, to become accustomed to the pressure of a boot and, as we all know, new boots can be quite sufficiently uncomfortable even for those who have always been in the habit of wearing them.

On the 7th February 1850, it was ordered that, except the Bass Drummer, no Drummer, Fifer or Bugler was to play in the Band on parade. Drummers were permitted to play in the Band when off duty, such employment to be perfectly voluntary on their part, and no Drummer was to be transferred from one Company to another with a view to keeping him with regimental headquarters.

On the 12th April 1850, revised rules regarding regimental Bands were issued, and the rates of subscription for officers of various ranks were laid down. It was ordered that all Band questions should be decided regimentally by a majority of two-thirds of the number of subscribers.

On the 9th May 1850, the following General Order was issued :—

"The practice at the several Stations of the Army, in respect to allowing the white linen Jacket or Ungreka to be worn during the hot weather, being dissimilar, and the Commander-in-Chief being desirous that the indulgence should be extended generally to the Troops (European and Native) at all Stations, His Excellency directs it to be notified that the white Jacket or Ungreka may be worn on all Regimental or General duties (except when otherwise specially ordered by local authorities) at the discretion of Commanding Officers according to the state of the weather—the local Commanding Officer regulating the periods during which it shall be worn by Troops on *general* duty or at Brigade Field Days, etc.

The Commander-in-Chief is also pleased to approve of European Officers being permitted to wear a white Jacket when white is worn by their men; or during the periods prescribed for white Trousers in the "Dress Regulations," on all occasions on which the cloth Jacket or Frock Coat would otherwise be worn.

On all occasions of *Duty*, the white Jacket is to be worn hooked or buttoned with stock. At other times, and at the ordinary Regimental Mess it may be worn open with a Waistcoat and black silk neck tie.

Patterns of the white Jacket and Waistcoat authorised for Officers have been deposited for reference in the Adjutant-General's Office, Fort Saint George, and Lithographed Drawings will be sent as early as practicable to the Head Quarters of Divisions and Forces.

The cloth Frock Coat or Jacket with Sword Belt or Sash is the appropriate dress for evening rides.

At General Courts-Martial, during the hot season, the "Undress" cloth Jacket and appointments may be worn instead of the "Dress."

There were three newspapers published in Madras at this time, called respectively the *"Athenæum,"* the *"Madras Circulator and General Chronicle,"* and the *"United Service Gazette."*

1851.

In 1851, the shoulder belts from which the bayonets were suspended were given up, and waist-belts, with frogs, were supplied instead.

On the 21st March 1851, a G. O. announced that the Queen had been pleased to signify her assent to a measure that had been proposed by the Court of Directors of the E. India Coy., of granting a medal to the surviving officers and soldiers of the Crown, who were engaged in the following services in India:—

Indian War Medal. 1799—1827. (Ribbon, pale blue).

	Clasps.	
Storm of Allighur, September 4, 1803		Allighur.
Battle of Delhi, September 11, 1803.		
Battle of Assye, September 23, 1803.		Assye.
Siege of Asseerghur, October 21, 1803.		
Battle of Laswarree, November 1, 1803.		
Battle of Argaum, November 29, 1803.		Argaum.
Siege and Storm of Gawilghur, December 15, 1803.		Gawilghur.
Defence of Delhi, October 1804.		
Battle of Deig, November 13, 1804.		Battle of Deig.
Capture of Deig, December 23, 1804.		Capture of Deig.
War in Nepaul 1816.		
Battle of Kirkee and Capture of Poona, November 1817.		
Battle of Seetabuldee and Battle of Capture of Nagpoor, November-December 1817.		
Battle of Maheidpore, December 21, 1817.		
Defence of Corygaum, January 1, 1818.		
War in Ava, 1824-26.		
Siege and Storm of Bhurtpore, January 1826.		

This order also permitted the medals given by the Company for the Mysore War and Seringapatam to be worn.

1852.

The 4th M. N. I. does not seem to have received percussion muskets, in lieu of the old flint-locks, until the 30th March 1852.

On the 8th June 1852, new rules for wound pensions to N. C. O's. and men were published.

According to the Madras Army List, some time in 1852, when Lieutenant-Colonel Budd was commanding the regiment, the colour of the regimental facings was changed from *orange* to *deep green,* the lace remaining *gold* as before, but I am inclined to think that this is merely an error in the Army List, as in the following year the original *orange* facings reappear.

The death of Field Marshal the Duke of Wellington was announced to the Madras Army by a General Order, dated the 29th October 1852, and 83 minute guns were fired at all the Military Stations in the Presidency.

1853.

By General Order No. 355, issued by the Governor-General in Council, on the 29th April 1853, it was determined that service in the Native Army prior to the completion of the age of sixteen should not reckon towards pension. The order was not made retrospective.

On the 17th June 1853, revised Regulations for Equipment were issued. From these we learn that one tent was allowed for 25 men in the infantry, and one tent for every 50 recruits. One lascar was allowed for every 4 tents. Parties on detachment consisting of less than 13 men were not allowed a tent, unless commanded by a Native Officer. One dooly was allowed for every 10 Europeans or 70 Native Soldiers. When on the march, a Native Regiment was allotted one medicine chest, with 5 bearers to carry it. In calculating the amount of transport required for baggage, a country cart was estimated at 800 lbs.; a carriage bullock, 123 lbs.; a "Cowry Cooly," 82 lbs., and a Common Cooly, 72 lbs.

On the 11th October 1853, a General Order fixed the price of porter for issue to European troops at Rs. 30 per hogshead or one anna per pint, and bottled porter was to be issued at 2 annas per quart, the empty bottles to be returned to the Commissariat department. The price was raised to 3 annas per quart in 1855.

New clothing regulations appeared on the 10th October 1853, by which the leather stock, which must have been a cause of much suffering and discomfort, was abolished both for European and Native troops.

On the 8th November 1853, the following General Order was issued by the Commander-in-Chief in India:—

"The Commander-in-Chief in India deems it a duty to publish to the Army the following Statement, showing the ruinous and fatal consequences which have ensued to so many good Soldiers who, misled by imaginary hopes of improving their condition, applied for their discharge and proceeded to Calcutta with the intention of emigrating to Australia.

His Excellency trusts that the fate of these unfortunate and misjudging men, added to the reports received from the Colony of the bad prospects of subsistence on first landing, the difficulties to be contended with, and the great amount of personal labour required to gain a livelihood there (such as few old Soldiers are able to undergo) will induce those who may be desirous of emigrating, to pause and consider well ere they give up their present comparative comfort, and hope of pension, for a future so uncertain and hazardous.

Eighty-six men obtained permission to proceed to Calcutta, and thence to Australia, during the months of October, November, December, January, February, March and April last, out of which number but 55 proceeded to their destination.

    7 having died en route to Calcutta.

    8 having died at Calcutta, awaiting embarkation.

    4 having been obliged to change their destination for want of funds, etc.

    4 having obtained permission to rejoin their Regiments.

    8 having embarked for Australia, but returned to the Presidency, the Vessel having grounded."

1854.

In 1854, the issue of packs instead of knapsacks commenced.

In this year the second India General Service Medal was instituted, worn with a ribbon of three red and two blue equal stripes. This replaced the medal of 1799—1827 (*vide* 1851), and remained in use till 1895, during which time 23 clasps were issued for it.

In February 1854, a letter appeared in the *Bombay Times*, which denounced, as having ruined the efficiency of the Native Army, the regimental system established in 1796, the Articles of War, and the general system of discipline. The letter was signed "John Jacob, Scinde Horse," and aroused the indignation of the Court of Directors, who informed the Governor-General that:—

"Any officer in the service is at liberty, and indeed in many cases is bound in duty, to communicate confidentially to the Commander-in-Chief of the Army to which he belongs the opinions he may entertain on points affecting the discipline or efficiency of the Troops; but he is not at liberty to denounce publicly the system established by the Legislature and by the Government he serves—Such conduct is entirely subversive of discipline, is calculated to excite discontent and insubordination in the Army, and we cannot express in too strong terms our disapprobation of the course which appears to have been taken on the present occasion."

In July 1854, the Governor-General notified that officers of Government, of whatever rank or class, should be absolutely prohibited from selling or being concerned in the sale of property, of any amount or description, to Native Princes and Chiefs, or to their relatives or ministers, or to any Native gentleman of rank or opulence, residing under the protection of the British Government. Up to 1832 such sales had been permitted, provided that the value of the property did not exceed Rs. 5,000.

On the 9th October 1854, **rates** of pay for Non-Commissioned Officers attached to Native Infantry Corps were laid down as follows, with effect from the 1st November:—

Rank.	Pay and Compensation for spirits. Rs. A. P.	Ration Money or Batta. Rs. A. P.	Total. Rs. A. P.
Serjeant-Major	44 7 10	6 5 4	50 13 2
Quartermaster-Serjeant.	38 7 10	6 5 4	44 13 2

1855.

On the 13th March 1855, the allotment of shotted cartridges for practice to Native Infantry of the Line was increased from 36 to 60 per man, with percussion caps and target materials according to the regulated proportion.

At this time no exchanges were permitted between officers of different branches of the service, nor between officers of the same branch above the rank of Cornet, 2nd Lieutenant, or Ensign.

On the 9th November 1855, orders were issued for a royal salute to be fired at every station in the Presidency in honour of the capture of the Town of Sebastopol, with its forts, arsenals and munitions of war.

1856.

From revised regulations regarding marches, issued on the 28th May 1856, it appears that the current price of sheep was then from 12 annas to one rupee, and of fowls from one anna to two annas each. Up to this date Tahsildars had been required to supply coolies, pots, firesticks and tent-pegs to troops on the march, without payment, but this practice was now brought to an end. Coolies were to be paid at the rate of 3 annas per 10 miles.

On the 5th September 1856, bandsmen were supplied with swords and sling belts instead of muskets, belts and pouches, but were to be instructed in musketry as before.

On the 18th September 1856, it was directed that the practice of wearing the sash with the blue frock coat or shell jacket should be discontinued. The sash was to be worn on all occasions with the coatee, and was to go twice round the waist and be tied on the right hip by Artillery and on the left hip by Infantry. The pendent part was to be uniformly 16 inches in length from the tie.

In October 1856, the adoption of tunics, waist belts and sashes, similar to those prescribed for officers of His Majesty's service, was authorised.

On the 23rd November 1856, an additional (7th) Captain and Lieutenant were allowed for each regiment of Cavalry and Native Infantry.

On the 5th December 1856, the Court of Directors sanctioned an allowance of Rs. 100 *per mensem* towards the maintenance of each regimental band in the Native Cavalry and Infantry, and Rs. 200 *per mensem* to each European Infantry Regiment, at the same time limiting the monthly band subscription to one day's net pay of regimental rank.

1857.

On the 7th May 1857, tunics were issued in supersession of the "coatee."

On the 17th June 1857, officers and soldiers of the East India Company's Service became eligible for the Victoria Cross, by Royal Warrant of H. M. Queen Victoria.

On the 20th November 1857, the establishment was increased to 1,000 Privates, and one Havildar and one Naigue added to each company. The strength of a company then was:—1 Subadar, 1 Jemadar, 6 Havildars, 6 Naigues, 2 Drummers or Buglers, 100 Privates.

The number of recruits enlisted for the Madras Army in the two years 1857-1858 was upwards of 17,000.

When, in 1857, the great Mutiny broke out, the Madras Army continued to be as ready and willing as ever to do its duty, and rendered very great assistance in putting down the outbreak. As has already been stated, the 4th M. N. I. was on foreign service at the time and took no part in these operations. Lieutenant-General Burton, an old Commandant of the regiment, bears the following testimony to the services of the old Coast Army:—

"It fought against the French, and against Hyder Ally and Tippoo Sultan; it fought under General Arthur Wellesley at Mahidpore, Amboor and Assaye; also in the Poligar War and against the robber hordes of Central India; likewise at Nagpore and at Sholinghur, where the 20th Madras Infantry behaved most gallantly, and bear to this day a *third* colour in memory of one captured from Hyder Ally; and in Burmah, in the former wars of 1824 and 1852, as well as in the recent campaigns of 1885—6—7, which, though not fruitful in honour, have yet been very much so in privations, hardships, and even hard knocks.

It shared with British Soldiers in the campaigns against the Bengal mutineers in Central India; also it has been more than once engaged in China. In these wars, and on many other occasions both within and without its own territory, the Madras army has always done good service. In Afghanistan, though kept back in favour of Bengal regiments which were pressed on to the front out of their turn, its men were second to none in endurance, cheerfully and healthfully bearing the rigour of so ungenial a climate. For many years past, until Sir Neville Chamberlain denounced the unfairness and impolicy of systematically keeping the Madras troops in the background, it was denied any opportunity of distinguishing itself, and was treated, especially after the mutinies, with spiteful contempt........ The Bengal papers have taken care to preserve silence on the laches of their own troops, but have industriously sought out and exaggerated all rumours affecting the Madrassees.

There is ample testimony to the bravery and good services of the Coast Army. Search the pages of Orme, of Malcolm in his " Political History of India "; read the lives of Clive and Coote; and greatest authority of all, the Indian despatches of the great Duke himself, and there will be found no want of just appreciation of the Madras Sepoy ....Once let the Madras army have a fair share of active service, and its turn in the front line with the men of the other presidencies, and it will perform its own advocacy in a sufficiently practical manner."

The following statement of servants' wages in India in 1857 was made out by a lady whose husband was serving in the 1st Madras Native Infantry:—

Khansama	Rs. 8-0-0	Ayah	Rs. 6-0-0
Khidmatgar	,, 7-0-0	2nd Ayah	,, 6-0-0
2nd Khidmatgar	,, 6-0-0	Durzi	,, 8-0-0
Cook	,, 8-0-0	Bhisti	,, 5-0-0
2nd Cook	,, 4-0-0	Two Punkah Men	,, 6-0-0
Masalchi	,, 5-0-0	Two do. (half month)	,, 3-0-0
Four Bearers	,, 16-0-0	Fowl Keeper	,, 4-0-0
Syce	,, 5-0-0	Dhobi	,, 12-0-0
2nd Syce	,, 4-0-0	Mali	,, 4-0-0
Two Grass-cuts	,, 6-0-0	Two Bearers (half April)	,, 4-0-0
Sweeper	,, 6-0-0		
		Total Rs.	127-0-0

1858.

On the 3rd September 1858, it was directed that all young officers should thereafter be required to do duty with a European Regiment for a period of six months before being permitted to join a Native Corps. Also that the command of a Native Regiment should not thereafter be permitted to be exercised by any Officer not considered qualified for such command by temper and tact, and by regard for the Natives, as well as by experience in the service. The principle of selection for all regimental commands, European or Native, was to be strictly applied in future.

On the 8th February 1858, similar resolutions were passed by the House of Lords and the House of Commons, of which the following is an extract:—

" That this House doth highly approve and acknowledge the high courage, the devoted loyalty, and the brilliant services of the Non-Commissioned Officers and Men of Her Majesty's Military and Naval Forces; of the European Troops in the service of the Honourable East India Company; and of the great body of those Native Corps throughout India who have remained faithful to their standards; and that the same be signified to them by the Commanders of the several Corps, who are desired to thank them for their gallant behaviour."

On the 21st September 1858, it was notified that appointment to the command of regiments would be strictly by selection.

On the 18th December 1858, knapsacks were finally abolished throughout the army (*vide* 1854).

1859.

On the 18th November 1859, an issue was made of an additional ammunition pouch, to be worn on the waist-belt.

The following is an extract from a Despatch from the Secretary of State for India, dated the 19th August 1859:—

"The Commander-in-Chief's Minute contains only a slight sketch of the important services which have been rendered by the Madras Army during the great contest in the North of India. It will be remembered in England that the first thing which encouraged us to take heart was the exhibition on the part of the Commanding Officer of the 1st Madras Fusiliers of a determination not to be put down by any obstacle. That Regiment turned the tide of events in the valley of the Ganges, in our favour. Throughout that death struggle, the Madras Army was our main Indian reserve. But the *great fact* has been the perfect fidelity of that Army, and the perfect loyalty of the twenty-three millions of persons, who inhabit this Presidency which enabled the resources of the South of India to be freely put forth in support of our hard-pressed countrymen in the North."

1860.

On the 3rd January 1860, the establishment was reduced to 700 Privates.

On the 26th October following, a further reduction was made, the establishment being now fixed at:—8 Subadars; 8 Jemadars; 41 Havildars; 40 Naigues; 600 Privates; 16 Drummers and Fifers; 24 Recruit Boys; 32 Pension Boys; 8 Puckallies; 1 Moonshee; 1 Armourer Maistry: 1 Assistant Armourer; 1 Chuckler; 1 Bellows Boy; 1 Chowdry; 2 Regimental Peons; 1 Second Tindal; 10 Lascars; 2 Toties.

The station in the Nilgiris now known as Wellington was so named by order of the Government of Madras in April 1860, its former name having been Jackatalla.

1861.

On the 10th April 1861, *the Indian Staff Corps* was inaugurated by a warrant for the formation of a Staff Corps in each Presidency, which was published by the Governor-General.

All officers of the Indian Army, under the substantive rank of Colonel, then holding staff appointments, were allowed the option of joining the Corps or of continuing to hold their appointments without joining it. Officers of the Indian Army not on the staff (but who had previously been permanently on it), were also eligible. Officers of the British Army in staff employ were allowed the option of transferring to the Corps. Officers who had held their staff appointments for less than one year were not to be permanently transferred unless they possessed certain qualifications to be specified hereafter. The option of joining was restricted to officers considered to be in all respects fit for it. Ensigns permanently appointed to the Corps were to have the rank of Lieutenant. Officers of 12 years' service of which 4 had been on the staff, were to be Captains. Those of 20 years' service, including 6 years on the staff, were to be Major, and those of 26 years' service, with 8 on the staff, to be Lieutenant-Colonels. Five years' service in the Corps as Lieutenant-Colonel entitled an officer too the brevet rank of Colonel, but the substantive rank of Colonel did not exist in the Corps.

Officers who were not qualified by previous employment on the staff having complained that this was an infringement of their rights, the Secretary of State announced, on the 6th August 1866, that officers of the old cadres of cavalry and infantry were at liberty to enter the Corps without any qualifying period of service on the staff and without having to pass any test.

On the 26th January 1861, it was decided to reduce the military establishment in Burma, and the troops were consequently withdrawn from all the minor stations in the Pegu and Tenasserim Provinces, thus reducing the military stations to Rangoon, Moulmein, Tonghoo and Thyetmyo.

On the 10th April 1861, the European Regiments of Her Majesty's Indian Forces were transferred to the list of regiments of the line, *viz.*:—

The 101st Regiment of Foot	(Royal Bengal Fusiliers).
102nd " " "	(Royal Madras Fusiliers).
103rd " " "	(Royal Bombay Fusiliers).
104th " " "	(Bengal Fusiliers).
105th " " "	(Madras Light Infantry).
106th " " "	(Bombay Light Infantry).
107th " " "	(Bengal Infantry).
108th " " "	(Madras Infantry).
109th " " "	(Bombay Infantry).

On the 3rd May 1861 the Governor-General fixed a uniform strength for Native Infantry Battalions throughout India. These were in future to consist of 8 companies each with 1 Subadar, 1 Jemadar, 5 Havildars, 5 Naicks, 2 Drummers and 75 Privates—a total for the battalion of 712 of all ranks.

At the same time the establishment of Native Infantry Battalions was fixed as follows:—

Under the Government of India	12	Battalions.
Bengal Army (including all Sikh and Punjab Regiments)	60	"
Madras Army	52	"
Pegu Sapper Battalion (temporary).	1	"
Bombay Army	30	"
Total	155	Battalions.

On the 13th November 1861, it was ruled by Government that soldiers of the Native Army who, with the permission of their Commanding Officers, accepted employment in the Police after having served as soldiers the prescribed period for military pension, should continue to be borne on the rolls of their respective Corps (as supernumeraries, so as to enable promotion to be made in their room if necessary) and returned as *"On Command Police."* The military pay of such men was to be included in their civil salaries, and the whole to be debitable to the Police. By this arrangement, the men were to retain their right to military pension when declared unfit for further military service and were liable to be remanded to their regiments for misconduct.

On the 23rd November 1861, Fife-Major George Johnston, 4th N. I., was awarded a silver medal for meritorious conduct since enlistment, with a gratuity equivalent to £10 payable on discharge, in addition to ordinary pension.

On the 16th December 1861, the Commander-in-Chief gave permission for pensioners to reside and draw their pensions with the regiment to which they belonged or with any regiment with which they had near relatives serving. They were only, however, to be allowed to reside in the lines by permission of the Commanding Officer.

1862.

On the 29th January 1862, orders were issued for the disbandment of eight of the fifty-two regiments of Madras Native Infantry on the 31st March following, and accordingly the 45th, 46th, 47th, 48th, 49th, 50th, 51st and 52nd M. N. I. were broken up on that date. (On this occasion, the following ranks were transferred from the 52nd M. N. I. to the 4th M. N. I.:—2 Jemadars, 4 Havildars, 13 Naigues, 2 Buglers, 112 Privates, 5 Recruit Boys and 8 Pension Boys).

On the 1st March 1862, the introduction of a new head-dress, consisting of a plain native turban of muslin or cloth, was sanctioned. It was left to the discretion of Commanding Officers to introduce it or not. In consequence, the 4th M. N. I. now wore crimson muslin turbans, in lieu of the old basket-work "pugree," those of the Native Officers being of finer cloth, with gold thread border and ends.

On the 26th April 1862, the Station Hospitals at Chicacole, Vizianagram, and Samulcotta were abolished.

On the 21st October 1862, the establishment of artificers in every regiment was abolished, and the Armourer Maistry, Assistant-Armourer, Chuckler, and Bellows Boy were consequently discontinued.

1863.

From July 1863, the wearing of sandals was discontinued, and shoes were introduced in their place.

1864.

On the 29th April 1864, it was ordered that sepoys should be eligible for the 1st rate of good-conduct pay after six, and the 2nd rate after ten years' service.

On the 30th April 1864, it was decided to reduce the strength of the Army by four battalions. The 42nd, 43rd and 44th N. I. were accordingly selected for disbandment as being the junior regiments in the Infantry, and the 18th N.I. was selected as the fourth battalion owing to a series of robberies, which revealed that several gangs of thieves were serving in it, a large number of men, from the Subadar-Major downwards, being implicated.

A draft of 5 Havildars, 2 Naigues, and 41 Privates was sent to the 4th from the disbanded 44th N. I. on the 1st July 1864.

On the 20th May 1864, 54 N.C.O.'s and men of the regiment were transferred to the pension establishment, including the Fife-Major, William Brailey.

On the 7th October 1864, the following General Order was issued:—

"Native Infantry—No. 91 —In assimilation with the orders in Her Majesty's British Forces, the Grenadier and Light Companies of Native Infantry Regiments will be discontinued, and the Companies will be numbered from 1 to 8 inclusive.

The several Companies will stand on parade habitually, according to the seniority of the Captains, or Officers Commanding them, from flank to centre, viz., the senior Captain on the right, next senior on the left and so on."

1865.

On the 26th January 1865, Government sanctioned the adoption by officers of Native Infantry Corps of the Red Serge Frock, which was to have the facings of the regiment, with badges of rank on the collar, Field Officers being distinguished by a row of gold braid at top and bottom, and company officers wearing the braid at the top only. Whenever worn, the sash was to be worn with it.

In February 1865, the regiment was issued with the new Enfield pattern muskets.

An order dated the 5th July 1865, sanctioned the issue of "Azemar's Silent Drums" to Native Regiments, at the rate of one per two companies. I regret that I am unable to explain what manner of drums these were.

On the 1st November 1865 a further reorganisation took place, the establishment of officers, and their staff pay, being fixed as follows:—

Commandant	Rs.	600.
Senior Wing Commander	„	270.
Junior Wing Commander	„	230.
Adjutant	„	200.
Quartermaster	„	150.
Doing Duty Officers (2)	„	100.

Each Wing Commander was allowed Rs. 80 in addition, for repair and upkeep of arms and equipment, and the Adjutant was granted an office allowance of Rs. 50. Every officer was to maintain a charger.

There was a Medical Officer with each regiment in addition to the above.

1866.

On the 18th January 1866, red fez-caps were introduced for ordinary wear, the red turbans being reserved for inspections and full-dress.

On the 23rd January 1866, the following memorandum was issued from Fort St. George:—

"The Commander-in-Chief sanctions Officers appearing in plain clothes at the Band or other places of public resort; but this indulgence will be withdrawn should Officers abuse it by wearing Shooting Jackets or Wide-awake Hats.
2. When Officers appear in Uniform, Swords are invariably to be worn.
3. This Memorandum does not cancel the existing order regarding Officers attending the *Morning* Service on Sundays in Uniform."

On the 27th March 1866, it was directed that officers of the Madras Army should thereafter be required to pass a test in Tamil, Telugu or Canarese, in addition to qualifying in Hindustani. The second language in the other Presidencies was Hindi.

On the 2nd June 1866, buff leather cap pouches were introduced instead of the cap pockets hitherto in use.

1867.

On the 5th February 1867, camp colours were introduced, which were to be of the same colour as the regimental facings.

On the 14th May 1867, it was announced that H. M. the Queen had approved of a proposal to substitute a Royal Crown on the Colours of Regiments of Native Infantry for the Lion and Crown—the crest of the East India Company. The alteration was to be made as demands for new colours were received.

1868.

New rules for furlough and leave were issued on the 1st July 1868, and these were again revised on the 1st December.

On the 7th August 1868, revised scales of daily working pay were sanctioned for Native troops, *viz.*:—Subadars, 8 annas; Jemadars, 6 annas; N.C.O.s and Rank and File, 2 annas. European Officers of Native Regiments, except the Sappers and Miners, under the grade of Field Officer, were to be paid:—Captains, Rs. 3; Subalterns, Rs. 2 *per diem*.

On the 11th September 1868, pack cloths were introduced, to contain the men's marching kit.

On the 9th December 1868, the "20 Rounds pouches" were abolished, and buff-leather "Ball Bags" introduced.

1869.

On the 5th February 1869, the white "trowsers", worn by the Native ranks in full dress, were abolished, and on the 26th October following, the red turban was discontinued as an article of head-dress, and the red fez-cap ordered to be worn as the one article of head-dress on all occasions in uniform.

Lieutenant-General E. F. Burton, in his book entitled *"An Indian Olio,"* writes as follows about the *taboots* or *taziahs* carried in procession at the Moharram festival:—

"The 4th Regiment Native Infantry, of which I had command in 1869, was specially noted for the beauty and elaboration of its *taboots*, and there being in that year a "Soldiers' Exhibition" at Madras, I induced the Mahomedans of the regiment to prepare a small one for exhibition, which they did, and it was sent to Madras, packed in several pieces in boxes, under charge of four of the best workmen in that particular way of the regiment. The result at Madras is shown in the subjoined extract from a Madras newspaper:—

'Madras, November 30, 1869.

'In the centre of the gallery, above the dais, was a wonderful, beautiful and characteristic specimen of native workmanship. It is a *taboot* worked in paper, silver and talc by the men of the 4th Regiment. It is about seven feet in height, and four in diameter at the bottom. It is a perfect marvel of delicate workmanship, and is also a marvel of land-carriage, for it was brought all the way from Hyderabad.

'Class XV.

'Miscellaneous Articles: First prize, the taboot of the 4th Regiment Native Infantry, forty rupees.'

So highly was this taboot or tazeeah thought of at Madras, that, there being a similar exhibition the next year at Meean Meer, in the Punjab, at which H. R. H. the Duke of Edinburgh would be present, I was directed to have it repacked and sent with its custodians by sea to Calcutta, and thence by rail to Meean Meer, which was done, and it was exhibited with great success, carrying off a prize of 100 rupees. The havildar in charge of the party was greatly delighted with the praise which was bestowed upon the work. He said, 'The Shahzada (Queen's son) examined it for a long time, and not only so but came back again after he had made the round of the exhibition, and examined it again.'

After exhibition the taboot was bestowed upon a fraternity of fakeers at Meean Meer, to be used by them, if they so pleased, at the next year's Mahorum. The two prizes were divided among the men (about a dozen) who had worked at it; the expenses, which, though carriage had been paid by Government, were over £12, were paid regimentally."

1871.

On the 5th September 1871, new pattern Colours were issued to the regiment.

General Burton writes as follows concerning an experiment made by him with regard to the footwear of the men of the regiment:—

"In 1871 I had command of the 4th Native Infantry at Secunderabad, and the route having been received for Bellary, one wing was marched under my Second-in-Command, and wore the regulation boots, when they started. Before they had made three marches the number of men "excused boots" by the Surgeon amounted to thirty daily, out of about 350 men, and increased to nearly double that number before they arrived at Bellary. Two-thirds, perhaps, of the boots were furnished by native contractors at Secunderabad; the remainder were "ammunition" boots, always to be bought in the bazaars of a large station where there is a strong British force.

I had obtained from a friend who had been in Afghanistan a pair of Afghan sandals, which have no toe-ring, but a strap coming from the hind part of the sandal and fastened over the ankle with a small buckle; also, instead of the hard piece of leather over the instep, an arrangement of soft plaited leathern straps. The front part of the sole was well turned up, so as to protect the toes from injury by thorns or stones.

This sandal was so pleasant and comfortable in wear that my friend used to put them on when he was out shooting; and having myself tried them, and become convinced of their advantages, I showed them to my regiment, and had them worn by some of the men at different times on parade; and they were so much liked that, as my headquarters wing was not to march for two months to come, I had a pair made up for each man in the wing. I may add that the cost was about one-third of that of boots—a great consideration with the sepoy.

Accordingly my wing marched all provided with these sandals, and there was not one case of sore or cut feet during the whole march!

Moreover, the men could double, and run at full speed also, without any fear of the sandals coming off.

On arrival at Bellary I reported the whole case to the Adjutant-General at Madras, and sent a pair of the sandals, with a request that the regiment might wear these Afghan sandals; I received a curt answer, returning the pattern, to the effect that, as the native army now wore boots, the Commander-in-Chief was not disposed to sanction any other foot-gear; so I gained nothing by my experiment but the satisfaction to feel that one wing of my corps had, for once in their lives, made an exceedingly comfortable march. 'Red-tape' had gained the day, and having considerable experience in office matters, I was in no way surprised or disappointed."

1872.

In 1872, the issue of Enfield rifles to all battalions was commenced. The 4th M.N.I. appear to have received theirs in May and June of this year.

On the 21st May 1872, waterproof kit bags were issued to the regiment.

About June 1872, a plain white tunic was substituted for the braided one hitherto worn.

On the 8th November 1872, it was ordered that pantaloons and high boots should be worn by all mounted officers together with the new-pattern spur.

By an order of the Governor-General in Council, dated 20th December 1872, the India Medal of 1854, with a clasp for *"Looshai"* was granted to all ranks who composed the Looshai Expeditionary Force.

1873.

On the 2nd June 1873, it was ordered that officers of infantry, when wearing the white tunic, should not wear a sash.

On the 22nd July 1873, it was laid down that officers who had retired from the service were to wear evening dress at dinner, when provided with passages on Her Majesty's Indian troop-ships.

1874.

In January 1874, a force consisting of one Cavalry Brigade, one Artillery Brigade, and two Infantry Divisions, was assembled at Bangalore for a camp of exercise, under the orders of H. E. Lieutenant-General (afterwards Field-Marshal) Sir F. P. Haines, K. C. B., the Commander-in-Chief. The regiment, commanded by Colonel W. A. Riach, which was then stationed at Bellary, was in the 1st Brigade (Colonel Knox Gore) of the 2nd Infantry Division (Major-General Blake).

In July 1874, with a view to reducing the excessive number of Field Officers in the Army, a scheme was promulgated, offering special terms for the retirement of 90 officers—40 from Bengal, 30 from Madras, and 20 from Bombay.

1875.

In May 1875, a recruiting party, under the command of Jemadar-Adjutant Syed Cowder, was despatched to Vellore, Krishnagiri and the surrounding country, and obtained 50 recruits.

1877.

On the 1st January 1877, Her Majesty Queen Victoria assumed the title of Empress of India, and a day's pay, including good conduct pay, was granted to every soldier of Her Majesty's army in India.

On the same day, Rs. 30 kit-money was sanctioned for every recruit, Rs. 4 half mounting allowance for every N.C.O., drummer and private, and good-conduct pay of Re. 1, Rs. 2, and Rs. 3 after 3, 9, and 15 years service respectively. Also, the pay of Native Officers was raised as follows:—4 Senior Subadars, Rs. 100; 4 Junior Subadars, Rs. 80; 4 Senior Jemadars, Rs. 50; 4 Junior Jemadars, Rs. 40. The allowance to Subadar-Majors was increased from Rs. 25 to Rs. 50.

The establishment of the Order of British India was increased from 200 to 350 members, of which 53 first-class and 53 second-class went to the Madras Army.

On the 12th March 1877, the pension rules were improved as follows:—

Superior rate after 32, instead of 40 years' service. Higher rates to Native Officers, *viz.*:—Subadar-Major and Subadar, ordinary Rs. 30, superior Rs. 50; Jemadar, ordinary Rs. 15, superior Rs. 25.

During this year Snider rifles were issued to the army.

On the 26th June 1877, the buff-leather accoutrements hitherto worn were abolished, and brown leather "Valise Equipment" introduced instead. The new equipment was not issued to the 4th M.N.I. until the 14th June 1879.

On the 25th September 1877, it was ordered that a cork helmet covered with white cloth, index seams bound with buff-leather at the bottom; and above the peak and going round the helmet a buff-leather band one inch wide, stitched top and bottom; with gilt spike and chin-strap, and with white pugree; should be worn by officers in Review order, Field Day order, and Marching order.

1878.

On the 8th March 1878, it was ordered that General Officers of the Indian Army, who had attained the age of 70 years, should be placed on the retired list, but such officers as were then holding appointments were permitted to complete the period for which they had been appointed.

1879.

In February 1879, exchanges between officers of the Indian Staff Corps and regiments of the line were restricted to subalterns.

In March 1879, a recruiting party, under Jemadar Adam Sherief, was sent to Vellore, Salem, North and South Arcot districts, when eleven recruits were enlisted.

1880.

In January 1880, officers of the British regiments serving in India were admitted as probationers for the Indian Staff Corps, provided that they had served one year with their present regiments, had less than seven years' service, and were under 27 years of age.

1881.

On the 28th February 1881, the Government of Madras requested the Commander-in-Chief to issue orders for one battery of Royal Horse Artillery and one regiment of Native Infantry to be moved from Bangalore to Mysore, to be present at the installation of His Highness the Maharaja, Sri Chamrajendra Wodeyar, G.C.S.I., and to act as the escort of the Right Honourable the Governor, who was to represent the Viceroy on that occasion. The regiment was selected for this duty, and left Bangalore on the 14th March 1881, arriving at Mysore on the 24th, and remaining there till the 28th. During this period, they found the Guards of Honour at the various ceremonies, and in recognition of the duties they had performed, each man of the regiment was presented with a khilat by order of the Maharaja, of a total value of two thousand eight hundred rupees. The regiment arrived at Bangalore again on the 4th April.

In May and September 1881, two recruiting parties, under Jemadar-Adjutant Gopaulsamy, visited the Vellore, Salem, and South Arcot districts, and enlisted 37 men.

By S.G.O. No. 96, dated the 13th September 1881, the 4th M.N.I. was permitted to add the word *"Afghanistan"* to its regimental colour, for service in the campaign of 1879-80. A silver medal was issued for this campaign, with a new ribbon of green with red edges, the medal for the first Afghan War of 1842 having been worn with the "rainbow" ribbon.

On the 20th September 1881, a revised scale of pensions to officers of the Staff Corps was published.

1882.

On the 9th May 1882, the tenure of regimental commands in the case of present incumbents was limited to seven years, or 55 years of age, whichever happened first, but for the future the age was fixed at 52.

Another General Order, of the same date, abolished eight regiments, and fixed the establishment of the remaining thirty-two regiments at 8 companies of 90 privates each, the regiment now consisting of: 8 Subadars; 8 Jemadars; 41 Havildars; 40 Naigues; 16 Drummers; and 720 Privates—a total of 833, all ranks. On this occasion the 4th M.N.I. received two Privates from the 34th M.N.I.; one Private from the 37th M.N.I.; 2 Naigues, 1 Drummer, and 32 Privates from the 38th M.N.I. —these regiments having been broken up.

On the same date, the number of European officers was altered to nine, while good-conduct pay was extended to Havildars and Naigues, of whom the former were to receive Rs. 1, 2, 3 and 4 after 2, 4, 6 and 8 years' service respectively; and the latter, Rs. 1 and 2 after 2 and 4 years' service respectively.

On the 22nd May 1882, the introduction of warm weather mess-dress was ordered.

On the 29th May 1882, the use of the saddle-cloth was discontinued.

On the 18th July 1882, new Royal Warrants were published for the pay, promotion and pension of officers of the Indian Staff Corps.

On the 4th September 1882, the facings of Native regiments were limited to three colours—white, green and yellow. Those of the 4th Regiment of Madras Native Infantry were *yellow*.

In November 1882, a recruiting party, consisting of two N.C.O.s and 10 men under the command of Subadar Moothoosamy, proceeded to Madura, Trichinopoly and Tanjore, and enlisted twenty recruits.

1883.

On the 24th February 1883, a recruiting party consisting of one Naigue and six men under the command of Havildar Ramasamy, visited Madras, Tiruvallur and vicinity, and obtained 47 recruits.

On the 7th May 1883, another party, consisting of two N.C.O.s and eight men under the command of Jemadar Mahomed Beg, proceeded to Ongole, Nellore, Guntur, Ellore and Masulipatam, where they obtained fifteen recruits.

On the 17th May 1883, the old scale of clothing was abolished, and a revised scale sanctioned as follows:—1 serge zouave jacket; 1 pair serge knickerbockers; 1 pair khakee gaiters; 1 khakee blouse; 1 pair khakee knickerbockers and gaiters; 1 khakee turband with band of the colour of the regimental facings and a fringe of the same colour as the turband.

A further order, dated 7th June, laid down the Orders of Dress as:—Review order: Marching order: Field Day order, and Drill order—and also specified the scale of necessaries to be maintained. The regiment obtained sanction from the Adjutant-General to continue wearing its own pattern of turban.

G. O. G. No. 409, dated the 13th June 1883, stated that:—"The Right Honourable the Secretary of State for India having sanctioned the conversion of the 4th Regiment of Madras Native Infantry into a Pioneer Corps, it will in future be styled the *4th Madras Native Infantry (Pioneers.)*"

On the 21st June 1883, the sabretache hitherto worn by infantry officers was abolished.

On the 24th October 1883, sanction was given for 4 men per company, not less than 5 feet 4 inches in height, to be enlisted, provided that they were carpenters or blacksmiths by trade, and in all respects except height perfectly fit for service.

1884.

In January 1884, it was notified that under certain circumstances the period of regimental command might be extended to nine years.

On the 8th July 1884, it was notified that in future all officers who failed to pass for promotion after twenty years' service as wing officer would be removed from regimental employ and placed on general duty.

The conversion of the 4th Madras Native Infantry into Pioneers necessitated certain alterations in their badges:—

I. *Collar Badges* (Cross Felling-axes) to be worn by British officers on the collar in all uniform; and by Native officers on the zouave jacket behind the badges of rank and on the collar of the khaki jacket.

II. *Cap Badges,* to be worn by British officers on forage caps, embroidered in gold, and in metal on helmets, glengharry, and active service and peace manœuvre caps; by Native officers and Rank and File on turbans; by Buglers and Bandsmen on glengharry caps and turbans; and on helmets by British officers, to be in keeping with the Native Ranks, who will wear it on their turbans.

On the 14th February 1884, the regiment, having become Pioneers, was armed with the short Snider rifle.

1885.

After the 1st January 1885, the number of persons admitted to live with a soldier in the regimental lines was limited to two adults, or one adult with his or her unmarried daughters and sons under 16, but discretion was given to Commanding Officers to make exceptions when absolutely necessary. Also, no recruit enlisted after that date was permitted to marry, or, if already married, to reside in the lines, for three years after enlistment. In June 1885, the 52-years' limit was made applicable to Wing Commanders.

The following is extracted from a letter, dated 5th June 1885, from Brigadier-General Godfrey Clerk, Adjutant-General, Madras Army, to the Officer Commanding 4th Regiment of Madras Native Infantry:—

"The 4th being a Pioneer Regiment, is no longer to carry Colors. The Commander-in Chief fully appreciating the sentiment of the regiment, sanctions the retention of the Colors by the regiment as regimental property. The Colors can be lodged in the mess-house."

S. G. O. No. 55 of 1885 ordered that the number of the regiment should be worn by British Officers on the shoulder straps of their khaki coats.

In this year, Drill Havildar Abdur Rahim, with a party of six men, enlisted 22 recruits in the Trichinopoly, Madura and Tinnevelly districts.

It may be noted that, in November 1885, the Belgaum Brigade was transferred from the Bombay to the Madras Army.

From this year, the regimental facings, which had hitherto been shown as *orange,* were described as *yellow,* and remained this colour till 1893 (*q. v.*).

1886.

On the 9th June 1886, a recruiting party, consisting of 2 Naigues and 12 Privates, under the command of Subadar Timiah *Bahadur,* left Trichinopoly and proceeded to the Northern Circars, where 41 recruits were enlisted, the party rejoining on the 9th August 1887.

A second party consisting of one Havildar, one Naigue and 10 Privates under the command of Jemadar Francis, proceeded to Bangalore, Vellore, Madras and its vicinity on the 8th September 1886, rejoining the regiment on the 31st January 1887, after obtaining 19 recruits.

On the 16th July 1886, the Commander-in-Chief directed that brass numerals, showing the number of the regiment, should be worn on the shoulder straps by Non-Commissioned Officers and men in regiments of Madras Infantry in their khaki as well as in cloth uniform.

In October 1886, the linked-battalion system was introduced, the 30 Infantry regiments being linked in threes, and the two Pioneer regiments together.

At the same time the periods of service for the second and third rates of good-conduct pay were reduced to 6 and 10 years. Also, the pay of Native Officers was re-arranged as follows:—

Two Subadars	Rs. 100 *per mensem*.	
Two Subadars	,, 80 ,,	Subadar-Major's allowance extra.
Four Subadars	,, 67 ,,	
Four Jemadars	,, 35 ,,	
Four Jemadars	,, 30 ,,	

Recruits enlisted elsewhere than at Headquarters were allowed pay from date of enlistment and free passage. Free conveyance by rail was granted to all Native Officers and men proceeding on furlough. The invalid pension after 15 years' service was abolished for all soldiers enlisted after 21 years. The superior rate of pension was to be continued.

1887.

From 1st January 1887, the annual half-mounting allowance was raised from four rupees to five rupees.

On the 14th February 1887, a recruiting party consisting of one Havildar, one Naigue and 14 privates, under the command of Subadar Ramasamy, proceeded to Bangalore, Vellore and Madras, rejoining the regiment on the 24th May 1888, in which period they enlisted 103 recruits.

On the 1st April 1887, the Reserve was organised.

On the 6th June 1887, another recruiting party, consisting of two Naigues and 10 Privates, under Subadar Gholam Husain, was sent to Madura, Tanjore and Tinnevelly districts, and obtained 24 recruits.

1888.

In this year 4 extra Artificer Non-Commissioned Officers were sanctioned, four Privates being reduced.

On the 25th May 1888, Subadar Tiruvengadam *Bahadur* relieved Subadar Gholam Husain on recruiting duty, and obtained 34 recruits.

On the 31st May 1888, the Adjutant-General sanctioned the issue of Martini-Henry Rifles in lieu of the short Sniders: these rifles were accordingly issued to the 4th Pioneers on the 4th September 1888.

1889.

The following General Order by the Government of India was published on the 26th April 1889:—

No. 378. The Most Honorable the Governor-General in Council has much satisfaction in notifying that Her Majesty the Queen-Empress has been graciously pleased to sanction the undernoted words being inscribed on the colors and appointments of the Corps named, in commemoration of their services during the Campaigns in the Carnatic and Mysore in 1780—84 and 1790—92:—

I. For Services during the Campaign of 1780-84, the word

"*Carnatic.*"

The 2nd Madras Lancers.

The Madras Sappers and Miners (Queen's Own).

The 1st, 2nd, 3rd, 4th, 5th, 6th, 7th, 8th, 9th, 10th, 12th, 13th, 14th, 15th, 16th, 17th, 19th and 20th Regiments of Madras Infantry.

II. For Services at the Battle of Sholinghur, on the 27th September 1781, the word

"*Sholinghur.*"

The 2nd Madras Lancers.

The Madras Sappers and Miners (Queen's Own).

The 3rd, 4th, 5th, 6th, 8th, 9th, 12th, 13th, 14th, 15th, 16th, 17th and 19th Regiments of Madras Infantry.

III. For Services during the Campaigns in Mysore, in 1790-92, the word

"*Mysore.*"

The 1st and 2nd Madras Lancers.

The 3rd and 4th Madras Cavalry.

The Madras Sappers and Miners (Queen's Own).

The 1st, 2nd, 3rd, 4th, 5th, 6th, 7th, 9th, 10th, 13th, 14th, 15th, 16th, 19th, 20th, 21st and 22nd Regiments of Madras Infantry.

1891.

On the 17th June 1891, Subadar Peddannah proceeded to Vellore and Madras and enlisted ten recruits, and Naigue Gangadaram enlisted 16 recruits at Bangalore.

From the 2nd November 1891 to the 22nd June 1892, while the regiment was in the Chin Hills, Subadar Solapuri enlisted 31 recruits at Family Headquarters in Bangalore.

In 1891, a third Madras Pioneer battalion came into existence, the 21st Regiment of Madras Infantry being converted into Pioneers, with the designation 21st Regiment of Madras Infantry (Pioneers).

1892.

S. G. O. No. 17 of 1892 ordered that regiments of Madras Infantry should in future wear brown boots on all occasions, and a subsequent order (No. 23) decided that Havildars of infantry regiments should carry a whistle.

G. O. No. 97 of 1892 prescribes the badges to be worn by the regiment:—

"The number 'IV' surmounted by an elephant and crossed felling-axes, surmounted by a laurel wreath, with names of engagements inscribed, and *Madras Pioneers* on a scroll underneath, the whole surmounted by a crown, shall be worn by all ranks on all head dress; Officers in silver, other ranks in brass."

Between the 4th October 1892 and June 1895, Subadar Abdulla Khan *Bahadur* enlisted 366 recruits from Vellore District and Madras and its vicinity.

1893.

By Adjutant-General's Circular, dated the 5th May 1893, the facings of the 4th Pioneers, which had hitherto been yellow, were altered to *white*.

Between the 5th March and the 24th December 1893, Subadar Ramasami enlisted 144 recruits in the Bellary, Trichinopoly and Tanjore districts.

Between the 13th March and the 18th July, Jemadar Syed Abdullah enlisted nine recruits in Salem district.

Between the 13th March 1893 and the 16th December 1894, Jemadar Harichandra Rao obtained 31 recruits in Chingleput and Tinnevelly districts.

The following General Order by the Government of India was issued on the 13th October 1893:—

"Medals, Burma.

No. 971. The Viceroy and Governor-General in Council has much pleasure in announcing to the Army that Her Majesty the Queen, Empress of India, has been graciously pleased to approve of the grant of the India Medal 1854 with clasps inscribed *Burma 1889-92* and *Lushai 1889-92* respectively, to all troops and followers who were employed in the operations detailed in Appendix A between the dates specified in Column 3 of that appendix. His Excellency the Commander-in-Chief is requested to issue the necessary subsidiary orders for submission of Medal Rolls in accordance with the instructions given in the War Office Army Order No. 154 of 1893."

Appendix A.

Name of Expedition or Column.	Clasps.	Dates of Operation.
Baungshe Column, Major R. H. Gunning, 4th Battalion, K. R. R. Commanding.	Burma. 1889-92.	25th December 1891 to 29th Feb. 1892 inclusive.
Lushai Expeditionary Force, under command of Colonel Tregear, 9th Bengal Infantry.	Lushai. 1889-92.	11th January 1889 to 5th May 1889 inclusive.
Operations undertaken to quell a general rising of the E. Lushai Clans, advance of a force under Captain Shakespear in S. Lushai Hills.	Lushai. 1889-92.	16th March to 13th May inclusive.

1894.

S. G. O. No. 26 of 1894 ordered that three small buttons, each half-an-inch in diameter, should be worn on the khaki blouse.

Between the 9th July and the 7th October 1894, Jemadar David enlisted three recruits at Madura.

Between the 31st March and the 31st December 1894, Subadar Abdul Aziz enlisted 97 recruits in Trichinopoly District, and in the same period Havildar Rangasami enlisted 23 men in Madura and Trichinopoly districts.

1895.

During this year there was a considerable amount of discussion as to whether Rifle regiments were to continue the practice of carrying out certain evolutions in ceremonial drill in a manner different to line regiments, for example, marching past with bayonets unfixed, and at the same time it was suggested that Pioneer regiments should preserve the distinctions in performing the manual exercises which had been accorded to them from time immemorial, but no orders were issued regarding Pioneer regiments, which continue to drill in the ordinary manner.

By G. O. C. C. No. 136, dated the 22nd March 1895, it was ordered that:—

"When Wing Officers of Native Infantry Regiments are mounted on non-ceremonial parades they will wear breeches or pantaloons with putties, ankle-boots and steel crane-necked jack spurs.

2. They will not wear spurs when dismounted on ceremonial parades in any order.

3. The putties will be of khaki colour when parading in khaki, and of blue colour when parading in red."

By S. G. O. No. 5 of 1895, permission was given for men of 5 feet 4 inches to be enlisted for Infantry, and of 5 feet 3 inches for Sappers and Pioneers, provided they were of exceptionally good physique or expert tradesmen, and at the same time the minimum chest measurement was raised from 32 inches to 33 inches.

Between the 1st August and the 31st December 1895, Jemadar Sriramulu enlisted 64 recruits in Chingleput and North Arcot districts.

Between the 8th and 31st December, Subadar Ramasami enlisted 4 men at Madura.

The third India (General Service) medal was issued in this year, with a ribbon of three green and two red, equal stripes. This medal remained in use till 1908, during which time seven clasps were struck for it.

Between the 1st January and the 28th February, Subadar Abdul Aziz obtained 19 recruits in Trichinopoly District.

From the 1st March to the 25th September, Havildar Rangasami enlisted 34 recruits in Madura District.

From the 7th April to the 31st December, Private No. 3230, Bulagapandayya Devan enlisted ten recruits in Tinnevelly District.

Between the 8th May and the 12th October, Naigue Kesavulu enlisted eleven recruits in Madras District.

The following note on life with the regiment, when at Trichinopoly in 1895, may be of interest to officers of a later generation. It was written by an officer who was serving with the regiment at that time:—

"In 1895, The IV Madras Pioneers were at Trichinopoly. It was organised in two Wings, each with two British Officers. Each Wing had four companies commanded by Native Officers.

The regiment had a name for good shooting. It was armed with the Martini rifle. One of the chief tests of efficiency was the bayonet exercise, which had to be done by the whole battalion at once in a fixed time. Half a minute over or under time meant the difference between a good and bad inspection report.

The regiment did about one hour's parade a day, and for the rest of the day was usually building lines.

A Sepoy's pay was Rs. 9, with a small allowance when the price of rice rose above a certain fixed rate. There were no free rations.

A favourite exercise of the O. C. Station, who was also Commandant, IV Pioneers, was "alarm" pratice. At any hour, usually at night, the alarm would be sounded, and the two regiments which garrisoned the Station raced for the *rendezvous*. The IV Pioneers, having a better intelligence system, through the O. C. Station's butler or otherwise, would arrive first, were praised for their prompt turn-out and marched home, while the unfortunate other battalion, the Wallajabads, was told off for being late.

The Officers' Mess was run in great style. Two guest-nights a week, and many late nights. The Senior Officer would sit long at the table after the wine had been round, and would tell yarns of Afghanistan and how he had outwitted various Generals, etc. Some junior officers would go to sleep at the table, but were not allowed to move till the senior officer rose. A boarded dance-floor was in the mess, which had been brought at great expense from Bangalore, when the regiment marched from there to Trichinopoly.

The Medical Officer was a Parsee, and he was Mess Secretary. A great whist-player, who instructed the last-joined Subaltern in a kindly way. He was a terror to any Sepoy suspected of malingering. His nickname, '20 grains' referred to his favourite remedy.

There were no motors or bicycles. Everyone had a pony or two, and all tried to play polo. There was no hockey, but occasional cricket. There were no married officers with the regiment.

The Subadar-Major—a 'Bahadur' for service in the Chin-Hills—was always in attendance on the Commandant. All the native ranks feared him, and nearly everything in the regiment was done through him. Two other native officers were distinguished for service in the Chin-Hills—one a 'Sirdar Bahadur' and the other a 'Bahadur.'"

1896.

By Madras Command Order No. 342 of 1896, the composition of the regiment was fixed provisionally at:—

1 Company, Muhammadans.

2 Companies, Tamils.

5 Companies, Mixed.

By S. G. O. No. 12 of 1896, the three buttons hitherto worn on the sleeves of the khaki coat were abolished, and it was ordered that the top edge of the flap of the breast pockets in the khaki coat should be on a line one inch below the second button.

Swords of a new pattern were introduced in this year, and also steel scabbards for all mounted officers, while steel spurs were to be worn by mounted officers in all orders except at Levees and at Mess, when brass spurs were to be worn.

Between the 1st January and the 15th June 1896, Jemadar Sriramulu remained on recruiting service, enlisting 116 men in North Arcot, Chingleput, Tanjore and Trichinopoly districts. From the same districts he obtained another 68 men between the 1st August 1896 and the 1st March 1897—altogether a very good record.

Between the 1st January and the 15th June 1896, Subadar Ramasami enlisted 27 recruits in the Madura, Ramnad and Tinnevelly Districts.

1897.

In January 1897, Colonel Porteous, the Commandant, on his departure from the regiment, presented a set of bagpipes to the Indian ranks.

On the 22nd February 1897, the Government of India sanctioned the location of the three Madras Pioneer Regiments at Bangalore, Trichinopoly and Belgaum, Bangalore to remain the regimental centre of the group, and the battalions carrying out a triangular relief every four years.

On the 16th February 1897 (Madras Command Order No. 110), a new scheme of recruiting for Madras Regiments was introduced, the area for recruiting for the three Pioneer Regiments being Tanjore, Madura, Ramnad and Tinnevelly Districts. Captain F. Churchill, 4th Pioneers, was appointed District Recruiting Officer.

In this year 30 recruits were enlisted, in addition to those brought in by Jemadar Sriramulu's party.

By G. O. C. C. No. 470 of 1897, the old pattern mess jacket was abolished, and a new pattern with roll collar, of the same facings as those of the regiment, was introduced. The following description of the new jacket was given in the following year (G. O. C. C. No. 13.) :—

"The following instructions are notified descriptive of the new obligatory pattern mess jacket, with roll collar, prescribed in the first paragraph of G. O. C. C. No. 470 of 1897 —

I. The roll collar is to be faced with cloth of the colour of the facings of the regiment.
II. The roll collar will be trimmed with plain white piping referred to in para 13 of G. O. C. C. No. 697 of 1896.
III. The cuffs of the jacket will be pointed.
IV. No buttons will be worn on any part of the jacket.
V. Badges of rank will be worn on the shoulder straps.
VI. Regimental badges may be worn on the lapels, but uniformity in a corps must be observed.
VII. Medal ribands will be worn commencing on the roll collar, and if numerous, to be continued in the same line on the jacket itself."

1898.

During this year the total number of recruits enlisted was 64.

By G. O. C. C. No. 885 of 1898 it was ordered that a pocket, measuring 5 inches by 4 inches, should be made inside the khaki coat of Native ranks, to contain the Field Service dressing packet.

Madras Command Order No. 639 of 1898 ordered that the Havildar-Major should be supplied with a Webley pistol.

In 1898 and 1899 the regiment had no less than three Indian officers serving, each with the order of British India, 1st class, which probably constituted a record. The officers were :—Subadar-Major Mahomed Salar, *Sirdar Bahadur;* Subadar Abdul Rahim, *Sirdar Bahadur;* and Subadar Abdullah Khan, *Sirdar Bahadur.*

1899.

A memorandum, dated the 28th July 1899, from the Deputy Adjutant-General, Madras Command (No. A/N.T. 11453), fixed the composition of the regiment at :—

2 Companies Muhammadans.

2 Companies Tamils.

4 Companies Mixed.

By Indian Army Circular No. 118 of 1899, the establishment of the Reserve, hitherto fixed at 160, was reduced to 60.

Madras Command Order No. 685 of 1899, ordered that the Recruit and Pension Boy establishment should be reduced by absorption to one-half of its present strength.

In 1899 a total of 91 recruits was enlisted for the regiment.

Although no Indian Sepoy could gain the Queen's South Africa medal (1899-1902) as a combatant, a certain number did so in non-combatant capacities. Havildar Syed Ali of the 4th Madras Pioneers received this medal, having been employed as a Pack Store Havildar with one of the hospitals during the campaign.

1900.

By Indian Army Circular No. 66 of 1900, the Double-Company system was introduced in place of the Wing System.

A Madras Command order (No. 820 of 1900) fixed the composition of the regiment provisionally at:—

- 1 Double Company Muhammadans.
- 2 Double Companies Tamils.
- 1 Double Company Mixed.

In this year 87 recruits were enlisted, and Captain N. M. C. Stevens, 21st Madras Pioneers, was appointed Recruiting Officer.

1901.

Madras Command Order No. 268 of 1901 announced that, "The Government of India have sanctioned the proposal that the appointment of Havildar-Major in Madras Infantry Regiments be abolished, with effect from the 1st April 1901."

Madras Command Order No. 483 of 1901 ordered that Native corps should not wear coloured kullahs, puggris and putties on Field Service or at manœuvres, but it was left optional with corps to wear these articles on all other occasions.

By Indian Army Circular No. 97 of 1901, one Double Company Officer was added to the permanent establishment.

Madras Command Order No. 549 of 1901 ordered that sashes should be worn by Havildars in khaki, in Drill Order and on duty generally. Madras Command Order No. 806 of 1901 directed that the *Old Stewart* tartan should be worn by pipers.

By G. O. C. C. No. 795 of 1901, it was directed that swords should not be worn by officers at musketry or field training, and that officers should carry carbines instead of swords at field manœuvres and on Field Service.

In this year 82 recruits were enlisted.

1902.

In January 1902 the regiment was re-armed with Lee-Metford rifles.

By G. O. C. C. No. 764, dated 10th October 1902, waist sashes were introduced for British Officers in place of shoulder sashes.

The number of recruits enlisted in 1902 was 100.

The following is a speech made by Lieutenant-General Sir George Wolseley, K. C. B., Commanding the Forces, Madras, at a parade of all the troops in Bangalore on the 17th July 1902, on the occasion of presenting his challenge shield to the 4th Madras Pioneers :—

'General MacCall, I have asked you to have this parade that I might have the pleasure of presenting in the presence of your Garrison, the shield, which I offer annually for competition amongst all the Native Corps in the Madras Command.

It has been won now in two annual competitions by the 4th Madras Pioneers, and in accordance with terms of the competition, has thus become the property of that gallant and distinguished Corps. And I trust that with the many other shooting trophies of that battalion, it may prove an incentive to others in future years, to maintain that standard of excellence to which the 4th Pioneers have now attained.

Owing to my lengthy tour in Burmah this year, I was unfortunately unable to be present on the day on which the competition was held, but I am informed by Major Bagnall, D.A.A.G. for Musketry in this Command, who superintended the contest, that the shooting of the 4th Pioneers, not only for the prize in question, but throughout the whole course of practical musketry for which the regiment was out in camp, was about the best he has ever seen.

Bearing in mind that you have won this shield two years out of the three that you have competed for it, that on the 3rd occasion you were second, and that this year you have won the prize given by His Excellency the Commander-in-Chief for competition amongst the whole of the Native Army in India, I think I may fairly congratulate you, my gallant comrades of the 4th Madras Pioneers, on having proved yourselves to be the best shooting battalion in His Majesty's Indian Army.

I wish to take this opportunity of telling you that this last year three Madras Regiments headed the list for H. E. the Commander-in-Chief's Prize. First came the 4th Pioneers, then the 1st Madras Lancers (who won my challenge shield in 1900) and then the 6th Madras Infantry, quartered at Nowgong. And in the contest for His Excellency's Prize to British troops, the Royal Warwickshire Regiment won that Prize, and was second for the challenge shield contested for by British troops in this Presidency.

I draw your attention to these facts because the conditions for H. E. the Commander-in-Chief's Prizes differ materially from those enforced for my challenge shield, thus, in my opinion proving that good shooting, is good shooting, whatever form the competition may take. There are, I know, some who still think that contests of this nature are no criterion as to the general shooting power of a Regiment, but experience, I think, goes to prove the contrary, as do these facts which I have just mentioned. The Commandant of a good shooting regiment is always able to produce a good team for any competition, but a really good team from a bad shooting regiment is unknown.

I am presenting a new challenge shield* for the ensuing year, and I only trust it will be contested for as keenly as has been the case hitherto, and that the best regiment may win it—as I know has been the case this past year.

Major Holloway, I have now the pleasure of presenting to you and your battalion this shield, and with it my warmest congratulations on having won it and my best wishes for the continued well-being of the gallant 4th Pioneers."

1903.

The number of recruits enlisted in the regiment in 1903 was 261.

Orders were issued by Madras Command that Pioneer regiments were to drill in every respect as ordinary infantry, the reason for this being that it had been suggested that they should adopt the drill of Rifle regiments.

On the 26th November 1903, a waterproof cape and warm drab serge coat were authorised, in place of the great-coat, for native ranks, and issued to the regiment as great-coats were worn out, commencing from April 1904.

On the 14th December 1903, the Regimental Centre, which had been transferred from Bangalore to Belgaum on the 1st February 1903, was again transferred from Belgaum to Trichinopoly.

On the same date, the composition of the regiment was fixed at 2 companies of Pariahs and Christians, 4 companies of Tamils, and 2 companies of Madras Musalmans. Double Companies were formed as follows:—

No. 1 (A and H Companies). Musalmans.
No. 2. (B and G Companies). Tamils.
No. 3. (C and F Companies). Tamils.
No. 4. (D and E Companies). Pariahs and Christians.

1904.

During this year, 156 recruits were enlisted for the regiment.

In January 1904, two Maxim machine guns were issued to the regiment, and 12 mules for these were received in April 1904.

On the 15th February 1904, the establishment of British Officers was raised to 12 (exclusive of the Medical Officer).

On the 26th April 1904, waist sashes were introduced for Native Officers in place of Shoulder Sashes.

---

*The new shield was again won by the 4th Pioneers and, on the retirement of Sir George Wolseley to England, was presented by him to the regiment as its permanent property. Sir George Wolseley was a brother of Field-Marshal Lord Wolseley.

In April 1904, 30 mules, for the carriage of Pioneer Equipment, were received from the Supply and Transport Corps, but were returned in September 1905.

In this year, the composition of Tamil companies was fixed as follows:—

(a) Two companies of the following, viz.—Agamudaiyan, Ambalakaran, Ilamagan, Kallan, Maravan, Vedan.

(b) Two companies of the following, viz.—Kammalan,* Kavarai, Lambadi,* Odde, Pallan,* Shanan,* Vanniyan or Palli, Vellala.

Native Christians were to be kept in one company, and 2 Chakkiliyan (shoe-makers) were to be enlisted for each company.

1905.

In this year, 86 recruits were enlisted for the regiment and, with effect from the 1st April, kit money was raised from Rs. 30 to Rs. 40.

On the 16th June 1905, the system of Artificers in Pioneer regiments was changed, and it was ordered that these should be sepoys, 16 in number.

On the 7th August 1905, Tindals and lascars were abolished, and the establishment of Naicks was raised from 40 to 46, a corresponding reduction being made in the number of sepoys.

On the 25th August 1905, new rates of clothing were introduced.

In December 1905, a new pattern of Pioneer Equipment (1905-Bandolier) was authorised, but was not actually issued to the regiment until August 1910.

1906.

In this year, 188 recruits were enlisted for the regiment, of whom over 100 were brought in by Subadar Sayyid Abbas from the Madura, Vellore, Salem and Trichinopoly districts.

On the 27th February 1906, the gradual adoption of the universal pattern of scarlet serge blouse for native infantry was sanctioned, in place of the red zouave jacket hitherto worn, for all regiments of the late Madras Command.

On the 9th April 1906, the designation of Drill Havildars of native infantry was changed to Havildar-Major.

---

* Limited to a maximum of 5 *per cent*.

On the 8th May 1906, an increase of 80 men (10 *per* company) in the strength of the regiment was authorised, thus raising it to a total of 912 of all ranks, and on the 24th September, the establishment of British Officers was increased from 12 to 13.

With effect from the 1st October 1906, kit money was raised from Rs. 40 to Rs. 60.

The following is an extract from a letter written by General Sir Archibald Hunter, G.O.C., Western Command, in 1906:—

"I have no fear that Madrasis would not do well on service, and I instance the case of the Madras Sappers and Miners in support of my belief in the capacity of this class of soldiers as specialists."

1907—1909.

The number of recruits enlisted for the regiment in these three years was 139, 117 and 144 respectively.

In 1908, the strength of the Reserve was raised from 70 to 90.

On the 16th February 1909, the establishment of British Officers was again raised from 13 to 14.

With effect from the 1st April 1909, the establishments of Recruit Boys and Pension Boys were abolished. The Recruit Boys wore the uniform of the regiment and were drilled and looked after by the Boy Havildar-Major. They were always smartly turned out and were very useful as orderlies and messengers. As a general rule, they enlisted in the regiment as soon as they were old enough.

On the 7th April 1909, it was ordered that British Officers should in future wear the khaki coat with an open collar, a white or khaki collar with a black tie being worn round the neck. The buttons were to be of brown leather.

On the 26th July 1909, scarlet cloth tunics were introduced for Indian Officers.

On the 20th December 1909, the title of Recruiting Staff Officer was changed to Recruiting Officer, and Recruiting Officers were grouped in one Department, instead of being attached to the Staff of a Division.

1910.

In this year, 91 recruits were enlisted for the regiment, chiefly from the Bangalore, Salem, North Arcot and Tinnevelly districts.

On the 30th May 1910, the appointment of Recruiting Officer for Madrasi Hindus and Christians was abolished, and his duties added to those of the Recruiting Officer for Madrasi Musalmans, with the title of Recruiting Officer for Madrasi Musalmans, Hindus and Christians. Captain C. V. Ommanney, 75th Carnatic Infantry, was given the appointment, with effect from the 17th September 1909.

1911.

In this year, 123 recruits were enlisted for the regiment mainly from the Salem, North Arcot and Bangalore districts.

On the 6th November 1911, the Government of India approved of the introduction of gold-laced slings and sword-knots, and white gloves, as worn by infantry officers of the British service, for use by British Officers of Indian infantry regiments dressed in scarlet, in place of brown leather slings and sword-knots, and brown gloves.

On the 20th November 1911, the adoption by the regiment of white gaiters, in lieu of khaki putties, for wear in review order, was sanctioned by H. E. the Commander-in-Chief, and on the 25th November, sanction was given for the adoption of a dark pagri, also for wear in review order.

1912.

In this year, 141 recruits were enlisted for the regiment, chiefly from the North Arcot, Salem, Tinnevelly and Chingleput districts, with a few locally from Secunderabad.

The following extract from Field Service Regulations (Operations), 1912, gives the accepted *rôle* of Pioneers:—

"In India, a Pioneer battalion forms part of the divisional troops. This battalion can be used if required, to supplement the engineer field companies in their duties. With exper assistance they can also be employed in the alignment of roads, plate-laying, and the repairing and laying of light railways.

In battle, however, Pioneers, being primarily fighting troops, will normally be used as such."

In August 1912, the regiment was re-armed with the Short M.L.E. Mark I rifle.

On the 30th October 1912, the Commanding Officer directed that N.C.O.s should wear whistles tucked under the khaki blouse between the first and second buttons and, when carrying clasp-knives, should wear them in the right-hand skirt pocket of their blouses, the lanyard passing under the belt.

1913.

In this year, 132 recruits were enlisted for the regiment. Captain C.G.M. Plumer, 61st (K.G.O.) Pioneers, was appointed Recruiting Officer, with effect from the 1st September 1913.

On the 3rd March 1913, a free issue of badges for Indian troops was sanctioned as follows:—

(a) A star to the three best sepoys, and to the three best N.C.O.s in each company, for judging distance.

(b) A badge for the best shot among the Havildars and Lance-Havildars in each battalion, and one for the best shot among the Naicks and Sepoys in each battalion.

1914.

In this year, 150 recruits were enlisted for the regiment. On the 2nd November, a payment of Rs. 3 *per* head was sanctioned for each approved recruit.

On the 14th March 1914, the system of keeping regimental accounts was fundamentally altered. Instead of pay-lists and muster-rolls being prepared monthly by the regiment, and submitted to the Divisional Disbursing Officer, the latter was to prepare a pay statement, to be kept corrected up to date by means of copies of all regimental orders affecting pay, which were to be submitted to him weekly. To enable this system to be adopted, the Military Accounts Department was completely re-organised.

On the 30th March 1914, a new pattern of service dress jacket was introduced for officers, cut similarly to a lounge coat, with waist seam and large pockets. At the same time, authority was given for field boots to be worn, in place of ankle boots and leggings, with the proviso that all the officers of a unit must be dressed alike in this respect. A light steel hunting-spur was also introduced in lieu of the steel jack spur: steel chains and black straps to be worn with black boots, and steel chains, brown straps and shields with brown boots.

On the 8th June 1914, it was ordered that, with effect from the 15th June following, the qualifying period of colour service for claiming discharge, or for transfer to the Reserve, which had hitherto been 3 years from date of attestation, should be altered to 4 years from date of enrolment, except in the case of special enlistments (bandsmen, clerks, mochis, etc.).

On the 24th August 1914, it was ordered that, with effect from the 1st September, Indian troops should be granted the option of drawing a money allowance in lieu of an issue of firewood in kind—this was to be a temporary measure for two years, or until further orders.

On the 31st August 1914, the combined establishment was increased by 70 men. From the 1st December 1914, it was ordered that the tenure of appointment of a Subadar-Major of the Indian Army should be limited to 7 years. Should his tenure expire before he had completed 32 years' service, the full pension of Rs. 50 *per mensem* was nevertheless to be granted, as well as the personal allowance of Rs. 50 *per mensem*, if recommended by the G.O.C. Division.

1915.

In this year, 329 recruits were enlisted for the regiment. Captain H. F. Murland was Recruiting Officer for the regiment from April 1915 to January 1916.

On the 27th February 1915, the combined establishment was fixed at 1,125. with a Reserve of 120.

On the 26th April 1915, the establishment was increased by the addition of one Jemadar for every complete 114 men in excess of 912. This promotion was to be permanent. One temporary Havildar and one temporary Naick were also allowed for every complete 20 men in excess of 912.

1916.

In this year, 541 recruits were enlisted for the regiment. Pensioned Subadar-Major Mir Abbas, *Bahadur,* was employed as an Assistant Recruiting Officer from November 1915 to December 1917, and again from July to December 1918.

On the 14th February 1916, the entertainment of the following artificer establishment (as a temporary war measure) was sanctioned for depots of Indian Pioneer regiments, in addition to the 24 artificers authorised for each unit:—

(1) For depots with an establishment of over 450:—Two at Rs. 10; two at Rs. 7; four at Rs. 4-8-0 *per mensem* each.

(2) For depots with an establishment of less than 450:— One at Rs. 10; one at Rs. 7; two at Rs. 4-8-0 *per mensem* each, extra artificer pay.

On the 15th February 1916, the following special allowances were sanctioned for Indian Troops serving overseas with Force "D" in Mesopotamia:—

Subadar-Major	Rs. 20-0 *per mensem.*		Naick	Rs. 3 *per mensem.*
Subadar	,, 15-0 ,,		Sepoy	,, 2 ,,
Jemadar	,, 7-8 ,,		Follower	Re. 1 ,,
Havildar	,, 4-0 ,,			

On the 15th May 1916, it was directed that service dress should be worn by all ranks for all purposes, except in mess order, during the continuance of the war. In mess order, officers in possession of mess dress were to wear it, and other officers service dress. Officers not in possession of mess dress were not required to provide themselves with it.

On the 19th June 1916, it was announced that, owing to the difficulty of obtaining khaki dyes, natural grey putties only would be supplied by the Army Clothing Department during the war, and that this pattern must be accepted by units.

On the 10th July 1916, it was announced that expenditure incurred on account of Pagri fringes and shoulder titles, issued to men of Indian units in the field, would be met by Government.

On the 25th September 1916, it was directed that the term "Double Company," as used in the Indian Army, should be discontinued. Battalions were hereafter to consist of 4 companies (A, B, C and D), and each company to consist of 4 Platoons (numbered 1 to 16 consecutively throughout the battalion). In the lines, each of the two Subadars of a company was to command two platoons; at drill and manœuvre, each platoon was to be commanded by an Indian Officer, either a Subadar or a Jemadar.

On the 9th October 1916, the following Regimental Order was published at Shaikh Saad, regarding the safe custody of rifles:—

"No. 974. In future rifles will not be chained to tent-poles as heretofore, but each man will be responsible for the safe custody of his own rifle. During the day-time such rifles as are not in use may be chained, but not between tattoo and reveille. Double Company Commanders may take any steps they think fit for the safety of their rifles. A narrow trench under each man's bedding is suggested, but other suggestions are invited."

It may be added that the suggestion made above was adopted, with the addition of strips of binding metal laid across the trench over the rifle. It speaks well for the care taken by the men that the regiment never lost a rifle by theft while in Mesopotamia, as everyone who served there can bear testimony to the marvellous skill in stealing of the local Arabs. Nothing—horses, camels, nor even the contents of General Officers' tents—being safe from them.

On the 11th December 1916, by order of the G.O.C. 3rd Corps, the regiment (in Mesopotamia) took over eight Lewis Guns. No one in the regiment had had any experience with this gun, with the exception of 2nd Lieutenants Banister and Fraser, who had just completed a 5-days' course. On the 14th December, the four machine-guns with the regiment were returned to the Ordnance Department.

1917.

In this year, 747 recruits were enlisted for the regiment. On the 16th April, Jemadar Perumal Pillai was granted a sword of honour, and No. 414 Lance-Naick Srinavasan and No. 28 Naick Gurusami were granted parchment certificates or sanads, in recognition of their good work in connection with recruitment during the war.

On the 1st January 1917, free rations on the following scale were granted to all combatant Indian ranks, except when on furlough or leave:—Atta or rice, 1½ lbs.; Dhall, 2 oz.; Ghi, 2 oz.; Potatoes, 2 oz.; Gur, 2 oz.; Salt, ½ oz. A messing allowance of annas 10 *per* man, *per mensem*, was granted in addition.

On the 19th February 1917, Naiks and drivers of equipment mules were granted the *status* of combatants as regards pay, pension, etc.

On the 12th March 1917, the Government grant for Officers' Messes was increased from Rs. 100 to Rs. 125 *per mensem*.

On the 4th June 1917, a bonus of Rs. 50 was sanctioned to each recruit, of which Rs. 10 was to be paid on enlistment, and the balance after the recruit had been passed by the medical officer. At the same time, appointments or promotions were offered as follows, for civilians or those serving :—

    As Jemadar for 100 passed recruits.
    „ Havildar „ 50 „ „
    „ Naick „ 30 „ „

On the 25th July 1917, the war establishment of the regiment was raised to 930 Indian Other Ranks.

With effect from the 4th August 1917, the following revised scale of pensions came into force:—

Rank.	Years' Service.					
	15	18	20	21	24	28
Sepoys	Rs. 5	Rs. 6				
Naicks		Rs. 7				
Havildars		Rs. 9		Rs. 11		
Jemadars			Rs. 24		Rs. 30	
Subadars and Subadar-Majors				Rs. 40	Rs. 45	Rs. 50

Subadar-Majors were to be allowed to retain their personal allowance of Rs. 50 *per mensem* on pension. The "superior" rate of pension was abolished, and new scales of wound, injury and special pensions were introduced.

On the 2nd October 1917, a ration allowance of annas 4 *per diem* was granted to Indian combatants on casual leave, in lieu of free rations.

On the 10th October 1917, eight more Lewis Guns were issued to the regiment, bringing the total on charge up to 16.

On the 22nd October 1917, a new system of clothing was introduced. Kit money was abolished and, with effect from the 1st October, free inital issues of clothing and necessaries were granted. Certain articles were given free on enlistment, and others on attestation.

During November 1917, the regiment exchanged its low-velocity for high-velocity rifles, which were of varying marks—Short L. E., Mark I*, Mark III, and Mark III*.

By the 28th November 1917, the strength of the regiment had risen to 1,128 Indian Other Ranks—much in excess of the War Establishment. This excess was found to put a great strain on tentage, transport, and interior economy in general, because no allowances were made to meet the excess.

1918.

In this year, 1,288 recruits were enlisted for the regiment.

Early in the year, it was directed that, as the grant of the *status* of "combatant" involved the conversion of specified classes from a "follower" service to a "combatant" service, men consenting to change their *status* must be formally discharged, and re-enrolled and attested as "combatants." This formal discharge was conditional on re-enrolment, and was not to affect continuity of service for reckoning continuous service on the active list for pension or gratuity. This procedure was made applicable to Equipment Mule Drivers of Pioneer units.

On the 12th February 1918, sanction was given for the construction of the following additional buildings in regimental lines, as funds became available:—Indian Officers' Club, with furniture; Durbar hall; quarters for mule drivers, standings for mules, etc.

From the 26th March 1918, water pakhals were supplied as a free issue.

On the 3rd April 1918, the regiment was issued with 5 Barr and Stroud range-finders and 24 grenade rifles.

About the same time, orders were given abolishing the practice of saluting with the left hand, and all ranks were directed to salute with the right hand only.

A provisional war establishment for a Pioneer battalion was fixed as follows:—

British Officers, including Medical Officer	13
Indian Officers	19
Warrant Officer	1
N.C.O.s	80
Drummers	16
Sepoys	637
Equipment Mule Drivers	12
Followers (Public 40, Private 33)	73
Horses	14
Pony	1
Mules in regimental charge	50
Mess Transport, animals	3
Attached Transport, Pack Mules	123
,, ,, Camels	67
,, ,, Personnel	68

Total Indians, 753.

The designation of "Colour Havildar" was now abolished and, in their place, 4 Company Havildar-Majors and 4 Company Quartermaster-Havildars were appointed.

A system of Station Hospitals was introduced for Indian troops, instead of the Regimental Hospitals, which had never been properly equipped, and it was announced that officers of the Indian Medical Service and Sub-Assistant Surgeons would no longer be attached to Indian regimental units.

During the spring of 1918, it was decided to raise a number of new regiments of Infantry and Pioneers, and the 64th Pioneers was ordered to provide a complete company, to proceed to the Advanced Base, where the 1/155th Pioneers, of which it was to form part, was to be formed. D Company, which was composed of the Sikhs received from the Sikh Pioneers, was selected for this purpose, and left the regiment on the 19th May, under Major T. B. Skinner, with a strength of 4 Indian officers, 203 Indian other ranks, and 15 followers.

The remaining companies of the regiment were then expanded to four, the war establishment being at the same time raised to 1,070 Indian other ranks. The re-organisation was completed at Hillah on the 26th May, the new organisation being as follows:—

Nos. 1 and 2 Platoons	Paraiyans.
No. 3 Platoon	Christians.
No. 4 Platoon	Paraiyans and Christians.
Nos. 5 to 14 Platoons	Tamils.
Nos. 15 and 16 Platoons	Musalmans.

1919.

In this year, 249 recruits were enlisted for the regiment. A sum of Rs. 2 *per* man was now paid to all recruiters bringing in recruits, to cover their subsistence up to the date of enrolment or rejection by an authorised enrolling officer. All initial bonuses for recruits, and also conveyance allowances, were abolished.

The following scale of war gratuities was granted for war service between the 4th August 1914 and the 3rd August 1919:—

Rank.	Minimum.	Monthly additions after 12 months.	Total Maximum.
Subadar-Majors and Subadars ..	Rs. 60.	Rs. 5.	Rs. 300.
Jemadars	,, 50.	,, 4.	,, 242.
N. C. O.s and Sepoys ..	,, 12.	Re. 1.	,, 60.
Public Followers	,, 8.	As. 8.	,, 32.

The following gilding-metal badges for certain N.C.O.s were introduced in this year:—

Battalion Havildar Major	Royal Arms,
Battalion Quartermaster Havildar	Crown and Wreath.
Company Havildar-Major	Crown.
Company Quartermaster Havildar	Crown and 3-bar chevrons (worsted).

The last-named to be worn on the right upper-arm, the others on the right forearm.

By Army Instruction (India) No. 783 of 1919 (as amended by No. 54 of 1923) the *British War Medal, 1914-19*, was granted to all ranks who served on duty in theatres of war during periods and within spheres defined in Instruction No. 53 of 1923, or who left their places of residence, and rendered approved service overseas, other than the waters dividing the different parts of the United Kingdom, between the 5th August 1914 and the 11th November 1918, both dates inclusive.

By Army Instruction No. 873 of 1919 (as amended by No. 53 of 1923), the *"Victory" Medal* was granted to all ranks who actually served on the establishment of a unit in a theatre of war, and between the periods as defined.

The establishment of British Officers was increased to 16 *per* battalion in this year, *viz.*:—Commandant; 2nd in Command; Adjutant; Quartermaster; 4 Company Commanders; 8 Company Officers.

As already remarked elsewhere, the regiment, while in Persia, maintained its reputation for hygiene and sanitation. On the 16th January 1919, it was visited by the A.D.M.S., Persian Line of Communications, who "seemed very pleased with everything he saw, especially the disinfecting and bathing facilities, and the healthy condition of the men." The entry in the War Diary concludes with the observation that the men had no time to be sick! Again, on the 26th August, Captain Blewitt, Sanitary Officer at Kermanshah, inspected the lines, and pronounced them the best on the whole Line of Communications.

In 1919, it was directed that Lieutenants who, on the date fixed as the termination of the War, had completed:—

3 and under 4 years' service for promotion, would be promoted on completion of 5 years' service.
2 ,, 3 ,, ,, 6 years' service.
1 ,, 2 ,, ,, 7 years' service.
Under one year's service ,, ,, 8 years' service.

The time-scale for promotion from Captain to Major, as introduced in 1917, was to remain in force for two years from the end of the War, when the period of 15 years laid down would be increased by one year. Thereafter this period would be increased by one year triennially until 18 years had been reverted to.

In 1919, revised rates of pay for British Officers were introduced, as follows:—

2nd Lieutenant .. .. Rs. 425.	Major .. .. Rs. 900.
Lieutenant .. .. „ 475.	„ (after 5 years) .. „ 950.
„ (after 7 years) .. „ 550.	Lieutenant-Colonel .. „ 1,150.
Captain .. .. „ 700.	
„ (after 9 years) .. „ 750.	

Exchange compensation allowance was abolished, and the former rates of staff pay were to be continued.

In 1919, a syllabus for the annual training of the personnel of Pioneer battalions in Pioneer duties was published. The object aimed at was to arrive at a high standard of technical training as Pioneers, combined with reasonable efficiency as Infantry.

With effect from the 1st April 1919, new rates of pensions for British Officers were introduced. These pensions were to consist of three parts:—(*a*) Service element, based on total service; (*b*) Rank element; (*c*) Indian element, for service in the Indian Army. The maximum pension for a Lieutenant-Colonel of 29 years service, and 4 years as Lieutenant-Colonel was £800 *per annum*.

1920.

In this year, 167 recruits were enlisted for the regiment.

In 1920, it was directed that an emblem of an oak-leaf in bronze should be worn on the riband of the *"Victory" Medal*, to denote that the wearer had been mentioned in despatches.

The grant of the *India General Service Medal, 1908,* was sanctioned for all ranks who took part in the operations against Afghanistan in 1919, with a clasp *"Afghanistan, North West Frontier, 1919."* In accordance with this order, certain officers, N.C.O.s and men of the regiment, who served with the 61st (K.G.O.) Pioneers in this campaign, became entitled to this medal.

The *1914-15 Star* and *"Victory" Medal* were granted to those who took part in the operations in the Kachin Hills, between the 31st December 1914 and the 28th February 1915. This included all those who were at Myitkyina, or north of that place. In addition, the *British War Medal* was granted to those who were with Major Bliss' column in the attack on Wawang village.

The strength of the Reserve was now fixed at:—Class I, 120; Class II, 80. Service in Class I was to be for not more than 5 years or until the age of 30, and training for Class I was to be carried out for one month every year, and for Class II for one month every alternate year. Class I Reservists were to be paid at the rate of Rs. 6, and Class II Reservists, Rs. 4 *per mensem*. No man was to remain in the Reserve after attaining 35 years of age.

With effect from the 4th August 1920, the pay of Indian ranks was increased as follows:—Subadars, Rs. 10; Jemadars, Rs. 5; N.C.O.'s and Sepoys, Rs. 4—and shortly afterwards, the following revised scales of pension were introduced:—

Rank.	Years' Service.					
	15.	18.	20.	21.	24.	28.
Subadar-Majors and Subadars	(Special) Rs. 45.	..	..	Rs. 55.	Rs. 60.	Rs. 75.
Jemadars	Rs. 25.	..	Rs. 30	..	Rs. 40.	..
Havildars	Rs. 9.	Rs. 12.	..	Rs. 15.	..	..

At an earlier date, it was recorded as noteworthy that the regiment had, in 1898-99, three Indian officers serving, each of whom had the Order of British India, 1st Class.

In 1920, the following five officers were serving, each with the Order of British India, 2nd Class, *viz.*:—Subadar-Major Krishnasami, *Bahadur*; Subadar Nanjappa, *Bahadur*; Subadar Narayanasami (I), *Bahadur*; Subadar Durugayya, *Bahadur*; and Subadar Viraraghavulu, *Bahadur*. In addition, the following officers were in possession of the Indian Distinguished Service Medal, *viz*:—Subadar Gopalsami, I.D.S.M.; Jemadar P. Narayanasami, I.D.S.M.; Jemadar Balagurusami, I.D.S.M.; and Jemadar Arogyasami, I.D.S.M.

With effect from the 1st October 1920, a new system of clothing and kit allowances was introduced. Subadar-Majors and Subadars now drew a consolidated quarterly allowance of Rs. 16-2-0; Jemadars, Rs. 13-2-0; Havildars, Rs. 11-13-0; and other ranks, Rs. 11-4-0.

1921.

In this year, recruiting was stopped, as the regiment was over strength, and was being re-organised. During the year, no fewer than 17 Indian Officers and 922 other ranks left the regiment on demobilisation, discharge, pension or transfer. One Indian Officer and 31 other ranks were received from the Training Battalion, and one Indian Officer and 144 other ranks from the 2/61st (K.G.O.) Pioneers and from Infantry regiments.

Revised rates of Family Pensions were introduced, *viz.*:—Subadar-Majors and Subadars, Rs. 50; Jemadars, Rs. 25; Other ranks, Rs. 8—and children's allowances were also granted, *viz.*:—Indian Officers, Rs. 4; other ranks, Rs. 2, for each child.

Shortly afterwards, the rates of pay for Indian ranks were revised as follows:—

Subadar-Majors, Rs. 200, with a personal allowance of Rs. 50; Subadars, Rs. 130 to Rs. 160; Jemadars, Rs. 75 to Rs. 100; Havildars, Rs. 25; Naicks, Rs. 15; Sepoys, Rs. 16. The rates of good service and good conduct pay were also revised, viz.:—Havildars and Naicks. After 2 years from date of promotion, Rs. 2; after 4 years, Rs. 4. Havildars only. After 6 years from date of promotion to Naick, Rs. 6.

Sepoys—After 2 years, Re. 1; after 4 years, Rs. 2; after 6 years, Rs. 3.

The grant of the *India General Service Medal, 1908,* with clasp *"Waziristan, 1919-21"* was authorised for all ranks who served under the orders of the G.O.C., Waziristan Force on the Takki Zam Line, north of, and including, Jandola, between the 18th December 1919 and the 8th April 1920, both dates inclusive. Certain officers and men of the regiment, who had served with the 2/61st (K.G.O.) Pioneers, were, consequently, granted this medal.

Rates of pay for British Officers were again revised, as follows:—

2nd Lieutenant .. .. Rs. 425.	Captain .. .. Rs. 750.
,, (after 2 years' service) ,, 475.	,, (after 15 years' service) ,, 850.
Lieutenant .. .. .. ,, 475.	Major .. .. .. ,, 950.
,, (after 7 years' service) . ,, 550.	,, (after 5 years as such).. ,, 1,050.
	Lieutenant-Colonel .. .. ,, 1,250.

Religious teachers were sanctioned for each religious class of the strength of not less than a Company, and the establishment of clerks was revised, as follows, contract allowances being henceforth abolished:—One Jemadar Head Clerk; 3 Havildars, 1st Grade; 2 Naicks, 2nd Grade; and 4 Sepoys, 3rd Grade. Grade pay, on a specified scale and in addition to ordinary pay of rank, was granted to these clerks.

A supply of lamps for lines, barracks and married quarters, was also sanctioned.

On the 3rd March 1921, orders were issued for the complete re-organisation of the Indian Army, and the three Madras Pioneer Battalions became one Group of 3 battalions, as shown below:—

1st Indian Pioneer Group.	61st (King George's Own) Pioneers (*1st Battalion*).	1 Company, Tamils.
		1 Company, Telegus.
	64th Pioneers (*2nd Battalion*).	1 Company, Paraiyans and Christians.
	1/81st Pioneers (*Training Battalion*) 2 Companies each:—	1 Platoon, Tamils.
		1 Platoon, Telegus.
		1 Platoon, Paraiyans and Christians.
		1 Platoon, Mixed.

The Regimental Centre, and location of the Training Battalion, were to be at Bangalore. The Training Battalion was to carry out recruiting and the training of recruits, to act as a depot to any Active Battalion proceeding on active service, and to have charge of reservists.

This organisation was brought into force with effect from the 1st October 1921, when Major H. F. Murland, with Subadar Gnanaprakasam and 6 other ranks, was transferred to the Training Battalion for two years, in exchange for Brevet Lieutenant-Colonel G. W. Cochran, D.S.O., with Subadar A. David, I.D.S.M., and 6 other ranks.

Instructions were issued, laying down the role, status and standard of training of Pioneer Regiments in India, viz:—

"Pioneer Regiments form part of the Divisional troops in war, and will be regarded as forming part of the technical troops of the District in which they are located in peace.
The role of these units is primarily that of Pioneers; Infantry duties form their secondary role."

The following establishments for peace and war were laid down in 1921:—

	Peace	War.		Peace	War.
British officers.	12	12	Public Followers.	38	38
Indian officers.	16	15	Private Followers.	..	19
Havildars.	36	34	Riding Horses.	7	7
Paid Lance-Havildars.	3		Ponies.	..	2
Naicks.	35	31	Pack Mules	31	32
Paid Lance-Naicks.	24		Bicycles.	6	6
Sepoys.	670	610			
Buglers.	16	12			
Artificers.		19			
Total Indian Combatants.	800	721			

1922.

In this year, 3 Indian officers and 94 other ranks left the regiment on discharge, pension, etc., and one Indian officer and 75 other ranks were received from the Training Battalion.

On the 31st March 1922, the class composition of the 1st Indian Pioneer Group was altered to 3 companies Tamils, Telegus, Pariyans and Christians (mixed). These were to be mixed in companies and platoons, and the proportion of the several classes to be maintained in future throughout the Group was to be: Tamils, 50 *per cent.*; Telegus, 15 *per cent.*; Paraiyans and Christians, 35 *per cent.*

Deferred pay, at the rate of Rs. *2 per mensem,* was introduced from the 1st April 1922. This was to begin:—

(*i*) In the case of men then in service, from the 1st April.

(*ii*) In the case of men enrolled after that date, from the date they received pay as combatants.

The concession was admissible only if the N.C.O. or soldier had rendered not less than 4 years' service, and was to be payable on discharge, in addition to pension or gratuity earned.

In this year, the system of allotting compassionate allowances to widows was revised and the method of allotting marks was altered. In future, half the annual allotment was to be awarded to widows of Indian officers, and half to widows of Indian other ranks.

Revised rules were also issued for the grant of disability pensions and gratuities to Indian combatants and non-combatants and also for the grant of family pensions. These rules and conditions were very lengthy, and space cannot be found for them here.

By *Gazette of India* Notification No. 1997, dated the 1st December 1922, the title of the battalion was altered to the "2nd Battalion, 1st Madras Pioneers."

1923.

The "Indianisation" of the regiment was announced by the following letter, dated the 6th March 1923, from the Adjutant-General in India:—

"I am directed to invite your attention to a pronouncement that was made in the Legislative Assembly, on February 17th, by His Excellency the Commander-in-Chief, on the subject of the Indianisation of eight units of the Indian Army. After the most careful consideration by His Excellency the Commander-in-Chief, in consultation with the General Officers Commanding-in-Chief, Commands, and with the approval of the Government of India, it has been decided that the Battalion under your Command shall be one of the units in question. Orders posting a certain number of young Indians holding the King's commission will be issued in due course by the Military Secretary, Army Headquarters.

2. The first consideration in selection of units was that they should hold a traditionally high standard of efficiency. It was, moreover, desirable that as many of the classes enlisted in the Indian Army as possible should be represented in the selected units. Enclosed will be found a copy of a statement which will shortly be presented to the Legislative Assembly, which gives full details of the scheme, and the proposed method of carrying it out. It is requested that this may be kept confidential until Monday, the 12th March.

3. The inception of the scheme will be momentous in the history of the Indian Army, and its success or failure is a matter of vital importance to the future of India. For its success the whole-hearted efforts of the young Indians posted to the selected units, and the loyal co-operation of the British Officers who will remain in these units during the period of development, will be above all things essential.

At the same time, great responsibility for the success or failure of this scheme lies in the hands of the Commanding Officer himself. His Excellency the Commander-in-Chief trusts that the Commanding Officer will do all that is in his power to ensure that the proposals of the Government of India are applied with the utmost tact and discrimination and that whilst maintaining the high standard of discipline and efficiency which has always characterised the Regiment, every care is taken to teach and to encourage the young Indians who are appointed.

4. His Excellency the Commander-in-Chief, who has been greatly impressed by the loyal manner in which the recent re-organisation of the Indian Army has been accepted and carried out by its British Officers and Indian ranks, knows that he can rely equally upon all ranks of these specially selected units to do their utmost to make effective and a success this first measure of Indianisation. It is a necessary outcome of the scheme of reformed Government in India, in sanctioning which His Majesty's Government have laid down that the traditional efficiency and reliability of the Indian Army should not be impaired."

The statement presented to the Legislative Assembly is not given here. It contained certain details regarding the number of officers in a regiment, etc., and stated that one Indian Company or Squadron Officer would be posted to each unit in 1923, and one *per annum* thereafter until, at the beginning of 1927, all Company or Squadron Officers of the Indianising units would be Indians. It also pointed out that the earliest date by which the eight units could be completely officered by Indian Officers would be approximately 22 to 23 years from the date of the inception of the scheme (*i.e.*, 1945 or 1946).

The following is a list of the eight units selected for Indianisation:—

Cavalry.
    7th Light Cavalry, late 28th Light Cavalry, Madras.
    16th Light Cavalry, late 27th Light Cavalry, Madras.

Infantry.
    2/1st Madras Pioneers, late 64th Pioneers.
    4/19th Hyderabad Regiment, late 98th Infantry, Hyderabad.
    5th Royal Battalion, 5th Mahratta Light Infantry, late 117th Royal Mahrattas.
    1/7th Rajput Regiment (Q.V.O.L.I.), late 2nd (Q.V.O.) Rajputs.
    1/14th Punjab Regiment, late 19th Punjabis.
    2/1st Punjab Regiment, late 66th Punjabis.

Pensions and gratuities for regimental followers were introduced in 1923.

Alterations in equipment for Pioneer Battalions (active) were made, as follows:—

(1) Light picks and shovels were to be withdrawn and replaced by axes, pick, 6½lbs., and shovels, R. E.

(2) Pioneer equipment, Indian Infantry, pattern 1905, was to be withdrawn, and certain additional items of bandolier equipment, pattern 1903, to be issued, to enable great coats and additional ammunition to be carried on the man. The whole of the bandolier equipment, pattern 1908, was to be replaced eventually by web equipment.

(3) Transport space for the large tools now to be issued, and which would be carried on regimental transport and not on the man, was to be provided by issuing equipment to enable each man to carry his own great-coat, and by transfer of an additional 20 rounds of ammunition, till then carried on the regimental reserve ammunition mules to the person of the man.

The war establishment was again modified, and now consisted of:—13 British Officers (including one attached); 16 Indian Officers; 1 Warrant Officer; 32 Havildars; 20 Artificers; 12 Buglers; 642 rank and file; 39 Public and 23 Private followers; 10 riding horses; 3 riding ponies; 32 pack mules; and 6 bicycles.

The *General Service Medal*, with clasp *"North-West Persia"* was granted to all ranks of "Norper Force," and also to those troops on the lines of communication from Quraitu, who served west of a line drawn north and south through Teheran between the 10th August 1920 and the 31st December 1920, both dates inclusive. The units employed on these operations included the 64th Pioneers.

New quarterly kit and clothing allowances for Indian troops and followers were introduced, with effect from the 1st April 1923.

New periods of enrolment for service as combatants in the Indian Army were fixed as follows:—In Army service, 5 years; in Reserve service, 10 years. But bandsmen, musicians, trumpeters, drummers, buglers, fifers and pipers, school masters, clerks, artificers, armourers, engine-drivers, farriers, carpenters, tailors and boot-makers were to enlist for 10 years in Army service.

The Reserve was once more completely re-organised. Space cannot be found here for the details, but I may mention that each Active Pioneer Battalion was allowed 55 Reservists in Class A (on Rs. 7 *per mensem*) and 100 in Class B (Rs. 4 *per mensem*).

A final revised scale of clothing and necessaries was issued, and a free issue of mosquito nets was sanctioned for troops and followers.

Regulations were issued governing the appointment of Colonels and Colonels-Commandant of units. Each Pioneer Group was to have a Colonel-Commandant, Field Marshals and General Officers not below the rank of Major-General were eligible for the appointment but, to be eligible, must have had some distinguished association with the regiment concerned.

In view of the re-numbering and re-designation, new shoulder-titles—"*1 Pioneers*"—were approved, and it was directed that, in future, collar-badges should be worn by officers only.

In India Army Order No. 923 of 1923, the 2nd Battalion 1st Madras Pioneers was included among Regiments which will not carry colours.

On the 5th September 1923, *Kullahs* were again taken into wear by the battalion, and pagris were tied in the same manner as was done by the 1st and 10th (Training) Battalions of the regiment, with the exception that the *shamla* was worn on the left front, instead of the right front, of the pagri.

On the 30th September 1923, when the peace establishments of Infantry and Pioneer battalions were reduced by 64 men each, 43 men were transferred to Class A Reserve.

1924.

The *Gazette of India* Notification No. 1366, dated the 10th October 1924, published the following extract from the *London Gazette,* dated the 9th September 1924:—

" The King has approved of the following appointments, or relinquishments of appointments, as Colonels-in-Chief of the amalgamated Regiments of the Indian Army:—

H. M. The King to be Colonel-in-Chief of the following Regiments:—

1st Madras Pioneers, in place of the 1st Battalion (King George's Own) Pioneers. "

In 1924, web rifle-slings were re-introduced; a scale of 18 mule water-tanks *per* battalion was laid down; and the following scale of bicycles, *viz.*:—2 for use in peace, 2 for mobilisation equipment, on unit charge, and 2 for issue on mobilisation.

Conditions were laid down, under which war medals were to be granted to authorised public and private followers. Under the terms of these instructions the regimental followers of the battalion became eligible for the British War and Victory medals.

With effect from the 1st April 1924, N.C.O.s and men actually in charge of the regimental equipment mules were granted extra duty pay at the rate of one rupee *per mensem.*

Improved rates of clothing allowance were authorised, *viz.*:—Rs. 12 *per* quarter for Havildars, and Rs. 11-10-0 *per* quarter for Naicks and Sepoys.

New rules for the working pay of artificers were introduced and the term "working pay" was changed to "Pioneer pay". This was to be drawn whenever ordinary pay was drawn, irrespective of the work or duty on which the man might be employed, and artificers were required to pass tests with the Sappers and Miners.

An additional Jemadar was appointed as Education Officer (on the peace establishment). The appointment was to be held for 4 years, and the duties were to be combined with those of Scouts Officer. With effect from the 1st November 1924, the British and Indian Army Schools of Education were amalgamated at Belgaum, the new school being designated "The Army School of Education, India."

It was decided that married accommodation in the lines was to be provided for seven *per cent.* of the total authorised establishment.

It was announced by Army Instruction (India) No. 1024 of 1924, that His Majesty the King had been graciously pleased to command that the *India General Service Medal, 1908,* in silver, with clasp *"Malabar 1921-22"* should be granted to the military forces which took part in the operations in Malabar in 1921 and 1922. The medal and clasp were to be granted to all troops which took part in the operations between the 20th August 1921 and the 25th February 1922, in Malabar, within the area bounded on the west by the sea; on the south by the Ponnani river; on the east by a north and south line from Gudalur to the Ponnani river; and on the north by an east and west line from Gudalur to the sea.

A ration allowance of annas four *per diem* was authorised for water-carriers, with effect from the 1st January 1925; and the following scale of emergency rations was fixed, *viz.*:—Biscuits, or atta, or Chenna chabena (parched gram), 1½ lbs; Sugar, 2 oz.; Tea, ration 4/7 oz. Units were given the option of selection.

1925.

In January 1925, it was directed that the following arms should comprise the equipment of a military officer, for the purposes of section 1 (*b*) of the Indian Arms Act, 1878:—

Officers holding commissions from H. M. the King.

    2 Swords. (One full dress pattern, and the other field-service pattern, when so required by the Dress Regulations for the Army).

    1 Revolver, and (of no special pattern, but must take Government ammunition of
    1 Pistol   ·455 bore).

    1 Dirk.
    1 Skeen Dhu. } (Highland Regiments only).

Officers holding commissions from H. E. the Viceroy.

    2 Swords   (as above)
    1 Revolver (Webley ·455 bore).
    1 Kukri   (Gurkha and Garhwali Regiments only).
    1 Dah   (Burman Regiments only).

This order was subsequently amended so as to permit officers holding commissions from H. M. the King to be in possession of 2 revolvers, or 2 pistols, or 1 revolver and 1 pistol, only one of which need take Government ammunition.

The issue of "Sam Browne" belts was sanctioned for regimental Havildar-Majors of Indian Infantry and Pioneer battalions.

A grant of Rs. 150 *per* battalion was sanctioned for the purchase of maps and instruments considered essential for imparting instruction in map-reading; and also a consolidated annual allowance of Rs. 1,000, to be known as "weapon training allowance," which took the place of musketry prize money and bayonet fighting allowances.

Instructions were issued as to the patterns of boots, leggings and spurs to be worn by officers, and directions given that, in India, the sword frog should only be worn with the "Sam Browne" belt when the sword was worn; also that service dress (drill) was the only service dress an officer of the Indian Army was to be required to provide, the provision of service dress (serge) being optional.

The annual Educational Training grant was fixed at annas 12 *per* man (Indian Officers and Indian other ranks), to be drawn quarterly in advance.

An issue was made of 3 steel helmets *per* battalion, for live grenade practice, also of one horse-clipping machine for each active Pioneer battalion, while tents, to be maintained on unit charge as mobilisation equipment, were issued, as follows:—

    To substantive Lieutenant-Colonels (and above) Tents, I.P. Officers (80 lbs.)
    To other Officers.   Tents, I.P. (40 lbs).

Durries, which hitherto had been public clothing, were henceforth to become the personal property of the soldiers to whom they had been issued.

Under the regimental system, all battalions of a regiment were required to wear the same badges. In order to distinguish one battalion from another, units were directed to wear, on the portion of the pagri just above the fringe, a distinctive coloured cloth band, with or without a metal or worsted number of the battalion. Training battalions were not to wear coloured bands. An allowance of one anna *per* man was sanctioned, to cover the cost. The colours for all regiments were to be as follows:—

1st battalions	Bright red.
2nd "	Orange.
3rd "	Violet.
4th "	Grass Green.
5th "	Navy Blue.
6th "	Black.

The standard length of pagris was fixed at 9 yards, and the standard width 32 inches.

Sanction was accorded in this year for the issue of the *India General Service Medal, 1908,* with clasp *"Waziristan 1921-24,"* to the military forces which took part in the operations in Waziristan between the 21st December 1921 and the 31st March 1924.

Orders were given that in future the term *"Adi-Dravida"* was to be adopted, in substitution for the term *"Paraiyan,"* when referring in official correspondence or publications to the class which had hitherto been known by the latter designation.

In this year, the pensions of officers (with the exception of General Officers) were reduced by 4 *per cent*.

The provision of an explosives magazine, and of a 30 yards range, for each Pioneer battalion, was sanctioned—to be provided as funds became available.

On the 30th September 1925, the Small Arms School at Satara was closed, and all weapon training was to be concentrated thenceforth at the Small Arms School, Pachmarhi.

The initial period of enrolment for all Class I followers was reduced to 5 years.

During the year, the Class A Reservists were called up for training by the Training Battalion. A staff was provided for this training by the 1st and 2nd Battalions, the latter, before moving to Mandalay, having left behind certain N.C.O.s for this purpose.

It has already been noted that the regiment has always had a fine record in rifle-matches, but in 1925 it excelled its previous efforts by winning nearly all the principal prizes at the South Indian Rifle Association's meeting at Bangalore in September. Captain A. H. Baker, who was in charge of the team, won all the pistol matches and the Pistol Championship. The Indian Army Championship (rifle) was won by No. 506, Pioneer Subbayya Konar, with No. 1891 Pioneer Kondayya, 3rd, and Jemadar Periyasami, 6th, and, besides a lengthy list of individual prizes, the regiment won the following team matches:—

The Cubbon Cup. Team:—Capt. A. H. Baker, Subadar Arogyasami, I.D.S.M., Jemadar Periyasami, No. 283 C.H M. Alagirisami, No. 745 NK. Arogyasami, No. 251 NK. Jesu, No. 1891 Pioneer Kondaya, No. 506 Pioneer Subbayya Konar.

The Indian Officers Cup. Team:—Subadars Arogyasami, I.D.S.M., and Balaraman, and Jemadar Periyasami.

On the 9th October 1925, the following order was issued:—

"Pioneers, Employment of:—Every effort will be made to enable Pioneer Battalions to take up contracts for work of a nature such as will afford training and experience for war.

Officers Commanding Pioneer Battalions will, therefore, always avail themselves of every opportunity for contract work in the vicinity of their Stations; in this General Officers Commanding and local authorities will give them all possible aid. The following natures of employment are cited as suitable: clearance of forest lands, construction of canals, roads and railways, and building of compound walls or similar manual work."

On the 25th November 1925, Officers of the Army were directed to wear mourning up to the 20th December 1925, on the occasion of the death of Her Majesty Queen Alexandra.

1926.

In this year, 3 Indian Officers, 13 N.C.O.s and 129 Pioneers were received from the Training Battalion, whilst 2 Indian Officers, 10 N.C.O.s and 29 Pioneers were transferred to the Training Battalion.

The following are extracts from the *Gazette of India* Army Department, dated the 19th February 1926:—

"No. 193. His Majesty the King has been graciously pleased to approve of the 1st Madras Pioneers bearing the distinction "*Afghanistan, 1919*" upon their Standard, Regimental colours and appointments respectively, in recognition of their services during the campaign known as the "3rd Afghan War."

"No. 194. His Majesty the King has been graciously pleased to approve of the grant to the 1st Madras Pioneers of the following Battle Honours in recognition of their services in campaigns during the Great War, 1914—1918:—

THE GREAT WAR.

"*Kut al Amara, 1917*", "*Baghdad*", "*Mesopotamia, 1916-18*", "*Persia, 1918*", "*N. W. Frontier, India, 1915*", "*Baluchistan, 1918*", "*Kilimanjaro*", *E. Africa, 1914-18.*"

With effect from the 15th February 1926, it was decided that all combatant ranks might be granted furlough up to two and a half months annually, with free passage by rail, or in the case of Burma by rail and sea, to and from the railway station nearest to their homes. Casual leave might be granted at discretion.

The peace strength of the battalion was fixed as follows:—12 British Officers; 17 Indian Officers; 720 Indian Other Ranks; 38 Followers, Class I; 7 Riding Horses; 32 Pack Mules.

The following is an extract from the *Gazette of India*, Army Department, dated the 18th June 1926:—

No. 790. His Majesty the King-Emperor has been graciously pleased to approve of the devices as detailed below, being borne as badges by the 1st Madras Pioneers:—

On buttons. In gilding metal, crossed axes encircled by the words 'Madras Pioneers.'

On collar of tunic and mess jacket. In silver, crossed axes.

On collar of service dress (for officers). In silver, as on collar of tunic and mess jacket.

On head-dress (helmet or pagri). In silver for British and Indian Officers, and in gilding metal for Indian Other Ranks. 'I' encircled by a band inscribed 'Seetabuldee' and 'Seringapatam.' Above the band the Assaye Elephant, and below the band a scroll inscribed 'Madras Pioneers.'

On cap. In silver, as on head-dress."

With effect from the 6th July 1926, free passages by rail, river and sea were granted to all classes of Indian combatants on completion of their army service.

Proficiency pay, at the rate of Rs. 2-8-0 *per mensem* (in place of good conduct pay) was made admissible to men enlisting on or after the 1st July 1926, but N.C.O.s of effective rank were not eligible, and would continue to draw good service pay.

On the 21st August 1926, approval was accorded to the wearing by the pipe band of the 2nd Battalion 1st Madras Pioneers of the *"Hunting Stuart"* Tartan and Pipe Streamers, consent having been given by His Majesty the King as Head of the Clan.

With effect from the 24th August 1926, Pioneer pay was made admissible to the full number of artificers authorised for a Pioneer Battalion by Peace Establishments.

On the 28th September 1926, it was directed that, at the discretion of the Commanding Officer, Indian troops might be permitted to keep two cotton shirts (in place) in lieu of one flannel shirt.

1927.

In this year, one Indian Officer, 13 N.C.O.s and 83 Pioneers were received from the Training Battalion, and one Indian Officer, 4 N.C.O.s and 10 Pioneers were transferred to the Training Battalion.

Leather rifle slings were again introduced in this year, in place of web slings, and amongst other changes in equipment, etc., the following may be mentioned:—4 Lewis guns for drill purposes were sanctioned for active Pioneer battalions; all service detonators, fuse and gun-cotton were to be held on deposit in Ordnance charge; the wearing of shorts was sanctioned on ceremonial parades in the hot weather; and it was directed that a khaki or drab cover was to be used on the blue forage cap in service dress, and a white cover in mess dress.

On the 19th May 1927, the following instructions were issued regarding the role in war, and the standards of, and responsibilities for, the training of Pioneer battalions :—

1. *Role of Pioneers.* Pioneers are primarily technical troops, and are maintained and trained in peace for their technical duties in War.

Pioneer Battalions are organised into 3 companies to suit technical requirements primarily. Consequently, they will only be employed as Infantry in an emergency or as a secondary role.

2. *Technical Training.* The syllabus of training for Pioneer recruits is contained in the Training Battalion Manual (Provisional) 1924. The syllabus of training in Pioneer duties for the trained soldiers of Pioneer Battalions is contained in G. S. T.-61. " Syllabus of Annual Field Works Training for Active Pioneer Battalions, India (Provisional), 1923," issued with I. A. O. 755-I of 1923.

In order to permit of the carrying out of the syllabus as prescribed in G.S.T.-61, which lays down that each company in a Pioneer Battalion will be struck off all other duties for a period of 10 weeks annually in order to carry out a course of technical training, a carefully devised programme, which will require the whole year to carry out effectively, is necessitated.

Every man in the Battalion, with certain exceptions mentioned below, will complete the course annually, unless unavoidably prevented from doing so, the reason for which must be given in the Annual Technical Report.

It is only by receiving the most careful consideration from higher formations that Pioneer Battalions will be able to attain this standard.

Registers will be kept by Pioneer Battalions showing how many days of the Annual Field Works' Course each man in the battalion completes.

The undermentioned may be exempted from the annual 10 weeks' course of technical training; but they will undergo a modified course of technical training, the scope of which will be determined by the O. C. Pioneer Battalion :—

(a) All personnel on the battalion headquarter staff.
(b) All personnel in the headquarter wing.

Pioneer Battalions will not normally be taken for brigade training, being reserved for the larger concentrations—inter-brigade manœuvres, etc.

3. *Training as Infantry.* A Pioneer Battalion will be not only capable of providing its own protection while employed on technical Pioneer work (*vide* F. S. R., II Section 43 (4) but also capable of being used as infantry in an emergency.

The 6 Lewis guns included in the H. Q. Wing are provided especially for the purposes of protection.

In order, however, to set free for technical work as large a number of the unit as possible, it will generally be advisable to provide protection from infantry or other means.

The training of the Pioneer Battalions as infantry will be carried out in accordance with the Infantry Training Manuals.

4. *Responsibility for training.* Pioneers will be trained under the orders of G. O.s C. Districts or Independent Brigades.

The Colonel-on-Staff, R. E., A. H. Q., will carry out the technical inspections of Pioneer units, *vide* para 4-A of A. I. (I). 538 of 1925, for the following purposes :—

    (*a*) To ensure that technical training is being conducted on the correct lines, and that the unit is efficient in its technical duties.

    (*b*) That technical equipment and stores are complete and maintained in a serviceable condition.

Copies of technical inspection reports will invariably be submitted to District or Independent Brigade Headquarters.

5. At all tactical training and exercises, Pioneers will primarily be employed in accordance with their technical role.

6. In peace Stations, as far as the exigencies of the service permit, Pioneer Battalions will, in view of their technical training requirements, be exempted from garrison guards and duties.

7. At inspections of Pioneer units, due consideration will be given to their dual role and duties and the high standard expected from purely infantry units will not be demanded of them.

8. I. A. O.s 464 of 1924 and 1026 of 1921 are cancelled.

In this year, revised scales of ordinary pension for Indian Officers were announced.

On the 24th June 1927, it was directed that the following percentage of specialists should be included in personnel transferred to the Class A Reserve :— Signallers, 5 *per cent;* Lewis Gunners, 10 *per cent.*

The war strength of the battalion was now laid down as :—12 British Officers; 17 Indian Officers; 706 Indian other ranks; 38 Followers, Class I; 21 Private Followers; 9 Riding Horses; 3 Riding Ponies; 32 Pack Mules; 6 Bicycles. *Attached* :—1 British Officer; 1 Warrant Officer; 3 Followers; 2 Animals.

New head-dress badges ("I" encircled by a band) were taken into wear from the 19th September 1927.

1928.

In this year, one Indian Officer, 13 N.C.O.s and 80 Pioneers were received from the Training Battalion, while 12 N.C.O.s and 53 Pioneers were transferred to the Training Battalion.

Revised furlough and leave rules for Indian ranks and enrolled followers were made effective from the 15th February 1928, as follows :—

    (*a*) *Furlough.* 3 months annually for a minimum of 50 *per cent.* of those of over two years' service, including free return passage.

    (*b*) *Leave.* 3 months annually at their own expense to all, having over one year's service, not granted furlough.

    (*c*) *Casual Leave.* At the discretion of Unit Commanders,

In this year, furniture was provided for regimental schools; non-prismatic binoculars were exchanged for prismatic; and British Officers were permitted to wear pith helmets of universal pattern, in the hot weather only, on all parades and duties except ceremonial parades.

On the 16th November 1928, the Madras Pioneers' War Memorial was unveiled at Bangalore by the General Officer Commanding, Madras District. The following extract from the *Madras Mail* gives a full account of the ceremony:—

"Major-General A. L. Tarver, C. B., C. I. E., D. S. O., Commanding the Madras District, this morning performed the ceremony of unveiling a fine memorial in carved grey granite to 350 officers and men of the five Battalions of the Madras Pioneers who fell in the Great War. Designed by Captain H. F. Tasker Taylor, more or less on the lines of the London Cenotaph, the north, south and east faces of the monument bear the crests of the 61st, 64th and 81st Pioneers, and on each panel is engraved the casualties incurred by each battalion. The fourth and west face bears the crest of the Madras Pioneer Regiment, which consists of the three Battalions mentioned, now designated the 1st-1st Madras Pioneers (King George's Own), the 2nd-1st Madras Pioneers, and 10th-1st Madras Pioneers.

The erection of the memorial in Bangalore appears to be particularly appropriate, as it has long been one of the Madras Pioneer stations and, under the present organisation, its Training Battalion is permanently located here.

The Pioneers paraded at full strength for the ceremony and when the General had been received by the senior Battalion Commander, and with the General Salute, he took his seat on a special dais, and Major A. H. Dawes, of the 1st-1st Battalion, delivered an address, in the course of which he said:—

' The five Battalions were the 61st (K. G. O.) Pioneers, the 64th Pioneers, the 81st Pioneers, the 2/61st Pioneers and the 2/81st Pioneers. The casualties suffered by each Battalion were as follows:—61st (K. G. O.) Pioneers; British Officers, 4; Indian Officers, 2; other ranks, 106. 64th Pioneers; Indian Officers, 3; other ranks, 67. 81st Pioneers; British Officers, 1; Indian Officers, 2; other ranks, 118. 2/61st Pioneers; other ranks, 28. 2/81st Pioneers; other ranks, 19.

The 61st (K. G. O.) Pioneers was raised in 1758, 170 years ago, at Fort St. George, as the 1st Battalion of Coast Sepoys. It is the oldest regiment in the Indian Army. During its long history, and prior to 1914, it had served with distinction in the wars of the Carnatic, Mysore, Seringapatam, Seetabuldee, Nagpore, Ava, Pegu, Central India, Afghanistan, Burma and China. In September 1914, the Battalion was mobilised and left, in October 1914, to join the East African Expeditionary Force. On November 3rd and 4th, 1914, it took part in the Battle at Tanga, on the east coast of Africa, where it was opposed by both German and African troops. In this action the Battalion behaved with the greatest gallantry in the face of the most difficult and adverse conditions. Their losses were heavy, including 2 British Officers, 2 Indian Officers, and over 100 rank and file killed. After this battle, the Battalion took part in the general advance under General Smuts in 1916, and was present at many actions from 1916 to 1918, serving with many Divisions in every part of East Africa. The Battalion returned to India in March 1918. At the outbreak of the Afghan War, in 1919, the Battalion was one of the first mobilised, and arrived at Jamrud on May 14th, 1919. It served through this short war, and remained on the Frontier, at Ali Masjid, until August 7th, 1920.

The 64th Pioneers was raised at Madras in 1759, as the 5th Battalion of Coast Sepoys. Thus it is only one year junior in age to the 61st (K. G. O.) Pioneers, and it is the third oldest Battalion in the Indian Army. The campaigns previous to 1914 in which this Battalion took part were the Carnatic, Sholinghur, Mysore, Assaye and Afghanistan. In December 1914 and January 1915, the Battalion took part in the operations against the Kachin rebels, whom they helped to suppress. The Battalion received the thanks of the Government of Burma for their conduct in these operations. In February 1916, the Battalion left for Mesopotamia. There it was employed on a great deal of hard work in the construction of trenches and roads between Shaikh Saad and the River Hai. In February 1917, it took part in the operations on the River Hai before Kut and was present at the battle of Shumran on February 23rd, when the British Force successfully crossed the river Tigris in the face of the enemy. During these operations, they lost one British Officer, one Indian Officer, and some 40 rank and file killed and wounded. In May 1919, the Battalion moved to N.W. Persia, while a detachment served in the Arab insurrection in August and September 1920.

The 81st Pioneers was raised at Chicacole in 1786, and was designated the 28th Madras Battalion. In the 142 years of its existence, it has taken part in the campaigns of Mysore, Seringapatam, Nagpur, Afghanistan, Burma, Tirah and the Punjab Frontier. Early in 1915, the Battalion moved to Nowshera, where it took part in several small operations against the Bunerwal tribe around Rustum. In 1917, the Battalion was employed on the construction of the Mohmand Blockade line. In March and April 1918, the Battalion took part in the punitive operations against the Murree tribe, and in June of that year proceeded to Bushire to join the Field Force there. In May 1919, the Battalion returned to India, and immediately joined the Field Army operating against Afghanistan, with which it took a very successful part at Thal against an attack by tribesmen.

The 2/61st Pioneers was formed at Dhond in 1918, by Colonel G. D. Bruce of the 61st (K.G.O.) Pioneers. Soon after it was raised, it was sent on service with the Derajat column, from whence it proceeded to South Waziristan, where it took part in the operations of 1919-20, including those of the Wana Column.

The 2/81st Pioneers was raised in 1917, and took part in the operations on the N. W. Frontier in 1919-20.

From the aforementioned short account of the services of the Madras Pioneer Battalions, it will be seen that they have taken an honourable part in a large number of the campaigns of the British Raj, and they have served in the field under such famous Generals as Sir Eyre Coote, Lord Cornwallis, the Duke of Wellington, Lord Roberts, General Maude, General Smuts, General Mackenzie-Kennedy and General Brooking, the latter two of whom are now the much respected Colonels of the 1/1st and 10/1st Madras Pioneer Battalions respectively.

In asking you, Sir, to unveil this Memorial, we feel that any such outward sign is but a poor tribute to those 350 of all ranks who gave their lives so willingly for the cause for which they fought, but we hope that those comrades of ours will rest content if they can feel that this Memorial to them will ever be an example to us of their patriotism, and of their loyalty to their King and Emperor, and of that spirit of sacrifice which inspired them to pay the extreme price. We are met here to do honour to their memory and to show, by this Memorial, that we realise and appreciate the greatness of their sacrifice.'

General Tarver replied as follows:—

'I cannot tell you how highly I appreciate the honour you have done me by asking me to preside at the unveiling of this Memorial. It is an honour which I feel immensely because of my long connexion with the Indian Army. I have loved them from the first day I joined them, and can realise what a really fine Army they are. If I may strike a more personal note, I may tell you that I now have three sons in the Indian Army following its noble career. Major Dawes has referred to the magnificent record of the Madras Pioneers. Now, what has created this record? The great war has certainly shown that the Indian Army can be trusted anywhere and everywhere, but what is it that inspires this wonderful spirit? In the last war they were not fighting for their own country, their gallantry did not amount to mere ambition. What was it then? It was to a very large extent the traditions of the Indian Army which inspired them. There was no question of loyalty. They were serving their King or the British Raj, and that was sufficient inspiration. And more than anything it has been the leadership of British Officers. From the days of John Company, the British Officer has been the inspiration. Should we not then acknowledge their reliance in the past, and their reliability in the future? Of course we must. This Memorial is a little thing in comparison with the great sacrifices they have made for the Empire, and this Memorial will be a perpetual inspiration to them to go on and fight for their King and country. Major Dawes has also said that it was very appropriate that this monument should be erected in Bangalore, where their Training Battalion is stationed. During the period of their youth, the men in training will derive the right traditions of the Madras Pioneers, their mother regiment, and you should make the most of the Memorial to impress upon them what loyalty and giving up their lives for their Regiment means, and they will join the Colours with that spirit which will never fail the Indian Army.'

The sentries at the corners of the monument stood with their arms reversed, there was a roll of the drums, the "Last Post" was sounded, and the Memorial veil dropped. The Pioneers presented arms, the "Reveille" crashed forth from the massed bugles, and then the General, and the senior Indian Officers present laid wreaths at the base of the Cenotaph. "God Save the King" concluded a very well-conducted ceremony."

On the 27th November 1928, instructions were received for a complete re-organisation of Pioneer Units, as approved by the Secretary of State, to be carried out, a later instruction fixing the 1st April 1929 as the date from which this was to take effect. The main details of the new scheme (as amended) were as follows:—

1. *Outline of New Organisation.*

(a) Indian Pioneer Units (other than the Hazara Pioneers) will be organised in three corps as under, with headquarters located as shown against each:—

    The Corps of Madras Pioneers   Bangalore.

1st (K. G. O.) Battalion.
2nd Battalion.

    The Corps of Bombay Pioneers   Kirkee.

1st (Marine) Battalion.
2nd (Kelat-i-Ghilzie) Battalion.

    The Corps of Sikh Pioneers   Sialkot.

1st Battalion.
2nd Battalion.

(b) Each corps will consist of:—Corps Headquarters; Two active battalions; Two training companies.

*   *   *   *   *   *   *   *   *   *   *

3. *Establishments.* The total peace establishment of each corps will be:—

(a) King's Commissioned Officers, 30; Subadars (including 3 Subadar-Majors), 17; Jemadars (including 3 Jemadar clerks), 22; Havildars, 72; Lance-Havildar, 1; Naiks, 60;. Lance-Naiks, 67. *Artificers.*—Havildars, 8; Naiks, 7; Lance Naiks, 8; Pioneers, 49. *Clerks.*—Havildars, 6; Naiks, 10; Pioneers, 16; Buglers, 31; Pioneers, 1,295; Followers, Class I, 60; Followers, Class II, 21; Riding Horses (Officers' Chargers), 16; Pack Mules, 72; Bicycles 14.

(b) The establishment of the Pioneer Reserve will remain temporarily as at present.

* * * * * * * * * * *

5. *Terms of Service.*

(a) Recruits will be enrolled for a particular corps of Pioneers.

(b) The period of enrolment will remain as at present, i.e., a total of 15 years' combined army and reserve service, except that the period of army service will be not less than 7 years.

The period of service in the reserve will be as follows:—

Class A Reserve:—Will comprise men who complete not less than 7, but not more than 10 years' army service or combined army and reserve service.

Class B Reserve:—Will comprise men who complete not less than 7, but not more than 15 years' combined army and reserve service.

All new enrolments will be on these terms.

(c) Subject to the maintenance of an even flow into the reserve, men who are being retained in the Pioneer units will be permitted to vary the terms of their original enrolment to agree with the new terms, the necessary variation of conditions as to discharge being made in their enrolment forms.

(d) Except as prescribed above, reservists of Indian Pioneer Corps will continue to be governed by existing regulations.

(e) For the purpose of the Indian Reserve Force Rules, 1925, contained in Regulations for the Army in India, Appendix XXVIII, the Officer Commanding Reservists will be the Officer Commanding the Headquarters of the Corps to which the Reservists belong. The Reserve Centre will be the Corps Headquarters.

6. *Surplus Personnel.*

Personnel serving with the colours, who are surplus to requirements under the new establishments, in their own units, and who cannot be placed, by voluntary transfer, in other units, corps or departments will be mustered out under the terms of Pay and Allowance Regulations........Jemadars with 20 years' service and over will receive the maximum pension admissible for their rank and grade. Subadar-Majors and Subadars with 21, 22 or 23 years' service will be granted the pension ordinarily admissible after 24 years' service. Those with 24 years' service and over will be granted the maximum pension admissible for their rank and grade.

The existing numbers and grades of clerks may be retained up to a maximum of 90 days from the date of this instruction, if considered necessary by Officers Commanding, in order to expedite re-organisation, disposal of records, etc.

7. *Allowances.*

Amendments to Pay and Allowance Regulations, showing the reigmental band, and contract allowances, authorised for units under the new organisation, will be issued in due course.

8. *Equipment.*

Revised scales of equipment are under preparation and will be issued shortly.

9. *Gazette Notification.*

A notification, constituting the new units as "Corps" for purposes of the Indian Army Act, has been published in Part I of the *Gazette of India* of 24th November 1928. . . . .

Orders were issued that, on re-organisation, training in Lewis gun and Signalling was to cease.

1929.

In this year, one Indian Officer, 9 N.C.O.s and 73 Pioneers were received from Corps Headquarters, and one Indian Officer, 8 N.C.O.s and 15 Pioneers were transferred to Corps Headquarters.

In 1927, the regiment had put forward a claim for the battle honour of "*Argaum,*" but the reply, dated the 14th January 1929, ran as follows:—

"The case has been very carefully considered, but in view of the length of time that has elapsed, and having regard to the policy adopted in similar cases by the Army Council, it has been decided that no useful purpose will be served by pursuing the regiment's claim to this ancient battle honour."

In this year, leather equipment, consisting of belt, frog and cartridge pocket, was issued in order to save wear and tear of web equipment; bayonets of ·476 bore muskets (used on guards) were hereafter to be carried fixed, and the frogs and scabbards were withdrawn; it was directed that hose-tops were to be worn on all occasions when shorts are worn, but not on field service; and the Educational Training Grant was reduced from 12 annas to 8 annas *per annum* for each Indian Officer and Indian other rank.

With effect from the 1st March 1929, higher rates of furlough pay, to include an additional Indian element, were granted to British Officers and, in July, railway concessions in Great Britain and the Irish Free State (1st Class return tickets for 1 1/3 single fares) were also granted to officers proceeding on leave or furlough.

With effect from the 24th June 1929, the new designation "2nd Battalion, Madras Pioneers" was used on official correspondence, on re-organisation.

On the same date, Commanding Officers were authorised to transfer Indian Soldiers prematurely to the Reserve, within the authorised establishment, on compassionate grounds, provided such had served for not less than 3 years with the colours.

With effect from the 1st August 1929, it was ordered that two separate banking accounts should be maintained for, (*a*) All public funds, (*b*) All regimental and private funds.

At the Southern Command Rifle Meeting in 1929, the Battalion won three cups and eight bronze medals. The Battalion also won the Inter-Battalion Rifle Shooting Challenge Shield for 1929, with a score of 915.

The following remarks, dated 23rd August 1929, were made by the G.O.C., Madras District, on the report of the Chief Civil Master Armourer on his inspection of the Battalion's rifles:—

"I am directed by the District Commander to convey his appreciation of the condition of the arms of the unit under your command as evidenced by the C.C.M.A.'s Report.

The report reflects great credit on all concerned."

Indian Officers and Indian other ranks, who had passed the preliminary examination in English, 1st Class, were permitted to sit for the preliminary examinations in Arabic, Persian and Turkish and, if successful, to draw an award of Rs. 400.

Indian Officers with honorary King's Commissions, holding the appointment of Subadar-Major, were admitted to double scale of pensions, when discharged from the service on completion of the tenure of their appointments.

In September 1929, it was laid down that the Battalion war strength on re-organisation should be:—British Officers, 11; Indian Officers, 13; Indian other ranks 627; Followers, Class I, 30; Followers, private, 22; Riding horses, 11; Pack mules, 36; Bicycles, 6.

Attached:—British Officer, 1; Warrant Officer, 1; Follower, Class I, 1; Follower, private, 1; Riding horse, 1; Riding pony, 1.

On the 10th September 1929, one Indian Religious Teacher for each religious class not less than the authorised establishment of a company, was laid down as the authorised scale for a Pioneer Battalion.

On the 5th October 1929, Indian troops were made eligible for the award of the Medal of the Order of the British Empire (Military Division) for:—

(a) Special services of a high degree of merit.

(b) Highly meritorious performance of ordinary duties.

(c) Acts of gallantry performed.

The award of the medal does not carry with it any financial benefits.

The following was laid down as the strength of Advance and Rear parties, when moving on relief in India:—

By Rail. 1 British Officer; 1 Indian Officer; 20 Indian other ranks.

By Road. 1 British Officer; 1 Indian Officer; 30 Indian other ranks.

1930.

In this year, one Indian Officer, and 108 Indian other ranks (including 95 recruits) were received from Corps Headquarters, and one Indian Officer, and 28 Indian other ranks were transferred to Corps Headquarters.

On the 25th March 1930, revised instructions were issued regarding the role in war and the standard of, and responsibilities for, the training of active Pioneer Battalions, as follows:—

"1. *Characteristics and role of Pioneers.*—Pioneers are primarily technical troops and are maintained and trained in peace for their technical duties in War.

Although trained as fighting troops, they should be employed as infantry only as a last resource; casualties are not easy to replace, and they may become needlessly involved in the fighting and lost for work which may have an important bearing on the operations.

When engaged in actual fighting, Pioneers should be allotted a definite task, such as the defence of a certain locality, the protection of an exposed flank or in very exceptional cases, the delivery of a counter-attack, etc. It is essential that they should be released as soon as possible, in order that they may resume their normal duties.

Pioneers are organised on a company basis, both for technical work and for fighting, and should be so employed. They have no Lewis or Vickers guns and no signallers.

Although they are capable of providing their own local protection while employed on Pioneer duties, it will generally be advisable to provide protection from other sources, in order to free as large a number of the unit as possible for technical work.

2. *Technical Training*—The syllabus of training for Pioneer recruits is contained in I. A. O. 241 of 1929. The syllabus for the annual field works training for active Pioneer battalions is issued by the General Staff at Army Headquarters.

In order to permit of the carrying out of this syllabus a carefully devised programme is necessary. This will be prepared in advance for the whole year, and approved by the C. R. E. of the District, if the battalion is in its war divisional area; the programmes of other battalions will be approved by the Chief Engineers of Commands.

Every man will complete the course shown in the syllabus annually, unless unavoidably prevented from doing so, with the following exceptions:—

(1) Personnel of battalion headquarters. (2). Personnel of Company headquarters. Reasons for the non-completion of the course by any other men will be shown in detail in the Technical Report.

Registers will be kept by Platoon Commanders showing how many days of the annual field works' course each man completes with the reason for non-completion of any portion.

Except at the request of the O. C. battalion, Pioneer Officers and men will only be called on to undergo courses contained in "Courses of Instruction (India)."

Battalions will normally be reserved for divisional or inter-brigade manoeuvres and will only be taken for brigade training when there is work for them in their technical capacity.

Apart from their annual course of field works, Pioneer battalions will be given every opportunity to carry out work for the M. E. S., etc., under the rules in R. A. I. Appendix XXVI.

Except in cases of emergency, they will not be employed on unskilled work which is not of a technical training nature; should such cases arise, working pay, as laid down in P. and A. Regulations Part I, para 88 (iii), will be admissible.

Nothing in the above is to be held to prevent the employment of Pioneers on any work for military purposes.

Such work will be carried out under the orders of the District or Independent Brigade Commander, who will decide what, if any, remuneration should be given.

3. *Training as Infantry.* Pioneers will be trained to act as infantry in order to carry out their duties as fighting troops, with the limitation laid down in para 1 of this order. Their training, therefore, will not extend beyond company training.

4. *Responsibility for Training.* Pioneers will be trained under the direct orders of the commander of the District or Independent Brigade in which they are serving at the time.

Officers will be given every opportunity of attending Brigade and District exercises. In addition to such exercises in their own area, the C. O. and Adjutant of a battalion not stationed in its war District will, whenever possible, atteend that District's exercises and manoeuvres under their war C. R. E.

The Brigadier, R. E., A. H. Q., will carry out the technical inspection of Pioneer units to ensure :—

    (a) That technical training is carried out on the correct lines and that the unit is technically efficient;

    (b) That technical equipment and stores are complete and maintained in a serviceable condition.

Copies of technical inspection reports will be sent to the Command concerned.

5. In all technical training and exercises, Pioneers will be employed as far as possible in accordance with their technical role.

O'.s C. Pioneer battalions will, however, take opportunities of attaching their officers to infantry and other arms, in order to improve their military knowledge generally and to further co-operation between Pioneers and other arms of the service.

6. Administrative inspection of Pioneer battalions will be carried out by the commanders of the Brigades, etc., in which they are serving,

7. I. A. O. 345 of 1927 is cancelled.

On the 28th April 1930, the normal class composition of the battalion was laid down as follows :—Tamils, 50 *per cent.*; Adi-Dravidas and Christians, 35 *per cent.*; Telegus, 15 *per cent.*

With effect from the 1st April 1930, the charpoy allowance was reduced from one anna to nine pies per man *per mensem*.

From the same date, both British and Indian units were authorised to maintain a combined fund, to be designated the "Unit Administration Fund," in respect of various funds hitherto separately maintained.

The monthly rate of kit and clothing allowances for Indian troops were amended as follows :—Indian Officers, Rs. 3-11-0; Havildars, Rs. 3-3-0; Indian other ranks, Rs. 3-1-0; Followers, Class I., Re. 1-11-0.

From the 28th June 1930, training with No. 36 live grenades was resumed.

From the 14th July 1930, the varnishing of bayonet scabbards with shellac, which had been introduced in February 1929, was discontinued, and the use of heel-ball and boning, at unit's expense, was substituted.

The following remarks, dated 12th July 1930, were passed by the District Commander on the C.C.M.A.'s Report for 1930:—

"The District Commander wishes to place on record his appreciation of the state of the arms and bicycles on your charge, as evinced by the C.C.M.A.'s report.

The report reflects great credit on all concerned."

With effect from the 1st July 1930, for a period of one year, a reduction was made in the service pensions, save disability pensions, of the officers of the Indian Army, the reduction applying only to officers below the rank of Colonel, and amounting to 7 *per cent.* in the rank and service elements.

On the 5th September 1930, the allotment of personal numbers (for use after mobilisation) to British and Indian Officers of the Indian Army was introduced.

On the 9th September 1930, measures were introduced to meet the prospective congestion in the higher and middle ranks of the officers of the Indian Army, certain concessions being offered to officers on retirement, with the object of reducing the block in promotion.

On the 16th September 1930, a change was made in the form of Jagirs granted to Indian Officers, *viz.*:—a cash payment amounting to Rs. 600 *per annum* (for three lives, reducible by one half on each succession, and known as "Jagir Allowance"), in place of Jagirs in the form of assignments or remission of land-revenue, and of special pensions granted to Indian Officers resident in Indian States.

On the 29th September 1930, sanction was accorded to the extension of the service of Indian other ranks due for discharge or transfer to the Reserve, to the extent necessary to enable them to be granted such furlough or leave as might be due to them.

On the 30th September 1930, an order was issued directing that service rendered by British Officers and Indian ranks in aid of civil power should be treated as military service and field service respectively for the purpose of disability and family pensions.

With effect from the 29th October 1930, the procedure of marking rifles and bayonets serially throughout the battalion was adopted.

The Battalion won the Inter-Battalion Rifle Shooting Challenge Shield for 1930 with a score of 887, while at the Southern Command Rifle Meeting, the Battalion won **three cups.**

Part III.

BRITISH OFFICERS, WARRANT OFFICERS AND NON-COMMISSIONED OFFICERS.

1759—1930.

[With Alphabetical Index]

Note.

This Part of the Records deals with the British Officers of the Regiment and, in addition, lists are given of the Colonels of the Regiment, and the European Non-Commissioned Officers.

It is intended to serve as a corollary to the Army List pages referring to the Regiment which have been procured by Colonel S. M. Rice, C.I.E., C.B.E., and are now in the Officers' Mess.

This Part, perhaps more than any other, suffers from the lack of contemporary documents, and is consequently not so complete as might be desired.

The officers have been dealt with more or less in chronological order, as they joined the Regiment, but an alphabetical index has been added to facilitate reference.

Colonels of the Regiment.

Note.—The appointment of Colonel was instituted in July 1796.

Colonel George Clarke, 1796.

Major-General Thomas Trent, 1797.

Major-General Joseph Bilcliffe, 1st January 1800.

Lieutenant-General Sir Thomas Bowser, K. C. B., 1st May 1804.

Lieutenant-General Daniel McNeill, 1820.

Major-General Sir Hopetoun S. Scott, K.C.B., 1st May 1824.

Colonel W. C. Oliver, 30th January 1834.

Colonel Alexander Grant, C. B., 14th February 1834.

Major-General Charles Augustus Walker, 26th May 1835.

Major-General John Munro, 24th December 1842.

Major-General George Hutton, 18th June 1858.

Major-General James Bell, 26th March 1860.

In 1924, H. M. the King became Colonel-in-Chief of the 1st Madras Pioneers.

The following officers are now Colonels of the Corps of Madras Pioneers:—

Major-General Sir Edward C. W. Mackenzie-Kennedy, K.B.E., C.B. (23rd April 1912). *Late 61st (K.G.O.) Pioneers.*

Major-General Sir Harry T. Brooking, K.C.B., K.C.S.I., K.C.M.G. (23rd July 1918). *Late 61st (K.G.O.) Pioneers and 81st Pioneers.*

British Officers.

Airey, George:—This officer entered the Company's service as an Ensign on the 26th March 1754, and was commanding the 5th Battalion of Coast Sepoys in the operations against Mahomed Yusuf at Madura in 1763 as a Captain, so that it appears probable that he was the first Commanding Officer of the regiment.

The following references to his services are extracted from *Orme's History*.

On the 14th December 1758, Lieutenant Airey was detached with four Companies of Sepoys by Captain Preston at Chingleput, and took a 13-inch mortar, which was being escorted by 150 Sepoys to assist the French, then besieging Fort St. George. He defeated the Sepoys between Sadras and Covelong, "but having no bullocks to draw off the mortar, ruined it as well as he could, and left it on the road."

On the 19th December 1758, he accompanied Captain Preston in an unsuccessful attempt to intercept the English prisoners captured in a sally from Fort St. George, who were being escorted to Pondicherry.

On the 19th February 1759, Ensign (*sic*) Airey had a narrow escape when making a sally from the Mount, then being attacked by the French, his party being scattered by French Cavalry and many cut down.

On the 3rd March 1759, "Captain Preston at Chingleput, hearing there was but a slight force in the fort of Carangooly, had detached Lieutenant Airey, with seven Companies of Sepoys, to surprise it; but they took a panic under the walls, not to be recovered by the bravery of their Officer, which encouraged the garrison to sally, who killed 25 of them in their flight."

On the 15th April 1759, while Colonel Monson was attacking "Conjeeveram Pagoda" in front, Lieutenant Airey, accompanied by Mahomed Yusuf, led a party over the rear wall and took the defenders of the gateway in rear, the "Pagoda" being then captured.

At the end of March 1760, "Captain Airey, who commanded in Chittapett, and from thence over Trinomaly, sent a detachment of Sepoys to enable the garrison there to take the field, which in a few days drove the guards out of Soolabaur, Tricalour and Trivaneloor."

On the 10th June 1760, "More Mysoreans arriving, they called in their parties, and being joined by 40 or 50 of the French troops from Thiagar, appeared before Tricalore on the 10th but the Frenchmen having brought only two or three small field-pieces, and the fort being of stone, the Sepoys within, who were three good Companies left there by Captain Airey, refused to surrender; and by the fire of their musketry from the walls obliged the enemy to retire."

Bowman, ———:—Lieutenant Bowman was in command of the 5th Battalion Coast Sepoys at the Battle of Tiruvannamalai on the 26th September 1767, when the battalion greatly distinguished itself: Captain Baillie was commanding the Sepoy Corps of Grenadiers at this time. As an Ensign, and presumably then serving with the 5th Battalion, he was wounded, at the second Siege of Madura, on the 20th June 1764.

A Captain Bowman was in command of the 3rd Circar Battalion in August 1770, and there was another Captain Bowman who was killed by a party of the Pychy Rajah's men in the Wynad in January 1797.

Baillie, William:—This was the Commanding Officer who gave the regiment its ancient designation *"Baillie-Ki-Paltan."* He entered the company's service from H. M.'s 89th Highland Regiment in 1764, on the departure to England of the King's troops serving in Madras, and it appears probable that he obtained command of the 5th Battalion of Coast Sepoys in November 1765, when the Army was re-organised. He was in command during the operations against Haidar Ali in 1767-1768, though occasionally absent when put in charge of the corps of Grenadiers. In 1771 he acted as Brigade-Major of the General Staff during the operations against Tanjore, and there is nothing to show that he had any further connection with the regiment thereafter. A full account of his disastrous defeat by Tippu Sultan and Haider Ali at Pullalur in 1780 is given elsewhere in these records.

The following is the inscription on his monument in the Lal Bagh at Seringapatam:—

"To the memory of Colonel William Baillie who, with a detachment of British troops under his command, after a noble and most gallant resistance to a superior force of the enemy on the plains of Periambaucum was ultimately compelled to surrender to the united armies of Hyder Ally and Tipoo Sultan on the 10th day of September 1780, and died in the fortress of Seringapatam on the 13th day of November 1782. This monument is erected and inscribed by his nephew John Baillie, Lieutenant-Colonel on the establishment of Bengal, and Resident at the Court of Lucknow. A. D. 1816."

There was a curious old drawing in the Officers' Mess, executed in 1781, which depicts the Colonel handing over his sword to Haidar Ali after the battle, but this was, most unfortunately, stolen from the Officers' Mess during the Great War.

Barton, Richard:—Lieutenant, 10th May 1768. Lieutenant Barton of the 4th Carnatic Battalion was wounded during the operations against Tanjore in 1771. He was serving with the regiment at Vellore in November 1774 and August 1775, and disappeared from the roll before the 1st January 1779.

Campbell, ———:—Lieutenant Campbell of the 4th Carnatic Battalion was wounded during the operations against Tanjore in 1771.

Campbells are exceedingly difficult to identify, as there were such numbers of officers of this name serving in India, many of whom lie buried in various places throughout the Madras Presidency.

Davis, ———:—Lieutenant Davis was also wounded while serving with the 4th Carnatic Battalion during the operations against Tanjore in 1771.

Edington, James:—Captain, 15th July 1770; Major, 7th May 1784; Lieutenant-Colonel, 7th February 1786. Captain Edington (or, as he signed his name, Eidingtoun) was in command of the 4th Carnatic Battalion in 1776, and in all probability had succeeded Captain Baillie in the command in 1771. He was still in command of the regiment at Vellore in August 1775, and acted as Adjutant-General in Madras in 1776. He was concerned in the dissensions which culminated in the arrest of the Governor, Lord Pigot, in that year, being one of the officers who actually arrested him, but at the trial which resulted, in 1780, he was acquitted, together with the other officers who had taken part. He was said to have received a bribe of 10,000 pagodas from the Nawab for his share in these proceedings, but no proof was ever forthcoming of this or any of the other alleged bribes.

In 1788, he was in command of the force sent to overawe the Nizam, and he left the service in 1789.

In 1771 he had married Miss Ann Weller, and in St. Mary's Cemetery, Madras, is the tomb of a Miss Catharine Eidingtoun, daughter of Colonel Eidingtoun who died on the 3rd June 1788, aged 16.

Alexander, James:—Lieutenant, 16th November 1772. Lieutenant Alexander was serving with the regiment in November 1774, but had left before August 1775.

There was a Robert Alexander, who became Member of Council in Madras in 1814, and who had a son, James William, who entered the Bengal Civil Service. Robert's uncle, James, was Member of Parliament for Derry, and became the first Earl of Caledon. A Colonel James Alexander, of the Madras establishment, was promoted to Major-General on the 28th June 1838.

Goddard, William:—Lieutenant, 9th September 1774. Lieutenant Goddard was borne on the rolls in November 1774, but disappeared from the list before August 1775. He may have been a relation of Thomas Goddard, of the Bengal establishment, who made a remarkable march from Bengal to the Mahratta country in 1779, and rose to the rank of Brigadier-General.

Meeke, Thomas:—Lieutenant, 12th December 1773. Lieutenant Meeke was also borne on the rolls in 1774, but his name had disappeared by August 1775.

Eagle, Archibald:—Ensign, 10th November 1770. This officer was also borne on the rolls in November 1774, but his name was removed before August 1775.

Lowe, Robert:—Ensign, 11th July 1771. His name was sometimes spelt "Low." He appears on the list for November 1774, but had left before August 1775.

Richardson, John:—Ensign, 14th March 1772. Ensign Richardson was also on the rolls in November 1774, but his name is absent from the list for August 1775. A Colonel Plampin Richardson commanded the 1st 18th N.I., and was married at Seringapatam in 1806, dying at Rameshwaram, where he is buried, on the 16th May 1813.

Crisp, John:—Ensign, 12th December 1773. Another officer whose only appearance on the rolls is in November 1774. A Major J. Crisp, of the 1st Native Veteran Battalion, was granted 3 years' furlough to Europe in 1836. If this was the same officer, he was certainly a veteran.

Weller, George:—Ensign, 4th January 1774. This officer also makes a brief appearance on the regimental roll in November 1774. I cannot trace him.

Phillips, James:—Lieutenant, 18th July 1770. Lieutenant Phillips' name appears on the list for August 1775, but had left before January 1779.

Prendergast, Thomas:—Lieutenant, 10th July, 1770. Appears on the roll of the regiment for August 1775, but is shown as doing duty as Adjutant at Fort St. George. He disappears from the list before January 1779. A Lieutenant James Prendergast of H. M. 74th Foot was killed at the assault on Seringapatam on the 4th May 1799.

Skryme, Francis:—Lieutenant, 18th February 1772. Lieutenant Skryme was Adjutant of the Regiment at Vellore in August 1775, but I have found no further trace of him.

McGill, Patrick:—Lieutenant, 21st November 1772. His name was on the roll of the regiment in August 1775, but disappeared before January 1779. An Ensign Alexander McGill of the Royals was buried at Wallajahbad on the 28th August 1808.

Grant, Lewis:—Ensign, 3rd June 1775. Was shown on the list of officers in August 1775, but his name does not appear in January 1779.

Mackay, Robert:—Ensign, 1775, after serving for eleven months as a volunteer in the Artillery: appointed Adjutant, 4th Battalion N.I., in March 1780; and served with the battalion throughout Sir Eyre Coote's operations till the end of 1782, when he became Lieutenant and was appointed *Aide-de-Camp* to Colonel Reinbold of the Hanoverians, who had two regiments under his orders in India. In the operations round Cuddalore in 1783 he served with a battalion of European Grenadiers. On the conclusion of peace, he was appointed to a native corps in one of the northern provinces, and in 1785 was made Captain-Lieutenant to a Corps (not specified) doing duty at Madras. In 1789, he was promoted to Captain, and given command of the Grenadier Company of a regiment of European Infantry at Vellore. In May 1789, he took command of the fort of Arni, remaining there during the campaign against Tippu Sultan, at the close of which he rejoined his regiment. Early in 1793, he was appointed to command a native corps in the subsidiary force of the Nizam, and served with it till 1797, when he was appointed Major to a regiment destined for the expedition to Manila, but the expedition was countermanded. In 1800, he was in command at Rayakota. In October 1802, he proceeded to England, after 29 years' service, arriving in March 1803. He was promoted to Lieutenant-Colonel Commandant on the 21st September 1804; Colonel, 25th April 1808; Major-General, 4th June 1811: and Lieutenant-General on the 19th July 1821.

Other Mackays who were serving in the Army at the same time were Donald, a Major in the Artillery, who was buried at Guindy racecourse. He was severely wounded at the siege of Cuddalore in June 1783, and died on the 17th September following. George Mackay, a Lieutenant in the 1st European Regiment, was commanding at Chingleput in 1780, when Colonel Baillie met with disaster. Aeneas Mackay was also a Lieutenant in the 1st European Regiment. A Lieutenant Hugh

Mackay died at Vallam, seven miles from Tanjore on the 12th September 1773, aged 25; and there was also an Ensign James Mackay.

Fraser, Charles:—Cadet, 1762: Captain, 28th June 1770: Lieutenant-Colonel, 7th May 1784: Colonel, 24th September 1790. This Captain Fraser commanded the 4th Battalion on the expedition to Mahé in 1779. He had served in the Royal Marines for six years before entering the service of the East India Company in 1762. I have no record as to the length of his service with the 4th, but he probably served with the regiment till he went home on furlough in 1781. He eventually became a General and commanded a Division of the Madras Army. There are conflicting statements as to the date of his death; his grandson says that he died in 1794, while Dodwell and Miles state that he died on the 5th May 1795, and J. J. Cotton, who is probably correct, says that he died on the 27th April 1795. His tombstone in the Masulipatam Fort Cemetery bears the following inscription:—

"Here lies the body of Colonel Charles Fraser, aged 56 years, who died at Masulipatam in command of the Northern Division of the Army. This stone is inscribed with filial reverence and affection by his son Hastings, 1814."

He was married to a Miss Isabella Hook at Campbelltown on the 16th December 1768. The above was a *Fraser of Ardachy*, descended from the third son of the sixth Lord Lovat, and while I am on the subject of Frasers, I shall append here, for reference, some notes on the Frasers who came to India, as there were several of the same name, and the subject is somewhat complicated. I am unable to say to whom I am indebted for these notes, as I have unfortunately lost the reference. The eldest son of the above Charles Fraser was Hastings, born at Vellore on the 25th August 1771, and named after Warren Hastings, who at that time was a Member of Council at Madras. It may be of interest to quote the letter written by the future Governor-General on this occasion:—

"Fort St. George, 15th January 1772."

"Dear Sir—I learnt with much pleasure from Mr. Anderson some time ago the Honor which you had done me in making me one of the Sponsors for your Son. I am much obliged to you and Mrs. Fraser for this Distinction though I cannot hope for some Years to have the Pleasure of seeing my Godson, or of being a Witness of his Growth and Improvements. I shall be glad, however, to be informed of the Progress he makes in both, and of his Health and shall be truly interested in his Welfare.

I have taken the liberty to send a piece of Shawl directed to you, which I request your Permission to present, as a mere Token of Affection to my young Namesake, and to plead a Right to his Acceptance of it from the Relation that you have given me to him.

I beg you will present my Compliments to Mrs. Fraser, and Believe me to be, with esteem.

Yours very faithfully,
WARREN HASTINGS."

Hastings Fraser was present at two sieges of Seringapatam, the capture of Pondicherry, and the Isle of Bourbon, where he commanded a brigade, and the officers of the 86th Regiment subscribed 100 guineas to present him with a sword, and the

Indian Corps gave him a service of silver plate "as a trifling mark of their esteem." He died at the age of 83, a General, C.B., and Colonel Commandant of H. M. 61st Regiment.

James Stuart Fraser, the 5th son of Charles Fraser, was born at Edinburgh in 1783. He was A.D.C. to Sir G. Barlow, Governor of Madras, and was made Resident in Hyderabad by Lord Auckland in 1839, retiring owing to a disagreement with Lord Dalhousie. He died at Twickenham in 1869, aged 85. His son, Hastings of the Madras Infantry (C.B. 1886; Lieutenant-General, 1892), behaved very gallantly during the Mutiny. He was Assistant Resident at Hyderabad for a time, and left India in 1884, dying at Bedford in 1892. He was author of *"Our Faithful Ally the Nizam,"* and also of a Memoir of his father.

As regards the *Frasers of Reelick,* descended from a natural son of the 4th Lord Lovat, James (11th of Reelick) was a Member of Council at Surat, and an oriental scholar. His eldest son had five sons, of whom four went to India. The eldest, James Baillie Fraser, wrote many books including a memoir of Colonel James Skinner, and the second, William, of the Bengal Civil Service, was Secretary to Sir David Ochterlony, Resident at Delhi, in 1805, with Elphinstone at Peshawar in 1811, and himself became Resident at Delhi in 1830, where he was shot dead in 1835 by an agent of the Firozepur Nawab, who was hanged.

The mother of the five Reelick Frasers was a *Fraser of Balnain.* This branch was also descended from Hugh, 4th Lord Lovat. Dr. William Mackinnon Fraser was Physician to the Prince Regent (George IV), and his 5th son, Hugh, was a Bengal Civilian, who died in 1842, of lockjaw caused by wounds inflicted by insurgents in Bundelkhand. One of Dr. Fraser's brothers, Charles, was a Major in the Bengal Cavalry, and A.D.C. to Marquis Wellesley. Two of his sons were in the Bengal Civil Service, one of whom, Simon, Resident at Delhi in 1857, was killed when starting to close the gates against the mutineers from Meerut. Of Dr. Fraser's sisters, one, Charity, married William Chambers, an oriental scholar, and was mother of Sir Charles Harcourt Chambers of the Bombay High Court; another, Jane, married, in 1770, Charles Grant (Bengal), thrice Chairman of the Court of Directors. Her sons were Charles, President of the Board of Control in 1830, and created Baron Glenelg, and Sir Robert, Governor of Bombay, 1835. Sir Robert's son was Sir Charles Grant, Foreign Secretary in India under Lord Ripon.

The daughter of an earlier Fraser of Balnain married Alexander Tytler, and from them are descended the Fraser-Tytlers.

The *Frasers of Leadclune* are descended from a younger son of the first Fraser of Balnain. The second Fraser of Leadclune married a Macdonald of Glencoe in 1692; their eldest son, wounded at Culloden, had a grandson, James, who was shot in a duel in India, and their second son was father of Sir William Fraser, created a Baronet in 1806. He was in the Company's naval service, and in command of the Indiaman *Lord Mansfield,* which was wrecked whilst coming out of the river into the Bay of Bengal. He became a Post Captain in the Royal

Navy. His son was high in the Company's service in China, and died unmarried in 1827. The third Baronet was his brother, Sir James John Fraser, whose son Lieutenant-General Sir Charles Crawfurd Fraser, was at the capture of Delhi in 1857, and won his V.C. in 1858 for rescuing an officer and some men from drowning in the Rapti, and the C.B. in the Abyssinian War.

Of the *Frasers of Culduthel,*—descended from the 4th Lord Lovat through his great-grandson, James,—Colonel Roderick Fraser, Bengal Infantry (born 1763) and his brother, Simon, killed in a duel in India, were both in the Company's service, and died unmarried. Their elder brother had a son, Colonel Fraser, who lost a hand whilst charging Dost Muhammad's Sowars at Parwan Dharra, fought at Chillianwalla and Gujerat, and died at Edinburgh in 1868, unmarried.

Of the *Frasers of Newton,* Major Thomas Fraser, Royal Scots, had two sons —Hugh, Judge at Delhi in 1835, who was 5th Fraser of Newton and died in 1843; and Alexander, a Bengal civilian, who died in 1850. Their sister married Thomas Porter Bonell Biscoe, Sudder Judge at Allahabad.

Colonel Hugh Fraser, of the *Frasers of Propachy and Torbeck,* was in the Bengal Engineers, and Chief Commissioner of Agra in 1857. He was awarded the C.B. for the capture of a stockade at Rangoon in the second Burmese War.

Of *other Frasers,* Sir Hugh Fraser entered the Madras Army in 1790 and became a K.C.B. He is said to have been a son of William Fraser of Inverness, who married a niece of Brigadier Simon Fraser (of Balnain) who was killed at Saratoga in 1777. General John Henry Fraser, a King's officer, lost a leg at the battle of Deig in 1804. Mill says that his death after the battle "was felt as a national calamity by every Briton in India."

Burr, Daniel:—Cadet, 1767; Ensign 3rd November 1768: Lieutenant, 19th September 1770: Captain, 18th July 1779: Major, 9th September 1789: Lieutenant-Colonel, 1st March 1795: Colonel, 13th July 1797: Major-General, 1st January 1805: Lieutenant-General, 22nd April 1815. He was attached to the 1st European Regiment at Trichinopoly in 1769, after seeing service with Colonel Wood's detachment. In June 1771, he was put in charge of Ayalur, a small fortress 45 miles west of Trichinopoly. He took part in the operations against Tanjore in 1771, and in those under General Joseph Smith in Ramnad in 1772, after which he was appointed to the 5th N.I. He again saw service in the Tanjore country in 1773, and commanded the 5th N.I. at Madura till October 1774, when he was appointed Adjutant of the 4th Circar Battalion at Aska. In January 1778 he was shot through both legs when on service in the Gumsur country. He was Adjutant of the 4th in 1779, and in March 1780 was appointed to command the *Sibbendies* in Ganjam district, joining Sir Eyre Coote's army in 1782, and taking part in the Siege of Cuddalore in 1783. He commanded the garrison at Vellore in 1789, and the troops in Guntur district in 1791—94. On promotion to Colonel, he was appointed to the 10th N.I., and went home on furlough from January 1798 till August 1799. He commanded in the

Molucca Islands in 1800, and the successful Ternate expedition in 1801, finally retiring to England in 1803.

I may note that Philippart defines "Sibbendies" as "a description of Native troops designed solely for the collection of the revenues, officered by Native invalid Commissioned and Non-Commissioned Officers and considered incapable of effective service."

Marshall, David:—Lieutenant, 14th October 1770. Shown on the regimental roll in January 1779 as of the Nabob's service, and gone home, so he probably never actually served with the 4th.

Lorrimore, Samuel:—Lieutenant, 12th February 1773. Shown on the regimental roll for January 1779, but I have no record of his services.

Munro, John:—Cadet, 1777: Ensign, 2nd July 1778: Lieutenant, 6th March 1782: Captain, 1st June 1796: Major, 20th June 1799.

Ensign John Munro of the 4th Carnatic Battalion was transferred to the Guntoor Local Corps in July 1779, when that corps was being raised. I have not been able to trace him further, except that he died on the 23rd December 1800.

Another John Munro was Quartermaster-General in 1809, and yet another was Colonel of the 4th in 1842.

Capper, Francis:—Ensign, 17th April 1778: Lieutenant, 11th January 1782: Captain, 6th August 1794: Major, 4th October 1798: Lieutenant-Colonel, 17th June 1800. Ensign Francis Capper was also transferred from the 4th Carnatic Battalion to the Guntoor Local Corps in July 1779. In 1800 he was a Major in the 2nd 4th, commanding the 3rd Brigade under Wellesley during the operations against Dhoondiah, when he specially distinguished himself, and as a Lieutenant-Colonel, commanding the 2nd 4th, he is shown as "absent on a secret expedition" in 1802. In 1809, he was Adjutant-General in Madras, and was at that time borne on the list of officers of the 1st 4th as Lieutenant-Colonel, being shown in a return dated the 1st January 1810 as "under suspension." An account of the part taken by him in the events leading to the mutiny of officers in 1809 will be found in Part I. He accompanied the Commander-in-Chief, General Macdowell, to England, and both of them were lost at sea, in the *"Lady Jane Dundas,"* on the 14th March 1809.

Dawes, Nathaniel:—Cadet, 1769: Ensign, 13th November 1770: Lieutenant, 26th December 1775: Captain, 2nd November 1783. As a Lieutenant he commanded the 4th Carnatic Battalion in the action against Haidar Ali near Virakanellur on the 23rd October 1781, and he appears to have been in command for the next ten years, dying at Bangalore during Lord Cornwallis' campaign against Tippoo Sultan in 1791. His tomb was formerly in the Fort at Bangalore, and bore the following inscription:—

"Sacred to the memory of Captain Nathaniel Dawes, Commandant of the fourth battalion of N. I., who died March 25th, 1791."

This tomb has, however, with many others, been swept away. In their place stands a modern cenotaph erected by the Mysore Government, at the suggestion of Major Vibart, R. E., to the memory of the officers and soldiers who fell at the siege, and who died in Bangalore in 1791 and 1792, the name of Nathaniel Dawes being included in the list.

An Ensign Dawes, of the 2nd Circar Battalion, was killed at Pullalur in 1780.

Wheller, John:—Ensign, 3rd January 1774. The name is so spelt in the *Madras Army List* for January 1779, but this may have been a misprint for "Wheeler." In this list he is recorded as "dead," so he may never have joined the regiment.

Coke, Thomas:—Ensign, 19th January 1776. Shown as belonging to the regiment in January 1779, but probably never joined.

Chalmers, John:—Ensign, 2nd September 1776. Shown as belonging to the regiment in January 1779, but does not appear to have joined.

Dundas, John Elphinstone:—Ensign, 3rd September 1776. Borne on the rolls in January 1779, but probably never joined.

Thompson, John:—Ensign, 1778. Was posted to the regiment in 1778, but must have gone to some other corps.

One George Nesbitt Thompson was junior advocate to the Company and Private Secretary to Warren Hastings in 1783. He had a son, Christopher Anstey, who died in 1831, when Collector of Nellore. Another George Thompson was a writer in 1776, and became Resident in Negapatam in 1800.

Watkins, John:—Ensign, 1778. Was posted to the 4th at the same time as the above, but I have no record of his services.

Turing, James:—Cadet, 1771: Ensign, 1st May 1773: Captain, 16th November 1783. This officer was commanding the 4th Battalion of Native Infantry in 1792 and 1793. He died on the 13th July 1793, whilst commanding the regiment, at Pennagaram in Salem district, where his tomb is still to be seen on the glacis of the old Fort, with the following inscription:—

"Captain James Turing, Commandant of the Garrison of Pinagra, and the 4th Battalion, Native Infantry."

There were several Turings, which is rather confusing, so I append a few notes on some of the other members of the family.

One Turing, when an Ensign, served with the force sent into the Mahratta country in 1775 under Colonel Keating, to assist the Peshwa, Raghunath Rao, against his rebellious subjects. Philippart says of him:—

" During the retreat of our advanced division, a Mahratta Officer of Cavalry came upon Ensign Turing, a gallant youth of sixteen, who lay upon the ground severely wounded; he ordered him to mount behind on horseback immediately; the young Officer declared it to be impossible from loss of blood, and the nature of his wounds: the Mahratta then ordered him to deliver his sash, as a token to his Commanding Officer that he had done his duty, which having complied with, he was instantly ran over by a troop of cavalry, and almost trampled to death. He was again severely wounded in Colonel Baillie's memorable action in the Carnatic, and finished his short career of glory in a subsequent engagement with the Sultaun of Mysore."

A Robert Turing is shown in the *East India Calendar or Annual Register* for 1795 as belonging to the 4th Battalion. His date of commission as Lieutenant is given as the 9th May 1784, and on the 11th July 1789 he became Brigade Major and Captain. He died at Madras in 1801, when Secretary to Government in the Military Department, and was buried in St. Mary's Cemetery.

Another Robert Turing was appointed Surgeon's Mate at Fort St. David in 1729. He was Surgeon at Vizagapatam in 1841, and one of the Presidency Surgeons from about 1753 to 1762 or later. A Dr. John Turing, Surgeon of the Company's Ship *Greenwich*, at Madras in 1729, may have been his brother.

Another John Turing entered the Civil Service in 1762, was Mayor of Madras in 1776, and a Member of Council 1782—89, and yet another, son of Sir Robert (?) Turing, who was a writer, died at Vizagapatam in 1809.

A William Turing, who entered the Civil Service in 1769, disappears from the lists after 1780.

Oliphant, William:—Cadet, 1780: Ensign, 26th October 1780: Lieutenant, 17th April 1786: Captain, 1st June 1796. Is shown as having proceeded to sea on six months' leave on the 3rd November 1792, and does not appear in any regimental return thereafter. A Lieutenant Oliphant is mentioned by Colonel Wilson as serving with the 5th Battalion, so he was probably transferred. This officer died at sea on the 19th August 1797.

Browne, John:—Cadet, 1780: Ensign, 30th May 1783: Lieutenant, 21st August, 1790: Captain, 10th December 1799. Is shown as Adjutant and doing duty with the regiment, 1788—95. From the 20th April 1795 to 1797, he was commanding the garrison of Virabadradurgam in Salem District, and, from the 7th August 1797, was doing duty with the Pioneers (now the Q. V. O. Madras Sappers and Miners) in the Baramahal. He died at Seringapatam on the 18th August 1808.

Barclay, Robert:—Lieutenant, 17th April 1786. Is shown as present with the regiment, in 1793, but does not appear in subsequent returns. He was invalided in 1796, and died at Vizagapatam on the 1st June 1805.

MacRae, Hugh:—Lieutenant, 7th June 1792. I have not been able to trace this officer. He was serving with the regiment in 1792-93 at Pennagram, Salem District, and in 1794-95 commanded the detachment of the regiment in garrison at Virabadradurgam, after which there is no further mention of him.

Muirhead, Alexander:—Lieutenant, 7th June 1792: Captain, 17th June 1800: Major, 27th June 1805. Is shown as having proceeded to Madras on sick leave on the 9th November 1792, and he was present with the regiment from 1794 to 1797, after which he no longer appears. He died at Onore on the 15th November 1809. *Philippart's East India Military Calendar* states that a Captain Muirhead commanded the 4th on the Expedition to Mahé, but I believe the 4th was commanded by Captain Fraser on this occasion, and Muirhead commanded the 20th Carnatic Battalion. This was in 1779, so that in any case it cannot have been this Muirhead.

Shadwell, Thomas:—Lieutenant, 7th June 1792. Is shown as serving with the regiment from 1792 to 1794, and was transferred to the 23rd N.I., on the 19th November 1794. His health appears to have broken down shortly afterwards and he was sent to Europe in February 1795, and recommended for Lord Clive's Bounty.

Lyon, Robert:—Ensign, 20th January 1789: Lieutenant, 7th June 1792; Captain, 10th December 1799. Only appears in the earliest available regimental record as having proceeded to Madras on sick certificate on the 29th May 1792. He died on the 7th November 1802.

Strut, J. R.:—Ensign, 4th August 1791. I have not been able to trace what happened to this officer. He was serving with the regiment at Pennagaram in 1792-1793.

Grant, Alexander:—Cadet, 1790: Ensign, 28th August 1791: Lieutenant, 6th August 1794: Captain, 17th May 1801: Major, 1st March 1809: Lieutenant-Colonel, 19th January 1816: Colonel Commandant, 1st May 1824: Colonel, 5th June 1829. This officer is shown on the 1st January 1793, as on his way to join the regiment. He was present up to the 31st October 1794, when he went to serve with the 23rd N.I., rejoining the 4th Battalion on the 17th November 1794. In 1795 he was commanding the detachment of the 4th Battalion at Kangundi, and was Adjutant of the regiment from 1796 to 1798, after which he disappears from the returns. In 1817 he is once more shown as Lieutenant-Colonel and Deputy Commissary-General, and finally appears in a return, dated the 1st January 1835, as Colonel Alexander Grant, C.B., and Colonel of the Regiment, but meanwhile he had died in Scotland. I had a note to the effect that he had died on the 6th December 1834, but have since seen a General Order, dated 1st October 1833, which states that authentic information had been received of the death of Colonel Alexander Grant, C.B., which would appear to refer to this officer.

Doveton, Gabriel:—Cadet, 1775: Ensign, 7th May 1776: Lieutenant 9th November 1780: Captain, 29th December 1789; Major, 1st June 1796: Lieutenant-Colonel, 4th May 1799: Colonel, 25th October 1809: Major-General, 1st January 1812. Is shown as posted to the regiment on the 22nd July 1793 but had not yet joined on the 1st January 1794, being on duty in Madras. He was present with, and commanding, the regiment in 1795-98, and again in 1801, proceeding to Europe on furlough on the 20th January of the latter year. He did not rejoin the regiment and I have no further particulars of his services.

He commanded the flank companies of the regiment at the storming of Nandidrug in 1791, and various references to him will be found in Part I, of these records. He died in London on the 9th April 1824.

As in the case of the Turings, there were several Dovetons. Lieutenant-Colonel Doveton who was given the care of Tippu Sultan's family at Vellore after the fall of Seringapatam in 1799 was, I believe, the John Doveton who eventually became Lieutenant-General Sir John Doveton, G.C.B., Commander-in-Chief in Madras in 1826. There is a huge well at Rayakota blasted from the solid rock with his own hands by a Colonel Doveton who I had supposed was Gabriel Doveton, as the latter served with the 4th for so long in the Baramahal, but Cotton says that it was John, though perhaps not on good authority.

A Major William John Doveton of the 36th M.N.I., was promoted to Lieutenant-Colonel on the 18th February 1861, and a Lieutenant-Colonel J. H. Doveton was Consular Agent at Pondicherry in 1873.

MacGregor, Malcolm:—Cadet, 1778: Ensign, 12th August 1778: Lieutenant, 1st April 1783: Captain, 1st June 1796: Major, 10th December 1799. Is shown as commanding the regiment, pending the arrival of Captain Doveton, on the 1st January 1794; and commanding the detachment at Chendraya-durgam from the 4th November 1794; after which he no longer appears in the returns of the 4th Battalion, but appears to have been transferred to the 10th Battalion. He was invalided on the 10th July 1802, and died on the 4th November 1804. There is a plain tombstone in the Fort cemetery at Masulipatam with the words *"Major Malcolm M'Gregor"* inscribed on it.

Symons, John Hilley:—Cadet, 1779: Ensign, 24th August 1780: Lieutenant, 17th April 1786: Captain, 1st June 1796: Major, 21st February 1802: Lieutenant-Colonel, 12th December 1804: Colonel, 9th October 1818: Major-General, 12th August 1819. This officer arrived in Madras on the 10th October 1780, and joined a party of cadets attached to a Madras battalion of European infantry, serving with the army, then encamped near Madras, under the command of Sir Hector Munro. In November he joined the 21st Carnatic Battalion, and served with them throughout Sir Eyre Coote's subsequent campaign, being wounded in the leg in the action at Virakanellur on the 23rd October 1781. On promotion to Lieutenant, he was posted to the 17th Carnatic Battalion, and on the outbreak of hostilities against Tippu Sultan in 1790, he was appointed Adjutant of a Revenue Corps, to render it fit for field service. In 1793, he accompanied Captain Gabriel Doveton, with a grenadier company of the 4th, as part of an escort to the sons of Tippu. On the 1st January 1794, he is shown as absent at Krishnagiri, on sick certificate, since the 24th November 1793. He was "on command" at Madras on the 1st November 1794, and proceeded to Kangundi on the 17th April 1795, to command the detachment, remaining there till 1798, when he disappears from the returns of the 4th. In 1799, he acted as Brigade-Quartermaster to Colonel Read's detachment, becoming Superintendent of Brinjarries during the campaign. In 1800, he was employed by Government on a mission to the Chittoor Pollams, in settling disputes among the Poligars; and, in 1801, in adjusting the supply accounts, and the accounts of the bullock department of the Army. He was next appointed judge and magistrate of a Civil and Criminal Court, established at Seringapatam for the good order and civil government of the fort and island, under the superintendence of Wellesley, who was at that time commanding the forces in Mysore and Malabar, and was subsequently appointed Superintendent of Police and given charge of the bazaars. During the Mahratta campaign, he acted as Agent for Draught and Carriage Cattle, and in 1808 was appointed Superintendent of Police at Madras. On the 11th March 1819 he proceeded to England on medical certificate. He died on the 1st June 1838.

Cormick, Michael H.:—I have not been able so far to trace the career of this officer. He became a Lieutenant on the 21st August 1790, and was serving with the regiment 1794-95, and commanding the detachment at Chendraya-durgam from the 17th April 1795 to 1798, after which his name disappears from the list.

Monin, Antony:—Cadet 1791: Ensign 19th May 1793: Lieutenant, 6th August 1794: Captain, 21st September 1804: Major, 23rd March 1816: Lieutenant-Colonel, 16th May 1822: Colonel, 15th June 1829: Major-General, 28th June 1838.

Is shown as having been appointed from the 2nd European Battalion on the 17th December 1793, but had not joined by the 1st January 1794, and as he makes no further appearance in the returns he must have transferred to another battalion. This is probably the same officer who was buried in the cemetery of St. John's, Trichinopoly, his tombstone being inscribed:—

"Major-General A. MONIN, who departed this life the 5th day of January 1839 in the 65th year of his age, deeply and deservedly regretted, having faithfully served in the King and Honourable Company's Service during a period of 60 years, R. I. P."

With regard to the above, Cotton remarks:—

"A curious instance of a child commission. The General's father was killed in action, and the grant of a commission to the child at the age of five was a way at that time of giving a family allowance."

In December 1834, he was Colonel of the 17th Native Infantry.

Clarke, George:—Lieutenant, 13th July 1770: Captain, 29th December 1777: Major, 17th April 1786: Lieutenant-Colonel, 14th December 1789: Colonel, 1st June 1796. This officer appears to have been the first Colonel of the 4th Regiment after the organisation of the Army in regiments of two battalions. In 1794, he was in command of the 5th Brigade at Madras, and went home on furlough in that year. He is shown as Colonel of the Regiment on the 1st January 1797, but had, as a matter of fact, been allowed to retire with the pay of his rank in 1796.

A Colonel Tredway Clarke, of the Madras Artillery, was promoted to Major-General in June 1813.

Flint, William:—Cadet, 1769: Ensign, 30th September 1770: Lieutenant, 5th May 1774: Captain, 23rd November 1782: Lieutenant-Colonel, 1st June 1796. This officer is shown as Lieutenant-Colonel of the 1st 4th M. N. I. (on furlough) on the 1st January 1797, but was transferred to the 1st 3rd M. N. I., in the following December. *Dodwell and Miles* state that he retired on the 5th May 1795, but this must be a mistake.

His heroic defence of Wandiwash in 1780-81 will be found mentioned elsewhere in these records.

Wilks says of him:—

" Strange as in these days the proposition may sound, this Lieutenant was an officer of very considerable experience: to a scientific knowledge of the theory, he added some practical acquaintance with the business of a siege: and to military talents of no ordinary rank, a mind fertile in resources, and a mild confidence of manner, which, as his troops were wont to say, rendered it impossible to feel alarm in his presence............He was justly deemed to be the centre of all correct intelligence. The model proposed by the experienced for the initiation of the young and aspiring; the theme of general applause; honourable in private life as he was distinguished in public conduct,—the barren glory remained to him of preserving the letters on service, written in Sir Eyre Coote's own hand, full of affectionate attachment and admiration. Colonel Flint is living, and in London. Fancy would associate with the retirement of such a man marks of public approbation, and dignified competency; but human affairs too often reflect an inverted copy of the pictures of the imagination."

Colonel Flint died in 1820.

Corner, Charles:—Cadet, 1775: Ensign, 25th November 1776; Lieutenant, 7th December 1780: Captain, 6th June 1793: Major, 29th November 1797: Lieutenant-Colonel, 10th December 1799: Colonel, 25th October 1809: Major-General, 1st January 1812: Lieutenant-General, 27th May 1825. This officer appears in a return, dated 1st January 1797, where he is shown as on Staff Duty, as Muster Master, Ceded Districts. He was transferred to the 2nd 2nd M. N. I., after attaining his Majority, on the 10th December 1797. He died on the 23rd December 1838.

An Ensign Corner of the 1st Carnatic Battalion was taken prisoner at Pullalur with Colonel Baillie and imprisoned at Seringapatam and this is in all probability the same man.

Innes, James:—Cadet, 1777: Ensign, 4th July 1778: Lieutenant, 7th March 1782: Captain, 1st June 1796: Major, 1st July 1799: Lieutenant-Colonel, 1st January 1803: Colonel, 1st January 1812: Major-General, 4th June 1814. Is shown as a Captain, commanding the detachment of the 1st 4th M. N. I., at Salem from the 12th June 1797 up to 1798, after which his name no longer appears.

An "Ensign Innis," 1st Carnatic Battalion, was shown as wounded and taken prisoner with Colonel Baillie in 1780, but it is not possible to say whether it was this Innes, who was known as James Innes *Junior,* or another, James Innes, *Senior,* who died at Madras in 1804. This James Innes died at Fort St. George on the 21st September 1818, but there does not appear to be any memorial to him there.

Munro, Thomas:—Cadet, 1778: Ensign, 20th May 1779: Lieutenant, 11th February 1786: Captain, 1st June 1796: Major, 7th May 1800: Lieutenant-Colonel, 24th April 1804: Colonel, 4th June 1813: C.B., 14th October 1818: Major-General, 12th August 1819: K. C. B., 26th November 1819.

This was the celebrated Major-General Sir Thomas Munro, *Bart*, Governor of Madras. It is doubtful whether he ever served with the 1st 4th M. N. I., but he was borne on the rolls of the regiment from 1796 to 1798, where he is shown as absent on Staff duty, as Assistant Collector, Ceded Districts.

He died at Gooty, in Anantapur District, on the 6th July 1827, and the following inscription is to be seen in the cemetery there:—

" Major-General Sir Thomas Munro, Bart. and K. C. B., Governor of Madras, died at Putticonda on the 6th July 1827 and was interred at Gooty on the 7th idem. His remains were afterwards removed to the seat of Government, and deposited in St. Mary's Church, Fort St. George."

Cotton says:—

" Munro died of cholera while on tour in his beloved Ceded District. The story goes that shortly before his death he was riding through a pass in the ghauts and imagined that he saw a garland of flowers stretched across the valley. This optical delusion is believed by the natives to have been a presentiment. At Pattikonda Government constructed a tope and tank to his memory; and at Gooty is the Munro Choultry, within which hangs an engraving of Shee's full-length portrait, copies of which also adorn the cutcherries at Bellary and Cuddapah. Munro was known in the Ceded Districts under the appellation of the Father of the People; and in the village of Bellaguppa, Rayadrug Taluk, Bellary District, the eldest sons of a shepherd's family were till recently named after him Munrolappa. Many local ballads were composed in his honour, some of which are still sung."

The inscription on his tomb in St. Mary's Church, Fort St. George, whither his remains were taken in 1831, runs as follows:—

" Near this stone are deposited the remains of Major-General Sir Thomas Munro, Bart, K. C. B., Governor of the Presidency of Fort St. George, who after 47 years of distinguished civil and military services, seven of which he passed at the head of that Government under which he first served as a Cadet, was suddenly called from his labours on the 6th of July 1827 at a moment 'when,' in the language of the Honourable Court of Directors, " he was on the point of returning to his native land in the enjoyment of well-earned honors from his Sovereign and from the Company, having recently manifested a new proof of his zeal and devotion in retaining charge of the Government of Madras after he had intimated his wish to retire therefrom and at a period when the political state of India rendered the discharge of the duties of that high and honorable station ' peculiarly arduous and important.' " Aetat. 65. Sir Thomas Munro was from the earliest period of his career remarkable amongst other men. All those who were associated with him at the commencement of his service, many of whom have since become illustrious in the annals of India and of their country, yielded to him with common consent that pre-eminence which belonged to the ascendency of his character. The resources of his mind rose superior to every emergency of civil government or military enterprise, and he united to those great qualities an unpretending modesty (that exalted sign of innate worth) which courted no applause and which would have obstructed his advancement had not his transcendent merits in the cabinet and in the field forced him into public notice and elevated him to the highest Office of this presidency."

Of Sir Thomas Munro Canning said:—

"Europe never produced a more accomplished statesman nor India, so fertile in heroes, a more skilful soldier."

There is an equestrian statue of him by Chantrey on the Island at Madras, and a portrait by Sir Martin Archer Shee in the Banqueting Hall. His father was a Glasgow merchant trading to Virginia.

Ormsby, Adam:—Cadet, 1780: Ensign, 26th September 1781: Lieutenant, 16th August 1788: Captain-Lieutenant, 29th November 1797. He first appears in the regimental returns as a Lieutenant, on detachment at Salem, on the 1st January 1797, and again in 1798 as a Captain-Lieutenant, after which there is no further mention of him and I have no other information about him except that he died on the 16th October 1800.

There was a Lieutenant of the Indian Navy of this name who was one of the first Europeans to explore parts of Mesopotamia and Arabia, and who wrote one or two books describing his experiences in Baghdad and other places.

Rhodes, William:—Cadet, 1781: Ensign, 15th October 1782: Lieutenant, 24th February 1790. Is shown as a Lieutenant on detachment at Pennagaram on the 1st January 1797, and again in 1798. He died in the latter year but from what cause, or where, is not on record.

Innes, John:—Lieutenant, 3rd April 1790. Is shown as on detachment in Salem from the 12th July 1798 to 1799 and makes no further appearance, as the John Innes, who was serving with the regiment in 1807 must have been another man. There is a tomb at Rayakotta, inscribed:—

"Captain John Innes, of the Honourable East India Company's Service, on their establishment of Fort St. George, aged 40 years."

And this was probably the man. The tomb is dated 20th March 1802, Cotton says that he was then serving in the 14th M.I.

Munro, Robert:—Lieutenant, 26th February 1789: Captain, 8th January 1796: Captain-Lieutenant, 29th November 1797. He is shown on the roll of the regiment in June 1797, but it appears probable that he served with the 2nd 4th and not with the 1st Battalion.

Batchelor, Edward:—Cadet, 1781: Ensign, 28th November 1782: Lieutenant, 21st August 1790: Captain, 26th December 1798: Major, 1st March 1805: Lieutenant-Colonel, 21st July 1808: Brevet-Colonel, 4th June 1814. Is shown on the regimental rolls for 1787-98 as on furlough, and in all probability he never joined the regiment, as he is not heard of again. He retired in England on the 14th April 1817.

Blackburne, William:—Cadet, 1782: Ensign, 5th June 1783: Lieutenant, 21st August 1790: Captain, 10th December 1799: Major, 25th February 1807: Lieutenant-Colonel Commandant of a regiment, 1824. This officer only appears in the regimental returns for 1797-98 as on furlough, and probably never joined. I have had some difficulty in tracing his record as there was another William Blackburne who was killed in the attack on the fort of "Loussoulgaurm" on the 8th October

1804. He arrived at Madras in June 1783, and served with the 24th Battalion in the operations of Colonel Fullarton, returning to garrison at Trichinopoly in 1785. In the following year, he was transferred to the 1st Battalion at Tanjore, where his knowledge of the Mahratta language procured him the appointment of Mahratta Interpreter. In June 1793, he proceeded to England, owing to ill-health, and, at the end of 1798, resumed his appointment at Tanjore. He received the thanks of the Governor-in-Council for his share in the negotiations leading to the treaty of 1799 with the Rajah of Tanjore, and two years later although only a junior Captain, he succeeded Mr. Torin as Resident. In 1806 he was, in addition, given charge of the estates of the Tondiman Rajah (Pudukotta). He resigned his appointment as Resident in 1823, and embarked for England on the 4th March, receiving the thanks of the Governor-in-Council for his eminent services. He died, with the rank of Major-General, on the 16th October 1839.

Another Blackburne who did good service in Madras was John, Collector of Madura, from 1847, to whom there is a monument in Madura town, "erected by a grateful people."

Smith, Henry Francis:—Ensign, 1793: Lieutenant, 12th December 1794: Captain, 8th September 1803: Major, 15th October 1811: Lieutenant-Colonel, 15th February 1818: Companion of the Bath, 8th March 1819: Colonel-Commandant, 1st May 1824: Colonel, 5th June 1829. This officer is shown as present for duty with the 1st 4th M.N.I., on the 1st January 1797, and then does not re-appear in the returns. He was present with the army throughout the operations for the conquest of Mysore, and in June 1799, in his endeavours to quell a mutiny at Gurrumcondah in one of Raymond's French Corps, of which he was Adjutant, he received five pike and bayonet wounds. He served in the Poligar wars of 1800, and received the thanks of Major-General Agnew for the zeal he displayed through the whole course of that campaign.

He commanded the 1st 14th N.I., in the Travancore War, and was commended by Sir T. Hislop, the Commander-in-Chief. For his services in the operations against the Pindarris in 1815—17 he received the thanks of Major-General Smith, the Hon. Mountstuart Elphinstone, and the Governor-General. He was present at the battle of Mahidpur on the 21st December 1817, where he distinguished himself greatly, being awarded a medal, and subsequently admitted to the Order of the Bath. In the two following years he commanded a Brigade, and his conduct was honourably mentioned by Sir John Malcolm and the Marquess of Hastings.

He died at Pondicherry on the 21st February 1834, and his tomb in the English Cemetery there bears the following inscription:—

"Ici repose Henri Francois Smith, Colonel, Compagnon du Bain, qui a ete 40 ans au Service de l' honorable compagnie des Indes, distingue par differentes marques d' approbation de ses chefs, et cheri dans la vie privee comme le superieur le plus doux et le meilleur des maris, et surtout ce qui vaut mieux devant Dieu, le plus humble des chretiens; age de 55 ans.

He had married, in January 1812, Miss Heloise Maissin, who died in 1841.

Mangnall, Kay:—Cadet, 1795: Ensign, 18th February 1796: Lieutenant, 7th May 1797. Was appointed to the 1st 4th on the 17th January 1797, from the 2nd 4th, and joined shortly afterwards, serving with the regiment till 1801, when he was killed in action on the 31st March at Panjalamkurichi. He, with Lieutenant William Fraser of the regiment, who was mortally wounded in the second attempt on Panjalamkurichi in May, was buried at that place, where there is a cemetery near Gavunagiri village in Ottappidaram Taluk.

Speaking of these actions against the Poligars, Colonel Welsh says:—

"No account of this service has been given to the public, and it was customary, while gallant fellows were falling covered with glorious wounds, to put down the casualty in the newspapers as if they had died in their beds, thus 'Deaths Lately to the Southward, Captain—— or Lieutenant——.'"

Trent, Thomas:—Cadet, 1766: Ensign, 14th November 1767: Lieutenant, 27th July 1769: Major, 17th April 1786: Lieutenant-Colonel, 6th February 1787: Colonel, 1st June 1796: Major-General, 1st January 1798. He was appointed Colonel of the 4th Regiment, in succession to Colonel George Clarke, in 1797, but did not join the regiment then, as he had proceeded to Europe on three years' furlough on the 28th February 1797. He retired on the Off-Reckoning Fund on the 8th April 1808, and died in London on the 22nd May 1825.

Little, Joseph:—Cadet, 1771: Ensign, 18th May 1773: Lieutenant, 27th November 1778: Captain, 13th December 1783: Major, 1st January 1796: Lieutenant-Colonel, 29th November 1797. This officer was appointed to the 1st 4th, as Lieutenant-Colonel, on the 10th December 1797, and proceeded to Europe on furlough on the same date. As he retired in June 1798, he cannot have served with the regiment at all.

Pierce, Frederick:—Ensign, 18th June 1786: Lieutenant, 7th June 1792: Captain, 10th December 1799: Major, 21st September 1804: Lieutenant-Colonel, 22nd November 1808: Colonel, 4th June 1814. This officer is shown on the roll, dated 1st January 1798, as belonging to the 1st 4th, but absent on staff duty as Secretary to the Military Board. As he does not appear in any other return, it may be presumed that he did not join the regiment.

He died at Belgaum on the 2nd January 1825.

Hawkins, John:—Ensign, 1793: Lieutenant, 19th December 1795: Captain, 9th October 1804. This officer was serving as a Lieutenant with the regiment on the 1st January 1798, after which he disappears from the list, and must have been transferred to some other battalion.

He died on board the *"Indus"* on the 6th July 1805.

Ormsby, Robert:—This officer was posted to the regiment on the 6th December 1797, but does not appear to have joined. I believe he is the Robert Ormsby who became a Cornet in the Cavalry on the 6th April 1796, and Lieutenant on the 29th November 1797. He was lost in the sinking of the *"Prince of Wales."* Possibly a brother of Adam Ormsby (*q.v.*).

Stanley, Richard:—Ensign, 1795: Lieutenant, 29th November 1797: Captain, 21st September 1804. This officer was present for duty on the 1st January 1798, but makes no further appearance in the list, and must have been transferred. He was cashiered on the 4th March 1808, but I have not discovered for what reason.

Bilcliffe, Joseph:—I have not been able to trace very much of this officer's career. He became a Major-General on the 3rd May 1796, and was Colonel of the 4th Regiment of Native Infantry from the 1st January 1800 to the 30th April 1804, during the whole of which period he was absent on furlough to Europe. In June 1766, as a Lieutenant, he was one of the officers sent by the Madras Government to assist the Government of Bengal when the officers of the Bengal Army mutinied, and he returned to Madras on the 1st September following. When the 19th Carnatic Battalion was raised, in April 1877, Captain Joseph Bilcliffe was made Commandant. He was a Lieutenant-Colonel Commanding a Brigade at the Siege of Pondicherry in 1793, and in the following year he was commanding the 4th Battalion European Infantry at Ellore. I have no particulars of his subsequent service.

Hill, Joseph Gulston:—Cadet, 1777: Ensign, 21st July 1778: Lieutenant, 14th March 1782: Captain, 1st June 1796: Major, 31st July 1799: Lieutenant-Colonel, 1st August 1803. This officer first appears in a return, dated 1st March 1801, as Major of the 1st 4th M.N.I., but he was absent in that and the following year, commanding the 1st Madras Battalion. He was commanding the battalion in 1803 when it was marching to join Sir Arthur Wellesley in the Mahratta country, but appears not to have been in command at the Battle of Assaye. (*Vide Part I, 1803 and account of James Nagle below*). He continued to command the regiment up to the year 1806, when he went to Europe on furlough, and in 1812 he was commanding at Seringapatam, where he died on the 5th April of that year. Seringapatam,—"that grave of thousands," as Colonel Welsh calls it, was notoriously unhealthy, and on the 31st March 1812, out of a brigade nearly 3,000 strong, only 834 officers and men were fit for parade. On the 28th March 1812, old Purniah, the former Dewan of Mysore, died, and Colonel Welsh writes as follows:—

> "Colonel Hill and Poorniah were old acquaintances; and the Colonel was himself dying, when Poorniah sent him word, 'That he was going to the land of his fathers'. He sent back a reply, 'That he was going the same road' and actually survived him only a few days. An old and gallant soldier, devoted to his profession and a keen drill, he was the first man in India that used the pendulum; and he had them, and chain lines, etc., made for him at a considerable expense. In short, drill was his hobby, but there was no unkindness with it; and he died beloved and lamented by all who knew him intimately."

J. J. Cotton says that the tomb of *John* Gulston Hill, who died on the 5th April 1832, is to be seen at Seringapatam. It is inscribed "Colonel J. G. Hill of 1st Battalion 13th Regiment." Cotton has evidently made a mistake in the name.

Darley, John:—Captain, 7th January 1796: Major, 17th June 1800: Lieutenant-Colonel, 19th May 1804. This officer is shown as belonging to the 1st 4th in 1809, in which year he was in Europe on furlough, but I do not think he ever served with the 1st Battalion as on his promotion to Major he was transferred to the 2nd 4th, of which he became Commanding Officer on the 30th May 1804.

Nagle, James:—Cadet, 1780: Ensign, 2nd September 1781: Lieutenant, 12th September 1787: Captain, 7th January 1796: Major, 20th May 1804: Lieutenant-Colonel, 16th July 1807. This officer sailed from England early in 1781, and was in the engagement with the French fleet at Port Praya. Shortly after his arrival in India, he was made a prisoner, when serving with Sir Eyre Coote, and did not regain his liberty till 1784. In 1789, he served with Lieutenant-Colonel James Stuart, and in 1790 with General Medows. He was with Lord Cornwallis throughout the campaign of 1791, and was present at the siege of Bangalore, and all the other operations of that year. In 1792, he accompanied Lieutenant-Colonel Maxwell during that officer's operations in the Tinnevelly district, and in 1793 was present at the siege of Pondicherry. In the following year he served at Nagpur, subsequently returning to Tinnevelly and took part in the expedition to Ceylon in 1796. He left Ceylon for Pondicherry in July 1797, and sailed with the expedition to Manila, which was, however, countermanded, whereupon he proceeded to Malacca with the 3rd European Regiment. In 1800, he returned to Madras and was posted to the 1st 4th which, in the absence of Lieutenant-Colonel Doveton and Major Hill, he commanded till 1802.

Sir John Philippart, in his *East India Military Calendar* states that

"This officer commanded the Corps in the Battle of Assaye, 23rd September, and he received thanks, in brigade orders, from Colonel Wallace, for his conduct in the action........ An addition to his arms was granted him, in consequence of his services at the battle of Assaye, etc., with the motto 'On with you.'"

Some remarks regarding the command of the regiment during this battle will be found elsewhere in these records.

He continued to serve with the 1st 4th throughout the Mahratta campaign, but at the end of 1804 he became very ill and sailed for England, where he arrived in March 1805, finally retiring from the service on the 22nd January 1808: Philippart says of him:—

"During the twenty-four years' service of this officer in India, sixteen of which were in the field and foreign service, he was employed at seven sieges, and in five engagements exclusive of a variety of Poligar and jungle fighting, and he is now totally deprived of sight."

I have found no record of the date of his death.

Bruce, Charles David:—Ensign, 23rd November 1782: Lieutenant, 21st August 1790: Captain, 7th January 1796: Major, 24th January 1805: Lieutenant-Colonel, 11th September 1809. This officer was posted to the regiment as a Captain on the 1st January 1800, but proceeded to Europe, on sick certificate, on the 13th

April 1800, remaining absent up to 1803, after which he was transferred to the 2nd Battalion of the 4th. He died at Fort St. George on the 24th January 1813.

Wilson, James:—Cadet, 1789: Lieutenant, 7th June 1792: Captain, 15th October 1799: Major 1804. He was posted to the 1st 4th M.N.I., as a Captain on the 1st January 1806, but was absent on staff duty, as Muster Master, Ceded Districts, from the 27th December 1800 till 1802. He served with the regiment in 1803, but went to sea for the benefit of his health on the 7th June 1803, and died in Bangalore on the 8th November 1805. There is no record of where he was buried.

Ceville, James:—Cadet, 1790: Ensign, 27th June 1791: Lieutenant, 6th June 1793: Captain, 17th June 1800. He joined the regiment as a Captain on the 17th June 1800, and served with it throughout 1801, and in 1802 was with the detachment at Madras. While still serving with it, he died on the 7th April 1803, but there is no record as to where he died.

Fraser, William:—Cadet, 1792: Ensign, 11th June 1793: Lieutenant, 6th August 1794. Though posted to the regiment on the 1st January 1800, he had not joined by the 1st March 1801, but must have done so immediately afterwards, as he was serving with the 1st 4th during the operations against Panjalamkurichi, and was mortally wounded at the storming of that place on the 21st May 1801, and died on the 26th (*See Note on Lieutenant Kay Mangnall above*).

Walker, Joseph:—Cadet, 1782: Ensign, 20th May 1783: Lieutenant, 21st August 1790: Captain, 17th June 1800: Major, 21st September 1804. Captain Joseph Walker of the 1st 4th commanded the detachment of the Madras European Regiment which formed part of the force despatched in January 1801 against the Dutch island of Ternate in the Moluccas and, on the withdrawal of the troops, was left in command with a small garrison. I have not found his name in any regimental returns. He died at "Chatterpore" on the 11th June 1806. In the cemetery at Ganjam is a tomb bearing the inscription:—

"Major Joseph Walker, 1st Battation 19th Regiment M.N.I., aged 24 years."

Maitland, John:—Captain-Lieutenant Maitland is shown as having been appointed Adjutant and Quartermaster of the 4th N.I. (both battalions) on the 1st January 1800, but I have not been able to find any further reference to him and he was not serving with the regiment in 1803.

Davis, William:—Ensign, 28th April 1793: Lieutenant, 6th August 1794: Captain, 21st March 1802. This is another officer whose name I have not found in the regimental returns, but a Captain Davis of the 1st 4th M.N.I., was transferred to the Pioneers (now the Sappers and Miners) on the 28th January 1803, and this is the man. There must have been two officers of this name as *Dodwell and Miles* call this one William Davis *Junior*. He died on the 26th May 1806.

Muat, George Alexander:—Cadet, 1794: Ensign, 25th January 1796: Lieutenant, 1st June 1796: Captain, 24th June 1803: Major, 22nd May 1807: Lieutenant-Colonel, 14th March 1813. He was posted to the 1st 4th on the 1st January 1800, and was Adjutant of the regiment from the 28th June 1800 till 1803, continuing to serve with it till the 28th October 1805, when he went on furlough, on medical certificate. He remained absent till 1807, when he appears to have joined the 2nd 4th as Major, and was serving with them up to 1813 after which I have no trace of him. He died at St. Thomé on the 23rd March 1822.

There was another Muat who, as a Lieutenant of the Sepoy Marksmen, was captured with Colonel Baillie at Pullalur in 1780.

Newall, David:—Cadet, 1795: Ensign, 13th March 1796: Lieutenant, 16th September 1797: Captain-Lieutenant, 7th August 1803: Captain, 20th May 1804: Major, 4th October 1810: Lieutenant-Colonel, 7th December 1817: C.B., 23rd July 1823: Colonel-Commandant, 1st May 1824. He landed in India in January 1797 and joined a regiment at Pondicherry, with which he embarked for Manila with the expedition which was abandoned after part of the force had been assembled at Penang. He remained in the Moluccas till 1803, taking part in the capture of Ternate in June 1801. He joined the 1st 4th, to which he had been posted on the 1st January 1800, in 1803, but too late to take part in the Mahratta campaign. In 1806 he is shown as absent on medical certificate, but on the 10th December became Inspector of Poligar Forts. He commanded the 1st 4th in the war against the Rajah of Travancore, where he received a severe wound in the arm, and was thanked for his services by Colonel Chalmers, commanding the Division and by the Governor of Madras in Council.

In 1810, he was transferred to the 2nd 4th, was present at the capture of the island of Bourbon on the 8th July 1810, and at the reduction of the Isle of France in December 1810, remaining there till 1812, when he was invalided to England. Returning in 1814, he saw service in the Ceded Districts till 1817, when he was appointed to the command of the garrison and fortress of Darwar. He was present at the sieges and capture of Gadag, Damal, Badami (?), Belgaum and Sholapur, at each of which places he received the thanks of Major-General Sir T. Munro, in Divisional Orders, for his energy and good conduct in the field, and also those of Sir T. Hislop, Commander-in-Chief of the Madras Army and of the Marquess of Hastings. During this period he was borne on the rolls of the 2nd 4th as a Lieutenant-Colonel.

At the end of 1820, he was appointed British Resident at the court of the Rajahs of Travancore and Cochin, and eventually died on the *"Cumberland"* on his way home on the 30th July 1827. Colonel Welsh, who knew him well, says of him:—

"Lieutenant-Colonel D. Newall from whom I parted in 1826, and who died a few months afterwards on his passage to England, was Resident while I was in command of the subsidiary force, and the greatest cordiality subsisted between us at all times. He was a kind-hearted, liberal man, and a particular favourite of Sir Thomas Munro, than whom no man ever possessed a clearer judgment."

Clapham, William:—Cadet, 1796: Ensign, 5th August 1797: Lieutenant, 29th September 1798: Captain, 21st September 1804: Major, 4th June 1817: Lieutenant-Colonel, 25th February 1824: Colonel, 5th June 1829: Major-General,

28th June 1838. He was posted to the regiment on the 1st January 1800, and served with it in the operations against Panjalamkurichi, where he was wounded in the groin. Continuing to serve with the regiment, he was absent, sick, in Madras from the 22nd July 1803: in garrison at Mysore with a detachment in 1805; commanding the detachment at Chomadi in the Wynad in 1806; present at Headquarters in 1807; absent without leave in 1810; present in 1811; on command 1813-14; Brevet-Major 1816; with the Field Detachment at Rajahmundry, 1817; acted in command of the regiment from 1819 to 1823; absent on furlough from 1824-26; commanding the regiment, 1828; after which there is no further mention of him. He died in August 1851.

Marriott, Charles Silwood:—Cadet, 1796: Ensign, 11th September 1798: Lieutenant, 29th December 1798. This officer was posted to the 1st 4th on the 1st January 1800, and continued to be shown in the annual returns up to 1804, but never joined. *Dodwell and Miles* say that he was "struck off, as not arriving on the 8th May 1804," but I do not know what caused his disappearance.

He may be the Charles Marriott who served with the 1st M. N. I. from 1797 till about 1816.

Birch, George:—Cadet, 1798: Lieutenant, 7th August 1799: Captain-Lieutenant, 9th November 1805: Captain, 16th July 1807. He was posted to the 1st 4th on the 1st January 1800, and served with it during the operations against Panjalamkurichi in 1801, where he was wounded, and up to 1804, when he became Adjutant of the 5th Extra Battalion, returning to the regiment in time to see service with it in the Wynad in 1805. In the following year, he was in command of the detachment at Edaterra in the Wynad, as Captain-Lieutenant, and in 1807 he was serving with the regiment at Calcaud. He died in Travancore on the 31st March 1809.

Robertson, William McD.:—Cadet, 1798: Lieutenant, 7th August 1799: Captain, 22nd May 1807: Major, 1st May 1824. He was posted to the regiment on the 1st January 1800, and went on command to Madras with Captain James Ceville on the 28th February 1801. He continued to serve with the regiment till 1810, when he went to the Madras Volunteer Battalion, with which he was still serving in 1813. He is shown as on furlough, on medical certificate, in 1816-17 and again in 1819—21. He was present with the regiment again in 1822 and is shown as still with it up to 1824, when he was acting in command. Colonel Welsh knew him, and writes as follows:—

"On the 4th November 1824, I set out in company with Lieutenant-Colonel Newall, Major Robertson, Captain Lethbridge and Mr. Dalmahoy, Assistant-Surgeon, in boats, on a shooting excursion up the backwater....................Our poor friend, Major Robertson, who had succeeded Captain Rand in command of the 15th Regiment, getting wet through in the Cochin Rajah's large boat with me during the night, laid the foundation of a disease which shortly afterwards killed him. At this time he was one of the healthiest looking men in India; and being of a robust make, with a countenance beaming with intelligence and good nature, of the most abstemious habits, and fond of exercise, he was the man I should have selected from a thousand, as a likely candidate for longevity. Poor fellow; he lingered for a few months, and breathed his last at the Nielgherries, on the 24th of April 1825, sincerely and deservedly regretted by all who knew him."

There is a tablet to his memory in St. Stephen's Church at Ootacamund, which bears the following inscription:—

"Major W. M. Robertson, late 15th Regiment N.I., who died 24th April 1825, and whose remains lie interred in the burying-ground attached to Stone House, aged about 42 years."

The 15th N.I. had, of course, previously been the 2nd Battalion of the 4th N. I.

Palk, Charles:—Cadet, 1799: Lieutenant, 15th July 1800. He was posted to the 1st 4th on the 15th December 1800, and went on command to Madras, with Captain Ceville, on the 28th February 1801. He appears to have been transferred to the 2nd Battalion of the 4th, as he was serving in garrison with them at Gooty in 1802. He died on the 14th December 1802, but there is no record as to where he died.

Palk was a name well-known in the Presidency, Robert Palk having been Governor of Fort St. George from 1763 to 1767, and a Thomas Palk joined the Civil Service in 1768.

Smith, Lewin Scott:—Cadet, 1799: Lieutenant, 15th December 1800: Captain, 9th January 1808. He joined the 1st 4th as a Lieutenant in 1800, and is shown as serving with it in garrison at Madras on the 1st January 1802. In 1804 he appears to have been transferred to another regiment. He retired in England on the 1st March 1819.

Weir, John:—Cadet, 1799: Lieutenant, 15th December 1800. This officer joined the 1st 4th at the end of 1800, and on the 1st January 1802 was serving with it in garrison at Madras, and it was there, presumably, that he died, on the 2nd September 1802, though there is no record of his having been buried there.

Moor, George:—Cadet, 1799: Lieutenant, 15th December 1800: Captain, 18th January 1813. This officer joined the regiment at the end of 1800, and was serving with it in garrison at Madras on the 1st January 1802. In 1804, he was absent, on medical certificate, but rejoined the same year and served with the regiment until 1812, when he went on furlough, on medical certificate. He was invalided on the 10th December 1813, and died at Nellore, on the 29th March 1820, where there is a tombstone in the cemetery, simply inscribed *"Captain George Moor."*

His name was spelt indifferently in the returns as Moor or Moore. He suffered from asthma, as the following certificate shows:—

"I do hereby certify that Lieutenant G. Moor of the 4th Regiment N.I. is unable to join his Corps from severe asthma.

PALLAMCOTTAH, D. PROVAN (?), APTCARY,
19th December, 1810. *Garrison of Pallamcottah."*

Maver, Robert:—Cadet, 1800: Lieutenant, 20th July 1801. He is shown as an Ensign serving with the regiment at Madras, on the 1st January 1802, but the date of his joining is not given, and his date of rank was "not known." He continued to serve with the 1st 4th up to the Battle of Assaye, on the 23rd September 1803, in which battle he was killed.

Bannerman, John:—Cadet, 1776: Ensign, 9th April 1778: Lieutenant, 8th January 1782. Captain, 6th August 1794: Major, 29th September 1798: Lieutenant-Colonel, 8th May 1800. He was posted to the 1st 4th as Lieutenant-Colonel on the 24th May 1802, but probably never joined as on the 1st January 1803, he is shown as absent on furlough, and in 1808 he was chosen as a Director of the Hon'ble East India Company at the election of that year. He died in England on the 6th November 1810.

Dalziel, John:—Cadet, 1800: Lieutenant, 20th July 1801: Captain, 8th January 1816: Major, 6th September 1829. He appears first in a return, dated 1st January 1803, when he was serving with the regiment. From the 3rd September 1803 he was absent on staff duty with the Provision Department, and went to Bengal on 4 months' leave on the 14th September 1804, but was back with the regiment in 1805 and was Adjutant from 1806 to 1816. In 1817 he is shown as a Brevet-Captain, absent on medical certificate. In 1821 he was Superintending Officer of Gentlemen Cadets at Fort St. George, in which employment he remained, though still borne on the roll of the 4th Battalion, till the 10th March 1831, when he retired in India.

Showers, Nathaniel Thornton:—Lieutenant, 6th August 1794: Captain, 15th December 1801. These dates are given by *Dodwell and Miles,* who say that Captain N. T. Showers died on the 23rd June 1803. An officer of this name, who must be the same man I think, was serving with the 2nd 4th in 1802 as Captain-Lieutenant, and appears in the roll of the 1st 4th on the 1st January 1804, as a Captain and on furlough, news of his death having probably not yet been received.

A Major-General Edward Melian Gullifer Showers, of the Madras Artillery, was promoted to Lieutenant-General on the 11th November 1851, and to General on the 4th March 1858.

Palk, Thomas:—Cadet, 1794: Ensign, 31st December 1795: Lieutenant, 8th January 1796: Captain, 8th April 1803. He was posted to the 1st 4th on the 1st January 1800 and is shown as a Lieutenant in the 2nd 4th on field service in 1802. Rejoining the 1st 4th, he became a Captain-Lieutenant on the 20th April 1803. He was absent, sick, at Adjanta from the 8th October 1803 to 1805, and died on the 1st April 1805. He was probably a brother of Charles Palk (*q. v.*).

Harris, William:—I have not been able to find out much about this officer. He was with the 2nd 4th at Gooty in 1802, having been promoted Lieutenant on the 1st December 1800. He was serving with the 1st 4th in 1804-05; was absent on detachment at "Pullingall" in 1806; absent on medical certificate from the 1st November 1806; present for duty in 1810; Captain-Lieutenant, and still serving, in 1811 and 1813: absent on furlough, on medical certificate, in 1814—16; became a Captain in the latter year, and was still on furlough in 1817 after which his name disappears, so presumably he either retired, or died in England, in that year. There is a medical certificate, dated Cuddalore, 22nd November 1813, showing that he suffered from a chronic affection of the liver.

Hargrave, William:—Cadet, 1801: Lieutenant, 2nd July 1803: Captain, 1st January 1819. This officer was posted to the 1st 4th on the 2nd July 1803, but did not join the regiment till some time in 1804, when he is shown as present for duty till 1807, and again in 1810-11. In 1812, he went on furlough, on medical certificate, and is still shown as absent up to 1817. He was present with the regiment again, as a Captain-Lieutenant, on the 1st January 1819, and died at Berhampur on the 28th November of that year.

Another Hargrave was Collector of Salem, and died there in 1830, aged 56.

Chillingworth, Joseph:—Cadet, 1802: Lieutenant, 9th May 1804. This officer joined the 1st 4th in 1804, and served with it up to 1806. He died at Seringapatam on the 15th December 1806.

Bowser, Thomas:—This officer was Colonel of the 4th Regiment of Native Infantry from 1805 to 1820. He joined the 1st Madras European Regiment as an Ensign in December 1773, and rose in it through every grade until promoted Lieutenant-Colonel in 1797. He was a full Colonel in 1805; Major-General, 1812; and Lieutenant-General, 1815.

He served at the siege and capture of Pondicherry in 1778, and two years later was present with Colonel Baillie's force at Pullalur, as a Lieutenant in Captain Ferrier's European Grenadiers. Here he "received a musquet ball in the leg during the engagement, and eight wounds with a scymitar after the surrender and was left for dead." He recovered consciousness and tried to get to Conjeveram on the 11th September, but was captured and taken before Haidar, and subsequently joined the other prisoners. He continued a prisoner in Bangalore fort, heavily ironed, till 1784.

He subsequently served in all the other wars in India, and in 1799 was in command of a detachment of the Hyderabad Subsidiary Force, which invested and captured Gooty, while he was present at the operations against Dhoondiah in 1800.

He acted as Commander-in-Chief in Madras from the death of Sir A. Campbell on the 11th December 1824 till the arrival of Sir G. Walker on the 3rd March 1826, having previously acted for a short time in June 1821. He departed for Europe early in 1826. A copy of his farewell Order to the Army has been given elsewhere in these records. On the 26th December 1826, he received the K. C. B.

Sir Thomas Bowser died in England, on the 14th July 1833, from a disease of the legs caused by the galling of the heavy irons while in captivity.

Scott, Robert:—Cadet, 1793: Lieutenant, 5th August 1795: Captain, 8th April 1803: Major, 9th November 1805: Lieutenant-Colonel, 4th October 1810: C. B., 14th October 1818: Colonel, 1st May 1824: Major-General, 22nd July 1830: K. C. B., 27th September 1831. This officer served originally with the 2nd 4th and was transferred to the 1st 4th on the 12th December 1805 but did not join till later as he was absent in Europe, on medical certificate, on the 1st January 1806. In the following year he was acting in command of the regiment, and is shown as Lieutenant-Colonel Commanding from the 21st October 1810 till 1811, and succeeded Lieutenant-Colonel William Blackburne (*q. v.*), as Resident at Tanjore in 1823. He died at Haddington, N. B., on the 21st December 1832. His name is occasionally spelt "Scot" in the returns, but he signed his name as "Scott." There were several other Scotts serving in the Presidency at the same time, including Captain John Scott, A. A. G. at Cannanore, who died in 1818, and Lieutenant-Colonel James George Scott, Commandant of Seringapatam, 1814—1818, afterwards a Major-General, whose "deserted bungalow" in that place has been made famous by "Aliph Cheem" (Captain Yeldham) in the *"Lays of Ind."*

A further note reads as follows:—

"It was a fortunate circumstance that Sir Walter Scott, the father of the 19th Century novel, had numerous personal connections with India, his brother-in-law having been Collector of Salem, and his eldest son having joined the Indian Military Service. It was noteworthy that this son had been in Bangalore before he left on the voyage home which was to prove fatal to him."

James Bristow mentions a Captain Scott, commanding the *Prince of Wales* Indiaman in 1771, who had lost an arm in a duel fought at Madras.

Williams, William:—Cadet, 1803: Lieutenant, 21st September 1804. This officer appears to have been posted to the 1st 4th on the 30th January 1805. He was absent at the sea-coast on sick certificate on the 1st January 1806, but had returned to duty before the 1st January following. He is shown as absent without leave in 1810, but was present for duty in 1811. In the following year he proceeded to England, on medical certificate, and died there on the 13th February 1815.

Walker, Andrew:—Cadet, 1803: Lieutenant, 21st September 1804: Captain, 9th August 1819. This officer was posted to the 1st 4th on the 30th January 1805, and was serving as Captain Clapham's subaltern at Chomadi from 30th November 1805. He was present at Headquarters on the 1st January 1807. In 1810, he was Aide-de-Camp to General Gowdie, and in the following year is shown as "A.M.B., Malabar," while from 1813 to 1819 he is shown as "M. B.,—Malabar,"—which was probably "Major of Brigade." He does not appear to have rejoined the regiment, and I have no further particulars of his career up to his death, at Bangalore, on the 22nd November 1831.

Lieutenant-Colonel James Walker of the 3rd M.N.I., who was killed in action near Rangoon in 1824, may have been a brother.

Sheen, Henry:—Cadet, 1803: Lieutenant, 21st September 1804. Henry Sheen or Sheene was posted to the 1st 4th on the 20th August 1805, and was on detachment at "Eddatorra" in the Wynad with Captain Birch from the 15th December 1805. He served continuously with the regiment up to the 2nd May 1818, when he died at Aska, in Ganjam District.

Stock, Arthur:—Cadet, 1800: Lieutenant, 29th December 1802: Captain, 4th June 1817: Major, 25th April 1824. This officer was serving with the 2nd 4th in

1802, but seems to have been posted to the 1st 4th on the 6th January 1803 though he does not appear in any return until the 1st January 1807, when he is shown as absent on Staff duty since the 9th September 1804, as Assistant Secretary to the Military Board. From the 19th June 1810 he was absent on furlough in Europe, and re-appears as Deputy-Paymaster of Vizagapatam in 1816—19. In 1819, he became Paymaster of the Northern Division and is shown in that employment up to 1824. He died at Ispahan on the 5th August 1831, but I have no information as to what he was doing in Persia.

Button, Philip:—Cadet, 1804: Lieutenant, 17th July 1805. He was posted to the 1st 4th on the 20th February 1806, and is shown as absent on furlough on the 1st January 1807. He appears to have remained absent, on medical certificate, up to 1814. *Dodwell and Miles* say that he was "struck off," so presumably he was never fit enough to return to India.

Innes, John:—Cadet, 1803: Lieutenant, 21st September 1804. This officer first appears in a return, dated the 1st January 1808, when he was present for duty, and he apparently continued to serve with the 1st 4th up to the 22nd December 1812, when he proceeded to Europe on furlough, on medical certificate, and died on the 28th January 1817.

Hammond, Anthony:—Cadet, 1805: Ensign, 17th June 1806: Lieutenant, 16th July 1807. First appears with the regiment as "present, sick," in a return, dated 1st January 1808. He was absent, on medical certificate, at Anjengo, from the 8th December 1809, and rejoined in 1810. He resigned his commission on the 15th March 1811. There is a certificate extant, dated Anjengo, 30th December 1809, which states:—

"This is to certify that Lieutenant A. Hammond of 1st Batt. 4th Regt. N. I. is so unwell as to be unable to join his Corps.

(*Signed*) JAMES ALEXR. MAXWELL,
Assist. Surgeon."

LePage, John:—Cadet, 1805: Ensign, 27th June 1806: Lieutenant, 16th March 1811. He was absent on furlough on the 1st January 1808, having been posted to the regiment in 1807. When he joined from furlough, he served with the 1st 4th until the 28th March 1813, when he died in India, presumably at Bellary, where the regiment was stationed at that time.

Wallis, Henry:—Cadet, 1805: Ensign, 27th June 1806: Lieutenant, 16th March 1811: Captain, 1st May 1824. He appears to have been posted to the regiment in 1807, and was absent on furlough, in the Presidency, on the 1st January 1808. He is returned as present on duty in 1810—11, 1813—14 and 1816. On the 1st January 1817, he was acting as Adjutant, and he was Adjutant from 1818 to 1822, being absent only for a short time from the 21st December 1819, when he was on Staff duty. On the 1st October 1822, he went on furlough, and is shown as still absent in 1824, after which he no longer appears in the returns. He died on the 28th May 1829, and had probably been transferred to the 2nd 4th (*i.e.*, 15th

N. I.), on promotion to Captain in 1824, as his tombstone in Coimbatore bears the inscription:—

"Henry Wallis, Captain, 15th Regiment. aged 42 years."

Moore, James:—Cadet, 1796: Lieutenant, 29th November 1797: Captain, 21st September 1804: Major, 19th February 1813. This officer appears as a Lieutenant in the 2nd 4th on the 1st January 1800, and again with that battalion as "Sick, absent," in 1802. He first appears on the strength of the 1st 4th on the 1st January 1810, when he was absent, sick, at Ganjam, and the following certificate is still extant:—

"I do hereby certify that Captain James Moore of the 1st Battalion 4th Regiment N. I. has been affected with Symptoms of Hepatitis for a considerable time and is now in a Debilitated State.—And it is my opinion that it is absolutely necessary that he should proceed to sea for the recovery of his health.

GANJAM,
4th of November 1809.

THOS. OWEN,
Garrn. Surgn."

He was present on duty with the regiment in 1816 and was acting in command in 1817, and he died at Bimlipatam on the 3rd June of that year where his tombstone in the Flagstaff Cemetery bears the following inscription:—

"Major James Moore, 4th Regiment M. N. I., aged 36 years, nineteen of which had been dedicated to the Service of the H. E. I. Company. Erected by the officers of both Battalions as a tribute to friendship and pledge of their sincere regard."

Duggan, Timothy Frederick:—Cadet, 1797: Ensign, 25th July 1798: Lieutenant, 26th October 1798: Captain, 1st April 1805. As a Lieutenant, this officer belonged to the 2nd 4th and was serving as Major of Brigade to Colonel Oliver in the Moluccas Islands in 1802. From the 20th October 1805, he was employed as Deputy Judge-Advocate in the Northern Division and it is in this employment that he is shown as serving when he first appears in the returns of the 1st 4th on the 1st Jaunary 1810. He went on furlough to Europe on the 4th December 1810, and died at Cork on the 11th April 1813.

Erskine, James:—Cadet, 1802: Lieutenant, 21st September 1804. This officer does not appear to have served with the regiment. On the 1st January 1810, he is shown as having been posted to the 1st 4th, but as being absent without leave; while from 1811 to 1814 he is shown as serving with the 2nd 12th N. I. He died at Bombay on the 12th November 1819. In Ranipet Cemetery, North Arcot District, there is a tombstone, dated 18th June 1814, which bears the following inscription:—

"G. W. J. Erskine. Lieutenant, 4th Light Cavalry, aged 32 years. This monument was erected as a token of fraternal affection by Lieutenant James Erskine, 4th Regiment N. I."

There was a John Erskine, Collector of Ongole and the Palnad, who died in 1792, and may have been the father of these two.

Pringle, Francis:—Cadet, 1806: Ensign, 3rd July 1807. He was present for duty with the 1st 4th on the 1st January 1810, and appears to have continued to serve in the regiment up to his death on the 3rd February 1811, but I have not discovered where he died, though the following certificate would seem to show that it was somewhere in Canara:—

"This is to certify that Lieutenant Pringle of the 1st Battalion 4th Regiment N. I. is unable to join his Corps in consequence of a Dysenteric complaint accompanied with affection of the Liver.

JOHN GRANT,

December 29th, 1810.   *Garrison Surgeon of Canara.*"

Sibbald, Andrew:—Cadet, 1806: Ensign, 3rd July 1807: Lieutenant, 28th March 1813: Captain, 12th July 1824. This officer joined the regiment in 1809, and appears to have served with it continuously up to 1822. He acted as Adjutant for a time in 1819-20, and proceeded on furlough, on medical certificate, on the 14th April 1822. After 1824 he disappears from the roll, and he died at Vellore on the 2nd August 1830. He was probably transferred to another battalion on promotion to Captain.

A Captain John Sibbald, of the 34th Chicacole Light Infantry, died at Cannanore in 1844.

Payne, John:—Cadet, 1806: Ensign, 3rd July 1807. He joined the 1st 4th in 1809, and served with the regiment till his death at Bellary on the 27th February 1813. He may have been a brother of Lieutenant George Payne, 1st 6th M.N.I., who died at Ellore in 1820. The latter had some reputation as a painter, and one of his paintings, a view of Gingee, hangs in a corridor of the India Office.

Forbes, Nathaniel:—Cadet, 1781: Ensign, 1782: Lieutenant, 21st August 1790: Captain, 26th December 1798: Major, 11th July 1802: Lieutenant-Colonel, 5th February 1805: Colonel, 4th June 1813: Major-General, 12th August 1819: Lieutenant-General, 10th January 1837. This officer was appointed to the 1st 4th, as Lieutenant-Colonel, on the 13th September 1812, but had not joined by the 1st January 1813, and thereafter appears no more in the returns of the regiment, so presumably he never joined. I have not traced to which regiment he belonged.

A Lieutenant B. J. Forbes of the 74th Regiment was killed in Colonel Maxwell's attack on Krishnagiri Fort on the 7th November 1791, and a Captain James Forbes was promoted to Major in the 2nd Madras European Light Infantry on the 11th November 1851.

Carter, Henry:—Ensign, 10th December 1808. This officer was serving as an Ensign with the 1st 4th on the 1st January 1813, but went to serve with the 1st 3rd M. N. I. later in that year. On the 12th December 1815, he was transferred to the 2nd 4th, and I have been unable to trace him further.

Walker, Thomas:—Ensign, 27th February 1811. This officer was present for duty with the 1st 4th on the 1st January 1813, but I can find no other mention of him. The date of his rank precludes him from being considered the same man as the Thomas Walker given later on (*q. v.*).

Van Heythuysen, Henry Thomas:—Ensign, 25th May 1811: Lieutenant, 14th February 1815. This officer joined the regiment in 1812, and continued to serve with it till 1823. He saw a good deal of field service in 1817-18 in the Northern Districts, and was in command of the detachment of the 4th at Sorokota in the latter year. In 1819, he was on recruiting service, and he was Quartermaster of the regiment from 1810 to 1823. He proceeded to Europe, on medical certificate, on the 15th July 1823, and did not rejoin the regiment. In 1834, he was serving with the Carnatic European Veteran Battalion, and in 1836, as a Captain, with the 1st Native Veteran Battalion. On the 24th June 1836, he was permitted to return to Europe and to retire from the service of the Honourable Company.

Martin, George:—Cadet, 1779: Ensign, 4th September 1780: Lieutenant, 17th April 1786: Captain, 2nd July 1796: Major, 24th August 1803: Lieutenant-Colonel, 23rd March 1805: Colonel, 4th June 1813. This officer was sent with a draft from the 1st 4th to the 2nd Extra Battalion (28th M. I.) in October 1798. He was appointed Lieutenant-Colonel of the 1st 4th on the 7th July 1813, and was absent on command at Advana, by order of Major-General Taylor, from the 7th December 1813. He never rejoined the regiment, but died at Bellary on the 17th June 1815.

Hall, Humphry Senhouse:—Cadet, 1804: Lieutenant, 17th July 1805: Captain, 25th February 1824. This officer first appears on the roll of the 1st 4th on the 1st January 1814, when he was absent, having proceeded on three years' furlough to Europe on the 4th September 1812. He was acting in command of the regiment in 1826, and died on the 15th July 1827.

Metcalf, John:—Cadet, 1812: Ensign, 6th July 1813: Lieutenant, 1st June 1817: Captain, 8th September 1826. He was posted to the 1st 4th in 1813, and was on service with the regiment in 1816—17. On the 15th September 1818, he proceeded on furlough, on medical certificate, and was still absent up to 1822. In 1826, we find him serving as Fort Adjutant at Bellary, but he was invalided in India on the 17th August 1827, and died at Madras on the 18th June 1833.

O'Reilly, Edward:—This officer was appointed to the 1st 4th as Lieutenant-Colonel on the 4th August 1814, and was commanding the regiment on the 1st January 1816, but died at Samulcotta on the 22nd March following. His tombstone in Samulcotta Cemetery is inscribed as follows:—

"Colonel Edward O'Reilly of the 1st Battalion, 4th Regiment, aged 58 years, 36 of which were spent with distinguished reputation in the Service of the Hon'ble Company."

I have not been able to trace any particulars of the earlier part of his service.

Jobson, James:—Cadet, 1800: Lieutenant, 20th July 1801: Captain, 11th December 1813. He was posted originally to the 2nd 4th, and was appointed to the 1st 4th on his promotion to Captain. He served with the regiment during the operations in the Northern districts (*vide Part I of these records*) in 1817-18, and died of fatigue and exposure at Berhampur on the 3rd June 1818, after having been selected to command the newly raised Ganjam Hill Rangers on the 9th February 1818. There is a tombstone to his memory in the cemetery at Bhapur, Berhampur Town, (Ganjam District) which is in the heart of the town and choked among houses, the inscription reading as follows:—

"Captain James Jobson, of 1st Battalion 4th N. I., who died after a few hours' illness from excessive fatigue in the zealous discharge of his duty against the rebels in the Moherry hills, aged 34 years."

Conway, Henry:—Cadet, 1802: Ensign, 17th April 1803: Lieutenant, 26th May 1804: Captain, 29th November 1819. He appears to have joined the 1st 4th in 1814 or 1815, and from the 22nd February 1815, up to 1818, was on field service with a detachment of the regiment. On the 6th September 1819, he became Cantonment Adjutant at Wallajahbad, and on the 7th February of the following year he was appointed Brigade-Major at Secunderabad, proceeding on furlough in 1812, and rejoining the regiment in 1822. In 1824, he was commanding a detachment of the 2nd N. V. Battalion at Nellore. He retired in England on the 6th January 1828.

Grant, Charles St. John:—Cadet, 1806: Ensign, 3rd July 1807: Lieutenant, 12th April 1813: Captain, 8th September 1826: Brevet-Major, 10th January 1837: Major, 15th June 1838. This officer does not appear to have actually served with the regiment, though he was borne on its rolls from 1815 to 1823, when he is shown as having been transferred to the 2nd 4th, but on the re-organisation of the Army in 1824, he was returned to the 4th M. N. I., disappearing finally from the list in 1826. On the 12th April 1813, he was posted for service with the Resident's Escort at Hyderabad, and remained in that employment certainly up to the date of his promotion to Major. In the cemetery at the back of the Hyderabad Residency, there is a tomb inscribed:—

"Charles Russell Falkland Murray Grant, the only child of Lieutenant Charles St. John Grant of the Resident's Escort, who died on the 4th September 1817, aged 10 months and 19 days."

Grant had married a Miss Mary Stoddard on the 12th December 1812.

He was serving as a Major in the 52nd M.N.I. at Sholapur in January 1839, and in command of the same regiment at Bangalore in 1842, in which year large numbers of men of that regiment were court-martialled for having refused to receive their pay without field batta, the latter having been discontinued by order of the Government of India. Most of them were sentenced to two years' imprisonment and sent to Salem Jail. In 1843, he was commanding the 18th N.I., but was subsequently transferred to the 42nd N.I. He died at Walthair on the 20th December 1852, being then a Lieutenant-Colonel.

Haleman, Francis:—Cadet, 1812: Ensign, 6th July 1813: Lieutenant, 14th August 1816: Captain, 19th September 1826: Major, 9th October 1830: Lieutenant-Colonel, 20th February 1836: Colonel, 27th August 1847. This officer appears to have been posted to the regiment in 1815 and served with it throughout the operations in the Northern Districts from 1815 to 1821, and up to 1824. He apparently went to the 15th N.I., with which regiment he was serving prior to his promotion to

Lieutenant-Colonel in 1836. He was court-martialled at Fort St. George on the 10th December 1834 for having come to blows with the Commander of the ship *Ganges,* thereby setting a bad example to the men and officers of the detachment under his command, and occasioning himself to be placed in arrest by a junior officer, and was sentenced to be suspended from rank, pay and allowances for seven calendar months. The President of the Court was Colonel Anthony Monin. (*q. v.*). He commanded the 14th N.I., in the war with China in 1842, when the Madras troops received the highest praise from Lieutenant-General Sir Hugh Gough, subsequently joining the 46th N.I., from which, on the 11th May 1843, he was transferred to the 16th N.I. He became a Lieutenant-Colonel Commandant on the 22nd September 1845, and was commanding the 25th N.I., in 1846-47. He died on the 2nd January 1854.

Watson, David:—Cadet, 1811: Ensign, 11th June 1812: Lieutenant, 15th August 1816. He appears to have been posted to the 1st 4th just before his promotion to Lieutenant in 1816, and served with it in the Northern Districts up to the 22nd September 1820, when he left for Europe, on medical certificate, but died at the Cape of Good Hope on the 11th December 1820. He was probably a brother of Thomas Watson. (*q. v.*)

Munro, John:—This officer was appointed Lieutenant-Colonel of the 1st 4th on the 18th August 1818, having been promoted to that rank on the 9th February of that year. At that time he was Resident of Travancore, and consequently he did not join the regiment. On the 19th January 1819, he proceeded to Europe on three years' furlough and we do not hear of him again till the 24th December 1842, when, as a Major-General, he became Colonel of the regiment, an appointment which he held up to the 4th March 1854. He had previously been Colonel of the 31st (Trichinopoly) Light Infantry. He appears to have died on the 26th January 1858.

Hunter, Robert:—This officer appears to have been posted to the 1st 4th on promotion to Captain on the 4th June 1818, but there is nothing to show that he ever joined as he proceeded to Europe on furlough on the 11th July 1818, and was still on furlough till 1821, on the 19th November of which year he was transferred to the 2nd 4th. He was still serving with them in 1824, and became Secretary to the Clothing Board in the following year, after which I have not been able to trace him.

Dyce, Archibald Brown:—Cadet, 1816: Lieutenant, 4th June 1817: Captain, 16th July 1827: Major, 19th March 1831: Lieutenant-Colonel, 10th April 1836: Lieutenant-Colonel Commandant, 7th September 1846: Colonel, 27th August 1847: Lieutenant-General, 26th June, 1860. He appears to have been posted to the 1st 4th on the 4th June 1817, but from the 5th August 1817 till 1821 (?) he was absent, acting as A.D.C. to Major-General Dyce. In 1823, he became Adjutant of the regiment, and on the 25th May 1824, was appointed Brigade-Major at Bangalore, an appointment which he held up to 1829. In 1832, he was acting in command of the regiment, and proceeded on furlough on the 15th January 1834. On the 27th July

1836, he was transferred to the 52nd Regiment of Native Infantry, and on the 3rd April 1838, from the 45th N.I. to the 1st N.I. On the 15th October 1839, he was transferred from the command of the 34th Chicacole Light Infantry to command the new 2nd Madras European Regiment, but appears to have returned to the 34th L.I., as, on the 2nd June 1842, he was transferred from that regiment to the 14th N.I. In June 1844, when he is shown as belonging to the 1st N.I., he was appointed to the command of Jaulnah. On the 27th July 1844, he was transferred from the 1st to the 52nd N.I., and on the 18th July 1845, was promoted to Brigadier, 1st Class, and put in command of the Hyderabad Subsidiary Force. On the 16th February 1847, he was appointed to command the Northern Division of the Army, *vice* Lieutenant-General Welsh, and on the 21st November 1862, (having then risen to the rank of Lieutenant-General), he was appointed Colonel of the 105th Regiment of Foot.

This Dyce was probably connected with the well-known family of that name which played a considerable part in the early history of the English in Northern India. The originator of the family in India appears to have been a Lieutenant David Dyce, who died at Fort William in 1789, leaving a son by an Indian wife. This son, George Alexander David (known as "General" Dyce) married a granddaughter of Walter Reinhardt (*alias* Zafir Yah Khan), who was husband of the Begum Sumru, and was himself Commandant of that forceful lady's army. He had one son, David Ochterlony Dyce Sombre, whom the Begum adopted as her heir, and whose wealth and eccentricity impressed London society for a time in the eighteen-thirties. A reference to the Begum Sumru will be found in Part I of these Records, at the end of the account of the battle of Assaye. Archibald Brown Dyce had, I believe, a son who was a well-known Shakespearean editor.

McNeill, Daniel:—Cadet, 1771: Ensign, 23rd October 1772: Lieutenant, 4th August 1778: Captain, 2nd November 1783: Major, 1st June 1796: Lieutenant-Colonel, 27th July 1796: Colonel, 1st January 1803: Major-General, 25th July 1810: Lieutenant-General, 4th June 1814. This officer, of whose services I have no record, was Colonel of the 4th Regiment of Madras Native Infantry from 1820 (when he succeeded Sir Thomas Bowser) to 1824. He died in London on the 21st October 1826.

There is a monument in Madras to a Brigadier Malcolm MacNeill who died in Rangoon in 1852.

Alcock, Francis:—Cadet, 1818: Lieutenant, 13th June 1819. This officer was appointed to the 1st 4th in 1819, but never came out to India, as he died in England in 1820.

MacLeod, Charles:—Cadet, 1794: Ensign, 12th January 1796: Lieutenant, 1st June 1796: Captain, 21st September 1804: Major, 23rd October 1815: Lieutenant-Colonel, 13th July 1821: C. B., 23rd July 1823: Colonel, 5th June 1829: Major-General, 28th June 1838. He was appointed Lieutenant-Colonel of the 1st 4th on the 23rd July 1821, but was absent on Staff duty as Deputy Quartermaster-General to the Hyderabad Subsidiary Force, in which employment he remained up to 1824, after which he disappears from the returns of the regiment.

Webbe, James Taylor:—Cadet, 1807: Ensign, 6th April 1810: Lieutenant, 2nd February 1814: Captain, 8th September 1826. He appears to have been posted to the 1st 4th in 1821, but was absent in Europe, on sick certificate, from the 15th September 1820, and presumably never joined the regiment as in 1824 he was serving with the 2nd 4th. He was invalided in India on the 15th February 1833. He probably belonged to the family of Josiah Webbe, a famous Madras Civilian and Resident of Mysore, who died in 1804.

Smith, William Hope:—Cadet, 1818: Lieutenant, 13th June 1819: Captain, 7th January 1828: Major, 20th February 1836. He was posted to the 1st 4th in 1821, but proceeded on sick certificate to Europe on the 13th July of that year, and as he was serving with the 2nd 4th in 1824, he appears never to have joined the 1st 4th. I can trace him no further.

Haldane, Edward:—Cadet, 1819: Lieutenant, 10th June 1820: Captain, 11th March 1831: Major, 28th May 1842: Lieutenant-Colonel, 3rd March 1848: Brevet-Colonel, 28th November 1854: Major-General, 18th March 1859. This officer joined the regiment in 1821; was acting as Adjutant in 1823, and as Quartermaster in 1827, proceeding to Europe, on medical certificate, on the 22nd January 1828. He was present for duty again in 1831, and acted in command in 1835. On the 13th December 1836, he was appointed to command the Resident's Escort in Mysore, and once more went to Europe on sick certificate in February 1839. In 1841, he rejoined the regiment from 1843 till the 17th July 1848, when he was transferred to the 42nd N.I., and in the following August proceeded to Europe on furlough. On his return, he was posted to the 43rd N.I., and on the 16th February 1850, was transferred to the 12th N.I. In January 1853, he proceeded to Europe, on medical certificate, from the 52nd N.I., and on the 7th March 1856, was transferred from the 1st Madras Fusiliers to command the 4th, being transferred again to the 37th Grenadiers on the 10th November 1856, when he was succeeded by Lieutenant-Colonel W. Cotton.

Ross, John Maitland:—Cadet, 1819: Lieutenant, 13th June 1819: Captain, 16th December 1832. This officer was posted to the regiment in 1821, but had proceeded to Europe on sick certificate on the 4th September 1821. He is shown as still absent up to 1824, when his name disappears from the list. He was transferred to the 5th N.I., as appears from the following inscription on a tablet in St. George's Cathedral, Madras:—

" Sacred to the memory of Captain John Maitland Ross, 5th Regiment N. I., who departed this life on the 18th May 1839, aged 36 years. His widow has erected this well deserved tribute to the memory of a kind and affectionate husband."

Stokes, John Day:—Cadet, 1817: Lieutenant, 28th October 1818: Captain, 18th August 1827: Major, 10th April 1836: Lieutenant-Colonel, 6th April 1841: Brevet-Colonel, 17th March 1851: Colonel, 29th August 1851: Major-General, 28th November 1854. This officer appears to have joined the regiment in 1822, and served with it till the 30th December 1825, when he went to Hyderabad on the staff of the Resident. He acted as Quartermaster of the regiment from 1823 till 1825. He rejoined the regiment for duty in 1830 (?) but from the 13th April 1831 he is shown as "under the orders of the Supreme Government," and on the 26th February 1833, he proceeded to Europe on furlough. On the 29th May 1835, he went to Mysore, and is shown as Resident of Mysore till 1841, when he disappears from the rolls of the 4th. In 1843, he was on the roll of the 7th N.I., and in October of that year proceeded to Europe, on medical certificate. In October 1848, he was transferred from the 35th N.I., to the 18th N.I., and in the following December, from the 18th N.I., to the 48th N.I. On the 3rd March 1850, he was again transferred to the 25th N.I., and on the 26th April 1850 was appointed a Brigadier of the 2nd Class and posted to command the Southern Division and Trichinopoly. He died on the 11th December 1862. (*Vide Oliver Day Stokes*).

Marshall, George:—Cadet, 1819: Lieutenant, 24th July 1821. He appears to have joined the regiment on promotion to Lieutenant in 1821, and served with it till the 7th March 1825, when he was cashiered. He was the second officer of that name to meet with this fate in 1825. (*Vide John H. Marshall*).

Faunce, Edmund Burrell:—Cadet, 1819: Ensign, 6th April 1820: Lieutenant, 17th September 1823: Captain, 3rd August 1830. He joined the regiment in 1821 and served with it up to 1824, after which his name drops out of the returns.

He was probably a brother of Major-General Robert Nicholas Faunce, to whose memory there is an inscription in the Agram Cemetery, Bangalore, and who was drowned in 1869, aged 64.

McNair, Archibald:—Cadet, 1820: Ensign, 13th February 1821: Lieutenant, 12th July 1824: Captain, 31st May 1831. He was appointed to the 1st 4th in 1821, but he did not join till 1822, and on the 2nd December 1823 he went on sick leave, and never rejoined. He was transferred to the 2nd Battalion, apparently, as his tombstone in Chittoor Cemetery bears witness:—

"Captain Archibald Macnair, late of the 15th Regiment, aged 33 years."

He died on the 11th July 1838.

Chauvel, John Edward:—Cadet, 1819: Lieutenant, 13th June 1819: Captain, 7th March 1829. He joined the regiment in 1822, but disappeared from the list in 1824, probably being transferred to the 15th N.I., on the re-organisation of the Army in that year. He died at Shamul (?) on the 30th May 1831.

A Captain Thomas Arthur Chauvel was invalided in 1834.

Marshall, John H.:—Cadet, 1820: Ensign, 13th February 1821. He was present for duty with the regiment on the 1st January 1823, and is shown as "in arrest" in 1824. He was tried by Court-Martial and cashiered on the 22nd February 1825, but I have not discovered what he was charged with. If George Marshall (*q. v.*) was his brother, they seem to have been an unlucky family.

Kirby, Hickman Rose:—Cadet, 1819: Lieutenant, 7th April 1820: Captain, 24th June 1830. He appears to have joined the regiment in 1823, and is shown as "in arrest" on the 1st January 1824. On the 1st September 1825 he went to Masulipatam on sick leave, and on the 9th February 1827 he went to Europe on medical certificate, not rejoining the regiment till 1831. On the 3rd January 1834, he again proceeded to Europe, sick, but returned to duty in December 1837, and was acting in command on the 1st January 1839. On the 15th March 1840, he took leave "to the Western Coast, on account of the severe illness of Mrs. Kirby and to see her embarked for Europe if necessary." A return, dated the 4th December 1840, shows that "Captain H. R. Kirby, K. S. F.", had again proceeded to Europe on sick certificate, on the 22nd November 1840, and he died in April 1842.

On the 12th March 1837, he was granted "Her Most Gracious Majesty's royal licence and permission to accept and wear the Cross of the National and Military Order of Saint Ferdinand of the first class, conferred upon him by the Queen Regent of Spain, in testimony of Her royal approbation of important services rendered in the action of the 6th June 1836." Two other officers of the Madras establishment, namely Captain E. Apthorp of the 2nd N.I., and Lieutenant R. Cannan of the 40th N.I., also received this decoration.

This action of the 6th June must have been fought by the British Legion, which displayed great gallantry before Bilbao, fighting on the side of the Queen Regent Cristina against Don Carlos, and these officers had no doubt volunteered for the Legion (which was commanded by Sir George DeLacy Evans), when on furlough in England.

Harris, H. L.:—Ensign, 27th April 1822. This officer was present for duty with the 1st 4th on the 1st January 1824, but I have not been able to find any further mention of him. He must have been transferred to another battalion when the re-organization took place in 1824.

Atkinson, Edwin Henry:—Cadet, 1823: Ensign, 14th May 1824: Lieutenant, 8th September 1826: Captain, 28th August 1835. This officer is shown as "appointed, but not joined" on the 1st January 1824, and must have gone to some other battalion, as his name does not reappear.

An Edward Atkinson (Cadet, 1821) died on the 20th August 1821, at the Isle of France, on board the L. S. *"Fort William."*

Scott, Hopetoun Stratford:—Cadet, 1791: Ensign, 24th June 1793: Lieutenant, 3rd October 1794: Captain, 13th September 1804: Major, 15th August 1805: Lieutenant-Colonel, 7th March 1810: C.B., 14th October 1818: Colonel, 12th August 1819: Major-General, 22nd July 1830: K. C. B., 27th September 1831: Lieutenant-General, 23rd November 1841: General, 20th June 1854.

Colonel H. S. Scott, C. B., became Colonel of the Regiment in succession to Lieutenant-General D. McNeill, probably on the re-organisation in 1824, but there is some doubt, as there are no returns available for 1825. He served at Pondicherry in 1793, and with the abortive expeditions to the Isle of France, and to Manila in

1797. He was present at the battle of Malavilly and the siege of Seringapatam in 1799, and joined the Hyderabad Subsidiary Force in 1800, taking part in the operations against the Mahrattas in the years 1803 to 1805. He commanded at Hyderabad in 1812-13, and commanded a brigade against the Pindarris in 1815-16. He was in command at Nagpur on the 26th November 1817 when, with a force of 1,350 men, he defeated the Rajah's forces, consisting of 20,000 horse, 8,000 infantry and 35 guns, and in the subsequent battle at the same place, he commanded the left column of the attack. On the 16th March 1818, he was appointed to the command of the Nagpur Subsidiary Force, remaining in that employment till 1822, when he was given command of the Travancore Subsidiary Force. In 1824, he proceeded on furlough to Europe. He continued to be Colonel of the 4th till the 30th January 1834, when he was transferred to the 33rd Regiment, from which he was removed on the 15th October 1839, and posted as Colonel of the newly-raised 2nd Madras European Regiment.

Jollie, Walter:—Cadet, 1793: Lieutenant, 19th February 1800: Captain, 9th November 1805: Major, 25th February 1824. This officer was serving with the 2nd 4th in 1802, and was appointed to the 4th Regiment M. N. I., as a Major after the re-organisation in 1824. As, however, he proceeded on furlough to Europe on the 27th August 1824, and died in London on the 6th September 1826, he never appears to have joined the regiment.

Baker, Benjamin:—There must have been two Bakers, and I have found it difficult to distinguish them. *Dodwell and Miles* give a Benjamin Baker (Cadet, 1805: Ensign, 27th June 1806: Lieutenant, 24th November 1808: Captain, 2nd January 1821), who was invalided on the 28th May 1822, and died at Guntur on the 24th October 1831, where there is a tombstone inscribed:—

" Captain Benjamin Baker, aged 45 years, and Mary his daughter, aged 8 months."

This, however, if correct, can scarcely be the Captain Benjamin Baker who was appointed to the 4th M. N. I., on the 1st May 1824, as the latter, who formerly served with the 2nd 4th, is shown as absent from the 6th June 1823, first (up to 1826) as Paymaster, Ceded Districts, and then as on furlough to Europe, on medical certificate, up to 1831, when his name disappears from the list altogether.

A Captain Baker was selected to command the 5th extra Battalion at Bangalore in 1819, but I do not know which this was.

There was a Captain William Way Baker in the 32nd M. N. I., son of Robert Baker, Montague Place, London, who died of cholera at Tumkur in 1839, and who was probably of the same family.

Watson, Thomas:—Cadet, 1805: Ensign, 27th June 1806: Lieutenant, 13th January 1812: Captain, 26th July 1826. This officer was also posted to the regiment on the 1st May 1824, but was absent from the 1st August 1823 up to 1830, as Paymaster, Presidency. On the 27th April 1830, he went on furlough, and he retired in India on the 18th March 1831.

(*Vide David Watson*).

Campbell, Robert Nutter:—Cadet, 1818: Lieutenant, 13th June 1819: Captain, 6th September 1829: Major, 5th April 1841. This officer was posted to the 4th on the 1st May 1824. He acted as Adjutant of the regiment from 1825 (?) to the 29th February 1827, when he proceeded to Fort Cornwallis on staff duty, under the orders of the Governor. He was then appointed Staff Officer and Paymaster on the Neilgherry Hills, returning to regimental duty in April 1834. In the following October, his services were placed at the disposal of the Resident in Travancore to command the Nair Brigade, an appointment which he resigned on the 11th May 1842. He was permitted to retire, on the pension of his rank, on the 28th May 1842, when he returned to Europe.

A Lieutenant-Colonel James Campbell, 11th M. N. I., possibly a brother, died at Vizianagram in 1844, aged 44 years; and an Ensign Henry Foster Campbell, 47th M. N. I., died at Chicacole in 1824, aged 23 years. There was also a David Campbell who was taken prisoner in the disaster to Colonel Baillie, and who became a Lieutenant-General in 1814.

Church, Charles:—Cadet, 1819: Ensign, 6th April 1820: Lieutenant, 25th February 1824. He was posted to the regiment on the 1st May 1824, and is shown as present for duty on the 1st January 1826, dying at "Capperpaud" (?) on the 5th May 1827.

Cramer, John Henry:—Cadet, 1820: Lieutenant, 8th March 1825: Captain, 19th March 1831. This officer also was appointed to the 4th M. N. I. on the 1st May 1824. On the 1st September 1825, he proceeded to Europe on sick certificate rejoining in 1828. On the 27th October 1830, he went on Staff duty, as Aide-de-Camp to the Right Honourable the Governor and, in 1831, was Military Secretary as well as A. D. C. He went on furlough, on medical certificate, on the 25th September 1832, and on his return in 1835 became Deputy Judge-Advocate-General at Trichinopoly from the 24th March. In 1836, he held a similar appointment in the Northern Division. From the 2nd January 1838, he acted as Deputy-Secretary to Government, and on the 8th October 1839, he was transferred to the newly-raised 2nd Madras European Regiment. On the 26th July 1842, when he is shown as belonging to the 2nd European Light Infantry, and Secretary to the Clothing Board, he was granted two years' leave of absence to the Cape of Good Hope, on medical certificate. He resigned his appointment on the Clothing Board in December 1846, when he proceeded to Europe, again on medical certificate, and retired from the service on the 15th July 1849.

Miller, William Armit:—Ensign, 27th April 1822: Lieutenant, 26th July 1826. This officer was posted to the regiment on the 1st May 1824. From the 28th February 1825, he did duty at Nagpur, with the Rifle Corps, and he went on furlough, on medical certificate, to the West Coast on the 30th June 1827, rejoining in 1829. He continued to serve with the regiment up to 1832, after which his name drops out.

Chinnery, William Charles:—Cadet, 1823: Ensign, 14th May 1824: Lieutenant, 8th September 1826: Captain, 10th April 1836. He was posted to the regiment on the 8th July 1824, and went on furlough in the Presidency on the 1st October 1825, rejoining in 1827. From 1827 to 1833 (?) he was Adjutant to the regiment, and subsequently became Quartermaster. He was a much court-martialled officer, being first tried at French Rocks on the 27th August 1838, when he was honourably acquitted, and again on the 28th December 1838, this time on the complaint of Lieutenant T. J. Fischer, 4th N.I. (*see below*) for having stated to a Dr. Maule that he had received a letter from Lieutenant Fischer "urging him to take the money that had been offered to him and to be off, that it was the eleventh hour, and that he had no time to spare," this assertion being a scandalous falsehood. He was acquitted by the Court, who remarked that in bringing the charge Lieutenant Fischer was not actuated by any illiberal or improper motive, but was merely desirous to clear his character from the injurious reports in circulation. He was again court-martialled at Cannanore on the 5th July 1839, on a charge not specified, when he was "most fully and most honourably acquitted." There was evidently a great deal of illfeeling at this time amongst the officers of the regiment, and Lieutenants Fischer and Colbeck, who appear to have been hostile to Captain Chinnery, were transferred for one year, by order of the Commander-in-Chief, the former to the 9th N.I., and the latter to the 32nd N. I.

A painter named George Chinnery resided in Calcutta for over twenty years, and died at Macao in 1850; and a Madras Civilian, John Chinnery, died, at the age of 40, in 1817.

Fischer, Thomas James:—Cadet, 1823: Ensign, 14th September 1824: Lieutenant, 8th September 1826: Brevet Captain, 14th September 1839: Captain, 3rd October 1839: Major, 3rd March 1848: Brevet Lieutenant-Colonel, 22nd August 1855: Lieutenant-Colonel, 15th September 1856: Companion of the Bath, 1st March 1861. He was posted to the regiment on the 4th March 1825, and served with it till the 6th February 1826, when he went to Nagpur to do duty with the Rifle Corps, rejoining in 1831, when he acted as Quartermaster. On the 6th February 1833, when acting as Adjutant of the regiment, he was tried by General Court-Martial at Fort St. George, on a charge of having, in an official letter addressed to the Adjutant-General of the army, falsely accused Lieutenant-Colonel G. M. Stewart (*q. v.*), Commanding Vellore, and Major A. B. Dyce (*q. v.*), Commanding the 4th N.I., of having committed forgery; also of having accused Major Dyce of falsifying documents with a view to getting Lieutenant Colbeck and himself into trouble; and of having aspersed the characters of Captain R. N. Campbell and Captain E. Haldane. He was found guilty, but as the court considered that the accusations made by him had not been made maliciously, he was only sentenced to be suspended from rank and pay for twelve calendar months, from the 13th March 1833. On the termination of his period of suspension, a year later, he rejoined the regiment, and on the 17th December 1834, he went on sick leave in the presidency, proceeding to Europe on the 20th January following. He rejoined in 1838, and took furlough in the Nilgiris from the 6th April 1839 till the 16th April 1841, "to join his family in the Hills, whether he was obliged to send them on account of sudden and severe illness." On the 30th September 1839, he was sent to the 9th N.I. for one year, owing to his quarrel with Captain Chinnery, subsequently rejoining the regiment. On the 13th July 1842, he went to act as Adjutant of Engineers, rejoined in 1843, and accompanied the regiment to China, where he acted in command for a time in 1844-1845. On the 15th June 1847, he was granted six months' leave to Salem and the Nilgiris, and on the 1st January 1849, he is shown as "in arrest by order of C. O., from 27th November 1848," (the C. O. then being Lieutenant-Colonel W. Justice), but in view of his subsequent career, the reason for his arrest cannot have been a very serious one. On the 29th January 1849, he left to do duty with the 1st Madras Fusiliers at Bellary, rejoining in May 1850, and was posted to the 18th N.I. on the 20th October 1856. He acted in command of the Madras Troops in Bengal in 1858, and was again with the 1st Madras Fusiliers, as a Brevet Colonel, in January 1861, when he was transferred to the 3rd Light Infantry. In 1862, he acted for a time in command of the Provinces of Malabar and Canara, and I have no further record of him till his death at Trichinopoly, where a tablet in St. John's Church is inscribed:—

"Thomas James Fischer, C. B., Lieutenant-Colonel, H. M. Indian Army, who departed this life at Trichinopoly on the 7th January 1864, aged 58 years. The paths of glory lead but to the grave."

He was a brother of George Frederick Fischer (1805—1867), Zemindar of Salem, who was the last of the great "adventurers" or non-official English in Madras. Their father was George Fischer (1774—1812) and their grandfather, George Frederick, was a ship's Captain. A son of Colonel Fischer, named James, died at Salem in 1873, aged 41 years.

Walker, Thomas:—Cadet, 1805: Ensign, 27th June 1806: Lieutenant, 1st April 1809: Captain, 1st May 1824. This officer was posted to the regiment in 1824, and was borne on the strength till he died, at Palavaram, on the 23rd June 1830, but he does not appear to have served with the 4th as, during that period, he was Paymaster of the Centre Division.

Rattray, James:—Cadet, 1824: Ensign, 6th May 1825: Lieutenant, 6th May 1827. He was posted to the regiment on the 23rd June 1825 and served with it till 1830, acting as Quartermaster for a time in 1828-29. On the 16th February 1830, he proceeded to the Nilgiris, on sick certificate, and died at Vellore on the 31st July 1831.

Glynn, John Edmund:—Cadet, 1825: Lieutenant, 16th July 1827: Captain, 8th October 1839. He appears to have been posted to the regiment on his promotion to Lieutenant in 1827, and served with it continuously till the 24th March 1840, when he became Fort Adjutant at Bellary. On the 21st January 1842, he proceeded to Europe on three years' furlough, but rejoined the regiment on the 31st December 1843. On the 8th March 1846, he went to the Nilgiris on sick leave, returning to duty in the following year, but on the 22nd May 1848 he had to proceed to Europe, on sick certificate, and he retired from the service on the 22nd October 1850.

Wood, Herbert William:—Cadet, 1825: Ensign, 8th January 1826: Lieutenant, 18th August 1827: Captain, 6th April 1841: Brevet Major, 1854 (?): Lieutenant-Colonel, 5th December 1856. He was appointed to the 4th on promotion to Lieutenant in 1827. On the 26th October 1830, he went to Europe on furlough, rejoining in 1833. He acted as Adjutant in 1838-39, and was confirmed as Adjutant in the latter year. He went to Bellary to act as Fort Adjutant on the 15th December 1841, rejoining some time in 1842. In 1844, he was at Wallajahbad, in charge of the details of the regiment, then serving in China. On the 11th October 1845, he proceeded on furlough to Europe, not returning till 1848. In August 1852, he was appointed to act as Paymaster, Ceded Districts, and he again went to Europe in 1854, and came out to Calcutta in charge of a party of recruits in 1855, rejoining the regiment in November of that year. He was permitted to retire from the service, on the pension of a Lieutenant-Colonel, on the 10th September 1856.

Powys, Philip Annesley Secundus:—Cadet, 1825: Ensign, 8th January 1826: Lieutenant, 11th March 1831: Brevet Captain, 1841: Captain, 20th April 1842. This officer was appointed to the 4th on the 25th October 1826. While he was serving with the regiment in 1835, he was concerned in two General Courts-Martial, the first of which will be found referred to elsewhere (*Vide William Lawless Seppings*). The second, which took place on the 16th September 1835, is of interest as showing the procedure adopted as regards the practice of duelling, which was frowned upon by the authorities. The President of the Court was Lieutenant-Colonel Richard Brunton, of H. M. 13th Light Dragoons (whose name is still preserved in Brunton Road, at Bangalore), and with him there sat one Lieutenant-Colonel, four Majors and eleven Captains, with an Interpreter and a Deputy Judge-Advocate-General. The following was the wording of the charge:—

"Lieutenant Robert Atkinson Joy of the 27th Regiment of Native Infantry, Lieutenant Henry Morland, also of the 27th Regiment of Native Infantry, placed in arrest by order of Colonel Patrick Cameron, Commanding Bangalore, and Lieutenant Philip Annesley Secundus Powys, of the 4th Regiment of Native Infantry, previously in arrest, charged by order of the Commander-in-Chief as follows, namely:—

Charge—That the said Lieutenant Joy, at Bangalore, on the twelfth day of August, in the year one thousand eight hundred and thirty-five, feloniously, wilfully, and of his malice aforethought, did make an assault upon Ensign Arthur Davies of the Left Wing of the Madras European Regiment, doing duty with 4th Regiment of Native Infantry, and then and there, against and upon the said Ensign Davies, feloniously, wilfully and of his malice aforethought, did shoot and discharge a Pistol, loaded and charged with Gun Powder and a leaden Bullet, and, then and there, with the Bullet aforesaid, so shot and discharged, feloniously, wilfully, and of his malice aforethought, did strike, penetrate and wound the said Ensign Davies, giving to the said Ensign Davies, in and upon the crown of his head, one mortal wound, whereof he, the said Ensign Davies, died, at the same place, on the sixteenth day of the same month, in the same year.

That the said Lieutenant Morland, and the said Lieutenant Powys, on the day and year aforesaid, at the place aforesaid, feloniously were present, aiding, abetting and assisting the said Lieutenant Joy to do and commit the felony and murder aforesaid.

So that the said Lieutenant Joy, the said Lieutenant Morland and the said Lieutenant Powys, in manner and form aforesaid, feloniously, wilfully and of their malice aforethought, did kill and murder the said Ensign Davies.

The above being within the provisions of the fourth Article of the Twenty-first Section of the Articles of War.

Head Quarters: Madras.
The Tenth of September,
One Thousand Eight Hundred
and Thirty-five.

By Order.
(*Signed*) T. H. S. CONWAY,
Adjutant-General of the Army."

In the result, the Court found all three officers guilty of so much of the charge as amounted to manslaughter, and sentenced Lieutenants Joy and Powys to twelve months', and Lieutenant Morland to six months', imprisonment, with a recommendation to mercy in the case of the last-named. H. E. the Commander-in-Chief ordered Lieutenant Morland to be released from arrest, and to be returned to duty, and the other two to be sent to the common Jail at Madras, to undergo their sentences. This, however, did not necessitate their removal from the service, as on the 9th November following Lieutenant Joy was posted to the Carnatic Veteran European Battalion, and was still serving in 1842, while Lieutenant Powys rejoined the 4th, with which he is shown as serving up to the 21st January 1841, when he proceeded to Europe on furlough, and as acting Quartermaster from 1837 to 1841. He rejoined from furlough in 1842, but had to leave again, on medical certificate, on the 26th March 1844. Up to 1849 he is still shown as absent on sick leave, but thereafter his name disappears from the list. He retired from the service on the 7th December 1853.

Stokes, Oliver Day:—Cadet, 1825: Ensign, 8th January 1826: Lieutenant, 19th March 1831. This officer appears, from his name, to have been a brother of John Day Stokes (*q. v.*), but unlike that distinguished officer, his ending was unfortunate. He seems to have been appointed to the regiment on the 25th October 1826, and served with it till the 12th January 1830, when he went on furlough, rejoining in the following year. On the 26th January 1836, he was appointed to command the Escort of the Resident in Mysore, and, on the 27th September following, was appointed Quartermaster and Interpreter of the 4th, *vice* Captain Chinnery. His last appearance in the regimental returns is on the 31st July 1837, where he is shown as "confined in the common Jail at Madras for two-and-a-half years by sentence of a General Court-Martial." While I have been unable to find the proceedings of the Court-Martial, the following extract from a letter from the Honourable the Court of Directors, published in General Orders, dated the 8th September 1838, goes some way towards solving the mystery, though it does not explain why Lieutenant Stokes fell upon Private Paupiah with his sword:—

"1. We have repeatedly expressed and enforced our intention of dismissing from the Company's Service ' every officer who shall be proved to have been guilty of cruelty to any Native, either by violently and illegally beating or otherwise maltreating him,' and we have desired the local Governments to be very particular in bringing to our notice any instance of that kind that may occur.

2. It is with deep regret that our attention has now been called to the cases of two Officers of your Establishment who were arraigned in June and July last before the same Court-Martial on separate charges of the murder of natives.

3. The first of these officers is Lieutenant Oliver D. Stokes of the 4th Regiment of Native Infantry, who was charged with 'wilful murder' in having 'struck with a sword on the left side of the neck of Paupiah, Private in the same Regiment, and thereby inflicted a mortal wound, whereof he, the said Paupiah, died at the same place on the same day.' Lieutenant Stokes was found guilty of 'so much of the charge as amounts to mauslaughter' and sentenced to be imprisoned for the space of two years and six months.

4. This decision was confirmed by the Commander-in-Chief, who directed that Lieutenant Stokes should be forwarded from Cannanore to the Jail of Madras, and that the period of his imprisonment should be calculated from the date of his reception there.

5. We have carefully perused and considered the whole of the proceedings on the trial of this officer and we are satisfied that the good of the service no less than justice to the Native Soldiers, imperatively requires that he should be immediately dismissed from the Company's Army.

6. We accordingly direct that you forthwith strike his name out of the List of the Army......."

In General Orders, dated the 30th January 1839, the following further letter from the Court of Directors was published:—

"1. Having brought to the notice of the Queen the peculiar circumstances under which Mr. Oliver Day Stokes committed manslaughter as declared by the sentence of the Court-Martial held upon him on the 22nd June 1837, we have the satisfaction to acquaint you that Her Majesty has been most graciously pleased, in compliance with the prayer of our petition, to grant to him a free pardon for his said crime.

2. The Royal Warrant granted for this purpose is herewith enclosed."

Colbeck, Henry:—Cadet, 1825: Ensign, 6th May 1825: Lieutenant, 1st August 1831: Brevet Captain, 1840: Captain, 28th May 1842: Major, 11th November 1851: Lieutenant-Colonel (on retirement from the Army), 28th November 1854. He was appointed to the 4th on the 1st June 1827, but on the 25th September following, proceeded to Europe on medical certificate, and apparently did not rejoin till 1831. On the 20th March 1833, he was posted to do duty with the Madras European Regiment. He went on furlough to Poona from the 20th November 1837 till the 20th March 1838, when he rejoined, and on the 30th September 1839, he was ordered by the Commander-in-Chief to join the 32nd N.I., owing to the dissensions among the officers of the 4th. He subsequently rejoined the 4th, and went on furlough to Bombay from the 23rd October 1841 till the 15th February 1842. On the 21st January 1845, he was granted 12 months' sick leave in India by the G.O.C. the Forces in China, and from the 26th October 1846 was acting Police Magistrate at Madras. He again returned to the 4th in 1847, and apparently remained with the regiment till the 15th November 1853 when, being then a Brevet Major, he was posted as fourth Captain to the newly raised 3rd European Regiment. He appears eventually to have become a permanent Police Magistrate as the following tablet in St. George's Cathedral, Madras, shows:—

"In memory of Clarence Harry, only son of Lieutenant-Colonel H. Colbeck, Senior Magistrate of Police. He was a Lieutenant in Her Majesty's 3rd Madras European Regiment, was mortally wounded in action at Banda and died on the 28th April 1858, aged 22 years. Also of Emma, wife of Lieutenant-Colonel H. Colbeck, and mother of the above, she was born on the 31st May 1809 and died at Bangalore on 16th July 1859."

Marret, Philip Thomas:—Ensign, 8th January 1826. This officer is shown as having been appointed to the regiment on the 20th June 1827, but, as his name does not re-appear in any returns, he must have joined some other Corps.

Dods, Joseph:—Cadet, 1826: Ensign, 5th March 1827: Lieutenant, 16th May 1832: Brevet Captain, 5th March 1842: Captain, 24th January 1845. He was posted to the regiment on the 4th September 1827, and served with it till the 12th May 1845, when he proceeded to Europe on sick leave. He had acted as Quartermaster for a time in 1830-31. On his return from furlough in October 1839, he was appointed to act as Quartermaster and Interpreter to the 24th Regiment, but rejoined the 4th at Singapore, as Quartermaster, in 1843, and was still serving in that capacity at Hongkong in 1845, but died in the same year, just after the regiment returned to Vellore.

Bowes, Frederick:—Cadet, 1800: Lieutenant, 20th July 1801: Captain, 17th August 1810: Major, 17th October 1819: Lieutenant-Colonel, 1st May 1824. Lieutenant-Colonel Bowes was posted to the command of the 4th on the 30th May 1828, and remained in command till the 24th April 1829, when he went to Europe on furlough, and does not appear to have rejoined the regiment. He was promoted to Major-General on the 28th June 1838.

Johnston, John M'Mahon:—Ensign, 31st August 1828: Lieutenant, 10th April 1836: Brevet Captain, 3rd January 1843: Captain, 2nd September 1845. This officer was posted to the regiment on the 1st September 1828, became Adjutant in 1833, and proceeded to Europe on sick leave on the 5th December 1838, rejoining in 1841. From the 9th June 1841 to 1843, he was acting D. A. A. G. to the Army and, rejoining in the latter year, once more became Adjutant. He died in September 1845.

A Colonel Francis James Thomas Johnston, of the Madras establishment, was promoted to Major-General on the 28th June 1838.

Steuart, George Mackenzie:—Cadet, 1802: Lieutenant, 1st January 1807: Captain, 19th January 1816: Major, 14th October 1823: Lieutenant-Colonel, 11th April 1826: Brevet Colonel, 18th June 1831: Major-General, 23rd November 1841: Lieutenant-General, 11th November 1851. This officer arrived at Madras in June 1803, and joined the cadet company at Tirupassur. In the following November he joined the 1st 1st M. N. I., at Madras, and was with that regiment when it mutinied at Vellore in 1806. He served in the Mahratta campaigns of 1812-13, and in 1814 proceeded to Europe on sick leave. He returned to India in 1817, and saw service against the Mahrattas in 1817-18. In January 1819, he was nominated to raise one of the six extra battalions, and received the approbation of the Commander-in-Chief for his celerity in recruiting the 2nd Extra Battalion to its full strength. In 1821, he took his battalion to Travancore, and, on its disbandment in the following year, was posted to the 2nd 1st Battalion at Trichinopoly, commanding that corps in Travancore in 1823. From June till October 1823, he was Secretary to the Clothing Board in Madras, subsequently commanding the 1st 1st M.N.I. On the reorganisation of the Army in May 1824, he was appointed Major of the 17th M. N. I. (formerly 2nd 1st M. N. I.) and took over command at Quilon.

On the 17th September 1831, he was posted to the 4th as Lieutenant-Colonel, and assumed command on the 18th October following. He left the regiment, however, on the 10th December, and assumed command of the garrison of Vellore on the following day. On the 13th January 1834, he was transferred from the 4th to the 5th N.I., and on the 10th March 1834, to the 20th N.I., retaining the command of Vellore. He was still in that appointment, as a Brigadier, in 1838. In 1843, he was commanding the Northern Division, and in October of that year was granted sick leave to the Neilgherry Hills and Western Coast up to the 1st February 1845. He resigned the command of the Northern Division in October 1844, and proceeded to Europe on furlough. He had been appointed Colonel of the 33rd Regiment on the 15th October 1839. His name is sometimes spelt "Stewart".

Seppings, William Lawless:—Cadet, 1828: Ensign, 16th May 1829: Lieutenant, 4th September 1838. This officer joined the regiment on the 23rd March 1831, and served with it till the 11th November 1839, when he proceeded to Europe on sick leave. He retired from the service on the 23rd September 1842. At Bangalore, on the 6th April 1835, he was tried by General Court-Martial, at the instance of Lieutenant P. A. S. Powys (*vide supra*), the charge being worded as follows:—

"I charge Ensign William Lawless Seppings of the Fourth Regiment of Native Infantry with
conduct unbecoming the character of an Officer and a Gentleman, in having, at Bangalore, on the morning of the twenty-sixth of April, One Thousand Eight Hundred and Thirty-five, on the Public Road, struck me, his superior Officer, a violent blow with his clenched hand in the face, I being at that time on duty as Officer of the day.

The above being in breach of the Articles of War.

BANGALORE, (*Signed*) P. A. S. POWYS, Lieutenant,
17th May 1835. 4th *Regiment Native Infantry.*"

The Court found him guilty of the charge, with the exception of "conduct unbecoming the character of an Officer and a Gentleman," and sentenced him to be reprimanded, remarking that they were induced to pass so lenient a sentence "in consequence of Lieutenant Powys having been the aggressor by laying violent hands on the Prisoner, by whom a blow was struck in a moment of Irritation, when under great excitement."

Lieutenant Powys seems to have been an extremely quarrelsome officer.

Lacon, John Edmund:—Cadet, 1828: Ensign, 1st August 1831. He joined the 4th on the 6th August 1831, and on the 19th March 1833, was posted to the Corps of Pioneers. On the 5th July 1833, he proceeded to Europe on sick leave, and I have been unable to trace his subsequent history.

Watt, James:—Ensign, 19th January 1833. This officer, who was then serving with the 4th, was, on the 21st December 1833, appointed to do duty with the 9th N.I. till further orders. In October 1834, he was serving with the 20th N.I., and on the 27th of that month, was posted to the 48th N.I.

Oliver, W. C.:—Colonel Oliver was posted to the Colonelcy of the regiment on the 30th January 1834, in place of Sir H. S. Scott, K. C. B., but on the 11th February following, he was transferred to the 41st N.I., and Colonel A. Grant, C.B., replaced him. He proceeded to Europe on furlough in June 1834. I have not been able to trace his record of service.

Metcalfe, Howe:—Ensign, 1st February 1834. This officer, then recently arrived in Madras, was, on the 16th June 1834, appointed to do duty with the 4th N.I. On the 27th October following, he was posted to the 29th N. I.

Anderson, William Wallace:—Ensign, 13th December 1833. This officer, then recently arrived in Madras, was, on the 2nd July 1834, appointed to do duty with the 4th. On the 27th October following, he was posted to the 25th N. I.

Showers, Howe Daniel:—Ensign Showers, then recently arrived in Madras, was, on the 9th July 1834, appointed to do duty with the 4th N. I. I do not know what became of him subsequently.

Sturrock, George:—Ensign, 13th December 1833. This officer also was, on the 18th July 1834, appointed to do duty with the 4th, and on the 27th October following, was posted to the 11th N.I.

Webb, Edward Arthur Henry:—Ensign, 13th December 1833: Lieutenant-Colonel, 18th February 1861. This officer was, on the 18th July 1834, appointed to do duty with the 4th N.I., and was posted to the 22nd N.I., in the same year. The only later reference to him that I have seen is his admission to the Madras Staff Corps, as a Lieutenant-Colonel, on the 10th June 1862.

Templer, Frederick:—Ensign, 14th July 1832. This officer, then doing duty with the 27th N.I., was, on the 18th July 1834, removed to do duty with the 4th. On the 13th September following, he was sent to do duty with the 13th N.I., and on the 27th October, was definitely posted to the 51st N.I.

Wyndham, Arthur:—Ensign, 24th November 1832: Major, 1st February 1861: Lieutenant-Colonel, 18th February 1863. This officer, then doing duty with the 27th N.I., was, on the 18th July 1834, posted to do duty with the 4th N.I., and was posted to the 2nd N.I., on the 27th October following. He was admitted to the Madras Staff Corps, as a Major, on the 10th June 1862.

Vardon, Frank:—Ensign, 22nd December 1832. This officer also did duty with the 4th for a short period in 1834, and was then posted to the 25th N.I.

Beadle, Denis Robert Hudson:—Ensign, 16th February 1833. Another new arrival in the Presidency, who did duty with the 27th N.I., and then with the

4th N.I., in 1834. On the 27th October of that year, he was posted to the 12th N.I., but to remain with the 4th until the arrival of his regiment at Bangalore.

St. George, William:—Ensign, 14th June 1834. This officer was also attached to the 4th for duty in 1834, and was posted to the 51st N.I., on the 19th January 1835.

Doria, Alexander:—Ensign, 27th May 1834: Major, 5th November 1858. This officer was appointed to do duty with the 4th N.I., on the 20th September 1834, and on the 19th January 1835, was posted to the 5th N.I., with which regiment he was still serving as a Captain in 1844. In 1856, he was Commandant of the 4th Cavalry, Hyderabad Contingent, and was removed from his command, and reverted to duty with the 28th N.I., by order of the Governor-General in Council, for having "interfered in a violent and angry manner with a large concourse of natives engaged in celebrating a marriage at Hingoli."

A Colonel R. A. Doria was Commandant of the 35th M.N.I. in 1873.

Morgan, John:—Cadet, 1800: Lieutenant, 20th July 1801: Captain, 8th November 1811: Major, 8th September 1826: Lieutenant-Colonel, 24th December 1831: Companion of the Bath, 1st August 1838: Lieutenant-Colonel Commandant, 23rd January 1843: Colonel, 10th November 1843. This officer appears in a return, dated the 1st January 1835, as Lieutenant-Colonel of the 4th, but absent on furlough in the Presidency from the 12th September 1834. He succeeded Lieutenant-Colonel G. M. Stewart (*q. v.*) on the 13th January 1834, and was evidently still with the regiment in March 1835, as he then appears as a member of a General Court-Martial at Bangalore, where the regiment was then stationed. He left Bangalore on four months' sick leave on the 25th September 1835. He was awarded the C.B., on the occasion of the Coronation of H. M. Queen Victoria. He was commanding at Masulipatam as a Brigadier in 1843, and proceeded to Europe on furlough in 1844. He was promoted to Lieutenant-General on the 27th January 1858, and to General on the 27th May 1866.

Sellon, Edward:—Cadet, 1832: Ensign, 8th February 1834. This officer was posted to the 4th N.I. on the 27th October 1834, having previously been attached for duty to the 29th N.I. At Bangalore, on the 11th May 1836, he was tried by General Court-Martial for "scandalous and infamous behaviour such as is unbecoming the character of an Officer and a Gentleman," in having made use of highly insulting and grossly abusive language to Lieutenants Herbert William Wood and Henry Colbeck of the 4th, and presented a loaded pistol at the former with intent to shoot him. The Court found him guilty and sentenced him to be discharged the service, but the Commander-in-Chief remitted the sentence, on the ground that he had evidently been insane at the time he committed the offence. He was pensioned on the 31st May following, and on the 11th June was given permission to reside and draw his pension at Cuddalore.

Shawe, Robert:—Ensign, 13th December 1834. This officer was attached for duty with the 4th on the 14th April 1835, and proceeded to Mangalore to join the

2nd N.I., on the 1st November following. He retired from the service, with the rank of Major, on the 31st December 1861.

Davies, Arthur:—Ensign, 13th December 1834. This officer was also attached for duty with the 4th, at Bangalore, on the 14th April 1835. On the 7th August following, he was posted to the Left Wing of the Madras European Regiment and directed to proceed to Kamptee to join that corps on the 1st October 1835. In the meanwhile, however, he was killed in a duel at Bangalore by Lieutenant Joy of the 27th N.I. Particulars of the resulting Court-Martial have already been given above. (*Vide Philip Annesley Secundus Powys.*)

Walker, Charles Augustus:—Colonel, 5th June 1829: Major-General, 28th June 1838. This officer became Colonel of the 4th on the 26th May 1835, in place of Colonel Alexander Grant, C.B., and held the appointment till his death, on the 2nd October 1842. Major-General John Munro succeeded him in the following December. I have, unfortunately, been unable to find any particulars of his services.

Green, John:—A Lieutenant-Colonel of this name appears to have been serving with the 4th at Bangalore in January 1836. He may have been posted from some other regiment to take the place of Lieutenant-Colonel John Morgan. I have not been able to trace him.

A Major Henry Green was serving with the 18th M.N.I. in 1852.

Walhouse, James Moreton:—Ensign, 17th January 1836. This officer was attached for duty, first to the 4th N.I., and then to the 19th N.I., in May 1836, and on the 30th July 1836, was posted to the 1st N.I. In 1838, he was serving with the Madras European Regiment.

Nuthall, Henry Robert:—Ensign, 17th January 1836. This officer was also attached for duty to the 4th N.I., in May 1836, and was subsequently posted to the 23rd N.I.

Dickson, George Collingwood:—Ensign, 17th January 1836. Another young officer attached for duty to the 4th N.I., and subsequently posted to the 28th N.I., on the 30th July 1836.

West, Arthur Robert:—Ensign, 16th January 1836. This officer was only attached to the regiment for a few days in May 1836. He was eventually posted to the 6th N.I.

Nelson, Frederick:—Ensign, 8th January 1836. Another officer who was attached for duty to the 4th on the 1st June 1836, and was finally posted to the 11th N.I., at Kamptee.

Fullerton, William Robert:—Ensign, 9th December 1835. This officer was also attached to the 4th for two months in 1836, and then posted to the 46th N.I.

Williamson, William:—Cadet, 1805: Lieutenant, 25th March 1807: Captain, 31st January 1821: Major, 21st March 1827: Lieutenant-Colonel, 22nd December

1832. This officer was posted to the 4th, from the 27th M.N.I., as Lieutenant-Colonel, on the 23rd November 1837, and joined on the 18th December following. In 1838, he was awarded a C.B., on the occasion of H. M. Queen Victoria's Coronation, and on the 7th August of that year was placed in command of the Provinces of Malabar and Canara. He was posted to the 46th N.I., on the 24th December 1839, and in 1842, when he was a Brigadier, commanding the Nagpore Subsidiary Force, he went on sick leave to Mangalore. He died on the 7th May 1855, being then a Major-General.

Two Captain Williamsons had fought, and died, in the wars in Mysore— James, Commandant of Bangalore, who died in 1790; and Henry, 4th Cavalry, who died in 1799,—and one of these may have been the father of the above.

Dunlop, George Wellington Nelson—Ensign, 14th February 1836: Lieutenant, 3rd October 1839: Captain, 24th September 1845. This officer joined the regiment on the 3rd November 1836, having been previously posted to the 18th N.I. He served continuously with the regiment up to the time of his death, in 1855, with two absences on furlough, from 1841 to 1843, and 1845—47. A tablet to his memory in St. John's Church, Trichinopoly, bears the following inscription:—

"Sacred to the memory of George Wellington Nelson Dunlop, Captain in the Fourth Regiment of Madras Native Infantry, who died of Cholera at Sattiamungalam on the 6th of January 1855, aged 41 years. And to the memory of Henry Beresford Podmore, Ensign in the Fourth Regiment of Madras Native Infantry, who died of Cholera at Uttacolapoor on the 31st of December 1854, aged 20 years. This tablet is erected by their brother officers."

A Major William Wallace Dunlop was serving with the 50th N.I., in November 1851.

Palmer, James Edward:—Ensign, 31st January 1837: Lieutenant, 8th October 1839: Captain, 3rd March 1848: Major, 15th September 1856. This officer joined the regiment on the 6th July 1837. On the 29th April 1840, he went to the 32nd M.N.I., to act as Quartermaster and Interpreter, rejoining in 1843. He was absent on sick leave for a time when the regiment was at Hong Kong (1844-45), and the following appeared in General Orders, on the 3rd July 1845:—

"With the sanction of Government, Lieutenant J. E. Palmer, of the 4th Regiment N. I., on leave of absence on medical certificate at Singapore, is permitted to remain at that Settlement until the 4th Regiment passes through the Straits of Malacca or, in the event of its coming by the Straits of Sunda, until an opportunity offers for his proceeding direct to India."

From the 29th July 1845 till 1848, he was Quartermaster of the regiment, acting as Adjutant, in addition, in 1847. On the 5th January 1855, he was appointed 2nd Assistant Civil Engineer, D.P.W., and posted to Bellary District, being then struck off the strength of the regiment.

He retired from the service on the half-pay of his rank on the 20th September 1856.

Tweedie, Maurice:—Major, 15th March 1832: Lieutenant-Colonel, 5th January 1839: Colonel, 19th March 1849: Major-General, 28th November 1854: Lieutenant-General, 6th April 1862. This officer was in command of the Resident's Escort at Tanjore, prior to the 11th June 1833, on which date he returned to the 20th N.I. On the 24th December 1839, he was posted to command the 4th, in succession to Lieutenant-Colonel Williamson, and on the 31st July 1842, proceeded to Bangalore on sick leave. He did not rejoin the regiment, being transferred to the 27th N.I. on the 12th January 1843, and in 1844 he was commanding the troops at Penang, Singapore and Malacca. On the 3rd May 1845, he was transferred from the 27th N.I. to the 43rd N.I., and I have no further record of his services. He died on the 14th December 1867.

There was another Colonel Maurice Tweedie, who arrived in India as an Ensign in 1856, and served in Central India during the Mutiny, subsequently joining the Oudh Police Department. He was a well-known killer of tigers, and wrote a chapter on the fauna of Oudh for the *Oudh Gazetteer*.

A Colonel William John Tweedie was Commandant of the 10th N.I., in 1873, and retired from the service, with the honorary rank of Major-General, on the 1st August 1875.

Owen, Henry Rees:—Ensign, 11th January 1838. This officer, who at the time was doing duty with the 38th N.I., was posted to the 4th on the 30th January 1839, but on the 8th November following was transferred, at his own request, to the 2nd Madras European Regiment. In 1842, he was serving, as a Lieutenant, with the 2nd Native Veteran Battalion.

Silver, Alexander Crombie:—Ensign, 12th June 1838: Lieutenant, 3rd October 1840: Captain, 22nd October 1850: Major, 20th September 1856: Lieutenant-Colonel, 1st January 1862: Colonel, 1st January 1874: Major-General, 1st October 1877. This officer, who had been attached to the 24th N.I., was posted to the 4th on the 30th January 1839. From 1841 to 1843, he acted as Adjutant, proceeding to the Nilgiris on sick leave on the 29th September of the latter year. He was also acting as Station Staff Officer at Singapore in 1843. He returned to the regiment in 1845, and was appointed Adjutant till 1849, with a short absence on sick leave in the Nilgiris in 1846. From 1853, he was "Acting Assistant and Civil Engineer to the Justices in Session," the duties of which appointment I am unable to explain, and in 1859 he was Agent for Army Clothing, with the honorary rank of Lieutenant-Colonel while commanding the Volunteer Guards. In 1867-68, he was Superintendent and Agent for Army Clothing, and in 1871—74 he was Secretary to Government in the Military Department. He was Major-General, Commanding the Northern District in 1878.

A Lieutenant John Leigh Goldie Silver, of the 34th Chicacole Light Infantry, was dismissed from the service, in September 1865, for intoxication on duty.

Gibbon, Septimus:—Lieutenant, 23rd November 1841. This officer was transferred, at his own request, from the 42nd N.I., to the 4th N.I., on the 8th

November 1839, but appears to have returned to his original unit shortly afterwards, if he ever joined the 4th, as he is shown as serving with it from 1842 to 1856. In December of the latter year he was tried by General Court-Martial at Poona, and dismissed the service, for having "introduced a certain lady into the society of the ladies of the station at a dance given by the 3rd Bombay Light Infantry, under the pretence that she was his sister-in-law."

Cleghorn, Allan Mackenzie:—Ensign, 12th June 1839: Lieutenant, 5th April 1841. He was first attached for duty to the 13th N.I., and then posted to the 4th on the 5th December 1839. He served with the regiment till the 14th June 1842, when he proceeded to Europe on sick leave, and never returned, as he died on the 4th November 1844.

In 1845, an Assistant Surgeon H. F. C. Cleghorn was in medical charge of the Nugger Division of the Mysore Commission.

Gordon, John Francis:—Ensign, 30th September 1840: Lieutenant, 16th July 1842. This officer appears to have joined the 4th in 1840, and served with it till 1843. There was a large number of Gordons serving in the Presidency at this time which is confusing. The last mention of him that I can discover is on the 15th November 1843, when he is shown as "placed in arrest," and he was permitted to resign the service in 1844, but I am not aware of the cause of his leaving the regiment.

Wood, Philip Raymond Jarvis:—Ensign, 10th August 1839: Lieutenant, 20th April 1842: Captain, 15th November 1853: Major, 31st December 1861. This officer was posted to the 4th on the 8th December 1839, and served with it continuously till the 23rd May 1847, when he went on sick leave to Cuddalore and the Eastern Coast, rejoining in 1848. From the 18th February 1859, he was absent on detachment at Prome, and went on leave in 1862. On the 26th April 1863, "being disqualified for the active duties of his profession," he was transferred to the Invalid Battalion.

Denton, James:—Ensign, 4th August 1840: Lieutenant, 28th May 1842. This officer joined the regiment in 1840 or 1841, and was serving with it at Hong Kong in 1845. In 1845-46, he was attached for duty to the 42nd M.N.I., for some time. He was tried by General Court-Martial at St. Thomas' Mount, on the 15th March 1847, on a charge of having absented himself without leave from the garrison of Vellore, and of having falsely stated to Major Haldane, then Commanding the 4th, that he had visited all the guards, etc., during his tour of duty as Regimental Orderly Officer of the Day, whereas he had failed to do so. He was found guilty, and sentenced to lose three steps in the regiment, by being placed on the list of Lieutenants next below Lieutenant J. F. A. Plant. He was again court-martialled at St. Thomas' Mount, on the 28th October 1847, for having absented himself without leave from parade (at Vellore) and for having at the same time and place incapacitated himself from the performance of his duty by drinking intoxicating liquor to excess. He was found guilty, and sentenced to be suspended from rank, pay and allowances for a period of nine months. On the 1st January 1849, he is shown as "to appear before a Medical Committee," and he appears to have died in the following month, but I do not know where.

In the first issue of these Records, not knowing what had become of James Denton of the 4th, I had identified him with a Major James Denton, whose tombstone, in Cannanore Cemetery, dated the 12th July 1868, is inscribed:—

"James Denton, Major in the Madras Army, aged 80 years, after a service to his Queen and country of 60 years."

The latter, however, who, according to Cotton, was "a man of herculean physique, who obtained his commission through the ranks," was a man who "in consideration of his merits and his services" was granted a commission as Lieutenant on the Veteran Establishment in May 1837, and rose to the rank of Major in 1855, when he was Deputy Commissary of Ordnance at Cannanore.

Brine, John Jones:—Ensign, 25th December 1840: Lieutenant, 23rd September 1842: Captain, 7th December 1853: Major, 27th April 1863: Lieutenant-Colonel, 25th December 1866 (?). This officer joined the 4th on the 18th May 1841. He seems to have been serving in the Forest Department some time later, as is evidenced by an order permitting him to resign his appointment as Assistant Conservator of Forests, Annamallai, on the 28th May 1862, and to rejoin the regiment, with which he continued to serve till he retired on the 15th September 1868. He was officiating Commandant in 1865-66.

The following is an extract from the *Army and Navy Gazette,* dated the 11th June 1910:

"64th PIONEERS.—The death took place on the 31st ult., at Torquay, of Colonel J. J. Brine who retired from the 4th Madras Native Infantry 42 years ago. The deceased officer, who was a son of the late Captain J. Brine, R. N., was in his 86th year, and he was probably the oldest surviving officer of the regiment."

Jones, William James:—Ensign, 11th August 1841: Lieutenant, 18th April 1844: Captain, 6th January 1855: Major, 11th August 1861: Lieutenant-Colonel, 12th September 1866: Colonel, 9th October 1874. He was posted to the regiment on the 22nd November 1841, and served with it continuously up to the 7th April 1847, when he went to Europe on sick leave. In July 1859, he is shown as "to appear before a Medical Committee." He was present for duty from 1862 to 1865, and is shown as a Brevet-Major of the 38th N.I., Officiating Senior Wing Commandant with the 4th, in November 1865. On the 19th December 1866, he went on sick leave, being then 2nd in Command of the regiment, and he proceeded to Europe, on medical certificate on the 18th November 1868, having meanwhile been promoted to Lieutenant-Colonel. He did not rejoin till December 1870, when he was still 2nd in Command, and he became Colonel and Commandant of the regiment in 1874, but, continuing to be in ill-health, he eventually went to Europe on two years' furlough from the 24th March 1875, and retired from the service on the 6th October 1876.

Edwardes, H. J. B.:—This officer was attached to the 4th for duty, from the 1st March to the 24th May 1842, when he was posted to the 18th N.I., with the rank of Ensign.

Strahan, William Abingdon Otto:—Ensign Strahan of the 8th N.I., was attached for duty to the 4th from the 10th March to the 27th November 1842, when he left to join his regiment at Vellore. He was transferred to the Corps of Sappers and Miners in October 1846, but rejoined the 8th N.I., in November 1847. In October 1848, Captain Robert Mackenzie of the 8th N.I., was tried by General Court-Martial at Secunderabad for having tried to promote a duel between Lieutenant Strahan and Ensign Hailes, and was sentenced to suspension from rank, pay and allowances for three months. Lieutenant Strahan, it may be noted, had died on the 27th September 1848, but from what cause I do not know.

Plant, John Floyd Alexander:—Ensign, 23rd December 1841: Lieutenant, 4th November 1844: Captain, 10th September 1856: Brevet-Major, 23rd December 1861. This officer joined the regiment on the 24th May 1842, and was present for duty till the 20th November 1848, when he proceeded to Europe on sick leave. In November 1856, he again went to Europe on sick leave, being then Fort Adjutant at Trichinopoly. He was still on the regimental list till the 1st February 1865, when he was placed on the retired list.

William Charles Plant (*q. v.*) was probably his brother.

Harkness, Charles Thomas:—Ensign, 30th January 1842: Lieutenant, 24th January 1845: Captain, 15th September 1856: Major, 30th January 1862: Lieutenant-Colonel, 30th January 1868: Colonel, 30th January 1873: Major-General, 25th November 1875. This officer was posted to the regiment on the 14th June 1842, and served with it till the 2nd April 1844, when he is shown as absent on command on the Transport *"Defiance,"* but rejoined in the same year. On the 28th April 1848, he was appointed Quartermaster and Interpreter. From the 12th December 1848 to the 15th April 1849, he was absent on sick leave "to the Western Coast and Hoonoor," and, on the 19th July 1853, was appointed Adjutant of the regiment. From about 1859 to 1864, he acted as Quartermaster and, on the 1st November 1866, proceeded to Europe on furlough, after which he did not rejoin the regiment. He is shown in General Orders, dated the 4th February 1873, as having elected to remain in Europe and, on the 25th November 1874, was granted the honorary rank of Major-General on retirement.

A Captain George Harkness was serving with the 25th N.I., in 1853.

Shand, John:—Captain, 16th May 1854. Ensign Shand was attached to the 4th for duty in June 1842, but only for a few days, being then posted to the 17th N.I. He subsequently joined the 51st N.I. with which he was still serving in 1855, and shown as employed on the Coimbatore roads, so was presumably with the D.P.W. for the time being. On the disbandment of the 51st N.I., in 1862, he was transferred to the Hyderabad Contingent, and in 1863 was officiating as Commandant of the 1st Infantry.

Cuming, William Herbert:—Ensign, 12th June 1842. This officer was attached to the 4th for duty in September 1842, and in the following month was posted to the 1st N.I. In 1855, he was serving under Major-General R. J. H. Vivian, commanding a Turkish contingent, presumably in the Crimean War.

Bird, William Cornelius John Frazer:—Ensign, 12th June 1842. This officer was attached to the 4th for duty at the same time as Ensign Cuming and was then posted to the 40th N.I. In 1853, he was Cantonment Adjutant at Jaulnah, and he died on the 1st March 1861, being then a Captain in the 40th N.I.

Holland, Charles:—Ensign, 11th June 1842: Lieutenant, 2nd September 1845. He joined the 4th on the 5th October 1842, and served with it until the 7th October 1844, when he went to Europe on two years' sick leave, from Hong Kong, rejoining in 1846. He left the regiment on detached duty with a company on the 10th October 1848, but rejoined in 1849, and continued to serve until the 20th May 1851, when he went on 18 months' sick leave. He rejoined in 1852, and two years later became Temporary Executive Officer, D. P. W., and left the regiment.

Lawder, James:—Ensign, 10th August 1842: Lieutenant, 3rd September 1846. This officer was posted to the 4th on the 28th October 1842 but on the 3rd February following, was removed to the 28th N.I., at his own request. In 1855, he was Assistant Secretary to the Military Board.

Another James Lawder, on the General List, was promoted to Lieutenant on the 1st January 1862.

Newlyn, William Rouse:—Lieutenant, 17th June 1846: Major, 3rd February 1862. Ensign Newlyn of the 19th N.I. was removed from the 17th N.I., to do duty with the 4th N.I., on the 14th December 1842. He appears to have subsequently served with the 19th N.I., and then joined the Commissariat Department, being appointed Deputy Assistant Commissary-General on the 23rd February 1855. He was admitted to the Madras Staff Corps, as a Major, on the 10th June 1862, and appointed Assistant Commissary-General on the 23rd December following.

He died on the 16th July 1863.

Cary, Robert Ormsby:—Ensign Cary, doing duty with the 17th N.I., was, on the 14th December 1842, transferred to do duty with the 4th N.I., and a fortnight later was posted to the 13th N.I.

Hitchens, Benjamin Robertson:—Cadet, 1806: Ensign, 3rd July 1807: Lieutenant, 4th August 1810: Captain, 8th January 1826: Brevet-Major, 10th January 1837: Lieutenant-Colonel, 29th June 1842: Brevet-Colonel, 27th October 1852: Colonel, 2nd January 1854: Major-General, 28th November 1854. This officer succeeded Lieutenant-Colonel Tweedie on the 12th January 1843, but did not actually serve with the regiment, though he is still shown as Lieutenant-Colonel of the 4th up to 1847, during which period he was on staff duty as Stipendiary Member of the Military Board, and Member of the Marine Board. On the 23rd October 1847, he was transferred from the 4th to the 2nd European Light Infantry.

Tireman, George Joseph Stainton:—Ensign, 28th December 1842: Lieutenant, 24th September 1845: Captain, 20th September 1856: Major, 28th December 1862. This officer joined the 4th on the 15th June 1843, and served with it until the 2nd May 1847, when he proceeded to Europe on sick leave. In 1852, he was Acting Assistant to the Superintendent of Roads, and in 1854, he was appointed Sub-Assistant Commissary-General. He was admitted to the Madras Staff Corps, as a Captain, on the 10th June 1862, and became a Deputy Assistant Commissary-General, on the 23rd December following. He was finally struck off the strength of the regiment from the 1st November 1865, and retired from the service on the 3rd December 1867.

Babington, Richard Clarke:—Ensign, 9th December 1843: Lieutenant, 3rd March 1848: Captain, 23rd November 1856: Major, 9th December 1863: Lieutenant-Colonel, 13th June 1873: Colonel, 9th October 1874. This officer first joined the 48th N.I., and was posted to the 4th on the 11th June 1844, but did not join till the following year, being on furlough in Europe. On his return, on the 6th September 1845, he joined the regiment at Vellore, and in April 1846, was granted four months' sick leave to the Eastern Coast and Saint Thomé. In 1849, he went on two years' sick leave, and from 1853 was working with the D. P. W., becoming an Assistant Executive Engineer on the 18th February 1858, and an Executive Engineer in 1862 (?). He was admitted to the Staff Corps on the 10th June 1862, and on the 8th July 1864, was appointed Executive Engineer in the Rangoon Division. He was serving with the regiment in 1874, and officiated as Commandant in the following year. He became Commandant in 1877, and went on furlough to Europe on the 17th January 1879, being succeeded by Colonel Hodding on the 1st July 1880.

There were several other Babingtons in the Madras Army at about the same time, including Major William Knox Babington, who was serving with the 17th M. N. I., in 1852; Colonel David Babington, Madras Infantry, who was promoted to Major-General on the 17th August 1864; and Lieutenant-Colonel John Henry Melville Babington, who was in the Madras Staff Corps in 1863.

Renton, Robert:—Ensign, 27th February 1844: Major, 27th February 1864: Colonel, 27th February 1875. This officer was attached for duty to the 44th N.I., from the 5th July 1844, and to the 49th N.I., from the 29th November following. On the 31st December 1844, he was posted to the 4th N.I. (then in China) and directed to remain with the 49th N.I., till further orders. On the 27th March 1845, he was transferred, at his own request, to the 21st N.I., and consequently never joined the 4th. In 1861 and 1862, he was Commandant of H. H. the Rajah of Mysore's Escort, and was admitted to the Madras Staff Corps in the latter year. In May 1864, he was appointed to be Magistrate of the town of Mysore, in addition to his duties as Commandant of the Raja's Troops, and proceeded to Europe, on medical certificate, in 1865. He continued to be Town Magistrate of Mysore till the 1st October 1877, when he retired from the service, with the honorary rank of Major-General.

Macdonald, John Collins:—Ensign, 11th January 1845: Lieutenant, 15th February 1849: Captain, 1st January 1862: Major, 29th September 1872: Brevet-Colonel, 11th January 1876. This officer was posted to the regiment on the 2nd April 1845, but did not join till the following year, having been ordered to do duty with the 2nd European Light Infantry for eight months from the 24th June 1845. He was acting Quartermaster of the regiment in 1848-49, and on the 14th September 1849, was appointed to act as Quartermaster and Interpreter of the 41st N.I. He rejoined the regiment on the 1st July 1853, as Quartermaster and Interpreter, and left on staff duty as Sub-Assistant Commissary-General on the 25th March 1857. On the 8th April 1861, he was appointed a member of the Presidency Military Hindostanee Examining Committee, and was transferred to the Staff Corps in 1862.

He finally left the regiment on the 1st November 1865. He was a Deputy-Assistant Commissary-General in 1876.

Jenkins, Alexander:—Ensign, 14th June 1845: Captain, 1st October 1861. This officer, who was doing duty with the 21st N.I., was posted to the regiment on the 30th September 1845, but on the 2nd October following, was re-posted, at his own request, to the 2nd N.I.

Stiles, George Harcourt:—Ensign, 13th June 1845: Lieutenant, 22nd October 1850: Captain, 27th April 1863: Brevet-Major, 13th June 1865. This officer was also posted to the 4th on the 30th September 1845, but did not join for some time, as he had not arrived from Europe. From the 9th April 1856, he was Adjutant of the regiment, till the 16th January 1863, when he was permitted to resign the appointment, and on the 5th February following he proceeded to the Nilgiris, and subsequently to Europe, on sick leave. He was transferred to the Staff Corps on the 12th September 1866.

Dent, William McKerrell:—Ensign, 3rd July 1845. This officer was posted to the regiment on the 20th November 1845, but did not join at once, as he was doing duty with the 2nd N.I. He was present, but on the sick list, in November 1846, and on the 13th December of that year he proceeded on sick leave to Europe, where he is still shown up to 1848, after which his name drops out.

Turner, Charles James Alexander:—Ensign, 13th December 1845. This officer was posted to do duty with the 4th N.I., on the 7th April 1846, and directed to join the regiment, with leave of absence to visit Chittoor for two months *en route*. He was subsequently posted to the 29th N.I., and directed to join that regiment at Madras on the 22nd July 1846.

Jacob, Vickers Gilbert:—Ensign, 4th February 1846. This officer was posted to the 4th, then at Vellore, on the 15th June 1846. He never joined, being transferred to the 44th N.I., on the 19th June 1846. He was still serving with that regiment in 1855.

Grant, Douglas Gordon Seafield St. John:—Ensign, 13th June 1846: Captain, 18th February 1861: Brevet-Colonel, 13th June 1877. This officer was attached to the 4th for duty on the 30th June 1846, and on the 15th December following, was posted to the 9th N.I., but on the 4th January 1847, he was transferred, at his own request, to the 44th N.I. From his name, it would appear to be probable that he was a relation of Charles St. John Grant (*q. v.*), and a Lieutenant Charles Doveton Wetherall Seafield Grant, who was serving with the 50th N.I. in 1846, was presumably his brother.

Griffin, Francis Blackburn:—Ensign, 20th March 1846. Ensign Griffin was attached for duty to the 17th N.I., on the 7th May 1846, and was posted to the 4th on the 23rd June following. He died on the 15th July 1846.

Williams, Watkin Lewis Griffies:—Colonel, 29th January 1854: Major-General 28th November 1854. This officer was transferred from the 3rd L.I., to the 16th N.I., on the 13th October 1846, and was posted to the 4th as Lieutenant-Colonel on the 23rd October 1847, in succession to Lieutenant-Colonel Hitchens, but was absent on sick leave to Europe from the 1st March of that year, and never served with the regiment. On the 19th April 1848, he was transferred to the 1st Madras Fusiliers, and was succeeded by Lieutenant-Colonel E. Haldane.

Walker, George Andrew:—Ensign, 23rd June 1846: Lieutenant, 15th November 1853: Captain, 1st February 1865: Lieutenant-Colonel, 23rd June 1872: Brevet-Colonel, 23rd June 1877. This officer was posted to the regiment on the 15th December 1846, but did duty with the 27th N.I., till the 23rd March 1847, when he proceeded to join the 4th, serving with it till the 24th January 1853, when he left on staff duty, as Sub-Assistant Commissary-General, remaining with that department till the 1st November 1865, when he finally left the regiment. He was transferred to the Madras Staff Corps on the 10th June 1862, and in 1865, was Assistant Commissary-General, Nagpore Field Force.

Justice, William:—Lieutenant-Colonel, 20th September 1842: Brevet-Colonel, 10th May 1853: Major-General, 28th November 1854: Lieutenant-General, 6th December 1866. This officer was serving with the 38th N.I., in 1843, and on the 27th July 1844, was transferred from the 52nd N.I., to the 1st N.I., in place of Lieutenant-Colonel A. B. Dyce (*q. v.*). He was posted to the 4th, from the 28th N.I., on the 17th July 1848, *vice* Lieutenant-Colonel E. Haldane, and joined the regiment on the 3rd August following. He continued in command till the 18th March 1850, when he was transferred to the 49th N.I., being succeeded by Lieutenant-Colonel R. Budd. On the 6th June 1853, he was transferred from the 34th L.I., to the 7th N.I., and in September of that year, was Brigadier Commanding Malabar and Canara, being subsequently transferred to the command of Masulipatam. He died on the 27th October 1868.

Salter, Patrick:—Ensign, 11th December 1847: Lieutenant, 7th December 1853: Brevet Captain, 18th February 1861: Captain, 12th September 1866: Lieutenant-Colonel, 11th December 1873. This officer was originally attached for duty to the 52nd N.I., and was posted to the 4th on the 5th June 1848, joining in the following August. He proceeded to Europe on furlough on the 6th October 1859, and does not appear to have returned till 1863. In 1867, he was officiating Second in Command, and in 1872, was serving, as a Major, with the 25th N.I.

A Lieutenant John Henry Salter of the Madras Artillery, who died in 1831, is buried at Begur, near Nelamangala, in Bangalore District, and there was a Major-General F. Salter serving in the Madras Army in 1838.

Macdonald, Charles Edward William Chambers:—Ensign, 11th January 1848. This officer, who arrived at Madras on the 30th April 1848, was attached for duty to the 12th N.I., and was posted to the 4th on the 5th June following, but with orders to remain with the 12th N.I., till October. On the 8th September 1848, however, he was re-posted to the 27th N.I., and consequently never joined the 4th.

Smith, Henry Delves Broughton:—Ensign, 11th January 1848: Lieutenant, 27th May 1853: Captain, 22nd May 1862. This officer was originally appointed to do duty with the 2nd European Light Infantry in May 1848, and on the 5th June, was posted to the 24th N. I. with orders to remain with the 2nd E. L. I., till the 1st October 1848. On the 19th August 1848, he was permitted to effect an exchange with Ensign R. Menzies of the 2nd E. L. I., at his own request, but on the 8th September following, was posted to the 4th N. I. He was again transferred to the 2nd E. L. I. on the 18th April 1849, and eventually directed to join that corps in May 1849. He did not serve again with the 4th. In 1865, he was Executive Engineer, D.P.W., in Oudh, and was granted furlough on medical certificate.

Palmer, William Charles:—Ensign, 22nd August 1848: Lieutenant, 31st August 1854. This officer first did duty with the 15th N.I., and was posted to the 4th on the 19th February 1849, but with orders to remain with the 15th N.I., till the 30th June. He served with the regiment till the 9th March 1854, when he went on command as an Executive Engineer, 4th Class. He was admitted to the Staff Corps, as a Captain, on the 10th June 1862, in which year he became an Executive Engineer, 3rd Class, and his name was finally removed from the roll of the 4th from the 1st November 1865.

He was probably a brother of James Edward Palmer of the 4th (*q. v.*).

Fuller, William Henry Lawrence:—Ensign, 20th December 1848: Lieutenant, 6th January 1855: Brevet Captain, 18th February 1861: Captain, 16th June 1867. This officer was attached for duty to the 14th N.I., on the 7th February 1849, and was posted to the 4th on the 13th August following. In July 1853, he was granted one year's furlough, and from the 29th December 1857 till about May 1860, he was commanding the depot of the regiment at Rangoon. On the 1st May 1863, he was granted three years' furlough in India, and on the 12th September 1866, was admitted to the Staff Corps.

Budd, Richard:—Brevet-Major, 28th June 1838: Lieutenant-Colonel, 11th November 1843: Brevet-Colonel, 7th May 1854: Major-General, 10th February 1856: Lieutenant-General, 19th October 1868: General, 8th July 1874. This officer was serving as a Captain, with the 32nd N.I., in 1833-34, and, as a Major, with the same regiment in 1843, but was then acting as Superintendent of the Bangalore Division of the Mysore Territory. In March 1844, he was posted to the 2nd European Light Infantry, which he commanded till the 15th October 1846, when he was transferred to the 10th N.I. He then, apparently, went to the 12th N.I., as, on the 18th March 1850, he was transferred from that regiment to the 4th, in succession to Lieutenant-Colonel Justice, and continued to hold the appointment till the 23rd October 1853, when he was transferred to the 39th N.I., and again transferred, on the 2nd October 1855, to the 11th N.I. On the 26th October 1855, he was appointed a Brigadier of the 2nd Class, and to command Bangalore. An order striking him off the strength of the 8th N.I. appeared on the 5th June 1856.

On the 27th February 1861, the Commander-in-Chief, Sir Patrick Grant, K.C.B., having embarked for Europe, the command devolved upon Major-General Budd as next senior officer, and he accordingly acted as Provincial Commander-in-Chief till relieved by Sir J. Hope Grant on the 26th December 1861, being afterwards appointed to command the Southern Division. He was placed on the retired list, with the rank of General, on the 1st October 1877.

There was a Colonel William Henry Budd serving in the Madras Infantry in 1861.

Carr, Robert:—Ensign, 20th December 1849: Lieutenant, 15th June 1853. This officer was attached for duty to the 21st N.I., on the 4th February 1850, but was removed to the 4th N.I., on the 8th March following, and remained with the regiment till September, when he was posted to the 37th Grenadiers.

Weston, Charles:—Ensign, 20th January 1850. This officer was attached for duty to the 21st N.I., on the 7th March 1850, but on the 18th May, was removed to the 4th, remaining with the regiment till the 19th December, when he was posted to the 1st Madras Fusiliers as a second Lieutenant.

A Lieutenant George Edward Weston was serving in the Presidency in 1862.

Smithers, Otway Francis:—Ensign, 20th January 1850: Captain, 11th October 1861. This officer arrived at Madras on the 2nd March 1850, and was attached for duty to the 15th N.I. He was posted to the 4th in January 1851, and in 1853 proceeded to Europe on sick leave. On the 15th November 1853, he was posted to the newly-raised 3rd Madras European Regiment at Bellary. The next reference to him which I can trace, is in 1865, when he was attached to the 4th for duty from the 1st November. In 1868, he was officiating Quartermaster of the regiment. In 1878, he was serving in the 14th N.I., as a Lieutenant-Colonel.

Prescott, William:—Lieutenant-Colonel, 28th August 1843: Colonel, 15th April 1854: Major-General, 15th September 1855: Lieutenant-General, 22nd April 1868: General, 10th April 1874. This officer was appointed to command the 4th, in succession to Lieutenant-Colonel R. Budd, on the 23rd October 1853. From the 15th April 1854, he was Brigadier, commanding Trichinopoly, and he was struck off the strength of the regiment on the 21st January 1856. In March 1856, being then on the Unattached List, he was permitted to reside and draw his pay at Trichinopoly and Madras, but, a month later, he proceeded to Europe on medical certificate.

Jennings, Charles James:—Ensign, 10th September 1853: Major, 10th September 1873. This officer was first posted to the 21st N.I., on the 2nd November 1853, and subsequently to the 4th, on the 15th February 1854, but was transferred to the 15th N.I., and never joined, nor served with, the regiment.

Podmore, Henry Beresford:—Ensign, 10th December 1853. This officer, who joined the 4th, on the 15th February 1854, died of cholera at Uttacolapoor, while on the march with the regiment from Mercara to Trichinopoly, on the 31st December 1854. There is a tablet to his memory and that of Captain Dunlop in St. John's Church, Trichinopoly. (*Vide George Wellington Nelson Dunlop*).

A Richard Pakenham Podmore was serving in the Madras Army in 1836, and an Ensign Robert Podmore died in 1838.

Hutton, George:—Major-General, 4th July 1856. This officer was transferred from the 13th N.I. to the 48th N.I., on the 3rd March 1850, being then a Lieutenant-Colonel, and subsequently served with the 2nd European Light Infantry, from which he was removed on promotion to Major-General. He became Colonel of the regiment, in succession to Major-General John Munro, on the 18th June 1858. He died at Vizianagram, where he had been permitted to reside, on the 28th August 1861. His tombstone in the Cantonment Cemetery at Vizianagram bears the following inscription:—

"Major-General George Hutton, aged 67 years, after 50 years' Service in H.M.'s E. I. Service."

There was a William Forbes Hutton serving in the Madras Army in 1836.

Cotton, William:—Major, 7th January 1843: Lieutenant-Colonel, 4th September 1849: Colonel, 28th November 1854: Lieutenant-General, 31st December 1861. This officer was serving with the 10th N.I., in March 1843, and was commanding the 37th Grenadiers prior to his transfer to the 4th. He succeeded Lieutenant-Colonel Prescott in command of the regiment on the 10th November 1856, and held the appointment until 1859.

William Forbes Cotton of the 4th (*q. v.*) was his son.

Davidson, Alfred Augustus:—Ensign, 1st April 1854: Lieutenant, 10th September 1856: Captain, 1st August 1866. This officer was posted to the 4th on the 28th June 1854, but was appointed to do duty with the 51st N.I. He went on sick leave to Tranquebar and the Eastern Coast on the 1st January 1855, and joined the 4th on the 16th May 1855. On the 18th December following, he proceeded to Europe on sick leave. From the 5th August 1862 till the 1st November 1865 (when he was transferred from the regiment) he was absent on staff duty with the Nair Brigade in Travancore.

Mackenzie, Colin:—Ensign, 20th June 1854: Lieutenant, 15th September 1856: Brevet Captain, 20th June 1866: Captain, 14th August 1868. This officer was posted to the regiment on the 30th September 1854, and from the 20th January 1858 till 1862, he was absent on sick leave in Europe. In 1863, he became Adjutant of the regiment, and held the appointment till he went on furlough on the 24th December 1866, proceeding to Europe on the 25th August following. He does not appear to have returned as, after being shown as "absent without leave from the 25th November 1870", he makes no further appearance.

There was a more distinguished officer of this name on the Madras establishment at an earlier date—Colonel Colin Mackenzie, C. B., who died at Calcutta in 1821, when Surveyor-General of India.

Another Colin Mackenzie (Major, 30th January 1856: Lieutenant-Colonel, 7th October 1860: Lieutenant-General, 1st October 1877) served with the 48th and 45th M. N. I. and was awarded a C.B. in 1867; and a Major Simon Fraser Mackenzie was shown as belonging to the 2nd Madras Cavalry in 1852.

Phelips, Robert Hoskyns:—Ensign, 20th October 1854: Lieutenant, 20th September 1856: Brevet Captain, 20th June 1866: Major, 20th October 1874: Lieutenant-Colonel, 20th October 1880. This officer was posted to the 4th on the 2nd March 1855, but did duty with the 44th N.I. till the 15th November following. He proceeded to Europe on 18 months' sick leave on the 16th July 1857, and was again compelled to go on a year's sick leave to the Nilgiris on the 15th October 1863. He went on furlough on the 28th October 1865, rejoining on the 27th February 1866, and again from the 10th November 1866 to the 9th January 1867, after which he again proceeded to Europe on sick leave till the 1st January 1870, and never rejoined the regiment.

A Major H. R. Phelips was in charge of pensioners at Guntur in August 1875.

Houghton, Richmond:—Ensign, 9th December 1854: Major, 9th December 1874. This officer was posted to the 4th on the 2nd March 1855, but did not arrive in India till the 11th April following, when he was removed, at his own request, to the 46th N.I., and consequently never served with the regiment. He was admitted to the Madras Staff Corps, as a Lieutenant, on the 10th June 1862, and the only other reference to him which I have seen is in April 1875, when as a Major and Superintendent, British Burma Police, he embarked at Rangoon on furlough.

Shelley, Harry Byam:—Ensign, 5th March 1855. This officer arrived at Madras on the 11th April 1855, and was directed to do duty with the 31st L.I. On the 22nd May 1855, he was posted to the 4th, but on the 1st June, was transferred, at his own request, to the 32nd N.I. On the 10th July 1855, he was again transferred, at his own request, to the 31st L.I. He never actually served with the regiment. On the 8th March 1862, he was court-martialled at Waltair for having unauthorisedly entered the house of Charles Thomas Longley, Esq., M.C.S., called for brandy and water, and assaulted one of the servants, and for having been drunk, and was sentenced to be cashiered.

Rivers, Francis James:—Ensign, 4th May 1855. This officer was attached for duty to the 31st L.I., on arrival at Madras on the 11th April 1855, and on the 7th August, was posted to the 4th, but ten days later, was removed, at his own request, to the 34th L.I.

Plant, William Charles:—Ensign, 9th June 1855: Lieutenant, 23rd November 1856: Major, 9th June 1875. This officer was attached for duty with the 4th on the 14th June 1855, and posted to the 34th L.I. on the 7th August following, but ten days later, was transferred to the 4th. He was serving with the detachment at Prome from the 21st December 1857 till the 7th June 1860, when he became Assistant Magistrate at Rangoon. He was appointed to the Madras Staff Corps in 1862, when he was Assistant Commissioner, Henzada, and in April 1863, became Assistant Commissioner, Thayetmyo. In 1864, he was Assistant Commissioner at Prome, and in 1865, officiating as Deputy Commissioner and Superintendent of Police, Sandoway, after which I have no further record of him.

He was, presumably, a brother of John Floyd Alexander Plant of the 4th (*q. v.*).

Russell, William:—Major Russell of the 18th N.I. was posted to the command of the 4th on the 21st January 1856, *vice* Colonel Prescott, who had been promoted to the rank of Major-General. I have not been able to find out much about him. In 1853, he proceeded to Europe on sick leave, and presumably rejoined the 18th N.I. on his return. He was transferred to the 2nd N.I. on the 7th March 1856, his place being taken by Brevet-Colonel Haldane (*q. v.*), and does not appear ever to have joined the 4th. He was promoted to Colonel, after his retirement, on the 17th April 1857.

McNeill, Duncan:—Ensign, 8th December 1855. This officer, on his arrival in the Presidency in December 1855, was attached for duty, first with the 49th N.I., and next with the 11th N.I. On the 26th February 1856, he was posted to the 4th, but on the 28th March following, was transferred, at his own request, to the 26th N.I.

Graham, David:—Ensign, 12th December 1856. This officer was posted to the 4th on the 20th February 1857, but his name disappears from the list after April 1858, and I do not know what became of him.

Anderson, William:—Ensign, 4th March 1856: Lieutenant, 23rd November 1856: Captain, 29th September 1872. This officer was posted to the 4th in 1856, after having been attached for duty to the 14th N.I. and 6th N.I. From the 24th January 1859 till the 9th January 1862, he was absent on sick leave to Europe, and in 1873 was still shown as belonging to the regiment.

Thomas, E. Hastings:—Ensign, 16th August 1856. This officer was posted to the 4th on the 28th October 1856, joining in the following December, and served with the regiment till 1860, when he must have been transferred to some other corps.

Oakes, George Henry:—Ensign, 4th March 1857: Lieutenant, 30th August 1860. This officer was posted to the 4th on the 21st April 1857, and was transferred, at his own request, to the 39th N.I. on the 30th August 1860.

Just about this time (1860—66) officers were constantly being transferred from one regiment to another, owing to the introduction of the Staff Corps, and consequent reorganisation.

One Thomas Oakes joined the Madras Civil Service in 1770, since when many of his descendants have served in the Indian Army.

Cotton, William Forbes:—Ensign, 20th January 1857: Lieutenant, 31st December 1861. This officer was posted to the 4th on the 26th May 1857, and from the 31st January 1859, was serving with the detachment at Prome. He died, while serving with the regiment at Madras, on the 30th October 1862, his tomb in St. Mary's Cemetery bearing the following inscription:—

"William Forbes Cotton, Lieutenant, 4th Regiment M.N.I., son of Lieutenant-General William Cotton, Madras Army, aged 26 years."

Lieutenant-General William Cotton (*q. v.*) had been a Commandant of the 4th.

Bell, James:—Lieutenant-Colonel Commandant, 30th May 1849: Colonel, 28th March 1850: Lieutenant-General, 8th January 1865. This officer was a Lieutenant-Colonel Commanding the 1st Madras European Regiment at Secunderabad in 1842 and, in 1849, when borne on the rolls of the 11th N.I., was appointed to be a Brigadier of the 2nd class and to command Masulipatam. On the 23rd October 1855, his services were placed at the disposal of the supreme Government for appointment to the command of the Pegu Division, in succession to Major-General Sir S.W. Steel, K.C.B., he being at that time in command of the Hyderabad Subsidiary Force, and in February 1861, his appointment came to an end, and he proceeded to Europe on furlough. On the 26th March 1860, he was appointed Colonel of the 4th, in succession to Major-General Hutton, and continued to hold the appointment till the 1st November 1865. He was placed on the retired list, as a full General, on the 1st October 1877.

A Robert Bell, who became a Lieutenant-General in 1819, was Commandant of the Madras Artillery from 1805 to 1820.

Bird, John Francis:—Brevet Lieutenant-Colonel, 23rd November 1841: Lieutenant-Colonel, 15th April 1853: Brevet Colonel, 3rd August 1855: Major-General 31st December 1861. This officer being then a Captain and Brevet Major in the 22nd N.I., was appointed D.A.A.G., Southern Division, on the 8th November 1842, and was posted to the command of the 22nd N.I. on the 6th June 1853, but was transferred to the 28th N.I. on the 26th November following. He was absent on furlough in Europe throughout 1853, and on the 17th June 1859, succeeded Colonel Cotton in command of the 4th, holding the appointment till the 31st December 1861, when he retired from the service with the rank of Brevet Colonel, but was subsequently granted the rank of Major-General from the same date.

Warden, James Hale:—Captain Warden of the 13th N.I. was attached to the 4th for duty as Quartermaster and Interpreter from the 20th November 1860, till the end of 1861. He became a Brevet Colonel in 1877.

Campbell, J.:—Captain and Brevet Major J. Campbell of the 50th N.I. was removed from doing duty with the 34th L.I. on the 9th February 1861, and posted to do duty with the 4th, but I have not been able to find out anything about him.

Power, A. G. C.:—Ensign Power was attached for duty with the 4th from February till the 17th September 1861, when he was transferred for duty with the 23rd L.I.

Bird, Francis Paske Harvey:—Lieutenant Bird was attached for duty with the 4th for a short time in 1861, and on the 1st May of that year, was ordered to join his own regiment, the 2nd European Light Infantry, at Trichinopoly.

Taylor, Ralph Neufville:—Captain Taylor of the 17th N.I. was attached for duty with the 4th for three months from the 20th June 1861.

Whyte, A. C. V.:—Ensign Whyte was also attached for duty with the 4th for a short time in 1861, and on the 14th October of that year, was transferred for duty with the 23rd L.I.

McGoun, Thomas:—Major, 22nd August 1853: Colonel, 6th September 1862. Lieutenant-Colonel McGoun was posted to command the 4th, in succession to Colonel Bird, on the 1st January 1862, but did not join the regiment, being employed on the staff as Auditor-General and Controller of Military Finances till his death on the 19th April 1868. A tablet to his memory in St. Andrew's Church, Madras, reads:—

> "Major-General Thomas McGoun of the Madras Army, who died at Marseilles, on his way to England, in the 62nd year of his age, after an almost uninterrupted service in India of 42 years. He served with his Regiment (6th Madras Native Infanty) in Goomsur in 1837, and was present with it at the storming of Chin Kiang Foo and other engagements in the Chinese War of 1841-42. His services were especially conspicuous in the Judge-Advocate and Military Finance Departments, in the former for 20 years, and in the latter (specially appointed Controller by the Government), from 1860 until his death."

His wife, Mary Elizabeth McGoun, died in 1867, and there is a fine monument to her memory in St. Andrew's, Bangalore.

Dobbie, R. S.:—Ensign, 11th January 1838. This officer did not belong to the 4th, but was attached to the regiment for duty, as a Major, from the 1st January 1862. He was still with the regiment, and in command, on the 1st January 1864, but left, presumably to return to his own regiment, the 39th N.I., between that date and April 1865.

Another officer of the same name—George Staple Dobbie,—who arrived in Madras as a cadet in 1836, was posted to the 44th N.I. He subsequently served with the corps of Sappers and Miners (1839), in the D.P.W. as Executive Officer (1855) and with the 44th N.I. (1862).

Young, G. A.:—Lieutenant Young, on the disbandment of the 52nd N.I., was posted to the 24th N.I. in May 1862, and was attached for duty with the 4th from the 26th November 1862 till some time in 1864. In May 1863, he was granted a certificate of qualification in surveying.

Kilgour, Frederick:—Major, 11th July 1877. Lieutenant Kilgour, on the disbandment of the 52nd N.I., was attached for duty to the 4th from the 17th May 1862 till some time in 1863. He is shown in August 1873 as a Captain in the Staff Corps and probationary Assistant Superintendent of Police, 1st Class.

Mottet, Arthur Charles:—Lieutenant, 1st January 1862: Major, 4th September 1879. This officer was attached to the 4th for duty from the 2nd September 1861 till the 7th December 1865, when he proceeded to Europe on sick leave till the 13th October 1868.

Mottet, Henry Edward:—Captain, 20th December 1862. Lieutenant H. E. Mottet was nominated to act as Quartermaster and Interpreter of the 4th from the 26th November 1861 till further orders. In the following December, he was officiating Fort Adjutant at Fort St. George, subsequently transferring to the Commissariat Department (17th January 1862), and then to the Mysore Commission (26th March 1864). He was Deputy Commissioner of Shimoga District in 1878.

A Lieutenant Gustave Henry Mottet of the 19th N.I. died on the 23rd March 1861, and a Captain Edward Adolphe Mottet was serving with the 42nd N.I. at about the same time.

Nicholls, Henry James:—Lieutenant Nicholls was attached to the 4th for duty from the 24th December 1861 up to 1865. I have not been able to find out anything about him.

In St. Mary's Church, Fort St. George, there is a tablet to the memory of "Anne Lilly Nicholls, wife of Henry James Nicholls of the 25th Regiment M.N.I.," who died in 1837, aged 20, but, from the date, this must have been another officer of the same name.

Johnston, Charles James:—Ensign, 4th January 1862. This officer was attached for duty to the 69th Foot in May 1862, and to the 4th from the 17th September following till the 2nd August 1863, when he was transferred for duty at the Civil Engineering College, Madras.

Hudleston, W.:—Lieutenant Hudleston of the 2nd N.I. was attached to the 4th for duty from the 12th November 1861 to the 3rd December 1862. This may have been the Wilfred Hudleston, who was promoted to Lieutenant-Colonel on the 13th June 1875.

There were several Hudlestons in the Madras Civil Service; one William; another, John (1766); and another, John Burland, Collector of Tinnevelly, who died in 1823. A Lieutenant John Hudleston of the 18th N.I. was court-martialled at Cannanore on the 12th March 1861 for intoxication and breaking his arrest, and was sentenced to be cashiered, but was pardoned by the Commander-in-Chief, General Budd (*q. v.*), on account of his inexperience and youth—he was only 19 years of age.

The same officer was again court-martialled at Kamptee in March 1865, and severely reprimanded, for having remained in Bombay for several months, after having been ordered to join the 1st N.I. Sir J. G. LeMarchant, then Commander-in-Chief, ordered the Court to reconsider their sentence, which in his opinion was entirely inadequate, but the Court stuck to their point, and the sentence was "confirmed, but disapproved." A Lieutenant-Colonel J. Hudleston was Superintendent of Family Payments and Pensions in 1875, and a Lieutenant E. Hudleston was Adjutant of the 50th N.I. in January 1862.

Gosling, Henry Monteith:—This officer was attached for duty to the 1st Royals in 1862, and was similarly attached to the 4th, being then a Lieutenant in the 50th N.I., from 1863 to 1866.

There were three other Goslings in the Presidency; one, George Robert, of the Madras Civil Service, who died in 1825; another, Henry Charles, of the 7th N.I. and, later commanding the 10th N.I., 1862-66, who retired from the Army as a Major-General; and Lieutenant-Colonel, W.C.F. Gosling, A.A.G., Royal (Madras) Artillery in 1868.

Stevens, Joseph Fisher:—Lieutenant-Colonel, 1st January 1862. This officer was a Lieutenant, and Adjutant of the 18th N.I. in 1844, and appears to have served with that regiment until he was promoted to Lieutenant-Colonel, when he was posted to command the 6th N.I. On the 27th September 1864, when he was on sick leave in Europe, he was appointed to command the 4th, in place of Lieutenant-Colonel McGoun. He returned to India on the 30th December 1865, as Commandant of the 4th, and retired from the service on the 30th April 1866.

Magan, Tilson Shaw:—Captain, 8th April 1873: Major, 9th October 1879. This officer was attached for duty with the 4th in 1865, and posted to the regiment on the 30th October 1866, serving with it till the 17th June 1867, when he proceeded to Europe on 18 months' sick leave. He was serving with the 25th N.I. in 1873, and never rejoined the 4th.

Jones, Robert:—Brevet Major, 14th November 1861: Major, 23rd March 1863. Major and Brevet Lieutenant-Colonel Jones of the 3rd L.I. was appointed Senior Wing Commandant of the 4th on the 15th March 1866, when he was on furlough in Europe, but never joined, nor served with, the regiment.

Burton, Edmond Francis:—Ensign, 18th September 1839: Lieutenant, 31st March 1842: Captain, 7th March 1848: Major, 18th February 1861: Lieutenant-Colonel, 18th September 1865: Brevet Colonel, 18th September 1870. Lieutenant-Colonel E.F. Burton was appointed Commandant of the 4th M.N.I. on the 15th March 1866, and remained in command of the regiment till the 9th September 1872, when he proceeded to Europe on two years' furlough. He had commenced his service with the 13th M.N.I., with whom he was serving, as a subaltern, at Samulcotta (Samalkot) about 1840. From 1858 to 1865 he held a staff appointment at Kamptee. On his return from furlough he did not rejoin the 4th, but became Commandant of the 8th M.N.I. which was stationed at Sitabaldi in 1875. Having become a full Colonel in 1870, in 1878 he was appointed General Officer Commanding the Northern District, with headquarters at Walthair, but only held this appointment for about two months, when it was altogether abolished. He was then given the command on the Western Coast, with headquarters at Cannanore. In 1882, he was, for a short time, in command of the Hyderabad Subsidiary Force, and was instrumental, by making a forcible representation to the British Resident, in getting the game restrictions at Hyderabad modified, these having been made so rigorous that officers of the force could get practically no shooting at all. In the same year, 1882, he was given temporary command of the Burma Division, and shortly afterwards retired to England with the rank of Lieutenant-General. He was a great *shikari* and while in Secunderabad with the 4th he kept an elephant to take him out on his many shooting excursions. After his retirement he wrote two interesting books, both of which had considerable success in their day and are still to be met with occasionally. The first was entitled, "*Reminiscences of Sport in India*" and the second, "*An Indian Olio.*" I have no record of the year of his death. He was awarded a good-service pension on the 1st April 1877.

Whitlock, William Henry:—Captain Whitlock, of the 5th N.I., was attached to the 4th M.N.I. for duty as Officiating Wing Officer from the 1st December 1868. Promoted to Major in 1869, he continued to serve with the regiment till 1872 when, presumably, he returned to his own corps. He became Colonel on the 20th September 1880.

Marsack, Augustus Becher:—Lieutenant, 18th November 1846: Captain, 9th March 1861: Major, 18th February 1863. This officer, on the 22nd September 1842, was transferred from the 36th N.I. to the 15th N.I. as fifth Ensign, and was still serving with the latter in 1844, when he proceeded to Europe on sick leave. In 1853, he acted as Interpreter to the 31st L.I., and was then appointed 2nd Assistant Civil Engineer in the D.P.W. He became a Superintendent of Police on the 25th November 1859, and on the 20th February 1863, he was appointed Military Joint Magistrate at Trichinopoly, and in 1865, proceeded on 20 months' leave on medical certificate. He was posted to the 4th, as a Major and Wing officer, on the 1st April 1867, and was officiating Second in Command. He was promoted to Lieutenant-Colonel in 1868, and served with the regiment until the 20th April 1871, when he proceeded to Europe on two years' furlough, and did not rejoin the regiment thereafter, though he returned to India in 1873. A Major Edward Becher Marsack of the 13th N.I., who died in August 1861, was presumably his brother.

Blenkinsop, Edward George:—Lieutenant, 1st January 1862: Captain, 27th May 1875: Major, 20th September 1879: Lieutenant-Colonel, 1885: Colonel, 1889. This officer entered the service on the 20th September 1859, and joined the regiment as a Lieutenant on the 24th August 1867, becoming Adjutant shortly afterwards, an appointment which he retained till 1879. On the 24th March 1872, he went to Europe on two years' sick leave, and had another two years' furlough from the 30th August 1880. In 1885, he was officiating 2nd in Command of the regiment, and he officiated as Commandant in the following year. On the 5th November 1891, he retired, and he died at Clifton in 1910.

His services with the regiment in Afghanistan, and on the Periyar Project, will be found referred to elsewhere in these records.

Rennick, R. H. F.:—Lieutenant Rennick of the Royal Artillery was posted to the 4th M.N.I. as Quartermaster on the 30th May 1868, but does not appear ever to have joined. In 1869, he is shown as a probationer for the Bengal Staff Corps.

An Ensign James Rennick of the Palamcottah Light Infantry died on active service in Ganjam in 1836, and an R. H. Rennick was Deputy Inspector-General of Hospitals in 1870.

Brereton, S. W. T.:—Captain, 1869. Lieutenant Brereton, Staff Corps, was attached to the 4th M.N.I. in 1868, was Quartermaster of the regiment in 1869-70, and appears to have left it in 1871. I have not been able to trace his subsequent history.

Ellis, William Charles:—Lieutenant, 1st January 1862. This officer was attached to the 4th M.N.I. in 1868, but there is nothing to show whether he ever did duty with the regiment or not, as he proceeded to Europe on sick leave on the 22nd January 1868, and retired from the service on the 7th September 1871, being then a Brevet-Captain.

One H. L. A. Ellis, 1st Bengal Light Cavalry, 2nd-in-Command of the Governor's Body Guard, and A.D.C. to the Governor-General, who may have been a brother of the above, died at Madras in 1852.

Hornsby, A. W. H.:—Lieutenant Hornsby was posted to the 4th M.N.I. from the 19th Foot on the 21st September 1869, but left the regiment in 1870 and I have not discovered what became of him thereafter.

Carr, William George:—Captain Carr was appointed 1st Wing Subaltern of the 4th M.N.I. on the 20th January 1870, but never joined the regiment, and the appointment must have been cancelled.

Gabbett, Joseph:—Captain J. Gabbett, 95th Foot, was posted to the 4th M.N.I. on the 18th November 1870, but the order must have been cancelled, as he never joined the regiment.

He was promoted to Major, in the Madras Staff Corps on the 30th March 1875.

Maltby, Francis Crichton:—Lieutenant, 14th October 1871: Captain, 16th October 1878. This officer was posted to the 4th on the 28th November 1870, and served with it till he was transferred to the 16th N.I. as Quartermaster in 1874. He proceeded to Europe on two years' furlough in 1875.

A Captain E.P. Maltby was an Assistant Commissioner in the Mysore Commission in 1873.

Desborough, Lawrence Cameron:—Lieutenant, 29th June 1861: Captain, 13th April 1873. This officer was serving with the 51st N.I. in 1861—64, and was posted to the 4th in April 1870, when he was absent on sick leave to Europe, but after remaining nominally on the strength of the regiment till the end of 1871, he no longer appears, and he never joined for duty.

A Major S. H. Desborough, possibly a brother of the above, was killed at St. Thomas' Mount in 1878, by a fall from his horse, which collided with a buffalo.

Barnett, James Herbert Marsh:—Captain, 13th April 1873: Major, 13th June 1877. This officer joined the regiment as officiating Quartermaster, from the 16th N.I., on the 30th March 1871. He proceeded to Europe on two years' sick leave on the 1st August 1875, and on his return he was placed on general duty in Bangalore. He rejoined the regiment as Second in Command and Wing Commander on the 8th December 1881, and on the 27th July 1885, proceeded to Europe on a year's leave on medical certificate, rejoining in 1887. He was Commandant of the regiment from the 23rd May 1886 until his retirement on the 8th July 1890. I have no record of the date of his death.

Robertson, Norman Donald:—Captain N. D. Robertson was posted to the 4th M.N.I. on the 10th January 1871, when he was absent on sick leave to Europe. He was present for duty with the regiment from 1872 till 1874, but as his name does not re-appear after the 1st January 1874, he must either have died or been transferred to another regiment in that year.

Riach, William Alexander:—This officer, then belonging to the 12th N.I., was appointed D.A.Q.M.G., Ceded Districts, from March 1862, and retained that appointment till September 1865. In 1872, being then a Colonel, he officiated in command of the 4th while Colonel Burton was on furlough, and Colonel W. J. Jones on the sick list. He was appointed Commandant of the 3rd L.I. on the 1st January 1874.

Thomas, G.:—Major, 1878. This officer was posted to the 4th on the 7th March 1862, being then a Captain. He was absent on furlough in India from the 4th October 1873 till the 3rd April 1874, and proceeded to Europe on two years' sick leave on the 23rd August 1874. On his return, he served with the regiment till 1879, when he again went to Europe, and did not rejoin the regiment.

Lavie, Robert Comyn:—Major, 1st January 1874: Lieutenant-Colonel, 20th December 1874: Brevet Colonel, 20th December 1879. This officer was posted to the 4th as officiating Second in Command on the 2nd October 1875, but only served with the regiment till some time in 1877, after which I do not know what became of him. His previous service had been with the 3rd L.I. and 6th N.I.

Bruce, J. C. W.:—Lieutenant-Colonel Bruce was appointed to the 4th as Wing Officer on the 31st December 1874, but does not appear ever to have joined, or served with, the regiment.

Baugh, Guillum Scott:—Lieutenant Baugh joined the 4th from the 2nd Battalion 12th Foot, on the 11th May 1874, and on the 24th March 1875, left Palavaram with the detachment of the regiment, under Colonel Babington, which proceeded to Rangoon. He appears to have left the regiment in 1876.

Hodding, George Carr:—Captain, 16th July 1864: Major, 13th April 1873: Lieutenant-Colonel, 10th February 1877: Colonel, 1881: Brigadier-General, 1886. This officer was a Lieutenant in the 20th N.I. in 1861, and became Adjutant of that regiment in February 1862. He was still serving with the 20th in 1873, and joined the 4th on the 2nd October 1875. He became Commandant on the 1st July 1880, and was in command during the Afghan War. He left the regiment in 1886, on being appointed to the command of a district with the rank of Brigadier-General.

Porteous, James Edward:—Lieutenant, 2nd May 1868: Captain, 22nd September 1877: Major, 1885. Lieutenant-Colonel, 1891: Brevet Colonel, 1896. This officer joined the 4th M.N.I. on the 22nd May 1875. He acted as Quartermaster of the regiment until the 24th July 1880, when he went to Europe on 18 months' sick leave. On the 11th January 1886, he went on Staff duty as Officiating D.A.Q.M.G., Southern District, and on the 2nd February 1887, he became D.A.Q.M.G. to the Nagpore Force, being subsequently appointed District Staff Officer, 2nd Class, Secunderabad District. On the 5th November 1891, he was appointed Commandant of the regiment, and remained in command until the 26th January 1897, when he went to England on leave, pending retirement, finally retiring from the service on the 4th November 1898. He distinguished himself during the Afghan Campaign of 1879—90. On his departure from the regiment, he presented a set of bagpipes (which are still maintained), to the Indian Officers and men of the regiment. Before joining the regiment he had seen service during the campaign in Abyssinia in 1867-68.

Many representatives of this family have served in Madras, and all were descended from the Craiglockhart branch of the Hawkshaw family of Porteous. Thomas Porteous, Provost of Edinburgh in 1695, had a grandson, Henry, who migrated to St. Helena in 1802, and there married a daughter of Captain Knipe of the St. Helena Regiment in 1808. This Henry Porteous became a great friend of the interned Emperor Napoleon, and died in 1819, leaving four sons, all of whom entered the medical profession, the third, Henry William, joining the Madras Medical Service, in which he eventually became Inspector-General of Hospitals. His son, Colonel Charles Arkcoll Porteous, C.I.E. (1839—1928), after a distinguished career during the Mutiny with the 27th M.N.I., in the Cawnpore district, became Inspector-General of Police in Madras.

Grant, James Murray:—Captain, 1st January 1862. This officer was serving with the 15th N.I. in 1862, and was admitted to the Madras Staff Corps on the 10th June of that year. On the 10th August 1876, he, being then officiating Commandant of the 24th N.I., was appointed Second in Command of the 4th, but never joined, nor served with, the regiment.

A Colonel C. D. Grant of the Madras Staff Corps retired on pension in April 1873.

Wetherall, Pritzler James Pakenham:—Lieutenant-Colonel Wetherall was posted to the 4th on the 12th August 1877, as Second in Command, but I am not certain whether he ever joined the regiment as, from the 9th August 1877, he was officiating Commandant of the 41st N.I.

Godson, John:—Major, 4th July 1875. This officer served originally with the 52nd N.I. and, on the disbandment of that unit in 1862, was posted to the 31st L.I. On the 27th March 1877, he was posted to the 4th as Wing Commander, and served with the regiment in Afghanistan in 1879—80, where he died from fatigue and exposure.

Passy, DeLacy Dayrell:—Lieutenant, 19th October 1872: Captain, 1884. This officer was posted to the 4th M.N.I. from the 67th Foot, on the 7th August 1876. He became Quartermaster on the 1st February 1878, and acted as Adjutant from 1879 to 1883. He served with the regiment in Afghanistan, 1879-80. In 1885, he died of cholera, whilst working with the regiment on the Sind-Peshin Railway.

Wilmot, Henry Eardley:—2nd Lieutenant, 12th February 1877: Lieutenant, 4th March 1878. This officer, who belonged to the 38th N.I., was attached to the 4th from the 14th October 1879, but ceased to do duty with the regiment in the following year.

Coningham, Walter:—2nd Lieutenant, 12th December 1857: Major, 12th December 1877. Major Coningham was attached to the 4th M.N.I., as Officiating Wing Commander and 2nd-in-Command, on the 8th November 1880, but left the regiment, to which he never belonged, in 1881.

Welch, M. E. H. O.:—2nd Lieutenant, 20th July 1870. Lieutenant Welch of the 9th N.I. was only attached to the 4th N.I. for a few months from the 25th October 1880, and acted as Quartermatser.

Kaye, Arthur E. C.:—2nd Lieutenant, 11th February 1875. Lieutenant Kaye, 109th Foot, was also attached to the 4th N.I. for a few months from the 24th November 1880, as Officiating Wing Officer, on probation.

Hudson, H. S.:—2nd Lieutenant, 2nd February 1876. Lieutenant Hudson, Royal Artillery, was attached to the 4th for a few months from the 4th November 1880, on probation.

Hatton, Arthur:—2nd Lieutenant, 1st September 1876.

Mackenzie, Donald:—2nd Lieutenant, 1st September 1876.

Longford, W. J.:—2nd Lieutenant, 19th September 1877.

The above three Lieutenants, with Lieutenant G. B. Stevens (*q. v.*), were all attached to the 4th M. N. I., from the Royal Marine Light Infantry, on the 20th November 1880, as Officiating Wing Officers, on probation, but all left the regiment within a few months.

Clerk, Robert Mildmay:—Ensign, 4th March 1861: Lieutenant, 30th July 1862: Brevet Captain, 9th December 1872: Captain, 4th March 1873: Major, 1881: Lieutenant-Colonel, 1887.

This officer was attached to the 4th as Officiating Wing Commander on the 23rd October 1880, and was permanently posted to the regiment, as a Major, in 1881, when he was still Officiating Wing Commander and Acting Quartermaster. He accompanied the regiment to Aden in 1882, and became Railway Transport Officer of the Indian Division at Cairo. For his work in this appointment he was highly complimented by Major-General MacPherson, Commanding the Indian Division. On the 1st April 1883, he was appointed D.A.A.G., Eastern District, and from the 25th October 1886 officiated as A.A.G., Army Head-Quarters. On the 23rd November 1888, he was transferred to the 25th M.I.

King, H. T.:—2nd Lieutenant, 1st May 1878. This officer was attached to the 4th M.N.I., from the 103rd Foot, on the 22nd October 1880, but was only with the regiment for a few months.

Stevens, George Borlase:—2nd Lieutenant, 19th September 1877: Lieutenant, 1880: Captain, 19th September 1888: Brevet Major, 5th October 1892: Major, 1897: Lieutenant-Colonel, 19th September 1903: Honorary Brigadier-General, 1917. This officer joined the Royal Marine Light Infantry in 1877, and was posted to the 4th on the 20th November 1880. He was Adjutant of the regiment from 1884 to 1888, and served with the Egyptian Expeditionary Force in 1882, and in the campaigns in Burma in 1886—88, on special duty, and as Staff Officer and Assistant Inspector of Mounted Infantry, taking part in the operations of the 1st Brigade, for which he was mentioned in despatches. His distinguished services with the Lushai (1889) and Chin Hills (1890—92) Expeditionary Forces will be found narrated elsewhere in these Records, and he received a Brevet-Majority in 1892. He became Commandant of the regiment on the 5th November 1898, and remained in command till the 10th May 1905, when he proceeded to England, retiring from the service on the 4th November 1910.

He rejoined the Army for service during the Great War of 1914—18, became Brigade Commander in 1915, and was Corps Water Patrol Officer in the Ypres Area, 1917—1919. He retired, with the honorary rank of Brigadier-General on the 9th October 1919, and died on the 5th April 1929.

He was a son of Surgeon-Major John Borlase Stevens, Inspector-General of Hospitals in the Madras Presidency.

Holloway, Edward Leigh:—2nd Lieutenant, 10th April 1880: Lieutenant, 1st July 1881: Captain, 22nd February 1891: Major, 25th February 1900: Lieutenant-Colonel, 5th November 1905: Brevet Colonel, 5th November 1908. This officer joined the 4th on the 26th April 1882, and was permanently posted to it on the 1st July following. He served with the regiment at Aden in 1882, and officiated as Quartermaster from 1885 to 1889. In 1891-92, he served with the regiment in the Chin Hills and, in 1894-95, officiated as D.A.A.G. for Musketry, 2nd Circle. He became Second in Command on the 5th November 1898, officiated as Commandant in 1901-02, and became Commandant on the retirement of Lieutenant-Colonel Stevens on the 4th November 1905. He retired from the service on the 4th November 1910.

During the Great War of 1914—18, he raised, and commanded for some time in England, a battalion of Pioneers.

Keate, C. R.:—2nd Lieutenant, 22nd January 1881: Lieutenant, 1st July 1881: Captain, 1892. This officer joined the 4th Pioneers from the Leinster Regiment on the 4th May 1883. He officiated as Adjutant from 1886 to 1888, and served with the regiment in the Chin Hills in 1890-91. On the 28th January 1892, he was transferred to the 31st Burma Regiment, as a Captain.

Burrows, G. V.:—2nd Lieutenant, 21st June 1879. Lieutenant Burrows was attached to the 4th N.I. on probation, from the Royal Irish Rifles, on the 26th June 1882, but left the regiment in the following year.

Churchill, Folliott:—Lieutenant, 22nd October 1881: Captain, 22nd October 1892: Major, 10th July 1901: Lieutenant-Colonel, 23rd March 1905. This officer was attached to the 4th from the Oxfordshire Light Infantry on the 11th June 1883, and was permanently posted to the regiment on the 23rd May 1886. From the 13th September 1886 to the 22nd November 1887, he was attached to the 1st Madras Pioneers for service with the Burma Field Force. He officiated as Adjutant of the 4th in 1888-89, and served with the regiment in the Chin Hills, where he was highly complimented for his skill in constructing roads. He continued to serve with the regiment till the 23rd March 1905, when he became Commandant of the 81st Pioneers. He died in England, shortly after retiring from the service, in 1910.

Aplin, Stephen Lushington:—Lieutenant, 1st September 1883. He was posted to the Royal Marine Light Infantry on the 1st September 1883, and was attached to the 4th Pioneers, on the 13th January 1887. From the 26th August 1888, he did duty with the 29th Madras Infantry in Burma, and on the 31st May 1889 he was transferred to the 25th Madras Infantry. He subsequently joined the Burma Commission, and was Commissioner of the Mandalay Division when the regiment arrived at Mandalay in 1913 for work on the Putao Road.

Wilkieson, Claude W.:—Lieutenant, 10th March 1883: Captain, 10th March 1894. He was attached to the 4th Pioneers, from the Cheshire Regiment on the 26th February 1886 and was permanently posted to the regiment on the 10th June 1887. He acted as Quartermaster till 1887. From the 17th September 1888 to 1890, he did duty with the 15th Madras Infantry in Burma, and on the 19th November 1890, he proceeded to Europe on one year and three months' leave. He was transferred to the 1st Madras Pioneers on the 13th August 1895.

Swan, Charles Tarrant:—Lieutenant, 25th August 1886: Captain, 25th August 1897: Major, 25th August 1904: Lieutenant-Colonel, 17th September 1911. This officer joined the 4th on the 26th January 1888 from the Royal Berkshire Regiment, having originally been posted to the 1st Madras Pioneers. He was employed with Colonel Blenkinsop on the Periyar Project in the following year, and was permanently posted to the regiment on the 5th November 1891. He served with the regiment on the Lushai Expedition of 1889, and in the Chin Hills in 1891-92. He was Quartermaster from the 1st April to the 20th October 1892, when he became Adjutant, holding that appointment till 1897. In 1898, he became Adjutant of the Nilgiri Volunteer Rifles, and in 1900, saw service in China, as Orderly Officer to General Cummins, Commanding the 4th Brigade. He was transferred to the 61st Pioneers on the 6th November 1910, but rejoined the regiment on the 17th September 1911, and became Commandant *vice* Colonel Batten, who returned to the 61st Pioneers. He commanded the regiment in the Kachin Hills in 1913—15, being mentioned in despatches, and in the campaign in Mesopotamia, till he was invalided to England, and finally retired from the service on the 22nd March 1920.

He was Master of the Ootacamund Hounds for two seasons, in the nineties.

Holmes, Gilbert Vallentin:—2nd Lieutenant, 5th February 1887: Lieutenant, 12th April 1888. This officer was attached to the 4th Pioneers (from the Essex Regiment) on the 12th April 1888, and became permanent on the 9th July 1890. He served with the regiment in Lushai and the Chin Hills, and on the 22nd May 1895 he was transferred to the Bhopal Battalion, subsequently serving with the 43rd Erinpura Regiment.

Rainey, E. F.:—2nd Lieutenant, 5th February 1887: Lieutenant, 17th October 1888. This officer was attached to the 4th Pioneers, from the West India Regiment, on the 31st March 1889, and served with it on the Periyar Project in that year. He proceeded to the Chin Hills with the Right Wing of the Regiment in 1890 and on the 26th June 1891, he was transferred to the 12th Burma Infantry (now the 92nd Punjabis), subsequently joining the Burma Commission.

Mears, Arthur:—2nd Lieutenant, 30th January 1889: Lieutenant, 21st November 1890. This officer was attached to the 4th Pioneers from the Royal Lancashire Regiment on the 3rd May 1890, and proceeded to Burma to join the Right Wing in the Chin Hills. He was transferred to the 2nd Madras Infantry in 1892, and subsequently joined the Survey of India.

A Captain Arthur Mears of the Madras Staff Corps was transferred to the half-pay list on the 15th February 1872.

Bruce, F.:—2nd Lieutenant, 4th May 1887. This officer was posted to the 1st Madras Pioneers from the Welsh Regiment in 1888, and was attached to the Lushai detachment of the 4th Pioneers for a short time from the 28th December 1888.

Groves, J. M. S.:—2nd Lieutenant, 4th March 1891. This officer joined the 4th Pioneers from the 18th Hussars on the 14th September 1892, and died at Bangalore on the 16th May 1894.

Rice, Sidney Mervyn:—2nd Lieutenant, 28th January 1893: Lieutenant, 28th April 1895: Captain, 28th January 1902: Major, 28th January 1911: Lieutenant-Colonel, 28th January 1919. He was attached to the 4th on the 2nd April 1894, and permanently posted to the regiment on the 15th February 1895. He became Quartermaster on the 1st May 1896, and Adjutant on the 1st July 1900, and was Station Staff Officer, Trichinopoly, from the 1st January 1900 till the 4th December 1901. He was specially mentioned in Madras Command Order No. 306, of 1902, for shooting, and from April 1903 till May 1904, was D.A.A.G. for Musketry, 2nd Circle, Madras Command. From the 1st June 1904 till the 24th June 1907, he was Brigade Major, Bangalore Brigade, and was then admitted to the Staff College, Quetta, from which he graduated on the 20th December 1908. From 30th January 1909 till the 1st October 1911, he was Brigade-Major, Jhansi Brigade, and here he had the great misfortune to suffer amputation of a leg, as the result of being mauled by a panther—an accident which debarred him from further service as a regimental officer, to the great loss of his regiment. From the 28th April 1912 till the 8th November 1916, he was a D.A.Q.M.G. at Army Headquarters, Simla, and A.Q.M.G. from the 9th November 1916 till the 8th April 1917, being decorated with the C.I.E. on the 1st January 1917, for meritorious services in connection with the Great War. For many years he acted as Secretary of the United Services Institution at Simla. His next appointment was at Shahjehanpur, as Assistant Superintendent of Army Clothing, and here he remained till February 1918, when he became A.A. and Q.M.G., Northern Command, at Rawalpindi till, on the outbreak of the war with Afghanistan, he was appointed A.A. and Q.M.G., North-Western Frontier Force, at Peshawar, his valuable services in this connection being twice mentioned in despatches, and rewarded with a C.B.E. on the 1st January 1920. From 23rd September 1919 till the 25th May 1921, he was an A.Q.M.G., Southern Command, at Poona, and on the 28th May 1921, he retired from the service.

Until handicapped by the result of his accident at Jhansi, he was a fine polo and hockey player, and a magnificent shot, a fact to which a great number of trophies in the Mess can bear witness, and he was further endowed with a genius for imparting some of his own skill to others.

On retirement he proceeded to Oxford where, after three years spent in study, he graduated in Forestry.

He was a son of Mr. Lewis Rice, C.I.E., Director of Archæology in Mysore.

Scott-Elliot, Charles Reginald:—2nd Lieutenant, 28th January 1893: Lieutenant, 28th April 1895: Captain, 28th January 1902: Major, 28th January 1911: Lieutenant-Colonel, 5th May 1917. This officer joined the regiment on the 9th April 1894, and was permanently posted to it on the 3rd September 1895. He served in the Tirah Campaign of 1897-98 as Assistant Superintendent of Army Signalling, Kurram Movable Column, and with the Expeditionary Force to China in 1900. In 1905, he was transferred to the 81st Pioneers, and served with that regiment up to the outbreak of the Great War. He served in France and Belgium from September 1914 till December 1916, and subsequently succeeded Colonel Batten (*q. v.*) in command of the 61st (K.G.O.) Pioneers in East Africa, where he served till February 1918. During the War, he was twice mentioned in despatches, and awarded a Brevet Lieutenant-Colonelcy. He served in the Afghan Campaign of 1919, being mentioned in despatches, and eventually retired from the service on the 5th November 1921.

Ross, R. J.:—2nd Lieutenant, 19th April 1893. This officer was attached to the 4th Pioneers on the 20th July 1894, and died on the 19th June 1895.

Watson, Spencer Burton:—2nd Lieutenant, 10th October 1894: Lieutenant, 10th January 1897: Captain, 10th October 1903: Major, 10th October 1912: Brevet Lieutenant-Colonel, 3rd June 1916: Lieutenant-Colonel, 20th August 1920. This officer joined the 4th on the 20th December 1895, from the Unattached List. In 1897-1898, he was on Famine duty in the Central Provinces, and in 1898 was with the regiment on the Ootacamund Lake Reclamation Scheme. He was Adjutant of the regiment from the 1st October 1902 to the 13th May 1906, and was with it on the Coonoor—Ootacamund Railway work in 1905—08. He was attached to the 121st Pioneers in April 1911, and rejoined the regiment in the September following. He was with the regiment on the Myitkyina Road in 1913-14, and was on leave in England on the outbreak of the Great War. From August 1914 to February 1915, he was attached, first to the 3rd Battalion, Suffolk Regiment, and subsequently to the King's Liverpool Pioneers, and on the 7th March 1915, joined the 107th Pioneers in France, with whom he served at Neuve Chapelle and Festubert, and whom he subsequently accompanied to Mesopotamia. He was mentioned in despatches and awarded a Brevet Lieutenant-Colonelcy on the 3rd June 1916. In September 1916, he rejoined the 64th Pioneers in Mesopotamia, commanded the depot at Bangalore from December 1916 to January 1917, and again returned to the regiment in March 1917. In May 1918, he was selected to raise and command the 1st Battalion, 155th Pioneers, with whom he served on the Egyptian Expeditionary Force from 1918 to 1920, being mentioned in despatches, and awarded the Order of the Nile, 3rd class. On the 20th August 1920, he became Commandant of the 64th, with whom he served in N.W. Persia in 1920-21, and in Waziristan in 1923-24. He became unemployed on the 20th August 1921, and finally retired from the service on the 20th February 1925. He was a fine rifle and revolver shot, and in charge of many successful regimental teams at the South Indian Rifle Association Meetings.

Geddes, Malcolm Henry Burdett:—2nd Lieutenant, 16th January 1895: Lieutenant, 16th April 1897: Captain, 16th January 1904: Major, 16th January 1913. This officer was posted to the 4th on the 16th September 1896, and officiated as Quartermaster in 1899. In 1900-01, he was on plague duty in Bombay, and on return to the regiment, again officiated as Quartermaster till 1904, when he was attached to the Supply and Transport Corps, commanding the 41st Pony Cadre, and subsequently the 23rd Mule Corps. Rejoining the regiment in 1905, he commanded the depot at Belgaum from 1906 till the regiment returned from Ootacamund on the 4th October 1907. On the 16th August 1912, he proceeded to England on leave on medical certificate, and died in 1914, shortly after the outbreak of the Great War.

Keble, J. A.:—2nd Lieutenant, 14th August 1895. This officer was attached to the 4th Pioneers on the 1st November 1896, and was transferred to the 14th Madras Infantry on the 31st May 1898. He accompanied a draft of the regiment to Ali Musjid to join the 21st Madras Pioneers, then serving with the Tirah Expeditionary Force, on the 7th March 1898, and did not rejoin the 4th.

Marshall, W. F.:—This officer was posted to the 4th Pioneers as a 2nd Lieutenant on the 27th March 1898, but died at Ootacamund on the 21st June following, whilst working on the Lake Reclamation Scheme.

Mackie, Ralph:—2nd Lieutenant, 4th August 1897: Lieutenant, 4th November 1899: Captain, 4th August 1906: Major, 4th August 1915: Lieutenant-Colonel, 1st February 1921. This officer joined the 4th on the 24th November 1898. In 1901, he became officiating Quartermaster, and retained that appointment till 1906. He was Adjutant from 1906 to 1910, and served with the regiment in the Kachin Hills, 1913—15, and in Mesopotamia in 1916, towards the end of which year, he was invalided back to India, and was then selected to raise and command the 2nd Battalion, 81st Pioneers. When that battalion was disbanded, he was transferred to the command of the 2nd Battalion 61st (K.G.O.) Pioneers, then serving on the N.W. Frontier. He saw service in the campaign against Afghanistan in 1919 (mentioned in despatches,) and in Waziristan, with the Wana Column, in 1921. On the disbandment of the 2/61st (K. G. O.) Pioneers, he became Commandant of the 75th Carnatic Infantry, and remained in that appointment till he retired from the service on the 1st March 1926.

Malet, Robert James:—2nd Lieutenant, 22nd January 1898: Lieutenant, 22nd April 1900: Captain, 22nd January 1907: Major, 1st September 1915: Lieutenant-Colonel, 1st February 1921. This officer joined the regiment on the 29th March 1899, and served with it continuously till 1915, being present with it in the Kachin Hills in 1913—15. On the 29th December 1915, he was appointed G.S.O. 2., Presidency Brigade, and remained in this appointment till the 1st July 1918, being mentioned in despatches and awarded the O.B.E. He was then selected to raise and command the 2/88th Carnatic Infantry, a battalion composed of Coorgs and Nayars, and, on that unit being disbanded, he became Commandant of the 73rd Carnatic Infantry. He saw service in Waziristan in 1923-24, and was mentioned in despatches, eventually retiring from the service on the 1st March 1926.

Meiklejohn, Walter Lloyd Sinclair:—2nd Lieutenant, 20th July 1898: Lieutenant, 20th October 1900. This officer was posted to the 4th Pioneers from the Unattached List on the 8th October 1899. In 1901, he was in command of the depot of the 1st Madras Pioneers, and in 1902 he joined the Supply and Transport Corps at Wellington, subsequently transferring to the 106th Hazara Pioneers.

Bowen, C. E.:—2nd Lieutenant, 16th November 1887: Captain, 16th November 1898. Captain Bowen was posted to the 4th Pioneers on the 15th August 1900 and was borne on the strength of the regiment until 1903. He was in the Burma Commission, so his connection with the regiment was only nominal, as he never served with it.

Johnson, Maurice Eustace Stanley:—2nd Lieutenant, 27th July 1898. This officer was posted to the 4th Pioneers from the Unattached List on the 18th October 1899, but on the 16th October 1900 he was transferred to the 23rd Wallajahbad Light Infantry, subsequently joining the 48th Pioneers.

Harvey-Kelly, Harvey St. George Hume:—2nd Lieutenant, 17th January 1900: Lieutenant, 17th April 1902: Captain, 17th January 1909: Major, 1st September 1915: Lieutenant-Colonel, 9th November 1923. This officer joined the regiment on the 28th March 1901 and, with Captain Marsden, was attached to the 32nd Sikh Pioneers for service with the Tibet Expedition of 1903-04, rejoining the regiment on the 4th November 1904. He officiated as Quartermaster from the 13th May 1906 till the 31st October 1907, and in June 1909, left the regiment for employment in the Burma Military Police, serving continuously in various commands with that force till January 1917. He commanded the regimental depot at Bangalore from the 6th June 1917 till the 26th September 1919, when he proceeded to join the regiment on service in N.W. Persia, where he officiated in command for various periods. He again saw service with the regiment in Waziristan in 1923, and on the 4th September of that year, was appointed Commandant of the 10th (Training) Battalion of the regiment, eventually retiring from the service on the 9th May 1928.

James,_____:—Lieutenant James was posted to the 4th Pioneers on the 27th December 1902, but was only borne on the strength of the regiment for a few days being transferred to the Supply and Transport Corps on the 8th January 1903.

Marsden, Edmund:—2nd Lieutenant, 20th January 1900: Lieutenant, 20th April 1902: Captain, 20th January 1909. This officer joined the regiment on the 31st March 1903, and was attached to the 32nd Sikh Pioneers for service on the Tibet Expedition of 1903-04, and the remainder of his service was spent with the regiment till his death at Myitkyina on the 26th May 1915, to which reference will be found elsewhere in these Records.

The following is an extract from the *"Cheltonian"* for October 1915:—

"Far away in North Burma, far from the trenches of Flanders, but none the less doing his duty as a soldier, there has passed away one whom all who knew him loved and admired. Captain E. Marsden was the eldest of the family of athletes and scholars well known to several generations of Cheltonians. He passed young into Sandhurst, and so never got into the XI here; but he was a very fine bat (the best we have ever turned out that did not get his colours) and among the best ten that we have produced in the last 25 years. He was a beautiful lawn-tennis player—only just below really first-class standard. He had been making a road for military purposes in North Burma, and although he had had a severe attack of malaria at Christmas, he was obliged to remain up there, as the authorities could not send up men to relieve him, as would have been the case in normal times. They had one or two expeditions to make through the jungle, of a punitive character, against native tribes. All this must have rendered him unable to withstand the attack of malaria which came upon him as he was on the march back to his regiment in a healthier place.

The following is an extract from a letter sent to his father by the Colonel of the Regiment:—

'I can hardly tell you how deeply I feel his loss as a personal friend, as well as the whole of the regiment, to whom he had endeared himself by his sterling qualities of sportsmanship, good temper and unassuming demeanour. The Service loses a first-class officer, who would have gone far. He behaved with the greatest gallantry in action at Wawang on the 28th and 29th of January of this year, and I had the greatest pleasure in bringing his conduct to notice for suitable reward.'

As unassuming as he was brilliant as an athlete, sterling and true in all that he did, he will be mourned and missed by all his many friends, but by none more than by those who knew and remember him best on the O. C. cricket weeks at Market Drayton. He was born in 1881, and was at College as a day boy from January 1896 to December 1898, when he passed for Sandhurst. He received his first commission in 1900, was made a Captain in 1909, and served with the 64th Pioneers. He took part in the Tibet Expedition of 1903-04, and entered Lhasa, receiving a medal and clasp."

Breithaupt, Edward Avenel:—2nd Lieutenant, 18th January 1902: Lieutenant, 18th April 1904. This officer joined the regiment at Bangalore on the 11th April 1903, and served with it till the 6th May 1905, when he was transferred to the 63rd Palamcottah Light Infantry. He rejoined the regiment on the 23rd February 1928, and became Commandant of the 1st Battalion, Madras Pioneers, on the 16th May 1928.

Murland, Howard Ferguson:—2nd Lieutenant, 27th August 1902: Lieutenant, 27th November 1904: Captain, 27th August 1911: Major, 27th August 1917: Lieutenant-Colonel, 27th August 1928. This officer joined the 64th at Bangalore on the 7th January 1904, from the Unattached List, having been attached to the 1st Battalion Essex Regiment. He officiated as Adjutant from the 28th February to the 25th October 1908, and as Quartermaster from the 1st April 1909 to the 12th May 1910. He was Adjutant of the regiment from the 13th May 1910 to the 12th May 1914. He was on recruiting duty from April 1915 to February 1916, when he accompanied the regiment to Mesopotamia, where he was severely wounded, near Kut-al-Amara, in February 1917. He was D.A.A.G., 9th (Secunderabad) Division, from the 13th July 1918 to the 12th May 1919; D.A.A. and Q.M.G. to the Deputy Inspector-General of Communications, Quetta (during the war with Afghanistan) from the 20th May to the 5th July 1919; and D.A.A.G. (2), Baluchistan Force, from the 6th July to the 8th October 1919. He commanded the depot, 2/61st (K.G.O.) Pioneers, from the 24th January to the 10th May 1921, and was D.A.Q.M.G., Waziristan Force, from the 19th May to the 25th July 1921. He rejoined the regiment on the 3rd August 1921, and was transferred to the 81st Pioneers, then being re-organised as the Training Battalion, 1st Madras Pioneers, on the 1st November 1921, remaining with that battalion till the 1st December 1924, when he rejoined the 2nd Battalion, then under orders for Mandalay. He proceeded on two years' leave in India, pending retirement, on the 17th November 1926, and eventually retired from the service on the 17th November 1928.

Harris, Hugh Anstruther:—2nd Lieutenant, 8th January 1901: Lieutenant, 5th March 1904. This officer joined the regiment on the 5th March 1904, and served with it till the 20th September 1905, when he was transferred to the 79th Carnatic Infantry.

Rogers, Archibald Clement Campbell:—2nd Lieutenant, 21st January 1903: Lieutenant, 21st April 1905. This officer joined the regiment on the 19th April 1904, and remained on the roll till the 30th November 1910. He had the misfortune to sustain serious injuries to his eyes, as the result of an explosion whilst experimenting with fulminates, and was placed on the retired list, on permanent half-pay, on the 1st December 1909. During the Great War (1914—18), he was attached to the Political Department in Mesopotamia.

Hemsley, Charles:—2nd Lieutenant, 19th August 1903: Lieutenant, 19th November 1905: Captain, 19th August 1912: Major, 19th August 1918. This officer was attached to the 1st Lincolnshire Regiment from November 1903, and was posted to the 86th Carnatic Infantry on the 8th November 1904, but was transferred to the 64th Pioneers on the 24th November following. He was Quartermaster of the regiment from the 1st November 1907 till the 5th December 1912, when he became A.D.C. to the G.O.C. 9th (Secunderabad) Division. He rejoined the regiment in February 1916, and accompanied it to Mesopotamia. On the 15th November 1916, he was appointed G.S.O. 3 to the 3rd Indian Army Corps. From the 1st September 1917 till the 2nd March 1919, he was Brigade-Major, 50th Indian Infantry Brigade, and acted as temporary G.S.O. 2., 18th Infantry Division from the 16th October till the 17th November 1918. From the 3rd March to the 1st May 1919, he was attached to the General Staff, G.H.Q., Mesopotamia Expeditionary Force. From the 15th November 1919 to the 31st October 1920, he was G.S.O. 2. (Operations) at G.H.Q., officiating as G.S.O.I. (Operations) from the 15th November 1919 to the 28th March 1920. He was at the Staff College, Quetta, from the 1st November 1920 to the 22nd December 1921, and was appointed G.S.O. 2., Bombay District, on the 18th December 1922. On the 8th May 1925, he was appointed Second in Command, 10th Battalion, 2nd Bombay Pioneers (Marine Battalion), and subsequently became Commandant of the Hazara Pioneers. During the campaign in Mesopotamia, he was four times mentioned in despatches and, on the 26th August 1918, was awarded the D.S.O.

Smith, Maurice Castle:—2nd Lieutenant, 16th December 1903: Lieutenant, 16th March 1906: Captain, 3rd July 1912: Major, 3rd July 1918. This officer joined the regiment on the 25th June 1905, after having seen service in the South African War in 1902 (Queen's medal and two clasps), and served with it till 1914, when he became Instructor at the School of Musketry, Pachmarhi. For his services in this capacity, he was mentioned in despatches and awarded the O.B.E. He rejoined the regiment after the War, and was transferred to the 4/19th Hyderabad Regiment, retiring from the service on the 14th June 1924.

Bliss, James Arthur:—2nd Lieutenant, 3rd May 1890: Lieutenant, 3rd August 1892: Captain, 3rd May 1901: Major, 3rd May 1908: Lieutenant-Colonel, 3rd May 1916: Colonel, 7th June 1920. This officer joined the regiment from the 81st Pioneers on the 5th July 1905, on appointment as Double Company Commander, Captain Scott-Elliot being transferred to the 81st in his place. He first served with the Middlesex Regiment, and joined the 21st Pioneers on the 4th December 1891, with which regiment he saw service on the Chin Hills Expedition of 1892-93 (medal with clasp) and in Tirah, 1897-98, being present at the actions of Chagru Kotal and Dargai, and the operations in the Bazaar Valley, 25th to 30th December 1897 (India medal 1895, with three clasps). His services were brought to notice in connection with famine duty in the Central Provinces in 1899-1900, and he was one of the few officers of the Indian Staff Corps who took part in the South African War, where he acted as Adjutant of Imperial Yeomanry (Queen's medal and five clasps). He proceeded to Tibet with the expedition of 1903-04 (Medal), and was officer in charge of H.M. the King's Indian Orderly Officers in 1912 (M.V.O. 4th Class). He served with the regiment in the Kachin Hills in 1914-15, and received the thanks of the Government of India for services in connection with the suppression of the rising in 1915, and accompanied the regiment to Mesopotamia in 1916, in which year he succeeded Lieutenant-Colonel Swan as Commandant. He was seven times mentioned in despatches, and was awarded the D.S.O. and the Serbian Order of the White Eagle, 4th Class (with swords), and continued to serve with the regiment till the 19th August 1920, when he retired from the service. In 1922, he became a Justice of the Peace for the county of Oxfordshire.

Story, John Alexis:—2nd Lieutenant, 5th August 1905: Lieutenant, 5th November 1907: Major, 5th August 1920. This officer joined the regiment on the 23rd December 1906, and served with it till the 15th February 1908, when he was transferred to the 61st (P.W.O.) Pioneers. The remainder of his service was spent with that regiment, and he was awarded the M.C. for his services with it in East Africa, during the Great War. He retired fom the service on the 5th August 1923.

Burne, Frank Owen Newdigate:—2nd Lieutenant, 17th August 1907: Lieutenant, 17th November 1909: Captain, 17th August 1916: Major, 17th August 1922. This officer joined the regiment on the 19th November 1908. He was Quartermaster from the 6th December 1912 till the 12th May 1914, and Adjutant from the 13th May 1914 till the 18th May 1918. ·He served with the regiment throughout the Great War, being twice mentioned in despatches, and awarded the M.C. He served on the staff of Persian Line of Communications from the 8th March 1920 till the 15th June 1921, and was mentioned in despatches. He served with the 10th Training Battalion of the regiment from the 30th October 1922 till the 16th December 1924, rejoining the 2nd Battalion on the 17th December 1924. He retired from the service on the 1st July 1927.

Hare, Ivan Lancelot O'Hara:—2nd Lieutenant, 25th January 1908: Lieutenant, 25th April 1910: Captain, 1st September 1915: Major, 25th January 1923. This officer joined the regiment on the 30th March 1909, and served with it till the 15th August 1917, being in command of the regimental depot from the 1st February 1916 till the 15th August 1917. He then joined the 2/107th Pioneers, with which he saw service with the Egyptian Expeditionary Force in 1918. From May to July 1921, he commanded the depot of the 2/12th Pioneers, and was re-posted to the 64th on the 8th July. In December 1921, he became Assistant Commandant, Lashio Battalion, Burma Military Police, and rejoined the regiment on the 5th August 1925. On the 1st January 1929, he returned to the Burma Military Police as Commandant of the Rangoon Battalion.

Cassidy, Vivian Clemons:—2nd Lieutenant, 20th January 1909: Lieutenant, 20th April 1911: Captain, 1st September 1915: Major, 20th January 1925. This officer joined the regiment on the 9th April 1910, and served with it till the 2nd November 1914, when he was transferred to the Supply and Transport Corps, with which he served in Burma till 1917, when he proceeded to Belgaum, and subsequently to Bandar Abbas, South Persia, with Force "J." He was invalided to India in 1918, and to England in 1919, returning as D.A.D.S. and T., first to the Kohat-Kurram Force, and next to Northern Command at Rawalpindi. He subsequently commanded the 38th Mule Corps and 82nd Transport Corps, and in 1925 took command of No. 24 Divisional Troops Transport Company.

Batten, Frederick Graeme:—2nd Lieutenant, 6th May 1885: Captain, 6th May 1896: Major, 6th May 1903: Lieutenant-Colonel, 5th November 1910. Major Batten joined the regiment on the 4th November 1910 from the 61st (P.W.O.) Pioneers, and succeeded to the command on the retirement of Colonel Holloway. He remained in command of the regiment till the 17th September 1911, when he became Commandant of the 61st (P.W.O.) Pioneers. He commanded that regiment in East Africa during the Great War, and was awarded the D.S.O. He died in England in July 1925.

Skinner, Thomas Burrell:—2nd Lieutenant, 3rd July 1903: Lieutenant, 4th October 1905: Captain, 26th September 1910: Major, 26th September 1916. Captain Skinner joined the regiment on the 19th December 1910, on transfer from the 61st (P.W.O.) Pioneers. His first service was with the Militia during the South African War, 1901-02 (Queen's medal and five clasps). He served with the West Riding Regiment from July 1903 to May 1905, when he was transferred to the 77th Moplah Rifles. In December 1906, he joined the 61st (P.W.O.) Pioneers. From March to September 1910, he officiated as Adjutant, Hyderabad Volunteer Rifles, and commanded the 2nd Battalion, Nayar Brigade, from April 1913 till November 1914, when he was appointed Recruiting Officer, first for the Coimbatore, and then for the Malabar District. He rejoined the regiment in February 1916, and proceeded with it to Mesopotamia, serving with it till April 1918, when he was posted to the newly-raised 1/155th Pioneers. With that regiment he served with the Egyptian Expeditionary Force in Palestine till January 1919, when he proceeded to France as D.A.Q.M.G. to the D.G.R. and E., Indian Section. He joined the 61st (K.G.O.) Pioneers as Second in Command on the 19th September 1920 and, from the 1st October 1920 till the 6th February 1921, commanded the depot of the 2/32nd Sikh Pioneers, rejoining the 64th on the 15th February 1921. From August to October 1921, he acted as D.A.Q.M.G. during the operations in Malabar and, in February and March 1923, served as Liaison Officer during the Police operations in the Agency Tracts. He proceeded to Waziristan with the regiment in 1923 and, on the 11th November 1924, joined the 1st Battalion as Second in Command. On the 2nd December 1925, he was posted to the Training Battalion, and he retired from the service on the 10th November 1929.

Deane, Henry Harold Rookhurst:—2nd Lieutenant, 8th September 1909: Lieutenant, 8th December 1911: Captain, 1st September 1915: Major, 8th September 1925. This officer joined the regiment on the 6th March 1911, and served with it till November 1912, when he became personal assistant to Sir Michael O'Dwyer, Agent to the Governor-General in Central India. He rejoined the regiment in April 1914, and served with the depot of the 61st (K.G.O.) Pioneers from March 1915. He proceeded to England on sick leave in December 1915, and took command of the regimental depot in December 1916. From March 1917 till September 1918, he was a Platoon Commander at the Cadet College, Quetta, and at the Staff School, Saugor, till December 1918, when he became a D.A.Q.M.G. at Army Headquarters. He served with the 2/128th Pioneers in June and July 1919, and with the 2/12th Pioneers from July 1919 till February 1920. From February to August 1920, he commanded the depot of the 1/81st Pioneers and, from August to December 1920, the depot of the 64th. He became Adjutant of the regiment on the 29th August 1921, and held that appointment till the 18th February 1925, when he was admitted to the Staff College, Quetta; from which he graduated in December 1926. On the 15th September 1926, he was transferred to the 3rd Battalion, 16th Punjab Regiment and, on the 1st February 1929, was appointed G.S.O. 2., Lucknow District.

Urmson, Denis George Severn:—2nd Lieutenant, 11th December 1909: Lieutenant, 11th March 1912: Captain, 1st September 1915: Major, 11th December 1925. This officer served with the Kent R.G.A. (Militia) and Kent R.F.A. (Reserve) from 1907 to 1909, when he was gazetted to the R.F.A. He joined the regiment on the 20th February 1914. He became Quartermaster in October 1914, and accompanied the regiment to Mesopotamia in 1916. In 1917, he became Staff Captain, 12th Infantry Brigade and, in 1919, Brigade Major, 56th, and subsequently 34th, Infantry Brigades. From November 1920 to April 1921, during the Arab Revolt, he was Brigade-Major, 51st Infantry Brigade, subsequently rejoining the regiment. He was three times mentioned in despatches. From October to December 1921, he was Brigade-Major during the operations in Malabar. On the 30th January 1923, he was transferred to the Indian Army Service Corps and, in February 1925, was admitted to the Staff College, Quetta, from which he graduated in December 1926. On the 27th May 1929, he was appointed D.A.D.S. and T., Peshawar District.

Wilson, L. D.:—2nd Lieutenant Wilson, I.A.R.O., was attached to the regiment, in Burma, from the 12th March till the 17th September 1915.

Aylward, Douglas:—2nd Lieutenant Aylward, I.A.R.O., was attached to the regiment from the 12th August 1915 till the 17th April 1919 when (as a Captain) he was released from the service on demobilisation and went to Kenya. He served with the regiment throughout the campaign in Mesopotamia, was mentioned in despatches, and awarded the M.C.

Elliot, C.:—2nd Lieutenant Elliot, I.A.R.O., was attached to the regiment from the 26th October 1915 till September 1916. On the departure of the regiment to Mesopotamia, he remained at the depot.

Rossel, Henry George Theodore:—2nd Lieutenant, 11th August 1915: Lieutenant, 11th August 1916: Captain, 11th August 1919. This officer joined the regiment on the 6th November 1915, and served with it till the 27th October 1923, when he was transferred to the Military Farms Department. He served in the campaign in Mesopotamia till the end of 1920, being mentioned in despatches, and then did duty at the regimental depot in Bangalore.

Slade, Meade:—2nd Lieutenant, 15th November 1915: Lieutenant, 15th November 1916: Captain, 15th November 1919. This officer joined the regiment on the 27th November 1915, and accompanied it to Mesopotamia. On the conclusion of the Great War, he completed his qualification as a Barrister-at-Law and, on the 6th December 1922, was admitted to the Indian Civil Service, and posted to Burma.

Smith, D. C. Sidney:—2nd Lieutenant Sidney Smith, I.A.R.O., joined the regiment on the 26th January 1916, and accompanied it to Mesopotamia, where he was mentioned in despatches. Before joining, he had served in the campaign in German South-West Africa. At the end of 1918, he proceeded to Vladivostock with the Knox Mission, subsequently rejoining the regiment. On the 15th April 1923, he retired as surplus to establishment.

Banister, F.:—2nd Lieutenant Banister, I.A.R.O., joined the regiment in Mesopotamaia on the 9th November 1916, and served with it till the 30th April 1919, when he was demobilised, and became British Consul at Hamadan, North-West Persia. He was mentioned in despatches in 1919, and awarded the M.B.E.

Glover, W. S. C.:—Captain Glover was attached to the regiment from the 34th Sikh Pioneers in Mesopotamia from the 1st April till the 12th July 1916, as a railway engineer, while the regiment was laying a light railway from Shaikh Saad to the Sinn position. He was then transferred to the Railway Department of the Mesopotamia Expeditionary Force.

Stonehewer, E. H.:—2nd Lieutenant Stonehewer, I.A.R.O., was attached to the regiment in Mesopotamia from the 18th September 1916 till the 20th March 1919, when (being then a Captain) he was released from army service on demobilisation.

Fraser, H. W. M.:—2nd Lieutenant Fraser, I.A.R.O., was attached to the regiment in Mesopotamia from the 18th September 1916 till the 19th May 1918, when he was transferred to the 1/155th Pioneers, then being raised for service in Palestine.

Curle, Victor:—2nd Lieutenant Curle joined the regiment in Mesopotamia from the 81st Pioneers on the 19th October 1916, and served with it till the end of 1918, when he proceeded to Vladivostock, as an Instructor, with the force under Colonel Knox. He afterwards rejoined the 81st Pioneers, subsequently retiring as surplus to establishment, and settling in Canada.

Findlay, M. A.:—2nd Lieutenant Findlay, I.A.R.O., served with the regimental depot from the 29th September 1917 till the 23rd May 1921, when he was released from the army on demobilisation, having meanwhile been promoted to the rank of Captain.

MacMahon, J. J.:—2nd Lieutenant MacMahon, I.A.R.O., was attached to the regimental depot from the 29th September 1917 till the 27th May 1918, when he was transferred to the Military Works Service.

Deed, L. H.:—2nd Lieutenant Deed, I.A.R.O., was attached to the regiment in Mesopotamia from the 21st October 1917 till the 26th April 1919, when he was released from army service. In June 1919, he was mentioned in despatches.

Barnes, Thomas James:—2nd Lieutenant, 4th July 1915: Lieutenant, 4th July 1916: Captain, 19th March 1920. This officer joined the regiment in Mesopotamia on the 30th November 1917, and has served with it continuously since that date. His services were brought to the notice of the Government of India for exceptionally able and gallant conduct while in command of a platoon during the operations in Malabar, particularly near Nilambur on the 24th September 1921, when a party of the Dorsets and the 64th, under Brevet Lieutenant-Colonel Herbert, was ambushed. An account of this will be found in Part I. He was posted to the 10th Battalion for a tour of duty from the 11th September 1926 till the 6th February 1929, when he rejoined the regiment.

Mills, F. C. R.:—Lieutenant Mills joined the regiment in Mesopotamia on the 8th December 1917, and served with it till the 15th July 1922, when he retired from the army as surplus to establishment, and settled in South Africa.

Mills, W. S.:—Lieutenant Mills (no relation of the above) joined the regimental depot on the 9th December 1917, and served with it till the 6th March 1918 when, as an acting Captain, he was transferred to the 2/81st Pioneers.

Johnstone, C. W. H.:—2nd Lieutenant Johnstone joined the regiment in Mesopotamia on the 30th January 1918, and served with it till released from army service on demobilisation, on the 28th January 1919.

Shute, P. E.:—Lieutenant Shute, Royal Engineers, was attached to the regiment in Mesopotamia from the 21st to the 28th May 1918, when he was transferred to the 2/128th Pioneers.

Taylor, J. F. S.:—2nd Lieutenant Taylor served with the regimental depot from the 29th May 1918 till the 8th May 1919, when he was released from army service on demobilisation.

Huffton, P. H.:—2nd Lieutenant Huffton served with the regimental depot from the 29th May to the 16th June 1918, when he was released from army service on demobilisation.

Daldy, A. J.:—Lieutenant Daldy joined the regiment in Mesopotamia on the 20th May 1918 and served with it till he retired, as a Captain, surplus to the establishment, on the 15th September 1922.

Foster, M. R.:—2nd Lieutenant Foster, I.A.R.O., served with the regimental depot from the 31st May till the 25th July 1918.

Ward, F. H. T.:—2nd Lieutenant Ward, I.A.R.O., was attached to the regimental depot from the 8th June to the 27th July 1918, when he was transferred to the 2/61st (K.G.O.) Pioneers.

Sultana,———**:**—2nd Lieutenant Sultana was attached to the regimental depot from the 3rd to the 20th June 1918, when he was transferred to the Officers' Training School, Bangalore.

Carey, A. B.:—2nd Lieutenant Carey, I.A.R.O., was attached to the regimental depot from the 19th July 1918 to the 8th May 1919, when he was released from army service on demobilisation.

Cornwell, R. B.:—Lieutenant Cornwell, I.A.R.O., joined the regiment in Mesopotamia on the 8th August 1918 and, on the 18th April 1919, was released from army service on demobilisation.

Scott, E. H.:—Lieutenant Scott, I.A.R.O., was posted to the regimental depot on the 19th August 1918 and, on the 3rd September 1919, was transferred for duty with a Labour Corps.

Fairclough, J. E. B.:—2nd Lieutenant Fairclough was attached to the regimental depot from the 19th August 1918 to the 18th September 1919, when he was released from army service on demobilisation.

Worthington, Roger Francis:—2nd Lieutenant, 31st August 1918: Lieutenant, 31st August 1919: Captain, 31st August 1923. This officer joined the regimental depot on the 14th September 1918 and, in January 1920, joined the 107th Pioneers in East Persia. From September 1920 to March 1921, he served in Persia with the Khorasan Levies, subsequently joining the 2/107th Pioneers at Jhansi. In May 1921, he proceeded to Mesopotamia as Quartermaster of the 2/76th Punjabis. He rejoined the regiment at Bangalore on the 1st December 1921, and was Quartermaster from December 1922 to November 1924, which included the period of its service in Waziristan. He did duty with the 10th (Training) Battalion from the 7th February 1926 till the 6th February 1928, when he was seconded for duty with the 14th Battalion (I.T.F.), rejoining on the 12th October 1930.

Williamson, V. C.:—2nd Lieutenant Williamson was attached to the regimental depot from the 21st September to the 20th November 1918, when he was released from army service on demobilisation.

Jennings, L. W. B.:—2nd Lieutenant Jennings, M. C., was posted to the regiment on the 24th September 1918, and served with it till the following year, when he was attached to the 1/61st (K.G.O.) Pioneers for service on the North-West Frontier. On the 2nd September 1922, having meanwhile been promoted to Lieutenant, he was admitted to the Indian Forest Department.

Bryant, L.:—2nd Lieutenant Bryant, Indian Army (temporary commission) was attached to the regimental depot from the 5th October 1918 till the 9th June 1919, when he was transferred to No. 1 Mule Depot at Sialkot.

Wood, ———:—2nd Lieutenant Wood, I.A.R.O., was attached to the regimental depot from the 5th October 1918 till the 4th April 1919, when he was released from army service on demobilisation.

Donne, A. J.:—2nd Lieutenant Donne, I.A.R.O., was attached to the regimental depot from the December 1918 till the 10th April 1919, when he was released from army service on demobilisation.

Smith, J. Coleman:—Lieutenant Coleman Smith served with the regimental depot from the 23rd March 1918 till the following year, when he was attached to the 1/61st (K.G.O.) Pioneers for service on the North-West Frontier. On the 7th August 1922, he retired from the army as surplus to establishment.

Corley, L. C.:—2nd Lieutenant Corley, I. A. R. O., was attached to the regimental depot from the 20th December 1918 till the 30th September 1919, when he was released from army service on demobilisation.

Batchelor, C. F. F.:—2nd Lieutenant Batchelor, I. A. R. O., was posted to the regiment on the 23rd December 1918, and served with it in Persia till the 13th April 1919, when he was released from army service on demobilisation.

Mangin, Etienne Bessonnet:—Captain Mangin, M.C., was transferred to the regiment for duty, from the 48th Pioneers, on the 13th December 1918, and served with it in Mesopotamia till the 26th July 1920, when he was transferred to the 107th Pioneers, having meanwhile been promoted to Major.

Doig, E.W.:—Lieutenant Doig was attached to the regiment from the 1/61st (K.G.O.) Pioneers on the 26th March 1919, and rejoined his regiment, as a Captain, on the 17th December 1920.

LeMay, A.C.:—Lieutenant LeMay was attached to the regiment from the 1/61st (K.G.O.) Pioneers on the 26th March 1919, and served with it in Persia. On the 31st October 1919, he was released from army service on demobilisation.

Kemble, Thomas Aubery:—2nd Lieutenant, 29th August 1906: Lieutenant, 29th November 1908: Captain, 29th August 1915: Major, 29th August 1921. Captain Kemble joined the regiment in North Persia on the 12th April 1920, his previous service having been with the 81st Pioneers. During the rebellion in Malabar, he was Base Commandant at Tirur from September 1921 to February 1922, and he was with the detachment at Bellary from July to November 1922. He took command of the regimental depot in October 1923, and was transferred to the Training Battalion, for a two years' tour of duty, on the 1st December 1924, rejoining the regiment on the 1st October 1926. On the re-organisation of Pioneer Battalions, he was transferred to Corps Headquarters, as 2nd-in-Command, on the 1st February 1929.

Hutchinson, G. W.:—Lieutenant Hutchinson joined the regiment in Persia on the 9th December 1920 and, on the 23rd March following, was transferred to the Wireless in Iraq.

Malby, J.:—Lieutenant Malby was attached to the regimental depot from the 19th December 1919 till the 1st April 1921, when he was released from army service on demobilisation.

Robertson, S.:—Lieutenant Robertson, I.A.R.O., was attached to the regimental depot from the 24th March to the 31st August 1920, when he was released from army service on demobilisation.

Anderson, T. A.:—Lieutenant Anderson, I.A.R.O., was attached to the regimental depot from the 8th to the 26th April 1920, when he was released from army service on demobilisation.

Moody, B. C.:—Lieutenant Moody, I. A. R. O., was posted to the regiment on the 10th April 1920, and served with it in Persia till the 28th May 1921, when he was transferred to the Arab Levies in Iraq.

Knight, F. M. C.:—Lieutenant Knight, I. A. R. O., was attached to the regimental depot from the 10th May 1920 till the 12th April 1921, when he was released from army service on demobilisation.

Driver, H. S.:—Lieutenant Driver, M.C., I.A.R.O., was attached to the regimental depot from the 10th May to the 10th October 1920, when he was released from army service on demobilisation.

Bowden, Spencer Albert:—2nd Lieutenant, 1st March 1917: Lieutenant, 1st December 1918: Captain, 10th November 1922. This officer joined the regiment on the 19th August 1921, and served with it till the 25th June 1925, when he acted as Executive Officer, Nowshera Cantonment, rejoining the regiment on the 15th December 1925. On the 31st March 1926, he left the regiment to become acting Executive Officer, Rangoon Cantonment. During the Great War, he served in France from the 26th September 1917 till the 2nd July 1918, being once wounded. From April to July 1918, he was Intelligence Officer, 76th Infantry Brigade.

Ford, John Meredith Randle:—2nd Lieutenant, 7th November 1906: Lieutenant, 7th January 1909: Captain, 7th November 1915: Major, 7th November 1921. Captain Ford, O.B.E., M.C., joined the regiment from the 61st (K. G. O.) Pioneers on the 4th October 1920, and served with it till the 13th November 1921, when he rejoined the 61st, and was subsequently transferred to the 1st Battalion, 3rd Sikh Pioneers.

Kelk, B. M.:—Captain Kelk joined the regiment from the 2/61st (K.G.O.) Pioneers on the 26th November 1921, and served with it till the 3rd October 1922, when he retired from the army as surplus to establishment.

Cox, Henry Francis:—2nd Lieutenant, 24th December 1920: Lieutenant, 24th March 1923. This officer was posted to the regiment on the 7th March 1922, and served with it till the 24th February 1923, when he was transferred to the 3rd Sikh Pioneers.

Cochran, George Walker:—2nd Lieutenant, 8th May 1901: Lieutenant, 8th August 1903: Captain, 8th May 1910: Major, 8th May 1916: Brevet Lieutenant-Colonel, 3rd June 1918: Colonel, 3rd June 1922. Brevet Lieutenant-Colonel Cochran, D.S.O., joined the regiment as 2nd-in-Command on the 1st November 1921, and served with it till the 26th March 1922, when he was transferred to the Training Battalion, and subsequently became Commandant of the 2nd Battalion, 2nd Bombay Pioneers (Kelat-i-Ghilzie). His previous service was with the 81st Pioneers, and he served with great distinction on the staff throughout the campaign in Mesopotamia, where he was wounded, many times mentioned in despatches, and awarded the D.S.O., and a brevet of Lieutenant-Colonel.

Stewart, A. R.:—Lieutenant A. R. Stewart was posted to the regiment on the 14th August 1922, and retired, as surplus to establishment, twelve days later.

Monypenny, R. d'A.:—Captain Monypenny served with the regiment from the 20th March 1919 till the 27th July 1922, when he retired as a surplus officer. He saw service with the regiment in Persia.

Hamilton, L. S.:—Captain Hamilton served with the regiment from the 20th April 1918 till the 1st August 1922, when he retired, as surplus to establishment, subsequently joining the Royal Air Force. He saw service with the regiment in Persia and in Malabar.

Raven-Hill, L. E.:—Captain Raven-Hill, a son of the well-known *Punch* artist, joined the regiment from the 2/81st Pioneers on the 6th February 1921, and served at the depot till the 12th August 1922, when he retired as surplus to establishment.

Tipping, Richard Percy Macrae:—Captain Tipping joined the regiment on the 23rd January 1923, on relinquishing the appointment of Staff Captain, Allahabad. He was transferred to the 1st Battalion on the 9th November 1927. During the Great War, he saw service in the Tochi Valley in 1915: the Mahsud Expedition of 1916: Mesopotamia, 1917-18: Palestine, 1918: and Asia Minor, 1919.

Fennell, Alfred Ernest Slater:—2nd Lieutenant, 8th January 1901: Lieutenant, 8th April 1903: Captain, 31st March 1910: Major, 31st March 1916: Brevet Lieutenant-Colonel, 3rd June 1919: Lieutenant-Colonel, 5th May 1925. This officer was posted to the regiment on the 15th May 1923, his former regiment having been the 81st Pioneers. He was 2nd-in-Command from the 9th November 1923, and succeeded Colonel Watson as Commandant on the 5th May 1925. On the 1st March 1929, he was appointed Recruiting Officer, Burma. He had served with the 32nd Sikh Pioneers on the Tibet Mission of 1904, and joined the Burma Military Police on the 1st July 1908, holding various commands till the 22nd June 1915, when he proceeded to England. In November 1915, he became 2nd-in-Command of the 19th Welch Regiment (Pioneers), 38th Division, and served in France from the 3rd December 1915 till the 17th January 1916, when he was recalled by the India

Office and, after a month as 2nd-in-Command of the 16th Sherwood Foresters, returned to the Burma Military Police. On the 17th March 1917, he rejoined the 81st Pioneers, then serving in the Mohmand Blockade and, from the 8th April 1918 till the 25th May 1919, commanded the depot of his regiment at Bangalore (brevet of Lieutenant-Colonel). He then returned to the Burma Military Police.

Oung, Tun Hla:—2nd Lieutenant Oung was posted to the regiment on the 11th November 1923, and served with it till the 8th July 1924, when he was transferred, first to the 7th Cavalry, and subsequently to the 20th Burma Rifles.

Baker, Arthur Hillman:—2nd Lieutenant, 16th August 1916: Lieutenant, 16th August 1917: Captain, 16th August 1920. Captain Baker was posted to the regiment from the 107th Pioneers on the 19th December 1923. He was Adjutant of the regiment from the 19th February 1925 till the 19th June 1929 and, in 1930, passed the examination for admission to the Staff College, Quetta. During the Great War he served in France with the Middlesex Regiment from the 23rd January 1917 till the 24th March 1918, being mentioned in despatches and once wounded.

Mallannah, Satyavant Shrinagesh:—2nd Lieutenant, 30th August 1923: Lieutenant, 30th November 1925. This officer joined the regiment on the 13th October 1924, being the first King's commissioned officer to join in accordance with the scheme for Indianising certain battalions. He officiated as Quartermaster from the 15th June 1925, and was confirmed in that appointment on the 1st December 1927, holding it till the 31st March 1929. He was seconded for duty with the 11th Battalion (I.T.F.) on the 7th May 1930.

Khan, Sahibzada Anis Ahmad:—2nd Lieutenant, 30th August 1924: Lieutenant, 30th November 1926. This officer joined the regiment on the 2nd November 1925.

Thackwell, Arthur Charles Austen:—2nd Lieutenant, 28th January 1903: Lieutenant, 28th April 1905: Captain, 15th June 1911: Major, 15th June 1917. Major Thackwell, M.C., was posted to the regiment as 2nd-in-Command on the 5th May 1925, but remained with the Nayar Brigade till he retired from the service on the 9th December 1927. He saw service in the South African War from January to September 1902, and joined the 81st Pioneers on the 5th November 1904, with which regiment he continued to serve till the 20th November 1914, when he joined the 61st (K.G.O.) Pioneers in East Africa, where he was awarded the M.C. On the 30th November 1916, he rejoined the 81st Pioneers and, from June to August 1917, served on the Mohmand Blockade and, from March to May 1918, with the Marri Field Force. He served with the Bushire Expeditionary Force from June 1918 to May 1919, and took part in the Afghan War from July 1919 to May 1920. On the 6th February 1923, he became Commandant of the Nayar Brigade.

Southgate, Compton:—2nd Lieutenant, 1914: Lieutenant, 4th November 1914: Captain, 8th January 1915. Captain Southgate, M.C., was posted to the regiment from the 81st Pioneers on the 7th November 1922. He served in France as Adjutant, 14th Northumberland Fusiliers (Pioneers), and later as Staff Captain, 62nd Infantry Brigade, from the 9th September 1915 till the 26th June 1918, being mentioned in despatches and awarded the M.C. He served with the 2/81st Pioneers from the 5th September 1918 till May 1920, including the Afghan War of 1919, and then joined the 1/81st Pioneers. He was Staff Captain, Southern Command, from the 14th May to the 31st October 1921, and Staff Captain, Poona District, from the 1st November 1921 till the 24th February 1925. He graduated from the Staff College, Quetta, in December 1927. He was G.S.O. III., G.S. Branch, Army Headquarters, from April 1929 to March 1930, when he was appointed G.S.O. II.

Ashford, Ernest:—2nd Lieutenant, 5th January 1918: Lieutenant, 20th December 1919: Captain, 1st October 1924. This officer was posted to the regiment in November 1922. He served with the 2/4th Wiltshire Regiment from August 1914 to September 1916, and with the Indian Ordnance Department till January 1918, seeing service in Mesopotamia from November 1916 to November 1918, and being mentioned in despatches. He joined the 1/81st Pioneers in November 1918, and served with that unit in Persia, 1918-19, and on the North-West Frontier (Afghanistan) in 1919. On the formation of the Training Battalion, he became Quartermaster, and retained that appointment till March 1925. He officiated as Adjutant from the 17th April 1926 to the 16th January 1927 and, on the 26th January 1928, was seconded for duty with the 14/3rd Madras Regiment. On the 20th June 1929, he rejoined the regiment, and was appointed Adjutant from that date.

Wallis, Cedric:—2nd Lieutenant, 5th November 1914: Lieutenant, 5th August 1916: Captain, 4th August 1919. Captain Wallis joined the regiment from the 10th (Training) Battalion on the 16th November 1925. During the Great War, he had the misfortune to lose the sight of one eye, while taking a despatch at night at full gallop, when A.D.C. to the G.O.C., 38th Infantry Brigade, and was consequently only in France for a short period in 1915. He joined the Guides Cavalry on the 10th May 1917, and proceeded with that regiment to Mesopotamia in April 1918, where he joined the Political Department. He was First Assistant to the Chief Political Officer, Mosul Division, from January 1919 to April 1920; Assistant to H. B. M.'s Consul, and officiating as H. B. M.'s Consul at Ahwaz, in Persia, from November 1920 to October 1921; H. B. M.'s Vice-Consul at Dizful, on special duty in Khuzistan from October 1921 to October 1922. He became Company Commander, 14/3rd Madras Regiment (Coorg Territorials) on the 28th September 1923, and joined the 10/1st Madras Pioneers on the 26th January 1925. On the 7th February 1929, he was transferred to Corps Headquarters, officiating as Adjutant from the 20th August 1929, and was confirmed in that appointment on the 20th February 1930.

Khurana, Mehtab Singh:—2nd Lieutenant, 29th January 1925: Lieutenant, 24th April 1927. This officer was posted to the regiment from the Unattached List having been attached to the 2nd Queen's Royal Regiment, on the 8th April 1926. He officiated as Quartermaster from the 25th May to the 3rd December 1928.

Singh, Baljit:—2nd Lieutenant, 3rd September 1925: Lieutenant, 3rd December 1927. This officer was posted to the regiment from the Unattached List, having been attached to the 2nd Lincolnshire Regiment, on the 13th October 1926.

Ghose, Sushil Kumar:—2nd Lieutenant, 4th February 1926: Lieutenant, 4th May 1928. This officer was posted to the regiment from the Unattached List, having been attached to the 2nd Yorkshire Regiment, on the 22nd April 1927. On the 3rd March 1930, he was posted to Corps Headquarters for a tour of duty.

Nance, Walter Joseph:—2nd Lieutenant, 25th January 1908: Lieutenant, 25th April 1910: Captain, 25th January 1917: Major, 25th January 1923. Major Nance was posted to the regiment from the 1st (K.G.O.) Battalion on the 5th November 1928, on the re-organisation of Pioneer battalions. He was attached to the 2nd Royal Berkshire Regiment in 1908, and joined the 81st Pioneers on the 8th April 1909. He was Station Staff Officer, Belgaum Brigade, from the 1st April 1913 to the 15th March 1914, Quartermaster of his regiment from February 1915 to April 1916, and officiating Station Staff Officer, Nowshera, from December 1916 to November 1917, when he became Adjutant of his regiment, holding this appointment till March 1919. From the 7th June 1919, he acted as 2nd-in-Command till the 23rd February 1920, when he was appointed Commandant, 5th Infantry and Engineer Company, South Persian Rifles, and, on the 1st June 1921, became Brigade Commander, Fwis Brigade, South Persian Rifles. On the 20th November 1922, he joined the 11/3rd Madras Regiment (I.T.F.), remaining with that unit till April 1926, when he was appointed D.A.D.A. and T., Army Headquarters. On the 27th January 1928, he joined the 1st (K.G.O.) Battalion, 1st Madras Pioneers. He saw service on the North-West Frontier from the 16th August to the 25th September 1915 and from the 1st July 1919 to the 21st February 1920; with the Mari Punitive Field Force from the 9th March to the 8th April 1918; and with the Bushire Field Force from July 1918 to May 1919, being mentioned in despatches.

Hamilton, Archibald Francis:—2nd Lieutenant, 27th January 1904: Lieutenant, 27th April 1906: Captain, 27th January 1913: Major, 27th January 1919: Lieutenant-Colonel, 1st March 1929. Major Hamilton, M.C., was posted to the regiment, as officiating Commandant, on the 27th November 1928, on the re-organisation of Pioneer battalions, and became Commandant on the 1st March 1929. He was posted to the Bedfordshire Regiment on the 27th January 1904, and attached to the 2nd Royal Scots on the 25th March 1904. He joined the 61st (K.G.O.) Pioneers on the 20th August 1905, and became Adjutant of that regiment on the 30th July 1911. During the Great War, he served in East Africa from November 1914 to March 1918, being twice mentioned in despatches and awarded the M.C. He acted as Staff Officer to the I. G. C., East Africa, from the 29th December 1915 to the 3rd March 1916, and was attached to Headquarters, 2nd Division, from the 14th to the 31st March 1916. He was Special Service Officer from the 1st April to the 27th July 1916; Staff Captain, 1st East African Infantry Brigade, from the 28th July 1916 to the 24th February 1917; and Brigade-Major from the 25th February to the 8th November 1917. He acted as temporary 2nd-in-Command of the

2/10th Jats from the 1st August to the 5th November 1918, and of the 2/63rd Light Infantry from the 6th November 1918 to the 3rd May 1919. He served on the North-West Frontier with the 1/61st (K.G.O.) Pioneers from July to December 1919, and commanded the depot from the 20th December 1919 to the 25th August 1920, when he rejoined the battalion in Waziristan, officiating as Commandant from May to November 1922. On the 3rd March 1923, he joined the 10th (Training) Battalion for a tour of duty and, on the 27th November 1925, was appointed Administrative Commandant, 14/3rd Madras Regiment.

Walawalkar, Bhalchandra Pandurang:—2nd Lieutenant, 2nd February 1928; Lieutenant, 2nd May 1920. This officer was posted to the regiment from the Unattached List, having been attached to the 2nd Northumberland Fusiliers, on the 22nd March 1929.

Bahadur, Rana Jodha Jung:—2nd Lieutenant, 11th November 1913; Lieutenant, 11th February 1916; Captain, 25th August 1920. Captain Rana Jodha Jung Bahadur, M.B.E., M.C., was posted to the regiment from the 1st Battalion, 3rd Sikh Pioneers, on the 1st April 1929, on the reorganisation of Pioneer battalions. He was first commissioned in the Indian Land Forces in 1913, and was attached to the 2/3rd Gurkha Rifles for training from the 1st August to the 30th September 1913, and to the 1st Sappers and Miners from the 15th October 1913 to the 14th February 1914. On the 15th February 1914, he was appointed Commandant, Tehri-Garhwal Indian State Sappers, and joined the 1/39th Garhwalis on the 11th December 1914. On the 7th October 1919, he joined the 2/23rd Sikh Pioneers and, on the 1st January 1922, the 1/3rd Sikh Pioneers, being transferred to the 12/2nd Bombay Pioneers, and attached to the 10/3rd Sikh Pioneers, on the 21st December 1925. On the 20th February 1930, he left the regiment for a tour of duty with Corps Headquarters. During the Great War, he served in Egypt from February to March 1915; in France and Belgium from March to November 1915; in Mesopotamia, from September 1917 to October 1918; and also on the North West Frontier (Afghanistan) from May to October 1919, and in Waziristan from the 30th January to the 31st December 1923, and from the 23rd January to the 6th April 1925. He was twice mentioned in despatches in France, and twice wounded, and was awarded the M.C. in 1915, and the M.B.E. (Military Division) in 1919. He attended the Delhi Coronation Durbar in 1911, and became Honorary A.D.C. to H. E. the Viceroy on the 5th April 1916.

Alphabetical Index of British Officers.

Name	Page		Name	Page
Airey, George	372		Bruce, F.	446
Alcock, Francis	405		Bruce, J. C. W.	441
Alexander, James	374		Bryant, L.	458
Anderson, T. A.	460		Budd, Richard	430
Anderson, William	434		Burne, Frank Owen Newdigate	453
Anderson, William Wallace	418		Burr, Daniel	378
Aplin, Stephen Lushington	445		Burrows, G. V.	445
Ashford, Ernest	463		Burton, Edmund Francis	438
Atkinson, Edwin Henry	408		Button, Philip	399
Aylward, Douglas	455			
Babington, Richard Clarke	427		Campbell, ——	373
Bahadur, Rana Jodha Jung	465		Campbell, J.	436
Baillie, William	373		Campbell, Robert Nutter	410
Baker, Arthur Hillman	462		Capper, Francis	379
Baker, Benjamin	409		Carey, A. B.	458
Banister, F.	456		Carr, Robert	431
Bannerman, John	396		Carr, William George	440
Barclay, Robert	381		Carter, Henry	401
Barnes, Thomas James	457		Cary, Robert Ormsby	426
Barnett, James Herbert Marsh	441		Cassidy, Vivian Clemons	453
Barton, Richard	373		Ceville, James	392
Batchelor, C. F. F.	459		Chalmers, John	380
Batchelor, Edward	387		Chauvel, John Edward	407
Batten, Frederick Graeme	454		Chillingworth, Joseph	397
Baugh, Guillum Scott	442		Chinnery, William Charles	411
Beadle, Denis Robert Hudson	418		Church, Charles	410
Bell, James	435		Churchill, Folliott	445
Bilcliffe, Joseph	390		Clapham, William	393
Birch, George	394		Clarke, George	384
Bird, Francis Paske Harvey	436		Cleghorn, Allan Mackenzie	423
Bird, John Francis	435		Clerk, Robert Mildmay	444
Bird, William Cornelius John Fraser	426		Cochran George Walker	461
Blackburne, William	387		Coke, Thomas	380
Blenkinsop, Edward George	439		Colbeck, Henry	415
Bliss, James Arthur	452		Coningham, Walter	443
Bowden, Spencer Albert	460		Conway, Henry	403
Bowen, C. E.	449		Corley, L. C.	459
Bowes, Frederick	416		Cormick, Michael H.	384
Bowman, ——	372		Corner, Charles	385
Bowser, *Sir* Thomas	397		Cornwell, R. B.	458
Breithaupt, Edward Avenel	451		Cotton, William	432
Brereton, S. W. T.	440		Cotton, William Forbes	435
Brine, John Jones	424		Cox, Henry Francis	460
Browne, John	381		Cramer, John Henry	410
Bruce, Charles David	391		Crisp, John	374

	Page.		Page.
Cuming, William Herbert	426	Fuller, William Henry Lawrence	430
Curle, Victor	456	Fullerton, William Robert	420
Daldy, A. J.	457	Gabbett, Joseph	440
Dalziel, John	396	Geddes, Malcolm Henry Burdett	448
Darley, John	391	Ghose, Sushil Kumar	464
Davidson, Alfred Augustus	432	Gibbon, Septimus	422
Davies, Arthur	420	Glover, W. S. C.	456
Davis, ——	373	Glynn, John Edmund	412
Davis, William	392	Goddard, William	374
Dawes, Nathaniel	379	Godson, John	443
Deane, Henry Harold Rookhurst	454	Gordon, John Francis	423
Deed, L. H.	457	Gosling, Henry Monteith	438
Dent, William McKerrell	428	Graham, David	434
Denton, James	423	Grant, Alexander	382
Desborough, Lawrence Cameron	441	Grant, Charles St. John	403
Dickson, George Collingwood	420	Grant, Douglas Gordon Seafield St. John	428
Dobbie, R. S.	436	Grant, James Murray	442
Dods, Joseph	416	Grant, Lewis	375
Doig, E. W.	459	Green, John	420
Donne, A. J.	459	Griffin, Francis Blackburn	429
Doria, Alexander	419	Groves, J. M. S.	446
Doveton, Gabriel	382		
Driver, H. S.	460	Haldane, Edward	406
Duggan, Timothy Frederick	400	Haleman, Francis	403
Dundas, John Elphinstone	380	Hall, Humphry Senhouse	402
Dunlop, George Wellington Nelson	421	Hamilton, Archibald Francis	464
Dyce, Archibald Brown	404	Hamilton, L. S.	461
		Hammond, Anthony	399
Eagle, Archibald	374	Hare, Ivan Lancelot O'Hara	453
Edington, James	373	Hargrave, William	397
Edwardes, H. J. B.	425	Harkness, Charles Thomas	425
Elliot, C.	455	Harris, Hugh Anstruther	451
Ellis, William Charles	440	Harris, H. L.	408
Erskine, James	400	Harris, William	396
		Harvey-Kelly, Harvey St. George Hume	450
Fairclough, J. E. B.	458	Hatton, Arthur	443
Faunce, Edmund Burrell	407	Hawkins, John	389
Fennell, Alfred Ernest Slater	461	Hemsley, Charles	452
Findlay, M. A.	456	Hill, Joseph Gulston	390
Fisher, Thomas James	411	Hitchens, Benjamin Robertson	426
Flint, William	385	Hodding, George Carr	442
Forbes, Nathaniel	401	Holland, Charles	426
Ford, John Meredith Randle	460	Holloway, Edward Leigh	444
Foster, M. R.	457	Holmes, Gilbert Vallentin	446
Fraser, Charles	376	Hornsby, A. W. H.	440
Fraser, H. W. M.	456	Houghton, Richmond	433
Fraser, William	392	Hudleston, W.	437

	Page.		Page.
Hudson, H. S.	443	MacDonald, Charles Edward William Chambers	430
Huffton, P. H.	457	MacDonald, John Collins	428
Hunter, Robert	404	McGill, Patrick	375
Hutchinson, G. W.	459	McGoun, Thomas	436
Hutton, George	432	MacGregor, Malcolm	383
Innes, James	385	Mackay, Robert	375
Innes, John	387	Mackenzie, Colin	432
Innes, John	399	Mackenzie, Donald	443
		Mackie, Ralph	449
Jacob, Vickers Gilbert	428	MacLeod, Charles	405
James, —-	450	MacMahon, J. J.	457
Jenkins, Alexander	428	McNair, Archibald	407
Jennings, Charles James	432	McNeill, Daniel	405
Jennings, L. W. B.	458	McNeill, Duncan	434
Jobson, James	402	MacRae, Hugh	381
Johnson, Maurice Eustace Stanley	449	Magan, Tilson Shaw	438
Johnston, Charles James	437	Maitland, John	392
Johnston, John M'Mahon	416	Malby, J.	460
Johnstone, C. W. H.	457	Malet, Robert James	449
Jollie, Walter	409	Mallannah, Satyavant Shrinagesh	462
Jones, Robert	438	Maltby, Francis Crichton	440
Jones, William James	424	Mangin, Etienne Bessonnet	459
Justice, William	429	Mangnall, Kay	389
		Marrett, Philip Thomas	416
Kaye, Arthur E. C.	443	Marriott, Charles Silwood	394
Keate, C. R.	445	Marsack, Augustus Becher	439
Keble, J. A.	448	Marsden, Edmund	450
Kelk, B. M.	460	Marshall, David	379
Kemble, Thomas Aubery	459	Marshall, George	407
Khan, Sahibzada Anis Ahmed	462	Marshall, John H.	407
Khurana, Mehtab Singh	463	Marshall, W. F.	449
Kilgour, Frederick	437	Martin, George	402
King, H. T.	444	Maver, Robert	395
Kirby, Hickman Rose	408	Mears, Arthur	446
Knight, F. M. C.	460	Meeke, Thomas	374
		Meiklejohn, Walter Lloyd Sinclair	449
Lacon, John Edmund	417	Metcalf, John	402
Lavie, Robert Comyn	441	Metcalfe, Howe	418
Lawder, James	426	Miller, William Armit	410
Le May, A. C.	459	Mills, F. C. R.	457
Le Page, John	399	Mills, W. S.	457
Little, Joseph	389	Monin, Antony	384
Longford, W. J.	443	Monypenny, R. d'A.	461
Lorrimore, Samuel	379	Moody, B. C.	460
Lowe, Robert	374	Moor, George	395
Lyon, Robert	382	Moore, James	400

Name	Page	Name	Page
Morgan, John	419	Rattray, James	412
Mottet, Arthur Charles	437	Raven-Hill, L. E.	461
Mottet, Henry Edward	437	Rennick, R. H. F.	440
Muat, George Alexander	392	Renton, Robert	427
Muirhead, Alexander	381	Rhodes, William	387
Munro, John	379	Riach, William Alexander	441
Munro, John	404	Rice, Sidney Mervyn	446
Munro, Robert	387	Richardson, John	374
Munro, *Sir* Thomas	386	Rivers, Francis James	434
Murland, Howard Ferguson	451	Robertson, Norman Donald	441
		Robertson, William McD.	394
Nagle, James	391	Robertson, S.	460
Nance, Walter Joseph	464	Rogers, Archibald Clement Campbell	451
Nelson, Frederick	420	Ross, John Maitland	406
Newall, David	393	Ross, R. J.	448
Newlyn, William Rouse	426	Rossel, Henry George Theodore	455
Nicholls, Henry James	437	Russell, William	434
Nuthall, Henry Robert	420		
		St. George, William	419
Oakes, George Henry	434	Salter, Patrick	429
Oliphant, William	381	Scott, E. H.	458
Oliver, W. C.	418	Scott, *Sir* Hopetoun Stratford	408
O'Reilly, Edward	402	Scott, *Sir* Robert	397
Ormsby, Adam	387	Scott-Elliot, Charles Reginald	447
Ormsby, Robert	389	Sellon, Edward	419
Oung, Tun Hla	462	Seppings, William Lawless	417
Owen, Henry Rees	422	Shadwell, Thomas	382
		Shand, John	425
Palk, Charles	395	Shawe, Robert	419
Palk, Thomas	396	Sheen, Henry	398
Palmer, James Edward	421	Shelley, Harry Byam	433
Palmer, William Charles	430	Showers, Howe Daniel	418
Passy, De Lacy Dayrell	443	Showers, Nathaniel Thornton	396
Payne, John	401	Shute, P. E.	457
Phelips, Robert Hoskyns	433	Sibbald, Andrew	401
Phillips, James	375	Silver, Alexander Crombie	422
Pierce, Frederick	389	Singh, Baljit	464
Plant, John Floyd Alexander	425	Skinner, Thomas Burrell	454
Plant, William Charles	434	Skryme, Francis	375
Podmore, Henry Beresford	432	Slade, Meade	456
Porteous, James Edward	442	Smith, D. C. Sidney	456
Power, A. G. C.	436	Smith, Henry Delves Broughton	430
Powys, Philip Annesley Secundus	413	Smith, Henry Francis	388
Prendergast, Thomas	375	Smith, J. Coleman	459
Prescott, William	431	Smith, Lewin Scott	395
Pringle, Francis	400	Smith, Maurice Castle	452
		Smith, William Hope	406
Rainey, E. F.	446	Smithers, Otway Francis	431

	Page.
Southgate, Compton	462
Stanley, Richard	390
Stevens, George Borlase	444
Stevens, Joseph Fisher	438
Steuart, George Mackenzie	416
Stewart, A. R.	461
Stiles, George Harcourt	428
Stock, Arthur	398
Stokes, John Day	406
Stokes, Oliver Day	414
Stonehewer, E. H.	456
Story, John Alexis	453
Strahan, William Abingdon Otto	425
Strut, J. R.	382
Sturrock, George	418
Sultana, ――	458
Swan, Charles Tarrant	445
Symons, John Hilley	383
Taylor, J. F. S.	457
Taylor, Ralph Neufville	436
Templer, Frederick	418
Thackwell, Arthur Charles Austen	462
Thomas, E. Hastings	434
Thomas, G.	441
Thompson, John	380
Tipping, Richard Percy Macrae	461
Tireman, George Joseph Stainton	427
Trent, Thomas	389
Turing, James	380
Turner, Charles James Alexander	428
Tweedie, Maurice	422
Urmson, Denis George Severn	455
Van Heythuysen, H. T.	402
Vardon, Frank	418
Walawalkar, Bhalchandra Pandurang	465
Walhouse, James Moreton	420
Walker, Andrew	398

	Page.
Walker, Charles Augustus	420
Walker, George Andrew	429
Walker, Joseph	392
Walker, Thomas	401
Walker, Thomas	412
Wallis, Cedric	463
Wallis, Henry	399
Ward, F. H. T.	458
Warden, James Hale	435
Watkins, John	380
Watson, David	404
Watson, Spencer Burton	448
Watson, Thomas	409
Watt, James	418
Webb, Edward Arthur Henry	418
Webbe, James Taylor	406
Weir, John	395
Welch, M. E. H. O.	443
Weller, George	374
West, Arthur Robert	420
Weston, Charles	431
Wetherall, Pritzler James Pakenham	443
Wheller, John	380
Whitlock, William Henry	439
Whyte, A. C. V.	436
Wilkieson, Claude W.	445
Williams, William	398
Williams, Watkin Lewis Griffies	429
Williamson, V. C.	458
Williamson, William	420
Wilmot, Henry Eardley	443
Wilson, James	392
Wilson, L. D.	455
Wood, Herbert William	413
Wood, Philip Raymond Jarvis	423
Wood, ――	459
Worthington, Roger Francis	458
Wyndham, Arthur	418
Young, G. A.	436

Warrant Officers and Sergeants.

Of the many British Sergeants who served with the Regiment, the only men whose names I have been able to trace are the following:—

1. Sergeant-Major T. P. Smaasen,* who was transferred from the Regiment de Meuron† to the Honourable Company's service on the 26th September 1805.

2. Quartermaster-Sergeant G. Himbler, who was tried by Court-Martial, on the 1st January 1811, for "insolence, disobedient of orders, and for being drunk," and was sentenced to be reduced to the ranks, and to receive 300 lashes.

3. Sergeant-Major Longdon, who was serving with the 4th in 1834.

4. Quartermaster-Sergeant Cunningham, who died in 1834, whilst holding the appointment.

5. Quartermaster-Sergeant J. Flood, who succeeded Cunningham, having previously been Sergeant-Major of the Ootacamund Convalescent Depot.

6. Quartermaster-Sergeant Gwynne, who was serving with the 4th in 1836—1839. He was with the regiment at Cannanore in 1838, and was pensioned on the 17th December 1839. On the 21st April 1836, he had been appointed to act as "Road Sergeant" by the Officer Commanding, Mysore Division, and during his absence—

7. Gunner Richards, "A" Troop, Horse Artillery, was appointed to act as Quartermaster-Sergeant of the 4th.

8. Sergeant-Major J. McDonnell, who exchanged from the 4th, on the 8th February 1838, with

---

* One John Smaasen was Assistant-Surgeon to the Regiment de Meuron, when the latter was quartered at Arni after talking part in the Siege of Seringapatam in 1799. There is a monument to his wife, Jeromana Smaasen, in the Fort Cemetery at Arni.

† The Regiment de Meuron was a Swiss corps which surrendered to the British when Ceylon was captured from the Dutch in 1795. The regiment was transferred to the British East India Company by a deed executed at Neuchatel in March 1796. Although raised in Switzerland, the corps was not under control of any of the cantons, and the officers were nominated by the Count de Meuron. The Colonel-Commandant was the Colonel's brother and most of the other officers were connected with him. It was composed of 10 companies, about 800 strong, when it arrived in Madras Presidency. In 1808 the regiment was disbanded, when 133 men were transferred to the artillery, on which occasion the Court of Directors remarked: "In consideration of the long and faithful service of the Regiment de Meuron under the British Government in India, and of the deficient state of your artillery corps we do not object to the transfer of a part of that regiment to the corps alluded to, notwithstanding our disinclination, on general principles, to any large proportion of foreigners being admitted into that corps."

It may be noted that Brigadier de Meuron was commanding the troops at Madras in 1800.

9. Sergeant-Major Farrell, who was Store Sergeant at Cannanore. He died in 1839.

10. Sergeant-Major George Hardy, who was appointed to act as Sergeant-Major of the 4th, on the death of Farrell, in 1839.

11. Sergeant-Major Thomas Coffin, who was appointed to the 4th on the 26th December 1839, having been promoted from the rank of gunner in the A Company, 2nd Battalion Artillery. He was appointed Quartermaster-Sergeant of the 10th N. I. on the 23rd September 1842. In 1846, when Sergeant-Major of the 17th N. I., he was appointed Cantonment Sergeant-Major of Secunderabad.

12. Sergeant-Major Thomas Taylor, who was promoted from the rank of gunner in the 1st Battalion Artillery, was appointed Sergeant-Major of the 4th (*vice* Coffin) on the 23rd September 1842, and held the appointment till 1857, when he was transferred to the Ordnance Department as Acting Sub-Conductor.

13. Quartermaster-Sergeant Frederick Potter, who rejoined the 4th at Wallajahbad on the 23rd December 1844, with details from foreign service under Captain H. W. Wood. He had been Sergeant-Major of the 4th up to the 18th December 1839, when he was appointed Quartermaster-Sergeant in place of Gwynne (*q. v.*), transferred to pension. On the 9th November 1855, he was promoted to Acting Sub-Conductor in the Ordnance Department.

14. Quartermaster-Sergeant Thomas Ambler, who had been a Sergeant in the 1st European Infantry, was appointed to the 4th on the 13th November 1855, *vice* F. Potter (above) and was made permanent in the appointment on the 2nd June 1856.

15. Quartermaster-Sergeant William Ellery, who was transferred from the 74th Highlanders on the 19th December 1863.

16. Sergeant-Major George Brown, late 4th M.N.I., who was awarded a silver medal and a gratuity of £5 on the 30th May 1863, at which time he was drawing his pension at Coimbatore.

17. Quartermaster-Sergeant Thomas Harte, who had been a Sergeant in the 1st Battalion 18th Royal Irish Regiment, was appointed to act as Quartermaster-Sergeant of the 4th in April 1865.

18. Quartermaster-Sergeant John Butler, who was transferred from the 4th to the Garrison of Fort St. George in February 1873.

Part IV.

INDIAN OFFICERS

1759—1930.

Note.

This section of the records is in many ways incomplete as it has been found difficult, and in many cases impossible, to trace the services of Indian Officers, so that what follows is, to a great extent, merely a list of names and dates.

Great assistance has been given by Pensioned Subadar-Majors Mir Abbas, *Bahadur,* and Sayyid Abbas, *Bahadur,* in tracing the names of officers who served with the regiment during the past forty years.

The spelling of the officers' names is as given in contemporary returns, and no attempt has been made to modernise it.

Native Commandants.

The appointment of Native Commandant was instituted when the Madras Army was first formed into battalions in 1759, and was abolished in 1785.

So far, the only Native Commandant of the 4th Battalion whose name I have been able to trace is:—

Meer Sally. He was killed at the Battle of Arni on the 2nd June 1782. After the battle Sir Eyre Coote issued a complimentary order concerning him, which will be found recorded in Part I. His eldest son, Tippu Sahib, was promoted to Jemadar and his second son, Mahomed Sahib, to Havildar.

Indian Officers.

Name.	Jemadar.	Subadar.	Subadar-Major.	Remarks.
Tippoo Sahib	June 1782	?	..	Son of Meer Sally, Native Commandant. (q. v.)
Monsur Ally	..	?	..	Transferred to the 2nd/4th, 24th January 1797.
Bahauder Beg	..	1st Feb. 1789.	..	Was Senior Subadar in 1808.
Shaik Boodeen	..	1st Feb. 1789.	..	Invalided, 31st December 1809.
Shaik Emaum	..	1st Feb. 1789.	..	Invalided, 31st December 1809.
Said Mahomed	..	30th Oct. 1798.	..	Invalided, 31st December 1809.
Ramoo	..	23rd Sept. 1803.	..	Left before 1813. Was Senior Subadar in 1811.
Ramswamy	..	12th Aug. 1804.	..	Was Senior Subadar from 1813 till he left in 1817 or 1818.
Boot Sing	..	1st Jan. 1805.	..	Left before 1808.
Ram Sing	..	1st Jan. 1805.	..	Left in 1817 or 1818.
Tandavorayah	..	9th Oct. 1804.	1819	Senior Subadar from 1817, and the first Subadar-Major of the regiment from 1819 till he was struck off on the 21st November 1824.
Golam Hussain	..	2nd Mar. 1806.	..	Left in 1822.
Shaik Mohideen	13th July 1804.	..	..	Left before 1808.
Chinganah	?	..	..	Pensioned, 31st December 1805.
Shaik Hussain	12th Aug. 1804.	1st Jan. 1808.	..	Pensioned, 31st December 1819.
Shaik Adam	10th Oct. 1804.	1st Jan. 1808.	..	Left in 1816.
Venket Ram	10th Oct. 1804.	29th Dec. 1808.	..	Left in 1818.
Arjoonah	10th Oct. 1804.	..	..	Never became Subadar, and was invalided, 31st December 1819.
Moodeenah Beg	1st Jan. 1805.	1st Jan. 1810.	..	Left in 1822.
Homed Khan	1st Jan. 1805.	1st Jan. 1810.	1824 ?	Left in 1826. I believe he succeeded Tandavorayah as Subadar-Major.

Name.	Jemadar.	Subadar.	Subadar-Major.	Remarks.
Shaik Homed	9th Oct. 1804.	1st Jan. 1812.	..	Left in 1826(?).
Said Ebram	9th Feb. 1806.	6th Nov. 1816.	..	Left about 1818.
Said Hussain	2nd Mar. 1806.	22nd Sep. 1817.	..	Pensioned, 3rd December 1825.
Kistan Sing	23rd Jan. 1807.	..	..	Left before 1813.
Nuzeef Khan	1st Jan. 1808.	1st Jan. 1818.	..	Pensioned, 3rd December 1825.
Peermauloo	1st Jan. 1808.		..	Left about 1818.
Said Emaum	29th Dec. 1808.	1st Jan. 1818.	1826 ?	This officer may have succeeded Homed Khan as Subadar-Major for a short time, but this is doubtful, as I think he was still serving in 1829, and Venketsawmy became Subadar-Major in 1827.
Shaik Adham	1st Jan. 1810.	1st Jan. 1818.	..	Pensioned on full pay, 10th January 1834.
Abdul Cawder	1st Jan. 1810.	..	..	Left about 1815.
Soorat Sing	1st Jan. 1812.	..	..	Left in 1818 (?)
Lutchmen Sing	1st Jan. 1812.	..	..	Left in 1813.
Anap Sing	18th April 1813.	..	..	Left in 1819.
Shaik Hussain	1st Jan. 1814.	..	..	Left in 1819.
Peermanandam	16th Nov. 1816.	1st Jan. 1820.	..	Left in 1829 (?).
Ramasawmy	22nd Sept. 1817.	16th Mar. 1822.	..	Left in 1829 (?).
Syed Ismall	1st Jan. 1818.	21st Nov. 1824.	..	Left in 1836 (?).
Venkoo	1st Jan. 1818.	..	..	Invalided, 31st December 1819.
Mahomed Gouse	8th Feb. 1818.	4th Dec. 1825.	..	Left in 1836 (?).
Chillembram	6th Oct. 1818.	..	..	Left in 1821.
Gooroovapah	13th Nov. 1818.	..	..	Left in 1821.
Mahomed Sahib	1st Feb. 1819.	4th Dec. 1825.	..	

This officer was transferred to the pension establishment on the 15th November 1836, on the full pay of his rank, in consideration of his long and faithful services, extending to a period of 40 years.

Name.	Jemadar.	Subadar.	Subadar-Major.	Remarks.
Shaik Homed	16th June 1819.	..	..	Left in 1824.
Shaik Meeran	1st Jan. 1820.	..	..	Invalided on the 31st December 1823.

Name.	Jemadar.	Subadar.	Subadar-Major.	Remarks.
Cuddumbanada	1st Jan. 1820.	..	..	Left in 1826 (?).
Ramasawmy	1st Jan. 1820.	11th Mar. 1826.	..	*Appears to have been the first Jemadar Adjutant (1821-26).* Left in 1836 (?).
Venketsawmy	..	1st Feb. 1819.	1st May 1827.	Joined from the 2nd Extra Battalion on the 1st December 1821.

This officer was transferred to pension, on Rupees 40 *per mensem* and the Staff allowance of his rank on the 12th November 1839. He appears in General Orders, in July 1835, as President of a Native General Court-Martial at Bangalore, to the proceedings of which he appended a cross, being illiterate.

Name.	Jemadar.	Subadar.	Subadar-Major.	Remarks.
Nutter Beg	1st Feb. 1819.	..	..	Joined from the 2nd Extra Battalion on the 1st December 1821, and died on the 16th December 1822.
Mahomed Pautcha.	1st Feb. 1819.	..	..	Joined the 1st 4th in 1821, and was pensioned on the 31st December 1822.
Shaik Modeen	1st Jan. 1820.	..	..	Was posted to the 1st 4th in 1822 and died on the 28th December 1822.
Koossal Sing	17th Dec. 1822	1st Jan. 1827.	..	Left in 1836 (?).
Shaik Hoosain	29th Dec. 1822	17th Jan. 1829.	..	Left in 1836 (?).
Runno Sing	1st Jan. 1823.	11th Jan. 1834	..	Left in 1836 (?).
Vencatachellam	1st Jan. 1824.	31st Dec. 1835.	..	Pensioned on Rs. 40 *per mensem* on 3rd April 1838.
Hoosain Khan	21st Nov. 1824.	1836 (?)	1st July 1840	*Jemadar Adjutant. 1826-1836 (?)* Succeeded Venketsawmy as Subadar-Major. Left in 1842.
Ramasamy	1st Mar. 1825.	..	..	Pensioned on half pay, 19th February 1833.
Venketrajah	4th Dec. 1825.	..	..	Left in 1832 (?).
Coopah	4th Dec. 1825	15th Nov. 1836.	12th Feb. 1842.	Succeeded Hoosain Khan as Subadar-Major. Pensioned on Rs. 40 *per mensem*, plus the staff allowance of his rank on 24th October 1845, when he was succeeded by Shaik Adam.

Name.	Jemadar.	Subadar.	Subadar-Major.	Remarks.
Shaik Bram	1st Jan. 1826.	1837 (?)	..	Pensioned on Rs. 25 *per mensem* on the 5th August 1842.
Cantaveriah	11th Mar. 1826.	..	..	Pensioned on half pay on the 27th March 1834.
Anantaram	1st Jan. 1827	1836 (?)	..	*Jemadar Adjutant*, 5th April 1836.

Subadar Anantaram was court-martialled at Cannanore, on the 9th January 1839, on a charge of giving false evidence before a court-martial held at French Rocks on the 31st August 1838, for the trial of Captain W. C Chinnery of the 4th N. I., but was acquitted. On the 30th September 1839, following on a further court-martial held on the same officer, he was, by order of the Commander-in-Chief, transferred to the 41st N. I., with effect from the 30th October 1839, owing to his having "possessed and exercised a very undue inflence in the 4th Regiment."

Name.	Jemadar.	Subadar.	Subadar-Major.	Remarks.
Ramasamy Naick	17th Jan. 1829.	..	..	Left in 1831.
Akeel Homed	..	10th Nov. 1831.	..	Joined the 4th in December 1828 (?). Pensioned on the 31st December 1835.
Shaik Adam *Sirdar Bahadur*	1832 (?)	1836 (?)	24th Oct. 1845.	*Order of British India, 2nd Class, 1851. Order of British India, 1st Class, 1853.* Pensioned on Rs. 40 *per mensem*, with the staff allowance of his rank, on the 30th November 1855.

Shaik Adam is shown as Subadar-Major in the Madras Army List up to the 1st April 1852. On the 1st January 1853, "*Sunkerlingam, Sirdar Bahadur*" is shown as having been Subadar-Major of the regiment since the 9th January 1843, but there must have been some clerical error, as Shaik Adam once more appears as Subadar-Major (dated 24th October 1845) in the Army List for the 1st April 1854.

Name.	Jemadar.	Subadar.	Subadar-Major.	Remarks.
Shaik Madar	11th Jan. 1834.	1837 (??)	..	Pensioned on Rs. 40 *per mensem* on the 3rd July 1855.
Shaik Homed	28th Mar. 1834.	3rd April 1838.	..	*Jemadar Adjutant*, 31st October 1837. Pensioned on Rs. 40 *per mensem* on the 20th October 1848.
Shaik Ghooroo	31st Dec. 1835.	16th Aug. 1839.	..	Pensioned on Rs. 25 *per mensem* on the 13th May 1842.
Mootoosamy	1836 (?)	12th Nov. 1839.	..	*Jemadar Adjutant, 1838—1840.* Left in 1850 (?).

Name.	Jemadar.	Subadar.	Subadar-Major.	Remarks.
Syed Hoosain	15th Nov. 1836.	12th Feb. 1842.	..	*Acting Jemr. Adjutant, 1843.* Struck off in 1845.
Shekh Emaum	1837 (?)	1st Mar. 1842.	..	Pensioned on Rs. 40 *per mensem* on the 11th January 1850.
Setwajee	1837 (?)	13th May 1842.	..	Struck off in 1845.
Ramasamy	1837 (?)	5th Aug. 1842.	..	Pensioned on Rs. 40 *per mensem*, 24th December 1847.
Moonegah	1837 (?)	..	..	..

This officer was transferred from the 4th to the 33rd N. I., with effect from the 30th October 1839, by order of the Commander-in-Chief, at the same time as Subadar Anantaram was transferred to the 41st N. I., and for the same reason.

Name.	Jemadar.	Subadar.	Subadar-Major.	Remarks.
Moncapah	3rd April 1838.	?	..	*Jemadar Adjutant, 1840-43.* Pensioned on half pay on the 20th October 1843.
Seetiah	?	?	..	..

This Officer was transferred from the 41st N. I. to the 4th by order of the Commander-in-Chief, he "having been found to exercise an undue influence" in the 41st N. I. He was what used to be known as a "*Palki Subadar*", that is to say he had been presented by the Honourable East India Company with a palki or palankin, in which he was entitled to be carried.

Name.	Jemadar.	Subadar.	Subadar-Major.	Remarks.
Shekh Ismail	?	..	..	Transferred from the 33rd N. I. to the 4th, as a Jemadar, on the 30th October 1839, *vice* Jemadar Moonegah.
Moonesamy	16th Aug. 1839.	20th Nov. 1844.	..	Pensioned on Rs. 40 *per mensem* on the 17th April 1857.
Abdool Sherriff	16th Aug. 1839.	24th Oct. 1845.	..	Pensioned on Rs. 25 *per mensem* on the 19th March 1847.
Ramah	12th Nov. 1839.	..	..	Pensioned on half pay on the 22nd November 1842.
Jait Ram	1841 (?)	2nd May 1845.	..	Left between 1847 and 1862.

Subadar Jait Ram was tried by an European General Court-Martial at Trichinopoly, on the 6th March 1855, for having entered into a pecuniary transaction with Private Kunkiah by lending him rupees four and receiving four annas interest. He was found guilty, and sentenced to be suspended from rank, pay and allowances for one month.

Name.	Jemadar.	Subadar.	Subadar-Major.	Remarks.
Shekh Hassen	12th Feb. 1842.	19th Mar. 1847.	..	Pensioned on Rs. 25 *per mensem*, 24th December 1847.
Shekh Ally	1st March 1842.	?	..	Struck off in 1847.
Polenaidoo	1st March 1842.	24th Dec. 1847.	..	Pensioned on half pay of his rank, 27th June 1854.
Khader Saib	13th May 1842.	24th Dec. 1847.	..	*Jemadar Adjutant*, 1844. Pensioned on Rs. 25 *per mensem*, 1st February 1850.
Bawa Saib	5th Aug. 1842.	..	..	Struck off in 1844.
Rutten Sing	22nd Nov. 1842	20th Oct. 1848.	..	*Jemadar-Adjutant*, 1844-1848. Left before 1859.
Buckt Sing	20th Oct. 1843.	11th Jan. 1850.	..	Pensioned on half pay on the 7th September 1860.
Essapah	15th July 1844.	1st Feb. 1850.	30th Nov. 1855.	Succeeded Shaik Adam as Subadar-Major. Pensioned on Rs. 40 *per mensem*, and the staff allowance of his rank, on the 14th March 1862.
Soobiah	26th Nov. 1844.	26th Oct. 1851.	..	Pensioned on Rs. 25 *per mensem* on the 27th June 1854.
Palanyandy	2nd May 1845.	7th Jan. 1854.	..	Pensioned on Rs. 40 *per mensem* on 6th May 1859.
Shekh Homed	24th Oct. 1845.	22nd June 1855.	..	Pensioned on Rs. 40 *per mensem* on the 21st January 1859.
Syed Peer	19th Mar. 1847.	27th June 1854.	..	Pensioned on Rs. 40 *per mensem*, 14th Mar. 1862.
Mahomed Saib	12th Sep. 1847.	27th June 1854.	..	Pensioned on half pay on the 7th September 1860.
Shekh Russool	24th Dec. 1847.	?	..	Left in 1849 or 1850.
Mahomed Esuff	24th Dec. 1847.	?	..	*Jemadar Adjutant*, 1849. Left about 1850.
Mootoosamy	20th Oct. 1848.	3rd July 1855.	..	No record.
Kassim Khan	11th Jan. 1850.	28th Nov. 1855.	..	Pensioned on half pay, 6th April 1863.
Mahomed Yacoob	1st Feb. 1850.	30th Nov. 1855.	..	Pensioned on half pay, 14th March 1862.
Nursing Bawn	26th Oct. 1851.	..	..	..

Name.	Jemadar.	Subadar.	Subadar-Major.	Remarks.
Sheikh Sillamon	28th July 1853.	17th April 1857.	14th Mar. 1862.	*Jemadar Adjutant*, 1855. Pensioned on Rs. 40 *per mensem*, 1st Dec. 1868 and was succeeded as Subadar-Major by Abdul Wahab. Became Subadar in the 2nd Extra Regt. N. I.
Sayannah	7th Jan. 1854.	1st Aug. 1857.	..	Pensioned on Rs. 25 *per mensem*, 6th April 1863.
Mahomed Ugber	27th June 1854.	21st Jan. 1859.	..	Pensioned on Rs. 25 *per mensem*, 7th June 1864.
Mahomed Sallar	27th June 1854	..	..	..
Tautiah	19th Dec. 1854.	6th May. 1859.	..	Pensioned on Rs. 25 *per mensem*, 14th March 1862.
Abdul Wahab	29th Dec. 1854.	7th Sept. 1860.	1st Dec. 1868	Pensioned on Rs. 40 *per mensem*, 21st December 1874, and was succeeded as Subadar-Major by Shaik Booden.
Mahomed Eusoff	22nd June 1855.	7th Sept. 1860.	..	Pensioned on Rs. 40 *per mensem*, 25th Mar. 1862.
Gassee Ram	3rd July 1855.	14th Mar. 1862.	..	Pensioned on Rs. 25 *per mensem*, 7th June 1864.
Noor Khan	28th Nov. 1855.	14th Mar. 1862.	..	Pensioned on Rs. 25 *per mensem*, 20th December 1867.
Errah Sing	30th Nov. 1855.	25th Mar. 1862.	..	*Jemadar Adjutant*, 1859. Pensioned on Rs. 40 *per mensem*, 21st December 1874.
Fakeer Odeen	23rd Dec. 1856.	6th April 1863.	..	Pensioned on Rs. 25 *per mensem*, 7th June 1864.
Nagapah	17th April 1857.	?	..	Pensioned on half pay, 18th November 1861.
Gholam Mohideen	1st Aug. 1857.	?	..	Pensioned on half pay, 14th March 1862. (Was Jemadar in 2nd Extra Regt. N. I.)
Shaik Booden, *Sirdar Bahadur*	6th Jan. 1857.	7th Mar. 1862.	21st Dec. 1874.	Transferred from the disbanded 52nd N. I. in August 1862. *Order of British India, 2nd Class, 1877, 1st Class, 1878.* Pensioned on Rs. 50 *per mensem*, 1st September 1878, and was succeeded by Mohideen Khan.

Name.	Jemadar.	Subadar.	Subadar-Major.	Remarks.
Hoosain Khan	?	15th May 1862.	..	Transferred from the 52nd N. I. in August 1862. Pensioned on Rs. 40 *per mensem* on the 1st March 1876.
Shaikh Homed	?	?	..	Pensioned on Rs. 12-4-0 *per mensem*, 7th June 1864.
Rutten Singh	21st Jan. 1859.	?	..	Pensioned on Rs. 12-4-0 *per mensem*, 7th June 1864.
Shaikh Bram	7th Sept. 1860.	7th June 1864.	..	Pensioned on Rs. 25 *per mensem*, 20th December 1867.
Coopoosawmy	7th Sept. 1860.	7th June 1864.	..	Pensioned on Rs. 40 *per mensem*, 1st August 1872.
Mohideen Khan, *Bahadur*	7th Mar. 1862.	20th Dec. 1867.	1st Sept. 1878.	Transferred from the 52nd N. I. in 1862, *Order of British India, 2nd Class*, 1881. Pensioned, 1883, and succeeded by Gopalsamy.
Narainsamy	7th June 1864.	21st Dec. 1874.	..	Pensioned on Rs. 50 *per mensem*, 1st September 1878.
Meer Hoosain	7th June 1864.	?	..	Not traced.
Rungiah	25th Mar. 1862.	1st Dec. 1868.	..	*Jemadar Adjutant*, 1862, Pensioned on Rs. 25 *per mensem*, 20th May 1875.
Coopiah	20th Dec. 1867.	21st Dec. 1874.	..	Pensioned on Rs. 50 *per mensem*, 1st September 1878.
Shaikh Survur	14th Apr. 1862.	1st Aug. 1872.	..	Transferred from the 52nd N. I. in 1862. Pensioned on Rs. 25 *per mensem*, 20th May 1875.
Abdul Rhyman	15th May 1862.	20th May 1875.	..	Transferred from the 52nd N. I. in 1862. Pensioned in 1879.
Verdiah	14th Mar. 1862.	20th Dec. 1867.	..	Pensioned on Rs. 40 *per mensem*, 12th January 1877.
Mahomed Oosman	25th Mar. 1862.	..	..	Pensioned on Rs. 20 *per mensem*, on the 1st August 1872.
Condiah	20th Dec. 1867.	20th May 1875.	..	Left in 1878.

Name	Jemadar.	Subadar.	Subadar-Major.	Remarks.
Govindoo	1st Dec. 1868.	1st Mar. 1876.	..	Left in 1879.
Syed Khader *Bahadur.*	6th Oct. 1869.	1st Feb. 1877.	..	*Order of British India 2nd Class, 21st July 1880.* Left in 1881.
Mahomed Kasim	1st Aug. 1872.	1st Sept. 1878.	..	Left in 1882.
Ramasawmy	1st Aug. 1872.	..	..	Pensioned on Rs. 25 *per mensem,* 10th October 1878.
Venketsamy	21st Dec. 1874.	1st Sept. 1878.	..	*Jemadar-Adjutant, 1878.* Left in 1881.
Mootoosamy	21st Dec. 1874.	1st Sep. 1878.	..	Left in 1883.
Adam Sherif	20th May 1875.	21st Oct. 1878.	..	Died on Sind-Peshin Railway Work, 1886.
Veeragaloo	20th May 1875.	20th Sept. 1879.	..	Left in 1880.
Mahomed Kassim	1st Mar. 1876.	..	..	Left in 1881.
Mahalingum	1st Feb. 1877.	..	..	Left in 1883.
Narain Singh	1st Sept. 1878.	20th Sept. 1879.	..	Left in 1883.
Mohideen Sheriff	1st Sept. 1878.	11th Dec. 1880.	..	Pensioned, in 1885.
Gopalasamy, *Bahadur.*	1st Sept. 1878.	1st May 1881.	21st Sept. 1883.	*Jemadar-Adjutant 1878-1881. Order of British India, 2nd Class 31st October 1883.* Pensioned, 20th January 1886.
Rangasamy	10th Oct. 1878.	..	..	Left in 1881.
Abdul Nubbee	21st Oct. 1878.	1st Nov. 1881.	..	Pensioned, 26th December 1885.
Mootoo Kistnah	20th Sept. 1879.	16th Jan. 1882.	..	Left in 1883.
Syed Adam	20th Sept. 1879.	25th Jan. 1883.	..	*Acting Jemadar-Adjutant. 1881-83.* Pensioned, 1886.

General Burton, in "*An Indian Olio*", makes the following mention of this officer:— "The next march onward is Kundy (in the Deccan), where is the very best of snipe-shooting. The people of this place are very uncivil and troublesome; and on one occasion, when a friend of mine was staying in the public bungalow, they came down upon him and attacked him and his people, amomg whom were a native Corporal and two men of my regiment (4th Pioneers), whom I had lent to him to help him in his shikar. The Naigue afterwards Subadar Syed Adam, and his two men behaved exceedingly well, and though severely handled, drove the villagers off and saved my friend, who was also taking his own part in the row, from probably a savage beating. The villagers were heavily punished by Sir Salar Jung, and I promoted Syed Adam to the rank of Havildar. He was, and I doubt not still is, a good specimen of a Mahomedan native soldier, and well deserved the commission which he afterwards obtained."

Name.	Jemadar.	Subadar.	Subadar-Major.	Remarks.
Mahomed Yacoob	11th Dec. 1880.	..	..	Left in 1884.
Appow	1st May 1881.	..	..	Left in 1884.
Abdul Khader	11th Sept. 1881.	11th July 1883.	..	Pensioned, 1886.
Gassi Ram	21st Oct. 1881	..	..	Pensioned, 1888.
Tiroovengadam, *Bahadur*	1st Nov. 1881.	21st Sept. 1883.	..	*Order of British India, 2nd Class, 29th May 1887.* 'Pensioned', 1889
Mahomed Beg, *Sirdar Bahadur*	16th Jan. 1822.	21st Sept. 1883.	21st Jan. 1886.	*Order of British India, 2nd Class, 8th May 1886.* *Order of British India, 1st Class, 1887.* 'Pensioned', 19th Nov. 1890.
Timmayya, *Bahadur*	25th Jan. 1883.	10th Feb. 1885.	..	*Order of British India, 2nd Class, 1st July 1886.* 'Pensioned', 10th February (?) 1888.
Gholam Hoosain	11th July 1883.	26th Dec. 1885.	..	Pensioned, 1888.
Mahomed Uqber	7th Aug. 1883.	21st Jan. 1886.	..	Pensioned, 1891.
Shaikh Homed	21st Sept. 1883.	..	..	*Jemadar-Adjutant* 1884—1886. Died on Sind-Peshin Railway Work, 1886.
Sungalee	21st Sept. 1883.	25th Jan. 1886.	20th Nov. 1890.	Succeeded Mahomed Beg as Subadar-Major. Pensioned, 1892.
Ramasamy, *Bahadur*	22nd Feb. 1884.	1st Mar. 1886.	..	*Order of British India, 2nd Class, 28th March 1891.* Pensioned, 1893.
Syed Khader	21st June 1884.	26th Oct. 1886.	...	Pensioned, 5th December 1889.
Francis	10th Feb. 1885.	..	..	Pensioned, 1887,
Abdul Rhymon	26th Dec. 1885.	11th Feb. 1888	..	Pensioned, 1891.
Mahomed Salar, *Sirdar Bahadur*	21st Jan. 1886.	26th Dec. 1888.	16th Aug. 1892.	*Jemadar-Adjutant, 1886—88. Order of British India, 2nd Class, 2nd June 1893, Order of British India, 1st Class, 1897.* Pensioned, 1899.

The following extract from the "*Madras Mail*", dated 30th March 1903 gives some particulars of his services:—

The 4th Madras Pioneers—Death of a Worthy Native Officer.—We regret to announce the death at Trichinopoly on the 27th instant of Honorary Captain Muhammad Salar, Sirdar Bahadur, late 4th Madras Pioneers. The deceased was a very distinguished officer, who throughout his service had filled every post of distinction and trust that it was possible for him to hold in the regiment with conspicuous success and to the entire satisfaction of every Commanding Officer under whom he served. His record shows 32 years with an exemplary and unblemished character and he well earned the distinction of the 1st Class Order of British India, the promotion to Honorary Captain on retirement, and a Jagir for his distinguished services. Throughout his long service he only spent 8 months on leave and 18 days in hospital. His ancestors have served in his late regiment since it was raised in 1759. His field and War Services include Afghanistan, 1879—80, Chin Hills, 1890—92, and Pioneer work all over India. His unfailing resource and steady perseverance were a brilliant example to all ranks and his unexpected death at the comparatively early age of 53 comes as a blow to his old regiment in which he was beloved by all."

As mentioned above, he was granted the rank of Honorary Captain on retirement (London Gazette, dated 7th December 1898) and he was also granted a Jaghir (23rd November 1901) value Rs. 400 *per annum*.

Reference to him will be found in Part V. of these records (1897—98).

Name.	Jemadar.	Subadar.	Subadar-Major.	Remarks.
Mootoosamy	24th Jan. 1886.	..	..	Struck off in 1889.
Abdul Sattar Khan.	25th Jan. 1886.	..	..	Was shot dead by a Sepoy on the glacis of Fort St. George, while en route to the Chin Hills, in November 1890.
Abdul Rahim, Sirdar Bahadur	1st Mar. 1888.	6th Dec. 1889.	1899	Jemadar-Adjutant 1888-1889. Order of British India, 2nd Class, 1892. Order of British India, 1st Class, 1895. Died while still serving, in 1899, just after he became Subadar-Major.

This officer was mentioned for good service in the Chin Hills in 1890—91, and with the Kanhaw Column in 1882, the Commanding Officer of the latter remarking:—

"I cannot speak too highly of this Native Officer's good work. His unflagging energy and unfailing resource have been conspicuous, and I would beg that his good work be recommended for suitable recognition." And again, in connection with the affair at Botaung:—" I would again specially bring to notice the valuable services of Subadar Abdul Rahim, 4th Madras Pioneers. It is due to this Native Officer's skill and energy that the raft by which the Botang garrison was brought across the dangerous Manipur river was made and worked. His coolness under fire and his capacity for work have been of the greatest use to me."

General Order by the Government of India, dated 14th October 1892:—

No. 922, The Governor-General in Council is pleased to sanction the admission to the order of British India, as supernumeraries on the Madras list, until absorbed by the occurrence of vacancies, of the undermentioned Native Officers, in recognition of the good service rendered by them during the recent operations in Burma and the Chin Hills............ Madras.

To the 2nd class, with the title of "*Bahadur*."
Subadar Abdul Rahim, 4th Regiment of Madras Infantry (Pioneers).
Jamadar Abdullah Khan,   do.   (*vide below*).

This Officer was subsequently awarded an assignment of land revenue of Rs. 250 *per annum* from land in Vellore, North Arcot district. (30th December 1897).

Name.	Jemadar.	Subadar.	Subadar-Major.	Remarks.
Moonisamy.	26th Oct. 1886.	..	..	Pensioned in 1892.
Peddanah.	1st June 1887.	20th Nov. 1890.	..	Pensioned in 1893.

This officer was a son of Subadar Seetiah of the 4th.

Name.	Jemadar.	Subadar.	Subadar-Major.	Remarks.
Abdul Sherif.	11th Feb. 1888.	..	..	Pensioned in 1893.
Moonisamy.	15th Feb. 1888.	25th Nov. 1890.	..	Pensioned in 1892.
Abdul Aziz.	26th Dec. 1888.	28th Oct. 1891.	..	Pensioned in 1895.
Mir Abbas, *Bahadur*	16th June 1889.	28th Oct. 1891.	21st May 1899.	Jemadar Adjutant, 1889-1891. *Order of British India, 2nd Class,* 1901. Pensioned in 1907.

This officer was specially promoted to Jemadar for good service on the Lushai Expedition in 1889. In 1903, he was selected as Orderly Officer to His Majesty King Edward VII, and proceeded to England with the first contingent of King's Orderly Officers. On the 18th July 1903, he was presented with the Royal Victorian Medal by H. M. the King in person. During the Great War (1914-18), he did excellent service as an Assistant Recruiting Officer. He died at Trichinopoly in August 1924.

A fine portrait of him, painted by Mr. G. Spencer Watson (now A. R. A.) and presented by him to the Officers of the regiment, hangs in the Officers' Mess.

Name.	Jemadar.	Subadar.	Subadar-Major.	Remarks.
Abdullah Khan, *Sirdar Bahadur*	26th Nov. 1889.	16th Aug. 1892.	..	Jemadar Adjutant. 1891-1892. *Order of British India, 2nd Class,* 1892. *Order of British India, 1st Class,* 1897. Pensioned in 1905.

This officer was mentioned by Colonel Mainwaring, Commanding Southern Chin Hills, for specially good service in the Chin Hills in 1890-91, and by Generals Palmer and Stewart, C. B., for good service with the Newengal-Lushai Column in 1892. Captain Rose, commanding the latter column, wrote as follows in his report:—"Jemadar Abdullah Khan, IV Pioneers, is a most hard working, intelligent Native officer, who throughout did most excellent work." While to Captain Stevens he wrote:—"I should be glad if you would let your Colonel know the excellent work done by Jemadar Abdullah Khan and the men of his column on detachment with me: they worked most splendidly under very trying circumstances, and I never heard a complaint from start to finish." He died in Madras, shortly after retiring on pension. (For the order granting him the Order of British India, *vide* Subadar Abdul Rahim).

Name.	Jemadar.	Subadar.	Subadar-Major.	Remarks.
Solapuri	6th Dec. 1889.	1st Mar. 1893.	1907.	Pensioned in 1908.

This officer was a very fine rifle and revolver shot, and his name will be found on most of the musketry cups in the Officers' Mess. He died in October 1922.

Name.	Jemadar.	Subadar.	Subadar-Major.	Remarks.
Venkatachellam ..	20th Nov. 1890.	1st Dec. 1903.	..	*Acting Jemadar-Adjutant, 1893-95.* Pensioned in 1908.

This Officer proceeded to Australia with the Indian Army Contingent in 1900-01, to take part in the Australian Jubilee celebrations.

Sulaimon Sharif ..	25th Nov. 1890.	..	..	*Jemadar-Adjutant 1891.* Pensioned in 1893.
Ramasamy ..	28th Oct. 1891.	1st Feb. 1894.	..	Not traced.
Streeramooloo ..	28th Oct. 1891.	..	..	Pensioned in 1899.

This officer was granted a wound pension, his eye having been injured with a piece of bullet, while he was on duty in the butts.

Harichandra Rao ..	26th July 1892.	1st Jan. 1895	..	Pensioned in 1907.

The promotion of this officer to Jemadar was specially sanctioned by H. E. The Commander-in-Chief for good service in the Chin Hills.

Saiyid Abdullah ..	16th Aug. 1892.	..	..	Pensioned in 1896.

The promotion of this officer to Jemadar was also specially sanctioned as above.

Varadarajulu ..	1st Sept. 1892.	26th Jan. 1899.	..	*Jemadar-Adjutant, 1897-99.*

This officer served in China with the 1st Madras Pioneers in 1900-01. I have been unable to trace what became of him.

Abdul Aziz ..	1st Mar. 1893.	21st May 1899.	..	Died on sick leave in 1900.
Gurappa ..	1st Dec. 1893.	10th July 1900.	..	Pensioned in 1903. Died about 1907.
David ..	1st Feb. 1894.	..	..	Pensioned in 1902.
Rangayya ..	1st Mar. 1894.	..	..	*Offg. Jemadar-Adjutant, 1895-97.* Discharged by Sentence of a General Court-Martial in 1897.
Dharmayya ..	1st Jan. 1895.	..	..	Pensioned in 1902.
Sayyid Abbas, *Bahadur* ..	1st Jan. 1896.	1st Jan. 1904.	19th Nov. 1908.	*Jemadar-Adjutant, 1899-1904.* Order of British India, 2nd Class, 1911. Pensioned in 1911.

This officer did excellent service as an Assistant Recruiting Officer during the Great War (1914—18).

Name.	Jemadar.	Subadar.	Subadar-Major.	Remarks.
Muniratnam	6th April 1897	1st Jan. 1904.	..	Pensioned in 1907.

This officer served in China (1900-01) with the 1st Madras Pioneers. During the Great War (1914—18), he rejoined the Army and did good service as Subadar of a Labour Corps.

Name	Jemadar	Subadar	Subadar-Major	Remarks
Shaikh Amin	26th Jan. 1899.	18th Jan. 1904.	27th Mar. 1912.	Pensioned on the 15th May 1914.

This officer was specially promoted to Havildar for good service in the Chin Hills. He was a fine shot, and his name appears on most of the musketry cups in the Officers' Mess. During the Great War (1914—18), he joined the regimental depot at Bangalore for duty.

Name	Jemadar	Subadar	Subadar-Major	Remarks
Ramasami	2nd Mar. 1899.	..	..	Struck off in 1902.
Muhammad Yusuf	21st May. 1899.	16th April 1906.	..	Pensioned in 1909.
Venkatasami	10th July 1900.	7th June 1906.	..	*Jemadar-Adjutant*, 1904-7. Pensioned in November 1913. Died in 1921.
Srinavasulu	10th July 1900.	..	..	Died, while serving with the regiment, at Bangalore in 1904.
Sivaprasad Pande	22nd July 1902.	..	..	Pensioned in 1907. Died in 1923.

This officer was the only Brahmin officer on record as serving with the regiment.

Name	Jemadar	Subadar	Subadar-Major	Remarks
Krishnasami, *Bahadur*	8th Oct. 1902.	26th July 1907.	15th May 1914.	Order of British India, 2nd Class, 1917. Pensioned on the 11th January 1920.

This officer was transferred to the IV Pioneers from the Queen's Own Sappers and Miners in 1902. He was Subadar-Major of the regiment throughout the operations in which it was engaged during the Great War (1914—18), being awarded the Order of British India, 2nd Class, for distinguished conduct in the field. He was promoted to the rank of Honorary Lieutenant on the 1st July 1920.

Name	Jemadar	Subadar	Subadar-Major	Remarks
Muhammad Sikandar	1st Jan. 1904.	1st Nov. 1907.	..	*Offg. Jemadar-Adjutant*, 1907. Pensioned in 1915.

This officer served with the regiment in the operations in the Kachin Hills.

Name	Jemadar	Subadar	Subadar-Major	Remarks
Francis	1st Jan. 1904.	26th May 1908.	..	Pensioned in 1914.
Audinarayanasami	18th Jan. 1904.	19th Nov. 1908.	..	*Jemadar-Adjutant*, 1908-1909. Pensioned in 1912.

Name.	Jemadar.	Subadar.	Subadar-Major.	Remarks.
Kuppusami	5th July 1904.	..	..	Pensioned in 1908.
Saiyid Munawar	16th April 1906.	1st Oct. 1909.	..	Pensioned on the 5th February 1917.

This officer served with the regiment in the operations in the Kachin Hills, and during the campaign in Mesopotamia till the end of 1916.

Name.	Jemadar.	Subadar.	Subadar-Major.	Remarks.
Abdul Latif	7th July 1906.	..	..	Pensioned in 1910.
Muttukaruppan	25th July 1907.	..	..	Pensioned in 1911.
Anantadri Nayudu.	25th July 1907.	2nd Mar. 1912.	..	*Jemadar Adjutant* 1909—1912. Pensioned on the 15th November 1920.

This officer served with the regiment in the operations in the Kachin Hills, and during the campaign in Mesopotamia till the end of 1916, after which he rendered excellent service at the regimental depot. He was promoted to the rank of Honorary Lieutenant on the 1st July 1920.

Name.	Jemadar.	Subadar.	Subadar-Major.	Remarks.
Subrahmani	1st Nov. 1907.	..	..	Pensioned in 1909.

This officer served with a Labour Corps in Mesopotamia during the Great War, and retired with the rank of Subadar.

Name.	Jemadar.	Subadar.	Subadar-Major.	Remarks.
Munisami	17th Mar. 1908.	..	..	Pensioned in 1912.
Nanjappa, *Bahadur*.	26th May 1908.	27th Mar. 1912.	15th Nov. 1920.	*Order of British India, 2nd Class,* 1918. Pensioned on the 1st Nov. 1922.

This officer served with the regiment in the operations in the Kachin Hills, and during the campaign in Mesopotamia, being mentioned in despatches and awarded the Order of British India, 2nd Class, for devotion to duty in the field. In 1922, he was selected to proceed to England as one of the Indian Orderly Officers to H. M. King George V, and received the Royal Victorian Medal. This was the second occasion on which an officer of the regiment was selected for this honour. For some years past he has been nominated by His Excellency the Governor of Madras to membership of the Madras Legislative Council.

Name.	Jemadar.	Subadar.	Subadar-Major.	Remarks.
Narayanasami (I), *Bahadur*	19th Nov. 1908.	13th Dec. 1913.	1st Nov. 1922.	*Jemadar Adjutant*, 1912-14. *Order of British India, 2nd Class,* 1919. Pensioned on the 1st January 1925.

This officer was a remarkably fine shot and from the beginning of his service up to the date of his retirement was in practically every regimental rifle and revolver team. He proceeded to England in 1911, to represent the regiment at the Coronation of H. M. King George V, and was granted the Coronation Medal. He served with the regiment in the operations in the Kachin Hills, and throughout the campaigns in Mesopotamia and Persia, being mentioned in despatches and awarded the Order of British India, 2nd Class, for devotion to duty. He was in Malabar for a short time, on inspection duty, in 1921, and served with the regiment in Waziristan in 1923-24. I may add that he has since (in 1931) been granted a jagir award of Rs. 600 *per annum*, for three lives, in recognition of his good work while serving in the Army.

Name.	Jemadar.	Subadar.	Subadar-Major.	Remarks.
Sayyid Saduddin	1st Oct. 1909	..	..	Died while serving with the regiment, in 1912.
Musa Raza Khan	10th Dec. 1909	1st June 1915	..	*Jemadar Adjutant,* 1914-15.

This officer is served with the regiment throughout the operations in which it took part during the Great War till the 2nd February 1917, when he was killed in action near the River Hai, in Mesopotamia.

Durgayya, *Bahadur.*	28th May 1910.	4th May 1914	..	Order of British India, 2nd Class, 1919. Pensioned on the 1st Feb. 1920.

This officer served with the regiment in the operations in the Kachin Hills, and during the campaigns in Mesopotamia and Persia, being mentioned in despatches, and awarded the Order of British India, 2nd Class, for devotion to duty.

Narayanasami (II)	5th April 1911.	15th May 1914.	..	Pensioned on the 19th November 1920, and died a few days later.

This officer served with the regiment in the operations in the Kachin Hills and during the campaigns in Mesopotamia and Persia, where he was mentioned in despatches (in 1918) as specially deserving of mention.

Krishnamurti	2nd Mar. 1912.	8th Aug. 1916.	..	*Jemadar Adjutant,* 1915-16. Pensioned in 1919.

This officer served with the regiment in the operations in the Kachin Hills and during the campaign in Mesopotamia and in Persia.

Anthony David, I. D. S. M.	13th July 1911,	17th Feb. 1918.	..	Pensioned on the 1st January 1925.

This officer joined the regiment at Jhansi from the 81st Pioneers, on mobilisation for Mesopotamia in 1916, and served with it continuously thereafter. He was mentioned in despatches in 1918, and awarded the I. D. S. M. for devotion to duty in the field.

Muthuvelu	27th Mar. 1912.	8th April 1917.	..	Pensioned on the 9th October 1921.

This officer served with the 1/61st (K. G. O.) Pioneers in East Africa from 1915 to 1919 and subsequently rejoined the regiment in Mesopotamia in 1920.

Thandavarayan	10th April 1912.	..	..	Died, while serving with the regiment, in the Kachin Hills in 1914.
Viraraghavelu, *Bahadur.*	1st Oct. 1912.	11th Feb. 1916.	..	Order of British India, 2nd Class, 1918. Pensioned on the 7th April 1921.

This officer served with the regiment in the operations in the Kachin Hills, and throughout the campaigns in Mesopotamia and Persia, being three times mentioned in despatches (in 1917, 1918 and 1919), and awarded the order of British India, 2nd class, for distinguished service in the field.

Name.	Jemadar.	Subadar.	Subadar-Major.	Remarks.
Gopalasami, I. D. S. M.	13th Dec. 1913.	8th April 1917.	..	Pensioned on the 23rd February 1921.

This officer served with the regiment in the operations in the Kachin Hills, and joined the 1/61st (K. G. O.) Pioneers in East Africa in 1915, where he was awarded the I. D. S. M. He rejoined the regiment in Persia in 1920.

Name.	Jemadar.	Subadar.	Subadar-Major.	Remarks.
Shamsuddin	4th May 1914.	19th May 1918.	..	Pensioned on the 8th October 1921.

This officer served with the regiment in the operations in the Kachin Hills, and throughout the campaigns in Mesopotamia and Persia.

Name.	Jemadar.	Subadar.	Subadar-Major.	Remarks.
Isvar Rao	15th May 1914.	..	..	

This officer was transferred on the 4th March 1918, as a Subadar, to the 2/81st Pioneers, then being raised by Lieutenant-Colonel R. Mackie of the 64th, previous to which he had been serving with the regimental depot.

Name.	Jemadar.	Subadar.	Subadar-Major.	Remarks.
Narayanasami (III).	18th Sept. 1914.	..	..	Died, while serving with the regiment at Thayetmyo, in 1915.
Abdul Aziz	1st June 1915.	..	..	Died on active service with the regiment in Mesopotamia, on the 16th November 1916.

This officer was a son of Subadar-Major Abdul Rahim, *Sirdar Bahadur*, of the 4th.

Name.	Jemadar.	Subadar.	Subadar-Major.	Remarks.
Gnanaprakasam	20th July 1915.	15th Nov. 1920.	..	Pensioned on the 16th November 1925, and died nine days later.

This officer served with the regiment in the operations in the Kachin Hills, and throughout the campaigns in Mesopotamia and Persia. He served with the Training Battalion from 1921 to 1923.

Name.	Jemadar.	Subadar.	Subadar-Major.	Remarks.
Punyakoti	11th Aug. 1915.	19th May 1918.	..	Pensioned on the 1st January 1921.

This officer served with the regiment in the operations in the Kachin Hills, and was then transferred to a Signal Company rejoining the regiment in 1916, for service in Mesopotamia. He was invalided in 1918, and spent the remainder of his service at the regimental depot.

Name.	Jemadar.	Subadar.	Subadar-Major.	Remarks.
Perumal Pillai	10th Oct. 1915.	..	..	Pensioned on the 30th June 1920

This officer was on recruiting duty for the regiment from 1915 to 1918, and was awarded a sword of honour for his services in this connection. He rejoined the regiment in Persia in 1919.

Name.	Jemadar.	Subadar.	Subadar-Major.	Remarks.
M. Anthony	11th Jan. 1916.	..	..	Died, while serving with the regiment in Mesopotamia, on the 18th May 1916.
Muhammad Abdul Karim	11th Feb. 1916.	19th Nov. 1920.	..	Pensioned on the 8th October 1921.

This officer served with the regiment in the operations in the Kachin Hills, and during the campaign in Mesopotamia subsequently serving at the regimental depot from 1917 to 1920, when he rejoined the regiment in Persia.

Name.	Jemadar.	Subadar.	Subadar-Major.	Remarks.
Dharmalingam	19th May 1916.	1st Jan. 1921.	..	*Indian Adjutant*, 1916-21. Pensioned on the 8th July 1925.

This officer served with the regiment in the operations in the Kachin Hills, and during the campaigns in Mesopotamia and Persia, being mentioned in despatches in 1918. He also saw service with the regiment in Malabar in 1921, and in Waziristan in 1923-24.

Name.	Jemadar.	Subadar.	Subadar-Major.	Remarks.
P. Narayanasami I.D.S.M.	9th Aug. 1916.	23rd Feb. 1921.	..	Pensioned on the 16th March 1924.

This officer served with the regiment in the operations in the Kachin Hills. He joined the regiment in Mesopotamia in November 1916, and remained with it till the end of the campaign, being mentioned in despatches and awarded the I.D.S.M. in 1917, for distinguished service in the field. He served with the regiment in Waziristan in 1923-24.

Name.	Jemadar.	Subadar.	Subadar-Major.	Remarks.
Narayanasami (IV)	9th Aug. 1916.	..	..	

This officer served with the regiment in the operations in the Kachin Hills, and was subsequently transferred, in August 1918, to the 2/80th Carnatic Infantry, then being raised.

Name.	Jemadar.	Subadar.	Subadar-Major.	Remarks.
Vadamalai	9th Aug. 1916.	..	..	Pensioned on the 20th February 1921.

This officer served with the regiment in the operations in the Kachin Hills, and throughout the campaigns in Mesopotamia and Persia.

Name.	Jemadar.	Subadar.	Subadar-Major.	Remarks.
Puniakoti Mudali	28th Sept. 1917.	..	..	Pensioned in 1921.

This officer served with the regiment in the operations in the Kachin Hills, and throughout the campaigns in Mesopotamia and Persia, being mentioned in despatches in 1918.

Name.	Jemadar.	Subadar.	Subadar-Major.	Remarks.
Balaraman	3rd Dec. 1917.	1st Nov. 1922.	..	Pensioned on the 1st October 1927.

This officer served with the regiment in the operations in the Kachin Hills, and throughout the campaigns in Mesopotamia and Persia, being mentioned in despatches in 1919. He also served with the regiment in Malabar in 1921, and in Waziristan in 1923-24.

Name.	Jemadar.	Subadar.	Subadar-Major.	Remarks.
Muhammad Hussain	1st Feb. 1918.	..	..	

This officer served with the regiment in the operations in the Kachin Hills, and proceeded to Mesopotamia with the regiment. He was invalided in August 1916, and joined the regimental depot, being transferred, as a Subadar, to the 2/81st Pioneers, then being raised, on the 10th March 1918.

Name.	Jemadar.	Subadar.	Subadar-Major.	Remarks.
Babu	1st Feb. 1918.	..	..	Pensioned on the 15th May 1920.

This officer served with the regiment in the operations in the Kachin Hills, and subsequently in Mesopotamia till 1917.

Name.	Jemadar.	Subadar.	Subadar-Major.	Remarks.
Balagurusami, I.D.S.M.	17th Feb. 1919.	8th Oct. 1921.	..	Pensioned on the 18th February 1926.

This officer served with the regiment in the operations in the Kachin Hills, and throughout the campaigns in Mesopotamia and Persia, being mentioned in despatches, and awarded the I. D. S. M., in 1919, for devotion to duty in the field. He also served with the regiment in Waziristan in 1923-24.

Name.	Jemadar.	Subadar.	Subadar-Major.	Remarks.
Ahmad Khan	20th Feb. 1918.	..	..	Pensioned on the 17th November 1920.

This officer served with the regiment in the campaign in Mesopotamia.

Name.	Jemadar.	Subadar.	Subadar-Major.	Remarks.
Sauriappan	1st April 1918.	..	..	Pensioned on the 20th July 1921.

This officer served with the regiment in the operations in the Kachin Hills, and with the regimental depot till 1919, when he was transferred to the 2/61st (K. G. O.) Pioneers.

Name.	Jemadar.	Subadar.	Subadar-Major.	Remarks.
Muhammad Burhan.	1st April 1918.	..	..	Pensioned on the 7th August 1921.

This officer served with the regiment in the operations in the Kachin Hills, and in the campaign in Mesopotamia till 1917, when he was transferred to the regimental depot.

Name.	Jemadar.	Subadar.	Subadar-Major.	Remarks.
Saurinayagam	1st Apr. 1918.	9th Oct. 1921.	..	Pensioned in 1925.

This officer served with the regiment in the operations in the Kachin Hills, and throughout the campaigns in Mesopotamia and Persia. He also served in Waziristan in 1923-24.

Name.	Jemadar.	Subadar.	Subadar-Major.	Remarks.
Shaikh Jamaludin	9th May 1918.	..	..	Pensioned on the 12th October 1921.

This officer served with the regiment in the operations in the Kachin Hills, and throughout the campaigns in Mesopotamia and Persia.

Name.	Jemadar.	Subadar.	Subadar-Major.	Remarks.
Narayanasami (V)	19th May 1918.	..	..	Pensioned in 1921.

This officer served with the regiment in the operations in the Kachin Hills and throughout the campaigns in Mesopotamia and Persia.

Arogyasami, I.D.S.M.	19th May 1918.	1st Jan. 1925.	21st Dec. 1927.	*Indian Quartermaster, 1922-25.*

This officer served with the regiment in the operations in the Kachin Hills, Mesopotamia and Persia, being mentioned in despatches in 1919, and awarded the I.D.S.M. for devotion to duty in the field. He also served with the regiment in Malabar in 1921, and in Waziristan in 1923-24.

Munisami (I)	1st June 1918.	..	..	Pensioned on the 16th December 1921.

This officer served with the regiment in the operations in the Kachin Hills, and in Mesopotamia till 1917, when he was transferred to the depot, rejoining the regiment in Persia in 1919.

Ramasami	1st June 1918.	..	..	Died at the regimental depot on the 23rd September 1918.

This officer served with the regiment in the operations in Kachin Hills, and with the 1/61st (K. G. O.) Pioneers in East Africa from 1915, rejoining the depot in 1917.

Chinnappan	1st Aug. 1918.	..	..	Pensioned on the 16th October 1921.

This officer served with the regiment in the operations in the Kachin Hills and subsequently at the depot. He was with the regiment in Persia for a short time in 1920.

Tirumalai	1st Sep. 1918.	..	..	Pensioned on the 20th July 1921.

This officer served with the regiment in the operations in the Kachin Hills, and subsequently at the depot. From 1919 to 1921, he served with the 2/61st (K.G.O.) Pioneers.

Balasundaram	5th Sep. 1918.	16th Mar. 1924	16th July 1927.	*Indian Adjutant 1920-24.*

This officer joined the regiment as Schoolmaster on the 22nd June 1912, and subsequently joined the combatant ranks. He served in the operations in the Kachin Hills, and then at the depot till 1919, when he was attached to the 1/61st (K.G.O.) Pioneers, rejoining the regiment in Persia in 1920. He served in Waziristan in 1923-24. On the 21st December 1927, he was seconded to the Cantonment Department.

Munisami (II)	23rd July 1919.	..	..	Pensioned on the 3rd November, 1927.

This officer served with the regiment in the operations in the Kachin Hills, Mesopotamia and Persia, being twice mentioned in despatches in 1919.

Name.	Jemadar.	Subadar.	Subadar-Major.	Remarks.
Ramannah	26th May 1918.	..	..	Pensioned on the 1st April 1929.

This officer served in Mesopotamia with the 83rd Wallajahbad Light Infantry from 1918 to 1920, and was transferred to the 64th on the 1st October 1921. He served with the regiment in Waziristan in 1923-24.

Govindasami	5th June 1919.	8th July 1925.	..	*Indian Adjutant, 1924-25.*

This officer served during the Great War at the depot of the 2/81st Pioneers. He joined the 2/1st from the Training Battalion in 1922, and served with the regiment in Waziristan in 1923-24.

Arunachalam, I.D.S.M.	19th Oct. 1920.	..	..	Pensioned on the 9th August 1927.

This officer served with the regiment in the operations in the Kachin Hills, Mesopotamia and Persia, being awarded the I.D.S.M. for distinguished conduct in the field. He also served with the regiment in Malabar in 1921, and Waziristan in 1923-24.

Ayyalu Naidu	20th Feb. 1921.	..	..	Pensioned on the 1st July, 1927.

This officer served with the regiment in the operations in the Kachin Hills, Mesopotamia and Persia.

Sangili (I)	1st Apr. 1921.	16th Nov. 1925.	..	Pensioned on the 10th May 1930.

This officer served with the regiment in the operations in the Kachin Hills, and in Mesopotamia and Persia till 1920, when he was transferred to the depot. He was mentioned in despatches, and awarded the M. S. M. in 1918, for meritorious service in the field.

Kadirvelu	16th Jan. 1922.	..	..	

This officer served with the regiment in the operations in the Kachin Hills, Mesopotamia, Persia and Waziristan.

Muhammad Jaffar Hussain.	18th Apr. 1922.	..	..	Pensioned in 1926.

This officer enlisted originally as a Schoolmaster and on the formation of the Indian Army Educational Corps, became the first Education Jemadar to serve with the regiment. He was present during the operations in the Kachin Hills.

Parthasaradi	1st Nov. 1922.	..	..	Invalided on the 1st May 1923.

This officer served with the regiment in the operations in the Kachin Hills, Mesopotamia and Persia.

Ramasami	1st May 1923.	18th Feb. 1926.	..	*Indian Quartermaster,* 1925.

This officer served with the regiment in the operations in the Kachin Hills, Mesopotamia and Persia and Waziristan in 1923-24

Name.	Jemadar.	Subadar.	Subadar-Major.	Remarks.
Virabhadra Goundan.	16th Mar. 1924.	1st Oct. 1927..	..	*Indian Adjutant*, 10/1st M. Prs., 1927.

This officer served with the regiment in Mesopotamia in 1916. and subsequently with the 2/81st Pioneers on the North-West Frontier in 1919.

Ramachandra Rao.	2nd July 1924.	..	..	*Indian Adjutant*, 1924-27.

This officer was transferred to the regiment on the 1st October 1921, from the 83rd Wallajahbad Light Infantry, with which regiment he served in Mesopotamia and Persia in 1918—20.

Tambusami, I.D.S.M.	18th May 1917.	19th Aug. 1920.	1st Jan. 1925..	Pensioned on the 16th July 1927.

This officer was transferred to the regiment, as Subadar-Major, from the 1/61st (K. G. O.) Pioneers, with which regiment he had served throughout the campaign in East Africa, and subsequently on the North-West Frontier. He was awarded the I. D. S. M. for distinguished service in East Africa.

Periyasami	..	1st Jan. 1925.	16th July 1927.	..	*Indian Quartermaster*, 1926-27.

This officer served with the regiment in the operations in the Kachin Hills, and in Mesopotamia, and Persia from 1917 till the regiment returned to India.

Francis	..	3rd June 1925.	..	..	*Indian Adjutant*, 1927-28.

This officer served with the regiment in the operations in the Kachin Hills, and with the 1/61st (K.G.O.) Pioneers in East Africa from 1915 to 1918, when he rejoined the regimental depot.

Loganathan	..	8th July 1925.	..	..	*Indian Quartermaster*, 1927-29.

This officer served with the 1/81st Pioneers on the North-West Frontier from 1915 to 1918, and at Bushire in 1919-20, being transferred to the regiment from the Training Battalion in 1924.

John Sandon	..	1st Sept. 1920.	16th Aug. 1925.	..	*Indian Quartermaster*, 81st Pioneers, 1921.

This officer was transferred to the regiment from the Training Battalion on the 16th August 1925. He served with the 81st Pioneers on the Mari Expedition of 1918, with the Bushire Field Force, 1918-19, and on the North-West Frontier (Afghanistan), 1919-20. He was awarded the M.S.M. at Bushire in 1919, and mentioned in despatches in 1920.

Kumarasami	..	18th Feb. 1926.	..	..	..

This officer served with the regiment in the operations in the Kachin Hills, and in Mesopotamia, Persia and Waziristan.

Name.	Jemadar.	Subadar.	Subadar-Major.	Remarks.
Sangili (II)	15th Oct. 1926.	..	..	*Educational Jemadar, 1926-30. Indian Adjutant 1929-30.*

This officer served in Waziristan from 1919 to 1921 with the 2/61st (K. G. O.) Pioneers, and with the regiment in Malabar in 1921.

Doraisami	1st July 1927.	..	..	

This officer served with the regiment in the operation in the Kachin Hills, in Mesopotamia from 1916 to 1917, and on the North-West Frontier (Afghanistan) with the 61st (K. G. O.) Pioneers in 1919. He served with the regiment in Persia in 1920-21.

Ondimuthu	16th July 1927.	..	..	

This officer served with the regiment in the operations in the Kachin Hills, in Mesopotamia in 1916, and in Waziristan in 1923-24. He is a son of Jemadar Muttukaruppan of the 64th.

Ersu Nukayya	14th Feb. 1918.	15th April 1920.	..	

This officer was transferred to the regiment, as a Subadar, on the 21st December 1927 from the 1/3rd Madras Regiment, on the disbandment of that unit. He served in Waziristan from 1921 to 1923.

Arogyasami	9th Aug. 1927.	..	..	*Indian Adjutant 1928.*

This officer served with the regiment in the operations in the Kachin Hills, in Mesopotamia in 1916, in Persia in 1920, and in Waziristan in 1923-24.

Sangili (III)	1st Oct. 1927.	..	..	*Indian Adjutant and Educational Jemadar 1930.*

This officer served with the regiment in the operations in the Kachin Hills, in Mesopotamia and Persia, and in Malabar in 1921.

Alagirisami	3rd Nov. 1927.	..	..	Pensioned on the 1st January 1929.

This officer was transferred to the regiment from the Training Battalion on the 15th December 1923. He served with the 81st Pioneers on the Rustum Field Force in 1915, the Mari Punitive Force in 1918, the Bushire Field Force in 1918-19 and on the North-West Frontier (Afghanistan) in 1919-20.

Munisami, I.D.S.M.	18th July 1928.	..	..	

This officer served with the regiment in the Kachin Hills, and in Mesopotamia till 1919, also in Malabar in 1921. He was awarded the I. D. S. M. in 1919, and in 1922 proceeded to England as orderly to Subadar-Major Nanjappa, *Bahadur.*

Jagannathan, I.D.S.M.	1st July 1918.	19th May 1923.	..	*Indian Adjutant, 1st (K.G.O.) Pioneers 1920.*

This officer was transferred to the regiment from the 1st (K. G. O.) Battalion, Madras Pioneers, on the 9th July 1930. He served with the 61st (K. G. O.) Pioneers in East Africa in 1914—17, being awarded the I. D. S. M., and twice mentioned in despatches; on the North-West Frontier (Afghanistan) in 1919-20; and in Waziristan in 1922-23 and 1924-25.

Part V.

PIONEER WORK.

1883—1930.

Note.

This part of the records aims at giving a summary of the Pioneer Work carried out by the regiment from the year 1883, when it became a Pioneer battalion, to the year 1930, and forms an *addendum* to Part I. By "Pioneer Work" is meant principally work carried out in peace-time, by contract or otherwise, with a view to giving all ranks practice in performing the duties they will be called upon to carry out on field service, while at the same time enabling the men to earn working-pay, to the benefit of recruiting.

While the facts and figures given here can scarcely be expected to appeal to the ordinary reader, it is hoped that they will be of value to the future officers of the regiment.

1883.

The question as to the formation of the Madras Pioneer battalions appears to have first arisen just after the return of the 4th Madras Native Infantry from the campaign of 1879-80 in Afghanistan. During that campaign the 4th and the 32nd Sikh Pioneers were frequently stationed together, and the former were constantly called upon to carry out what was really the work of a Pioneer battalion,—for example the construction of a road to the Snow Mountains,—Colonel Ross Thompson, R. E., expressing his entire satisfaction with their work.

Application was accordingly made to H. E. the Commander-in-Chief, then Sir Neville Chamberlain. The suggestion was favourably received, and, pending the receipt of sanction from the Secretary of State for India, the Commander-in-Chief intimated that men should be enlisted for Pioneer Work. Sanction was received from England in 1882, and the order for the conversion of both the 1st and 4th M.N.I., into Pioneers appeared in the following year (13th June 1883).

As soon as the order was received, two books were kept open for a period of six weeks, one for the names of those men who wished to become Pioneers, and the other for those who preferred to serve in an Infantry battalion, and the latter were gradually transferred to other corps. At the same time Captain J. E. Porteous was sent to the Punjab to gain some insight into the methods of the 23rd and 32nd Sikh Pioneers.

The first work carried out by the 4th Madras Pioneers, as such, was on the 28th November 1883, when they marched from Bangalore to Krishnarajapuram, in order to prepare a site for a Camp of Exercise. The work was completed on the 8th December, when the regiment returned to Bangalore.

1884.
The Agram Entrenchment.

From the 1st March to the 30th September 1884, the regiment was employed in constructing a fortified work on the East side of Bangalore, called the Agram Entrenchment, the work comprising both skilled and manual labour, and at the end of this year it was summoned to assist in carrying out a much more important project.

1884—1886.
The Sind-Peshin State Railway.

Towards the end of 1883, it became evident that the Russians, under a General named Alikhanoff, were coercing the people of Merv and its neighbourhood, so as to form a starting-point for more advanced operations, and to come within striking distance of the positions that lay between Merv and Herat. On this fact becoming obvious, the Government of Lord Ripon decided to hasten on the construction of the railway connection with Quetta. This had been projected by Lord Lytton, who, in

1879, had sent Sir Richard Temple, the Governor of Bombay, to Baluchistan, to examine the possibilities of the various passes leading to the Peshin plateau.

The projected railways were two in number; a broad-gauge line was to be constructed for heavy traffic through the Harnai passes, and a light line (by Colonel Lindsay) through the Bolan pass. Both were to start from Sibi at the foot of the mountains, diverging there to unite at Quetta, the two lines forming an oval, with the stations of Sibi and Bostan at the opposite ends. The length of the Harnai line was about double that of the Bolan line, which was to have steeper gradients and to carry only light traffic. The limit of the gradients of the Harnai line was fixed at 1 in 45 and the minimum radius for curves was 600 feet.

It was decided that the work should be carried out under the Military, and not under the Public Works, Department, and Colonel James Browne, R. E., who had been selected as engineer of the Harnai line, and who had already made a great reputation both as an engineer and a political officer and had great control over the wild tribes of the borderland, was to work under the direct guidance of the Commander-in-Chief, Sir Donald Stewart.

In October 1883, Browne started his operations for the construction of the railway but, on reaching Sibi, found that the work had suddenly been transferred from the Military, to the Public Works Department under a special Public Works Member of Council, which hampered him considerably from the very commencement.

During the remaining months of the cold weather of 1883, a certain amount of work was done on the lower part of the line, but the time was mostly spent in arranging for the collection of workmen and materials.

It will be as well to describe briefly the engineering task which was to be carried out. **Engineering Features.** Sibi is about 300 feet above sea-level, and at the summit near Kach, 120 miles from Sibi, the height is 6,500 feet. The construction of a broad-gauge line over so great a height in so short a distance was a task hitherto unknown in any part of the world, except in Peru. The country from Sibi to Garkhai was a rugged wilderness of rocks and stones, with scarcely a blade of grass the whole way, except for a few small patches near Harnai and Sharigh. The people were continually engaged in inter-tribal warfare. As regards the climate, the intense heat of the rocky gorges, on the lowest parts of the line, was only a little less endurable than the bitter cold of the upper passes in winter. Midway, near Harnai and Sharigh, the more equable climate was discounted by the presence of malaria and pestilence.

The principal engineering difficulties were:—

    (1) *The Nari Gorge;* which extended for some 14 miles from where the Nari river debouches on the plains. The whole of this wild gorge is formed by the tortuous channel of the river, which was some 300 yards wide in flood, with a depth of 10 feet and great velocity. The line crossed this river five times in the course of the 14 miles.

(2) *The Gandakindaf Defile;* which was only about 8 miles long, but involved two tunnels, through most treacherous material, and four large bridges.

(3) *The Chappar Rift;* which was a chasm about 21 miles long, joining two parallel valleys. The gradient of the bed was 1 in 20, so the entrance at the lower end had to be arranged for at a great height above the bed of the stream, so as to enable the line to issue at a proper level at the upper end. This involved a number of tunnels (aggregating over a mile in length) and one large bridge, 290 feet above the stream below.

(4) *The Mud Gorge;* in the summit portion, comprised five miles of narrow valley between precipitous mountains, filled with soil of an exceedingly treacherous nature and with a fairly steep longtitudinal slope.

Colonel Browne decided that during the cold weather, from October to April, attention should be directed to the works in the Nari Gorge and Gandakindaf Defile, while in the summer months the difficult portions in the higher parts of the line would be negotiated. He was supplied with troops in addition to the local labour almost from the commencement.

During the summer of 1884, attention was chiefly paid to the survey and tunnel work in the Chappar Rift, the alignment of the summit portion and much of the earthwork there, and the survey of the last 33 miles into Quetta. There was a good deal of sickness, fever and scurvy among the workmen and the troops, 60 *per cent* of the Sappers being in hospital, but on the whole the work had gone on without much hindrance.

In the autumn of 1884, fresh troops were sent up, comprising three full battalions of Pioneers,—the 4th Madras Native Infantry (Pioneers), the 23rd Sikh Pioneers, and 32nd Sikh Pioneers.

The 4th Pioneers move to Harnai. The 4th Pioneers left Bangalore on the 5th October 1884, with Colonel Hodding, Commandant; 8 other British Officers; 13 Native Officers; 2 Hospital Assistants; 34 Havildars; 15 Drummers; 683 Rank and File; 30 Public and 65 Private followers. With them went a party of the Queen's Own Sappers and Miners. A depot was left at Trichinopoly, under Major H. E. D. Bayley, 30th M. N. I., and Subadar-Major Gopalsamy also remained behind. The regiment reached Karachi on the 29th October 1884, and was forced to halt there for some time, owing to the prevalence of cholera further up the line. While halted, a certain amount of private work was done by the men.

At last they arrived at the Nari Gorge, in November 1884, and here it was found that the local labour had gone on strike and was very troublesome, so the regiment was set to loading and unloading trains, as well as doing all the platelaying and laying of points and switches. Their arrival was very timely, as otherwise the whole work in the Harnai would have been at a standstill.

This work continued till about the middle of December, when the regiment moved on by stages to Sunari, arriving on the 27th December, and here much good work was done, greatly to the satisfaction of Browne, who was now a Brigadier-General.

Great difficulties were met with owing to constant outbreaks of sickness, especially cholera, amongst the local work-people, and in November 1884 all the Afghans deserted in a body, while many of the engineering staff died. Matters were not improved by sudden floods in April and May 1885, caused by an unprecedentedly heavy rainfall, which swept away bridges and did an infinity of mischief.

The 4th Pioneers continued to work at Sunari until the beginning of April, when they moved to Bhostan, otherwise called Haji Harun Khan, in the Peshin Valley, arriving there with the 23rd and 32nd Pioneers on the 7th April 1885. They had throughout been remarkably free from sickness, and this record was maintained during their stay at Bhostan, where they worked until November 1885.

During this year, when war seemed imminent with Russia, the regiment was visited by General Sir Donald Stewart, Commander-in-Chief in India, who was accompanied by the Members of the Viceregal Council, and who remained with the regiment for three days. The following extract from one of Colonel Hodding's fortnightly reports to the Quartermaster-General at Ootacamund, dated Camp Bhostan, Peshin Valley, 15th November 1885, is of interest:—

"Sir Donald Stewart, the Commander-in-Chief in India, inspected the regiment on the first November, and His Excellency expressed himself as highly satisfied with everything he saw, and said that he could duly communicate the fact to Sir Frederick Roberts when he met him to make over charge in Bombay. Sir Donald Stewart also said that wheresoever he had been and all along the route, His Excellency had heard nothing but the most excellent accounts of the regiment. His Excellency also expressed himself as greatly pleased with the camp and all the arrangements connected therewith, and which His Excellency considered reflected great credit on all concerned, as we had made a pattern camp in the wilderness."

As winter was fast closing in, and already 18 degrees of frost had been registered—which is not very pleasant for men living in tents,—the 4th Pioneers left Bhostan on the 23rd November 1885 and, moving down the pass, marched to Panjah, where they arrived on the 29th. Here they remained at work till the 5th January 1886, being strengthened during their stay at Panjah by the arrival of Lieutenant G. B. Stevens with a party of about 50 men, who had left Trichinopoly on the 18th November.

Up to this time the health of the regiment, as has already been observed, had been remarkably good, but now their misfortunes were to begin. On the 7th January 1886, they arrived at a horrible place called Dal-o-jal (which means "life or death"—in other words it is doubtful if a man will survive one night there), and here they remained until the 6th February 1886. The only flat place available for a camp was the site of a cemetery where the victims of a cholera outbreak had been buried, and one officer who was present has recorded the fact that "when we drove in our tent-pegs, the fumes from the ground were too awful." In the first three weeks spent at this pestiferous spot over 30 officers and men died, including Captain de L. D. Passy, Subadar Shaikh Adam, and Jemadar-Adjutant Shaikh Hamid, while Colonel Barnett and Surgeon-Major McCarthy subsequently died, undoubtedly from the effects of the climate there.

The number of sick became so serious that it was decided that the regiment should be withdrawn, and accordingly they moved to Gandakindaf on the 7th February; Sibi on the 10th February; and Karachi on the 17th. From Karachi they sailed for Bombay on the *S. S. Tennasserim* on the 19th February, and reached Trichinopoly on the 26th February 1886.

The opening ceremony of the Harnai Railway did not take place till the 27th March 1887. General Browne received a K. C. S. I., and was shortly afterwards appointed Quartermaster-General in India.

The following is extracted from the Proceedings of the Madras Government, dated 9th July 1885 (No. 3718):—

Working Parties.

Read the following paper:—

No. 1174. From Brigadier-General Godfrey Clerk, Adjutant-General, to Lieutenant-Colonel A. Kenny Herbert, Officiating Secretary to Government, Military Department, dated Ootacamund, 1st July 1885 (No. 1510, N.A.):—

"I am directed by the Commander-in-Chief to forward herewith, for the information of Government, a copy of the correspondence noted in the margin (A.G. in India's No. 1779—D. and Engineer-in-Chief, Sind-Peshin State Railway, No. 53-C.), bringing to notice the good work done by the 4th Regiment Madras Infantry (Pioneers) in connection with the Sind-Peshin Railway and the excellent spirit which the regiment has shewn.

2. His Excellency feels sure that Government will agree with him in thinking this report most satisfactory in every way and as reflecting great credit on Colonel Hodding and his Officers."

From Major-General T. D. Baker, Adjutant-General in India, to His Excellency the Commander-in-Chief of the Madras Army, dated Simla, 12th June 1885, No. 1779-D:—

"I am directed to forward, for Your Excellency's information, the accompanying extract from the report by the Engineer-in-Chief on the work done by the three Pioneer Regiments employed on the Sind-Peshin Railway, and to convey the Commander-in-Chief's appreciation of the good work done by the 4th Madras Pioneers and the excellent spirit which the Regiment has shown."

Extract of a letter from Brigadier-General J. Browne, R.E., C.B., C.S.I., Engineer-in-Chief, Sind-Peshin State Railway, Northern Section, to the Adjutant-General in India, dated 15th May 1885, No. 53-C:—

"I have the honour herewith to forward, for the information of His Excellency the Commander-in-Chief the following reports on the three Pioneer Regiments employed during the winter on this Railway.

* * * * * *

9. The *4th Madras Pioneers* were detained at Nari till the 20th December as cholera was raging up the line. They were employed, two companies at a time, in platelaying and laying down sidings in Nari Station-yard, as also in loading and unloading railway material, an useful accomplishment.

On Marching to Suneri, the regiment was employed on making about a mile of bank some twelve feet high; thus inuring the regiment, which has only lately been made a Pioneer Regiment, to the earth work which is the A. B. C. of their trade. This heavy bank was successfully accomplished, each man making from 7 to 8 annas a day. The spirit in this regiment is good and keen. A portable engine, weighing eight tons, having got stuck in the river shingle, two companies of the regiment turned out and dragged it up over ten miles in one day, returning back to camp the same distance that evening, under their Colonel's direction, up hill and down dale, across shingle beds and awkward corners, which showed that the men's hearts were in the job as well as their hands.

10. The health of the three Regiments has throughout been excellent, and they were comfortably rationed, clothed and sheltered. They were marched up to Peshin with camels obtained from the country people, through the Railway authorities, who indeed have to supply all the transport for the troops, and most of their food, without reference to either the Political or Transport Departments at Quetta. The regiments not being on Kabul scale and marching with 15 days' supplies required about 1,500 camels, which were taken up by contract at so much per camel, thus saving all grazing guards and other arrangements for preventing the straying of camels, which give troops extra trouble and fatigue. Each regiment was provided with 52 camels in permanent regimental charge to bring rations from different depots when in standing camp.

11. The amount of crime was practically nil and the amount of drill given to the regiments was very small, although in all probability their efficiency has not been hereby impaired. I trust in health and physique, intelligence, contentment, heart for fighting and trained capacity for hard work, the regiments have in no way deteriorated from their connection with the Sind-Peshin Railway.

12. In conclusion, I would heartily thank the Commanding Officers for the way in which they have taught and encouraged their men to work and have done all in their power to promote the completion of the Railway."

No. 175. *Order thereon*, 9th July 1885:—

"The Right Honourable the Governor in Council concurs in His Excellency the Commander-in-Chief's opinion, and resolves to communicate the foregoing correspondence to Her Majesty's Secretary of State for India."

Government of Madras, Military Department, 21st November 1885, No. 6614.

Working Parties.

Read the following:—

No. 338. Extract from a Military Despatch from the Right Honourable the Secretary of State for India, dated 22nd October 1885, No. 78:—

"Para 14. I have perused with much satisfaction the correspondence forwarded by your Government in respect to the work done by the 4th Madras Infantry (Pioneers) in connection with the construction of the Sind-Peshin Railway."

No. 339. *Order thereon*, dated 21st November 1885:—

"Communicated to the Provincial Commander-in-Chief, with reference to Proceedings of Government No. 3718, dated 9th July 1885.

(*Signed*) A. KENNY HERBERT, *Lt.-Col.*,
Offg. Secretary to Government."

1886.
Line Building, Trichinopoly.

On their return to Trichinopoly from work on the Sind-Peshin Railway, the regiment was employed, during the year 1886, on the construction of lines for the 30th Madras Infantry, which were completed before the end of the year.

1889.
Lushai Hill Tracts.

As has already been recorded elsewhere in these records, a detachment, under the command of Captain G. B. Stevens, was despatched from Trichinopoly on the 3rd January 1889, to join the Lushai Expeditionary Force, and returned to Trichinopoly on the 9th May 1889.

During this period, an immense amount of work was done, the men only having one day's holiday. Roads were constructed, and a fort was built at Lungleh in the Lushai Hills, while it was made evident to the authorities that the services of a party of Pioneers with all such expeditions and columns in the hill tracts were absolutely essential, if the country was to be properly opened up.

The Colonel Commanding the Lushai Expeditionary Force expressed his satisfaction with the excellent work done by the detachment in a Farewell Order, which will be found elsewhere.

1889.
The Periyar Project.

On the 3rd October 1889, a detachment of 270 men of the 4th Pioneers, under the command of Major E. G. Blenkinsop, with Subadar-Major Mahomed Beg, *Sirdar Bahadur*, left Trichinopoly, in order to work on the Periyar Project. This was an irrigation scheme, by which a large dam was to be thrown across the valley of the Periyar, and the work, as far as the Pioneers were concerned, appears to have been entirely earthwork. The party rejoined regimental headquarters at Bangalore in 1890.

The following is an extract from the *History of the Periyar Project,* by Mr. Mackenzie, the Engineer-in-Charge:—

"In 1889 and again in 1890 detachments from the First and Fourth Pioneers were lent for service at the Periyar. While labour was scarce, bad, and ill-organised, the Pioneers were of great service and the officers made a welcome addition socially. Certain drawbacks, however, attached to the arrangements. The men being, of course, under the orders of their own officers only, were sometimes difficult to supervise effectually unless working in large bodies, which was not always practicable; while exigencies of military service sometimes clashed with the interests of the works. After 1890, therefore, the services of the Pioneers were not utilised, and labour having by this time become more regular and abundant, the loss was not markedly perceptible."

With regard to this, it may be remarked that on all the many other occasions where the regiment has been employed on civil works, the executive engineers have invariably congratulated themselves on the fact that the work was so thoroughly supervised regimentally that they were saved all the trouble caused by the unfortunate tendency of some civil contractors to increase their profits by scamping the work.

The following is an extract from the Report on the Progress of the Periyar Project Works for October and November 1889, read in G. O. No. 633, I, Public Works, dated 17th December 1889:—

"2. The labour supply continued to increase steadily, and by the end of November there were more than 1 500 men in the two camps, including 300 Pioneers.

3. A fourth detachment of the latter, making up a total of 400, should have arrived during November, but were stopped on account of cholera in the Cumbum valley. These men have been found very useful, their superior physique as compared with the Madura coolies more than compensating for their extra cost."

The following is an extract from the Report on the Progress of the Periyar Works for the month of February 1890, read in G. O. No. 164, I, Public Works, dated 12th March 1890:—

"9. The detachment of Pioneers left on the 17th; their loss will be much felt, their services having been very valuable."

1890.
Line Building, Bangalore.

When the regiment moved to Bangalore in 1890, they were once more employed in line-building, and completed the construction of the South Lines at Agram. These are the infantry lines near the European cemetery, on the Hosur Road.

1890-1891.
The Chin Hills.

On the 20th November 1890, the Right Wing of the 4th Pioneers left Bangalore for special service in the Chin Hills. Two companies, under Captain Churchill with Lieutenant Holmes, proceeded to Fort White, and the remaining two Companies and Wing Headquarters, under Captain Stevens, with Lieutenant Rainey, to Haka.

The Right Wing.

The principal Pioneer work of this season was to cut a mule road from Fort White to Haka, a distance of about 80 miles, the task assigned to each of the two companies being to cut the road as far as the Manipur River, which was roughly half way between. The Haka party commenced the road on the 18th January 1891, and completed it on the 20th March, enabling a large column with transport to march to Falam and meet a similar column that had started from Fort White over the other portion of the road made by Captain Churchill's two companies.

The Fort White companies also cut a road from Fort White to Tiddim, and were employed on the erection of Tiddim Post. On the completion of this road, owing to disturbances in Manipur and the fear of a general rising of Chins, the wing, instead of returning to India as originally ordered, was kept on as an increase to the garrisons of the Chin Hills.

Through the ensuing rains, the headquarter companies concentrated at Haka and sent a detachment of 50 Rifles, under Lieutenant Rainey to Rowan. Captain Churchill's two companies were split up between Fort White and the posts on the road to the Kale Valley, and suffered very greatly from the deadly climate of No. 2 Stockade at which post the garrison had to be changed every fortnight, owing to their decimation by fever.

The following Pioneer works were carried out by the Haka companies during the rains:—

(1) The road from Haka to Kan (80 miles) repaired and cleared of jungle.

(2) The post at Rowan repaired, and a magazine built.

(3) The post at Haka repaired and strengthened, and extra buildings put up, including commissariat shed, cook-houses, and transport stables.

(4) Two complete temporary posts for a garrison of 50 Rifles, and accommodation for 100 Rifles passing through, with mule lines for 250 mules, erected at Bwelet and Yokwa by Jemadar Abdulla Khan. The excellence of this work was complimented by General Graham, Commanding Myingyan District.

(5) Roads made (at the request of the Political Officers) from Haka Post to Haka and Kotan villages.

(6) A complete chain of strong stockades round Haka Post.

The companies at Fort White, when not on garrison duty, constructed extra buildings, including a pukka stone Telegraph Office and Treasury, also extra barracks and Officers' quarters.

1891—1892.
The Chin Hills.

At the end of 1891, the two companies from Haka moved to Fort White, where the whole Right Wing concentrated while Haka was occupied by the Headquarters and Left Wing of the regiment, which had arrived from Bangalore.

The Right Wing.

During the ensuing open season, from December 1891 to May 1892, the following Pioneer work was carried out by the Right Wing:—

(1) New officers' quarters at Fort White.

(2) Temporary barracks at No. 5 Stockade.

(3) A signal station, with temporary post complete, at Kennedy Peak, including a mule-path down to the water 1,500 feet below the post, along the face of a precipitous cliff.

The following work was done by the 50 Pioneers with the Kanhaw column under the superintendence of Lieutenant Holmes:—

(1) A new mule-road from Kennedy Peak ridge to Tiddim (about 13 miles).

(2) A mule-road from Tiddim to Tunzan traced and cut out afresh including two strong temporary bridges across the Manipur river, distance about 20 miles.

(3) A mule-road traced and cut out from Tunzan to Lenacot (Linkang?) about 30 miles.

(4) Temporary posts constructed at Tunzan and Lenacot.

(5) A mule-track opened out from Lenacot to Tong-long, a distance of 70 miles, and another into the Manipur plain, 30 miles.

Headquarters and Left Wing. The Headquarters and Left Wing of the regiment left Bangalore on the 1st November 1891, and reached Pakkoku on the 14th November. From Pakkoku they marched on the 20th November, and arrived at Kan on the 10th December, repairing the roads and bridges en route. Halting at Kan till the 17th December, the march was then resumed, and Haka was reached on the 24th, a distance of 72 miles in 8 days, the work of improving the road being continued as before.

On arrival at Haka, road work was resumed and was carried on until the 20th April 1892, when the whole regiment set out to return to Bangalore, where they arrived on the 21st June 1892. Fuller details of the movements of the Left Wing have been given elsewhere in these records, where will also be found extracts from various reports conveying an expression of the satisfaction of the authorities with the good work done by the regiment.

1893—1894.
Line-Building, Bangalore.

In January 1893, the 4th Pioneers were once more set to work to build lines, this time on the northern side of Bangalore, beside Baidarhalli. These lines were completed before the regiment left for Trichinopoly in November 1894, and have ever since been occupied by the Pioneer regiment stationed in Bangalore.

1895.
Work at Paliyanpatti.

While the regiment was stationed at Trichinopoly in 1895, a detachment of four companies were sent off on the 12th September, under Captain F. Churchill, to Paliyanpatti, in Tanjore District, to dig ballast for the South Indian Railway Company. After a fortnight's work the detachment rejoined the regiment on the 25th September.

1896.
Floods at Trichinopoly.

In July 1896, owing to heavy rains, the river Kaveri was in flood and rose to a dangerous height. The rush of water eventually breached the Kodamurti-Woriur road in several places, and, at the request of the Collector of Trichinopoly, the regiment turned out on the 31st July to repair the breaches, the work being satisfactorily completed on the 3rd August.

At the same time the river breached the flood-bank on the island of Srirangam and part of the regiment was diverted to Melur, on the island, to repair this bank, which was effected between the 1st and 7th August.

The regiment received the thanks of the Board of Revenue for their services on this occasion.

1897-1898.
The Ootacamund Lake Reclamation Project.

The next work on which the 4th Pioneers were to find themselves employed was the scheme to fill in the upper part of the lake at Ootacamund. The lake consisted of two portions, divided by a bund, called the Willow Bund, carrying a road across the lake, and the result of filling in one half of it has been to provide Ootacamund with a large level stretch of ground, called the Hobart Park, alongside which the Gymkhana buildings have been erected, while the park itself was laid out with a race-course and cricket and polo grounds.

The following extracts from the Government papers, and report by Lieutenant-Colonel G. B. Stevens on the work done by the 4th Pioneers, give full details of what was done.

"*Government of Madras, Public Works Department.*"

G. O. No. 1697-W., dated 25th June 1897.

Buildings and Roads.
Civil Works.

Read the following papers:—

Telephone message from the Deputy Adjutant-General, Madras Command, to the Secretary to Government, Public Works Department, dated 19th June 1897, No. 675-B:—

"Government India sanction appointment 4th Madras Pioneers on lake reclamation at Ootacamund, on the understanding that there will be no expense to the State. Lieutenant-General Commanding Madras, however, doubts whether Madras Government will want them brought up in this weather as they could not do much work. Please reply very early as this information required before orders can issue for bringing up the troops."

From E. G. Barrow, Esq., Officiating Deputy Secretary to the Government of India, Military Department, to the Quartermaster-General in India, dated 17th June 1897, No. 1107-C. (*Distribution of Army—Movements of Troops*):—

"I am directed to acknowledge the receipt of your letter No. 2391-A, dated the 14th June 1897, and in reply, to say, for the information of His Excellency the Commander-in-Chief, that the Government of India sanction the employment, by the Government of Madras, of the 4th Madras Pioneers from Trichinopoly on lake reclamation at Ootacamund, on the understanding that there will be no expense to the State."

Copy of the above forwarded to the Chief Secretary to the Government of Madras for the information of His Excellency the Governor-in-Council.

(By Order)

(*Signed*) E. G. BARROW,
Offg. Dy. Secy. to the Govt. of India.

No. 1316, Public.

"Transferred to the Public Works Department."

(*Signed*) J. F. PRICE,
Chief Secretary.

25th June 1897.

Order—N. 1697-W., dated 25th June 1897:—

"The Government observe that the only expense to the State that will be incurred by bringing up the 4th Pioneers to Ootacamund for employment on the lake reclamation project will be the grant of Rs. 1,000 for sanitary arrangements referred to in paragraph 5 of the agreement printed in G. O. No. 1517 W., dated 11th June 1897, and this amount will be debited to the work.

2. It is understood that the monthly accounts of expenditure shew that there were large sums spent on the work in July, August and September 1896. It is evident from this that a good deal of work can be done during the monsoon. The troops, moreover, will be comfortably housed at Ootacamund, and will no doubt be able to take advantage of all breaks in the weather. His Excellency the Governor-in-Council, therefore, considers that there are sufficient reasons for bringing them up now, and His Excellency the Lieutenant-General Commanding the Forces will accordingly be requested to be so good as to issue the necessary order for their despatch to Ootacamund without delay."

(True Extract).

(*Signed*) D. McNEIL CAMPBELL, COLONEL, R. E.,
Secretary to Government.

Memorandum.

Showing details regarding the Employment of IV Madras Pioneers at Ootacamund on Special Work, 1897-98, and remarks thereon.

1. The question of the employment of the Regiment on the Ootacamund Lake Reclamation Scheme was first raised by Mr. Somers Eve, the Executive Engineer in Charge, on account of the difficulty of getting a constant supply of local labour, and the importance of a speedy completion of the work.

Reasons for Employment.

Mr. Somers Eve furnished me with a copy of the rates of payment of work and after
Contract. consultation a draft contract was drawn up for approval by all ranks of
the Regiment; it being clearly notified that the acceptance of it was
voluntary and that only volunteers would be allowed to proceed to Ootacamund.

There was no hesitation on the part of the men; the difficulty was to obtain volunteers to remain at the depot, Trichinopoly. The Regiment having for many years, when in Cantonments, been employed incessantly in line-building without, of course, remuneration, the idea of working pay was highly acceptable.

2. The sanction of Government having been accorded in G. O. No. 1097—W,
Employment of Regiment Sanctioned. dated 25th June 1897, and the terms of the contract between the Regiment and the Executive Engineer, Mr. Somers Eve, agreed to, arrangements were made to move the Regiment to Ootacamund, leaving a depot at Trichinopoly.

The strength of the depot at Trichinopoly was, including recruits, who, as they passed their drills, joined Headquarters at Ootacamund:—

British Officer	1.
Native Officers	4.
Rank and File	258.

3. On the 28th June 1897, an advance party, strength as below, left Trichinopoly
Move to Ootacamund. for Ootacamund to prepare the Ootacamund Jails for accommodation of the Regiment.

British Officer	1.
Native Officers	2.
Rank and File	61.

A week later, the Regiment moved up to Ootacamund in detachments, arrangements having been made with the South Indian and Madras Railways for the men to travel at reduced fares, provided they moved in parties of 60 or 120 at a time, special carriages being allotted to them. Officers travelled on Form E.

On the 13th July 1897, the strength of the Regiment at Ootacamund was:—

British Officers	7.
Native Officers	11.
Rank and File	541.

On the 15th September, a further party arrived from the depot of 1 Native Officer and 61 Rank and File, bringing the total Native Ranks at Ootacamund to 614.

4. The Regiment, as stated above, moved in detachments from Trichinopoly to
March to and from Ootacamund. Mettupaliyam by rail, and thence by construction line, in trucks which were placed at its disposal by the kindness of Mr. Weightman, Superintending Engineer, Nilgiri Railway, as far as Kullar. At Kullar the baggage was put into carts, and the whole marched to Ootacamund via Coonoor. At Coonoor each detachment halted a night in tents pitched on the Railway bank

close to the Coonoor chattram, arrangements having been made for cooks to be in charge of the tents and have food ready in the chattram for each detachment when passing through. The President of the Coonoor Municipality kindly had the chattram cleared for the Regiment on the dates required.

Similar arrangements were made for the detachments when returning from Ootacamund to Trichinopoly except that tents were not required, as each detachment did the march down from Ootacamund to Mettupalaiyam in one day, only halting a couple of hours at Coonoor for food.

I would note that the Nilgiri line having been taken over by the Madras Railway the courtesy that gave the men a free lift from Mettupalaiyam to Kullar on the way up was lacking on their return journey, and they had to march the whole way—one detachment did a record march, leaving Ootacamund at 4-30 a.m., and arriving at Mettupalaiyam at 3 p.m., on the same day.

N.B.—It having been ruled that work should stop on 1st October 1898 to permit the regiment being back at its Station for the Drill Season, the whole Regiment returned to Trichinopoly by the 10th of that month.

5. The Regiment was quartered in the old European and Native Jails. These **Accommodation.** buildings, with the aid of the money granted, were made very fairly comfortable. The proximity of the latrines and cooking-places was unavoidable, owing to the limited space, but by careful and constant supervision, the health of the men was not affected. The members accommodated were roughly 400 in the European Jail and 200 in the Native Jail. The Native Officers were comfortably housed in little bungalows close to the Jail. The Hospital was inside the European Jail in two large airy rooms. The men's rifles were kept in the inside hall of the European Jail in improvised racks that answered the purpose well, and were easily seen by one sentry. Water was laid on to the Jail in pipes from the main at regimental expense; the supply was sufficient and good.

6. The work on the Lake Reclamation Scheme consisted chiefly in removing earth **Nature of** from the south side of the Lake, and filling in and levelling the portion **the Work.** reclaimed, between the Willow Bund and Gymkhana, and also in the construction of stone and other drains for carrying off the water. A considerable quantity of stone had to be blasted and some heavy work was done in rectifying landslips, owing to springs appearing in the hill-side below the road. As the work progressed the *lead* increased, and in some cases the earth had to be carried nearly 400 yards. This was done by means of trollies on rails, which were utilized as far as the limited supply would permit. In consequence of the earth from the hill-side being required for the lake, the road had to be diverted and laid out afresh. Earth was also taken from the bed of the lake across the Willow Bund. In addition to this work, the main supply channel of the lake was deepened and widened, and a concrete culvert constructed to carry the road over it; the main drain was also relaid. These last two works were heavy and unpleasant, and were done in the rainy season without a grumble of any kind.

7. In April 1898, the work on the lake being nearly completed, the Regiment, at the request of the Executive Engineer, was also employed on the construction of the *Havelock Road*. Before taking up this work, the men were given the option which resulted in 108 men asking to return to Trichinopoly and 92 volunteering to replace them from the depot.

Work on Havelock Road.

The work on the Havelock Road was easy, consisting mostly of cutting a road 20 feet wide on the hill-side with a certain amount of blasting and stone-breaking. During the last month (September 1898) a heavy piece of work was done in reducing the gradient of the old road above St. Stephen's Church. The work was stopped on 1st October 1898.

8. The work was measured up monthly by the Executive Engineer and a monthly payment made to the Regiment. The total amount of Working Pay earned was as follows:—

Measurement of & Payment for Work.

For Lake Reclamation Work	.. Rs.	60,821 6 8
For Havelock Road	.. ,,	2,846 9 1
For Miscellaneous	.. ,,	2,602 0 11
	Total Rs.	66,270 0 8

The average rate paid to the Rank and File was Rs. 9-5-8 *per mensem*. Native Officers received supervision pay at the rate of 12 annas per working day, British Officers by common consent, owing to the fact that the expenses of the men were great and that Government had refused them the local rates of rice compensation, consented to forego working pay. I was able, however, at the conclusion of the work, to pay a certain sum into the Officers' Mess as a set-off against the expenses it had been put to.

9. The Regiment was actually employed at work 364 days, of 8 hours, between 15th July 1897 and 1st October 1898. Sundays were reserved as a day of rest and one day a week for "Strong-as-possible Parades." Work was occasionally stopped by wet weather. The Annual Inspection also necessitated a few days' stoppage of work: otherwise the work was incessant. I would add that each day the work was stopped meant a loss of about Rs. 170 to the Regiment and as it was the object to cover the cost of the messing with the working-pay, it was important to work as many days as possible.

Number of Working Days, etc.

10. The Regiment was messed by companies according to caste, the Messes being worked on the same lines as the Recruits' Mess. The cost of messing was high and averaged about Rs. 2-4-0 *per mensem* above the Trichinopoly rates. In some months, when bad weather interfered with the work, the men with difficulty earned enough working pay to cover the cost of messing. This did not matter much to bachelors but married men who sent their ordinary pay to provide for their families at the depot found it difficult.

Messing and Cost Thereof.

Whilst on this subject I would mention that rice compensation was refused to the Regiment on the ground that Government was not to be put to extra expense. This refusal was not anticipated as the compensation was understood to be an established right of the sepoy: as a matter of fact Government saved money by the regiment being at Ootacamund and not firing its annual course. The amount thus saved, exclusive of extra ammunition specially granted to the Regiment for collective practice, amounts to Rs. 6,420-5-0 whereas the difference between the Ootacamund and Trichinopoly rice rates for the whole period which has been refused on the score of extra expense, amounts only to Rs. 3,253-0-0.

11. The expenses of the Regiment may be summed up as follows:—

Regimental Expenses.
Railway Charges	Rs.	2,982 5 9
Cart Hire	„	753 8 0
Regtl. Deductions and Contingencies	„	5,561 13 1
Total Rs.		9,297 10 10

Note.—It has been the custom to set aside 15 *per cent.* of the regimental earnings for payment into the working fund but on this occasion, the expenses being very heavy, and the cost of living high, not more than 1½ per cent was available for the fund.

The following statement shows the monthly earnings and expenses throughout, and also the cost of messing monthly:—

Month.	Working Pay Issued.	Misc. Deductions and Expenses.	Total Working Pay Received.	Cost of Messing.
July, 1897	..	1,483 15 0	3,000 0 0	2,097 12 4
August	2,921 0 3	183 1 1	3,342 4 3	3,729 5 8
September	3,480 12 6	90 12 0	3,596 3 9	3,750 14 9
October	4,147 1 9	384 8 6	4,735 8 9	3,689 14 0
November	4,388 14 0	127 0 0	4,609 0 2	3,871 7 9
December	4,481 14 6	17 4 8	4,807 9 3	3,708 7 9
January, 1898	4,708 13 1	228 14 0	5,056 8 7	3,550 8 4
February	4,705 8 3	444 11 5	5,548 4 5	3,431 15 5
March	4,198 14 1	239 6 1	4,542 3 9	2,943 14 7
April	5,452 8 11	373 8 6	5,999 10 8	2,679 4 6
May	3,829 5 3	146 3 9	3,970 12 1	2,487 4 4
June	3,545 1 0	738 4 5	4,431 15 2	2,202 3 2
July	2,557 6 6	313 4 0	2,701 6 0	1,949 5 2
August	2,671 13 3	411 2 0	2,976 9 9	1,985 6 0
September	3,132 9 6	333 15 0	3,869 1 6	2,468 10 0
October	2,750 11 0	679 3 0	2,874 12 11	..
November	..	2,968 14 5	95 5 6	..
December	..	133 11 0	112 12 2	..
Total Rs. ..	56,972 5 10	9,297 10 10	66,270 0 8	44,546 5 9

12. The pay proper of the Regiment whilst at Ootacamund was drawn from the Madras Bank, to which, with the sanction of the Controller of Military Accounts, a sufficient assignment had been made. The pay of the depot was drawn at Ootacamund and remitted by transfer receipts to Trichinopoly, the acquittance rolls being prepared at Regimental Headquarters and transmitted to the Officer Commanding the Depot, before whom the men were paid.

Regimental Pay.

13. The health of the Regiment, in spite of the change of climate and the hard and frequently wet work, was good throughout; the average rate of admissions to hospital being 10·9 which is 10 per cent. less than the average at Trichinopoly for the past two years. The British Officers, however, suffered. 2nd Lieutenant W. Marshall, a promising young officer, died of enteric fever and Lieutenants S. M. Rice and M. H. B. Geddes were invalided; among the Native Ranks there were nine deaths (one by the explosion of an old mine) and 49 men were invalided.

Health.

14. The conduct of the men whilst at Ootacamund was good. Two Courts-Martial were held, the offences being absence without leave and anonymous letter writing; in the latter case the offender was convicted and awarded two years' imprisonment with hard labour.

Conduct.

15. I would sum up the results of the above experiment, or rather enterprise, as distinctly good in training the men in all-round work and it might, I think, with advantage be repeated; but I consider that volunteering on the part of men for this kind of work is objectionable; and that provided the question of the work being suitable or otherwise has been thoroughly gone into by the regimental authorities, orders for the work to be carried out should be issued. I also consider that compensation for dearness of food at local rates should invariably be given. This would prevent the men feeling that they were civilians on a private job and that they were being defrauded of their lawful earnings when taken on work for military duty, and also would enable them to be exercised more in their military duties such as Musketry, Field Training, etc., and not leave them dependent on the work for the extra cost of feeding themselves.

General Remarks.

16. I cannot close this Memorandum without expressing my satisfaction at the cordial feeling that has existed throughout the work between the Regiment and the Executive Engineer, Mr. Somers Eve. This is entirely due to this gentleman's tact and ability, and to the willing co-operation and support that I received from the British and Native Officers, among the latter of whom I would especially mention Subadar Major Muhammad Sallar, now Honorary Captain, for his untiring zeal and devotion to work. I append a list of the British Officers who served with the Regiment whilst at Ootacamund, and would record that for the last seven months of work the Regiment was ably commanded by Major Holloway, during my absence on leave.

G. B. STEVENS, LT.-COL.,
Commandant,
IV Madras Pioneers.

Trichinopoly,
31st March 1899.

List of British Officers who served with IV Pioneers, whilst on Special Work at Ootacamund.

Rank and Name.	Remarks.
Lieutenant-Colonel G. B. Stevens	On leave from March to September 1898.
Major E. L. Holloway	Offg. Commdt. of Regt. ditto.
Captain C. T. Swan	
Lieutenant S. M. Rice	Invalided 15th November 1897.
,, C. R. Scott-Elliot	Arrived 13th March 1898.
,, S. B. Watson	Arrived 20th January 1898.
,, M. H. B. Geddes	Invalided August 1898.
2nd Lieutenant J. A. Keble	Transferred to 14th M.I.
,, W. F. Marshall	Died 21st June 1898.
Captain A. E. Berry, I.M.S.	
,, F. L. Blenkinsop, I.M.S.	Temporary Medical charge.
,, T. G. Gibbard, R.A.M.C.	
Major M. T. Kelawala, I.M.S.	From 10-9-97 to 23-8-98.

Contract.

In the event of it being decided that the services of the IV Pioneer Regiment can be employed on the Ooty Lake Filling, the following are the draft terms of contract between the Officer Commanding and the Executive Engineer in charge of the work.

1. Payments. (a) Earthwork at Rs. 15 *per* 1,000 cubic feet.
   (b) Blasting Rock at Rs. 55 *per* 1,000 cubic feet.

2. Tools, Mamooties, Crowbars and Pickaxes will be supplied by D. P. W. as far as possible. Jumpers, Spoons and Explosives to be provided by the Pioneers. If supplied by the D. P. W. the rate of payment for work will be lowered proportionately. Providing that in no case will the Regiment be expected to pay more than Rs. 500 for tools (not explosives).

3. Plant will be provided by the D. P. W. as far as available and must be maintained by the Regiment.

4. Carriage of troops will be paid by the Regiment, but an advance for expenses in coming up will be made by the Executive Engineer, such advance to be recovered in three monthly instalments.

5. Quarters will be paid provided rent-free in the European and Native jails as personally shown to Colonel Stevens. Rs. 1,000 will be granted by the D. P. W. for the purpose of making latrines, forming beds, etc. This is to be spent at the will of the Commanding Officer subject to the condition that proper sanitary arrangements are made.

6. No other charge whatever will be met from D. P. W. funds, other than payments made for work done, tools, and the above lump sum. All other expenses to be met by the Regiment.

7. Payments to be made fortnightly or monthly as desired, but the monthly payment is to be a final one.

Measurements will be taken by the Executive Engineer or those deputed by him in communication with the Officer Commanding Regiment and the Executive Engineer's decision to be considered as final.

I concur in the above,

Ooty,
28th May 1897.
3rd June 1897.

(*Signed*) G. B. STEVENS, *Major.*
(*Signed*) J. F. SOMERS EVE,
Executive Engineer.

The following are extracts from the Proceedings of Government on the completion of the work:—

Government of Madras, Public Works Department.
G. O. No. 1400-W., dated 1st June 1899.

Buildings and Roads.
Civil Works.

Read—the following paper:—
Report on the completion of the filling in of the Ootacamund Upper Lake.
Estimate. Rs. 1,99,140.

The work was practically completed on 31st March 1899, though, owing to various reasons, there remained a few small pieces of work to be done which will cost some Rs. 500, bringing the total expenditure to Rs. 2,01,830, or about Rs. 2,700 in excess of the estimate. This excess is covered by No. 4191-C., Public Works Department, of 23rd September 1898.

2. Reasons for savings and excesses on the various sub-heads of the estimates are given in the completion report, but broadly speaking considerably more money has been spent on (*a*) filling up depressions in the reclaimed portion which have repeatedly occurred, and (*b*) altering the upper road and improving it with its drainage owing to heavy land-slips in the steep slope.

3. It will no doubt be necessary, for some years to come, to fill up depressions as they occur, in order to make the reclaimed ground healthy and useful. After the ground has thoroughly settled, the centre portion will have to be drained. A small portion near the Hobart School has been so drained with 2 inch pipes, 20 feet apart; and this land, which was previously a bog, is now sound ground.

4. The permanent level of the lower lake has been lowered by order of Government one foot six inches; and I think the most conservative Toda cannot say it has spoilt the appearance of the lake. I would strongly urge that in a year's time the lake be lowered another foot or foot and a half, the main stream deepened, and the Hobart Park and upper portion of the reclaimed ground well drained. These cannot be effectively done unless the lake is lowered, and I am convinced the ground will never be really a healthy recreation ground until the sub-soil water is lowered.

5. The completion of this work in the time is chiefly due to the assistance of the IV Pioneers, who worked on this and other works from the beginning of July 1897 to 1st October 1898.

6. It is impossible for me to exaggerate the good work this Regiment did and the excellent effect this imported labour had on local labour in Ootacamund.

7. With the exception of some Rs. 1,500, spent on making the old jail suitable for their barracks, the men worked at the same rates as those given to the local labour, and they certainly did all the most difficult work.

8. I venture to request that the services of this Regiment at Ootacamund may be brought to the special notice of Government.

9. My particular thanks are due to Major Stevens, the Commanding Officer for the greater part of the time, and to Captain Holloway who commanded for the remaining time, also to Captain Swan, Lieutenants Rice and Watson. To the ready co-operation and kindly tact and keenness displayed by the officers, and ever ready assistance rendered by the remaining officers both European and Native, I ascribe the success which undoubtedly attended this experiment of the employment of military labour under a Civil Engineer. Under similar circumstances, the IV Pioneers are the first lot of men I shall apply for; and I feel proud to think they will readily come to me.

10. In addition to the above named officers, I beg to bring prominently to notice the services rendered by Subadar-Major Muhammad Sallar. I feel sure Major Stevens will not object to my describing him as the backbone of the regiment as far as work is concerned. His slightest wish was law with the men on the work and it is no exaggeration to say that he was always on the work and that where he was, good work was done. I can give him no better praise than to express my wish that we had a few men of his calibre in the Public Works Department.

11. In addition to the lake work, the men were employed on laying main sewer, altering the iron pipe sewer through the upper lake, building roads, road work. Some of these works were far from easy or pleasant, and there was never a grumble heard.

12. I append a note by the Commanding Officer, IV Pioneers. The Regiment was treated absolutely on the piece-work system, and from a Public Works Department point of view, this is, I think, the only system that should be employed. Tasks must be set daily and carefully checked. This is not difficult as there is a lot of superintendence available in the Regiment. From the Public Works Department view also volunteering is the better plan, as it ensures an anxiety to put the men on the work.

26th April, 1899. (*Signed*.) J. F. SOMERS EVE,
Executive Engineer.

No. 268/W.

'Copy submitted to the Chief Engineer, Public Works Department.

The difficulties attending the execution of large works on the hills have been most successfully overcome by the employment of the IV Pioneers, whose cordial co-operation has enabled Mr. Eve to complete the filling in of the lake in a very satisfactory manner.'

Camp Ootacamund, (*Signed*.) A. H. GARRETT,
14th May, 1899. *Suptg. Engineer, IV Circle.*

Order——No. 1400/W., dated 1st June 1899:—

'Government has perused this report with satisfaction.

2. The good services of the IV Pioneers, in connection with the Lake Reclamation Project at Ootacamund, will be brought to the notice of the Lieutenant-General Commanding the Force.'

(True Extract.)

(*Signed*.) W. B. DEWINTON,
Secretary to Government.

No. A/N T. 11130. Ootacamund,
22nd July 1899.

To the G. O. C., Southern District.

'Forwarded for information and favour of communication to the officer Commanding IV Madras Pioneers.

2. Sir George Wolseley has perused this report with pleasure.'

(By Order)
(*Signed*) G. SIMPSON, *Brigr.-General, D. A. G.*

Through O. C., Trichinopoly,
   The O. C., IV M. I. (Pioneers).
      Trichinopoly.

'Forwarded for information.
   (By Order)
(*Signed*) W. R. ROUTH, *Colonel,*
   A. A. G., Southern District.

1901.
Boer Prisoners-of-War Camp.

From the 25th March to 13th June 1901, the 4th Pioneers, which was still stationed at Trichinopoly, was employed on the construction of a camp for Boer prisoners-of-war. The work consisted of erecting huts, constructing a barbed wire entanglement round the camp, digging wells, and various other minor works.

For this the Regiment received the thanks of the G.O.C., Southern District. (*A. A. G. Southern District, No. 876/13, dated 1st April, 1901*).

From the 7th October to the 17th November 1901, the Regiment was again employed on the construction of additional huts for a second batch of prisoners.

The following officers were employed on this work:—

British Officers.	Subadars.	Jamadars.
Major E. L. Holloway	Mir Abbas, *Bahadur, Subadar Major.*	Varadarajulu.
" F. Churchill	Abdullah Khan, *Sirdar Bahadur.*	Dharmayya.
Lieut. S. M. Rice	Solapuri.	David.
" M. H. B. Geddes	Venkatachalam.	Sayyid Abbas.
" R. Mackie	Hari Chandra Rao.	Muniratnam.
" R. J. Malet	Gurappa.	Shaik Amin.
2nd Lieut. H. St. G. H. Harvey-Kelly	Abdul Aziz.	Muhammad Yusuf.
		Ramasami.

1903.
Bellary-Royadrug Feeder Line.

In May 1903, a detachment of 300 men under Captain C. R. Scott-Elliot was sent to Bellary to assist in the construction of the Bellary-Royadrug Feeder Line. The work consisted of making a railway bank across the bed of a large tank near Bellary and there was no other work besides the earth work. The rate was Rs. 5 *per* 1,000 cubic feet all round, which was very low and barely paid expenses.

The Railway granted the concession of a return fare for single rates, with a free baggage-wagon for every 100 men. Government paid for the move and made no deductions from the working pay.

The work was completed in the course of the month.

The following officers were employed on this work:—

British Officers.	Subadars.	Jemadars.
Capt. C. R. Scott-Elliot	Hari Chandra Rao	Shaikh Amin.
2nd Lieut. E. A. Breithaupt	Solapuri	Venkatasami.
		Srinavasulu.
		Sivaprasad Pande.

1904.
Bangalore.

From the 3rd May to the 5th July 1904, the regiment was employed on the construction of a foot-path round the general parade ground at Bangalore. This work was carried out under the orders of Brigadier-General John Eccles Nixon, without remuneration, as, under the orders of the Commander-in-Chief, every Pioneer Regiment was to carry out one month's labour yearly *gratis*.

On the 1st May 1904, a detachment of 65 rank and file, under Subadar Sayyid Abbas, proceeded to Yelahanka, near Bangalore, to prepare a camp for G Battery, R. H. A. The work consisted of clearing jungle, levelling ground, constructing stables, gun-sheds, cookhouses, etc. Working pay as military rates was drawn. The party returned on the 7th June 1904, and received the thanks of Captain Lawless, Commanding G Battery, and of Colonel Daniell, C. R. A., for its good work.

1905—1907.
Coonoor-Ootacamund Railway.

From the 1st January 1905 to the 1st October 1907, the regiment was employed on the Coonoor-Ootacamund Railway. Full particulars as to the work performed will be found in the following report.

Report on Employment, etc.

The following is a copy of a letter No. 124 M. W., Government of India, Military Department, dated Fort William, 14th January 1905.

Sanction for Employment.

To

THE QUARTERMASTER-GENERAL IN INDIA.

SIR,

I am directed to acknowledge receipt of your letter No. 3605 A, dated 22nd December 1904, and in reply to say that the Government of India sanction the employment of the 64th Pioneers on the construction of the Coonoor-Ootacamund Railway Extension, subject to the concurrence of the Hon'ble the Resident in Mysore, in the temporary reduction of the Garrison at Bangalore. The work will be done on the contract system, and the Regiment will receive payment for labour at full contract rates. From his receipts, the Officer Commanding the Troops will be required to meet all extra expenditure connected with transport, movement, extra clothing, water-supply, conservancy, etc., and repair and maintenance of tools, and cost of tear and wear of tents. The occupation of the British Depôt hut barracks at Wellington by the Regiment in the monsoon months may be arranged for under the orders of His Excellency the Commander-in-Chief, but any additional expense involved must be met by the Regiment. No portion of the extra expenses incurred by reason of the employment of troops on this work shall be borne by the Military Estimates.

2. The Regiment will, if possible, be allowed to remain undisturbed until the completion of the work, but no guarantee can be given to this effect. If the Battalion is required for Military service elsewhere, no compensation will be given on account of its removal.

I am, etc.,

(Signed) W. A. LIDDELL, Major, R.E.,
for *Secretary to the Government of India.*

The following report by Lieutenant-Colonel E. L. Holloway gives full particulars of the work done on this contract:—

British Officers 10, Native Officers 11, Rank & File 635. In accordance with the above sanction which had previously been telegraphed, the regiment, strength as per margin, left Bangalore on 19th December 1904, and after 14 days' march, arrived at Camp Yellanhalli on 1st January 1905. An advance party of 50 Rank and File with one Native Officer, under Major C. T. Swan, proceeded by rail to prepare camping ground, etc.

Camp Yellanhalli. The camp was situated on a knoll about 1,000 yards from the village of Yellanhalli, a post changing station five miles from Ootacamund. The only disadvantage of the camping ground was scarcity of water. This difficulty was overcome by laying a $\frac{3}{4}$ inch pipe 1,200 yards, and storing water in 300 gallon tanks, of which six were very kindly lent by the Rose and Crown Brewery Company.

Hutting. Sheds with corrugated iron roofs were built for store-houses, cook-houses, magazine and hospital, otherwise all ranks were housed in tents.

At the end of May 1905, half the regiment moved into Ootacamund. There the men were housed in vacated dwellings, on railway land, and in the old European Jail. In 1907, Bishops-down House, a large house in poor repair, was leased and used as a Barrack.

Health. During its stay in the Nilgiris, the health of the regiment, after the men had once got accustomed to the cold, was very good.

For the first four months the average daily number of men in hospital was 27 or nearly 4 per cent. For the second four months 12·66 or 2 per cent. For the third four months 5·77 or ·8 per cent. During the year 1906, 5·79 or ·8 per cent, and from January to September 1907, 7·41 **or** 1·15 per cent. The majority of cases in hospital were due to minor accidents on the work.

Casualties. There were in all 14 deaths:—Pneumonia, 7; from accidents on work, 3; other diseases, 4.

Of the accidents on work, two men received fatal injuries from a buried boulder, which slipped out of the hill cutting near where they were carrying earth. The third man was killed by injuries received from a log falling on him while he was employed in cutting wood.

Discipline. Discipline was good, the number of minor offences being small. In 1905, seventeen men were convicted by summary Courts-Martail. Of these, six for offences which happened at the depot of the regiment at Bangalore. In 1906, four, and one by Civil power. In 1907, two.

Discharges. The total number of men discharged in 1905 to 1907 was 216. Of these 106 were discharged under I. A. W., IV. 2, "As unlikely to become efficient soldiers."

Enlistments. In all 371 recruits were enlisted. The strength of the regiment was increased by 80 in 1906. The regiment was brought and kept up to full strength without much difficulty.

Work taken up. The work allotted to the regiment on its arrival at Yellanhalli was sixty chains (6,000 feet) long, chain 220 to 280, the heaviest work on this Section being a cutting 80 feet deep. At the end of May 1905, half the regiment moved into Ootacamund and took up chains 530 to 603. The heaviest works on this Section were a cutting 50 feet deep at Mungena Corrai, a similar cutting at Fernhill Palace Gates, the bank over the lake, and levelling for station yard at Mettucherry. Fourteen chains were also taken up near Lovedale (chains 420 to 434).

Not including petty works, noted below, the actual amount of work done by the regiment was :—

Total length taken up, 174 chains or 3 miles, 520 yards.

The excavation done was classified as follows (see Schedule of Rates attached) :—

Class A.	@ 6/	per mile Cubic feet	..	425,812
Class B.	@ 7/8	,,	,,	.. 6,855,913
Class C.	@ 15/	,,	,,	.. 2,036,917
Class D.	@ 25/	,,	,,	.. 212,348
Class E.	@ 40/	,,	,,	.. 171,481
Class H.	@ 60/	.,	,,	.. 280,340
		Total Cubic Feet	...	9,982,811

Lead varied from 1 chain (100 feet), for which no extra rate was allowed, to 14½ chains, paid at 6 annas per thousand cubic feet per half chain after the first chain. The longest lead was in Mettucherry, levelling for station yard and making the bank over the lake. Here 14½ chains lead was paid on 1,050,000 cubic feet of earth. Lines for trollies were laid for any lead over three chains, when trollies were available, otherwise spoil was carried as much as possible in wheel-barrows; baskets were never used, except for every short leads, or in places where the steepness of the ground rendered other transport impossible. It was found that the latter method of carrying earth did not pay.

Minor works. Besides the work noted above, many minor works were undertaken, such as:—Building bridges and culverts; making and metalling roads, laying and up-keep of trolly lines, manufacture of wheel-barrows, baskets and tools, felling timber, stone-walling and pitching, making side-drains in cuttings, etc.

The chief minor works were a stone masonry bridge to carry road over railway near chain 240, and a culvert near Fernhill, of which the dimensions were:—Length, 185 feet; inside measurement, 3 ft. by 4 ft.—3,955 c. ft. concrete in cement, 987 c. ft. concrete in lime, 1,869 c. ft. 1st class masonry in lime, 1,734 c. ft. 1st class masonry in cement.

Hours of Work. The Work Hours were 8 A.M. to 11-30 A.M. and 1 to 4-30 P.M. The men worked in squads of ten under a N.C.O. as a rule, each squad being given a task, after completion of which they were allowed to go.

Earnings. The total amount of money earned by the regiment was Rs. 1,86,506-0-10, which was distributed as follows:—

	Rs.	A.	P.
Pay, B.O.'s N.O.'s Rank and File	1,46,936	13	2
Hutting, Conservancy, etc.	2,637	9	5
Explosives	7,388	8	9
Tools & their Up-keep (not including Labour)	7,820	3	5
Movements, Rail Fares, etc.	4,701	11	11
Lime and Masonry Expenses	3,036	6	5
Pay of Locally Hired Labour	2,337	4	6
Miscellaneous	2,256	15	11

Number of men working. The daily average number of men employed on work was 466, exclusive of Native Officers.

Working Pay. The men were paid, on the average, 5 annas a day; artificers, from 6 to 8 annas; Native Officers 12 annas. About 24 days' work was done in the month.

Training of Field Engineering. Good practice in Field Engineering was obtained from the many temporary culverts and bridges necessitated by the trolly lines, which themselves gave good practice in plate-laying, the working of points and crossings, etc. The principal temporary bridges constructed were:—The bridge over the Railway near Mungena Corrai, which was used for road traffic for 18 months.

A bridge for trollies, built over the North Lake Road to lead earth from Mettucherry to Lake Bank. This bridge was 390 feet long, with 14 spans, trestles dogspiked, and sleeper stacks.

Tools. Much has been written on the subject of the equipment carried by the men of Pioneer Regiments. Experience on the Coonoor Ootacamund Railway has convinced me that the light tools carried by the men in heavy leather cases are absolutely useless for heavy earthwork. No contractor would dream of buying such tools. I consider that the working efficiency of a Pioneer Regiment would be increased 50 per cent., with the issue of heavy picks and more shovels in place of mamooties. Each Section should have a mule to carry its tools, the men themselves carrying only a light hasty-entrenching tool, for use when employed as ordinary infantry. This would mean an increase of 32 mules per Battalion, but it would be well worth it.

As regards boring tools, I would strongly recommend the substitution of, 7/8 inch octagonal boring bars and hammers, in place of the jumpers issued at present. The men can do at least 50 per cent., more work with smaller bars and hammers than they can with jumpers. They are also much lighter to carry and easier to temper. Such bars should be cut into lengths from 5 feet downwards.

Data for future employment of a Pioneer Regiment on contract work.

The total amount earned by the regiment in 33 months' work was Rs. 1,86,506.

Deduct—Explosives   Rs. 7,388
            Lime, etc.   „   3,036
            To local labour   „   2,337

                                                          Rs.   12,761

                                                    Balance Rs. 1,73,745

This sum represents in soft earth, Class A., 289,575,00 cubic feet.

The work of 466 men in 33 months of 24 working days = 369,072 men for one day. Dividing $\frac{289,575,00}{369,072}$ each man excavates 78 cubic feet a day and carries same 100 feet; he is paid 5 annas a day—369,072 x 5=Rs. 1,15,335. (The actual working pay, paid to rank and file, was Rs. 1,15,801).

Balance to pay expenses of tools, move, etc., and B.O.'s and N.O.'s pay for supervision is Rs. 58,410 or 33 per cent.

From these figures we can assume that the Commanding Officer of a Pioneer Regiment is safe in taking up work with soft earth at Rs. 6 per mille as a basis on which the rates are calculated, to pay his men annas 5 per diem and to make a profit of 33 per cent, to pay for supervision, move, tools and miscellaneous expenses. Also that a Pioneer Regiment, with 466 men on work, can excavate and carry 100 feet, 875,000 cubic feet of soft earth in a month of 24 working days. Working from this basis the approximate amount of work possible in hard earth or with longer lead can be found, provided that the rates for different classes of soil, rock, etc., are fairly calculated.

The correctness of these figures, taken from work extending over nearly 3 years and worked down to an average, can be checked in this way :—Suppose a man excavates 78 cubic feet and carries it 100 feet in a day; it takes 13 men to move 1,000 c. ft., *i.e.*, to earn Rs. 6. Their pay at 5 annas is Rs. 4/1 which gives a profit of Rs. 1/15 or about 30 per cent. In practice men can do more than 78 c. ft. in soft soil with 1 chain lead. The difference goes in pay to men employed in mending tools, making baskets, wheel-barrows, etc.

                                (Signed) E. L. HOLLOWAY, Lt.-Col.

BELGAUM, 1*st December* 1907.   *Commandant, 64th Pioneers.*

SCHEDULE OF RATES.

Class.	Schedule of Rates.	Unit of Calculation.	Rate. Rs.	A.	P.
	Earthwork.				
	Excavation in cuttings, including lead up to 100 feet in length and lift up to 4 feet in height, and dressing of formation and slopes, &c., in cuttings.—				
A	Soft earth, not requiring picks	c. ft. 1,000	6	0	0
B	Hard earth, requiring continuous use of picks	,,	7	8	0
C	Soft or disintegrated rock	,,	15	0	0
D	Rock requiring 25 per cent. blasting	,,	25	0	0
E	Large boulders of hard rock requiring 50 per cent. blasting	,,	40	0	0
F	Hard rock in mass	,,	60	0	0
	Extra rate on earth excavated from a cutting and used to form a bank, to cover work in forming and dressing slopes. (This rate applies only to actual quantity of earth excavated from a railway cutting of ordinary width)	,,	2	0	0
	Earth work in filling in banks excavated from borrow pits, including lead up to 100 feet in length and lift up to 4 feet in heigth, and dressing of formation and slopes and earth required to allow for shrinkage—				
A	Soft earth	,,	6	0	0
B	Hard earth	,,	7	8	0
	Extra for every complete length of 50 feet of lead, additional beyond first 100 feet	,,	0	6	0
	Extra for every complete lift of 4 feet additional above the first 4 feet	,,	0	6	0
	Hire of tramways or other plant supplied by Engineer-in-Chief, will be charged for at a rate per mensem equal to 2 per cent. of the actual value of the plant, the cost of carriage of all such plant, from depôt at Coonoor to site of works to be borne also by the Contractor.				

The Following is a List of the Officers Employed on this contract :—

British Officers.	Subadars.	Jemadars.
Lieut.-Colonel G. B. Stevens	Subadar-Major Mir Abbas, *Bahadur*.	Jemadar Muhammad Yusuf
Major E. L. Holloway		,, Venkatasami
,, F. Churchill	Subadar Solapuri	,, Sivaprasad Pande
,, C. T. Swan	,, Venkatachellam	,, Krishnasami
Capt. J. A. Bliss	,, Hari Chandra Rao	,, Muhammad Sikandar.
,, S. B. Watson	,, Sayyid Abbas	,, Francis
,, M. H. B. Geddes	,, Muniratnam	,, Audinarayanasami
Lieut. R. Mackie	,, Shaikh Amin	,, Kuppusami
,, R. J. Malet		,, Sayyid Munawar
,, H. St. G. Harvey-Kelly		,, Abdul Latif
,, E. Marsden		
,, E. A. Breithaupt		
,, H. A. Harris		
,, H. F. Murland		
,, A. C. C. Rogers		
,, C. Hemsley		
,, M. Castle Smith		
2nd Lieut. J. A. Story		

An appreciation of the services rendered by the regiment, on the Coonoor-Ootacamund Railway, by Government of Madras, was recorded in the following letter:—

Government of Madras, P. W. (Railway) Department
Proceedings No. 1630 Railway, *Dated the 1st October* 1907.

Read the following paper:—

Letter from the Engineer-in-Chief, Coonoor-Ootacamund Railway to the Secretary to the Government of Madras, P.W.D. (Railway), dated the 14th October 1907, No. 3151.

ORDER—No. 1630 RAILWAY, DATED 31ST OCTOBER 1907.

A copy of the letter No. 3151, dated the 14th October 1907, from the Engineer-in-Chief, Coonoor-Ootacamund Railway, read above, will be forwarded to the Assistant Adjutant-General, 9th (Secunderabad) Division, with an expression of this Government's appreciation of the services rendered to the Government Railway by the 64th Pioneers.

2. A copy of these proceedings will be forwarded to the Railway Board for information, with the intimation that the Commanding Officer's report, referred to in paragraph 3 of the Engineer-in-Chief's letter will be forwarded on receipt.

G. A. ANDERSON,
Secretary to Government.

Letter from the Engineer-in-Chief, Coonoor-Ootacamund Railway. To the Secretary to the Government of Madras, P.W.D. (Railway), dated the 14th October 1907, No. 3151.

I have the honour to inform you that in compliance with the orders of the Lieutenant-General Commanding the IXth Division, the 64th Pioneers left this station for Belgaum on the 2nd October. The greater part of the work allotted them has been completed and the Regiment has been paid in full for the work done to the end of September. A detachment remains under Capt. Watson to complete the works remaining as a separate contract.

2. I take this opportunity of bringing to your notice the tact, zeal and ability displayed by Major Swan, the Officer Commanding, and his Officers and the excellent behaviour of the men of the regiment. Major Swan has been in charge of the work for the greater portion of the time the regiment has been employed on the Railway and it is due to his determination to see the work through that the regiment has been permitted to remain until the back of the work has been broken and that a detachment has been left to complete it. With regard to the men of the regiment he informs me that while quartered at Ootacamund there has been not a single case of desertion, and practically no crime and that the health of the Regiment has been better than at any time for the past ten years and this in spite of the men having worked in all weathers in a particularly inclement climate. The Railway is greatly indebted to the regiment for their services.

3. Major Swan informs me that he is writing a note on the actual amount of work done by the regiment on the Railway. This if issued by the Railway Board would be of great use in future cases of the employment of Pioneer labour on Public Works, since owing to the want of knowledge of the Pioneers' methods of work and of the number of men available after allowing for furlough, training of recruits, etc., it has not been possible to make any reliable estimate of the amount of work a Regiment is capable of in a given time.

4. The regiment is I understand satisfied with the financial results of their labours and they have now an experience second to none of earthwork, blasting, temporary bridging and heavy masonry which should add greatly to their military efficiency should such services be required of them on active service.

On the departure of the regiment for Belgaum, a detachment was left behind, under the command of Captain S. B. Watson, which continued to work till the 4th April 1908. Full details will be found in the following report by Captain Watson.

REPORT ON THE WORK OF THE DETACHMENT, 64TH PIONEERS, ON THE COONOOR-OOTACAMUND RAILWAY, 1ST OCTOBER 1907— 30TH MARCH 1908.

1. On the departure of the regiment from Ootacamund for Belgaum a detachment **Strength.** was ordered to remain to complete the work. Strength of detachment:—

    2 British Officers.
    4 Native Officers.
    1 Hospital Assistant.
    256 N.C. Officers and men selected from those who volunteered to remain at Ootacamund.

2. In order to complete the work as fast as possible, a large number of local coolies **Local Labour.** were employed in conjunction with the men of the detachment, on earthwork and in carrying materials, sand, mortar, stone, etc., for the masonry. In this way trained Pioneers were made available for other work requiring skill.

3. The work extended for nearly two miles from Ootacamund towards Coonoor. **General Description of Work.** It included the completion of the banks and cuttings which the regiment had left unfinished, a masonry retaining wall and various other works such as rough bridging and shoring up the sides of cuttings.

    No platelaying was undertaken, as men could not be spared from other more urgent work.

4. The average number of sick was 4·8. This number was due mainly to minor **Sick.** injuries to hands and feet. There were no serious accidents. There was one death from pneumonia.

5. The main portion of the detachment was quartered, with all the rifles, in a house **Quarters.** rented at Rs. 70 per mensem; the remainder lived some in the Old Native Jail and some in native houses on railway land.

6. The discipline of the detachment was good. There was no serious crime. It is **Discipline.** to be noted to the credit of the men that no trouble arose with the large number of coolie women who were constantly at work close to them.

Statement of Receipts and Expenditure.

Receipts.	Amount.	Expenditure.	Amount.
	Rs.		Rs.
Earthwork	12,750	Working pay of detachment	15,268
Bridging and shoring	1,710	House rent	420
Masonry	16,154	Explosives	440
Turfing and planting	753	Tools	205
Miscellaneous work	863	Movements, Rail fares, &c., to Bangalore (Bangalore to Belgaum paid by Government.)	780
Total from Coonoor-Ootacamund Railway.	32,230	Stores, lime, sand and metal	9,273
Sale of tools and stores	1,081	Local labour	4,673
Miscellaneous	236	Hire of carts for sand and stone, &c.	1,508
		Miscellaneous, stationery, &c.	123
		Balance profit to regimental funds	857
Total ..Rs	33,547	Total ..Rs.	33,547

Working pay.

7. Rates of working pay were:—Native Officers, Rs. 1-2-0 daily; Artificers, As. 9 and 10 daily; N.-C. Officers and men, As. 8 daily. This was reduced to As. 6 for the last 3 months, but a bonus was paid afterwards making up the rate to As. 8.

As an explanation of the high rate of working pay, it may be noted that the men were largely employed on work requiring skilled labour, and that the cost of messing is always high at Ootacamund—on an average Rs. 2 per mensem more than at Belgaum.

A total of Rs. 382 was paid to the Hospital Assistant, clerk, sick, cooks and others not directly employed on the work.

Working Hours and Days.

8. Hours of the work were from 8 A.M. to 11-30 A.M. and 1 to 5 P.M. or until tasks were finished.

Work was carried on every day except a few wet days, Sundays and a weekly half holiday. Masonry work was continued on Sundays. Many men worked willingly 6½ days a week.

Total number of working days and men, excluding Native Officers, was 27,904. This does not include 2,100 men who contracted to supply sand and stone.

Tasks. 9. The men worked usually in squads of ten. Tasks were given, so many cubic feet per squad.

Men digging and washing sand and those quarrying and dressing stone were paid on the contract system according to the quantities supplied.

Earthwork Rates. 10. Rates for earthwork were the same as given to the regiment. (Appendix A).

Details of excavation by the detachment and local labour.

```
                                                        c. ft.
    Spoil re-handled  @ Rs.  2-0 per 1,000 c. ft. ..   29,711
        Do.           @  ,,  4-8    ,,     ,,     ..  111,000
    Class A.          @  ,,  6-0    ,,     ,,     ..   18,460
        Do.  B.       @  ,,  7-8    ,,     ,,     ..  796,460
    Special Wet       @  ,, 10-0    ,,     ,,     ..    6,314
        Do.           @  ,, 12-8    ,,     ,,     ..  107,261
    Class C.          @  ,, 15-0    ,,     ,,     ..   58,665
                                                      ───────
                                         Total    1,127,871 c. ft.
                                         =    ..   Rs. 8,926
```

Lead and Lift. Add for lead, lift, ramming and dressing .. Rs. 3,823

Total receipts on earthwork.. Rs. 12,749
Deduct work done by local labour .. Rs. 3,820

Balance by detachment .. Rs. 8,929

The maximum lead was 1,650 ft. Maximum lift 24 ft. Average lead about 600 ft. Average lift about 12 feet.

```
                                         c. ft.
    Total on which lead was paid  ..  1,019,965
        Do.         lift    do    ..    248,032
```

Baskets. 10. Baskets were used for short leads up to 50 ft. or where the ground was too wet or steep for wheel barrows.

Wheel Barrows. Wheel barrows (*vide* Appendix B) were used up to 300 ft.

Trolleys. Trolleys and rails for any lead over 300 feet but their use depends on the amount of labour required to lay the line and cost of materials, sleepers, etc. The trolleys contained about 13 c. ft. of earth. Rails were 40 lbs. and 50 lbs., 24 ft. and 30 ft., respectively. The latter were too long and heavy for easy laying. The pattern of switch used is described in Appendix C. No charge was made to the detachment for hire of trolleys or rails as the regiment had already paid this.

Description of Soil. 11. The majority of the earth was Class B, a hard clay with a large proportion of hard grit. In wet weather it melted into slush and became difficult to work in.

Cuttings. Sides of cuttings were cut to a slope of ¾ to 1. At any steeper slope slips frequently occurred. It was found best to take out the sides of cuttings in steps 4 ft. high and not less than 3 feet broad. This height is convenient for a man to work with a pick and the width sufficient for men to pass with baskets.

12. The bridging and shoring gave good practice in handling heavy rails and timbers and use of dog-spikes.

Bridging and Shoring.

13. The masonry at Manjinikorai consisted of two retaining walls of 1½ inch lime concrete with a facing of third class masonry and a concrete invert. The higher of the two walls was designed to be 30 ft. high, 14 ft. thick at the base, and 2 ft. thick at the top. A contract for a length of 300 feet, for which 60,000 c. ft. of concrete and 13,000 c. ft. of third class stone facing were required, was undertaken by the detachment but could not be completed, mainly owing to the difficulty of obtaining from local contractors regular supplies of materials, such as 1½ inch metal and stone. Another cause of delay was the difficulty of removing slips in the wet clay soil and shoring up the sides of the cutting.

Masonry.

The quantities put in were:—

1½ inch line concrete .. 43,919 c. ft.
3rd class stone facing .. .. 5,297 „

Total number of days and men, about 5,500 (exclusive of 2,100 supplying sand and quarrying stone). It is difficult to be exact, as a large number of men were working at the same place at earthwork, shoring and masonry simultaneously, This figure includes men carrying materials from the road side to the work, mixing mortar, ramming, etc., and masons laying stone.

Total number of coolies on this work 2,651, cost Rs. 853.

Four Pioneers, with 10 women coolies, put in 180 c. ft. in a day.

Tasks. Ten Pioneers, without coolies, put in 160 c. ft.

The tasks included lead of materials from road side to the mixing platforms and thence to the wall, an average distance of 400 feet, and an average lift of 4 feet. These tasks were arrived at after some months of work. The supply of material at first was too uncertain to make regular tasks possible. Latterly 500 to 800 c. ft. of concrete was laid daily, and 100 to 120 c. ft. of stone facing.

14. Explosives were used for quarrying stone for masonry and for getting out rock which coolies broke into metal for concrete. Blasting was always superintended by a British officer, usually Lieutenant H. F. Murland.

Explosives.

15. Some tools were left with the detachment by the regiment, but a few, such as steel boring bars and iron mortar pots, had to be purchased.

Tools.

16. The detachment on leaving Ootacamund was conveyed free by train to Coonoor and travelled over several portions of the line which had been completed by the regiment. The detachment marched from Coonoor to Mettupalaiyam, as no concession could be given by the Railway for that portion of the journey.

Railway Expenses from Ootacamund.

From Mettupalaiyam to Belgaum the detachment was conveyed by rail at the ordinary rate for Military traffic, *viz.*, 4 as. 6 p. per vehicle per mile.

17. To sum up the results of this six months' work of the detachment. The officers, British and Native, had a useful practical experience of contract work and of the management of local labour. In addition the whole detachment had practical instruction in rough masonry work and learnt something about concrete. This latter material is likely to be used more than ever in the future, so it is right that Pioneers should have some knowledge of it.

Summary of Results.

S. B. WATSON, CAPTAIN,
64th Pioneers.

APPENDIX A.

SCHEDULE OF RATES.

Class	Description of Work.	Unit.	Rate. Rs.	A.	P.
	Earthwork.				
	Excavation in cuttings, including lead up to 100 ft. in length and lift up to 4 feet in height, and dressing of formation and slopes, &c., in cuttings.—				
A	Soft earth, not requiring picks	c. ft. 1,000	6	0	0
B	Hard earth, requiring continuous use of picks	,,	7	8	0
C	Soft or disintegrated rock	,,	15	0	0
D	Rock requiring 25 per cent. blasting	,,	25	0	0
E	Large boulders of hard rock requiring 50 per cent. blasting	,,	40	0	0
F	Hard rock in mass	,,	60	0	0
	Extra rate on earth excavated from a cutting and used to form a bank, to cover work in forming and dressing slopes. (This rate applies only to actual quantity of earth excavated from a railway cutting of ordinary width)	,,	2	0	0
	Earth work in filling in banks excavated from borrow pits, including lead up to 100 ft. in length and lift up to 4 ft. in height, and dressing of formation and slopes and earth required to allow for shrinkage—				
A	Soft earth	,,	6	0	0
B	Hard earth	,,	7	8	0
	Extra for every complete length of 50 feet of lead, additional beyond first 100 feet	,,	0	6	0
	Extra for every complete lift of 4 feet additional above the first 4 feet	,,	0	6	0
	Hire of tramways or other plant, supplied by Engineer-in-Chief, will be charged for at a rate per mensem equal to 2 per cent. of the actual value of the plant, the cost of carriage of all such plant, from depot at Coonoor to site of works to be borne also by the Contractor.				

MISCELLANEOUS RATES.

Description of Work.	Unit.	Rate. Rs.	A.
Concrete in lime mortar consisting of 2 parts of ballast passing a 1½ inch ring to 1 part mortar. Mortar to be 1 of lime to 2 of clean approved sand	100 c. ft.	29	0
3rd class masonry in face work in lime mortar with headers every 4 ft. the average thickness of facing to be 1 ft. 4 in. Courses generally to be 1 ft. thick	100 c. ft.	42	0
Coping. 1st class masonry in lime	100 c. ft.	75	0
Brickwork (for pillars), in lime mortar, rough work	100 c. ft.	21	0
Brickwork in cement, excluding cost of cement	100 c. ft.	15	0
The above rates include all lead and lift on all materials.			
Turfing	100 sq. ft.	1	0
Lead on stone carried by men	100 c. ft. per 100 ft. distance.	0	8
Lead on stone by cart over 200 yards	100 c. ft. per mile.	3	8
Dry stone work in revetment	100 c. ft.	8	8
Dry stone side drains, section 3 sq. ft., lead not more than 600 ft.	per 100 running ft.	30	8
Dry stone culverts, 2 ft. x 2 ft. opening, stone on three sides only	per running ft.	2	0
Ditto of smaller vent	Do.	1	8
Spreading, watering, rolling, sectioning metal on roads 3 in. thick, excluding cost of materials	100 sq. ft.	0	10
For each additional 1 in.	Do.	2 as. 6 p.	
Daily labour As. 8 per man			
In wet weather, As. 10; on Sundays or holidays, Re. 1			
Carpenters, Masons, Blacksmiths and other skilled labour, Re. 1 per man, and Re. 1-4 per maistri (N. C. Officers).			
Removing tree stumps	per ft. girth.	1	0
or if over 7 inch diameter	each	2	0
Ramming earth	per 1,000 c. ft.	2	5

MISCELLANEOUS NOTES FROM 3¼ YEARS OF WORK ON COONOOR-OOTACAMUND RAILWAY.

I.—RATES.

In the following notes the daily rate of working pay is taken at 6 as. per diem.

Concrete in lime, Rs. 29 per 100 c. ft.

Quantities of Materials required per 100 c. ft. of concrete.

1½ in. metal	...	100 c. ft.
Sand	...	33⅓ ,,
Lime, unslaked	...	8⅓ = 16⅔ c. ft. of slaked lime.

Labour varies according to lead, a rough average is 6·25 men per 100 c. ft.

The rate when materials could be obtained regularly, gave a profit of 20 per cent.

Third class masonry, Rs. 42 per 100 c. ft.

This was roughly dressed stone with one square face in lime mortar. Rate for stone at quarry, Rs. 15 per 100 c. ft. Stone easy to split was scarce. The rock where found in masses did not lie in convenient layers. Blasting was little used. Small boulders gave the best results as they were easily spilt with wedges and hammer.

Coping, 1st class masonry in lime mortar, Rs. 75 per 100 c. ft.

This rate is very low. Rs. 100 would probably be a fair rate. 12 men can lay 100 c. ft. in 1 day, mixing their own mortar.

Turfing, Re. 1 per 100 sq. ft. Where the turf can be cut within 200 yds. of the bank, one man can cut and lay 100 sq. ft. in 1 day.

Lead on stone carried by men, As. 8 per 100 c. ft. per 100 ft. distance. 8 men can carry 100 c. ft. of rough stone, 1,800 ft. in 4 days. A poor rate.

Lead on stone by cart. *Vide* note on carts.

Dry stone revetment, Rs. 8-8 per 100 c. ft. 537 men built 4,775 c. ft. including bringing stone ¾ mile in 84 carts (that is, the equivalent of 84 carts for 1 day). The rate is a good one.

Rough stone side drains, Rs. 30 per 100 ft. Where stone is plentiful within 600 ft. 10 men can make 100 running ft. of drain in 3 days, including digging and carrying. Average section of drain 3 sq. ft. Rs. 40 to Rs. 50 was given in other places to allow for lead and cost of quarrying stone.

Dry stone culvert 2 ft. x 2 ft., Rs. 2 per running ft. 15 men including diggers, carriers and masons built 28 running ft. in 5 days.

Metalling roads, As. 10 per 100 sq. ft. 500 ft. x 12 ft. 3 in. were laid by 100 men including watering and ramming. The metal was stacked within 200 ft. The rate is a bad one.

Removing tree stumps, Re. 1 per ft. girth, or Rs. 2 each, if over 7 in. in diameter. The rates were fair, but hardly paid for big roots over 10 ft. in diameter. Blasting was tried but not found successful owing to the cost and large quantity of explosives required. It was cheaper to dig round the root and haul it away with ropes.

II.—BLASTING.

The rock was hard granite in solid masses with occasional cracks and flaws. The best charge was Nobel's gelignite in cartridges weighing 1 oz.—1 cartridge to every foot depth of bore hole.

Gelignite.

The best depth is 3 ft. The general rule being that the distance back from the face should not be greater than the depth of the hole.

Dynamite is not so effective as gelignite, and is the same price Rs. 1-10-6 per pound. Gelignite requires a No. 6 detonator, Rs. 5-1-9 per 100. No. 3 is strong enough for dynamite and cheaper, Rs. 3-4-3 per 100.

Dynamite.

A charge of wet guncotton broken up and pressed into a bore hole and a gelignite or dynamite cartridge placed on top as a primer was very effective. The hole was filled with guncotton up to 18 inches from the top and the gelignite cartridge placed on top. This charge in a 3 ft. hole was a big one, but effective as it shattered the rock into small pieces which could be easily carried away.

Guncotton.

Guncotton primers would not fit into holes made with $\frac{7}{8}$ in. bars. They were soaked in water, broken up and used as wet guncotton.

English gunpowder was tried but was effective only on small boulders up to 6 ft. in diameter. The charge was 3 to 8 oz. The small diameter of the bore holes did not allow of larger charges of powder.

Gunpowder.

A new explosive, "Ammonal," was tried and found to be about as effective as gelignite. It has advantages, as it will not detonate if hammered and will not burn, but it is rendered useless by damp or wet. It is detonated with a No. 6 detonator.

Ammonal.

Common safety fuze made by the Swansea Safety Fuze Co. was used. Price 5 as. 3 ps. per coil of 24 ft. In very wet places waterproof fuze was used. This is more expensive. The end of the fuze where placed in the detonator should be greased to keep the wet from the end of the fuze.

Fuze.

No fuze less than 18 inches long should be used. After cutting the end so as to expose the powder it is a good plan to place a pinch of gelignite on the end of the fuze which makes it easier and quicker to light.

Where several charges have to be fired at once, fuzes must be cut of different lengths. A difference of 2 inches is sufficient if there are three or four men to light the fuzes at once. Not more than 12 charges should be fired at a time.

Electric firing. Electric firing was not much used owing to numerous missfires caused by defective fuzes. It frequently happened that, of several charges connected in series, all would explode except one, which would be buried under the debris of the other charges and so could not be discovered at once and was likely to cause an accident.

The service electric fuzes were not available.

Tamping. The best is clay or any kind of earth that will bind well, when pressed into a hole. Water tamping was not often used owing to the extra cost of waterproof fuze.

Cost. The cost of explosives,—that is, gelignite—with No. 6 detonaters and ordinary fuze, is Rs. 25 to 30 per 1,000 cubic feet in solid rock cuttings.

III.—BORING.

One man with a 4 lbs. hammer and $\frac{7}{8}$ in. bar can bore 4 ft. in 1 day, and uses from $2\frac{1}{2}$ to 3 pints of water. At a depth below 3 ft., the bar is apt to stick, so that it is usually not worth while to make holes deeper than $3\frac{1}{2}$ ft.

The bars used were Edgar Allen's octagonal drill steel $\frac{7}{8}$ in. £ s. d. brand, class V.C., price Rs. 21 per cwt. at Kolar. (1 cwt. = about 50 ft.) About 2 in. of steel are wasted in tempering, etc., for every 4 ft. of boring.

When bars are too short for boring, that is, less than 1 foot long, they can be cut up for chisels and wedges for dressing and splitting stone.

The regulation $1\frac{1}{2}$ in. hole jumping bars were little used. Working with them, two men together make a 4 ft. hole in one day.

These rates of boring are for regular daily tasks of trained men. In a competition for a prize for one day these rates might be doubled.

Cost of boring. 1 man 4 ft. 1 day = 6 as.

Therefore 1 ft. costs 1 an. 6 p., add cost of $\frac{1}{2}$ in. steel bar wasted at 7 as. 6 p. per ft., total cost of 1 ft. of boring = 1 an. 10 p.

The cost of boring, including cost of steel bars and tempering, with the cost of labour getting out rock with crow bars and breaking up with hammers is Rs. 30 to 35 per 1,000 c. ft.

A fair rate for cuttings in solid rock (granite) would therefore be Rs. 75 per 1,000 c. ft., this would include a lead up to 50 ft. only and 4 ft. lift.

The rate of Rs. 60 paid to the regiment was profitable only in cuttings on the side of a hill where the rock only required to be rolled over the side and there was no lead.

Rates for lead and lift of rock should be three times the rates for earth.

IV.—MISCELLANEOUS.

Carts. Carts were hired from the Engineer-in-Chief at the rate of Rs. 30 per mensem.

An Army Transport cart with two bullocks carries:—

    Sand   ..   ..   17 to 18 c. ft.

    Metal 1½ inch   ..   17 to 18 c. ft.

    Dressed stone   ..   5 to 6 c. ft.

    Rough stone sufficient to make 12 c. ft. of revetment.

It will work, in the hills, 6 days a week, 12 miles a day, that is, 6 miles loaded and 6 miles unloaded. Wooden boxes must be made for the carts. Size 5½ ft. x 2¾ ft. x 1 ft.

Baskets. One man can make 6½ baskets in a day, cutting his own brushwood. At Ootacamund wattle was used for this. About 75 baskets are required per week for 100 men digging and carrying. This number varies with the state of the weather and nature of soil. Baskets rot quickly if used in the wet.

Measurements. Measurements were taken by the Engineer-in-Charge monthly by cross-sections at every 50 ft. along the line with measuring tape and Abney's level and monthly payments were made. It is important that these payments should be made regularly as a check on the progress of the work and to show if the rates are profitable or otherwise.

For these measurements a Pioneer officer requires an Abney's level and a dumpy level with a levelling staff, and a planimeter will be found useful for measuring areas of cross-sections on the plan.

Supervision. The length on which the regiment is working should be divided into sections and an officer placed in charge of the section. He should keep a record, in a separate book, of all orders and measurements affecting his portion of the work and of the number of men employed on it daily who will often belong to several diifferent companies. The usual present state of companies will be separate from this.

Accounts. An account of receipts and expenditure should be kept showing under separate headings: working pay, tools, explosives, movements, etc.

S. B. WATSON, CAPTAIN,
64th Pioneers.

BELGAUM,
5—11—1908.

E. L. HOLLOWAY, COLONEL,
Commandant, 64th Pioneers.

1907—1909.
Line Building at Belgaum.

On its arrival at Belgaum in 1907, the regiment commenced rebuilding its lines, some details of which will be found in the following report by Major C. T. Swan:—

Work 1907—08 (1¼ years.) I took over line building on the 12th December 1908—on that date two Blocks had been completed and a third commenced.

2. The rate of building had been slow, nearly an hour daily being wasted through a defective system of telling off working parties. From want of super-

Progress. vision little work was done; for instance, one item:—Masons laid about 10 feet per man *per diem* in sun-dried brick, whereas 45 cubic feet is a light task and 60 cubic feet has often been exceeded.

3. No. 1 Block had cost Rs. 2,600 and No. 2 Block, Rs. 2,550, for materials only exclusive of contingencies, and No. 3, if continued on the same scale,

Cost. would certainly not have cost less. The sanctioned estimate (our own) was Rs. 1,771—in other words we were exceeding our own estimate at the rate of roughly Rs. 800 per block, and the men were getting nothing for labour. This was a grave state of affairs, and there is little doubt that, had it continued, the officers concerned would have been called upon to make good the excess.

4. The chief reason for this excess was a gradual departure from the standard plan on which the estimate was based. To a certain this was due to the

Reasons for excessive cost. advice of the Garrison Engineer, who, it should have been remembered, was not concerned with the cost. In addition, there was considerable waste, and old materials were not utilised to the extent they might have been.

5. During December, the greater part of the regiment was employed at Pirandwadi, during January the whole regiment was in camp at Bacchi, and to the 15th

Work done in 1909. February at Poona. Since that date two companies have been struck off duty at a time for musketry, and the other Double Companies were at the disposal of their Commanders at least once a week. Notwithstanding all this, between the 12th December 1908 and 18th June 1909, seven blocks of Bachelors' Quarters, and two blocks of Cook-houses have been completed at an average rate of 21 days per building or 13½ working days, as there are only 4½ working days in each week.

6. The average cost per Block (including the excess in numbers 1, 2 and 3) works out to Rs. 1,535 for materials, exclusive of contingencies; for cook-houses,

Cost. it is within the sanctioned estimate of Rs. 553.

7. The men have been paid over Rs. 4,200, which includes half the cost of their

Working Pay. food while in camp at Bacchi and Poona.

8. The Pioneer Reserve Fund has benefited considerably.

BELGAUM,
21st June 1909.

(Signed) C. T. SWAN, MAJOR,
64th Pioneers.

1910.
Aurungabad.

Under the authority of G. O. C. 6th (Poona) Division, Telegram No. 847-A., dated the 17th February 1910, a detachment under Major J. A. Bliss left Belgaum on the 21st and 22nd February 1910, consisting of one B.O., 3 N.C.O.'s and 251 Rank and File, to rebuild the lines of the 34th Poona Horse at Aurungabad.

On the departure of Major Bliss on leave in May, Lieutenant M. Castle Smith, who joined the detachment in March, was left in command until the 31st August 1910, when the detachment rejoined the regiment.

The following Officers were employed on this work:—

British Officers.	Subadars.	Jemadars.
Major J. A. Bliss	Subadar Krishnasami	Jemadar Munisami
Lieut. M. Castle Smith	,, Francis	

Details of the work will be found in the subjoined report by Lieutenant Castle Smith.

REPORT ON A CONTRACT TAKEN UP BY THE 64TH PIONEERS IN 1910, AT AURANGABAD WITH MESSRS. JAFFER JUSUFF & CO., POONA.

A detachment was sent under Major J. A. Bliss to Aurangabad to build new lines for the 34th Poona Horse. It arrived there on the 21st February 1911 and commenced work on the 23rd February 1911.

Strength. The strength of the detachment was:—
    1 British Officer.
    3 Native Officers.
    250 N.C.O.'s and Men.

These included No. 4 Double-Company and men taken from other Double-Companies to make up the number.

On the 15th March, Lieutenant M. Castle Smith joined the detachment from Belgaum, taking over the command on Major Bliss going on leave on the 23rd May.

Labour. On arriving at Aurangabad the detachment found that the work had been going on under civil management for five months and although the books of the contractor showed a big expenditure on overseers, coolies, carts, etc., there was very little to show for it.

Major Bliss was asked to superintend the whole work after the detachment had been there a short time. This he did, sacking over 50 native overseers and so reducing the number to half-a-dozen. These men had to report any petty contractor for bad work but were not allowed to touch it until it had been inspected by a British Officer. With this arrangement numerous petty contractors took up small contracts for one or two blocks and worked very fairly well.

There was never any trouble between our men and the coolies, civil masons, etc., who were working alongside them.

Quarters. The detachment lived in tents pitched about half-a-mile from the work until about the middle of June when it moved into two blocks of syces' lines which had just been completed. Although these quarters were rather small yet the men were kept dry and seemed fairly comfortable.

Discipline. The discipline of the detachment was good. There was no serious crime.

Working Pay. Daily rates were given by the contractor throughout, 20 per cent. being deducted and put to the credit of the regiment.

The following were the rates:—

British Officers	Rs. 40	per mensem.
Native Officers	Re. 1	per diem.
Rank and File	As. 5	per diem.

These rates were raised on the 7th March to the following:—

Major Bliss	Rs.	175	per mensem.
Lieut. M. C. Smith	,,	150	,, ,,
Subadar Krishnasami	,,	60	,, ,.
,, Francis	,,	50	,, ,,
Jemadar Munisami	,,	30	,, ,,
N. C. O.'s and Masons	As.	7	per diem.
Rank and File	,,	5	,, ,,

At the same time the difference in Rice Compensation between Aurangabad and Belgaum was paid by the contractor.

The contractor defrayed all travelling expenses of the detachment, also the journey expenses of the Officer Commanding for one visit of inspection by him during the stay of the detachment.

Two men per hundred drew working pay and prepared the men's food. Bhistis and sweepers were provided by the contractor. Cost of tools, explosives, etc., were also defrayed by the contractor.

Working hours and days. Hours of work.—7 a.m. to 11 a.m., and 2 p.m. to 6 p.m., or until tasks were finished.

One half-holiday weekly and Sundays were non-working days. Before the rains, when the contractor wished the work hurried on, the men worked 6½ days a week.

Work. The work consisted in building Sowars' quarters, N.O.'s quarters and stables, etc.

These were built, on a stone-in-mud foundation and plinth, of sun-dried bricks 9 inches x 3½ inches x 4 inches, with the end walls facing the monsoon quarter of pukka brick.

Special men were brought from Bombay to make the roofs. If more of our men had been available they could have done the roof-work quite easily.

The stone for the plinths and founds was quarried by the men of the detachment. Gelignite was used to start with but, owing to the trouble and delay in getting it, country powder was used latterly. This was very poor stuff and usually broke up the rock into large pieces which had to be broken up by hammer and wedges, etc., causing a lot of extra labour. The quarry was in the bed of a river about a mile from the work.

Good experience was gained in brickmaking. The only baked bricks obtainable were so bad that the detachment started their own kilns and were most successful.

Profits. The profits on the return of the detachment after a little over six months' work on the 1st September 1910 amounted to Rs. 2,667. This represents as near as possible 20 per cent. of the pay drawn as the expenses incurred were extremely small.

In conclusion I must put in a good word for Messrs. Jaffer Jusuff & Co., who treated the detachment in the fairest manner and did everything they could for its comfort and welfare.

M. CASTLE SMITH, LIEUTENANT,
64th Pioneers.

NOTES ON THE FOREGOING REPORT BY MAJOR J. A. BLISS, 64TH PIONEERS.

The following points want to be watched in taking up similar contracts in future:—

Bricks. After the contract was started, the Poona Horse insisted that all bricks should be made from a particular earth only obtainable about 2½ miles from site. The mud for burnt bricks was found to contain a certain amount of lime kunker. When the bricks were burnt this became quick-lime and rendered the bricks useless.

Lime. Source of supply should be enquired into before taking up any contract. We had to collect it along nullahs in small nodules. It was very scarce.

Filling in of Plinths. The Poona Horse wanted to do this themselves with a view to saving money. This ought to be decided on at time of taking up contract, as otherwise earth taken from founds may be wasted.

Carts. Anywhere near the Nizam's Dominions, cartmen require advances before taking on work. After getting advances they usually bolt into the Nizam's Dominions and are no more seen.

545

The following letter was received from the Contractor:—

"Through the President, Bombay Cavalry Combine.

Aurungabad,

27th August 1910.

To the Officer Commanding,
    64th Pioneers,
        Belgaum.

Sir,

I beg to bring to your notice my appreciation of the work done by the detachment of your regiment that came to work on the construction of the new Cavalry Lines at Aurungabad. The British Officers, with Native and Non-Commissioned Officers and all the men were very regular in attendance to their work and willing to do everything and anything, and took interest in the work. Their behaviour throughout their stay was exemplary. Especially I bring to your notice the work done by Major J. A. Bliss, Lieutenant M. Castle Smith, Subadar Krishnasami, Subadar Francis, and Jemadar Munisami.

I beg to again bring to your notice specially the hard work done by Subadar Krishnasami, whose whole heart was in the work. He trained the men to do anything and everything. At the time of the arrival of the detachment there were only ten men to do masonry and bricklaying, but he gradually made the number to nearly fifty. He used to do the laying out, levelling and lining out of the buildings.

Major Bliss, Lieutenant Castle Smith and Subadar Krishnasami, besides managing their own men and supervising their work, supervised the work of civil bricklayers and workers, and with discretion exacted good work from them with theirs.

Especially in my absence they used to manage everything to my entire satisfaction.

I have to part with them with regret, as no building work can be carried out during the rains.

Yours Obediently,

JUSSUFF H. JAFFER,

Contractor, New Cavalry Lines."

"There is no doubt that the detachment of Pioneers has been of the very greatest use to the contractor, in fact I don't know what he would have done without them. Their conduct too, as he says, has been exemplary.

(*Signed*) C. M. DUCAT, COLONEL,

President, Bombay Cavalry Combine."

1912—1913.
Secunderabad.

Under the authority of Chief of the General Staff's letter No. 6134/1, dated 26th November 1912, to the G. O. C. 9th (Secunderabad) Division, the regiment was employed in various detachments from about the 6th October 1912 to the 15th March 1913 on H. H. the Nizam's Guaranteed State Railway.

REPORT ON THE WORK OF THE 64TH PIONEERS ON THE NIZAM'S GUARANTEED STATE RAILWAY, BROAD GAUGE, 6TH OCTOBER 1912 TO 15TH MARCH 1913.

The work consisted of
(a) Distribution and collection of material.
(b) Working a depot for wooden sleepers.
(c) Platelaying.

(a) *Distribution and collection of material.*

About 13,000 rails and 75,000 steel sleepers and other fittings were distributed over about 40 miles of line ready for relaying.

The rails weighed ½ ton each and were 39½ ft. long. A considerable number had to be unloaded from wagons with sides 5ft. high and were then particularly awkward to handle and gave good practice in weight lifting and the use of crowbars. There were two serious accidents. One man was killed and another had both legs broken. There were several minor injuries to hands and feet.

After some practice a party of one N. C. O. and 26 men could unload from a wagon 50—60 rails in an hour, but the number varied as the rails were jammed together and time was lost in loosing the first few rails.

The steel sleepers weighed 135 lbs. each. There was no difficulty with them but they were covered with tar and were nasty things to handle.

A company, or a company and a half, 60—90 men, manned a material train and unloaded. An Indian Officer was in charge of the train and kept account of materials unloaded. British Officers supervised the working of the trains and arranged for the supply of material, tools, camps and movements of the men. For a short time there were four trains working together.

This work and the collection of old material lasted for nearly five months. It soon ceased to be instructive.

(b) *The Sleeper Depot.*

Some 12,600 wooden sleepers were unloaded at Secunderabad and bored and adzed by a machine. Temporary stagings were built for unloading and a light trolley was laid for moving the sleepers in the depot. The engine and machine were driven by two civilians. All other work was done by the Pioneers. About 6,000 sleepers were adzed partly by hand.

About 60—140 men were employed for two months; the work was interrupted occasionally when the machine broke down.

(c) *Platelaying,* that is relaying the line with new rails and sleepers.

Two parties each of 140 to 200 men under a British Officer with a civilian Railway Chief Inspector worked for 2½ and 3 months respectively. Altogether 17 miles of line were relaid. It was found that after some practice, when the material was evenly distributed, 150 men could relay on an average ¼ mile a day, including replacing ballast and packing.

The work had to be carried out without interrupting the usual traffic. Only short periods, a half to two hours were available at a time during which the line was opened out and relaid. In the intervals the men were employed in filling in ballast, packing, distributing material, etc. They worked usually 9 hours a day with a rest on Sunday and half holiday on Saturday.

Over 400 N.C.O.'s and men were instructed. They were changed round so that all had a turn at each kind of work, *e.g.,* working with spanners, key hammers, straightening and lifting with bars, packing, etc.

General Remarks:

All ranks benefited by the work, receiving useful instruction and working pay. The men improved in physique. There was very little sickness. I am of opinion they were employed too long on the uninstructive work of unloading material.

S. B. WATSON, MAJOR,
64th Pioneers.

27th March 1913.

After the 15th March 1913, No. 4 Double Company remained out for another 1½ months to complete the station buildings at Mulkajgiri.

In addition to the work done on the railway, the regiment, during its stay at Secunderabad, did a considerable amount of other work, including the construction of a new Observatory, (with the exception of the dome and upper works) for H. H. the Nizam's Astronomer.

The following officers were employed on work at Secunderabad:—

British Officers.	Subadars.	Jemadars.
Lieut.-Col. C. T. Swan (*on inspection duty.*) Major S. B. Watson. „ M. H. B. Geddes. Capt. R. Mackie. „ E. Marsden. „ T. B. Skinner. Lieut. I. L. O'H. Hare. „ V. C. Cassidy.	Subadar Venkatasami. „ Krishnasami. „ Muhd. Sikandar. „ Francis. „ Sayyid Munawar. „ Anantadri Nayudu. „ Nanjappa.	Jemadar Musa Raza Khan. „ Durgayya. „ Narayanasami II. „ Krishnamurti. „ Muttuvelu. „ Tandavarayan. „ Viraraghavulu.

1913—1914.

Road Construction in the Kachin Hills.

Reasons for Employment.
In 1913, the Government of India was asked by the Government of Burma for the loan of a Pioneer regiment, in order to construct a road into the district of Hkamti Long which lies between the boundaries of China on the east, Tibet on the north, and Assam on the west. The Chinese had been encroaching on this part of the frontier, which had never been formally delimited, and in the previous year, a column of Military Police had been sent from Myitkyina, which penetrated to Putao, and killed or captured the whole of a party of Chinese, who were found to be surveying the country, and informing the inhabitants that they were now under Chinese rule.

The Government of Burma, therefore, which had hitherto made no attempt to administer Hkamti Long, decided to occupy that distant portion of its territories, which was to be known hereafter as the Putao District and to raise a new battalion of Military Police for its protection, to be termed the Putao Battalion.

The only means of communication between Myitkyina,—which was the terminus of the Burma Railway system and the headquarters of the most northern district hitherto brought under British administration,—and Putao, the principal village in Hkamti Long, consisted of a narrow track through dense jungle, following approximately the course of the Mali Hka or western branch of the upper waters of the Irrawaddy, and practically impassable during the rains.

Consequently, it was considered essential to construct a road which would at least be passable for loaded mules, and as local labour was not readily obtainable, the country being only sparsely inhabited by Kachins (whose best friends could not credit them with a desire for work), application was made to India, as already stated, for the services of a Pioneer battalion.

The Government of India accordingly sanctioned the loan of the 64th Pioneers to the Government of Burma for a period of two years, and orders to that effect were issued in October 1913.

Departure for Burma.
On the 6th November 1913, Lieutenant-Colonel C. T. Swan, Commandant of the regiment, left Secunderabad for Burma in order to discuss the arrangements to be made for the work with the Burma Public Works Department, and on the 11th November, the regiment followed, leaving Secunderabad in two trains, and arriving at Madras on the 13th November. A list of the British and Indian Officers who accompanied the regiment is given in the margin. Immediately on arrival at Madras, the regiment was embarked on the

British Officers.

Major J. A. Bliss, M.V.O.
" S. B. Watson.

Capt. R. Mackie.
" E. Marsden.
" H. F. Murland, *Adjutant.*
" M. Castle Smith.

Lieut. F. O. N. Burne, *Quartermaster.*
" I. L. O'H. Hare.
" V. C. Cassidy.

Major S. R. Godkin, I.M.S.

Indian Officers.

Subadar-Major Shaikh Amin.
Subadar Muhammed Sikandar.
" Krishnasami.
" Francis.
" Sayyid Munawar.
" Anantadri Nayudu.
" Nanjappa.

Jemadar Narayanasami I.
" Musa Raza Khan.
" Durgayya.
" Narayanasami II.
" Krishnamurti.
" Muttuvelu.
" Thandavarayan.
" Viraraghavulu.

R.I.M.S. Northbrook which sailed about 3-30 p.m., on the same day, and reached Rangoon on the evening of the 17th. On the following day, the regiment disembarked, and spent the night in the lines of the 79th Carnatic Infantry, the men being hospitably entertained by the Indian Officers of the 66th Punjabis, with whom they had been stationed in Belgaum a few years previously. On the morning of the 19th November, the regiment left Rangoon, in two trains, and arrived at Mandalay on the following morning, where Lieutenant-Colonel Swan resumed command. The regiment remained at Mandalay, occupying a portion of the lines of the 92nd Punjabis, for about a week. The Commissioner of Mandalay at this time was Colonel Aplin, who had commenced his service with the 4th Pioneers, and here also the regiment was visited by Captain Harvey-Kelly, Commanding the Shwebo Battalion, who had been serving with the Burma Military Police since 1908.

On the 22nd November, the regiment was inspected by Major-General Pilcher, C.B., Commanding the Burma Division, who expressed himself highly pleased with the appearance of the men, and congratulated Colonel Swan on commanding such a fine battalion and, on the 26th, the regiment left Mandalay in two trains, Major J. A. Bliss, M.V.O., remaining behind in command of the depot.

Myitkyina was reached late on the evening of the 27th November, after a journey which is particularly troublesome for troops owing to the necessity of crossing the Irrawaddy at Amarapura by ferry-boat, and the regiment encamped on the northern side of the station.

During the stay of the regiment at Myitkyina—in fact throughout its service in the Kachin Hills,—quinine parades were held twice a week, which no doubt had a considerable effect in reducing the number of men attacked by malaria, a disease which was to cause the death of a number of officers and men during the next two years.

Myitkyina.

On the 28th November, the regiment took over 36 Pioneer equipment mules, which Captain Hart, 15th Mule Corps, had brought from Maymyo. These mules were subsequently purchased from the military authorities by the Public Works Department.

On the 29th November, Colonel Swan proceeded to Watugyi, a Military Police post some 20 miles upstream, with Mr. Durie, the Executive Engineer, P.W.D. in charge, in order to make arrangements for the work to be commenced, returning on the following day.

Watugyi. On the 2nd December, the transport, consisting of some 300 Chinese mules, arrived and, on the following day, Numbers 1, 3 and 4 Double Companies, with Captains Mackie and Marsden, and Lieutenant Cassidy, marched to Watugyi (19 miles) leaving "D" Company at the 14th Mile, where a bridge was to be constructed across a stream. The road to Watugyi was supposed to be a cart road, but as the streams were unbridged and the road was in many places too narrow for carts, it could scarcely be said to fulfil its purpose, except as regards the first three or four miles, as far as Mankhin, where the Burma Gold-Dredging Company had established its headquarters. On the 3rd December, Captain Smith, with Major Godkin, I.M.S., and a small party of men, also proceeded to Watugyi, by launch, with part of the baggage and, on the 5th, Colonel Swan and Captain Murland followed.

On the 6th December 1913, the Double Companies at Watugyi commenced work, repairing, and in some places re-aligning, the existing road towards Myitkyina, and building timber-bridges over the numerous streams, while Mr. J. A. A. Morrison, P.W.D., began to mark out the line of the new cart road. It was intended that this should be completed, during the open season of 1913-14, as far as Nsop Zup, some 45 miles from Myitkyina, where a Military Police post had been established, the intention being to form a large ration depot at Nsop Zup, which was to be kept supplied by carts, and by boats on the river, from Myitkyina, while the Chinese mules were to work between Nsop and Putao (about 150 miles). The Government launches could not ascend the Irrawaddy beyond Watugyi, owing to a series of impassable rapids in the river just above that place.

On the 7th December, Major Watson arrived at Watugyi by road with No. 2 Double Company, and Lieutenant Hare came up by launch with the baggage, this Double Company having had to wait at Myitkyina until the mules of the other Double Companies returned for them.

Letpe. By the 16th December, most of the work within reach of Watugyi had been completed, and Mr. Morrison and Mr. Wells had got a considerable distance ahead with the alignment of the road, and were employing a number of Kachins to clear the jungle, a form of work at which they are particularly apt. On the 16th, therefore, No. 3 Double Company (Captain Smith) moved to a camp near Watu village, some 3½ miles ahead, and on the 17th, No. 1 (Captain Marsden) and 2 (Major Watson and Lieutenant Hare) Double Companies marched

6 miles to Letpe. A certain amount of rain had fallen, which made the jungle tracks very slippery and both mules and men had a difficult march, while the rain also interfered to some extent with the work. On the 18th December, two elephants arrived to assist in moving tree-trunks for the bridges and were sent up to Letpe.

On the 20th December, D Company moved to Watugyi, having completed the bridge over the large stream at the 14th mile, and on the 22nd, the whole of No. 4 Double Company (Captain Mackie and Lieutenant Cassidy) marched to a new camp about 2 miles beyond Letpe, while regimental headquarters moved to the camp at Letpe. There was heavy rain from the 22nd to the 25th December, and the temperature at night fell to 44 degrees.

On the 29th December, Captain R. J. Malet rejoined the regiment from Secunderabad, and took over the command of No. 3 Double Company.

Mile 28. On the 30th, No. 1 Double Company moved on to the 28th mile, and No. 2 Double Company joined No. 4, beyond Letpe, headquarters moving to the 28th Mile next day. On the 3rd January 1914, the Military Police column, *en route* to Putao, passed the 28th Mile, accompanied by Captains Burd, Morris, Mullaly and Smart. This column consisted of 2,300 mules, with 3 elephants carrying guns, in single file, and it may give some idea of the length of the column if I mention that it took no less than 2 hours 40 minutes for it to leave Nsop Zup. A large quantity of telegraph material was also being sent up at this time, as Putao was to be placed in telegraphic communication with Myitkyina.

The regiment was supplied with telephones, which could be connected up with the telegraph line, and this greatly lessened the difficulty of communicating with Myitkyina and with other camps.

Weshi. On the 10th January, G Company moved to Weshi, which was another small Military Police post, shortly afterwards abandoned, on the summit of a high hill not far from the confluence, where the Mali Hka and Nmai Hka rivers unite to form the mighty Irrawaddy. On the 11th January, Captain Smith, with C Company, and accompanied by Mr. Durie, set out for Nsop Zup, *en route* to Laza, where the Military Police column, on its way to Putao, was to establish a strong intermediate post. This company was to improve the track to Laza as much as possible and on arrival there was to construct the buildings required for the post.

A note on the itinerary of, and work done by, this company will be found elsewhere.

On the 12th January, there was more rain and, on the 14th, another Military Police column of 440 mules, under Captain Power, passed through Weshi on its way to garrison Laza. On the 15th, Captain Malet, who had meanwhile moved to Weshi, set out for the Hpungin Hka (some 5 or 6 miles ahead) with 60 men of F Company to repair the track at that point, which had been reported to be almost impassable. On the 17th January, Mr. Hertz, C.I.E., Deputy Commissioner of the new Putao District, passed through Weshi with an escort of Military Police, on his way to Putao.

On the 22nd January, regimental headquarters moved to Weshi, leaving only No. 1 Double Company at the 28th Mile. No. 4 Double Company was sent up to the Hpungin Hka, where a large bridge had to be constructed, while Captain Malet with his company, and Major Watson with No. 2 Double Company continued to work at Weshi.

On the 25th January, No. 1 Double Company moved to a fresh camp within 1½ miles of Weshi, and on the 3rd February, No. 2 Double Company moved to the Hpungin Hka.

On the 2nd February, Colonel Swan went to Myitkyina, to meet Major General Bunbury, Quartermaster-General in India, and Major-General Pilcher, and obtained sanction for the regiment to remain at Myitkyina during the rains, instead of going to Mandalay, as had originally been intended. He rejoined the regiment at Weshi on the 5th, and on the following day General Pilcher arrived, accompanied by Major Taylor (G.S.O. 2). On the 7th, the G.O.C. inspected the work at the Hpungin Hka, and next morning he left for Myitkyina, expressing himself very much pleased with all he had seen.

On the 9th February, Sir Otway Cuffe, Superintending Engineer, arrived from Myitkyina to inspect the work, with which he was quite satisfied, remaining until the following evening. Mr. Durie, Executive Engineer, returned from Laza on the 9th February, Mr. Morrison having gone to Laza in his place.

The Hpungin Hka. On the 12th February 1914, No. 1 Double Company moved to camp-half-way between Weshi and the Hpungin Hka and on the 15th, regimental headquarters moved to the Hpungin Hka. For the next few days there was a great deal of rain. On the 23rd February, Lieutenant Urmson joined the regiment and, on the 25th, No. 2 Double Company moved to Nsop Zup. On the 4th March, Captain Malet, with F Company, moved to a fresh camp within a mile of Nsop Zup, while Major Watson, with No. 2 Double Company, proceeded to Njip Zup and Tiang Zup, where there were streams to be bridged.

On the 9th March, Colonel Swan handed over command to Major Watson, and set out on leave to England, accompanied as far as Bhamo, by river, by Captains Mackie and Murland, who rejoined the regiment at the Hpungin Hka on the 19th.

On the 25th March, No. 4 Double Company set out for Myitkyina, in order to commence building lines for the regiment to occupy during the rains. D Company was left at Letpe, to cut bamboos and timber, which were to be floated down the river to Myitkyina. On the same day (25th) Major-General Raitt, C.B., who had succeeded Major-General Pilcher, in the command of the Burma Division, arrived at the Hpungin Hka, to inspect the regiment, and returned to Myitkyina on the 27th, Major Watson departing on leave at the same time. Towards the end of this month there was a considerable amount of rain.

On the 3rd April, all the available transport was sent off to Tiang Zup, and Lieutenant Hare, with No. 2 Double Company, returned to Nsop on the 4th. On the 6th April Nos. 2 and 3 Double Companies started to return to Myitkyina, a certain number of carts having arrived, and reached their destination on the 9th. No. 1 Double Company moved down as far as Watugyi, where they remained for some time, in order to collect material for linebuilding.

Return to Myitkyina.

Major Bliss had arrived at Myitkyina with the depot from Mandalay on the 7th April and, on the 11th, a site was chosen for the lines, and the work of clearing the site commenced on the 13th.

On the 16th April, Lieutenant H. R. Deane rejoined the regiment from Indore, where he had been acting as Political Assistant, and on the following day Captain Smith returned from Laza with his detachment.

Work proceeded on the lines throughout May, rafts of timber and bamboo being received twice weekly from Captain Marsden at Watugyi, while grass for thatching the roofs was obtained from near Rampur. On the 26th June, No. 1 Double Company rejoined the regiment from Watugyi, and by the end of July the main part of the lines had been completed, consisting of 14 blocks (holding 45 men each) 12 Indian Officers' quarters, quarter-guard, store, offices, magazine, cook-houses, covered mule-standings, and hospital.

By the 20th August, one more block, 2 Indian Officers' quarters, Bandmaster's quarters, band stand, followers' quarters and an additional store-room were ready, and 2 more Indian Officers' quarters and a school-room were finished by the 10th September. The addition of a mosque, on the 16th October, completed the work.

A schedule of rates paid for the different classes of work during the season 1913-14 is appended.

SCHEDULE OF RATES.

Myitkyina-Putao Road 1913—1914.

	Rs.	A.	P.
1. Earth excavation such as side-cutting per 1,000 c. ft. (up to width of 8 ft.)	5	0	0
do. do. do. do. (over width of 8 ft.)	6	0	0
2. Earth excavation and filling per 1,000 c. ft. (including lead up to 100 ft. and lift up to 5 ft.)	6	4	0
Extra per 50 ft. lead or 5 ft. lift.	2	8	0
3. Soft rock excavation, requiring picks, per 1,000 c. ft.	15	0	0
4. Loose rock excavation, requiring jumpers	25	0	0
5. Drilling holes in hard rock for blasting, including cost of tools, blacksmith, and clearing away debris, per ft.	12 As. to 1	0	0
6. Breaking selected river shingle for concrete. Per 100 c. ft. broken.	4	0	0

		Rs.	A. P.

7. Mixing and laying concrete, including supply of water and ramming Per 100 c. ft. — Rs. 4 A. 0 P. 0

8. Jungle clearing (including bamboos and small trees) 5 ft. wide, per mile — 10 0 0
    do. do do do. 100 ft. by 100 ft. — 4 0 0

Tree roots, bamboo roots and heavy jungle to be separately paid.

9. Rock blasting, including drilling holes, cost of tools and sharpening same, removing debris and dressing face, and explosives — 8 0 0

10. Dry stone work with stones from river bed, per 100 c. ft. — 5 0 0

11. Labour, per day — 0 8 0
    do Masons and carpenters, per day. — 0 12 0

MEMO BY EXECUTIVE ENGINEER.

1. The object is to open the road to cart traffic as far as Weshi, not to be make a cart road. (N.B.—The road was eventually open for carts to Nsop).

2. Trees and bamboo clumps which can be avoided by carts should not be removed.

3. When the road dips into a nullah, it should be given an inward slope, so as to drain into the nullah. In other cases the object should be to get water off the road as quickly as possible: it should therefore be given an outward slope. Where cross-drains are necessary on the road, they should be about 6 in. deep, with side slope of 1 in 10. They should be avoided if possible.

4. The width of cutting in sidelong ground should not be more than 12 ft. The formation width in channel cutting not more than 10 ft. Embankments and stone causeways 12 ft. wide.

5. Cutting up to 4 ft. high can be left vertical; above that they should be sloped ½ to 1.

6. Jungle need not ordinarily be cleared more than 15 ft. on either side of centre line. In future this will be done by Kachins when the road is aligned.

7. In steep sidelong ground all trees above the road cutting within 10 ft. of the edge should be cut down but not uprooted. Also any tree which is likely to fall across the road should be cut down and removed.

8. The rates for jungle-clearing include trees up 6 in. diameter and the rates for side cutting include the removal of roots and stones except in special cases, such as a big bamboo root which does not come away with the earth.

9. The size of bridge timbers should be calculated by the formula $6 d^2 = \frac{W. L.}{100}$ where b = breadth in inches, d = depth in inches, W = weight at centre in lbs., and L = span in feet.

10. An officer representing the 64th Pioneers will witness the first measurement, which will be made by a P.W.D. Gazetted Officer. Subsequent measurements can be made by the Section officers, and be checked by the P.W.D. In cases of dispute the final decision regarding accuracy of measurements will rest with the Executive Engineer, and the final decision regarding rates rests with the Superintending Engineer, Mandalay Circle.

No. 65.
16th December 1913.

(Signed) G. A. DURIE,
Executive Engineer.

RATES.

The following table of rates was arrived at during measurements carried out by **Mr. J. A. Morrison**, representing the P.W.D. and Captain H. F. Murland, representing the 64th Pioneers:—

					Rs.	A.	P.
Rate	A		Soft Earth		6	0	0
1/4 15/-	,,	3/4 6/-			8	4	0
1/2 15/-	,,	1/2 6/-			10	8	0
1/4 25/-	,,	3/4 6/-			10	12	0
3/4 15/-	,,	1/4 6/-			12	12	0
Rate	B		Soft Rock		15	0	0
1/2 25/-	,,	1/2 6/-			15	8	0
1/4 25/-	,,	3/4 15/-			17	8	0
1/2 25/-	,,	1/2 15/-			20	0	0
3/4 25/-	,,	1/4 6/-			20	4	0
3/4 25/-	,,	1/4 15/-			22	8	0
Rate	C		Loose Rock		25	0	0

REPORT ON THE WORK OF THE DETACHMENT (C COMPANY, 64TH PIONEERS) UNDER CAPTAIN M. CASTLE SMITH.

11th January—17th April 1914.

(Based on Captain Smith's Diary.)

This detachment, which accompanied Mr. G. A. Durie, P.W.D., marched to the Hpungin Hka on the 11th January 1914, and reached Nsop Zup on the following day. The 13th was spent in repairing the road towards the Hpungin Hka, and making small bridges and stone crossings. On the 14th the detachment marched to Kumtat (7 miles) and on the 15th reached Supka Ga (14 miles), where a halt was made owing to the exhaustion of the mules, of which two had died on the march.

On the 17th, the march was resumed to the Daru Hka (7 miles), one more mule dying *en route*, but fortunately the rations of the detachment represented one mule load daily, which minimised the misfortune. The Wama Hka (9½ miles) was reached on the 18th with the loss of one mule, and Ngagatawng (2 miles) on the next day. On the 20th another mule died on the road to Kraong-Kong Ga (10 miles), where a halt was made on the 21st for the mules to graze.

Gumchen-Ga (9 miles) was reached on the 22nd, and Laza (8 miles) on the 23rd. Here a site on a hill 2,632 feet high had been purchased from the Kachins for two hundred rupees, in order to build a Military Police post, and work was started on huts for rations and a hospital on the 24th January. The 26th was spent in clearing jungle, and on that day Mr. Hertz, C.I.E., with a column of 500 mules, arrived at Laza.

Laza.

On the 27th, work was started on a large P. W. D. go-down 60 ft. x 18 ft., and quarters for the Assistant Superintendent, with Cook-house and servants' go-down, and on the next day a site was marked out for a court-house and lines for the Civil Police. On the 30th, the telegraph-line reached Laza, and the mules were sent off to Myitkyina to bring up more rations.

Mr. Morrison, P.W.D., arrived on the 1st February, and set out for Bumkhang on the 4th, to examine the road, while Mr. Durie left for Myitkyina on the 3rd. On the 5th the weather, which had hitherto been fine, changed, and the almost constant rain made the work very unpleasant. Mr. Morrison returned from Bumkhang on the 14th, and Captain Power of the Military Police on the 20th, by which time a considerable number of buildings had been completed, the local Kachins assisting in thatching the roofs.

On the 22nd February, Captain Smith, with Jemadar Krishnamurti and a party of about 25 men, accompanied by Mr. Morrison, and six Gurkhas (to relieve the party of guard duties) set out towards Bumkhang, to improve the road. The party camped at Sumpraung (7 miles), two mules dying on the march, and on the following day completed one foot-bridge, and commenced a bridge (94 feet, in two spans) over the Raung Hka, 2 miles further on. Camp was moved to the Raung Hka on the 24th, when the bridge was completed, and two more bridges were built on the 25th and 26th, when the party moved to Kumtat (3 miles). The road was almost impassable and everywhere deep in mud. At Kumtat, one bridge (35 ft. span) was built, and the road improved to Dawan-Ga.

On the 28th February, the party marched to the (Upper) Hpungin Hka (8 miles), and remained there till the 2nd March, when it marched another 7 miles to Tingla, where a 67 ft. bridge, and a road diversion, were constructed.

On the 4th March, the return to Laza was commenced, and the party arrived there on the 7th, and resumed work on the buildings. Mr. Leonard, Assistant Commissioner, and Captain Power, Military Police, were now living at Laza and, on the 11th March, Mr. Durie returned from Myitkyina. The weather was very bad, which made the work of improving the road north of Laza very difficult.

On the 17th March, Mr. Durie left Laza, and Mr. Morrison set off towards Myitkyina to expedite the arrival of the ration mules. In the meantime, work was started by the detachment on the construction of post and telegraph offices and another set of quarters for the P.W.D., all of which were completed by the 24th. On the 23rd, Jemadar Krishnamurti, with 23 men, marched to join Mr. Morrison at the 96th mile, where work was to be commenced on the new road to the Daru Hka.

On the 26th March, the remainder of the detachment left Laza and reached the 95th mile (12 miles) on the same day. Hplai-Ga (8 miles) was reached on the 27th, after a stiff climb up the side of Hkran Bum, and the next day was spent in bridging and generally improving the road. On the 29th, the detachment marched to Kumgagatawng (5 miles), on the 30th to Kumpuga (5 miles), and on the 31st to Tingnugatawng.

Laisai-Ga was reached on the 1st April, where a considerable amount of bridging was necessary, and Kawapang on the 3rd, the detachment remaining there till the 7th, when they marched to the Daru Hka. This was their last day of work on the road.

The return march to Myitkyina was commenced on the 9th April, the itinerary of the detachment being Supka-Ga, 9th; Tiang Zup, 10th; Njip Zup, 11th; and Nsop Zup, 12th April. Myitkyina was reached on 17th April, when the detachment rejoined the regiment, with a most creditable record of work accomplished during its 3½ months' absence.

* * * * * *

Instructions for the employment of troops on civil work in peace time are given in the following copy of a letter No. 562-A, dated the 28th July 1910, from the Secretary to the Government of India, Army Department, to the Quarter Master General in India, Simla, which was received from Headquarters, Burma District, Maymyo, in December 1913:—

"In substitution of the orders contained in late Military Department No. 4225-M.W., dated the 29th December 1904, the Government of India are pleased to promulgate the following revised rules for the employment of troops on railway, public and military works including roads, under the Railway Administration, Public Works Department or Military Works Services.

2. Military labour should be employed on railway, public and military works, on a system as nearly similar to the Contract system as is possible. The Railway Administration, the Public Works Department and the Military Works Services will pay rates not exceeding those at which similar work in the same locality is being, or could be, satisfactorily carried out by a civil contractor, the Engineer-in-Chief or the Commanding Royal Engineer being the sole authority for deciding that such rates are not excessive, and the considerations that will guide him being precisely the same as in the case of an ordinary civil contract. Payments will be made direct to the Officer Commanding the Troops employed who will determine the amounts to be paid to the men, and also will, as in the case of a civil contractor, be required to meet from the payments for labour all extra expenditure incurred in connection with their employment including compensation for dearness of provisions, and all charges connected with transport, movement, extra clothing, hutting, water-supply, conservancy, etc., and repair and maintenance of tools and plant. Unless it be otherwise provided by special rule, no portion of the extra expenses incurred by reason of the employment of troops on these works shall be borne by the military estimates.

3. No working, engineer, or sapper pay shall be issued to any one employed with a unit engaged on railway, public or military works, or proceeding to or from such employment.

4. But in the case of Sappers and Miners the issue of working pay debitable to the Corps Grant, is sanctioned while a unit is employed under the Railway Administrations, the Public Works Department or the Military Works Services to:—

(b) British Non-Commissioned Officers;

(b) Bugle Majors, Colour, Drill and Pay Havildars, Havildar Instructors, Drill Naicks;

(c) Men employed upon instructional work, if there is no contract work available for them.

Provided they derive no benefit in the way of pay from the contract receipts.

5. Units employed under the Railway Administrations, the Public Works Department and the Military Works Services, can at any time be withdrawn from such employment should conditions of active service arise at any time during the period of their work such as to render their presence elsewhere necessary. Failing the existence of such conditions, there is no limit fixed as to the length of time a unit may be employed on contract work, and the ordinary rules governing the completion of a contract, once taken up, will apply.

6. During the course of any contract that extends beyond a period of six months, military training of the unit or units engaged thereupon must be carried on, sufficient for practical purposes of efficiency. In such cases not more than three quarters of any unit will be employed at any one time upon the actual contract work, although the whole unit will be moved to the site of the contract. The remaining quarter of the unit will be under military training at or near the locality where contract work is going on.

7. Contract work of the kind in question shall be regarded as Military duty for the purposes of the grant under paras 1054, 1056 (a) and 1065 (i), A.R.I. Volume 1, of injury pensions to men injured and of extraordinary family pensions to the heirs of those killed while in the performance of such work.

8. Should cases occur in which it may be desirable to modify the above provisions, they will be specially considered on their merits".

1914-1915.
Road Construction in the Kachin Hills.

The programme for the second season's work of the regiment in the Kachin Hills was, in the first place, to repair the ravages caused by the rains to the cart road already completed as far as Nsop Zup, and next, to construct a mule-road from Nsop to Putao. A list of the officers who served with the regiment during this season is given in the margin.

Lieut.-Col. C. T. Swan, *Commandant.*
Major J. A. Bliss, M.V.O. (No. 1 D. C.)
Captain R. Mackie (No. 4 D. C.)
    ,,   R. J. Malet (No. 3 D. C.)
    ,,   E. Marsden (No. 2 D. C).
    ,,   H. F. Murland.
    ,,   M. C. Smith (No. 4 D. C.)
Lieut. F. O. N. Burne, *Adjutant.*
    ,,   I.L O'H. Hare (No. 1 D. C.)
    ,,   D.G.S. Urmson, *Quartermaster.*
Major S. R. Godkin, I. M. S.

Mr. Durie had been transferred, and was succeeded as Executive Engineer by Mr. F. C. Lowis, C. I. E., who had recently constructed a road to Hpimaw on the Chinese frontier.

As regards the first part of the programme, the cart road itself had stood very well, but the bridges, which were almost all below high flood level, had for the most part been carried away, notably the crib-pier bridge over the Hpungin Hka which, though built some 20 feet above the cold-season, water level, had been submerged to the extent of 6 ft. or more, when a sudden spate in the river had overturned it completely.

The regiment had hitherto worked at contract rates, but owing to the difficulty of measuring up, and classifying the nature of the soil, in the case of a narrow hill-road which was only intended for pack animals, it was decided that work should hereafter be done at daily rates.

The Double Companies were to work independently, each being given a section of the road to complete, which done, it was to move on beyond the Double Companies ahead of it, and take up a new section. Ration depots were to be formed, as far as possible at points where the existing jungle-track crossed the line of the new road, and each Double Company, with the Chinese mules left with it for the purpose, was to keep itself supplied from the nearest depot.

The ration depots were to be kept supplied by means of 1,500 Chinese mules, working in 10 convoys of 150 mules each, which were to convey rations from the main depot at Nsop Zup. Captain Murland was placed in charge of the rationing, while, as regimental headquarters was to remain at Myitkyina, the Quartermaster was responsible for the supplies sent up from Myitkyina to Nsop.

As regards the medical arrangements, a Sub-Assistant Surgeon was attached to each Double Company, and the regimental Medical Officer was to make visits of inspection from time to time.

Work Commenced. The first Double Company to leave Myitkyina—No. 4—with Captains Mackie and Castle-Smith set out in three detachments on the 27th, 28th and 31st October, in order to repair the road to Nsop and renew the bridges, so as to enable carts to be sent up with supplies. This work was completed, including the construction of a new bridge over the Hpungin Hka, early in December and, on the 14th of that month, No. 4 Double Company moved to a camp some 3½ miles beyond Nsop Zup, Captain Smith having meanwhile been ordered to India, as a Musketry Instructor.

On the 26th December, Captain Malet with No. 3 Double Company left Myitkyina for Paukhong, where the first ration depot had been established. No. 2 Double Company, commanded by Subadar Anantadri Naidu (Captain Marsden, owing to an attack of malaria, being unable to leave Myitkyina) reached Nsop on the 2nd January 1915, and marched to Shingboi, on the Daru Hka, which was the second ration depot. The movement of these Double Companies had been delayed by rumours of an impending rising amongst the Kachins early in December, and an attack on Myitkyina was anticipated, but did not take place. The Kachins of the Hukawng valley, however, rose on the 1st January and the rising spread rapidly though the whole of the western portions of the Kachin Hills. Two Military Police columns were sent to operate against the Kachins of the Hukawng valley *via* Mogaung and Kamaing, and the 1st 10th Gurkhas were sent from Maymyo to garrison Myitkyina, thus enabling the Double Companies of the 64th to proceed to their work in the Mali Hka valley, where the Kachins had so far shown no signs of giving trouble. No. 1 Double Company, which had reached Nsop on the 1st January, was now in camp to the West of Supkaga and had commenced work on a section of the road between Nos. 3 and 2 Double Companies, while No. 4 Double Company had got as far as Njip Zup.

On the 12th January, B Company (No. 2 Double Company) left Shingboi for Kumpuga, which was the third ration depot. On the 16th, Mr. Lowis, who was at Kumpuga, received warning that the Military Police post at Laza was to be attacked by a large party of Kachins from the Triangle* and that should this be successful, an attempt would next be made on the working parties and ration depots. Kumpuga store was, therefore, prepared for defence, but the projected attack on Laza did not take place.

On the 20th January, No. 4 Double Company arrived in the neighbourhood of Kumpuga and commenced working towards Laisai Kong.

On the 23rd January, G. Company (No. 2 Double Company), which was still in camp at the ration store at Shingboi, received warning that a number of hostile Kachins had assembled at Wawang, a village some 15 miles to the north-east, and intended to attack the ration store on the night of the 24th. Information to this effect was sent to Myitkyina by telephone and, though no attack had taken place, Major Bliss was ordered, on the 27th January, to proceed with Captain Marsden (who had arrived at Shingboi on that date) and No. 1 Double Company, to clear up the situation at Wawang. Major Bliss, accompanied by Mr. Lowis as Political Officer, accordingly marched to Wawang on the night of the 28th, and after a very trying night-march, and meeting with considerable opposition, occupied Wawang early the following morning and burned the village at a cost of only three men wounded, Major Bliss himself shooting the *Agyiwa*, who was responsible for the rising†. The Double Company then returned to Shingboi, and a few days later a column, under the command of Lieutenant-Colonel C. T. Swan, 64th Pioneers, was sent up from Myitkyina, accompanied by Major Abbey, the Deputy Commissioner, and the principal offenders were captured, and order restored throughout this part of the country shortly afterwards.

On the 14th February, No. 1 Double Company passed through Shingboi *en route* to take up a new section of work in neighbourhood of Tingtuga near Pasiga. Here it was to work southwards to the Hpungsan Hka, drawing rations from a depot at Bumkhang.

At the end of February, No. 2 Double Company was near Kawapang, having completed a rather difficult section round the sides of Law Bum, the highest peak in this part of the country, and was working northwards to join up with No. 4 Double Company's section near Laisaikong.

---

* The country lying between the Mali Hka and the Nmai Hka is, from its shape, commonly called the Triangle. The Kachins call it *Nmaisin Long*. It has never been administered, and the inhabitants have a very bad reputation, having given shelter to numbers of fugitives from justice, and enslaved large numbers of their weaker neighbours.

† A fuller account of the rising at Wawang will be found elsewhere in these records.

No. 3 Double Company was still working between the Tiang Hka and the Daru Hka, while No. 4 Double Company had moved to Lewoga and was encamped near Machega, drawing its rations from a depot near Nta Galu, south of Lewoga.

By the middle of March, No. 3 Double Company was ready to move to a new section, and marched, *via* Laza, to Bumkhang, camping near the Ntsi Hka. Here it was first of all to join up with the work done by No. 1 (north of Pasiga), and then to work as far forward beyond Laon Ga as was possible during the remainder of the open season. From here on to Putao, some 30 miles, the country was more level, opening out into a wide valley, and Mr. Wells, P.W.D., was constructing this part of the road with local labour from Putao and Langtao.

By the 20th March, No. 2 Double Company was near Thinjanga, and No. 4 was near the junction of the Lailun Hka and Hpungin Hka.

The Double Companies were now all on their last sections of work, and were not required to make any more long marches to change camp—No. 2 was completing its section at the Sinan Hka, Nos. 4 and 1 were working to meet each other near the Hpungsan Hka, and No. 3 was pushing on north of the Ntsi Hka.

By the end of April, the road was practically completed, and transport was collected for the Double Companies to commence their march back to Myitkyina in the beginning of May. Unfortunately, the rains set in while the move was being carried out and the mules, having had a hard season's work, were all on the verge of breaking down—in fact, large numbers of them had already died—the result being that the companies suffered great hardships on the march, and were obliged in some cases to leave some of their tents and baggage behind at the ration depots, for want of transport. From the 8th May, it rained continuously till the end of the month, causing tremendous floods in all the rivers and, by the 25th, the bridges over the Daru Hka and Hpungin Hka had been carried away.

No. 4 Double Company was the first to reach Myitkyina, D Company arriving on the 16th May, and E Company two days later.

No. 2 Double Company was the next to arrive, coming in on the 27th May. Captain Marsden was attacked by malaria at the Daru Hka, on the way down: the men carried him as far as Nsop, where he was put on a boat, and reached Myitkyina on the 24th May, but died on the 26th, to the great grief of the whole regiment.

No. 1 Double Company reached Myitkyina on the 30th May, while No. 3 Double Company, which had perhaps the worst time of all, having further to march than the other Double Companies, did not arrive till the 4th June. Of their mules, 42 had died before half the march was completed, and the tents had to be left behind at Kumpuga: the one elephant with the Double Company broke down, and the men suffering from fever had to be carried by the other men until they either died or recovered.

On the 7th June, the first Double Company entrained for Mandalay, followed by the others in succession, and by the 15th the whole regiment was at Mandalay, this bringing their two years' service in the Kachin Hills to an end.

The following is a list of the officers employed on work in the Kachin Hills in 1914-1915.

British Officers.	Subadars.	Jemadars.
Lieut.-Col. C.T. Swan, *Commandant*. Major J. A. Bliss, M.V.O. Capt. R. Mackie " R. J. Malet " E. Marsden " H. F. Murland " M. Castle Smith Lieut. F. O. N. Burne *Adjutant.* " I. L. O'H. Hare " D. G. S. Urmson, *Quartermaster.* Major S. R. Godkin, I.M.S.	Subadar Major Krishnasami " Muhd. Sikandar " Sayyid Munawar " Anantadri Naidu " Nanjappa " Narayanasami I " Durugayya " Narayanasami II " Muza Raza Khan	Jemadar Krishnamurti " Viraraghavulu " Muthuvelu " Gopalasami " Shamshuddin " Isvara Rao " Narayanasami

REPORT ON WORK 1914-15. NSOP-PUTAO ROAD.

Lieutenant-Colonel Swan's Report on the work done was as follows:—

Rationing. In October and November ration depots were established at Nsop, Paukong, Shingboi, Kumpuga and Bumkhang. Captain H. F. Murland was appointed Supply and Transport Officer and carried out these onerous and responsible duties in a most efficient manner. Rations were carried by boat from Myitkyina to Nsop thence by Chinese pack mules along the old track to the various depots, about two months supply being stored in each, and subsequently replenished as required.

Work on cartroad. (2) On 26th October, No. 4 Double Company under Captain Mackie left to repair the cart road between Myitkyina and Nsop including a new 150 ft. bridge over the Hpungin Kha on wooden crib peers 25 ft. above water level.

The road was open for cart traffic early in December.

Work on Muletrack. (3) Nos. 1, 2 and 3 Double Companies left Myitkyina at the end of December and work was commenced about the 8th of January on a six foot mule track with a gradient of not more than one in seven on the new alignment between Nsop and Putao. This was completed as far as Namyak, 148 miles from Nsop, by 15th May. I attach a copy of the Executive Engineer's letter on work done.

The following are rough figures:—

Total mileage............148.

Cost per mile to P.W.D. for regimental labour Rs. 375.

Average No. working days....100.

Average No. working men....550.

Average turnout per man per diem 220 c. ft.

The men worked frequently over 10 hours a day in order to get the road through.

General. (4) There was considerable delay and interference with the work about the end of January due to the disturbed state of the Kachin Tribes and No. 1 Double Company under Major J. A. Bliss, M.V.O., was instrumental in quelling the beginning of what would undoubtedly have developed into a general rising of the tribes, by the attack and burning of Wawang village under the direction of the Civil Officer, Mr. Lowis.

The work done throughout was of a most arduous nature and weather conditions were extremely adverse. Major Bliss reports rain on 55 days out of 94 since his arrival at Bumkhang early in February. From the beginning of May, rain was torrential and incessant and the detachments were practically never dry on the march down. All the rivers were in flood and had to be crossed by rafts as temporary bridges had been washed away. This was an anxious and hazardous proceeding in many cases and I have much satisfaction in reporting that no loss of life occurred.

The last Double Company, under Captain Malet, reached Myitkyina on 6th June. His transport broke down completely and he was obliged to abandon his tents at Kumpaga to be brought in later by elephants (if available).

I beg to bring to notice the extremely good work of Major Bliss, Captain Mackie, Captain Malet and Captain Murland and of the following Indian Officers. Subadar-Major Krishnasami, Subadar Sayyid Munawar, Subadar Anantadri Naidu, Subadar Narayanasami II.

I much regret to report the death of Captain Marsden due to exposure and malaria. He was a most valuable officer and behaved with the greatest gallantry in action at Wawang. His work on the road was particularly good.

I trust the General Officer Commanding will favourably recommend for suitable recognition by Government the Officers whose names I have submitted.

I attach (*a*) Sketch of the country.

(*b*) Road report.

(*c*) Copy of letter from Executive Engineer Mr. Lowis, C. I. E.

MANDALAY,
July 1915.

(Signed) C. T. SWAN, LIEUT.-COLONEL,
Commandant, 64th Pioneers.

The following is a copy of a D.O. letter, dated Putao, June 6th, 1915, from Mr. Lowis to Lieutenant-Colonel C. T. Swan, 64th Pioneers:—

Dear Colonel Swan,

I wish to express my great appreciation of the work done by Officers and men on the Putao Road during the last working season.

It was entirely due to the Pioneers that such a length of road was able to be completed during the year, and there is now a mule road along which pack animals can travel the whole year round, as the small remaining portion between Namyak and Putao is all on the level and pack animals can easily get along the existing road during the rains.

I am afraid all the Double Companies which did not start until May 15th had a bad time getting down the road, owing to rain which was quite unprecedented in my experience. It may interest you to know the total length of the road from Insop to Namyak river comes to 148 miles, so that if only more of the road had been aligned last year and the whole four Double Companies been able to start work at the end of November, the road would have been completed right through to Putao in the one season.

1916—1917.
Mesopotamia.

In February 1916, as narrated in Part I, the regiment proceeded on field service to Mesopotamia. During this campaign it was ceaselessly employed on work and, consequently, its history so far as Pioneer Work is concerned, is inseparable from the remainder of its activities, so that it will only be necessary to include here such detailed notes and reports on work as would have unnecessarily interrupted the sequence of events.

NOTES ON THE CLOSING OF THE BREACH IN THE BUND AT UMM MOSAHR (5 MILES S. W. OF BAGHDAD), APRIL 1917.

On the night of the 24th/25th April 1917, this bund, which was holding back some miles of flood water from the Euphrates, was badly breached with the result that the Feluja road, and the Decauville railway were immediately flooded and rendered impassable.

The following is a brief summary of the work undertaken and methods employed in closing this breach:—

The work was carried out by the 64th Pioneers; 3 Sections 20th Company, 3rd Sappers and Miners; one Company, 34th Sikh Pioneers; the 4th Labour Corps; and about 70 local Arabs for part of the time.

The faces of the breach were first of all revetted with ballies and corrugated iron, to prevent further widening. Then the Sappers started a pier of five rows of stakes from a point on the up-stream side of the bund and some 30 yards from the breach; sand-bags were laid down on the outsides, and dry earth in the middle.

Simultaneously, the Arabs started a pier on the other side of, and also some 30 yards from, the breach, which was formed by rolling large "sausages" of earth and brushwood, bound round with rope, into the water.

These two piers were to meet, forming a ring bund outside the breach.

When the ends of these two piers, however, had reached a point some 25 yards apart, it was found that the volume of water rushing through between them was too strong to give any chance of its being held up; also, the water was about 15 feet deep and very turbulent. It scoured away the inside of the rings, especially on the Arabs' side, rendering further work on this line fruitless. Several spells of high north-westerly wind increased the volume and force of the water.

The work of the regiment was to bring up sandbags and earth for the Sappers and Arabs. Decauville line was laid from the piers to the nearest points where earth was obtainable, with contractors' switches in lieu of points and crossings. Trains of 4, 5 or 6 tip-wagons at a time were man-handled from the borrow-pits to the end of each pier, and additional frames were laid as the pier progressed. Sandbags were also filled at a point by the edge of the flood water 100 yards away and ferried across to the bund in a guffa.

The following notes were made while this work was in progress:—

Number of sandbags that one man can fill in an hour........18.
Average amount of earth in sandbag......................·6 cubic ft.
Average number of trolleys passed up from borrow-pit to breach per hour (over a lead of about 300 yards)   56.
(Each trolley held 40 filled sandbags or 1 cubic yard of earth).
Average number of sandbags dumped at the breach per day (12 hours)   24,500.
    or approximately   14,700 C. ft.

After abandoning work on the two piers, soundings were taken from a pontoon, and it was found that, on a radius of some 75 yards from the breach, the water was only about 2 or 3 feet deep.

The east (Sappers') pier was then continued on this line. While this work was proceeding, the force of the current was found to be scouring out the pier at one point, which had, consequently, to be thickened on the outside.

By the time the pier had reached a point more than half-way round the semicircle a large volume of water was held up, and only some 6 inches of water was running in over the shallows where the work was uncompleted.

The remainder of the opening was then closed in one day (13th May) by rabbit-netting, brushwood, and sandbags, and thus the breach was finally closed—though there was a small leakage

The trolley line was continued right round the new pier, and earth was fetched from both ends and tipped outside the sandbags, thus stopping the leakage.

After this had been effected, the filling in of the breach in the original bund was taken in hand.

REPORT ON WORK OF THE 64TH PIONEERS ON HINAIDI—BAQUBA RAILWAY.

B and C Companies, 64th Pioneers, began work on May 21st, 1917. They were first employed on earth work, and work in the yard at Hinaidi—such as digging wells, making frames, and digging ramps to the river.

Eventually other labour was found for yard work, and preparation of material.

Captain D. Aylward, who was in command of the detachment, made all preliminary arrangements, for linking with the Engineer in charge, and organised the various working parties. Captain F. O. N. Burne took over from him on the 25th June 1917.

C Company found the linking parties, and B Company parties for packing and levelling, while a labour Corps completed the earth work right through. The line is 2 ft. 6 in. gauge of 21 lb. rails. The greater part of the rails are in lengths of 12 ft.—a small portion being 12 ft. 3 in. These are made up in frames with 6 iron sleepers keyed or bolted to the rails.

A few 25 lb. rails in 24 ft. lengths, with wooden sleepers were used only when the stock of frames had been exhausted.

The total of the line from Hinaidi to Baquba is 35 miles 862 yards. The linking was completed in 34 working days. Railhead reached the yard at Baquba on the 10th July.

During the linking a detachment of about 200 men of the 2/6th Gurkha Rifles under Lieutenant R. H. Lynes, accompanied B and C Companies, and carried frames and unloaded trucks, etc.

This is arduous work, especially in hot weather, when the metal attains a burning heat. There is a knack in taking the frames off a wagon quickly, and carrying them up to railhead without delay. This the Gurkhas soon acquired, and were of great assistance all through.

The actual length of line that can be laid in one day depends almost entirely on the state of the material, and punctuality of construction trains. This material was prepared in the yard at Hinaidi by infantry working parties. Frequently frames were not square or had rails of different lengths; rails were curved; bolts were not oiled or were insufficient in quantity; keys were missing from sleepers; and many fishplates were bent. These defects all made for delay. The condition of the material improved towards the end.

The construction trains generally arrived up to time during the first 30 miles. After that, these trains had difficulty in getting over the distance in time. The weight of material was very heavy for the engine, especially as the line had been newly laid, and was badly in need of maintenance.

Also it was difficult to get enough water for engines en route, as tanks were not ready.

There were also occasional troubles in the machinery of the engines, which caused much delay.

Lastly, there was no communication along the line by which the railway staff at Hinaidi, could ascertain the whereabouts of the train.

There was much delay and some wastage of material caused by accidents. Most of the material was brought out on trains of 20 to 22 G. S. wagons (3 ton trucks).—22 frames were loaded on each wagon, making a heavy and unwieldy load. Most of the construction trains had to leave Hinaidi and travel a long distance in darkness.

Any load that was not well balanced soon began to shift under the swaying of the train, but it was not possible for the guard, to see what was happening.

As a result, in nearly every train, at least one load of frames was shot off on to the side of the track, and the wagon had to be uncoupled and taken off the rails.

Under favourable conditions, *viz*: when trains were punctual, and material good and sufficient, 1½ miles of line was laid in a day.

For the first 20 miles the men worked in two reliefs. As there was not enough rolling stock to send out all the material in the mornings, about 1 mile of line was put down in the mornings, and another train load—about ½ mile—in the afternoons and evenings. This was unfortunate as the conditions on a hot weather afternoon are unpleasant.

One of the difficulties experienced was that of moving camp without hindering work. It was impracticable to work at a distance greater than 10 miles from camp, as the long journey out and back on a slow train in addition to a hard morning's work adds considerably to the fatigue of the working parties, and is a waste of time.

At the same time the engineer in charge was anxious to move camp as seldom as possible, as each move meant a diminished day's work.

Only two camps were made between Hinaidi and Baquba and on days of the moves work was continued. After the linking had started, work was continuous—only one day's rest being given.

The health of the men remained very good throughout, though the conditions under which they were working were often trying.

They frequently left camp at 3 or 4 a.m., and did not reach camp again until 1 p.m. and sometimes even later. Only four men were transferred to hospital during the linking, one of whom was slightly injured in an accident. Their fitness may be attributed to the interest taken by all in the work; to the provision of E. P. tents; good rations; the excellent water of the Diyala river; and the good camp sites along its banks.

F. O. N. BURNE, CAPTAIN,
Commanding Detachment 64th Pioneers.
Hinaidi—Baquba Railway.

On the 13th August 1917, Regimental Headquarters and A Company arrived at the Diyala for work on the river bunds. The following memorandum from the Engineer-in-Chief explains the nature of the work to be undertaken:—

"It is intended to make a bund in continuation of the city bank to protect the camps and depots south-east of Baghdad and the Kut-Baghdad railway in the event of an overflow on the left bank north of Baghdad. This bund is intended to direct water into the Diyala river, the bund of which would only be cut on the water reaching its bank. In the event of the flood being in sufficient volume to reach the Diyala, it would greatly increase the amount of water passing down this stream, and it is therefore necessary to protect the enclosed area by raising the flood banks down to the mouth of the Diyala.

2. Your battalion will raise the right bank bund to a height of two feet above high flood level. The exposed face of the bund to be revetted with brushwood throughout.

3. The ground levels at various points along this bank are entered on the plan, also the high flood levels at the bend and at the mouth of the Diyala.

4. You should arrange with the controller of Native labour for as much Arab labour as can be obtained, both for constructing the bund and collecting camel thorn. The revetment work should be done as far as possible by Arab.

5. You will report weekly progress on the work and the number of local labour employed."

The dimensions of the bund were to be 4 feet broad at the top, with a slope of ½ on each side. When completed the total length of bund revetted was 4 miles 895 yards, the proportion of brushwood used to length of bund revetted being estimated at approximately 100 loads to 50 running yards.

The following is a copy of the specification for earthwork on the Eastern Bund (Baghdad to Diyala River), together with a memorandum, dated the 27th September 1917, from the works Directorate, Baghdad, showing the work to be carried out by the regiment.

EASTERN BUND (BAGHDAD TO DIYALA RIVER), SPECIFICATION FOR EARTHWORK.

1. The whole site on which new earthwork will rest, to be cleared of grass, brushwood, roots, etc., and well roughened, preferably with picks or "pharwas" in longitudinal lines, before the new earth is laid on. Where the site is sloping, e.g., on slopes of old bunds, it should be cut in horizontal steps to form a proper bond with the new earthwork and prevent slipping.

2. All clods to be broken. This should be done as far as possible in the borrow pits before the earth is taken to the bund.

3. Earth to be spread in layers about 6 inches deep. Ramming will only be done under special instructions from the O. I/c Bunds.

4. Borrow pits to be not less than 50 feet from either front (north east) or rear (south west) toe of bund. At this distance pits in front must not exceed 4 feet in depth, while pits behind must not exceed 2 feet in depth. At 70 feet or more behind the bund the depth of pits may be increased to 4 feet.

(*Note*:—Pits on the rear side of a bund are theoretically objectionable. In this particular case they are a necessary evil, but as far as possible the greater share of the earth should be obtained from in front of the bund).

MEMORANDUM.
REF: EASTERN BUND (BAGHDAD TO DIYALA RIVER).

1. The A.C.N.L., or his representative will supply Arab labour (3rd Arab Labour Corps) for the above named bund, and will be responsible for:—

   (a) the supply of labour and the rates at which it is paid,
   (b) driving the labourers,
   (c) their discipline,
   (d) seeing that they comply with the sanitary rules, and
   (e) making payments to them.

2. The Officer in charge Bunds will fix the alignment and levels for you and will give you any other particulars required. He is supplying you with type sections of the bund and specifications giving the engineering requirements, also with information as to the arrangement of borrow-pits.

3. The work to be done by your regiment will consist of the following items:—

   (a) Preparing the site.
   (b) Setting up profiles.
   (c) Marking out borrowpits.
   (d) Supervising the placing of the earth in the bund, *i.e.*, seeing that the work is done in accordance with the specification, with clods broken and earth put in layers, etc.
   (e) Measuring up borrowpits, passing them when finished, and issuing certificates or chits to the labour for finished pits. The labourers will then obtain payment from the O/C Labour Corps on these certificates.
   (f) Final dressing.

4. In addition to the above it will probably be necessary for your men to do the brushwood revetment when that work starts. Arrangements for brushwood supply are being made.

NOTES ON ROAD MAKING AND REPAIRING ON FALLUJA—BUSTAN ROAD, JULY—SEPTEMBER 1917.

The general idea was to make a more or less "pucca" road from a point 3½ miles from Falluja to Seria Post (breach in Sakhlawiya Canal Bund).

Work consisted of (i) Road construction, (ii) Road repair, (iii) Well digging.

1. *Road construction.* Previous to arrival, most of the road from 3½ miles from Falluja to Sakhlawiya had been constructed but owing to lack of water was breaking up and required repair. The road beyond Bustan had not been started.

2. Method of road construction. The road was roughly prepared—6 in. to 9 in. of broken up brick was laid on road—over this 4 in. of mud (dry). Water was then poured over the mud and rammed down with wooden rammers. The idea was, the wet mud and brick would consolidate and the road would then only require watering to be maintained.

Unfortunately there was no water, so wells had to be dug at frequent intervals along the road.

Local labour (Arabs with their donkeys) was employed by contract to fetch the brick. They were paid at rates varying from Rs. 2 to Rs. 6 per "form" (25 cubic feet) according to the distance the bricks had to be carried. The bricks were collected on either side of the road ready for spreading.

In my opinion, if, before the bricks had been spread (or even after) water had been poured over the road, so that the bricks instead of sinking into a dry dust bed, sank into wet mud, the road would have consolidated better.

Road repair between Falluja and Sakhlawiya.

Three methods were adopted:—

(i) *To fill up holes and repair bad places* in road only. This was found unsatisfactory, as the road soon became very uneven and the other holes appeared at either end of the repaired places.

(ii) *To add 3 in. of brick and 4 in. of mud and water and ram*—in fact remake the road adding 3 in. of brick. This, owing to lack of Arab labour (and hence bricks) was too slow and hence had to be altered. But undoubtedly this method was by far the most satisfactory, as the road thus made would require less than half the upkeep otherwise required. Eventually the method adopted was to water and ram the whole of the existing road, repairing where necessary at the same time, and removing the dust first if too thick. This method was found fairly satisfactory but only about 200 yards of road could be done daily owing to the lack of water carts and the fact that the first wells dug were situated over 100 yards from the road instead of being quite close to it.

As the road west of Sakhlawiya had never been properly watered and rammed, the mere watering of the road would have been insufficient; whereas when once properly watered and rammed, watering alone would be sufficient, *if kept up daily.* If not kept up, then the road will require continual repairing which means slow work. Hollows and large nullahs require continual repair and require 3 in. to 6 in. extra bricks on them. Small water courses should be filled with brick, not earth and a camber given to the road over them.

To keep the road watered, 5 wells per mile (*i.e.* approx. 350 yards apart) are necessary. Water carts need not then be used at all, as watering can be done by hand, *if wells are near road (i.e.* within 10 to 20 yards). 7 men per well working 6 to 8 hours would be able to keep 350 yards road watered once a day.

(iii) *Well digging.* Wells dug were 9 ft. in diameter at top. In nearly all cases soft sand was struck about 16 ft. below the surface, necessitating revetment of some sort. This stratum of sand appeared to be of considerable depth in most cases.

Owing to the total absence of any material, wells were revetted with a frame work of fascines made of brushwood.

The following method was found best:—

(i) Make up fascines about 9 in. diameter, measure diameter of well at the point at which revetment is required.

(ii) Make a cylinder of fascines about 4 ft. high and lower it into position. Each layer of fascines should be pegged to one below it as well as tied.

More fascines are added afterwards if required. This will minimise the falling in of the wells of soft sand. The deepening of the well is continued from inside the fascine. Even with fascine revetment the sides may start falling in, because, as the well gets through the sand, and reaches water, a certain amount of silt (sand) comes up from underneath or through the fascines causing the soft sand above the fascines to fall down. Unless these crevices are filled up, the wall above the layer of sand will also fall in. The filling up of these crevices with brushwood seems to be all that is necessary.

REPORT ON THE WORK OF B AND C COMPANIES, 64TH PIONEERS, ON THE SHAHRABAN RAILWAY EXTENSION. 25TH OCTOBER TO 28TH NOVEMBER 1917.

This extension of the 2 ft. 6 in. railway was first intended to run from Shahraban across the Ruz canal to the foot of the Jabal Hamrin, a distance of 6 miles, but was afterwards continued to near the foot of Table Mountain, a total of $8\frac{1}{4}$ miles.

As the work was at first not considered very urgent, Major Burn, R. E., who was in charge, arranged that the detachment with a working strength of about 340 men should do all the work, including survey, earthwork, bridges and platelaying.

2. *Survey.* Captain D. Aylward, 64th Pioneers, did the survey and put in pegs for alignment and levels.

3. *The earthwork* was begun on 25th October. On 30th October, as the work was then ordered to be pushed on urgently, a half battalion of infantry and some Arabs were told off to work with the Pioneers. Various half battalions continued the work until 5th November when half the 102nd Grenadiers took over and remained on the work until 25th November. A Pioneer officer with a few N.C.O.s and men marked out and supervised the infantry work. After a few days the infantry task rose from 30 to 60 c. ft. per man. The task for a Pioneer being 90 to 100 c. ft.

The Arabs were superintended by a Jemadar and a few men of the 64th. When well driven they did a certain amount of useful work but could not be depended on. Their numbers varied from 50 to 200 and as many came from long distances they always arrived late. Their own tools were few and in bad condition and the tools lent them did not suit them.

4. *Bridges.* There were some small bridges from 6 to 20 ft. span. They were simple girders on crib piers made of sleepers. For the smaller bridges, girders were made of several rails wired together. The only bridge of interest was that over the Ruz canal. Captain Aylward carried out this work with Subadar Nanjappa and a party of B Company. A road bridge 23 ft. span, with 8 girders on old brick abutments was rebuilt.

Crib piers of sleepers were placed on the abutments. Walls of bricks and sand bags were built to complete the abutments. The girders were raised on the cribs and roadway replaced 8 ft. above its old level.

Work was continued after dark by flare light. The flares were lent by the Motor Transport Company. The 5 carpenters with the detachment had heavy work boring and adzing sleepers, etc.

When complete, the bridge was passable for railway and road traffic, including caterpillars. It was open for road traffic after 3 days work but was closed again for a day, later on, for laying the rails.

5. *Platelaying* was under Lieutenant Curle with C Company. Owing to the irregular supply of material, it was not possible to lay any given length of track every day. The material was of various types, 25 lbs. and 21 lbs. rails, 24 ft. and 12 ft. long, wooden sleepers and steel sleepers. A large number of the rails were bent. The steel frames of rails and sleepers were made up and adjusted by a party of Pioneers at Shahraban. The material was collected and loaded on the construction train by Mr. Birrell, Permanent Way Inspector. He was most careful and prompt in sending out material complete with the proper bolts, spikes, etc. The greatest length linked in one day was 1¼ miles of steel frames. This with a party of only 130 Pioneers, helped for ½ day only by 50 Arabs carrying material, was a good day's work. The points and crossings were all put in by Captain Aylward. Linking as far as the first site of Table Mountain station was completed on 16th November.

6. *Packing and straightening* was done at first roughly and the whole length was packed and repacked two or three times. Some Arabs helped by heaping up earth for the packing. Straightening was difficult owing to the bent rails. The jim crow was used in the worst places.

7. The earth work for a further extension of 1,630 yards, including sidings, up to the 2nd site of Table Mountain station was completed on 28th November. This included a cutting 8 ft. deep which made some heavier work for the 102nd. Three culverts and a crossing were put in by Captain Aylward. But the linking could not be completed as no material arrived up to the time the detachment left.

(Signed) S. B. WATSON, Lt.-Col.,
O. C. Detachment 64th Pioneers.

1918.
Falluja-Dhibban Railway.

The earthwork for this railway was very heavy, particularly at the canal north of Sakhlawiya, where a high embankment was constructed by A and B Companies. This bank, when completed, was 20 feet high, 18 feet broad at the top, with sides sloping ½ to 1, and length about 300 feet. It involved 287,789 cubic feet of earth in 3,488 men days, an average of 83 cubic feet per man *per diem*, with a lead of 100 feet.

No trolleys nor wheelbarrows could be obtained, and baskets and sacks were used for carrying the earth. It was found that one man with a basket could carry nearly as much as two men with a sack. The baskets were large and rather too heavy.

From the 22nd January, infantry working parties from the 6th Jats and 97th Infantry, approximately 470 strong, assisted with the earthwork. Their average daily task *per* man was at first a little over one-third of that performed by a Pioneer, but they were eventually able to do 80 to 100 cubic feet per man daily.

REPORT ON LINKING 4 FT. 8½ IN. GAUGE RAILWAY FROM FALLUJA TO DHIBBAN, FEBRUARY 1918.

This section of the Railway was started on the morning of the 1st February 1918 by A and C Companies minus a small party from C Company, 64th Pioneers, who were completing earthwork. The work was started at chainage 194100 just north of Falluja station. The parties were detailed at the start roughly the same as Khan Sahib Muhammad Zaman's men had been, except that the sleeper carriers were cut down. Total strength of party employed on first day was 30 N.C.O.s and 474 men. Work was slow at first till the men had got into the way of handling this material and it was also greatly delayed owing to the first ¼ mile being on a high bank along which all the material had to be carried without moving up the construction train. The ¼ mile was completed by 3 p.m. having started work at 8-30 a.m. On 2nd February, working parties were changed a good bit but actual numbers were about the same, but as condition of bank was much better 5,508 ft. were linked by 3-30 p.m. On the 4th February, all parties were altered, the total being 37 N.C.O.s and 486 men, these being distributed as per attached table and which was kept to, all the way through. We had asked for 1¼ mile of material for this day and 1¼ mile for the 5th, but were told that only one mile per day could be supplied on account of shortage of labour for loading in Depot. On the 6th instant one mile of track was actually finished off in 4½ hours but all material was off loaded and laid in 3¼ hours.

On the 7th, the crossings were laid for the Sakhlawiya siding and line laid nearly up to the Sakhlawiya canal and, on the 8th, A Company and nearly all C Company moved camp by train to Sakhlawiya, where the siding was linked up and main line up to the Sakhlawiya canal, and two girders which were to span it, were off loaded. On the 9th, this bridge was completed and also nearly ¾ mile track completed. This brought line up to chainage 837312. On the 11th, we were delayed in starting owing to engine not arriving in time to bring material out from Falluja. It eventually arrived at 9-20 a.m. and we linked 4,968 ft. and finished at 3 p.m.

This was last of the material available, and on the 12th and 13th, the whole of A and C Companies turned out for packing, working in opposite directions from the Sakhlawiya canal bridge. There was a big lift across the 20 ft. high bund near Sakhlawiya village as the earthwork had sunk about 18 in. On the 14th, a fresh supply of material turned up and we started from the curve opposite Shaik Habib. One mile material was sent, but owing to 2 road-crossings and many water canals which made rail carrying difficult, it took 5½ hours to complete 5,400 ft. On the 15th, we had reached a lower embankment with out-water channels, and, starting at 8-30 A. M., we completed 3,700 ft. by 10-45 a.m. On the 16th, we again had good country and a much better bank and one mile was completed in 4 hours 10 minutes. We also completed the first cross-over in Dhibban Station. On the 17th, Dhibban Station and S and T siding were completed except for about 200 ft. at the very end on account of shortage of material, but the station and siding were in working condition by 3 p.m. on the 17th. Linking was done on 14 days; average distance per day 4,160 ft. only, owing to supply of material being short.

During the whole period of linking the casualties have been very few considering the heavy material handed. Out of 500 men, one man had his foot squashed and 3 men have had squashed finger tips, all very slight. One man unfortunately died; he had been knocked down 2 days previous to his death by a sleeper falling on his head when unloading. Subadar Viraraghavulu was in charge of the linking and Jemadar Dharmalingam of the spiking, both doing excellent work; Subadar-Major Krishnasami had complete charge of the completion of line behind the material train and here he did excellently, necessitating no supervision. The P.W.I., Ward, gave us great help. The material was sent out in very good condition but it would not delay work so much if the construction engine was a bit more reliable. Lieutenant D. C. Sydney-Smith was a great help at railhead, where he supervised the actual linking, and Lieutenant V. Curle, in charge of the unloading and carrying of material, also did his work well.

(*Signed*) D. AYLWARD, CAPTAIN,
Officer-in-Charge Linking.

Linking Parties 4 ft. 8½ in. Gauge, Falluja to Dhibban, February 1918.

Gang Number.	Work.	I.O.s	N.C.O.s	Men.	Tools.	No. of Tools.	Remarks.
No. 1	Spit locking centre line			3	Pegs, Rope & Picks	2	
	Spacing sleepers	1	1	4	Spacing Rods	2	
	Cutting paths for rail carriers			4	Mamooties	4	
No. 2	Placing rails		2	8	Square	1	
					Bars	4	
					Gauge	1	
	Inserting expansion pieces	1		2	Expansion pieces & Baskets		
	Rail marking			1	Marking Rod and Chalk		
	Linking		2	24	Spanners	16	
					Bars	8	
	Blacksmith			1	Hammer and Chisel		
No. 3	Spiking Load		3	12	Hammers spiking	4	
	,, Rail				Bars	2	
	,, Off	1	4	10	Augers	3	
	,, Rail				Gauges	4	
	Augering sleepers			3	Wooden blocks	7	For placing under bars to lift sleepers
	Adjusting sleepers			4			
No. 4	Rough straightening in front of train.		1	6	Bars	4	N.C.O. in charge to see that all joints are safe for train to pass over
					Spanners	2	
No. 5	Off loading rails (closed trucks)	1	2	36	Bars	8	I. O. to check length of every rail before off loading
	Off loading rails (open trucks)		1	8	Bars	8	
	Off loading sleepers		1	12	Nil		
	Carrying Rails	1	8	128	Slings	16	
	,, Sleepers		8	128	Nil		
	Distributing bolts & fish plates		1	12	Baskets	6	

Behind Material Train.

Gang Number.	Work.	I.O.s	N.C.O.s	Men.	Tools.	No. of Tools.	Remarks.
No. 6	Bolting			16	Spanners	16	
	Extracting expansion pieces			2	Bars	2	
	Adjusting sleepers			5	Hammers 14 lbs.	2	
	Spiking	1	5	50	Bars	16	
					Hammers	18	
					Gauges	3	
					Augers	6	
	Straightening		1	8	Bars	8	
	Feeders			1	Baskets	1	
	Picking up loose material			2			

REPORT ON LINKING BAGHDAD TO HILLA RAILWAY, APRIL AND MAY 1918.

This line was started on 2nd April, but on that date there was no engine available for construction owing to breakdown on the Falluja Line. All material had to be hand-shunted, and work was eventually stopped on account of rain. 2,916 ft. were linked; working party of 653 total, detailed as in column (1) on attached list.

The next day 1½ miles were linked, and 1¾ miles on the 4th, taking 7 hours actual working each day. This distance was continued daily, the time taken being decreased to 5 hours work daily till Awairij was reached, where linking was held up by a bridge which was not ready to link over. Material was carried over the gap for Awairij station and linked up on the 7th.

On the 8th, the regiment moved camp to Awairij and completed station sidings. On the 9th, linking was continued and there was nothing to delay work till Mahmudiya canal was reached on the 12th.

On the 11th and 12th, 2 miles were linked each day, with working party as per column (2) on attached list, work being completed in 5 hours 40 minutes and 6 hours 30 minutes on the two days respectively.

On the night of 12/13th, the girders were put across the Mahmudiya canal by Lieutenant Butcher and his Bombay Khalassis, the facing points and siding were put in Mahmudiya station on 13th, and the regiment moved camp on the 14th completing station crossings, etc......

The 15th was a holiday.

Mahmudiya to Khan Haswa, a distance of 12½ miles, was linked between 16th and 22nd, there being nothing beyond a few rail girder bridges to delay work, working strength being kept about 660. Only a few alterations were made in working parties, such as reducing the railcarriers by 2 gangs on the 18th.

On the 21st, General Lubbock, Director of Railways, inspected the work.

On the 23rd, the crossings and sidings at Khan Haswa were linked and the regiment moved camp on the 24th. The 25th was a holiday.

From Khan Haswa to Khan Nasiriya, all was plain sailing, there being only one girder bridge over the Musaiyib canal at chain 197,000. In order to reach Musaiyib canal on 29th, one and a quarter miles of material was sent out on one train; this was completed in 3 hours 35 minutes, and the girders were put in during the afternoon.

On the 30th, Khan Nasiriya crossing was put in and, on the 1st May, the regiment moved camp there and completed sidings and bridge. The 2nd May was a holiday.

From here onwards the earthwork had all been done by Arabs and was very lumpy and uneven, and in consequence delayed linking to a certain extent. On the 6th May, 2 rail girder bridges and 3 loading ramps were made, besides 7,524 ft. track laid on a very bad high bank, and in consequence it took 5 hours 10 minutes to link this distance.

Khan Mahawil was reached on the 7th May. Further progress was delayed till the 12th May, while a pile bridge of 40 ft. span was erected by Lieutenant Bender, with No. 9 Platoon and the Bombay Khalassis, over the canal. During this time the material was carried forward and the station completed.

Linking was resumed late on the morning of the 12th, but from here onwards linking became very difficult, owing to shortage of men, cultivation cuts, and numerous culverts, etc. On the 16th, no more material was available, and this day was observed as a holiday.

On the 17th, the regiment was employed on boxing the line between Khan Mahwil and Khan Nasiriya. On the 18th, linking was resumed and on this date 5,040 ft. only were laid owing to the sleepers being now pinkadoe wood, weighing 200 lbs. each, whereas the old ones were anything from 120 to 150 lbs. only. It took 6 hours to link.

On the 19th, the Nil Canal was reached and the regiment moved camp. From 18th to 24th May only one mile of material was sent out daily owing to shortage of trucks and so parties were detailed as in column 3.

Hilla Station was reached on the 25th May, the regiment moving up to Hilla on the 26th.

From this date till 14th June the whole regiment was employed on construction of Hilla Station. This work included earthwork for narrow gauge, unloading narrow gauge rolling stock, making bricks for station buildings, level crossings, roads, etc.

During the whole period of linking, between 2nd April and 25th May, there were only 27 casualties, the only serious one being where a man had his leg broken by a rail dropping on it when unloading; all the remainder of the casualties were squashed fingers and toes, etc., except one or two men who were hurt by falling down when carrying sleepers.

The men's health was good all through, and the weather was good till the last few miles were being linked, when it began to be a bit warm after 11 a. m.

The whole of this work was carried out under favourable conditions most of the time; the arrangements for the supply of material were well carried out by Captain Bowen; trains arrived to time, and all the railway staff did all they could to help. We again had Inspector Ward at railhead with our linking parties, where he gave great assistance.

During the progress of the work, the regiment was visited by General Marshall, G.O.C.-in-C., and staff, and on another occasion by General Stuart-Wortley, D.Q.M.G.

The work was supervised by Officers and N.C.O.s as follows:—

For the first 3 days' work on this line, Subadar Viraraghavulu *Bahadur* was in charge of the linking at railhead till he went on leave, when Subadar David took over from him on the 6th April.

No. 4469 Havildar (now Jemadar) Saurinayagam, No. 910 Naick (now Jemadar) Arogyasami, No. 409 Naick (now Havildar) Arogyasami, No. 256 Sepoy Abdul Majid, No. 590 Sepoy Gabriel and No. 277 Sepoy Appadurai were conspicuous in this gang.

Jemadar Balaraman managed the distribution of material and Jemadar Dharmalingam the spiking parties, both doing excellent work.

Lieutenant Sydney Smith had control of all the railhead parties, linking, spiking, etc. Captain Stonehewer and Lieutenant Deed were in charge of unloading and carrying up of sleepers.

Subadar-Major Krishnasami *Bahadur* was again in sole charge of the party working behind the train, completing spiking, bolting and straightening, where he again did excellent work with no need of any supervision of any sort.

The unloading of rails was supervised by Subadar Narayanasami I for the first 30 miles when he took over the spiking gangs from Jemadar Dharmalingam, who was going on leave, and handed over the control of rail unloading to Havildar Syed Hussain who did excellently, always working hard to get his trucks unloaded in record time, keeping his gang under good control and succeeding in unloading 60 miles of track with only 2 serious casualties, one broken leg and one squashed toe.

Havildar Chinnathambi again was left away behind by himself to do the straightening and with eight men in his gang did good work,—considering the condition of some of the rails he did very good straightening.

No. of Gang.	Linking gangs Baghdad-Hilla.	Col. 1. N.C.O.s	Col. 1. PTES.	Col. 2. N.C.O.s	Col. 2. PTES.	Col. 3. N.C.O.s	Col. 3. PTES.
1	Spitlocking centre Line Spacing Sleepers Cutting Paths	1	3 4 4	1	3 8 6	1	3 8 6
2	Placing Rails Inserting Liners Rail marking Linking Blacksmiths (Placing liners in position.)	2 2	8 2 1 32 2	2 2	8 2 1 32 2	2 2	8 2 1 32 2
3	Spiking Load Rail do. Off Rail Augering Sleepers	3 4	12 16 3	4 5	16 20 3	3 4	12 16 3
4	Adjusting Sleepers Rough straightening Tightening and checking joints	1	4 4 2	1	8 4 2	1	4 4 2
5	Off loading Rails	2	16	2	22	2	22
6	Off loading Sleepers	1	12	1	12	1	12
7	Off loading Bolts, Spikes and Fishplates.	1	14	1	16	1	16
8	Carrying Rails	10	160	11	176	9	144
9	Carrying Sleepers		200		250		180
	COMPLETING LINE BEHIND TRAINS:—						
	Spiking Augers Adjusting Sleepers do. Spikes, etc. Spanners Removing expansion Straightening Collecting materials Carpenters	6 1 1	48 6 5 2 16 2 8 2 2	6 — 1 1	54 6 — 2 16 4 8 — 1	5 — 1 1	45 5 — 2 12 4 8 — 1
	Total	35	590	38	682	33	554

Average = 609

1919—1921.
Persia.

While it formed part of the Army of Occupation in Persia, the regiment carried out a great deal of Pioneer Work, which will be found detailed in Part I of these records.

1923—1924.
Waziristan.

The work carried out by the regiment, while on the North-West Frontier, is described in the following report:—

REPORT BY THE COMMANDING OFFICER ON THE WORK OF THE 2ND/1ST MADRAS PIONEERS IN WAZIRISTAN 1923-1924.

(1) The Battalion arrived in Waziristan on 19th September 1923. As the move was temporary, for probably four months, a depot was left in Bangalore to look after stores, records, accounts, lines, etc. This and the number of men required in camp on various duties, guards, drivers, specialists and sick, seriously reduced the number available for road making.

(2) Signallers, Lewis Gunners, Buglers, etc., were employed on the road except for 1 or 2 days a week. Latterly all were continuously on road work.

The average number actually on work was 400, out of an average of 532 in Waziristan.

(3) The first task was on the Jandola-Kotkai-Sararogha road, making road diversions, a cutting at Kotkai and culverts, whilst two detachments were maintained at Jandola and Kotkai to keep in repair the river crossings.

(4) On the 15th December 1923, the road in the Shahur Tangi was begun. This was rock-cutting on precipitous hillsides. The rock was limestone of varying hardness. Using 1½ in. bars, a pair of men could jump 5 to 6 feet in 4 hours; with 7/8th in. bars and a 7 lbs. hammer, a pair of men could bore 6½ to 8 feet in 4 hours. If well tamped, gunpowder was effective, but gelignite was preferred as being quicker to load and more suitable in small bore holes; though to secure a clean face when there was a deep drop to formation level, gunpowder was found best. I consider that some 7/8th inch boring bars and 7 lbs. hammers should be included in the field service equipment of a Pioneer Battalion.

(5) The average number of men admitted to hospital sick from 19-9-23 to 9-12-23 was 11'7. This was mainly due to malaria. Detachments at Jandola and

Kotkai suffered considerably from this. The sick rate fell noticeably later. From 10-12-23 to 14-4-24 it was only 4 and most of these cases were due to small injuries received on work.

Although at one time at Kotkai, the detachment there had 25 per cent sick or attending hospital and unfit for work on the road, this percentage compared very favourably with that of other Units.

(6) In spite of the difficult conditions in the Shahur Tangi, the Battalion was lucky in escaping with few serious accidents.

When tamping a gunpowder charge, a Havildar was killed and one man seriously injured. The cause of the explosion remained unexplained.

3 men were seriously hurt by failing boulders.

(7) All ranks gained valuable experience in road-making, use of explosives, construction of perimeter camps and sangars and in road and camp protection duties. The benefit to the Battalion of transfer to Waziristan was invaluable from a fighting and working point of view. No amount of training in South India can equal the practical lessons learnt on the Frontier under active service conditions.

(8) The Battalion now is a unit well-trained for active service on the Frontier except that it still needs more training in piqueting and tactical operations.

1926—1927.
The Putao Road.

Various opportunities for Pioneer Work presented themselves to the regiment while stationed at Mandalay in 1926. The Federated Malay States had asked for the loan of a Pioneer battalion; the Burma Railways were making extensions in many places; and there was road-work, under the P. W. D., on the N. E. Frontier.

After due consideration, it was decided that the last-named (*viz.*—work on the Myitkyina-Sumpra Bum cart road) offered the best possibilities for good training, more especially as there was a chance of trouble in the Triangle, where troops were to be sent, for the first time, to release slaves, in which case the regiment might have an opportunity of seeing active service. As we have seen, this was familiar ground, the regiment having already constructed a mule-road to Putao in 1914-15.

Lieutenant-Colonel A. E. S. Fennell, therefore, after interviewing the Chief Engineer, sent Major F. O. N. Burne, M. C., on a tour with Mr. Farquhar Tait, the Executive Engineer, Putao District, to reconnoitre the alignment of the new road, and report on the possibilities of the contract and, on the latter's return, an agreement was made with the P. W. D. to undertake the work.

An advance party, consisting of Captain R. P. M. Tipping, with Subadar John Sandon and 30 rank and file, left Mandalay on the 15th October 1926, to arrange for a ration dump at Myitkyina, and to find contractors for the supply of vegetables, meat, etc., at the various working camps on the new road.

On the 30th October 1926, A and B Companies left Mandalay by special train, and were followed by the H. Q. Wing and C Company on the 11th November. From Myitkyina, the companies marched separately, to simplify camping arrangements and, by the 15th November, all had reached their working camps.

Within a week of their arrival, they had the misfortune to be attacked by a severe epidemic of influenza, which raged equally through all the camps and, out of 258 cases, there were 12 deaths. In addition, there was continuous rain, which was quite unexpected at that time of year.

However, in spite of this, good progress was made with the work and, by the 25th February 1927, approximately 10½ miles of road had been completed.

By the 2nd April, a further 4½ miles of road was finished, showing an average of 203 cubic feet per man which, considering the difficult nature of the soil, was a very satisfactory result.

In addition to the 15 miles of road, 40 temporary bridges were constructed, and also one permanent bridge of four 20-foot spans. Two permanent masonry buildings were erected at Sumpra Bum, except for the roofing, one of these being a large house (to cost Rs. 23,000) for the Assistant Superintendent and Political Officer.

During the work, some interesting experiments were carried out. One of these was to find out the greatest output possible, and one company worked by sections for eight hours daily (with a one-mile march each way) for five days. The best section averaged 328 cubic feet per man daily (in medium earth) and the weakest section averaged 189 cubic feet per man.

Another experiment was to find out the maximum outturn of a company, working continuously by platoons for 24 hours. There were three platoons, which relieved each other at intervals of four hours. The material to be excavated was hard sandstone, in which the normal task was 50 cubic feet per man. In the 24 hours the company excavated 7,239 cubic feet of sandstone, or an average of 121·6 cubic feet per man for eight hours' work.

The following is an extract from the report of the Superintending Engineer, North-East Circle, Maymyo:—

"12. *Pioneers.* The 2nd/1st Madras Pioneers have done very well and would have completed much more work, had bad weather and influenza not interfered so disastrously when the regiment first moved up to their camps. The work is excellent. They are cheerful and fit, and I have every confidence of their connecting up the two parts of their work before they have to return to Mandalay. Arrangements are being made by the Executive Engineer, Putao, to transport the regiment back to Myitkyina between 25th March 1927 and 6th April 1927. On the latter date the last man will have reached railhead."

Before proceeding on this contract, the regimental Contract Fund guaranteed a minimum of nine annas per day working pay for each man. In the result it was found possible to pay each man an extra bonus of four annas daily.

The following is a list of officers employed on this contract:—

British Officers.	Subadars.	Jemadars.
Lieut.-Col. A. E. S. Fennell.	Tambusami, I.D.S.M.,	Ramannah.
Major T. A. Kemble.	*Subadar-Major.*	Ayyulu Naidu.
,, F. O. N. Burne, M. C.	Balasundaram.	Munisami.
Captain R. P. M. Tipping.	Arogyasami, I.D.S.M.	Periyasami.
,, A. H. Baker.	Govindasami.	Ramachandra Rao.
,, E. Ashford.	J. Sandon.	Loganadan.
Lieut. S. S. Mallannah	Sangili I.	Kumarasami.
,, S. Anis	Ramasami.	
,, Mehtab Singh.		
2nd Lieut. C. Baljit Singh.		
Captain T. R. Birmani, I.M.S.		

The General Specification for the work was as follows:—

1. Jungle Clearing:—50 feet broad on either side of the alignment peg, as directed. Trees near the edges of cuttings should be felled, as directed.

2. Excavation:—The road shall be formed according to the drawing of Hill Section Road on P.W.D. type plan No. 2 of 1924, except that no catch-water drain or road-side drain shall be made without special orders, and when the hill-side slope is steeper than 35 degrees, the excavation shall be 12 feet inwards, or such extra breadth as the Executive Engineer may order, at a slope of 1 in 20 from the alignment peg.

The side slope of the cutting shall be ½ to 1, or as directed by the Executive Engineer.

Earth from excavations shall be deposited as directed by the Executive Engineer or his representative, and before borrow-pits are dug, permission of the P.W.D. Officer-in-Charge shall be obtained.

No borrow earth-work shall be paid for when the material can be obtained at less expense by carriage from a neighbouring cutting.

"Witnesses" or "Deadmen," 2 feet wide, shall be left at regular intervals of 20 or 30 feet, or such distance as the Executive Engineer may specify. If this is not done, the work shall be measured according to the Executive Engineer's directions, whose ruling in this case shall be final.

After final measurement and before final payment, all such witnesses shall be removed.

3. Dry Stone Masonry:—Dry stone masonry shall be carried out according to Marryat's Specification No. 40. In places where the stones are corbelled out to carry the road over an opening, it is essential that vertical joints shall in every case overlap.

The General Terms of the Agreement were as follows:—

1. All expenses in transporting the battalion kit, rations, extra rations and rum, including equipment of medical, personnel and followers, from Mandalay Barracks to the site of work, and back to Mandalay Barracks, shall be paid by the Public Works Department.

2. The Public Works Department shall pay the fares of all officers and other ranks once each way between Mandalay and the site of work. In the event of any officers or men requiring to travel in either direction more than once, the cost of their transport and fares shall be met by the battalion out of the profits accruing from the work.

3. The whole staff of Pioneers and men shall be housed in their own tents, free of cost to the Public Works Department.

4. The Public Works Department shall supply all tools and gear required for the actual work, but the battalion shall keep them in repair free of charge and return them to the Executive Engineer on completion of the work. Tools lost shall be paid for by the battalion.

5. The battalion shall work at the rates entered on the Piece-Work Agreement. The payment shall be made monthly, or at such other suitable periods as are agreed upon between the Commandant and the Executive Engineer, Putao Division.

6. If the gross earnings of the battalion are less than what they would have received had they worked at the daily rates given below, then the battalion shall be paid the difference between the earnings at contract rates and the amount calculated at daily rates for the period. The daily wage rates are:—

For British Officers	Rs. 6/-
„ Subadars	Rs. 2/-
„ Jemadars	Re. 1/8
„ Qualified Artificers	Re. 1/4
„ N.C.O.s and men	As. 12

All of above at half rates when travelling between Mandalay and site of work, or when prevented from working by sickness.

These daily rates shall not be paid on Sundays or holidays.

Followers shall receive annas four per day for the whole period of absence from Mandalay.

The Officer Commanding shall supply the Executive Engineer with a monthly statement of total liabilities calculated on this basis.

The Piece-Work Agreement was as follows:—

No. of Item.	Class and description of work to be executed.	Unit of calculation.	Rate of Payment.
			Rs. A. P.
i.	Excavation in all classes of earth-work and soft rock, not requiring blasting: boulders, stones and roots included. [*N.B.*—Lift will not be paid for extra]	100 c. ft.	1 10 0
ii.	Extra for lead, 100 cubic feet, on receipt of written orders from Sub-Divisional Officer in charge	100 r. ft.	0 4 0
iii.	Jungle clearing, including all bamboo clumps, and trees up to 12 inches diameter	10,000 s. ft.	3 0 0
iv.	Tree felling and removing over 12 inches diameter, girth measured 2 feet above ground	Foot girth.	0 8 0
v.	Dry stone masonry, including collection of stone, rough dressing and laying	100 c. ft.	10 0 0
vi.	Rock blasting, including drilling holes and removing debris, and cost of explosives	100 c. ft.	10 0 0
vii.	All artificers, and any others, working at any work unspecified in items (i) to (vi) above, will be paid at daily wage rates as given in general terms of Agreement, para. 6, for days on which they work]		
viii.	Log wooden bridges, as per plan, 12 feet wide	R. ft.	*2 0 0

* This was subsequently altered to Rs. 15 per running foot.

1927—1928.
The Hukawng Valley.

Early in June 1927, the battalion was asked by the Public Works Department if it were willing to undertake the construction of a road at the entrance to the Hukawng Valley in the Kamaing District.

As the project offered work of a more varied nature than was the case in the previous season, it was considered that the opportunity of gaining still further experience in the construction of a hill road should not be missed.

Sanction was finally accorded by Headquarters, Burma Independent District, in August 1927, and negotiations were opened with the P.W.D.

A provisional agreement, on the lines of the previous year's contract, having been arranged, Major Hare was sent to Myitkyina to discuss terms with Mr. J. B. Nottage, the Executive Engineer, Myitkyina Division, and, if possible, go over the line with him but, owing to the flooded state of the country, this was found to be impossible.

A contract was eventually agreed upon but, owing to the floods and consequent difficulty of fixing camp sites, it was not possible to complete final arrangements for the commencement of work until the end of November.

On the 4th December 1927, an advance party left Mandalay, in order to form a ration dump and erect cook-houses, etc., for the battalion, and arrived at 9th Mile Camp, Pakhren Bum, on the 9th December.

On the 15th December, A and B Companies arrived at this camp, and on the following day, the advance party left for Mataing Hka Camp by the Civil Road, a distance of 20 miles. On the 24th December, the H. Q. Wing and C Company arrived at Kamaing, the former proceeding to 9th mile camp, and the latter to Mataing Hka.

In the meantime, the P.W.D. surveyors had completed a preliminary alignment, and the work was divided into sections and allotted to companies, Company Commanders being made responsible for the detailed survey, and also encouraged to propose alterations to the line, where capable of improvement. The country offered considerable difficulties, these hills west of the Nam Kaung Valley being uninhabited, and consequently there are no Kachin tracks, so that elephant paths and bison tracks afford the only means of traversing the dense jungle.

For convenience, the line was chained in two sections:—
 (1) Zero at Pakhren Bum to R. D. 35,000, at Hkause Chaung.
 (2) Zero at Hkause Chaung to R. D. 19,000, at Mataing Hka.

The work on these sections was finally completed in four stages, as follows:—

1st Stage—(December 18th, 1927 to February 26th, 1928).

The opening of a 16' to 20' road passable for motor traffic, from Pakhren Bum to Mataing Hka—a distance of 10½ miles.

The work on this stage consisted of:—
 (i) Heavy side-cutting on Pakhren Bum, and Hill 1165 south of Mataing Hka.
 (ii) Clearing a 16' track, of trees, stumps, kaing grass, rocks, etc., between these hills and north to Mataing Hka.
 (iii) The crossing of the Hkause Chaung—a gap of 270 ft., with a bank 195 ft. long, and 22 ft. in height; and a trestle bridge of 75 ft. span and the same height.

This necessitated the following work being done:—
 (a) 6 miles side-cutting, including four big double cuttings.
 (b) ¼ mile embankments, from borrow-pits and hill-sides.
 (c) 4 miles of service tracks along sections where banks were required to bring the road above flood level.

Platoon camps were formed, named respectively Bison, Horeb, Hkause Chaung and Elephant camps, using battalion pack transport. This was found to be well worth while, as long marches to work were thus avoided.

2nd Stage.—(*February 27th to March 22nd, 1928*).

The work on this stage consisted of the construction of banks across kaing grass and low-lying wooded areas, and the continuation to Sasing Hka (3 miles).

The original alignment north of Mataing Hka having been abandoned, the P.W.D. carried out a fresh survey and fixed a certain number of obligatory points, between which the battalion was responsible for the alignment.

The aim was to avoid the low ground north of Mataing Hka, and skirt the high ground of the valley slopes, the road thus being a little longer and more difficult to construct, but the cost of maintenance would be less, and it would be well above flood level.

For the work on this stage, B Company was moved to Sasing Hka, 3 miles north of Mataing Hka and, by the 22nd March, all banks on the Pakhren Bum—Mataing Hka section had been raised above flood level, with the exception of the 5,000 feet of bank at Hkause Chaung.

The work done was as follows:—

(*a*) 2 miles of side-cutting, south of Sasing Hka.
(*b*) 2 miles service track on road alignment.
(*c*) ¾ mile embankments.
(*d*) 2 miles service tracks, through kaing areas, to Sasing Hka camp.

3rd Stage—(*March 23rd to April 15th, 1928*).

Work on this stage consisted of the continuation to Hwelon Hka (2½ miles) at a reduced width of 14 feet, and raising the bank south of Hkause Chaung by means of a Decauville track.

Up to now, the policy of the P.W.D. had been to complete a road, 16 to 20 feet wide, to Sasing Hka. On the 15th March, however, it was seen that, by reducing the width to 10 to 14 feet, Hwelon Hka could be reached and, sanction having been obtained for this change, companies were moved as follows:—

(i) C Company to Hwelon Hka, *via* the Civil Road and a service track.
(ii) H. Q. Wing (2 Groups) to Sasing Hka.
(iii) Headquarters to Hkause Chaung.

On the 6th April 1928, the road to Sasing Hka was opened for motor cars and, a few days later, a mule track was through to Hwelon Hka. On the 18th April, B and C Companies, with 90 carts, marched back to Mogaung along the road they had made.

The work done was as follows:—

- (a) 3 miles side-cutting.
- (b) 2 miles service track to Hwelon Saddle camp.
- (c) ¼ mile embankments at Hkause Chaung with Decauville, using 8 tip wagons.

Final Stage—(April 15th to April 26th, 1928).

Completion of the Hkause Chaung bank, and of rock blasting on Pakhren Bum. A few days before the departure of B and C Companies, the two groups of H. Q. Wing at Sasing Hka were brought back to Headquarters camp to assist in the Hkause Chaung bank. Ten more trucks had now arrived, and it was possible to employ 1½ companies on this work.

By the 25th April, the bank was completed to its correct height, allowing for sinkage. It was 5,000 feet long, and required three-quarters of a million cubic feet of earth.

Owing to the delay in the arrival of explosives from Rangoon, very little blasting was done during the second and third stages. Rock work on Pakhren Bum was completed during this stage by H. Q. Wing group at Signal Hill.

Actual Results.

A new road was cut through a trackless and uninhabited district, across swamps and along steep hill-sides, covered with impenetrable jungle. Of the sixteen miles completed, eleven miles were on sidelong ground, one and a half miles across flooded areas, and three and a half miles on level ground above flood level. In addition, four miles of service tracks were made to connect the Civil Road with camps north of Mataing Hka.

The road was to be continued with Kachin labour as far as Shaduzup and will ultimately go to Maingkwan in the Hukawng Valley. If labour can be raised in the Hukawng and work started from that end, no difficulty should be experienced in getting the road through. There would then remain a distance of only 120 miles to Ledo, in Assam, to link up by road the railway systems of India and Burma.

The total amount earned by the regiment on this contract for actual work done was Rs. 88,319-0-0.

The following is an extract from a letter, dated the 17th March 1928, from the Chief Engineer, P. W. D., Buildings and Roads Branch, Burma, to the Officer Commanding, 2nd Battalion 1st Madras Pioneers:—

"During my recent inspection of the Hukawng Valley road, I was immensely pleased with the work carried out by the Regiment, both as regards the alignment of the constructed road between the obligatory points given by my department, and the general quality and quantity of work per man.

I would also like to record my opinion that the arrangements made with regard to the high percentage of the men actually working, in comparison with the total camp strength, has been most satisfactory."

The following remarks, dated 7th September 1928, were written by the Engineer-in-Chief, Army Headquarters, on the technical training report on the battalion for the previous year:—

"A very satisfactory year's training, well thought out and carefully organised.

The Hukawng Valley contract was particularly valuable, and afforded the best possible training for all ranks. The report on the contract is excellent, and the organisation and execution of the work show that this battalion is technically highly efficient."

The following is a list of officers employed on this contract:—

British Officers.	Subadars.	Jemadars.
Lieut.-Col. A. E. S. Fennell.	Arogyasami, I.D.S.M.,	Ramannah.
Major I. L. O'H. Hare.	*Subadar-Major.*	Francis.
Captain C. Southgate, M.C.	Govindasami.	Loganadan.
,, C. Wallis.	J. Sandon.	Sangili II.
,, A. H. Baker.	Sangili I.	Arogyasami.
Lieut. S. Anis.	Veerabadra Goundan.	Sangili III.
,, Baljit Singh.	E. Nukayya.	Alagirisami.
,, S. K. Ghose.		
,, G. D. Rai, I.M.S.		

1929.

On the 6th July 1929, the battalion was inspected by Colonel R. C. R. Hill, D. S. O., Officiating Brigadier R. E., who reported that it was "a well-trained battalion, technically fit for service."

From the 26th to the 29th September 1929, No. 6 Company carried out digging operations at Pinya, as part of a Madras District Headquarters Tactical Exercise. The G. O. C. District wrote, through the D. A. Q. M. G., as follows:—

"The General has asked me to tell you how very pleased he was with the work done by your company under Captain Tipping in digging and wiring the reserve company area of the Pinya position and the machine-gun emplacements.

The company worked tremendously hard, and made a first-class job of the task.

Will you please convey his congratulations to the officer commanding, and all ranks of the company.

Incidentally, the measures taken to reduce to a minimum compensation for damage to crops were most effective."

1930.
Magadi Road Contract Work.

Early in 1930, negotiations were opened by the Commandant, Lieutenant-Colonel A. F. Hamilton, M. C., with the Chief Engineer, Mysore Government, which resulted in the battalion being offered a contract for road-work in connection with the Tippagondanahalli project, which was intended to supply water to Bangalore.

Although the original application for sanction to take up this contract was submitted on the 6th June, it was not until the 26th November that the final sanction of the Chief of the General Staff was obtained, the agreement having had to be submitted a second time to Army Headquarters, in order to obtain sanction for a few trifling alterations in the wording of the agreement.

The actual work undertaken was a portion of a deviation of the Magadi Road (Bangalore District) from miles 15½ to 21½, comprising an approximate length of 6 miles of the new alignment.

The new road, which followed the hills bordering the Arkavati River, afforded excellent practice in hill road-making with an appreciable amount of rock-blasting and masonry work on small bridges and culverts. The artificers of the battalion also gained valuable experience in the sharpening and maintenance of tools.

Owing to station guards and duties, it was not possible for the whole battalion to be sent out at one time. It was, therefore, arranged for companies to proceed independently, each company being allotted a portion of the work.

The companies marched out to the camp site (23 miles) in one day and, while in camp, the men were employed on road-work 5 days a week, of 8 hours each, the sixth day being reserved for military training. The ground in the vicinity of the camps, being of a hilly nature, afforded an excellent opportunity for practising mountain warfare.

In November 1930, a serious outbreak of cholera occurred in a neighbouring coolie colony, but fortunately the precautions taken averted an outbreak in the camp. The weather on the whole was good, though heavy rain was experienced soon after the commencement of work.

The amount of work completed was as follows:—

	Earth, boulders and stone.	Quarry stone.	Soft rock.	Rock blasting.	Rubble removing.	Metalling.
No. 4 Coy.	403,066 c. ft.	14,728 c.ft.	15,361 c. ft.	24,458 c. ft.	13.205 c. ft.	428 c. ft.
No. 5 Coy.	166,545 c. ft.	2,000 c.ft.	16,422 c. ft.	11,025 c. ft.	...	120 c. ft.
No. 6 Coy.	87,816 c. ft.	1,837 c.ft.	47,097 c. ft.	27,830 c. ft.	...	...

In addition, No. 6 Company cleared 18,000 r. ft. of jungle, and cleared 14,802 c. ft. of debris, besides doing 1,411 c. ft. of revetments, while each company constructed culverts to the value of Rs. 227-5-0.

The total amount of work completed was thus:—

No. 4 Coy. 471,246 c. ft. averaging 52 c. ft. per man (= output in ordinary soil of 107 c. ft.)
No. 5 Coy. 195,808 c. ft. ,, 49 ,, ,, (,, ,, 103 c. ft.)
No. 6 Coy. 198,793 c. ft. ,, 52 ,, ,. (,, ,, 107 c. ft.)
A grand total of 865,847 c. ft.

The total receipts of the regiment amounted to Rs. 14,622-6-0, and the following daily rates of working-pay were paid to companies:—Company Commanders, Rs. 4; Company Officers, Rs. 2; Subadars, As. 14; Jemadars, As. 10; Havildars, As. 8; Naiks, As. 6; Lance-Naiks and Pioneers, As. 5.

The following (dated 26th October) is an extract from the *Times of India*, referring to this contract:—

"Nothing interests Bangalore residents more than the new water-supply scheme. Great hopes are reposed in the dam which is being built across the Arkavati river, 20 miles from Bangalore, and constant visits are paid to watch its progress. When, about two years from now, the dam is built and the water flows to the city through pipes made at the Mysore iron-works in N.W. Mysore, the chronic water shortage will be finally settled and the city will be able to expand to its natural dimensions. This is only a part of the scheme. The love of the Mysore authorities for the beauty spots of the State amounts almost to an obsession, and every effort will be made to exploit the beautiful hill-girt lake that the dam will form, and turn it into a week-end Spa for Bangalore residents and a pleasure resort for visitors to the State. It has now been definitely decided to provide facilities for bathing and boating, and to stock the lake with trout—presumably rainbow trout, such as flourish in the Nilgiris. No doubt there will be a travellers' bungalow, and possibly even a hotel, and the source of the Bangalore water will thus become one of the most delightful week-end resorts in India........

A new road round the hills is being made, and as the work of building this road supplies conditions similar to what Pioneers expect to encounter on active service, the help of the Madras Pioneers from Bangalore has been lent for the formation of the road. The heavy final stages of road-building will be left to the 3,000 workmen, including many Pathans, already encamped near the dam.

The Madras Pioneers are the oldest regiment in the Indian Army. The road-making is being done by two companies of the 2nd Battalion, which has been "Indianized", to use one of the most dreadful words ever invented by officials. The Indian name of this battalion is *"Baillie-ki-Paltan"*, and commemorates Colonel Baillie of sad memory, the victim of Hyder Ali Khan of Mysore. Colonel Baillie did not raise the Battalion, though he commanded it for some years, and it was not present at his defeat, though it took part in the operations of Sir Eyre Coote which avenged the defeat.

Of the two companies that are at present in camp, one marched the whole 23 miles from Bangalore yesterday. The officers marched with the men, and no one fell out, though one man had to be helped part of the way."

The following officers were employed on this contract:—

British Officers.	Subadars.	Jemadars.
Captain A. H. Baker.	Arogyasami, I.D.S.M.,	Kadirvelu.
„ S. S. Murcott.	*Subadar-Major.*	Loganathan.
(*Attached from 1st (K.G.O.) Bn.*)	Jagannathan, I.D.S.M.	Doraisami.
Lieut. S. M. Shrinagesh.	J. Sandon.	Sangili II.
„ Anis Ahmedkhan.	Ramasami.	Ondimuthu.
„ Mehtab Singh.	Veerabadra Goundan.	
„ Baljit Singh.	Ersu Nukayya.	
„ B. P. Walawalkar.		

The following are the terms of the agreement made with the Executive Engineer, New Bangalore Water Works Division, Thippagondanahalli:—

"Whereas the Officer Commanding is desirous of taking up work on about two miles of the Bangalore-Magadi Deviation Road, it is hereby mutually agreed between the parties hereto as follows:—

The contract is to last for a period not longer than 3 months from the date of the commencement of the contract, and is terminable at the end of the first month or any subsequent month if the conditions of work are not satisfactory to the Executive Engineer in respect of the cost of the work.

Should the exigencies of the service necessitate, the contract will terminate at once, on such a contingency arising.

The Executive Engineer agrees to pay the following daily rates for each unit consisting of:—

    2 British Officers   Rs. 6/- *per diem* each.
    4 Indian Officers   Re. 1/8 „ „
  12 Non-Commissioned Officers   As. 12 „ „
 190 Pioneers   As. 10 „ „

The Executive Engineer agrees:—

(*a*) To provide all tools, baskets, charcoal, etc., required, subject to the payment of the cost of the articles and centage charges as per rules in force;

(*b*) To supply all explosives;

(c) To pay for transport for men, baggage, etc., to and from the site of the contract, the cost not exceednig a total of Rs. 750 for both ways. Half the cost of transport will be paid as soon as the men and baggage reach the work spot, the other half being payable after the work is completed;

(d) To permit the Officer Commanding to cart water to the extent of 1,000 gallons daily from the water storage tanks installed.

The Executive Engineer also agrees to pay for tentage hire a sum not exceeding Rs. 200 *per mensem*, or such less sum as such cost of hire may come to. The hire will be paid in one lump sum after the termination of the contract.

The Executive Engineer further undertakes to pay at the end of the contract 5 *per cent* on the full value of the contract to the Officer Commanding towards the liability to Government under Appendix XXVI, para 4, Regulations for the Army in India, the value being determined on the total amount paid under Clause 2 *supra*.

In return for the above considerations, the Officer Commanding undertakes to construct, according to plans and specifications furnished by the Executive Engineer, such portions of the Bangalore-Makadi Deviation Road as may be allotted to him, and to finish it in a workmanlike manner to the satisfaction of the Executive Engineer and to hand it over within the maximum period of 3 months.

The Officer Commanding undertakes to conform to all the technical instructions given by the Executive Engineer or any of his authorised representatives.

The Officer Commanding also undertakes to ensure the good behaviour of his men and to see that none of the members of his Battalion come into any conflict with other local labour or staff employed on the works, or the inhabitants of the neighbouring villages.

The Officer Commanding shall furnish fortnightly bills for the wages of the men employed according to the rates agreed to above, which will be paid by the Executive Engineer after scrutiny.

In witness whereof, the Officer Commanding, 2nd Battalion, Madras Pioneers, has hereunto set his hand and seal this 8th day of October 1930 and the Executive Engineer, New Bangalore Water Works Division, has hereunto set his hand and seal this 5th day of October of One thousand nine hundred and thirty (1930).

(*Sd.*) H. R. VENKATASUBBA RAO,   (*Sd.*) W. J. NANCE, MAJOR,
Executive Engineer,   *Commanding 2nd Battalion,*
New Bangalore Water Works Division.   *Madras-Pioneers.*"

Bibliography.

The following are some of the works which have been consulted for these Records:—

1. "*A History of the Military Transactions of the British Nation in Indostan,* from the year 1745. To which is Prefixed a Dissertation on the Establishments made by Mahomedan Conquerors in Indostan." By Robert Orme, Esq., F. A. S., *London*: Printed for F. Wingrave, Successor to Mr. Nourse in the Strand, 1803. Madras: Re-printed by Pharaoh and Co., Atheneum Press.—*Mount Road,* 1861. The Fourth Edition. Revised by the Author. 3 vols. large 8vo.

2. "*Historical Sketches of the South of India,* in an Attempt to trace the History of Mysoor from the Origin of the Hindoo Government of that State to the Extinction of the Mohammedan Dynasty in 1799, founded chiefly on Indian Authorities collected by the Author while officiating for several years as Political Resident at the Court of Mysoor." By Lieutenant-Colonel Mark Wilks. Second Edition, *Madras,* 1869. 2 vols. 8vo.

3. "*The History of Ayder Ali Khan, Nabob-Bahader:* or New Memoirs concerning the East Indies. With Historical Notes." By M.M.D.L.T.* General of Ten Thousand Men in the Army of the Mogul Empire, and formerly Commander-in-Chief of the Artillery of Ayder Ali, and of a Body of European Troops in the Service of that Nabob. In Two Volumes, 12mo. *London:* Printed for J. Johnson, No. 72, St. Paul's Church-Yard. 1784.

4. "*A View of the English Interests in India*: and an account of the Military Operations in the Southern Parts of the Peninsula, during the Campaigns of 1782, 1783 and 1784. In two letters; Addressed to the Right Honourable the Earl of........and to Lord Macartney and the Select Committee of Fort St. George." By William Fullarton of Fullarton, M.P., F.R.S.S., of London and Edinburgh, and late Commander of the Southern Army on the Coast of Coromandel. *London:* Printed for T. Cadell in the Strand; and W. Creech, Edinburgh, 1787. 1 vol. 8vo.

5. "*Historical Record of the Honourable East India Company's First Madras European Regiment*: containing an account of the establishment of Independent Companies in 1645; their formation into a Regiment in 1748; and its subsequent Services to 1842." By a Staff Officer† *London:* Smith, Elder and Co., 65 Cornhill, 1843. 1 vol. 8vo.

6. "*History of the Madras Army,* from 1746 to 1826, with an Account of the European Artillery, Engineers, and Infantry up to their Amalgamation with the Royal Army in 1861, and of the Native Cavalry and Infantry up to 1887." Compiled by Lt.-Col. W. J. Wilson, Ret. List, Madras. *Madras,* 1888, 4 vols. and 1 vol. maps, 8vo.

7. "*The Military History of the Madras Engineers and Pioneers,* from 1743 up to the Present Time". Compiled by Major H. M. Vibart, Royal (Late Madras) Engineers. *London:* W. H. Allen and Co., 13 Waterloo Place, S. W., Publishers to the India Office. 1881, 2 vols. 8vo.

8. "*Manual of the Salem District,*" by F. J. Richards, I.C.S. (Then in the press).

9. "*Memoirs of the War in Asia from 1780 to 1784.* Including a Narrative of the Imprisonment and Sufferings of our Officers and Soldiers." By an Officer of Colonel Baillie's Detachment.‡ The Second Edition. *London:* Sold by J. Sewell, Cornhill; and J. Debrett, Piccadilly. 1789. 1 vol. 8vo.

10. "*A Narrative of the Military Operations on the Coromandel Coast,* against the Combined Forces of the French, Dutch, and Hyder Ally Cawn, from the Year 1780 to the Peace

---

* Either De La Touche or De La Tour, probably the latter, as James Bristow refers to " M. le Maitre de la Tour."

† This history was, I understand, written by General Neill.

‡ Originally ascribed to Alexander Read, A. D. C. to Colonel Baillie, but now accepted as having been written by William Thomson, L. L. D.

in 1784; in a Series of Letters. In which are included many useful cautions to young gentlemen destined for India; A description of the most remarkable manners and customs of the East Indians; and an account of the Isle of France." Illustrated with a view of Port Louis in the Isle of France; and correct plans upon a large scale of the fortifications of Trinquamallee, and of all the Battles fought by the army under Lieutenant-General Sir Eyre Coote, K.B., and other Commanders, during that War.

By Innes Munro, Esquire, Captain in the late 73rd or Lord Macleod's Regiment of Highlanders. *London*: Printed for the Author by T. Bensley; and sold by G. Nicol, Bookseller to His Majesty, Pall-Mall, 1789. 1 vol. 4to.

11. "*The Life of Gen. the Right Hon. Sir David Baird, Bart, G. C. B., etc.*" Anonymous. *London*, 1832. 2 vols. 8vo.

12. "*Madras District Manuals. North Arcot.*" Compiled by Arthur F. Cox, M.C.S. New Edition, revised by Harold A. Stuart, I.C.S. *Madras*. 1895. 2 vols. 8vo.

13. "*History of the British Army.*" By the Hon. J. W. Fortescue.

(I regret that I have no copy available at the moment to record full particulars of this, the most admirable of all military histories.).

14. "*A Narrative of the Campaign in India, which terminated the War with Tippoo Sultan in 1792. With maps and plans illustrative of the subject, and a view of Seringapatam.*" By Major Dirom, Deputy Adjutant-General of His Majesty's Forces in India. *London*: Printed by W. Bulmer & Co., 1793. 1 vol. large 4to.

15. "*Major-General Sir Thomas Munro, Bart, K. C. B. Selections from his Minutes and other Official Writings*". Edited, with a Memoir, by Sir A. J. Arbuthnot, K. C. S. I., C. I. E., London, 1881. 2 volumes.

16. "*A View of the Origin and Conduct of the War with Tippoo Sultan*". By Lieutenant-Colonel Alexander Beatson, A. D. C., to the Governor-General and Surveyor-General to the Army in the Field. *London*, 1800. 1 vol. 4to.

17. "*A Manual of the Tinnevelly District in the Presidency of Madras*". Compiled by A. J. Stuart, M.C.S. *Madras*. 1879. 1 vol. 8vo.

18. "*Military Reminiscences of Forty Years' Active Service in the East Indies.*" By Colonel James Welsh. *London*, 1830. 2 vols. 8vo.

19. "*The Despatches of Field-Marshal the Duke of Wellington, During his Various Campaigns in India............*" Compiled from Official and other Authentic Documents by the late Colonel Gurwood, C.B., K.C.T.S., Esquire to his Grace as Knight of the Bath, and Deputy Lieutenant of the Tower of London. *London*: John Murray 1852. 8 vols. large 8vo. [*Vols. I and II only dealing with India*]

20. "*Medals of the British Army and How they were Won*". By Thomas Carter. *London*. 1861. 3 vols. 8vo.

21. "*Notes on the Battle of Assaye,*" from a lecture at the Indian Staff College, by Colonel Bird, D.S.O.

22. "*Wellington's Campaigns in India*". By Major R. G. Burton, 94th Russell's Infantry. Division of the Chief of the Staff, Intelligence Branch. *Calcutta*: Superintendent of Government Printing, India. 1908. 1 vol. [*For Official Use Only*].

23. "*Malabar*". By William Logan, M.C.S., Collector and Magistrate of the District, etc. *Madras*. 1887. 2 vols. 8vo., and extra vol. of documents.

24. *"Malabar Series: Wynad: its People and Traditions"*. By Rao Bahadur C. Gopalan Nair, Deputy Collector, Malabar. *Madras.* 1911. 1 vol.

25. *"History of the Political and Military Transactions in India during the Administration of the Marquess of Hastings. 1813—1823"*. By Henry T. Prinsep, of the Bengal Civil Service. *London.* 1825. 2 vols. 8vo.

26. *"The Ganjam District Manual"*. By T. J. Maltby, Late Madras Civil Service. Edited by G. D. Leman, M.C.S., Agent to the Governor and Collector of the District. *Madras.* 1882. 1 vol. 8vo.

27. *"History of the Ganjam District"*. By T. J. Maltby, M.C.S. Printed in the Ganjam Collectorate Press by G. Venkatakrushnama Chetti. 1877. 1 vol. fcp., paper covers.

28. *"Selections from the Records of the Madras Government No. XXIV: Reports on the Disturbances in Purla Kimedy, Vizagapatam and Goomsoor, in 1832—36"*. By Mr. G. E. Russell, Senior Member of the Board of Revenue and afterwards Member of Council at the Madras Presidency. *Madras,* 1856. 2 vols. 8vo.

29. *"Strictures on the Present Government, Civil, Military and Political, of the British Possessions in India; including a View of the Recent Transactions in that Country, which have tended to Alienate the Affections of the Natives: in a Letter from an Officer, Resident on the Spot, to his Friend in England"* *London*: Printed for J. Hatchard, Piccadilly, and T. and R. Hughes, Ludgate Street. 1808. (Pamphlet).

30. *"The Life of Hyder Ally: with an Account of his Usurpation of the Kingdom of Mysore, and other contiguous Provinces. To which is annexed a Genuine Narrative of the Sufferings of the British Prisoners of War, taken by his Son, Tippoo Saib."* By Francis Robson, Late Captain in the Hon. East-India Company's Forces. *London: Printed for S.* Hooper, No. 212 High Holborn. 1786. 1 vol. 8vo.

31. *"A Statement of Facts, delivered to The Right Honourable Lord Minto, Governor-General of India, etc., etc., on his Late Arrival at Madras."* By William Petrie, Esq., Senior Member of the Council at Madras. With an Appendix of Official Minutes. *London:* Printed for J. J. Stockdale, 41 Pall Mall. 1810. (Pamphlet).

32. *"A Short Account of the Mutiny of the Army of Bengal in 1766; Being preparatory to the Publication of an Accurate and Authentic Account of the Late Mutiny at Madras."* London: Printed for Edmund Lloyd, Harley Street, Cavendish Square. 1810. (Pamphlet).

33. *"An Accurate and Authentic Narrative of the Origin and Progress of the Dissentions at the Presidency of Madras: Founded on Original Papers and Correspondence."* London: Printed for Edmund Lloyd, Harley Street, Cavendish Square. 1810. (Pamphlet).

34. *"Observations on the Disturbances in the Madras Army in 1809."* In two Parts. By John Malcolm, Lieutenant-Colonel in the Honourable East India Company's Madras Army, Resident at Mysore, and late Envoy to the Court of Persia. *London:* Printed for William Miller, Albemarle Street, and John Murray, Fleet Street. 1812. (Pamphlet).

35. *"A Manual of the Salem District in the Presidency of Madras."* Compiled by H. LeFanu. *Madras,* 1883. 2 vols. 8vo.

36. *"The Second Afghan War, 1879-80."* Abridged Official Account. Produced in the Intelligence Branch, Army Head Quarters, India. *London:* John Murray, 1908. 1 vol. 8vo.

37. *"Madras District Manuals: South Canara."*

38. *"The Image of War, or Service on the Chin Hills."* By Surg. Capt. A.G.E. Newland, I. M. S., 2nd Burmah Bn., with an introductory historical note by J. D. Macnabb, Esq., Political

Officer, S. Chin Hills. Illustrated with 191 Photographs by the Author. *Calcutta:* Thacker, Spink & Co. 1894.

39. *"Frontier and Overseas Expeditions from India."* Compiled in the Intelligence Branch Division of the Chief of the Staff, Army Headquarters, India. Vol. V, Burma. *Simla,* 1907. 1 vol. 4to. [*For Official Use Only.*]

40. "*The Life and Times of General Sir James Browne, R.E., K.C.B., K.C.S.I. (Buster Browne)*" By General J. J. MacLeod Innes, R.E., V.C. *London:* John Murray, 1905. 1 vol. 8vo.

41. "*An Indian Olio.*" By Lieutenant-General E. F. Burton, Madras Staff Corps. With Illustrations from Sketches by the Author and by Miss C.G.M. Burton. *London:* Spencer Blackett, 1 vol. 8vo. 1881 (?)

42. "*Alphabetical List of the Officers of the Indian Army,* with the dates of their respective promotion, retirement, resignation, or death, whether in India or in Europe, from the year 1760 to the year 1834 inclusive. Corrected to September 30th, 1837." Compiled and edited by Messrs. Dodwell and Miles, E. India Army Agents, 69 Cornhill. Dedicated by permission to the Hon. Court of Directors of the East India Company. *London:* Longman, Orme, Brown and Co., 1838. 1 vol. 8vo.

43. "*List of Inscriptions on Tombs or Monuments in Madras, Possessing Historical or Archæological Interest.*" By Julian James Cotton, I.C.S. *Madras*: Government Press, 1905. 1 vol. Folio.

44. "*Memoir and Correspondence of General James Stuart Fraser of the Madras Army.*" By his Son, Colonel Hastings Fraser, Madras Staff Corps, 2nd Edition, *London,* 1885. 1 vol. 8vo.

45. "*The East India Military Calendar; containing the Services of General and Field Officers of the Indian Army.*" By the Editor of the Royal Military Calendar (Sir John Philippart), *London.* Printed for Kingsbury, Parbury and Allen, Leadenhall Street, 1823—26. 3 vols. 4to.

46. "*A Narrative of the Sufferings of James Bristow,* Belonging to the Bengal Artillery, During Ten Years' Captivity with Hyder Ally and Tippoo Saheb." *Calcutta,* printed: *London,* Reprinted for J. Murray, No. 32 Fleet Street, 1793. 1 vol. 8vo.

47. "*Notes on Medals Awarded to Indian Troops between 1778 and 1922,* (with special reference to the Q. V. O. Sappers and Miners)." Compiled by Lieutenant-Colonel R. L. McClintock, C.M.G., D.S.O., R.E., Commandant, Q.V.O.S. and M. *Bangalore*: Printed at the Sapper Press. 1922. 1 vol. fcp.

48. "*Memories of Madras.*" By Sir Charles Lawson. *London*: Swan, Sonnenschein and Co. Ltd. 1905. 1 vol. 8vo.

49. "*Indian Records Series—Vestiges of Old Madras. 1640—1800.* Traced from the East India Company's Records Preserved at Fort St. George and the India Office and From Other Sources." By Henry Davison Love, late Lieutenant-Colonel, Royal Engineers, and Bt.-Colonel, Hon. Fellow of the University of Madras. Published for the Government of India. *London*: John Murray, Albemarle Street, 1913. 3 vols. and Index vol. 8vo.

50. "*The Campaign in Mesopotamia, 1914—1918.*" (History of the Great War, Based on Official Documents). Compiled, at the request of the Government of India, under the direction of the Historical Section of the Committee of Imperial Defence, by Brig.-Gen. F. J. Moberly, C.B., C.S.I., D.S.O., P.S.C. *London.* H. M. Stationery Office. 1923. 4 vols. 8vo.

For the earlier edition of these records, much assistance was given by Mr. F. J. Richards, I.C.S., and, for the present issue, by Lieutenant-Colonel Hamilton, Major Burne, Major Deane and Captain Ashford, while I am also greatly indebted to Lieutenant-Colonel Crosthwait of the Survey of India for kindly undertaking the preparation of the maps and plans.

Reviews of the 1922 Edition.

RECORDS OF THE IV MADRAS PIONEERS, 1759—1903. (NOW THE 64TH PIONEERS) BY MAJOR H. F. MURLAND, 64TH PIONEERS.

Quarterly Journal of the Mythic Society (Bangalore), October 1922:—

"This handsomely turned-out quarto volume of over 300 pages is a substantial contribution to the history of early British military activities in South India; and Major Murland deserves the gratitude both of those who are interested in the history of this gallant and faithful old regiment and of those who delight to wander through the mazes of Indian history in general. The wideness of his researches, often through records that are not easily come by, and the care and thoroughness with which the work has been done, merit the highest commendation. In following the fortunes of the regiment over parts of three centuries, Major Murland has set himself to indicate the politics of the times, the movements of armies on both sides of the fields of war, and the issues of the various campaigns that come under review. The present writer knows of no single volume or series of volumes in which such information, succinct and exact, has been brought together. It is rather a matter of regret that the "Records" are published for private circulation only; and therefore the presentation of a copy to the Mythic Society by the 64th Pioneers gains the more both in grace and intrinsic value. Rather more than half the book is taken up by the story of the campaigns in which the regiment participated, together with the tale of its doings as a Pioneer regiment in civil undertakings; then follows a series of most interesting extracts which illustrate the interior economy of the regiment; and the book is closed with some account of the British and Indian officers who have been connected, through the period covered, with the life and doings of the regiment. It would be hard to say which of these is the most valuable contribution to history, for each has a unique interest and value.

The names of the British officers bring to our memory the great family names of the Turings, the Dovetons, the Munros, and many others. Old sepoys name the regiment after Baillie, "Baillie-Ki-Paltan", famous for his great, but ill-supported, stand against Hyder and Tippu at Pollilur in 1780 and for his heroic fortitude during imprisonment in Seringapatam, till death relieved his sufferings, but it appears clear that he did not himself raise the regiment. The credit of that rests with George Airey, probably its first commanding officer. Honour further clings to the regiment in that Flint, who defended Wandiwash for 167 days in 1780—81, was at least nominally its Lieutenant-Colonel in 1797: while we doubt not that the memory of Thomas Munro's enrolment for two years with the regiment is highly treasured. Probably many of our readers will desire to see the old drawing, preserved in the regimental officers' mess, which represents Baillie handing his sword to Hyder after the battle of Pollilur.

Since the history will be available to members of the Mythic Society in its library, little need here be said of the history of the four British campaigns against Hyder Ali and his son Tippu, nor of the war against the Mahrattas by Wellesley. Enough to say that readers can rely both on the general outline of history, and also on its details; a careful study of the latter can hardly produce a single correction, and none that is important. Local members of the Society will delight to note that the present 64th—formerly the 5th, and then the 4th battalion, with at first "Coast Sepoys", then "Carnatic Battalion", afterwards "Madras Native Infantry", as its descriptions—was present in Mysore in 1768 under the renowned Colonel Joseph Smith, again at the Capture of Bangalore and the Siege of Nandidroog, and did heavy convoy work in the Campaign of 1799 under the direction of Captain Alexander Reed. One of its Commandants, Captain Nathaniel Dawes, died at Bangalore in March 1791, just after the Siege, and was buried in the fort itself, but his tomb like many another has been swept out of recognition.

The amazing fidelity and service of the Indian Sepoy of South India is revealed again in these records. When the fortunes of the British were suffering eclipse in 1780—84, when the Civil authorities and the Military leaders were hopelessly at variance and consequently the troops were again and again more than half starved and almost helpless for lack of stores and ammunition, when leaders hesitated and bungled away their chances of victory, then the sepoys kept faith and fighting spirit to an extent that elicits wonder and admiration. Smith, Coote, Wellesley, all in their turn testify to the bravery and endurance of their sepoys. Perhaps the time when their lamp shone brightest was when numbers of those who had escaped from the disaster of Baillie, and had made their way to the army that did not make its way to them, still marched and fought with the most gallant. Major Murland rightly does not attempt to indicate the worth of all this, because it is beyond description; he contents himself with the bare record of facts and of the statements of eye-witnesses.

Readers of old records of military doings in India must often have been struck to find how very young numbers of the British troops and officers were. Tippu could find about sixty youths in captivity in the neighbourhood of Bangalore in 1783, and sent them off to be included in his "Cheylah" battalions: Here is a record of two boys, neither more than fifteen years of age, in charge of companies at the siege of Pondicherry in 1778; a fact possibly due to the old system which sometimes granted a deceased father's commission to his son even, as in the case of General Monin, buried at Trichinopoly, at the tender age of five years. Other reasons lay in the difficulty in securing recruits for India, so that recruits were found in the immature, and often, alas, in the gaols of the country.

We note with great interest in the record of the interior economy of the regiment, the system, started in 1785, of granting the pay of a sepoy who had been killed or had died in the service to one of his sons, who when he was ripening into manhood, must either enlist or be struck off the regimental roll. The system seems to have worked well, for two years after its initiation the numbers of two "recruit boys" per company was increased to forty per regiment, and that again shortly after to fifty. How much of regimental tradition, pride of service, mutual affection, must have been fostered by this old system!

It is interesting to laymen in matters military to note the frequency of the changes in details of regimental equipment, clothing, pay, etc., through the years. Military tailors have ever had keen eyes, and changeable tastes. We note that the best leaders were ever the most careful of their men, even of their finances. Smith, *e.g.*, recommended in 1770 that commanding officers should not stop "more than four, or at most five, rupees from any sepoy" for his clothing. "Slops" that clothing is called later in the same year, a term, that is now unknown to modern English generally, but is retained in the rural districts of North England to describe, when used in the singular, an "overall" or "smock", and when in the plural, a man's nether garments, specially of a "sloppy" cut.

The dress of British soldiers and their officers in those early days must have been a burden to the flesh in days of battle and long marching. William Hickey is quoted here as witnessing to the fact that "officers in India dress precisely the same (in point of coat at least), as in Europe, and although certainly absurd in such extreme heat, actually button the lapel close up to the throat." The drawings which represent the 18th century soldier in India bear the same testimony to the use of very unsuitable Western clothing by the Eastern campaigner. Small wonder that the climate claimed vast numbers of victims. On the other hand a study of the dress of the sepoys as described in 1780 shows that it was as simple and efficient as it was picturesque.

Much more has been marked down for comment, but the reviewer must be content thus far to commend these fascinating "Records" to the Mythic Society's readers, being sensible that this but poorly indicates the great worth of the compilation that Major Murland has given us.

F. G. (OODWILL)."

The "Pioneer" (Allahabad), 19th November 1922:—

"The Great War upset a good many popular opinions, some of which were lacking in any right to popularity. Amongst the latter was the Simla-born habit of discounting Madras troops, now, one trusts, buried and dead for ever. The habit was, up till 1914, notorious; for the moment we are concerned with one of its effects, which was to relegate to temporary oblivion the enormous share which the Madras Army bore in the British conquest and consolidation of India. At one time every fresh little expedition, west of Peshawar, was glorified by pen, pencil and voice; whilst such names as Assaye and Sholinghur were neglected like old and dusty files. Now that the Great War has itself upset that false balance of perspective all wars are taking a truer position in the national regard, and the old glories grow less faded, as they should justly do.

Major Murland's excellent production contributes notably to this effect, and in the records of a single battalion we may read much of the history which has made the India of to-day. As he shows us in his more strictly historical chapters, the IV Madras Pioneers were really born of the war against France in 1744. That war found Britain in India absolutely unprepared, and from John Company's feverish efforts to make good the deficiency, sprang the three great Presidency Armies. Not until the fifties of the eighteenth century did units arise as we know them to-day, and the IV Madras Pioneers, formed in September 1759, rank as one of the most senior units of the Indian Army. From then on, as the compiler sets forth, they were engaged on active service of one kind and another for almost seventy years without much real respite. Blooding themselves with Coote at Wandiwash, which victory, it has been said, gave us India, they pieced together one long record of honourable fighting, against the French, against Haidar Ali, against Tippu Sultan, in the great Mahratta War of 1803. Thereafter lesser affairs occupied them until the Coorg War of 1834, and only then came a period of peace until the Second Afghan War took them to the Khyber. Of later wars they were engaged in the Lushai and Chin Hills expeditions in 1889—92, and they found a considerable draft for China in 1900. It is a fine record.

All this military history of the battalion has been most readably set forth by Major Murland, not in the dryness of mere consecutive text, but with plentiful excerpts from contemporary letters, diaries and despatches. The result is an attractive narrative, which is at once enlightening and interesting. This record occupies about half the book. After it comes a brief chapter on the battalion's Pioneer work from 1883 to 1903, and we note that the IV Madras Pioneers performed yeoman work towards the construction of the Harnai Valley railway line, one of the greatest feats of modern engineering, and one which set the seal on Russia's Indian projects.

Next a chapter of considerable length is devoted to the usually uninteresting subject of 'Interior Economy.' In this case, however, the dryness of the title belies totally the nature of the contents, The chapter is one of the most interesting of the book. A chronological collection of facts, records, extracts from letters, and orders, it affords at times a deep insight into the conditions under which our armies of old had to soldier. For instance, in these days where every subaltern has his motor-cycle and his club bill it calls for considerable reflection to read that Sir Thomas Munro, as a cadet, was 'three years in India before he was master of any other pillow than a book or a cartridge pouch, and his bed consisted of a piece of canvas stuck on four cross sticks.' Again, let those who believe that red tape is a modern invention read of a Court-Martial on a sepoy in 1828, who had fired at his native officer. The third charge, in all solemnity, was:—"For making away with one round of ball cartridge, the property of the Honourable Company!" It is these sidelights which create the atmosphere, and these are only instances.

The book closes with a detailed chapter recording all the British Officers of the battalion, and with lists of the British Warrant Officers and Sergeants and Indian Officers.

There exists at times an idea that regimental records are of interest to the regiment alone. This is not true, and Major Murland's compilation should go a long way to disabusing it. The records of his battalion bear a goodly share in British and Indian history, and he has presented them in very attractive form. While his work should find a place in every military library, it has a marked claim upon the general reader as well."

The " Madras Mail," 25th August 1922:—

"It is no small thing if a historian, whose chief aim is to trace the growth, and record the spirit and achievements of a regiment, can make the politics, the wars, and the wide issues of past generations live before the present day reader. Major Murland, who for years past has been gathering materials for the history of the 64th Pioneers—first the Fifth, then the Fourth Madras Infantry, and from 1883 a "Pioneer" regiment—has given us, in a concise form not otherwise easily obtainable, a readable and reliable account of the early struggles of the British for existence and for mastery in South India, while recording the development and doings of his own regiment in particular. It reminds us of the well-known histories of the 13th and 19th Light Dragoons, both of which regiments did years of service in the long past in India. The latter regiment was for many years the only British Cavalry regiment in the country, and its early story deals with several of the campaigns in which the Pioneers also were engaged.

This is not a book for those who seek mere amusement, or even history as turned into romance by Henty. But for such as would have the services of a guide through the misty decades of the late eighteenth century, and would better know Colonel Joseph Smith, the redoubtable Coote, Cornwallis and Wellesley, Major Murland is a reliable and instructed scribe. We hope that the book is intended for more than private circulation, for it deserves a wider public than those interested in the fortunes of a single regiment. The form of the book reflects credit on the local publishers; but we could have wished for more thorough proof reading and press correction, the slips of which even "Corrigenda" has not nearly recorded.

Another hand is responsible (*N.B.—This was not the case.—H.F.M.*) for the record of the internal history of the regiment, most interesting records of its clothing, accoutrements, and the details of sepoy life. Also for the lists of its officers from the earliest days, which is vastly more to those who perceive than a list of dates of service and promotions and decease. It is worth noting at the outset that the name of the heroic Colonel Baillie is identified with the regiment, if not from the raising of the battalion, yet as its commander from 1765 to 1771.

British authority in South India had scanty sway in 1759, when the fifth started its long and always honourable career. Every sepoy regiment was sorely tried in the dark days of the first Mysore War, and the still darker days of the second. Yet the record of duty done, of actions fought, of country held, faith maintained, is amazing. Far too little has been said in history of the fidelity, courage and endurance of the Madras Troops of those beginning days of Empire. Those who speak of Madras Troops in comparison with the fighting races of the North with contempt, or but a modicum of respect, indicate but their ignorance of the Dravidian fighting man and of his actual fighting achievements on the field of battle.

It was September 1767, says Major Murland, when the Pioneers received their first baptism of fire under Colonel Joseph Smith, after years of preparation and standing by. Smith, himself one of the greatest soldiers who have commanded in India, says of them after the battle of Chengama: 'Marched 27 hours without the least refreshment for man or beast, who were never unloaded in the midst of this fatigue; the troops were *Chearful* though extenuated, and I can with the utmost pleasure assure the Honourable Board that during the action every corps of sepoys behaved with a regularity scarce to be expected, and with as much firmness as could be wished.' Hear Innes Munro, as he tells of the murderous fight of Baillie at Pollilur, and of the conduct of the sepoys, who escaped to the main army; "Many of Colonel Baillie's sepoys fought hard in General Munro's army next day, which was no small mark of their loyalty and courage." And take the witness of Coote after Porto Novo, a battle which decided, in 1781, whether or not the British light in South India should be extinguished, to the valour of his sepoys: 'The spirited behaviour of our Sepoy Corps did them the greatest credit, No Europeans could be steadier; they were emulous in being foremost on every service it was necessary to undertake.' It is not surprising, with this story of their staunchness and hard fighting, that by 1780 Hyder Ali had 15,000 of his infantry trained in European fashion.

The description given of the campaign in 1768 in the east of the Mysore country is clear, concise, correct. The 5th had the good fortune to be under the command of Colonel Smith, of whom Hyder learned to have a very wary respect, and were saved the blunderings of his colleague Colonel Wood. Colonel Wood deserved his trial and cashiering in 1769 for misappropriation and misconduct in the field; yet pity must not be withheld his memory, for he had done many soldierly things in earlier days.

Major Murland tells the story of the campaign which captured Bangalore, though he cannot trace the doings of his own corps in that siege. We note that he follows Mackenzie in locating the site of the British camp during the siege as on the north-west of the town; and probably this is correct, though ancient authorities are in conflict. But then it is obvious from their writings that some of them are not Orientals in their knowledge of the points of the compass. We thank the author for this story, new to us after much reading of the subject, of the siege of the fort of Bangalore: 'It is recorded in the private diary of Bell, Commissary of Stores to the army, who was present at the siege, that having enquired of an Irish Sub-Conductor, who came from the trenches for ammunition, what prospect there was of completing the breach, the latter replied, 'Breach or no breach, depend upon it they will get in. Sure it is open at the top.''' We take leave to point out a little slip regarding General Harris' march to Seringapatam in 1799, in that it is said that 'Harris reached Bangalore on the 14th March.' The line of march on this campaign was thirteen or so miles south of Bangalore, which was in sight of the army; but on this occasion the army did not touch Bangalore at all, as witness both Beatson and Allen.

Those who are interested in local history will be pleased to note that the present Pioneers were part of the brigade under Major Gowdie which besieged and captured Nundydroog, the first of the great Droog fortresses of Mysore that was captured by the British in the Third Mysore War. It had held up Hyder Ali for nearly three years before it surrendered through force of starvation, yet it was captured by the mixed force of British and Indian troops in about three weeks; and its capture sent a thrill throughout the country then held by Tippoo. We note that the compiler of this great record often turns aside to give information on minor matters, and always matters of great interest. The little stories and footnotes given are often valuable as filling up and adding interest to the picture. He refers to the story which will ever make Hosur of pathetic interest, of the imprisonment and death there of Hamilton and two other British captives. Hosur was much in the way of the 64th during the campaign of 1799, as they moved to and fro on convoy duty under Captain Alexander Read—another name of early times to be held in much honour—who was charged with convoys from the low country to the army. The version given is that Hamilton's death was the work of a chuckler's knife; but there is another, and probably more true, that 'Father' Hamilton was given time to say his prayers, and then his head was cut off by a sword stroke. His influence on the families of the garrison surely procured him this more honourable and soldier-like death.

The history travels far and visits many fields after this time. The regiment was at Assaye, hence September 23 is their regimental day. Afghanistan and Burmah too later saw their valour. But these records are more easily gettable otherwhere, and with this later story, as with the tale of civil works performed by the regiment after it became a Pioneer regiment, we may not deal. Some will like to be reminded that it was due to the work of the 64th Pioneers that the great boon of the level stretch of Hobart Park—now, alas, largely deserted by the gymkhana, was rescued from the lake for the good of Ootacamund and her visitors. Pity it is that the present generation hardly realises anything even of the past generation; 1897-98 is ancient history to multitudes, let alone the days of the raising of the 5th Infantry, the hard days of 1759."

www.ingramcontent.com/pod-product-compliance
Lightning Source LLC
Chambersburg PA
CBHW080537230426
43663CB00015B/2618